Roy Bainton, author of *A Brief History of 1917: Russia's Year of Revolution* and *The Long Patrol*, among other books, travelled around the world while serving in the Merchant Navy. He has written extensively for newspapers and magazines and has been a regular contributor to BBC Radio 4 and to the magazine of the unexplained, the *Fortean Times*.

The Mammoth Book of

UNEXPLAINED PHENOMENA

ROY BAINTON

ROBINSON

RUNNING PRESS
PHILADELPHIA · LONDON

Constable & Robinson Ltd
55–56 Russell Square
London WC1B 4HP
www.constablerobinson.com

First published in the UK by Robinson,
an imprint of Constable & Robinson Ltd, 2013

A copy of the British Library Cataloguing in Publication
Data is available from the British Library

UK ISBN: 978-1-78033-795-1 (paperback)
UK ISBN: 978-1-78033-796-8 (ebook)

First published in the United States in 2013 by Running Press Book Publishers,
A Member of the Perseus Books Group

Books published by Running Press are available at special discounts for bulk purchases in
the United States by corporations, institutions, and other organizations. For more
information, please contact the Special Markets Department at the Perseus Books Group,
2300 Chestnut Street, Suite 200, Philadelphia, PA 19103, or call (800) 810-4145,
ext. 5000, or e-mail special.markets@perseusbooks.com.

US ISBN: 978-0-7624-4809-8
US Library of Congress Control Number: 2012942533

9 8 7 6 5 4 3 2 1
Digit on the right indicates the number of this printing

Running Press Book Publishers
2300 Chestnut Street
Philadelphia, PA 19103-4371

Visit us on the web!
www.runningpress.com

Printed and bound by CPI Group (UK) Ltd, Croydon, CR0 4YY

This book is dedicated to the memory of
Ken Campbell (1941–2008),
actor, clown, man of vision

He is in love with the land that is always over
the next hill and the next, with the bird that is never
caught, with the room beyond the looking-glass.

He likes the half-hid, the half-heard, the half-lit,
the man in the fog, the road without an ending,
stray pieces of torn words to piece together.

Arthur Seymour John Tessimond (1902–62),
from "Portrait of a Romantic"

CONTENTS

INTRODUCTION:

E=mc² OR NOT?

There are known knowns. These are things we know that we know. There are known unknowns. That is to say, there are things that we know we don't know. But there are also unknown unknowns. There are things we don't know we don't know.

Donald Rumsfeld (1932–)

Donald Rumsfeld's bizarre utterance sat uncomfortably in the world of politics and international terrorism, and it may well be a puzzling quotation to open any written work. Yet when adapted for use in this book, those six staccato sentences possess an eerie resonance. What *do* we know?

Already, as I write, the towering genius of Albert Einstein is being challenged. The speed of light has been regarded as the universe's ultimate speed limit and the central plank of Einstein's theory of special relativity is the idea that nothing can exceed it. However, in its complexly titled report "Measurement of the Neutrino Velocity with the Oscillation Project with Emulsion-tRacking Apparatus (OPERA) Detector in the CNGS Beam" submitted to Cornell University, the world's largest physics laboratory near Geneva, CERN (the European Organization for Nuclear Research or, in French, Organisation Européenne pour la Recherche Nucléaire), has carried out experiments that suggest that neutrinos (subatomic particles) have gone faster than the speed of light. If similar experiments back this up, then the pillars of physics as we know them could come tumbling down. Finding the elusive, nigh-on incomprehensible Higgs boson is one thing, but exceeding the speed of light is something else. However, other scientists have already reacted to this possibility with caution. At the University of Surrey, Professor Jim Al-Khalili, a popular broadcaster, has expressed his incredulity by putting his public image on the line, saying, "If neutrinos have broken the speed of light I will eat my boxer shorts on live TV." Shades of Laurel and Hardy there, but that's science.

In addition, some scientists working with CERN's Large Hadron Collider – the world's largest atom smasher – think that it could be the first machine capable of enabling matter to travel backwards in time. This notion revolves around M-theory, a "theory of everything" that accommodates all the known properties of subatomic particles and forces, including gravity, but instead of the four dimensions we're used to, M-theory requires ten or eleven. *Eleven* dimensions? We're into the twilight zone here. The thought is staggering. So the idea of time travel, belatedly the province of science-fiction writers and Hollywood, as we shall see, is already under serious discussion. This will be examined when we come to the conundrum of UFOs. Are they time-travelling tourists? Anything seems possible. Whatever is revealed, proven or otherwise, at least Albert Einstein always expressed magnanimity among his peers, as evidenced by his statement "No amount of experimentation can ever prove me right; a single experiment can prove me wrong." If, however, we are eventually able to travel back in time, we might consider the entry for "time" in Ambrose Bierce's *Devil's Dictionary*:

PAST, n. That part of Eternity with some small fraction of which we have a slight and regrettable acquaintance. A moving line called the Present parts it from an imaginary period known as the Future. These two grand divisions of Eternity, of which the one is continually effacing the other, are entirely unlike. The one is dark with sorrow and disappointment, the other bright with prosperity and joy. The Past is the region of sobs, the Future is the realm of song. In the one crouches Memory, clad in sackcloth and ashes, mumbling penitential prayer; in the sunshine of the other Hope flies with a free wing, beckoning to temples of success and bowers of ease. Yet the Past is the Future of yesterday, the Future is the Past of to-morrow. They are one – the knowledge and the dream.

For the purposes of this book and for the scientific layman, and that includes this writer (the bottom of his class for mathematics at every school he attended), everything around Albert Einstein is crucial. That said, we need not become bogged down with the often perplexing intricacies of physics. There are plenty of books and websites if maths is your thing. However, we are about to embark on a voyage into all manner of anomalies from near-death experiences, spiritualism and ghosts to UFOs, coincidences, synchronicity and bizarre biology. All these subjects are part of our universe and, as such, in ways which most of us, excusably, might fail to comprehend, will be connected to such subjects as Space Time, Time Dilation, Chaos and Quantum Theory. So, let's offer some basics before we move on. First of all, what does $E=mc^2$ mean? It's simply Einstein's equation formulated in his special theory of relativity. E stands for Energy, m stands for Mass, c is the speed of light. It states that energy is equal to mass multiplied by the speed of light squared. It demonstrates that mass and energy are two forms of the same thing and can be interchanged. The energy released by the sun or by an atomic bomb is an example of the effect of mass-energy equivalence.

Space Time is a physics model connecting three-dimensional space and one-dimensional time to form the idea of space-time continuum. This enables physicists to render the laws of physics easier to grasp, so that we mere mortals might have a faltering grip on how the universe works on the big level, for example the stars, and right down to atoms. How many dimensions are there in Space Time? There isn't a fixed number, but usually four dimensions are worked with: three of space and one of time. Yet as we've already learned, this limitation is already being challenged. Albert Einstein, through his relativity theory, is usually associated with Space Time, but it was Hermann Minkowski, Einstein's teacher, who came up with the idea in the hope of making the theory of special relativity clearer.

Time Dilation posits that as you move through space, time itself is measured differently for the moving object than the unmoving object. As we approach the speed of light, this effect becomes apparent and might enable us to travel into the future faster than we normally do. One of the earliest predictions of relativity, in short, time dilation allows motion in space to actually alter the flow of time. It has been claimed that this manner of time travel is completely allowed by the known laws of physics, but we could only go into the future, not the past. Time dilation could suggest enthralling ways of extending life. Science fiction uses the idea because it allows humans to live long enough to travel between galaxies and stars.

Quantum Mechanics represents a collection of scientific principles that, together, try to explain the behaviour of matter and its interactions with energy on the scale of atoms and atomic particles.

Chaos Theory suggests that the big, complex systems in nature, for example the weather, possess an underlying order, but remain unpredictable and chaotic. Very tiny changes can have major effects (look up the "butterfly effect": for example, the flapping of a butterfly's wings in one location may affect the weather on the other side of the earth).

Do all these complex areas have connection to or an impact on unexplained phenomena? All we can really say is … perhaps. They are the mysteries of science that are still in the process of being unravelled and, no doubt decades from now, any one of these theories might come into play if we ever get to understand ghosts, UFOs and other aspects of the paranormal.

We are in a period of human history that is referred to by many spiritual and religious gurus as "The Quickening". In short, this means that things are beginning to move phenomenally fast. In 1977, when I was still using a typewriter and carbon paper, and travelling miles each week to access information in a public library, Ken Olsen, President of the Digital Equipment Corporation (now part of Hewlett-Packard), offered the opinion that "There is no reason for any individual to have a computer in his home." Less than four decades later, the typewriter is the equivalent of a chisel and a stone tablet, and the library is at my fingertips. Back then, the all-singing, all-dancing computer was simply a space cadet's dream as portrayed so perceptively in Stanley Kubrick's *2001: A Space Odyssey*. There is probably more technology in your mobile phone than there was in Neil Armstrong and Buzz Aldrin's *Eagle* landing craft when NASA went to the moon in 1969.

As the decades roll on, science will gather even more speed and no doubt many of the weird events outlined in this book may well leave the realm of the unexplained. But for now, they exist as a serious compendium of abnormal enigmas, and as such continue to exercise their grip on human imagination, sustaining our passion for romance and mystery.

This is a book about the things we can't explain, and a few of the things we *think* we can explain, yet still leave us puzzled. For example, as I write this, the UK newspaper the *Daily Mail* offers this weird report dated 15 December 2011:

IT'S RAINING APPLES! TRAFFIC GRINDS TO A HALT AS "MINI TORNADO" DUMPS A HAIL OF FRUIT

FREAK STORM "CAUSED BY WIND VORTEX" LIFTED FRUIT FROM GARDEN OR ORCHARD

After a series of storm warnings, drivers in the evening rush hour were prepared for almost anything. Except, that is, for it to start raining apples. Scores of them battered car roofs and windscreens before landing in the road at a busy junction in Coundon, Coventry. The deluge of fruit brought traffic to a standstill at 6.45 p.m. on Monday. A 20-yard stretch of the B4098 was left strewn with green slush after the incident. One motorist, who was travelling with her husband, said: "The apples fell out of nowhere. They were small and green and hit the bonnet hard. Everyone had to stop their cars suddenly." Brian Meakins, 63, was stunned when he opened his front door and found his garden full of smashed apples. The retired forklift truck driver said: "At first I assumed kids must have thrown them because we do get the occasional egg and apple thrown but there's way too many for that."

On 4 February 2012 the *Guardian* featured a bizarre report of a fall of mysterious blue balls of a gel-like substance from the sky in a Dorset garden. A local science lab had found them to be similar to sodium polyacrylate or "waterlock", the kind of stuff they put in babies' disposable diapers. They also fell in

Bournemouth, where resident Steve Hornsby said that the sky above his house turned dark, then yellow, and the balls came down in a violent hailstorm. Because such inexplicable, illogical events fall outside the parameters of mainstream science, they are classified as phenomena, but even then, science can't always leave it at that. Research assistant Josie Pegg, who studies aquatic ecology and examined the mysterious blue balls, put readers' minds at rest: "Perhaps someone was having a clear-out and chucked them over the fence." Scientific neatness, good house-keeping; another anomaly tidied up and filed away.

As human beings, we're conceited enough to believe that we are our planet's superior species. We're the ones who try to tame everything; we build the skyscrapers, make the roads, jumbo jets and the space shuttle. Spiders make webs and bees make honey, but we do everything else. This all adds an extra level of human confidence – we like to think that we can *explain* everything. After all, unlike chimpanzees, we have science. And so, just in case the media readership gets carried away with the inevitable drop-jawed "wow" factor engendered by any anomalous phenomena, the difficulty of falling apples must be explained, as follows:

> The explanation is down to a typical spell of British summer weather, where a few hot days are often followed by a thunderstorm. The phenomenon is believed to be down to a mini tornado which touched down elsewhere, sucking apples from the ground or from trees. Such a powerful vacuum could have travelled for many miles before the tornado's energy dissipated, depositing the fruit over Coventry. Another theory is that the apples could have fallen from the hold of a plane.

A senior meteorologist from British Weather Services, Jim Dale, was called upon to add his comments. He told us that the falling apples were probably the result of "returning polar maritime air". Mr Dale continues:

> Essentially these events are caused when a vortex of air, kind of like a mini tornado, lifts things off the ground, rising up into the atmosphere until the air around it causes them to fall

to earth again. Returning polar maritime air is such an unstable condition and it basically means air returning from the polar regions which is very unstable. We've all heard of fish and frogs falling from the sky, and apples is certainly unusual because they have some weight to them but it is not out of the realms of possibility.

Phew! Thank heavens for that explanation. For a moment, we all thought something weird was going on! After all, stuff's always falling from the sky. Yet some of it isn't as prosaic as little green apples. In Colombia in 2008 a red rain fell upon the small community of La Sierra, Chocó. It was analysed by a local bacteriologist who certified it as blood and this was further confirmed when a sample was sent to the nearest town, Bagadó. Inevitably, the local priest read this as a sign from God that people needed to change their sinful ways.

For Argentinean Christian Oneto Gaona, 6 April 2007 was quite a day. He not only witnessed a rain of spiders, but also became probably the first person in the world to catch this anomaly on camera. Along with some friends, for their Easter vacation Christian decided to take a hike up the San Bernardo Mountain in Salta Province. Around 5 p.m. on 6 April, they found the ground around them was blanketed with spiders, each measuring about four inches (10 cm) across, and they were of various colours. As the party progressed up the mountain, with spiders actually falling on them, they found more and more of the eight-legged horrors covering the ground. In this broad mountain valley, there was nothing above but the sky, and as they all looked up, there were masses more spiders falling down.

In 2009, scientists commissioned by *National Geographic* carried out tests on a rain of jelly that fell in Scotland, but failed to find any DNA in it. Jelly falls are not as rare as we would imagine. Reports of rains of what's become known as "star jelly" abound. One theory on offer is that the substance is regurgitated frog or toad ovaries, vomited by buzzards or herons because it is indigestible. Other explanations refer to the remnants of meteor showers or even fungus. In August 2007 fish also rained down in the streets of Great Yarmouth, Norfolk, after a mini-tornado at sea.

Throughout the decades, as far back as you'd like to look, you will find reports of weird stuff hitting the earth. On 18 August 2004, fish fell from the sky on to the village of Knighton, Powys, in Wales. If spiders are creepy, how about maggots? On 5 October 1967, thousands of maggots fell like rain over Acapulco, Mexico, after a heavy storm. In 1996 dozens of frogs were reported to be falling from the sky in Llanddewi, Powys, and again in Croydon, London, in 1998. Always, the scientists step forward because these things must be explained. Yet what do they make of angel hair? Angel hair falls have happened throughout history. Today it is described as a "siliceous cotton substance" and is claimed by the UFO community to be ionized air sleeting off an electromagnetic field dispersed from UFOs as they fly. It is described variously as a cobweb or a jelly, and is often reported on those holy occasions when the Virgin Mary is sighted (for example, the Miracle at Fatima in September and October 1917) but it soon disintegrates or evaporates. On 2 November 1959 in the city of Évora, Portugal, after a wave of UFO sightings, angel hair was collected and analysed through the microscope by a local school director. It was then examined by technicians from Portugal's armed forces and in the science faculty at the University of Lisbon. No firm conclusions were reached. What was established, however, was that angel hair was formed by a small organism featuring ten "arms" stretching from a central core. Some suggested that this might be a single-celled organism of some kind. OK – if we accept mini-whirlwinds, tornados and typhoons dumping frogs, fish and maggots on our shoulders, that's fine. Sceptics and debunkers rightly accuse total believers in ghosts and UFOs of being blinkered by their non-scientific acceptance of the unexplained and the paranormal, due to their deep desire for such things to be real. Yet it is those same elements that science omits in its mission to explain which maintain the high profile of these subjects.

Therefore, let us ask this question; when those apples fell over Coundon in Coventry, or the fish, the frogs, the spiders, how is it that meteorological "abduction" only selects *one* organism or item? Why were the apples not accompanied by leaves, some grass, the odd twig, a bit of earth? If the spiders were sucked up, why were the other members of the ugly bug ball left on the ground? And where are there such dense congregations of frogs to explain such a concentrated, four-legged amphibian downpour? Where are the weeds, the bits of water-lily, some mud, grass, the newts and tadpoles? And where in hell's name does the proposed "tornado" target itself to suck up enough *blood* to splatter a few acres elsewhere at random? What science adequately clarifies, we can accept. What it omits in its hypotheses, for sceptical convenience or lack of knowledge, simply leaves the ball in the air. How can the massed brains of the world's science faculty explain such anomalies as copper nails or an artefact resembling a spark plug, chipped out by miners from seams of prehistoric rock a mile underground? As the man we are about to meet, Charles Fort, once commented: "The fate of all explanation is to close one door only to have another fly wide open." Colin Wilson, in his 1978 book, *Mysteries*, sums up Fort's attitude thus: "Expressed in a sentence, Fort's principle goes something like this: People with a psychological need to believe in marvels are no more prejudiced and gullible than people with a psychological need not to believe in marvels."

These subjects have been entertaining us for decades. Without them there would never have been *The Outer Limits*, *The Twilight Zone*, *Doctor Who* or *The X-Files*, and both Steven Spielberg and Dan Brown, among others, would have some wide, empty spaces in their lives. Flying saucers are just one aspect of aberration, but even allowing for the possibility that UFOs could be a mass hallucination or a construct of our deep subconscious, they have a potential framework of logic; mechanical devices and technically advanced travellers from another world or dimension, they are currently an enigma yet are still something we may be able to explain in time. However, I recall my first jaw-dropping brush with the utterly baffling when, as a teenager in Yorkshire, I thumbed through a book in Hull's Central Library. Among reports of falling flesh and blood I was astounded to read a report from the Victorian era of a wedding party in a churchyard on a cold, foggy day. The cloud base was low and from this grim overcast sky, a rope descended. Sliding down the rope was a sailor, a Jack Tar of Nelsonian vintage. As he reached the ground in the churchyard, in view of the dumbfounded nuptial party, he collapsed, dead, and the rope was pulled back into the clouds above. The dead sailor was diagnosed as having expired from drowning. I cannot give you the precise provenance of this report, but let's meet the man who took my breath away all those years ago.

The Patron Saint of Strangeness

If the world of unexplained phenomena has a patron saint, then it has to be Charles Hoy Fort (1874–1932). Born in Albany, New York, of Dutch ancestry, he was a writer and researcher into anomalous phenomena. Although highly intelligent, with a deep interest in the natural world, he was not particularly bright at school. Yet Fort had a healthy curiosity about all things. He was a voracious reader, and through books he expanded his knowledge of the world day by day. When he was eighteen, a strong, hefty six-footer, he waved goodbye to New York for a while and embarked on his journey around the globe, saying it would "put some capital in the bank of experience". He trekked across the American west, sailed to Scotland and journeyed into England, but illness in South Africa (probably malaria) propelled him home, where he met up with Anna Filing, a friend from childhood. A Yorkshire girl, born and raised in Sheffield, England, she was married to Fort on 26 October 1896. She was twenty-six and he was just twenty-two. Opposites attract. Anna was a long way from the literary character of her husband. She wasn't much of a reader, and beyond her fascination with parrots, the cinema was her greatest passion. They lived frugally, with Charles doing a variety of day jobs, until in 1916 his uncle died and left him and his brothers Clarence and Raymond enough money for him to quit work and begin writing full-time. The following year Clarence died and his portion of the inheritance was shared between Charles and Raymond.

Fort struggled as a short-story writer and his success as a journalist was sporadic to say the least. But he did write no fewer than ten novels. Sadly, only one, *The Outcast Manufacturers* (1909), was published. It was well reviewed but a commercial flop. Two of his other manuscripts, oddly titled *X* and *Y*, which had unusual plots involving Martians controlling the earth and the possibility of an unknown civilization living in Antarctica, were championed by the great novelist Theodore Dreiser, yet even Dreiser's influence in the publishing world failed to get Fort a deal. The dismayed Fort threw X and Y on to the fire, so we shall never know what they really contained. However, by this time, he had spent much of his life in libraries and museums, as well as absorbing the contents of numerous newspapers each day. He spent twenty-six years amassing boxes of bizarre data, notes from journals and newspaper clippings, all dealing with weird and inexplicable events that science would reject and not explain. He put all this material to good use and wrote the work that would ultimately change his life, and with Dreiser's help, *The Book of the Damned* (1919) was published.

For two years, 1924–6, the Forts lived in London, not far from the British Museum on Marchmont Street, above a green-grocer's shop. *The Book of the Damned* and other works that followed, such as *New Lands* (1923), *Lo!* (1931) and *Wild Talents* (1932), were critically praised by some prominent literary practitioners, among them screenwriter, director, producer, playwright and novelist Ben Hecht, who unwittingly gave birth to a new noun when, reviewing *The Book of the Damned*, he wrote: "I am the first disciple of Charles Fort. He has made a terrible onslaught upon the accumulated lunacy of fifty centuries ... he has delighted me beyond all men who have written books in this world. Mountebank or Messiah, it matters not. Henceforth I am a *Fortean*" (my italics). As an Englishman, I like to ponder over Fort's 1920s London sojourn. There is something vaguely cinematic about the life of this fascinating American and his daily routine in that dark social valley between two great wars. He would start work at eight on his writing and files, then after lunch head off to the British Museum and British Library, where Karl Marx had spent many similar days of research, albeit utilizing vastly different shelves. After dinner Fort would sometimes walk in the park and talk to Londoners. What were those conversations like? And before the day was through, he would take Anna to see the latest movie.

A man of great wit and humour, Fort may well have found Donald Rumsfeld's weird words worthy of jotting down, for as he said, "We cannot define. Nothing has ever been finally figured out, because there is nothing final to figure out." His attitude to phenomena was arguably a healthy one, yet as to his sainthood, there are a few flaws. His dismissal of what he called "the priest-craft of science" often led him to some pretty odd conclusions; for example, he believed that the earth probably only rotated once every year, and that the moon was only 11,500 miles (18,507 km) distant with a diameter of 100 miles (161 km). Had he used some of the scientific methodology he sometimes despised, he might have reached the conclusion, based on tidal calculations, that for his tiny moon theory to work our satellite would need to have the density of lead multiplied ten times. But that was Fort's frustrating charm; he set out to enrage and affront the boffins, and his quirky style always leaves one smiling. He stated that the ideal was not to be a true believer, nor a total sceptic, and that "the truth lies somewhere in between". He knew that the many bizarre anomalies he collected would be brushed aside by science. Writing *The Book of the Damned*, he referred to his accumulated data as: "A procession of the damned. By the damned, I mean the excluded. We shall have a procession of data that science has excluded." Newcomers to his work will not find him a particularly easy read, but he is always entertaining. He appears by turns partisan and neutral, choosing not to challenge or support the provenance or veracity of many of his collected reports – he leaves it to us, the readers, saying, "Here it is – make up your own mind." This represents all the common sense you'll need as we trawl through the Sargasso Sea of strangeness in this book.

Some of the phenomena that inspired Charles Fort, such as frogs, fish, blood and jelly falling from the sky, could reasonably fit into the category "things we *think* we can explain". Hurricanes, typhoons, tornados may all play their part. The weird events they have been blamed for have been happening for centuries, and they keep on happening. A large shower of frogs fell over Hungary in 2010. In 2011, in Arkansas, over 4,000 red-winged blackbirds fell to earth; most were dead, others had damaged internal organs. In the same area 83,000 dead fish washed up on the banks of the Arkansas River. In Western Australia, thousands of assorted birds, pigeons, crows, wattles and honeyeaters fell dead from the sky. The question is: how – and why?

Yet these are events, although mysterious, with which science occasionally attempts to wrestle. There are many other phenomenal scenarios that fall way outside the borders of logic: near-death experiences, strange disappearances, the continuing riddle of UFOs, the spirit world, ghosts, spontaneous human combustion, synchronicity and coincidence. It's a long list.

In many ways, it seems apt that this book will appear in 2013, when the Mayans prophesied the end of the world as we know it to be in 2012. I am writing these first lines on 26 October 2011. American doomsday prophet Harold Camping was wrong when he predicted the world would end on 21 May 2011 and now he has been proved wrong again in thinking the "Rapture" would happen on Friday, 21 October. As one of those agnostic miscreants who would have been left behind, the sense of relief is enormous, although there was a bit of wind and rain last Friday.

However, the prophets and soothsayers are always telling us that we're not out of the woods yet. According to the skilful and meticulously produced videos of Keith Wyatt on such subjects at www.AwakeningAsOne.com, which certainly leave one pondering over the nature of faith, the Mayans may have been a year out, because according to predictions made earlier in 2011, Comet Elenin would bring great changes to the earth on Friday, 28 October 2011. Therefore if you're reading this, the Godly have all succumbed to the Rapture and you've been left behind or, once again, the mysterious Elders have got it wrong. Comet Elenin (astronomical title, C/2010 X1) was detected by Russian astronomer Leonid Elenin of Lyubertsy, Russia, in December 2010. Its approach fitted in well with the Mayan prophesy, and with those of Grandfather Martin of the Hopi tribe. This comet was regarded by the Hopi as one of two fateful stars, the blue Kachina and the red Kachina. The blue, Elenin, would be the harbinger of a global cataclysm, and once we had all found faith, the red Kachina, the redeemer, would arrive to begin a new age for humanity. However, Don Yeomans of NASA's Near-Earth Object Program Office at the Jet Propulsion Laboratory in Pasadena, reassuringly informs us that:

Elenin did as new comets passing close by the sun do about two per cent of the time: it broke apart. Elenin's remnants will also act as other broken-up comets act. They will trail along in a debris cloud that will follow a well-understood path out of the inner solar system. After that, we won't see the scraps of comet Elenin around these parts for almost 12 millennia.

So, thanks, NASA, I can continue writing.

I fell into the honeytrap of unexplained phenomena many years ago at the tender age of thirteen. Browsing in my local library after finishing my paper round, I came across a book by George Adamski (1891–1965), *Flying Saucers Have Landed*. Back then in the 1950s, our vision of the planets was coloured by the works of H. G. Wells, Jules Verne and Ray Bradbury. I was well and truly smitten. Every press report went into my scrapbook. Well into the 1970s, a huge amount of bestselling Adamski-inspired dross was published around the world. Outer space seemed to be teeming with wise golden beings determined to show us mere Earthlings the error of our atomic ways. Then came the "Was God an Astronaut?" period, with the prolific Erich von Däniken cleaning up with his attempts to convince us that ancient civilizations were regular space travellers and that the pharaohs had helicopters. Yet as the years passed, NASA, astronomy and science caught up and, despite YouTube and Photoshop, it's no longer possible (although many still try) to stick half a tennis ball on to a trash-can lid or a hub cap, dangle it from a tree on a fishing line and concoct a photograph of an "alien spacecraft". However, such self-obsessed chicanery made a number of authors a lot of money. Adamski's claims to have gone to Venus with his Nordic-type visitors in their one-piece Abba jumpsuits don't look so good now that we know that the planet has an atmospheric surface pressure ninety-two times that of earth, clouds composed of sulphuric acid and an average surface temperature of 461.85°C. Tough cookies, those Venusians.

Debunkers, such as the erudite sceptic and stage magician James Randi, who we shall meet later on, have a valuable role to play in at least one branch of phenomena – the paranormal. Scepticism is a requirement when entering the world of the unexplained because it keeps us grounded. The territory occupied by assorted mediums, spiritualists, prophets and fakirs is a minefield. In 1972 Randi publicly challenged the spoon-bender Uri Geller, accusing him of being nothing more than a charlatan or a standard magician in his paranormal acts. In 1991 Randi's book *The Truth about Uri Geller* led to Geller suing Randi for $15 million. The suit was against CSICOP (Committee for Scientific Investigation of Claims of the Paranormal), of which James Randi is a founder member. The case was dismissed in 1995 with Geller having to pay out $120,000 for filing a frivolous lawsuit. So, as we set off on this *Mary Celeste* of a voyage, let's keep Charles Fort in mind. Make your own interpretations. Be as cynical as you see fit, yet enjoy the sheer fun and wonder that the fascinating world of unexplained phenomena has to offer. As a safety belt, remember the observation of Sherlock Holmes: "The temptation to form premature theories upon insufficient data is the bane of our profession." The great Baker Street detective also said, "When you have eliminated the impossible, whatever remains, however improbable, must be the truth." Perhaps. Maybe … who knows. Incidentally, it is now Saturday, 29 October 2011. Although there was an earthquake in Turkey this week, yesterday's expected apocalypse did not happen. Well, at least not in this dimension. E=mc² or not? It's back to you, Mr Rumsfeld.

Roy Bainton

PART 1:

THE AGE OF UNREASON

If an elderly but distinguished scientist says that something is possible, he is almost certainly right; but if he says that it is impossible, he is very probably wrong.

Arthur C. Clarke (1917–2008)

It was the introduction of the printing press in *c.*1440 that made Europe's philosophers, writers and the propagators of new ideas realize that knowledge and the written word could be finally prised from the tight-fisted coterie of cloistered monks and scribes of Christendom. Through the printed page, knowledge could be rapidly dispersed to a wider world.

Eighteenth-century Europe saw a new, brave philosophical movement that has become known as the Age of Enlightenment or the Age of Reason. Intellectuals, mathematicians and philosophers led by such men as Isaac Newton (1643–1727), Voltaire (1694–1778) and John Locke (1632–1704) harnessed the power of reason in an attempt to promote science and advance society. The movement faced staunch opposition in the shape of centuries of ingrained superstition, religiously inspired intolerance and the abuse of politics. Some rulers, whilst remaining despots, took up some of these Enlightenment ideas, but by 1800 the sun had set on the Age of Reason, which would be replaced by Romanticism. Enlightenment stressed the superiority of reason, Romanticism emphasized emotion, intuition and imagination, all to such a degree that some Romantic thinkers have been accused of irrationalism.

It may sound extreme to call what we are now living in the "Age of Unreason". However, the two opposing camps experienced by the Enlightenment philosophers, science and religion, are still as entrenched as ever, fully armed, locked, loaded and facing one another from their opposing trenches across a no-man's-land of vitriolic argument and suspicion. If this book you are reading has a location, then you'll find it there, in no-man's-land. At one extreme we have deep-space probes and the Hubble telescope revealing the wonders of the universe. At the other, we have the Taliban, attempting to build a fossilized future from the past by seeking to recreate the twelfth century, whilst Western evangelists throw centuries of scientific advancement and research on to history's garbage dump in favour of creationism. That both these movements travel the world by jet plane, propagate their ideas via the internet, the iPhone, TV and radio, and with some seeking to utilize nuclear weaponry, all of which are the products of scientific research and technical genius, seems to be a paradox that has escaped them. But these are the views of one lone writer, and he, too, is guilty of Romanticism. Unexplained phenomena still hold us in the realm of shock and awe, and the juries of both science and the Godly remain "out" on the subject.

Outside of religion, where an afterlife is often promised, no one has yet discovered the ultimate secret of eternal life. Why do we die? How many years will we live? It used to be three score and ten – if you were lucky enough. Yet in the twenty-first century we are indeed living longer. We know so much more now about the human body. Many of the diseases that once ravaged the globe – bubonic plague, smallpox, for example – have been in the main consigned to the medical archives. Quite often, what medical science has historically deemed efficacious and utterly correct can seem ridiculous to future generations. The use of leeches, bloodletting and the crazy ingestion of mercury seem almost tragi-comic today, but not long ago such methods represented the pinnacle of research. Qin Shi Huang, the first emperor of unified China, is supposed to have died by ingesting mercury, which was intended to give him eternal life. One might imagine such an ancient debacle would have taught medicine a lesson. Centuries later, however, in the *Practitioner's Encyclopaedia of Medical Treatment* published in 1915 by Oxford Medical Publications, Mr McDonough FRCS tells his colleagues the following about how to deal with syphilis: "When a patient cannot get regular medical attendance, mercury should be taken internally in some form; if this method causes depression or sets up gastro-enteritis or diarrhoea, a suppository of 1 gr. of mercury salicylate in Oleum Theobromi 1/2 gr. inserted every night just before going to bed will often meet the difficulty." The well-meaning Mr McDonough assures his students that "three drugs only need be considered, mercury, iodine and arsenic". As if the Great War wasn't enough! If there was any transcendent punishment beyond a sexually transmitted disease for a hapless soldier, philandering with a mademoiselle behind the front line in France, the medical profession could provide it. Today, with our CT scanners, super drugs, lasers and laparoscopic surgery, our doctors would have appeared to Mr McDonough as Leonard "Bones" McCoy, portrayed by actor DeForest Kelley, does to us in the *Star Trek* movies. Yet cancer persists, malaria is still a major killer and heart disease continues to wreak havoc. There are strange locations, however, where possible cures still await discovery.

With its black stripes and iridescent scales, the zebrafish, a native of India's Ganges River, is a cute addition to any home aquarium. But this is a little fish with a big secret. One species of the zebrafish, *Danio rerio*, is offering us new hope in heart research. Astonishing though it is, if you cut out part of a zebrafish's heart, it will grow back again. A *regenerating heart*? It may seem like science fiction, but once researchers have finally figured out how this process takes place, it could mean a great stride forward in the repair of human hearts. The zebrafish's natural state is a gift to medical research, because it's translucent – we don't always need to cut into them; we can see what's going on inside their bodies. To enhance this beneficial state, in the city of Sheffield in England scientists in the field of genetics have been engineering these little Ganges wonders by lining their blood vessels with a fluorescent green protein that enables them to study their circulation more easily. At the University of Oxford the zebrafish has revealed another weird advantage. It possesses a substance known as fibroblast growth factor (FGF) which "instructs" embryo cells to become either blood vessel cells or heart cells. Scientists refer to this anomaly as a "switch", and they are searching for a way to click this on in human stem cells. If that's possible, then the humble zebrafish will be helping heart-attack victims by building new heart muscle cells. In Oxford, the suitably named Professor Roger Patient, who is leading this project, has expressed his confidence in the overall research, stating, "At the very least, our research will help the production of these cells in the laboratory for use in heart repair."

Hopefully, this non-human branch of stem cell research will keep the Baptists, Catholics, Methodists and Pentecostal faithful happy. Their opposition to such research has focused on human embryonic stem cells. The Southern Baptists are clear on their stance here: "The Bible teaches that human beings are made in the image and likeness of God (Genesis 1: 27; 9: 6) and protectable human life begins at fertilization." So, little fishes to the rescue. Over the past century man has developed all manner of scientific methods in his mission to explain the universe. We have carbon dating, we know that the Great Pyramid at Giza has been there for five millennia and that the dinosaurs died out millions of years before humanity emerged from the slime. We know that seams of coal are formed from the compressed sediment of forests that existed millions of years ago. From a purely scientific view, this all seems perfectly reasonable. We're living with electricity, the internet, the cell phone, TV, radio and nanotechnology, and satellites orbit the earth telling us where to go whilst we're studying our satnavs. The scientific human race has achieved all this. Yet there are many who exercise the human right to believe differently, even in the twenty-first century. Some would deem that the peculiar properties of the zebrafish are just another example of something called "intelligent design".

FAITH v. FACTS

It seems amazing, almost four centuries after the great astronomer and scientist Galileo (1564–1642) was ridiculed by the Vatican for suggesting *heliocentrism* – the fact that the earth revolves around the sun – that even a discussion on the dichotomy between religion and science can result in a threatening response. Some religions even respond by inflicting the curse of eternal damnation or prescribing death, despite all the repetitions in the great tracts of religion that proclaim God's mercy, understanding and compassion. Matthew 5: 39, "If someone strikes you on the right cheek, turn to him the other also", is conveniently overlooked by most zealots.

Eventually tried by the Inquisition, Galileo was found "vehemently suspect of heresy". He was forced to recant what he believed to be true and condemned to spend the rest of his life under house arrest. Yet whilst locked away in his house, he produced his finest work, *Two New Sciences*. These are now known as kinematics and the strength of materials. Of course, due to his pragmatism in recanting, Galileo was lucky. Unlike his brave predecessor, Gordiano Bruno (1548–1600), Galileo survived the Inquisition. Bruno stubbornly advocated the doctrine of the universe as we have come to understand it – infinity – and proudly maintained his theory of the "plurality of worlds"; in other words, the earth was not the be-all and end-all centre of the universe – there were others. Bruno stuck to his conclusions in the face of the Vatican's proud bigotry and was burned to a crisp at the stake in 1600. Such is the heroism science often requires.

There's nothing wrong with faith; it demands respect, it provides millions of people with immense comfort and, as the saying goes, faith can move mountains. Yet as Arthur C. Clarke observed, "A faith that cannot survive collision with the truth is not worth many regrets." However, if God made us all, he included scientists in the mix. If heaven is holding back countless hidden secrets that the angels expect us to work out for ourselves, then science could well be one of the main channels for such revelations. Yet reason and religion continue to be uneasy bedfellows.

A tool in Google Earth shows you the effect of climate change in your area. Using Google Earth's "Climate Change in Our World", you can look at climate effects under three different scenarios and see what temperature changes can be expected by the end of this century. Other new tools let you examine other aspects of climate change and suggest how we might adapt to this. The science is there and it's still in motion – and there is already serious melting of the polar ice regions. Yet to hear the GOP (that's the "Grand Old Party") one-time presidential front-runner, Republican Governor of Texas Rick Perry and some Tea Party-backed lawyers talking, it seems as if the Republican position on global warming is that it doesn't even exist. Perry, in his 2010 book *Fed Up*, called climate science a "contrived phony mess". And this is in twenty-first century America – whose cutting-edge science brought us the atomic bomb, space missions and the internet. Yet when we look closer at this denial of science, a survey by the Pew Research Center for the People and the Press, tracking what people believe about global warming, throws up even scarier statistics. The percentage of American evangelical Protestants who do not believe global warming is happening reached 50 per cent by October 2009. Republicans of all denominations believing the same reached almost 60 per cent, and even 26 per cent of the religiously unaffiliated US population refused to believe in global warming. Among those who suspect global warming *is* happening, less than 30 per cent of Republicans believe it has anything to do with human activity, as opposed to almost 60 per cent of Democrats, with the evangelists coming in around 33 per cent. Our technology is in overdrive, yet the minds of many men are obstinately stuck in first gear.

ONE TRUTH OR TWO?

In a BBC poll carried out in 2002, Sir Winston Churchill was voted as the greatest Briton of all time. On a political level, the illustrious war leader wasn't always everyone's cup of tea, but some of his aphorisms reveal a great mind at work. For example: "True genius resides in the capacity for evaluation of uncertain, hazardous and conflicting information." Even so, in 1957 he was so concerned about a reported encounter between a UFO and RAF bombers that he ordered it be kept secret for at least fifty years to prevent "mass panic".

As Charles Fort said, "I offer the data; you decide." Phenomena, the unexplained, politics, religion – it is anyone's privilege to believe or disbelieve. None of this is included here as political flag-waving for any church or party. It's simply present to demonstrate that the age of unreason through which Bruno and Galileo struggled is still with us. Beyond politics, it is that same unreason that crops up when a UFO is proved to be a weather balloon or a Chinese lantern. "Ah ... it's a CIA cover-up." No, not necessarily – it's a *weather balloon*! There are a lot of Republicans and good Christians with commendably open minds, and unreasonable inflexibility exists equally on the left-wing as much as it does the right, and in the world of the unexplained, even more so.

If they would delve a little deeper, the bane of many evangelists, Darwinism, might not seem so spiritually bereft. Although Darwin, who originally intended a life as a clergyman, lost his faith, if we look into the work of his contemporary and collaborator, Alfred Russel Wallace, we can see in his detailed

essay *The Scientific Aspect of the Supernatural* (1866) that laudable facility for an open mind that a frustrated Charles Fort found
so lacking in the scientists of his day.

Wallace prefaces his piece with a quotation from Sir John
Herschell (1792–1871): "The perfect observer in any department of science will have his eyes as it were opened, that they
may be struck at once by any occurrence which according to
received theories ought not to happen, for these are the facts
which serve as clues to new discoveries." Herschell, astronomer,
inventor, mathematician, experimental photographer, chemist
and botanist, and father of twelve children, also said, "We must
not impugn the Scripture Chronology, but we must interpret it
in accordance with whatever shall appear on fair enquiry to be
the truth – for there *cannot be two truths*." Will he be proved
wrong? If there are really eleven dimensions as opposed to four,
could there be a different version of the truth in each? Herschell
named seven moons of Saturn and four moons of Uranus, investigated colour-blindness and the chemical power of ultraviolet
rays. And they even named a crater after him on the moon.
What would he have made of the Large Hadron Collider?

So, if strange things are happening, let's keep an open mind.
If we're being visited by alien beings, even if there is, indeed, a
possibility of other dimensions, all we can do at this stage of our
existence is examine the ones in which we live, and go back to
the very basics. Who are we and how did we get here? Let's leave
our clumsy politics and observe some religious phenomena. Can
religion be regarded as part of "the unexplained"? The first
potential answer is that religion relies on *faith*. Therefore,
Christians will faithfully accept that a man, claimed as the Son
of God, was born to a virgin, could turn wine into water and
perform all manner of miracles. The first miracle, the five loaves
and two fish, known as "The Feeding of the 5,000", appears in
all four canonical gospels (Matthew 14: 13–21; Mark 6: 31–44;
Luke 9: 10–17; and John 6: 5–15). Then there's a second
miracle, with the seven loaves and fish, "The Feeding of the
4,000", in Mark 8: 1–9 and Matthew 15: 32–39, but Luke and
John leave it out. Add to these feats walking on water and the
keystone of Christian faith, the Resurrection, or delve even
further back in the Holy Bible to Moses and the parting of the

Red Sea, the visions of the prophet Ezekiel or the terrors of the Book of Revelation, and to the secular reader the term "unexplained phenomena" has true distinction. To the devoted Bible student, these events are articles of faith.

When it comes to religion's relationship with science, according to the prolific works of the Muslim scholar Harun Yahya, Islam provides extensive lists of miracles in the Qur'an. Just a few of the wide-ranging examples and explanations you will find in the study of the Qur'an include the ozone layer at the poles as the sun rises, cloning, heart massage, the expanding earth, quasars and the gravitational lens effect, and a warning that the sun will eventually expire. As for the solar system, how about this: "Do you not see how He created seven heavens in layers, and placed the moon as a light in them and made the sun a blazing lamp?" (Qur'an 71: 15–16). Not exactly Galileo, but centuries ahead of the stubborn Vatican in the sixteenth century.

Whereas many self-proclaimed "rational" people who adhere to the world's religions may snigger at the paranormal or the unexplained and fall about laughing at the notion of extraterrestrials (ETs), the pillars of their faiths are often constructed of the same phenomena, a richly embroidered tapestry of supernatural legend and miraculous magic. The massed congregations will accept anything their faith commands. As Ignatius of Antioch observed in the first century A.D, "Where the Bishop is, there let the multitude of believers be; even as where Jesus is, there is the Catholic Church." And wherever they all gathered, anything, from visions to miracles, could happen.

On 29 December, the fifth day of Christmas, after having honoured the martyrdom of St John the Evangelist, St Stephen and the Holy Innocents, England's Christians remember yet another martyr – St Thomas Becket (sometimes known as Thomas of Canterbury or incorrectly as Thomas à Becket). For those less familiar with what is a particularly English strand of history, Becket's tragedy was deemed important enough to inspire major playwrights and make it as far as Hollywood. The French writer Jean Anouilh (1910–87) wrote the play *Becket, or The Honour of God*, which was adapted by screenwriter Edward Anhalt (1914–2000) as the 1964 movie *Becket* released by Paramount Pictures. It won the Academy Award for Best

Adapted Screenplay. Starring Richard Burton as Thomas Becket and Peter O'Toole as King Henry II, it contains a variation on that line all British schoolkids were taught (at least back in my distant childhood), "Will no one rid me of this meddlesome priest?" With legendary thespians such as Burton and O'Toole involved, the movie has enjoyed a long shelf-life, with extensive restoration and newly restored prints re-released in 2007. There's even a 3D version, with a new Dolby soundtrack, and it came out on Blu-ray in 2008. So, Becket is important; yet beyond celluloid, he was already the subject of a bizarre religious cult.

Thomas Becket of Canterbury (1118–70) was made a saint in 1173, only three years after his murder, at a time when Rome and Santiago de Compostela in Spain competed as the most popular destination for pilgrims. Canterbury became number two on the pilgrim's tour charts. Astonishing claims and mythical magic made these places of pilgrimage. Legend has it that the apostle Saint James the Greater brought Christianity to the Celts in the Iberian Peninsula. In AD 44 he was beheaded in Jerusalem. Later, his remains were removed to Galicia, Spain. In the third century, after the Romans had been persecuting Galicia's Christians, his tomb was abandoned and its location forgotten. Now another legend arises, that a hermit called Pelayo rediscovered the tomb of St James in 814. How was this discovery made? Pelayo had seen "strange lights in the night sky". Bishop Theodomirus of Iria recognized this as a miracle. He informed King Alfonso II of Asturias and Galicia (791–842). Ever since, the cathedral at Compostela has been a top destination for Catholics.

The murder of Thomas Becket was just what Britannia's Christian pilgrimage business needed. Becket became a huge European cult. Soon, churches were being dedicated to Thomas as far afield as Iceland. He was a charismatic priest who had suffered a dramatic death. We all know about the four knights and his bloody assassination. He had fallen out with his erstwhile friend King Henry II over the relative rights of Church and State, and was sent into exile. Becket remained banished for seven years despite the mediations of Pope Alexander and King Louis VII of France. However foolhardy it seemed, he nonetheless decided to return home. His last words to King Louis were: "I am going to seek my death in England."

At this stage another phenomenal occurrence plays its part. Becket's death was predicted by a young man who had undergone a near-death experience. He had died and by some miracle had been resurrected. He claimed that during the short period he remained "dead" he had been led to the highest circle of the saints. Amidst the apostles he saw one empty throne. He asked the angels whose throne this might be and the heavenly host replied that it was reserved for a great priest from England. King Henry's rash intimation that Becket should be killed was ruthlessly acted upon by the assassins. Yet legend informs us that God's anger and vengeance brought the murderers madness, illness and death whilst others recorded that they all died "true penitents". There are other stories that some of them gnawed their fingers to shreds.

When the murderous knights had left the cathedral, every drop of Thomas's blood was collected. Pots were placed beneath his wounds. Not a drop of blood would be wasted, as it was to have miraculous powers. Still warm, it was smeared on the eyelids of a blind man who instantly recovered his sight. To make the blood go further, it was watered down. In what reads today like an early version of homeopathy, each minute drop was repeatedly diluted so that his blood lasted for centuries. Phials made of tin or lead were worn round the necks of Canterbury pilgrims and the diluted solution was applied for all manner of physical ailments. Petitioning Thomas in prayer also worked wonders – the deaf could suddenly hear, the blind saw, the dead were brought back to life and the lame could walk. Prayers to Thomas revealed the location of a lost horse, a missing loaf of bread was miraculously returned to its hungry owner and, after squeezing himself under railings to lie on top of Becket's coffin, an obese man, by the power of prayer, managed to squeeze himself free again. The miracles continued; a bird that had learned to speak had been taught the phrase "Saint Thomas, help me!" Whilst being chased by a hawk, the talkative fowl uttered the plea, the pursuing hawk fell dead and the bird escaped.

So is there a boundary between all these articles of faith and the modern fascination with the paranormal, UFOs, spiritualism and ghosts? What people are still prepared to believe would seem to confirm some kind of connection. If you thought the seemingly irrational beliefs of the Middle Ages were long gone, think again.

MEASURING A CIRCLE:
WHO MADE US?

It is difficult to keep Charles Fort at arm's length when attempting to study the world of the unexplained, but his highly quotable words can be irresistible: "Wise men have tried to understand our state of being, by grasping at its stars, or its arts, or its economics. But, if there is an underlying oneness of all things, it does not matter where we begin, whether with stars, or laws of supply and demand, or frogs, or Napoleon Bonaparte. One measures a circle, beginning anywhere." It's a big circle. There are a number of worldwide organizations who firmly believe in an idea touched upon by Fort: "We are property." That is, we're either being supervised (or even "farmed") by extra-terrestrials, or alternatively, we're descended from them. Ever since the first great UFO flaps of the 1940s and 1950s, from George Adamski onwards, contactees have been inundating us with messages concerning the watchful benevolence of the aliens. Because humanity is perceived to be making a hash of things, the Aetherius Society (www.aetherius.org) tells us that:

> The Cosmic Masters, our spiritual elders from other worlds, have come again to help us in our time of need. They have delivered their messages to the political and religious leaders, and have been ignored. They come now to you, with compassion and desire to help. They come with great hope, offering mystical tools of white magic that can give you the spiritual power available only to advanced adepts centuries ago.

Then we have the premier league of UFO enthusiasts, the Raelians, who have a message from space for us all. Their website (www.rael.org) informs us:

Thousands of years ago, scientists from another planet came to Earth and created all forms of life, including human beings, whom they created in their own image. References to these scientists and their work can be found in the ancient texts of many cultures. Due to their highly advanced technology, they were considered as gods by our primitive ancestors and often referred to as "Elohim" which in ancient Hebrew meant "Those who came from the sky".

Like many such convenient interpretations, this would not sit well with some Hebrew scholars. According to the *Dictionary of Deities and Demons in the Bible* (1999):

The word Elohim occurs more than 2,500 times in the Hebrew Bible, with meanings ranging from "god" in a general sense (as in Exodus 12: 12, where it describes "the gods of Egypt"), to a specific god (e.g. 1 Kings 11: 33, where it describes Chemosh "the god of Moab", or the frequent references to Yahweh as the "elohim" of Israel), to demons, seraphim, and other supernatural beings, to the spirits of the dead brought up at the behest of King Saul in 1 Samuel 28: 13, and even to kings and prophets (e.g. Exodus 4: 16). The phrase *bene elohim*, usually translated "sons of God", has an exact parallel in Ugaritic and Phoenician texts, referring to the council of the gods.

So it isn't that simple. But Elohim is ancient, arguable and mysterious, and therefore slots in nicely as an archaic prop for a new religion. Earth's conduit for the alien angels, Rael, is an ex-racing car driver, singer and songwriter, born as Claude Vorilhon on 30 September 1946 in Vichy, France, who was raised in Ambert by his aunt and grandmother. He's a big advocate for intelligent design, which we're about to examine.

Compared to the scattered infantry platoons espousing the non-existence of global warming, the massed ranks of creationism are a mighty Panzer Division, hell-bent on flattening Charles Darwin, Richard Dawkins and anyone else in their path. Their factions are legion: here's a list – if we start with the Flat Earthers we can progress (or regress, as your particular position dictates) to the Philosophical Materialistic Evolutionists, with Darwin at the helm:

Flat Earthers believe that the earth is flat. It's covered by a solid dome. Waters above this dome were responsible for Noah's flood. All this is a result of a very literal reading of the Bible, so when the good book mentions the "circle of the earth" or the "four corners of the earth" then that's good enough evidence that we're all horizontal. They don't have many followers these days, but you can get in touch at: International Flat Earth Society, Box 2533, Lancaster, CA, USA.

Geocentrists take us back to the days of Galileo. They'll agree that our planet is spherical, but for them, the earth doesn't move and the sun is not the centre of the solar system. Their theory on the flood coincides with that of the flat earthers and is once again a literal reading of the Bible. Both factions echo ancient Hebrew cosmology. Geocentrists are thin on the ground, but one of their champions, Tom Willis, managed to get the Kansas elementary school curriculum altered to exclude science methodology, evolution and earth history. Based in Cleveland, Ohio, you'll find them at http://www.csama.org.

Young Earth Creationists (YEC) are very influential. They also interpret the Bible literally and tell us that the earth is 6,000 to 10,000 years old. Adam and Eve's misbehaviour in the Garden of Eden resulted in our experiencing death and decay. The YEC interpretation of geology relies on Noah's flood. They insist all life was created in six days, but they're OK with a spherical earth and heliocentric solar system. Their seminal book, *The Genesis Flood* (1961) advances the ideas of the Seventh Day Adventist, George McCready Price. On page 232 the book suggests that earth's original soils were created appearing old. You'll find them at http://www.icr.org and Institute for Creation Research, El Cajon, CA, and several other locations. They even run the Creation Evidences Museum in Glen Rose, Texas.

"The Omphalos argument" was introduced in 1857 in a book by Philip Henry Gosse (1810–88). The idea here is that the earth was created young, but given an "appearance of age". Gosse, an English naturalist and advocate of natural science, is an interesting character. He's known for inventing the seawater aquarium and spent much of his time studying marine biology. Gosse's book *Omphalos*, attempts to merge the geological theories of Charles Lyell (1797–1875) with the Bible's account of creation. Lyell was a British lawyer and acclaimed geologist. He wrote the classic *Principles of Geology*, expounding James Hutton's concepts of *uniformitarianism* – suggesting the earth was shaped by slow-moving forces that are still current. Gosse is sailing in dangerous waters, though, because Lyell was a close and influential friend of Charles Darwin. Gosse's son, the critic and poet Edmund Gosse (1849–1926), wrote of his father as a somewhat tyrannical religious autocrat in his psychological masterpiece *Father and Son*. The Gosse position is that the universe was created young but with the necessary appearance of age. The family were devoted members of the Protestant sect, the Plymouth Brethren, which also had among its members the occultist Aleister Crowley, the adventurous drug user and practitioner of Magick, portrayed by the media of his day as "the wickedest man in the world". Crowley considered the Brethren's teachings and practices as essential for understanding his views.

Old Earth Creationists make some attempt at accommodating their religion with science. They generally accept that there was an ancient earth, although they firmly believe life was specially created by God, and they still base their beliefs on the Bible. "Gap creationism" (aka "restitution creationism") says that there was a lengthy gap between Genesis 1: 1 and Genesis 1: 2. After the gap, God created the world in the regulation six days. This appears as a pretty tidy outlook, because it accommodates both the biblical and Old Earth notions, so presumably everyone's happy.

Day-Age Creationists take the novel view that each of God's days of creation had a length of many thousands or even millions of years. They give mainstream science a nod because they think it can be paralleled with the events in Genesis 1. This is the position held by the Jehovah's Witnesses, which is set out in their publication *Life – How Did It Get Here? By Evolution or Creation?* (1985).

Progressive Creationists accept much of modern physical science, and even accept the Big Bang theory, although it is said to represent the power of God. However, Progressive creationists take a negative position on modern biology. They insist God sequentially created earlier organisms, which fossil records reveal, but that later organisms were specially created, and therefore not related to the ancient variety. There's more on this at www.reasons.org.

Intelligent Design Creationists follow the theory formulated in 1803 by William Paley. He used the analogy of a watchmaker to demonstrate that nature's adaptation and complexity represent God's benevolent and perfect design as a benefit for humanity. He had much influence on many scientists in his day, and even Darwin himself wrestles with the concept. However, modern intelligent design creationism (IDC) explores microbiology and mathematical logic in its attempts to verify Paley's original position. IDC has become an umbrella beneath which all manner of creationists can attack science, and their central belief is that the idea of evolution equals philosophical materialism (www.discovery.org/csc).

Evolutionary Creationists (ECs) do not believe that Adam was the first biological human – he was simply the first man to be spiritually aware. Their position is that nature is totally dependent on God's will and has no existence outside it. They will agree with Genesis, and the differences between theistic and evolution ECs are theological, not scientific. Many conservative (evangelical) Christians following evolutionary creationism view God as being more actively involved in evolution. They allow that the events of creation occurred, but not in time as we recognize it today (www.orot.com/ec.html).

Theistic Evolutionists include the Pope, and Theistic Evolutionism is even included on the curriculum in some Protestant seminaries. The position is that God creates through evolution. The level of God's intervention in this creation varies among Theistic Evolutionists. They accept a lot of modern science, but when it comes to the soul, science has to give way to God. How much God intervenes in the creation process is subject to fluctuating opinions.

Methodological Materialistic Evolutionists take the view that God stays out of evolution or at least doesn't get in the way. This branch is not altogether atheistic. Some Materialistic Evolutionists believe God created evolution. Materialistic Evolution has two strands: philosophical and methodological materialism. Methodological materialism simply describes our natural world with natural causes, leaving out the supernatural, neither denying nor affirming its presence.

Philosophical Materialistic Evolutionists (PMEs) are the *bête noir* of traditional biblical creationists, for whom Richard Dawkins, bestselling author of *The God Delusion*, almost equates to Beelzebub. He refuses to accept that the supernatural exists. To the PMEs, evolution – and everything else – is a natural process.

BEYOND THE BIBLE: NON-CHRISTIAN CREATIONISM

As with Christianity and the Bible, Islam today takes a literal view of the Qur'an. Muslims regard their holy book as the direct and unaltered word of Allah, and they consider Genesis to be a corrupted version of God's message. That said, accounts of the creation appear in several surahs or chapters (2: 109–111, 7: 52–7, 16: 1–17, 40: 66–70, 41: 9–12, 42: 28, 65: 12), and they accommodate several possible interpretations. As for the Buddhists, they seem happy with the theory of Evolution. Simple life forms evolved and changed until the creatures we know today existed. Even the Dalai Lama moves with the scientific times, as he is quite willing to accept scientific thought over Buddhist myths if new scientific discoveries throw up a conflict.

BUGS FROM SPACE

The term *Panspermia* originated in the writings of the fifth-century BC Greek philosopher Anaxagoras. Sir Fred Hoyle (1915–2001) and Chandra Wickramasinghe (born 1939) followed this hypothesis that bacteria trapped in space debris may lie dormant whilst traversing the universe, but if they land on a suitable planet they can become reactivated and begin the process of evolution. The jury is still out on this one, as many scientists doubt that bacteria can survive in space. Those who believe it can, however, suggest that life forms entering the earth's atmosphere could well be responsible for those most popular of media "we're all doomed" fixations – new diseases and epidemic outbreaks. See Fred Hoyle and Chandra Wickramasinghe, *Evolution from Space: A Theory of Cosmic Creationism* (1981; www.panspermia.org).

WHEN WORLDS COLLIDE

Meteorites, asteroids colliding with earth and worldwide volcanic eruptions all figure here. Catastrophic evolution suggests that evolution occurred suddenly, a result of extreme, planet-wide catastrophes. Geologist Michael Rampino at New York University, in an essay in the journal *Historical Biology* on 9 November 2010, claims that Charles Darwin's theory of gradual evolution is not supported by geological history. Rampino advocates a more accurate theory of gradual evolution, suggesting long periods of evolutionary stability were devastated by catastrophic mass extinctions of life, an idea originally put forward by Scottish horticulturalist Patrick Matthew (1790–1874). Matthew was a farmer who published the principle of natural selection as a mechanism of evolution twenty-five years before Charles Darwin and Alfred Russel Wallace, yet never got around to publicizing his theory. Darwin and Wallace knew nothing of Matthew's work when they published their ideas in 1858. See also Immanuel Velikovsky, *Earth in Upheaval* (1955).

THE HINDU VIEW

The Hindus have a variety of views on creation. Scriptures suggest humans have "devolved" or come down from a higher state of pure consciousness. Hindu creationists believe the universe may be billions of years older than current science suggests and that humans may have existed even trillions of years ago. Their view is probably the ultimate "ancient earth" creationism. However, the Hare Krishna people – the ones in the robes with the drums and bells, the International Society for Krishna Consciousness (ISKCON) – whilst not necessarily rejecting evolution altogether, have no faith in Charles Darwin's theory of evolution by natural selection.

THE GREAT SPIRIT: NATIVE AMERICA

Native American creationism encompasses a number of creation stories. Before delving into this, it is worth considering an example of the difficulties and obstacles that the descendants of America's original indigenous peoples face, surrounded as they often are by Christian fundamentalism, when attempting to research and preserve their own spiritual heritage. To the Conquistadors and the Pilgrim Fathers, blinded by their arrogant, religious self-assurance, the natives of the New World represented little more than uncultured savagery. Europeans considered themselves to be model patriarchal societies and decided that this was the only way to go for the "Indians". For example, assessing the new races he had discovered, Christopher Columbus reported back to King Ferdinand and Queen Isabella of Spain:

> They should be good servants and of quick intelligence, since I see that they very soon say all that is said to them, and I believe that they would easily be made Christians, for it appears to me that they had no creed. Our Lord willing, at the time of my departure, I will bring back six of them to your Highness that they may learn to talk.

Thus, the first Native American group Columbus came across, the 250,000 Arawaks of Haiti, he violently enslaved. Within half a century, only 500 Arawaks were left alive, and were extinct by 1650. The European view was that only the rich should own land, and their attitude to personal wealth and ownership contrasted vastly with those of Native Americans. The Indians did not believe property to be a personal possession to own; it was owned collectively by the tribe. They believed the land to be sacred, with everything on the earth given by the Great Spirit for all to share. A French Jesuit, writing in 1657, said, "Their kindness, humanity and courtesy not only makes them liberal with what they have, but causes them to possess hardly anything except in common." Yet the idea of a Native American culture, despite the fact that those indigenous people had lived there for around 15,000 years, had to be stamped out. The rest, if you read Dee Brown's *Bury My Heart at Wounded Knee*, is bitter, tragic history. As "political correctness" has appeared to blossom on the tree of "civilization" we imagine this might indicate that some belated respect for the Native American heritage has developed over the past half-century. Has it?

On 28 July 1996, Will Thomas and David Deacy, a couple of spectators at the annual hydroplane races at Kennington, Washington, found a skull on the bank of the Columbia River. Together with the rest of the unearthed remains, this became known as the Kennewick Man, a prehistoric (Paleo-Indian) discovery. Tests on what has proved to be one of the most complete ancient skeletons ever found have shown the bones to be somewhere between 5,650 and 9,510 years old. This triggered a decade-long struggle between lawyers, archaeologists and the federal government. The law stated that if human remains are found on federal lands, then according to the Native American Graves Protection and Repatriation Act, if a Native American tribe can establish that the remains were affiliated to their culture, then the tribe could lay claim to them. The Umatilla tribe stepped forward and sought custody, in order to be able to bury the skeleton according to tribal tradition. Their claim was contested. With an oral history stretching back some 10,000 years, the Umatilla have been around the Washington area for a long time. For the US government to contend that Kennewick Man was not a Native American appeared to be a rejection of the Umatilla's religion. Joseph Powell, an anthropologist at the University of New Mexico said that the skull was "unlike American Indians and Europeans" and hinted at a Polynesian origin. Considering the already tragic history of Native America, this kind of rejection seems par for the course, and to add insult to injury, the skeleton remains legally the property of the US Army Corps of Engineers, as the remains were found on land under its custody. Soldier Blue wins again. Kennewick Man's bones are still being studied, and on a more flippant note, the reconstruction of his features based around his skull reveals a dead ringer for Captain Jean-Luc Picard of *Star Trek*, as played by actor Patrick Stewart.

There are hundreds of different groups under the heading "Native Americans". In terms of creationism, many of these share a view that there were once giants walking the earth and that there was little or no difference between humans and animals. Once a golden age existed; when this ended in a blaze of fire, the result of worldwide volcanic activity, life forms began to shrink in size. But that's just one version. From nation to nation, Apache to Sioux, there are variations. Anyone who has read a decent western novel or seen a reasonable movie about Native Americans (thin on the ground though such films are) will be familiar with the Great Spirit, Wakan Tanka and the Four Winds, etc. For the Sioux, Wakan Tanka is a term meaning "divine" or "sacred". The Lakota Sioux, however, do not have a "One God", monotheistic religion. Many interpret Wakan Tanka more as "Great Mystery". Yet to attempt an overview of all the variations here would take several chapters. However, as a sample, here's a creation myth from the Cherokee.

Once there was a great ocean in which floated an island. It was suspended from the sky – which was solid rock – on four thick ropes. People did not exist and it was permanently dark. There were animals, however; so in order to see they took hold of the sun and set it on to a regular east–west path. The Great Spirit instructed the animals and the plants that they should remain awake for seven days and seven nights. But some were too tired and fell asleep. Among the plants which managed to stay awake were the cedar and the pine, so the Great Spirit gave them a reward – they could stay green all year round. The rest had to lose their leaves each winter. Those animals that had managed to stay awake, such as the mountain lion and the owl, received the gift of being able to go around in the darkness. After all this was settled, the humans appeared.

Elsewhere in the world, you'll find more creation myths than you can shake a stick at. The Finns believe a teal laid some cosmic eggs from which the sun, moon and everything else emerged. Then there's the Norse gods, the myths of the Mayans, Aztecs and Incas, the creation according to many Indian religions, the Greeks, the Romans, the Ancient Egyptians, the list goes on and on. Many, as we shall see, involve people from the sky. For example, in India's Vedic literature descriptions of flying machines called "Vimanas" are common. India's national epic, the Mahabharata, is a poem of vast length and complexity. According to Russia's Dr Vyacheslav Zaitsev, a contributing scientist to the magazine *Sputnik*, "the holy Indian Sages, the Ramayana for one, tell of 'Two-storeyed celestial chariots with many windows'. They roar off into the sky until they appear like comets." The Mahabharata and various Sanskrit books describe at length these chariots, "powered by winged lighting … it was a ship that soared into the air, flying to both the solar and stellar regions." Make of this what you will. Myth? Legend? Fanciful historical embroidery?

In general, most of current humanity accepts these stories of creation for what they are; but to those who take their holy books literally, the very word "myth" is an insult punishable by damnation or death. Many Orthodox Jews reject evolutionary theory. To them, the Bible is the truth. They feel that, if they agree with evolution, the current theory may well be overturned in a century or so, so they cannot reconcile Darwinism with the Bible. Some Orthodox Jews even ban any texts on evolution. The Orthodox Jewish scholar Natan Slifkin wrote books on science and the Torah, and had them banned in 2005 by prominent ultra-Orthodox Rabbis, because they regard Slifkin's views as a challenge to Jewish faith. Other Jews think differently and consider that the biblical version of creation doesn't stack up as it fails to explain the complexity of life, whilst they question the notion of a God who could have created a world with so many design faults. Of course, one doesn't need to be Christian, Jew, Native American or Muslim to tinker around with the creation or Darwin.

TOP GUN MEETS
SATURDAY NIGHT FEVER

According to various internet reports, it is alleged that in the late 1940s the science-fiction writer L. Ron Hubbard declared: "Writing for a penny a word is ridiculous. If a man really wants to make a million dollars, the best way would be to start his own religion." And so he did. It's called Scientology. It gets a real kicking across the globe from anti-cultists, so the best way to discover what its main tenets are is to go to the fountainhead at www.scientology.org. Here's the basics:

You are an immortal spiritual being.

Your experience extends well beyond a single lifetime. And your capabilities are unlimited, even if not presently realized.

Furthermore, man is basically good. He is seeking to survive. And his survival depends upon himself and his fellows and his attainment of brotherhood with the universe.

Does Scientology have a God? Definitely, as L. Ron Hubbard wrote in his *Science of Survival:*

No culture in the history of the world, save the thoroughly depraved and expiring ones, has failed to affirm the existence of a Supreme Being. It is an empirical observation that men without a strong and lasting faith in a Supreme Being are less capable, less ethical and less valuable to themselves and society ... A man without an abiding faith is, by observation alone, more of a thing than a man.

Scientology, with around nine million adherents, including such stars as Tom Cruise and John Travolta, claims to be the fastest-growing religion in the world. So far, so good. Unlike the rising vogue among many Christians for the total acceptance of biblical creationism, in Scientology, as its extensive and impressive website tells us: "this view flows from the theory of theta (the life force, or spirit) creating MEST" (Matter, Energy, Space and Time). In fact, it could be said that the creation of the universe is an inseparable part of that theory. The origins of theta and the creation of the physical universe set forth in Scientology are described in *The Factors*, written by L. Ron Hubbard in 1953 (price $250, yes, *two hundred and fifty* ... but free shipping). Since discovering *The Factors*, after revisiting the Scientology website, the book appears to have vanished, although at the time of writing I notice Amazon.com have two used copies available from $13.99.

In his description of alien interventions in our past lives and extra-terrestrial civilizations, L. Ron Hubbard used the term "space opera". Scientologists believe that we are immortal spiritual beings known as "Thetans". We're simply trapped here on earth in our "meat" body. When he passed away in 1986, his death was announced by the Church of Scientology to the effect that he had discarded his physical body and was now "on a planet a galaxy away". Yet to be fair, that's not a light year away from the Christian notion of going to heaven. As with most religions headed by a single charismatic leader, either dead or alive, it does seem remarkable that the thoughts and ideas of one person can be unquestioningly accepted by millions of people. Hubbard's story of humanity is heady stuff. For example, seventy-five million years ago, the leader of the Galactic Confederacy, Xenu, is said to have dumped several billion frozen people on the earth. These hapless frosty folk were piled around volcanoes, then came explosions from hydrogen bombs and the result was a race of wandering, disembodied alien souls – Body Thetans. Xenu is only one element of Scientologist beliefs in alien civilizations. Apparently we've been invaded by a legion of insect-like creatures about 6,000 BC known as the Fifth Invader Force.

There is no denying that as an author of science fiction, L. Ron Hubbard was a major figure in the genre. His books have sold millions, and have been translated into over twenty languages. Of course, that's no excuse for turning one of his bestsellers into a celluloid turkey – John Travolta's ill-starred *Battlefield Earth*. The sad, striking fact about what many regard as "the worst film ever made" (until *Human Centipede 2* came along) is that its British director, who won an Oscar for his work on *Star Wars*, had the somewhat incongruous name Roger Christian.

There are those who refer to Scientology as a "cult". Yet the dictionary reveals the following meanings of the word:

> a particular system of religious worship, especially with reference to its rites and ceremonies ... an instance of great veneration of a person, ideal, or thing, especially as manifested by a body of admirers ... a group or sect bound together by veneration of the same thing, person, ideal, etc. or a group having a sacred ideology and a set of rites centring around their sacred symbols.

The word comes from the French *culte* or Latin *cultus*, "worship". So if Scientology is a cult, why are Buddhism, Christianity and Islam "religions"? People choose what they want to believe in and that's their business. International banking is a cult with profit as its godhead. For those of us still wandering down the spiritual corridor of life, trying all the doors en route to find enlightenment, providing the Jehovah's Witnesses or the Mormons desist from knocking on our doors when we're watching TV, we're prepared to listen and learn – in our own time, thank you.

The Nabob of Godlessness, Richard Dawkins, unlike Salman Rushdie, appeared to be insulated by his fame when he claimed, "Science flies you to the moon; religion flies you into buildings." But there may well be elves in the woods and trolls under bridges though I have yet to see the evidence. However, I can't disprove it. Squirrels are good at hiding, too, and I've never seen a baby pigeon. If that makes me an agnostic, or in dire need of an exorcist, then Lucifer's on a roll.

Faith and religion aside, there is undoubtedly strangeness in our world. It's a bizarre, fascinating universe. Let's fasten our seat belts and take a look ...

PART 2:

HOT CHESTNUTS – UFOS

Our moods do not believe in each other.

Ralph Waldo Emerson (1803–82)

LOVING THE ALIEN

They're watching us more carefully ... Already they are becoming bolder, leaving imprints and other evidence of their landings on earth. When they are convinced that we can accept their reality they will formally make themselves known, and that will be fairly soon.

Gabriel Green (1924–2001),
candidate for the US Presidency,
on extra-terrestrial beings, in 1966

"To those who have, even more shall be given" (Matthew 13: 12). Look, I have a bone to pick with the aliens. I have been waiting to see a UFO all my life, and still they elude me. That doesn't mean I don't believe. But Victoria, the zillionaire, too-cool-to-smile spouse of international British soccer legend David Beckham, has been visited by what certainly seems to have been a UFO hovering above the Beckhams' palatial Los Angeles home. She went straight on to Twitter and tweeted "UFO hovering above our house last night!" The tweet was accompanied by a pretty impressive picture of what the media called "the extra-terrestrial sighting" (if, indeed, it was an ET). As if this level of celebrity wasn't enough for the Cosmic Masters, coiffeur supreme Ken Paves, Victoria's Beverly Hills hair-stylist, also saw it, and sent the ex-Spice Girl a tweeted warning: "UFO hovering above Beckham's house. Grab the kids @victoriabeckham and RUN-RUN @victoriabeckham RUN!"

Of course, some ill-informed sceptics were straight on the case to announce that what the sullen fashionista *Vogue* cover-girl had seen was the moon. Wrong. There's more to Mrs Beckham than Roberto Cavalli and posh perfume. The lesser members of Joe Public should have checked their lunar calendars, because the moon wasn't due out over LA on Halloween night, 2011. Then again, it could be a fashion statement; another LA glamour puss, "Skyscraper" chanteuse Demi Lovato, had seen one a couple of weeks earlier over Tinseltown and she, too, twittered. Victoria will not be outdone. As we shall learn, when celebrities see flying saucers, they make the news.

This frustrating yet highly entertaining subject, by necessity, occupies the larger part of this work because it is the most predominant of all modern phenomena. It encompasses many mysteries, has been examined, catalogued, recorded and argued over for the past seven decades, and grows new and more sinister branches with each passing year. In 2012 a new development in the strange changing nature of UFOs is continuing apace. The very shape of the prolific "flying saucer" image in dozens of new reports seems to have morphed from a disk into the now ubiquitous "flying triangle" with three lights. Early in 2012 more reports have come in of these from across Europe, with Belgium continuing to be a favourite location. Stealth bombers? Unknown new aircraft developments? They could be – but Stealth bombers don't hover and remain stationary in the sky.

Over the past fifty years, the graphic image of the flying saucer along with that of the grey-skinned, bulbous-headed, black-eyed alien have entered human mythology and must now surely share the status of the old-time witches on broomsticks, bogeymen, gargoyles and goblins. UFOs are the new, technical, nuts and bolts fables, representative of our electronic age, the true descendants of the fairies at the bottom of the garden and the *Flying Dutchman*. The extra-terrestrial hypothesis suggests that the sudden global emergence of the UFO, coinciding as it did with the advent of the atomic bomb in the mid-1940s, is generally regarded by ufologists as an indication of the interest shown in our planet by benevolent (or otherwise) races from across the universe. If this hypothesis has any credence, then it would appear that their sporadic incursions into our airspace prior to Nagasaki and Hiroshima were simply tourist jaunts. Once we earthlings developed the worrying ability to blow ourselves to kingdom come, the "space brothers" decided to monitor us more closely. This is, however, just one of numerous hypotheses.

There is also a dark undertow of conspiracy theories connected to the subject, which inevitably leads us to questions about governments, military research into anti-gravity, so-called "black operations" and the genuine mystery which is Nevada's Area 51. Our imaginations are fed by the possibility that in some cave, hangar or decommissioned missile silo, there may well be the cryogenically preserved remains of real aliens. There are many dedicated researchers who have been beavering away at this theme for decades and who have reached the conclusion that the aliens – origin unknown – are not simply curious tourists. Some suspect they are already here, among us, disguised in human form. Alongside the more open-minded are the growing legions of "New World Order" conspiracy theorists. The doyen of this group is the British ex-footballer David Icke. Whatever his critics say about him, one thing's for sure: Icke is sincere. He's utterly devoted to his theories and enjoys sold-out tours that attract millions of faithful fans around the globe. His blog is often witty and very entertaining, and watching him speak in his marathon full-day sessions, you can't fail to be impressed. Maybe he does know something. Prediction-wise, he certainly gets it right sometimes. For example, in his hefty 1999 book (one of many), *The Biggest Secret*, he predicts that the "New World Order" could well kick-off (courtesy of the shady Bilderberg Group) in 2012 – with "a global financial collapse" plus "conflicts and terrorism galore". Here we are, over a decade since that prediction, and he seems to be correct. Icke believes that the UFO phenomenon is a huge, manufactured scam. However, it is the sheer fantastic nature of Icke's wider claims that tend to deny him broader credibility. For example, that the British royal family, and most world leaders, aren't really human at all but shape-shifting alien amphibians – lizards. Whilst looking at most of our slimy politicians, shape-shifters or not, one could agree that there's something of the dank swamp about them, but Icke's claim, made early in his career as a prophet of doom, tended to convince many that his cheese had probably slipped off his cracker. Then he gives credence to a hoary old chestnut known as Project Blue Beam, a suggested conspiracy formulated by NASA to implement a New Age religion and a New World Order, via a technologically simulated Second Coming.

Blue Beam was the brainchild of a Canadian Quebec separatist, the late poet, writer and journalist, Serge Monast. It was supposed to happen in 1983. Surprise, surprise, it didn't. So, in the time-honoured fashion of most "prepare to meet thy maker" merchants, the date was altered to 1995. No show. Then again to 1996, but unfortunately, that was the year Monast succumbed to the Rapture, so sadly he never lived to see NASA's failure to deliver in the final year he settled on – 2000. How would NASA pull off this great holographic hoax? Proponents of the theory allege it would be done using the High Frequency Active Auroral Research Program (HAARP). This is an ionospheric research project, based in the Arctic, jointly funded by the University of Alaska, the US Air Force and the US Navy, and an organization known as DARPA – the Defense Advanced Research Projects Agency. Apparently, they would use the skies as an immense cinema screen and, using projected holograms and lasers, convince us all that fleets of UFOs were approaching and that the Lord was about to appear in the Second Coming. Then we would all be placed under martial law and would be required to bow down to one world religion. The amazing thing is that so many sane people are willing to accommodate such bizarre bunk without resorting to their common sense and delving a little deeper. As Marcus Tullius Cicero (106–43 BC) commented: "I wonder that a soothsayer doesn't laugh whenever he sees another soothsayer." They probably don't because few of them have much of a sense of humour.

UFOs: A Persistent Enigma

The Unidentified Flying Object must be the ultimate icon of Forteana. UFOs easily defy the sensible rule "seeing is believing". I haven't seen one, but despite a world-weary cynicism towards many other aspects of the unexplained, when it comes to flying saucers, I believe. Any devout sceptic attending the 3 April 2011 "Secret Space Program" conference at the Zonnehuis in Amsterdam may well have entered the venue with a cynical sneer, yet some of the revelations made by speakers such as America's Richard C. Hoagland and the UK's leading ufologist, Timothy Good, warrant serious consideration, not ridicule. Hoagland (although much maligned) is a former NASA consultant, space science museum curator and, during the historic Apollo Missions to the moon, was science advisor to Walter Cronkite and CBS News. Together with Timothy Good and other speakers he confirmed that the one-time jokey media subject of UFO/alien presence is a tangible and genuinely disturbing phenomenon, the true details of which are being deliberately kept secret from the public. The UFO lobby's position is this: the hidden details could have such far-reaching consequences for humanity that the subject has remained above top secret among world governments, especially in the United States, for decades. The cordon of security around UFOs surpasses even that of all forms of nuclear weaponry research and the level of disinformation spewed out by intelligence agencies as a smokescreen to confuse the public is immense. Possessing an attitude bordering upon agnostic in many aspects of the paranormal, accepting the contents of lectures and books by Good and Hoagland may suggest dumb gullibility. However, it is the frivolity engendered by the spoon-fed media around this subject over the past half-century that has managed to achieve a major aim of the official worldwide "cover-up" – the branding of anyone taking a close, serious interest in UFOs as some kind of credulous nut. Those like Good and Hoagland who have devoted decades to their research, however, have teased out of this cat's cradle of disinformation several tendrils of truth; for example, that the skilfully obscured budgets for so-called "black operations" and the research into bizarre, advanced technology are enormous, well into many billions of dollars – both public and corporate money. Yet although, as "one of us" – a genuinely puzzled non-scientific observer – Timothy Good's dedication and depth of knowledge deserves respect, we still have to remain wary of authors such as Hoagland. They start their writing career by raising valid questions and revealing genuine anomalies upon which they can speculate. Then, as their literary output increases, so does their readership's demand for sensation. Hoagland would appear to have inadvertently pandered to this demand with some of his current ideas, as will be revealed in a later section on astronomy.

Without doubt, many UFO/alien reports can be classed as baloney and are worthy of a good chuckle. But not all, by a long measure. There's an inner child in all of us, so as I sit here at my desk in the East Midlands I frequently gaze through the window and scan the sky, sending out telepathic messages in the hope that something solid and glittering (other than an Ibiza-bound airliner from East Midlands Airport) will appear and have me reaching for the camera. On Friday nights, after returning from the weekly shopping at the supermarket, I will sit in the dark in the garden with a bottle of beer and a cigar, head craned back, gazing at the stars. I feel that one day "they" will make an appearance. It hasn't happened yet, but it has happened to many thousands of others, even among some close friends. Yet that's a cosy romantic view of the subject. The deeper you dig, the romance dissolves into something totally disturbing. Little wonder that this is the greatest unexplained phenomenon of our age.

Despite all the tongue-in-cheek jiggery-pokery via Photoshop, the hoaxes and flashy YouTube videos cobbled together by an international cabal of PC nerds, sniggering over their mousepads in a million bedrooms, if we take just the 1 per cent of reports and sightings that are definitely unexplained, we still have a huge file of genuine phenomena. Since the advent of the increasingly sophisticated cell phone, with its built-in camera and video facility, even allowing for much of the ersatz ufology available on the internet, some of the footage, often shot spontaneously by puzzled members of the public, is truly amazing. There is definitely something "out there" – or, more disconcertingly, "in here".

There has been some speculation that UFOs are simply a product of our minds. Some investigations into the subject have reached the conclusion that what is referred to as the "right-brain" of an individual "reifies" the UFO, thus making the abstract idea or concept real; this reification leads to the objects being visible to other people. Although this idea, along with the concept of mass hallucination, cannot be totally dismissed, it does leave the prickly conundrum of half a century of photographs, and latterly video, often impulsively taken by startled individuals for whom the idea of a UFO may have been nowhere near their right or left brain.

Of course, when it comes to credibility for UFO reports, it certainly helps if the witness is one of the following: a policeman, a doctor, an academic, a prominent politician, a pilot, a scientist, a military leader or an astronomer. Fortunately, plenty of such witnesses exist, but in the main the aliens do seem to have an odd penchant for appearing to the ordinary Joe: lumberjacks, farmers, kids out on their bikes, motorists on lonely roads. It's an idea Steven Spielberg ran with in his masterful *Close Encounters of the Third Kind*, so the alien sense of mischief, appearing to some hapless old guy out walking with his dog, might explain why they've never landed on the White House lawn. Where would be the fun in that?

Before we levitate into orbit, it seems relevant at this juncture to set out the toolkit basics of ufology's lingua franca. The term "close encounters" has its origins in the US Air Force's early investigation into UFOs, Project Blue Book. As their scientific advisor, the USAF commissioned the astronomer Dr Josef Allen Hynek (1910–86). Hynek, horn-rimmed glasses, goatee beard, dedicated pipe-smoker, was the ultimate professor of ufology. However, it took him a long time to exit from the debunkers' camp. The USAF was constantly keen to propagate its theory that UFOs did not exist, and Hynek admitted that the time he spent debunking was enjoyable. Yet he became increasingly annoyed at the lack of scientific methodology demonstrated by the Air Force, as he slowly realized that a significant percentage of the reports he was called upon to study were genuinely inexplicable. Once he had left Blue Book, he conducted his own independent UFO research, developing the Close Encounter classification system, and is widely considered the father of the concept of scientific analysis of both reports and, especially, trace evidence purportedly left by UFOs. His system is included here for the sake of clarity:

CE1K: Close Encounters of the First Kind

In a CE1K, the UFO appears to be less than 500 feet (150 m) away from the witness and features of the object can be made out such as lights, windows, markings, doors, etc. However, the

UFO has no effect on the surrounding environment and leaves no quantifiable traces of its presence. An example of a CE1K is the Exeter case in New Hampshire, where several ground witnesses spotted a red, glowing object near the ground, but it left no trace.

CE2K: Close Encounters of the Second Kind

These are amongst the most compelling cases studied, since in a CE2K the UFO leaves trace evidence or causes effects in the environment and the witnesses. CE2Ks are very important in ufology, as there is some sort of physical evidence that is left that can be studied and analysed. Other characteristics of a CE2K case are interference with electrical equipment or car engines, effects on a person can be felt, and effects on animals. Why some close encounters are of the first kind and some are of the second kind remains a mystery. Examples of CE2Ks are the Valensole Case, the Coyne Case, the Falcon Lake Case and the Cash-Landrum Incident, all of which are well documented on the internet.

CE3K: Close Encounters of the Third Kind

This is where the witness actually observes occupants or animate objects onboard the UFO or around it. These are the proverbial "little green men" cases, although the occupants observed aren't necessarily little, green or men. These cases generally tend to be the hardest to prove, as the occupants seldom leave any sort of evidence. However, some very solid CE3K cases exist from reliable witnesses, such as the Kelly-Hopkinsville Incident, the Gill Sighting and the Socorro Case.

CE4K: Close Encounters of the Fourth Kind

More commonly known as an alien abduction, the CE4K is where the witness is taken aboard the UFO, usually against their will but sometimes at an invitation, where they are subjected to medical experiments, tests and strange scenarios created by their abductors.

There is also a CE5K. This occurs to many UFO witnesses in the days following their sighting and usually involves being visited by a strange character or characters, claiming to be government officials, who issue warnings and threats to persuade you not to speak of your experience. We'll look more closely at this bizarre mythos later.

Dr (aka Professor) Hynek was also the consultant Steven Spielberg employed for his 1977 movie, *Close Encounters of the Third Kind*, with a non-speaking appearance in the film towards the finale, when he steps forward from the crowd, smoking his pipe, to view the aliens disembarking from the "mother ship". Hynek died aged seventy-five on 27 April 1986 of a malignant brain tumour at Memorial Hospital in Scottsdale, Arizona. Ufology owes him much. As a passing point of interest, his son, Joel Hynek, is an Oscar-winning sci-fi movie visual effects supervisor, responsible for the design of the "camouflage" effect in the Arnold Schwarzenegger movie, *Predator*.

At the First International UFO Congress in Chicago, Professor Hynek put forward three hypotheses regarding the origin of UFOs. His third hypothesis amply demonstrates the adventurous range of his thinking.

I hold it entirely possible that a technology exists, which encompasses both the physical and the psychic, the material and the mental. There are stars that are millions of years older than the sun. There may be a civilization that is millions of years more advanced than man's. We have gone from Kitty Hawk to the moon in some seventy years, but it's possible that a million-year-old civilization may know something that we don't ... I hypothesize an "M&M" technology encompassing the *mental* and *material* realms. The psychic realms, so mysterious to us today, may be an ordinary part of an advanced technology.

As a reasoned, albeit speculative analysis of the UFO question, this could well prove in the years to come to be a major key in unlocking this persistent enigma (read more in Curtis Fuller, *Proceedings of the First International UFO Congress*, 1980). The possibility remains, however, that Hynek's hypothesis may well have been in active service with the US military. In an article by Tom Keller, an aerospace engineer, in the May 2010 issue of the *Mufon UFO Journal*, Ben Rich (1925–95), the former head of

Lockheed Skunk Works (the corporation's secret research and development arm) credited among military aviators as the "Father of the Stealth Fighter-Bomber", appears to have revealed some telling information about the military's possible connection with ETs and UFOs. If what Rich said just before he died was true, it could explain much:

> We already have the means to travel among the stars, but these technologies are locked up in black projects, and it would take an act of God to ever get them out to benefit humanity. Anything you can imagine, we already know how to do. We now have the technology to take ET home. No, it won't take someone's lifetime to do it. There is an error in the equations. We know what it is. We now have the capability to travel to the stars. First, you have to understand that we will not get to the stars using chemical propulsion. Second, we have to devise a new propulsion technology. What we have to do is find out where Einstein went wrong.

Asked how UFO propulsion worked, he responded with his own question; "Let me ask you. *How does ESP work*?" His interviewer suggested, "All points in time and space are connected?" Rich then said, "*That's* how it works!" It's intriguing, it's also vague (and it could be disinformation) but there just might be something there. However, if what Ben Rich said is valid ... *why* are we still using chemical propulsion to get into orbit?

Here, There and Everywhere

Mexico seems a popular destination for the ufonauts. Some of the mass sightings over Mexico City in recent years, available on YouTube, are truly mind-bending. *Inexplicata* is the journal of the Institute of Hispanic Ufology (IHU), which studies the paranormal sky anomalies in the Caribbean, South America and Spain. In 1994 members of the IHU met with European researchers at the Santo Espíritu del Monte monastery in Valencia. There, led by French investigator Pierre Delaval, they established the Project Delphos Manifesto. Project Delphos had one channel of research as its purpose; it aimed to prove that a great many UFO sightings were of an "inter-dimensional or Para physical nature – directly the opposite to the tenets of the ETH or Extra-Terrestrial Hypothesis". The initiative was spearheaded by the Commission d'Études Ouranos, which champions the belief that humankind has long been under the scrutiny of a non-human intelligence from another dimension or level of existence. Spain's Pedro Valverde and Ramón Navía, co-sponsors of the initiative, expressed the belief that "an extra-planetary force interferes in human affairs and with human minds, thwarting natural evolution since the beginning of time".

Even though some might regard this notion as hogwash, there remains the question: if UFOs are real, and they are not extra-terrestrial, then where *do* they come from? The suggestion emanating from the CERN experiments in Europe that other dimensions may exist is by no means a new idea. Schoolteacher Stephen Jenkins, the author of a truly disturbing book, *The Undiscovered Country* (1977), spent much of his time studying the mystery of ley lines in Britain and their connection to UFOs. He had some scary, bizarre experiences. Jenkins had also visited Tibet. His conversations with Tibetan Buddhist monks revealed that they believed that there were no fewer than six "realms of being", and that we mere mortals are only living in two of them. So what's going on in the other four? In May 1969, one of Britain's top military men, Air Marshal Sir Victor Goddard, discussed the puzzle of UFOs with the British Interplanetary Society. According to author Colin Wilson, in his book *Mysteries* (1978), "Goddard commented that there was no need to assume that UFOs were visitors from other planetary systems; they might come *from an invisible world that coincides with the space of our own*" (Wilson's italics). And before we even get to the subject of alien abductions, Goddard's suggestion is just one example of what makes this branch of the unexplained such engrossing territory to explore; we're dealing with something almost too huge to comprehend.

A BRIEF HISTORY OF UFOS

Though a good deal is too strange to be believed, nothing is too strange to have happened.

Thomas Hardy (1840–1928)

There are three camps in the UFO field. The largest is probably occupied by the gullible, the irrational – those ordinary innocents who want to believe at any cost. In the middle stand the rationalists; they seek to analyse and explain, and many of this camp's more astute occupants will go to extreme lengths in examining every case; what remains after they've filtered the primary sources is material they will dub as "unexplained" – that's when you can write a book about them. The third camp consists of the sceptics. They are powerful, rigorously thorough party-poopers hell-bent on a mission to debunk just about everything, no matter what, from spoon-bending to spiritualism, from ghosts to near-death experiences. The more prominent, academically qualified members of this latter camp will often come under fire from the first camp – the gullible – as being a sponsored part of that suggested worldwide, government and military-backed "cover-up" operation. So with each UFO report, both old and current, anyone with a serious interest in this subject should always visit the sceptics, pay careful attention and be prepared to have their own irrationality exposed. UFO reports are like dirty snowballs. They begin as a snowman's button – a bit of coal – and as they roll down the snowy hill of time they gather layer upon layer of fallacy. Be warned.

UFOs are no new phenomena. They have been making their appearance throughout recorded history, and since the mid-twentieth century they've become almost a daily event. The problem is where do we begin? We could simply list the most recent sightings, but in order to understand the way UFOs are perceived in the twenty-first century, we need to take on board Oliver Wendell Holmes' comment that "A page of history is worth a volume of logic." However, finding logic in UFO reports is not always easy.

Before the invention of photography, in which we still place so much faith when investigating UFO incidents, we simply had the written testimonies of such strange events buried in much larger texts, and sometimes appearing as mysterious images in medieval woodcuts such as one illustration featuring no fewer than forty UFOs that appeared over Basle in Switzerland on 7 August 1566. It was discovered in Zurich's central library by no less a luminary than the famed psychologist Carl Jung, who devoted much of his later studies to the phenomenon of UFOs. There's a strange depiction of what's claimed to be a "flying carpet" in the 1478–89 Cologne Bible. The Egyptians, in a scroll dated around 1500 BC, describe a circle of fire in the sky, followed by the arrival of others which landed, then took off again. There are some weird aboriginal cave paintings in Australia, and all manner of designs and assorted artefacts throughout South America, from stone spheres to anachronistic solid gold aeroplanes, all beloved of the von Däniken school of "Was God an Astronaut?" The Romans referred to UFOs as "burning shields". We have already touched upon the Vimana – the ancient Indian flying machines mentioned in the Mahabarata. Well, there's almost as much literature available on Vimanas as there is on the Wright brothers or Concorde. According to a book by David Hatcher Childress, *Vimana Aircraft of Ancient India and Atlantis* (2004), the "Vaimanika Sastra" (or "Vymaanika-Shaastra"), a manuscript discovered in a temple, features eight detailed chapters with diagrams, covering various kinds of aircraft, thirty-one essential parts of these vehicles and sixteen construction materials capable of absorbing light and heat. The technical drawings were added later by an engineering draughtsman, although sceptical Indian aeronautics experts give them the thumbs-down. However, if you want to answer Tom Waits's eerie question, "What's he *building* in there?" you could have a go at assembling your own Vimana, as Childress tells us that this document has been translated into English and is available by writing to the publisher: the book details are Maharishi Bharadwaaja, *Vymaanidashaastra Aeronautics* (edited by Mr G. R. Josyer, director of the International Academy of Sanskrit Investigation, Mysore, India: G. R. Josyer, 1979). You can save the shipping costs by just keying "Vymaanidashaastra Aeronautics" into a search engine and you'll discover various offers of a free download. However – and there's always a "however" in ufology – the one thing missing from the handy workshop manual is the propulsion method to get you levitated. But a smart Vimana would make a nice conversation piece in your garage or garden. Whilst you're online, take a look at the Great Stupa at Sanchi, India. It's been suggested that this immense building's design was based on a Vimana and an Indian flying saucer. As Charles Fort said: I offer the data. You decide.

BIBLICAL UFOS

If we go back half a millennium before the birth of Christ, we can read in the Old Testament of the Holy Bible (I'm using the King James Version) the peculiar Book of Ezekiel. Ezekiel was a Hebrew prophet exiled as a prisoner from Jerusalem to Babylon. I make no apologies for including the complete verses 1–28 from Chapter 1 of Ezekiel, because outside of their religious context, they are one of the most celebrated pieces of "ancient astronaut" lore available. Every ufologist of an archaeological bent will tell you that what Ezekiel experienced was a close encounter of the biblical kind, and one of NASA's major engineers, Josef F. Blumrich, in his book *The Spaceships of Ezekiel* (1974), suggests, in some technical detail, that what the prophet saw was indeed an interplanetary craft. Blumrich's prognosis makes for an engrossing read, but he is limited by his own scientific experience – he generally stays in the box of rocket propulsion, and although the algebraic calculations and diagrams are obviously the work of a highly skilled technician, four decades and countless new sightings on, the possible conclusion is that whatever powers UFOs, it certainly isn't NASA-style rocket fuel. Read on, and may the force be with you.

The Book of Ezekiel Chapter 1

1) Now it came to pass in the thirtieth year, in the fourth month, in the fifth day of the month, as I was among the captives by the river of Chebar, that the heavens were opened, and I saw visions of God.

2) In the fifth day of the month, which was the fifth year of king Jehoiachin's captivity,

3) The word of the LORD came expressly unto Ezekiel the priest, the son of Buzi, in the land of the Chaldeans by the river Chebar; and the hand of the LORD was there upon him.

4) And I looked, and, behold, a whirlwind came out of the north, a great cloud, and a fire infolding itself, and a brightness was about it, and out of the midst thereof as the colour of amber, out of the midst of the fire.

5) Also out of the midst thereof came the likeness of four living creatures. And this was their appearance; they had the likeness of a man.

6) And every one had four faces, and every one had four wings.

7) And their feet were straight feet; and the sole of their feet was like the sole of a calf's foot: and they sparkled like the colour of burnished brass.

8) And they had the hands of a man under their wings on their four sides; and they four had their faces and their wings.

9) Their wings were joined one to another; they turned not when they went; they went every one straight forward.

10) As for the likeness of their faces, they four had the face of a man, and the face of a lion, on the right side: and they four had the face of an ox on the left side; they four also had the face of an eagle.

11) Thus were their faces: and their wings were stretched upward; two wings of every one were joined one to another, and two covered their bodies.

12) And they went every one straight forward: whither the spirit was to go, they went; and they turned not when they went.

13) As for the likeness of the living creatures, their appearance was like burning coals of fire, and like the appearance of lamps: it went up and down among the living creatures; and the fire was bright, and out of the fire went forth lightning.

14) And the living creatures ran and returned as the appearance of a flash of lightning.

15) Now as I beheld the living creatures, behold one wheel upon the earth by the living creatures, with his four faces.

16) The appearance of the wheels and their work was like unto the colour of a beryl: and they four had one likeness: and their appearance and their work was as it were a wheel in the middle of a wheel.

17) When they went, they went upon their four sides: and they turned not when they went.

18) As for their rings, they were so high that they were dreadful; and their rings were full of eyes round about them four.

19) And when the living creatures went, the wheels went by them: and when the living creatures were lifted up from the earth, the wheels were lifted up.

20) Whithersoever the spirit was to go, they went, thither was their spirit to go; and the wheels were lifted up over against them: for the spirit of the living creature was in the wheels.

21) When those went, these went; and when those stood, these stood; and when those were lifted up from the earth, the wheels were lifted up over against them: for the spirit of the living creature was in the wheels.

22) And the likeness of the firmament upon the heads of the living creatures was as the colour of the terrible crystal, stretched forth over their heads above.

23) And under the firmament were their wings straight, the one toward the other: every one had two, which covered on this side, and every one had two, which covered on that side, their bodies.

24) And when they went, I heard the noise of their wings, like the noise of great waters, as the voice of the Almighty, the voice of speech, as the noise of an host: when they stood, they let down their wings.

25) And there was a voice from the firmament that was over their heads, when they stood, and had let down their wings.

26) And above the firmament that was over their heads was the likeness of a throne, as the appearance of a sapphire stone: and upon the likeness of the throne was the likeness as the appearance of a man above upon it.

27) And I saw as the colour of amber, as the appearance of fire round about within it, from the appearance of his loins even upward, and from the appearance of his loins even downward, I saw as it were the appearance of fire, and it had brightness round about.

28) As the appearance of the bow that is in the cloud in the day of rain, so was the appearance of the brightness round about. This was the appearance of the likeness of the glory of the LORD. And when I saw it, I fell upon my face, and I heard a voice of one that spake.

UFO, spacecraft, or indeed, the Lord himself and his angels? It all depends what you are looking for. Either Ezekiel did actually see the Heavenly Hosts, witnessed something really weird or maybe he'd been at the temple wine.

HOVER –
YOU'RE ON CAMERA ...

We had to wait until the nineteenth century and the invention of photography before we could see UFOs the way we see them now. 12 August 1883 is an important day in UFO history. Although by the nineteenth century the telescope had made huge advances and astronomers were making remarkable discoveries, the usual reaction if any interstellar anomaly was seen would be to declare it as a meteorite or a comet. But on that historic day in 1883, atop an 11,000-foot- (3,353 m) high mountain, at the Zacatecas Observatory in Mexico, the observatory's director, José Bonilla, was engrossed in a study of sunspots. His innovation was a camera attached to his telescope so that he could keep a record of the important images. Then he witnessed something very peculiar. Luminous shapes seemed to be passing across the sun's face. At first he imagined he was hallucinating, so he put his camera into action. He later reported that he had snapped images of spherical shapes making their trajectory across the sun, throwing out brilliant slipstreams of bright light, then becoming opaque and eventually dark against the glaring solar backdrop. He had taken the first ever UFO pictures, one of which he described as displaying a five-pointed star with a dark centre. Unwittingly, Bonilla had provided the first permanent and visible technical (as opposed to artistic) proof of something that had been puzzling stargazers for centuries. He had not exactly started a craze, but within the next seventy years, cameras around the world would be aimed at the heavens, and many of the images they caught are no closer to being explained than they were in 1883.

Ten years later, well into the age of the telephone, the telegraph and a burgeoning printed media, weird things start happening. In the Pacific Northwest, the headlines from 3 July 1893 in the *Tacoma News Ledger* newspaper (founded by R. F. Radabaugh in 1880 and today known as *News Tribune*, in Pierce County, Washington) proclaimed: "Electric Monster Sighted by Fisherman". You can read the full, detailed and chilling original report at www.ufosnw.com/documents/electricmonst/electricmonstnew.pdf, but here's the basic outline.

On 2 July 1893 several fishermen, including auctioneer William Fitzhenry, H. L. Beal, W. L. McDonald, J. K. Bell, Henry Blackwood "and two eastern gentlemen who are visiting the coast", had travelled on their sloop, the *Marion*, to Black Fish Bay. Asleep in their camp, they were awakened in the middle of the night by what they described as "an electric monster" that sent out waves of light and electrical charges whilst making a terrifying loud sound. Their watches stopped and some of the men were rendered unconscious as the others, terrified, ran off. Eventually the scared men went back to discover their friends had regained consciousness with no injuries.

This mysterious, detailed and sinister report is the first known documented encounter with a UFO in the Pacific Northwest. However, the full report contains many fantastic aspects, such as jets of illuminated water "like blue fire" and an electrical discharge making them feel as if "each man had on a suit of clothes formed of the fine points of needles". The complete report reads like a mix of the Loch Ness Monster combined with something mechanical, and it remains one of ufology's genuine curios.

MYSTERIOUS AIRSHIPS,
NOVEMBER 1896

From 1871 until the end of the nineteenth century there were dozens of strange reports around the world of mysterious, unidentified "airships". Of course, the balloon and the dirigible were, by 1900, in development. As early as 19 September 1783, the Montgolfier brothers in France had already sent the first living beings aloft in a balloon when the *Aérostat Réveillon* hauled up an attached basket containing a somewhat scared trio of farmyard balloonists: a sheep called Montauciel ("Climb-to-the-sky"), a chicken and a duck. But the reported celestial travellers of the great airship flap of 1896 were neither poultry nor mutton.

The innovative French writer Jules Verne, who arguably shares the title "the Father of Science Fiction" with H. G. Wells, had already fired the public's imagination for unorthodox travel, known as his *Voyages Extraordinaires* (extraordinary voyages), with *Journey to the Centre of the Earth* (1864); he then went extraterrestrial the following year with *From the Earth to the Moon*, before astutely predicting the atomic submarine in his *Twenty Thousand Leagues Under the Sea* (1869). Verne's big balloon-trip yarn, *Around the World in Eighty Days*, was a publishing sensation in 1872. Count Ferdinand von Zeppelin, who had been impressed by the Union Army's use of balloons whilst he was a military observer during the American Civil War, was already working on his dirigible designs. So, in the decades before the Wright brothers took off from Kitty Hawk, the idea of people in the sky was firmly lodged in the public's mind.

UFO sightings come in waves or, as we often glibly refer to them, "flaps". In the last decade of the nineteenth century the idea of the UFO as we now accept it was not current, so anything inexplicable seen in the air was inevitably referred to as an "airship".

The 1896 flap began with the newspapers the *San Francisco Call* and the *Sacramento Bee* reports of 18 November 1896, with these headlines: "Strange Tale of Sacramento Men Not Addicted to Prevarication" and "Viewed an Aerial Courser as it Passes Over the City at Night". Witnesses claimed to have seen a slow moving light over Sacramento on the overcast, rainy evening of 17 November. Its height was estimated at 1,000 feet (305 m). A dark shape beyond the light featured in many reports. Among the men "not addicted to prevarication" was George Scott, an assistant to the Secretary of State of California, who persuaded colleagues to join him on the observation deck above the State Capitol dome. R. L. Lowery, another witness, claimed he heard a voice from the craft issuing commands to go higher to avoid colliding with a church steeple. Lowery added, "in what was no doubt meant as a wink to the reader", that he believed the apparent Captain to be referring to the tower of a local brewery, as there were no churches nearby. Lowery seems to have seen more than anyone else, claiming that the airship was powered by two men on bicycle pedals, whilst above them was a compartment for passengers. Others said that the airship crew were singing as they drifted by with their bright light shining down from the craft's front end.

COWBOYS, ALIENS ...
AND ZEPPELINS

Soon, similar events were being reported across the United States. Some featured landings, and conversations held with what were said to be eccentric occupants. Many stories turned out to be hoaxes. The Wild West was replete with colourful campfire fabricators and some newspapers dismissed many stories as the "freemasonry of liars". One tall story in particular gained much attention, when some dubious fantasists in Aurora, Texas, claimed to have murdered the "spacemen" crew of an airship.

However, in April 1897, what could have probably been one of the first instances of aerial (as opposed to alien) abduction occurred when Alexander Hamilton reported that he'd seen a cow abducted by an airship at LeRoy in Kansas. This case has gone into UFO lore, yet the tale represents that stubborn unreason displayed by many convinced believers, because Hamilton eventually admitted to being a member of the LeRoy Liar's Club, and confessed he'd told a tall porky only a few days after the initial press reports.

However, the mysterious airships, with their powerful lights and strange buzzing noises, continued to dominate the skies and the newspapers for the next decade, appearing over Britain, New Zealand and elsewhere, until in 1912 Winston Churchill was asked to respond to a question asked by William Joynson-Hicks in the House of Commons, London, on 18 November. It concerned the mystery of an airship sighting over Sheerness in Kent on 14 October. According to *The Times* of 28 November 1912, J. E. B. Seely, the Minister for War, did not appear to have any information concerning a "Zeppelin dirigible passing over Sheerness on the night of October 14, about 8 p.m.". Churchill, who was at that time First Lord of the Admiralty, had no information either, but he made inquiries. He eventually reported to the Commons that he could not say whether it was an airship or an aeroplane, nor could he identify its nationality; he could only say that it was "not one of our own airships" and it was definitely "not British". Count von Zeppelin responded with his own declaration – it was "not German", although the German Zeppelin *L1* had made a flight that day over the North Sea, yet its logbook reports it had landed in Berlin sometime between 3.30 and 4 p.m., long before the Sheerness sighting. Zeppelin or UFO? We may never know.

Before what we'll refer to as the "classic" age of UFOs, which began in the 1940s, during the first half of the twentieth century there was no shortage of sightings, and many of the earlier ones were covered by Charles Fort in his books. Yet as ufology developed over the last half-century, the slipshod reporting style of the pre-internet age became less acceptable. Therefore I intend to skip over three decades to cut to the more celebrated events. If this leaves you feeling cheated, then you need to scan through a whole list of sightings in 1900–1940 online at www.bibleufo.com. Quite often the early reports lack authoritative provenance and include a lot of recycling and press embroidery, but they remain nonetheless engrossing.

THE LOS ANGELES INVASION, FEBRUARY 1942

On the night of 24–5 February 1942, air raid sirens sounded throughout Los Angeles County. Thousands of air raid wardens turned out and a total blackout was ordered. Multiple searchlight beams pierced the black firmament. At 3:16 a.m. the 37th Coast Artillery Brigade aimed their weapons skywards and began firing 12.8-pound anti-aircraft shells at what they believed to be enemy aircraft, possibly Japanese. Before the night was out, they would fire over 1,400 shells. Pilots of the 4th Interceptor Command were alerted but their planes never took off. At 4:14 a.m. the guns fell silent and the "all clear" was sounded, with the blackout order lifted at 7:21 a.m. None of the ammunition had any effect. What was it they had been firing at? Witnesses around LA had reported a large, dark hovering object, which had been drifting down the California coast. The local correspondent for the *Herald Express* reported that although the many shells fired at the object were on target, it remained undamaged and untroubled; it eventually moved off at a stately pace between Santa Monica and Long Beach before performing the usual UFO trick – disappearing.

As the defensive action had got under way, observers in Pasadena were seeing strange red lights on the horizon, moving in erratic patterns. The report sent by the US Chief of Staff, General George Marshall, to President Roosevelt concluded that no bombs were dropped, no planes were shot down and no American planes were in action. It stated that "as many as fifteen airplanes may have been involved, flying at various speeds ... from "very slow" to as much as 200 mph and at elevations from

9,000 to 18,000 feet". There were no military casualties, but several buildings were damaged by friendly fire, three civilians were killed by the anti-aircraft fire and as a result of the stress of the hour-long bombardment, three died of heart attacks. In the end, the whole incident was put down to "war nerves" – not surprising as, on 23 February 1942, the Imperial Japanese Navy's submarine *I-17*, under the command of Commander Nishino Kozo, surfaced and pumped sixteen shells (most of which missed) towards the Ellwood oil refinery near Santa Barbara. Britain's most balanced ufologist, Jenny Randles, reminds us perceptively in her book *UFOs and How to See Them* (1992) that those few days of LA panic were parodied in Steven Spielberg's film *1942*. As a trivial afterthought to that fact, the film starred John Belushi, who went on to star with Dan Aykroyd in *The Blues Brothers*. Aykroyd's character's name? Elwood.

On 11.11.11 (spooky!) a movie entitled *Battle – Los Angeles* was released, which according to the website www.reportthreats.org appears to be loosely inspired by the 1942 event. In this film, the earth is under attack. These are not Spielberg's benevolent, spindly aliens playing five harmless notes on a Casio keyboard – they're more the kind of tetchy critters we've already seen in *Independence Day*. As ever, the brave US Marines make their last stand, this time in Los Angeles. Strange how the inexplicable mystery of UFOs can echo western fears: al-Qaeda and the Taliban in flying machines? Hooray for Hollywood – a bit of celluloid milk and cookies, and we can all go to bed sans nightmares … but leave the light on, just in case.

TULAGI, THE SOLOMON ISLANDS, 12 AUGUST 1942

The testimony of Stephen J. Brickner, a sergeant with the 1st US Marine Division, makes its appearance throughout UFO folklore and is also featured in the hugely impressive book, *Above Top Secret: The Worldwide UFO Cover-up* (1988), by the dedicated British researcher Timothy Good. Brickner's actual words make fascinating reading.

The sightings occurred on Aug. 12, 1942, about 10 in the morning while I was in bivouac with my squad on the island of Tulagi in the southern Solomons, west of Guadalcanal. It was a bright tropical morning with high banks of white, fleecy clouds. I was cleaning my rifle on the edge of my foxhole, when suddenly the air raid warning was sounded. There had been no "Condition Red". I immediately slid into my foxhole, with my back to the ground and my face turned up to the sky. I heard the formation before I saw it. Even then, I was puzzled by the sound. It was a mighty roar that seemed to echo in the heavens. It didn't sound at all like the "sewing-machine" drone of the Jap formations. A few seconds later, I saw the formation of silvery objects directly overhead.

At the time I was in a highly emotional state; it was my fifth day in combat with the Marines. It was quite easy to mistake anything in the air for Jap planes, which is what I thought these objects were. They were flying very high above the clouds, too high for a bombing run on our little island. Someone shouted in a nearby foxhole that they were Jap planes searching for our fleet. I accepted this explanation, but with a few reservations. First, the formation was huge, I would say over 150 objects were in it. Instead of the usual tight "V" of 25 planes, this formation was in straight lines of 10 or 12 objects, one behind the other. The speed was a little faster than Jap planes, and they were soon out of sight. A few other things puzzled me: I couldn't seem to make out any wings or tails. They seemed to wobble slightly, and every time they wobbled they would shimmer brightly from the sun. Their colour was like highly polished silver. No bombs were dropped, of course. All in all, it was the most awe-inspiring and yet frightening spectacle I have seen in my life.

FOO FIGHTERS AND
GHOST ROCKETS, 1944–6

"Foo" was a bit of nonsense invented in the early 1930s by American cartoonist Bill Holman who used the words frequently in his "Smokey Stover" fireman cartoon strips in the *Chicago Tribune*. Holman said he'd "discovered" the word on the base of a Chinese figurine. But by 1944, as the Second World War raged, radar operators were using the term "foo" for any anomaly that crossed their screens. The US 415th Night Fighter Squadron first used the term "foo fighter" when they encountered mysterious aerial phenomena when flying over the Pacific and over Europe. For a while after 1944 it was generally thought that these rapidly manoeuvring balls of light, which accompanied aircraft, were some kind of new weapon invented by the Nazis. Some pilots reported foo fighters flying alongside them for over half an hour. Attempts to shoot them down were futile, and they would usually depart by zooming straight up into the sky. After the war, it was revealed that the Luftwaffe were just as mystified by these phenomena as the Allies, so the suspicion they were of Nazi origin was dismissed. Holman's cartoon character Smokey Stover had a catchphrase; "where there's foo, there's fire" so his "foo" might well have been derived from the French word for fire, "*feu*".

Immediately following the Second World War, beginning in the spring of 1946, close to a thousand sightings were reported of mystery rockets in the skies over Sweden. Described as silver, some with fins, metallic, issuing regular bursts of flame, with an estimated average speed of about 3000 km per hour, those which fell to earth usually crashed into lakes. When one did hit the ground, some debris was recovered. However, the origin of the rockets was never explained. On 3 January 1988, the Dutch historian Gerard Aalders published an article on the rockets in *Dagens Nyheter*, Sweden's largest morning newspaper, wherein one suggestion was that when the Russians had taken Germany's V2 rockets as war trophies back to the USSR, they had decided to experiment with them. There is one peculiar section of Aalders's article that deals with the analysis of a sample of the fragments found from one of the crashed rockets:

> 98% of the sample consisted of a thus far, unfortunately *unknown* material. Traces of nickel, copper and iron made up the remaining 2% of the secretive fragment. With the remaining 98% the experts were facing an enigma. Now suddenly the Russians seemed to have access not only to fantastic rockets but also to a new material that chemists couldn't analyse!

Dubbed by the media as "ghost rockets", they led to much international wrangling and cold war diplomacy, yet the projectiles remain a mystery to this day.

THE COMING OF THE PIE PLATES, JUNE 1947

24 June 1947 is a major milestone in the UFO story. On that day pilot Kenneth Arnold, a businessman who sold fire-fighting equipment, was flying his private CallAir mountain plane (NC33355) near Mt Rainier, Washington, when he spotted nine disk-shaped objects. Arnold described the motion of the objects as being "like a rock skipping over water". Thus the term "flying saucers" entered the twentieth-century lexicon. But here comes the inevitable "however" ... Because Arnold's bestselling book, *The Coming of the Saucers* (1952, written with the prolific writer/publisher Ray Palmer, a genuinely fascinating character – check him out at www.thelivingmoon.com), adopts the word "saucers", most ufologists have come to accept that Arnold coined the term. As ever, it was the press, who made his experience front-page news by 26 June 1947, who were actually responsible. Here's what they called Arnold's anomalies as they possibly mangled his words:

United Press: "They were shaped like saucers and were so thin I could barely see them ..."

Associated Press: "He said they were bright, saucer-like objects – he called them 'aircraft' ... He also described the objects as 'saucer-like' and their motion 'like a fish flipping in the sun' ... Arnold described the objects as 'flat like a pie pan'."

Associated Press: "like a fish flipping in the sun".

> *Chicago Tribune*: "They were silvery and shiny and seemed to be shaped like a pie plate ..."

The following day Arnold is reported in the *Portland Oregon Journal* as saying: "They were half-moon shaped, oval in front and convex in the rear ... there were no bulges or cowlings; they looked like a big flat disk." On the same day there were more sightings by other witnesses of a similar kind in Washington, Oregon and Idaho. So had the term "pie plate" been repeated often enough, that might well have become the UFO's regular name.

During the summer of 1947, it is estimated that around 1,000 reports of UFOs were made. The first big "flap" was on. Many of these sightings involved objects comparable to those sighted by Kenneth Arnold. By the time *Fate Magazine* came out in spring 1948, the term "flying saucer", featured on the front cover with Arnold's retold story, had become the catch-all term for any airborne anomaly.

Few cases have been the subject of as much rancorous argument and controversy as that of Arnold. In recent years it has been argued that what he really saw was a flock of pelicans or a flight of Navy test aeroplanes flying out of Whidbey Island Air Station in Washington State. The late sceptic Philip J. Klass suggested that Kenneth Arnold probably saw meteor fireballs. James Easton was the first to have the temerity to suggest Arnold had seen a flock of American white pelicans, the largest birds in North America. Many saucer fans have been outraged by Easton's conclusion, dubbing it "Pelicanism", which has in some UFO circles become a dismissive term for the attitude of determined sceptics who grasp at any other explanation of UFOs other than the ETH – the Extra-Terrestrial Hypothesis. There have been some serious academic attempts to dissect the Arnold sighting, such as the intricate 147-page investigation by Scotland's Martin Shough, entitled *The Singular Adventure of Mr Kenneth Arnold* (www.debunker.com/arnold.html). Shough is no "pelicanist" although, despite his thorough approach, he reaches no conclusions as to what Arnold *did* see. Harvard astronomer Donald Menzel was the leading light of UFO debunkers. In 1953 he said that what Arnold had seen was snow blown from the mountains south of Mt Rainier. Ten years later, he suggested the sighting was orographic clouds or wave clouds; by 1971, Menzel was proposing Arnold's UFOs were simply spots of water on his cockpit windscreen. Menzel, however, ignored the fact that Arnold had rolled down his window to rule out this possibility; he could *still see* the UFOs. Such bitter denunciation is rife throughout ufology, but it makes for entertaining reading.

For Kenneth Arnold, although he initially enjoyed his spell in the spotlight, the attention soon became annoying. He told the Spokane (Washington) *Daily Chronicle*: "I haven't had a moment of peace since I first told the story." A clergyman had phoned him to say that what he'd seen were "harbingers of doomsday" and that he had told his flock to get ready "for the end of the world". Then Arnold met a distraught woman in a café who shrieked at him, "There's the man who saw the men from Mars!" Arnold said she ran from the café and with a shudder began sobbing, saying she would "have to do something for the children". Arnold was already wound up by the whole business, telling the reporter, "This whole thing has gotten out of hand. I want to talk to the FBI or someone. Half the people look at me as a combination of Einstein, Flash Gordon and screwball. I wonder what my wife back in Idaho thinks." Perhaps it's little wonder that many pilots are told to remain silent after a UFO experience.

One thing's for sure – Arnold unwittingly instigated a whole new cultural genre which would lead to a spate of alien invasion movies, make millions for bandwagon writers (I hope I'm included) and culminate in TV's *X-Files* and dozens of magazines.

THE SUMMER OF 1947

Although it is a milestone, Kenneth Arnold's sighting was certainly not the first of 1947. Twenty years after that frantic summer, Ted Bloecher of the National Investigations Committee on Aerial Phenomena (NICAP) compiled a detailed report of almost 900 cases that arose during 1947, which includes a chronology of every sighting. It was updated in 2005, and the whole 190 pages can be studied at http://nicap.org/waves/Wave47. NICAP's dedication to this subject is staggering. In total, its website contains around a quarter of a million international reports, with a chronology stretching back into the nineteenth century.

June and July 1947 saw hundreds of UFO reports coming in across the United States. NICAP's extensive lists were collected from newspaper articles and some were collected from the official US Air Force's investigation, Project Blue Book. As the 1947 flap progressed, the sightings gradually increased from 15 June to early July and then steadily decreased.

UFDS – UNIDENTIFIED FLYING DOUGHNUTS: THE STRANGE CASE OF THE MAURY ISLAND AFFAIR, JULY 1947

Maury Island is a peninsula of Vashon Island, in Puget Sound, near Tacoma, Washington. On Monday, 21 July 1947, a few days before Kenneth Arnold made the news, a less celebrated yet uncanny event was experienced by a proficient sailor, Harold A. Dahl, his dog and his fifteen-year-old son, Charles, who were out in their boat patrolling the Sound. The Maury Island incident has been roundly dismissed by many in the UFO community as a hoax, yet its mere oddness, plus the repercussions and strange connections that followed, make it worthy of including in any catalogue of weirdness.

Dahl and his boss Fred Crisman salvaged driftwood floating in the sea in Puget Sound, helping to keep the waterways clear, and sold the salvaged timber to make a living. Dahl was a big, strong figure, well over six feet tall (1.83 m) and weighing around 230 pounds/104 kg (not that his description is crucial, but it adds some colour).

Around 2 p.m. six identical round objects appeared overhead. (The report to the FBI states four or five.) Dahl described them as having a hole in the centre, like a doughnut or an automobile inner tube. There were large portholes around the outer rim. Reports vary; some say there were portholes lining the *inside* of the ring. One of the doughnuts seemed to be in trouble and the other five encircled it closely. It began to lose height and started a perilous descent in the direction of Dahl's boat. Suddenly, the stricken craft began to eject chunks of material, which was thought to be some kind of slag, from the portholes. This detritus hit the boat's wheelhouse, killed Dahl's dog and damaged a light fitting, as well as injuring poor Charles, who required a visit to the hospital. Dahl said later that he'd taken several photographs of the UFOs (which were indistinct and inconclusive) and recovered some of the slag ejected from the malfunctioning craft, as well as sheaves of white, lightweight metal that fluttered down like paper from the troubled UFO. Some of the slag samples collected by Dahl were sent to Chicago and California for analysis, but legend has it that they "vanished", although a later report tells that a sample was sent to a local Tacoma mill and compared to generic slag from a smelter, the conclusion being that they were very alike.

So far, so good, and that might have been the end of the story. But it wasn't.

ENTER "THE MEN IN BLACK"

The next morning, Tuesday, 22 July 1947, Dahl claimed that a man dressed in a black suit, who he thought to be from the government, arrived at his house in a new 1947 Buick. This noir-clad visitor, the precursor of a sinister new cast of UFO characters, invited him to have breakfast at a local diner. It seems odd that one would go off at breakfast time to eat with a complete stranger, but Dahl accepted. The Man in Black knew all about the Maury Island incident and discussed it with Dahl. But the breakfast was rounded off with an ominous, veiled warning. Dahl realized that his visitor was issuing a threat, and that there might be forbidding consequences for him and his family if he continued to talk about the flying doughnuts.

Those who have experienced a visit from the Men in Black over the past fifty years are taken aback by the depth of detailed information they seem to possess about you, your family and the incident with which you were involved. This leaves people with the uncomfortable feeling that they have been under surveillance for a long time. There are, apparently, two types of these bizarre characters. There is the hail-fellow-well-met type, who seems to take things lightly and enjoy a laugh, yet others seem furtive and threatening. A high percentage of reports about MIBs describes them as being thin, often olive-skinned and Asian in appearance. Some are completely bald with no eyebrows, and seem to be unfamiliar with commonplace items such as cutlery, pens and even various foods. Others have a habit of using odd, anachronistic slang, decades out of date. Whichever kind one meets, however, it appears that their mission is clear – to tell you to stay quiet about your experience or even to convince you that you have not experienced any kind of phenomenon at all. So who are these sinister callers? Often they will show some form of identity claiming to be from some organization, such as the CIA, the FBI or the Air Force, whilst telling you that their job is to enquire about your UFO experience for research purposes. Yet they are frequently threatening. What usually happens is that when those who have been graced by the Men in Black contact the organization they claim to come from, to verify their identity, the answer comes back that no such person exists – and sometimes that they did once exist, but are now deceased. So, if you have a serious UFO experience, listen for the doorbell. It may be your turn next. We'll delve further into the MIB mystery later. Meanwhile, back to Maury Island and Harold Dahl.

Now it gets weirder. After breakfast with the Man in Black, Dahl began putting it around that his reported sighting had been a hoax, but he would later retract this, stating that he'd circulated the hoax story to protect his family. Later, for example, his son Charles left home and went to live in the wilds of Montana, although he may just have been an adventurous soul. According to other researchers, such as John Keel in his book *Our Haunted Planet* (1971), Dahl himself disappeared shortly after being interviewed by none other than the "flying saucer" man himself, Kenneth Arnold, who had been commissioned to look into the Maury Island affair by Ray Palmer of *Astounding Stories*. Keel tells us that, "Dahl … vanished … efforts by later investigators such as Harold Wilkins (1891–1960), a British author, have failed to locate him".

Now Dahl's boss, Fred Lee Crisman, enters the story. No stranger to mysteries, conspiracies and the paranormal, Crisman had already appeared in sci-fi pulp magazines and spent years peddling his story that he had encountered an underground race of aliens called the Deros – short for "detrimental robots". The Deros were already enjoying their time in the spotlight courtesy of Richard Sharpe Shaver, a writer whose name became synonymous with the "Shaver Mystery", which had been eagerly taken on board and published by *Amazing Stories* magazine. Fred Crisman is one of the most enigmatic characters to come out of the Maury Island affair. He's been cited as a CIA agent, among other things, and of all the great conspiracies around the shooting of President Kennedy on 22 November 1963, one legend persists that Fred Crisman was one of the three tramps arrested in Dallas immediately after JFK's assassination – some even suggest he was one of the men on the grassy knoll. Yet the official records say different; the tramps are listed by some JFK theorists as Harold Doyle, John Gedney and Gus Abrams. Others state they were Chauncey Holt, Charles Harrelson and Charles Rogers. Their story was that they were arrested immediately after the assassination. So why does Crisman's name crop up? Their arrest records exist, with "then and now" photographs and positive IDs for all three.

Let's take a breather and examine what we have so far:

- Six flying doughnuts, one damaged.
- A dead dog.
- An injured teenager.
- A damaged boat.
- Samples of mysterious doughnut "slag".
- The unidentified, threatening Man in Black.
- The arrival of Kenneth Arnold.
- The disappearance of Harold Dahl.
- The eventual departure of Charles Dahl.
- The blurred emergence of Fred Crisman.

Is there more? Oh, yes. Tacoma reporter Paul Lance, who helped Kenneth Arnold with his investigation, died shortly after the event. Next, we have a crashed plane, and despite what others have attempted to establish about Crisman, Britain's most respected UFO expert Timothy Good provides more information in his 2007 book, *Need to Know*.

Good tells us that the two pilots of an AAF B-25 bomber, Captain William Davidson and Lieutenant Frank Brown, were both killed when the plane, returning from Tacoma, Washington, crashed near Kelso on 1 August 1947. There were two survivors who escaped by parachute. The dead men were intelligence officers from 4th Air Force Headquarters at Hamilton Field, California. They had interviewed witnesses to

UFO sightings, pilots Kenneth Arnold and Captain Edward Smith, both of whom had become involved with the Maury Island incident. Davidson and Brown had been introduced to Fred Crisman by Arnold and Smith. Good states that Crisman's background was in counter-intelligence (including "black operations" for the CIA). Crisman presented the officers with large chunks of the recovered fragments in a heavy box. At McChord Field the box was loaded on to the B-25. In contrast to the fragments Arnold and Smith had previously been shown by Crisman, which had been metals of an aluminium type, these were different. As both Kenneth Arnold and Captain Smith had gone through some bizarre and unsettling experiences whilst investigating the Maury Island case, the puzzled men began to wonder if the B-25 crash might have had something to do with its cargo.

On page 111 of *Need To Know* there's a footnote:

Arnold, Kenneth and Palmer, Ray, *The Coming of the Saucers*, published by the authors, 1952. Those interested in this case, and in Crisman's extraordinary background – including his arrest in Dallas as one of the three "tramps" following the assassination of President Kennedy – should read *Maury Island UFO: the Crisman Conspiracy*, by Kenn Thomas, IllumiNet Press, PO Box 2808, Lilburn, GA 30048, 1999.

Another persistent tale is that Crisman was subpoenaed to attend as a witness by New Orleans Attorney General Jim Garrison in the trial of Clay Shaw, the only man ever to be tried for the assassination of JFK. The *Fortean Times Paranormal Handbook* offers this tasty morsel:

There is another, more tenuous link between Shaw and UFOs. In 1945, the German rocket scientist Werner von Braun surrendered to Major Clay Shaw and, under Project Paperclip (designed to secure advanced Nazi technology), was brought to the USA. Some believe that the "flying saucers" seen over Maury Island were creations of this alliance; and that this conspiracy went on to engineer the death of JFK, fake moon landings and create bogus aliens.

Some of the Maury Island UFO slag samples, apparently in a cigar box, were presented to *Amazing Stories* publisher Ray Palmer, who claimed that they were stolen from his Chicago office not long after he'd received them. Timothy Good goes on later in *Need to Know* to reveal that President Kennedy was well informed and deeply interested in the UFO situation, and as well as actually meeting ETs in California, he had a secret appointment with George Adamski, the famous UFO "contactee" whose story we will examine in some depth later. So, whatever we think of the Maury Island incident – hoary old chestnut, genuine sighting, hoax, myth, legend – if we consider its strange connections, when it comes to conspiracies, you certainly got value for money with the enigmatic Mr Crisman.

MEN IN BLACK II

Sadly, we need to forget the *Men in Black* movies (1997, 2002 and 2012) starring Tommy Lee Jones and Will Smith. With their jokey CGI aliens, oversized chromium plasma guns and facile plots, these films represent a missed opportunity to examine a genuine phenomenon, a bizarre central theme that runs throughout UFO lore. Truth or fiction, as well as Harold Dahl's visitation by what some believe to be first MIB, there exists a hefty catalogue of such narratives. Many of these reports are so fantastic that they are beyond any frame of reference and naturally will produce little more than incredulity. Some are well documented, many are apocryphal and a number can be termed downright lies.

Although the Harold Dahl episode is often referred to as the first MIB event, John Keel, in his fascinating books *Our Haunted Planet* and *The Cosmic Question* (1971 and 1978, http://galaksija.com/literatura/eigth_tower.pdf), reports the first MIB encounter as early as 1924, long before the great mid-century UFO flaps began. The story came from John Cole, a retired newsman in West Virginia. In 1924 a farmer in West Virginia's Braxton County witnessed an aeroplane crash in a forest. In the early 1920s there were very few planes around. The farmer said that the mysterious plane was without wings and silent, describing its size as "as big as a battleship". Cole called the local sheriff and he arrived with his men. They found the crash site, but were surprised to find half a dozen men already there. Some of them seemed oddly attired for such a location in the heart of a wild forest – some were wearing black suits and ties, others were in shiny overalls. They spoke in a strange, staccato way in an unknown foreign tongue.

The farmer related that some of the sheriff's men were carrying guns and one of them, upon seeing the odd party, exclaimed "By God, they're spies!" and raised his gun. The strangers were all small, not much beyond five feet (1.52 m) tall, olive-skinned, with an Asian appearance. Some of the MIBs hid in the wreck, but one came forward and took control, telling the sheriff that everything was all right; they were there to assess the damage and would issue a full report. The lawman had to admit that no crime had been committed and accepted the situation. Then that usual weirdness kicks into Cole's testimony:

> Here's the real funny part. While I was looking around I spotted a little thingamajig on the ground. I picked it up and decided to keep it. Don't know why I didn't turn it over to one of the foreigners. Anyway, I put it in my pocket. We all finally went away, leaving the foreigners to fuss with their contraption. It didn't look like much of a flying machine. In fact, I don't think it could fly at all. It was like the fuselage of a modern plane, with windows and all. But it didn't have any wings, tail or propellers. I'd say it was at least seventy-five feet long. It filled the whole clearing.

Cole went home to bed but was awakened at 3 a.m. by a loud knock on his door. He had a visitor:

> He was dressed in one of those broad-brimmed hats they used to wear, with those leg wrappings and all. It was a US Army uniform all right. I was in World War I ... except for his clothes he looked just like those foreigners from the airplane. Slant eyes, dark skin, but he was maybe a little taller.
>
> "You picked up something today," he said. "We need it back." I was half asleep and at first I couldn't think what he meant. Then I remembered the metal thingamajig. It was still in my coat pocket. I went and got it. He just grabbed it and walked off without a word.

The visitor had no car or, as was common in the area, even a horse. He just vanished into the night. Cole eventually returned to the crash site but everything had gone, although the trees were smashed where the craft had come down.

John Keel, one of ufology's most widely read and influential authors, became an original and controversial researcher, and is generally regarded as the originator of the term "Men in Black". To Keel, who died aged seventy-nine in 2009 and referred to himself as a "demonologist" rather than an ufologist, these sinister and threatening entities who assume human form to confront UFO witnesses originated from various fantastic sources. He could equally accept the possibility that they were ETs or, as he thought more likely, they could well be "intra-terrestrials" – entities from another dimension or even aliens living in secret bases on earth. However, those prominent cases that stand out do beg the question – why would someone make these stories up and stick doggedly by them? One of the most celebrated MIB events dates back to 1953 and involves a man called Albert K. Bender. But let's try for a commonsense balance before proceeding. Dr Aaron Sakulich, who runs the informative and highly entertaining website theironskeptic.com, is with me on the many contradictions inherent in MIB accounts, stating:

> Obviously, this paradox isn't 100% bulletproof. It's just hyperbole to show that you cannot, and must not, accept the testimony of witnesses as completely true just because you have no reason to suspect they are lying. If you believe every witness that claims involvement with aliens, as so many UFO enthusiasts are wont to do, you're going to be in for one hell of a logical headache. Albert Bender is a reliable witness, and his testimony stands in utter opposition to the testimony of other reliable witnesses. Who is right? Who is wrong?

With this in mind, a brief sample of these accounts is worth inclusion here.

In 1953, Albert K. Bender edited a small publication entitled *Space Review* and ran an organization called the International Flying Saucer Bureau (IFSB). The magazine and the IFSB's membership and circulation were not large. Readers and members were convinced that flying saucers were from outer space and that they, as members of the IFSB, were moving towards some kind of galactic enlightenment, and would soon be in possession of secrets that would change humankind. So they were more than a little puzzled and shocked when the October 1953 issue of *Space Review* hit their doormats. It contained these announcements:

> LATE BULLETIN. A source which the IFSB considers very reliable has informed us that the investigation of the flying saucer mystery and the solution is approaching its final stages. This same source to whom we had referred data, which had come into our possession, suggested that it was not the proper method and time to publish the data in *Space Review*.

> STATEMENT OF IMPORTANCE: The mystery of the flying saucers is no longer a mystery. The source is already known, but any information about this is being withheld by order from a higher source. We would like to print the full story in *Space Review*, but because of the nature of the information we are very sorry that we have been advised in the negative. We advise those engaged in saucer work to please be very cautious.

Bender then unexpectedly wound up the publication of *Space Review* and dissolved the IFSB.

When the news got around that he'd abruptly ended his UFO activities, the local press became interested. In a subsequent interview, he told reporters that he had been visited by "three men wearing dark suits" who issued an "emphatic" warning: stop publishing material about flying saucers. Bender claimed that in the MIB's presence he had been "scared to death" and for two days afterwards he could not even eat anything. Friends and associates tried and failed to get some adequate answers from him regarding his actions, yet Bender only gave vague answers or even refused to respond.

Many suspected that his story was simply a smokescreen to cover up the possibility that *Space Review* and the IFSB were losing money, and that he'd simply invented the Men in Black as a quick escape. However, over the years Bender stuck doggedly to his story and people began to think differently as similar experiences to his were being reported among the UFO fraternity. The general view among many was that the Men in Black were from the Air Force or the CIA. Their manner, their dress sense and their new vehicles suggested some government connection. However, as the reports piled up, Men in Black began to gather a strange air of the supernatural, and some suspected they had an extra-terrestrial or even a paranormal, psychic connection.

In 1963, ten years after his scary visitation, Albert Bender published a book entitled *Flying Saucers and the Three Men in Black*. It was eventually widely available from the Paperback Library (1968) but today remains out of print. This bizarre, almost unreadable tome did not tell us anything new, other than suggesting that the MIBs were, indeed, ETs, with glowing eyes. However, Bender elaborated and added something extra to UFO lore with "three beautiful women, dressed in tight white uniforms". Like their male counterparts, these ET sirens also possessed "glowing eyes".

The great majority of MIB reports are from the period 1966–70. The highest percentage originates in the USA, followed by the UK, and a small number in Europe. Some of the British reports are every bit as odd as their American counterparts.

There's a weird story in the March 1999 issue of Britain's *UFO Magazine*. Jerry Anderson (not to be confused with the TV *Thunderbirds* producer), a researcher with UFO Monitors East Kent (UFOMEK), was involved in looking into the Burmarsh UFO incident of 8 March. During his investigation, he received a letter purporting to come from the RAF, signed by a Wing Commander A. W. Ward. The letter told Anderson in no uncertain terms that he should stop investigating the Burmarsh event. However, Anderson was puzzled because the composition and syntax of the letter seemed at odds with what one might expect from an educated British Wing Commander. It read as if written by a foreigner. Anderson followed up on this, and discovered that there was indeed a Wing Commander Ward, and the airman wrote back to him, in grammatically correct style, and his reply was that he had never written to Anderson in the first place. He then had a visit from men claiming to be officials from the UK TV Licensing authority demanding to see his TV licence, a delight usually only visited upon those who dodged buying one. On 9 February 1999, the postman delivered a cassette of a phone conversation between Anderson and another UFO researcher, Chris Rolfe, which had taken place in January 1998.

Of course, occurrences such as this could easily be pranks carried out by tongue-in-cheek UFO sceptics with a bizarre sense of humour. One such case bound to raise a chuckle was reported in October 2011 in the *Fortean Times* in an article called "Britain's X-Files" by David Clarke. In January 2003, the UK Ministry of Defence (MoD) UFO desk received a report from a woman who said that in the early hours of the morning, with her mother, she had seen lights in the sky above their house in East Dulwich, south London. She'd called Peckham police because she feared the lights might have something to do with terrorism. With the lights still over the house, a patrol car duly arrived, but in addition to two policemen, it contained two men in space suits and sunglasses! They announced themselves as ... Mork and Mindy. These two astro-wags told the women that they shouldn't look at the lights in case they suffered from radiation. They were in possession of something like a Geiger counter, which kept on clicking. They were kindly gents, however; the woman had complained that her eyes were smarting from watching the lights, and they even offered to wash them for her with some special solution. Naturally, she declined the offer. Before they left, Mork and Mindy asked the women for their birth signs, and then issued the usual warning "not to talk to anyone about this and certainly not the press in case it caused panic". The MoD followed up the woman's report of this odd visitation, but the police denied taking Mork and Mindy out on patrol, and rejected all knowledge of a Geiger counter. Apparently the ladies were unaware of *Mork and Mindy*, the Robin Williams TV show, and have remained convinced that the local constabulary were simply out to make them look stupid. If all this is true, it does raise questions. Were the women fantasizing? If not, and if the cops were taking the mickey, where did two of them get space suits and a Geiger counter at three in the morning – in Peckham?

From Mork and Mindy to King Arthur is no great leap in ufology terms. Nick Redfern, also writing in *Fortean Times* in September 2004, tells the bizarre story of a man named Colin Perks, a King Arthur enthusiast who was searching for the mythical monarch's grave. Perks was lucky enough to then receive a visit from someone he referred to as "the most beautiful woman he had ever met", clad in "an expensive-looking black suit", who gave her name as Miss Sarah Key. (One wonders if this interloping beauty was a student of British politics, as there was a prominent Sara Keays who had dominated the media as the mistress of disgraced Conservative politician Cecil Parkinson.) The comely Miss Key seemed to know everything involved with Mr Perks's Arthurian quest in great detail and much besides. She told him she "represented the interests of a number of people within the British Government and the ruling establishment". Apparently, since the Second World War, her official masters had been carrying out their own occult research. Perks was warned that his occupation was "dangerous". He was told to abandon his research, and if he did not, he would "receive another visitor". Ravishing beauty or not, the determined Arthurian did not succumb to her threat. He carried on looking for Arthur. Sure enough, he did get another visitation. Not from the TV Licensing authority, either; he was duly terrorized by a seven-foot tall, leather-winged gargoyle entity complete with fangs and glowing red eyes. King Arthur's grave remains undiscovered.

There are many fascinating cases that could be included here, and the very best can be sourced at the excellent Magonia blog website, pelicanist.blogspot.com/2011/11/mib-encounters.html, where the balanced and thorough Gareth Medway has compiled an extensive list. But for the final word on the Men in Black, it is worth looking at one of the most peculiar and puzzling set of documents in ufology, the "O. H. Krill Papers".

No one really knows the identity of Krill. Some researchers have suggested that the name "Krill" is an expansion of an alien's name, KRLL, a hapless ET who was incarcerated at a US air base where he was kept alive by a sympathetic military physician. However, this suggestion falls down when you read the text. Some claim the initials "O. H." stand for "Omnipotent

Highness". But they're simply Tolkien in their sleep. The general consensus, especially among avid debunkers, is that the Krill Papers (which are quite extensive, and in four parts) are a major cynical fraud perpetrated upon the ufology community as disinformation and aimed at confusion. Who did it? The CIA? The USAF? The illuminati? No one knows. That said, they cover many aspects of the flying-saucer mystery in some depth and, if nothing else, make a fascinating read. The papers appeared online at the early stage of the internet's development in the 1980s, apparently from nowhere, and as their true origin, provenance or copyright ownership cannot be clearly established, I include here extracts from the Krill report on the Men in Black.

CONFIDENTIAL

A SITUATION REPORT ON OUR ACQUISITION OF ADVANCED TECHNOLOGY AND INTERACTION WITH ALIEN CULTURES

BY

O. H. KRILL

The Men in Black

All things considered, UFO research has become pretty much of a circus today, and the most intriguing and controversial sideshow skirting the edges is the question of the "silencers", or the mysterious "Men in Black." There is a strong subliminal appeal in these accounts of visits by mysterious dark-suited figures (I have been visited myself, as have others I've known) attempting to silence UFO witnesses. A typical situation would be that a witness has a UFO sighting or UFO-related experience. Shortly thereafter he is visited by one or more "odd"-looking men who relate to him the minutest details of his experience, even though he has as yet told no one for fear of ridicule or other reasons.

The men warn him about spreading the story of his experience around and sometimes even threaten him personally, sometimes obliquely, sometimes directly. Any evidence, if it exists, is confiscated in one way or another. Sometimes the visit is for some totally meaningless reason and the subject of UFOs is hardly mentioned, if at all. But again, the men all seem to look alike.

We actually seem to find ourselves in close proximity to beings who obviously must be directly connected in some way with the objects themselves or the source behind them, yet they seem to be functioning unobtrusively within the framework of our own everyday existence.

The classic conception of an MIB is a man of indefinite age, medium height and dressed completely in black. He always has a black hat and often a black turtleneck sweater. They present an appearance often described as "strange" or "odd". They speak in a dull monotone voice, "like a computer", and are dark-complexioned with high cheekbones, thin lips, pointed chin, and eyes that are mildly slanted.

The visitors themselves are often on absurd missions. They have reportedly posed as salesmen, telephone repairmen or representatives from official or unofficial organizations. Their mode of transportation is usually large and expensive cars – Buicks or Lincolns, sometimes Cadillacs, all black, of course. I might note at this point that their physical appearance also has included beings that have pale-greyish skin, and that some of them have been seen to have blond hair, yet they wear the clothing and drive the cars previously described.

Their cars often operate with the headlights off, but ghostly purple or greenish glows illuminate the interior. Unusual insignia have been seen emblazoned on the doors and the license plates are always unidentifiable or untraceable.

The fabric of their clothes has been described as strangely "shiny" or thin, but not silky – almost as if they have been cut from a new type of fabric.

Their often mechanical behaviour has caused them to be described by some as being like robots or androids (think back to the Dulce lab). [This is unverified, but according to www.abovetopsecret.com almost two miles beneath Archuleta Mesa on the Jicarilla Apache Indian Reservation near Dulce, New Mexico, is the top-secret laboratory, supposedly a joint United States government/alien biogenetics installation. Others exist in Colorado, Nevada, and Arizona.]

A lot of descriptions of some of these "folks" are pretty bizarre. A businessman's family in Wildwood, New Jersey, was visited by an unusually large man whose pants legs hiked up when he sat down, revealing a green wire grafted on to his skin and running up his leg.

There are other cases of MIB appearing on the other side of a wet, muddy field after a heavy rain, but having no mud whatever on their brightly shined shoes and in the bitter cold, out of nowhere, wearing only a thin coat. Their shoes and wallets all seem new and hardly broken in.

They are not alone. They seem to have faceless conspirators in the nation's post offices and phone companies. Researchers and witnesses often report their mail going astray at an unusually high rate and being bothered by bizarre phone calls where they are spoken to by metallic, unhuman-sounding voices. Unusual noises on the phone, intensifying whenever UFOs are mentioned, and voices breaking in on conversations, have all led many people to suspect that their phones are being tapped.

John A. Keel suggests that the UFO are part of the environment itself and come from another time-space continua; that most of the UFO phenomena is psychic and psychological rather than physical. Well, I personally would not define it that way, although those two components are certainly deeply involved in what's going on.

To illustrate a little how bizarre some of the incidents are regarding the MIB, I have assembled a short list of some of the more interesting factors in some cases:

- An ex-Air Force man is gassed and interrogated by MIB after he has learned classified NASA secrets.

- Close-up photos of UFOs were seized from a teenager who is also directly threatened by MIB.
- MIB sighted in the lobby of the US State Department leave a mysterious artefact.
- MIB pose as Air Force officers to silence witnesses.
- MIB tries to buy before-hours Coke and sings to birds in trees.
- MIB disintegrates a coin in a witness' hand and tells him that his heart will do the same if he talks.

Whoever the mysterious Krill was, his input to ufology must have been a gift to the makers of *The X-Files*. I've always been intrigued by "before-hours Coke". I never knew that Coca-Cola had its own licensing hours. Google the complete Krill Papers and be totally entertained ...

FACTS AND FABRICATIONS: WHAT MADE NEW MEXICO FAMOUS

In the second half of the nineteenth century, near a small settlement called Missouri Plaza in New Mexico, John Simpson Chisum, a cattleman acknowledged as "Cattle King of the Pecos", established what was then the largest ranch in the United States, the Jingle Bob Ranch at South Spring Acres. Chisum was what this part of the old West is *really* about; the great pioneer spirit, a genuine, hard-working and fearless three-dimensional reality, whose niece spent time canoodling on the front porch with none other than Billy the Kid.

Just five miles (8 km) down the trail from Jingle Bob Ranch, in 1869 Aaron Wilburn and an Omaha businessman, Van C. Smith, built two adobe buildings. In 1871, Smith filed a claim with the federal government for the land around the buildings and, on 20 August 1873, he became the fledgling town's first postmaster. Smith named the town after his father's Christian name; Roswell.

Today Roswell is the county seat of Chaves County in New Mexico, with a population, according to the 2010 census, of 48,366. It has ranches, dairy farms, manufacturing and distribution businesses, and it's a place well known for its petroleum industry. It is also the home of New Mexico Military Institute (NMMI), founded in 1891.

Ask anyone today about Roswell and the answer will have nothing to do with pioneering cattlemen, the Lincoln County Wars or even William H. Bonney. Roswell is the epicentre of every crashed UFO/aliens conspiracy there ever was. The so-called "Roswell Incident" has more wriggling legs than a box of centipedes, and to include every fine detail, every twisted claim, counter-claim, affirmation and denial could easily fill this book. In fact, there are already dozens of books, TV movies and documentaries on this subject. Even though the crash site of the alleged UFO was quite a few miles from Roswell and closer to Corona, the area's genuine, colourful history – great cattle barons and Billy the Kid – has been usurped by little green men. There are parts of this saga, even the new publications concurrent with this book, which deliver adequate evidence of the widespread gullibility of an insatiable ufology readership, which provides a lucrative media market for an ever-increasing pile of conspiracy dung.

THE ROSWELL STORY 1:
THE BASIC CHRONOLOGY

14 June 1947 (or, depending on conflicting accounts, "about three weeks" before 8 July): 30 miles (50 km) north of Roswell, William Ware "Mac" Brazel, a foreman on the Foster homestead, discovered some unusual debris. Interviewed by the local newspaper, the *Roswell Daily Record*, Brazel stated he and his son had seen a "large area of bright wreckage made up of rubber strips, tinfoil, a rather tough paper and sticks". He seems to have thought little about it, and left it there until 4 July when he returned to the site with his wife, son and daughter to gather the debris. There are conflicting accounts; one is that he gathered some up and hid it under a bush. Following this seemingly insignificant event, reports about flying disks came to Brazel's notice and he seems to have made a connection – could the stuff he'd found be related? Coinciding with the supposed crash, the *Roswell Daily Record* also states: "Mr and Mrs Dan Wilmot apparently were the only persons in Roswell who have seen what they thought was a flying disk. They were sitting on their porch at 105 South Penn. last Wednesday night at about ten o'clock when a large glowing object zoomed out of the sky from the southeast, going in a northwesterly direction at a high rate of speed."

7 July 1947 (or 6 July according to other reports): Brazel had a meeting with Roswell's Sheriff George Wilcox and indicated that he might have found a flying disc. Wilcox contacts Roswell Army Air Field (RAAF). Air Force Intelligence Officer Major Jesse Marcel and (possibly) two Counter Intelligence Corps agents, Sheridan Cavitt and Lewis Rickett, go with Brazel back to the site and retrieve more bits of the wreckage. "[We] spent a couple of hours Monday afternoon [July 7] looking for any more parts of the weather device," said Marcel. "We found a few more patches of tinfoil and rubber."

8 July 1947: RAAF public information officer Walter Haut issues a press release stating that the 509th Bomb Group had recovered a crashed "flying disk" from a ranch near Roswell. (Fast forward to 2002 on this entry!)

9 July 1947: Press reports indicate Commanding General Roger M. Ramey of the Eighth Air Force had claimed that what had actually been recovered by the RAAF was a radar-tracking balloon, not a "flying disk". At a press conference, debris said to be from the crashed object is displayed, confirming the weather balloon story. Apparently the balloon was part a classified programme named "Mogul". Colonel William H. Blanchard, commanding officer of the 509th, contacts General Ramey and Ramey has the object flown to Fort Worth Army Air Field in Texas. When it arrives, Warrant Officer Irving Newton confirms Ramey's assessment of the object as a weather balloon and its "kite", this being Air Force parlance for the radar reflector that tracks balloons from the ground. Fort Worth issues another press release, describing the object as a "weather balloon". Photographs of the debris are taken in General Ramey's office by reporter J. Bond Johnson of the *Fort Worth Star-Telegram* and other photographers. AWOL: big-headed, almond-eyed spindly-limbed three-foot aliens. One of the subsequent crucial conspiracy "cover-up" aspects of this case is the repeated claim that the recovered debris photographed that day wasn't the real UFO McCoy – it had been replaced with weather-balloon wreckage. However, according to Kal K. Korff of the Committee for Sceptical Inquiry (CSI);

> Colonel Thomas J. DuBose, who later retired as a brigadier general, was present when the wreckage was brought into Ramey's office. There's no disputing this fact, because DuBose met the B-29 personally when it arrived at Carswell AFB (Fort Worth) from Roswell carrying the debris that Marcel had collected. DuBose not only greeted the incoming plane, but hand-carried the wreckage remnants in a sealed canvas mail pouch, immediately escorting it to Ramey's office.

DuBose strenuously denies any switching of the material.

Story over? Everyone happy? For a couple of decades, yes. But meanwhile ...

22 March 1950: A report is lodged with the FBI by Special Agent Guy Hottel (apparently, this is available for inspection in the FBI's own reading room) suggesting that the Air Force recovered three flying saucers (each fifty feet in diameter) and nine three-feet (0.9 m) tall, human-shaped bodies. Agent Hottel seems to be uncharacteristically lax for an FBI man, because there is no location mentioned in his report.

8 December 1979: Journalist Robert Pratt of the *National Enquirer* interviews Jesse Marcel, the Air Force Intelligence Officer in the Roswell affair. Marcel now maintains that the wreckage material he had recovered "was nothing that came from earth". He describes tissue-thin, indestructible metal and "I" beams bearing some kind of hieroglyphics. The legend of Roswell is up and running.

So far we've had a bit of fun with this, but Roswell is an eternal bonfire, and just when it dies down, someone finds new kindling. Scepticism is healthy, but when what were previously regarded as utterly reliable official sources offer a complete turn-around, the mystery grabs you and drags you in again. On 26 December 2002, now retired and eighty years old, the RAAF's 1947 press officer, Walter G. Haut, put his signature on a revealing and starkly amazing affidavit, which you can see at www.ufos.about.com/od/uforelateddocuments/a/hautaffidavit.htm. Here are some extracts:

> **Paragraph 8**: Samples of wreckage were passed around the table. It was unlike any material I had or have ever seen in my life. Pieces which resembled metal foil, paper-thin yet extremely strong, and pieces with unusual markings along their length were handled from man to man, each voicing their opinion. No one was able to identify the crash debris.
>
> **Paragraph 12**: Before leaving the base, Col. Blanchard took me personally to Building 84 [Hangar P-3], a B-29 hangar located on the east side of the tarmac. Upon first approaching the building, I observed that it was under heavy

guard both outside and inside. Once inside, I was permitted from a safe distance to first observe the object just recovered north of town. It was approx. 12 to 15 feet in length, not quite as wide, about 6 feet high, and more of an egg shape. Lighting was poor, but its surface did appear metallic. No windows, port holes, wings, tail section, or landing gear were visible.

Paragraph 13: Also from a distance, I was able to see a couple of bodies under a canvas tarpaulin. Only the heads extended beyond the covering, and I was not able to make out any features. The heads did appear larger than normal and the contour of the canvas suggested the size of a 10-year-old child. At a later date in Blanchard's office, he would extend his arm about 4 feet above the floor to indicate the height.

If you continue to rake through the embers, you'll find other "death-bed confessions" from an ever increasing list of witnesses, such as the lady who claims she typed up the autopsy reports on the alien bodies, and a further example in 1989, when former mortician Glenn Dennis gave his account. True or fantasy? In the mid-1960s Senator Barry Goldwater, a brigadier general in the Air Force Reserve, asked his friend General Curtis LeMay about the rumours. Goldwater told the *New Yorker* (25 April 1988) that LeMay gave him "holy hell" and warned him never to bring up the subject again. Senators and generals – that's what we need for authenticity.

Roswell's historical landscape has become a territory of bitter division, a battlefield where the sceptics clash with the believers over and over again. If we take Charles Fort's dictum and remain as neutral observers, that's fine, but there's always a danger that being in the middle of the road one gets hit by traffic from both directions. Is there anything new on Roswell? The answer to that is always "yes". Try this for size. On 23 May 2011, the *Rapid City Journal* reported:

The world famous Roswell "incident" was no UFO but rather a Russian spacecraft with "grotesque, child-size aviators" developed in human experiments by Nazi doctor and war criminal Josef Mengele, according to a theory floated by investigative journalist Annie Jacobsen. Her book, *Area 51:*

An Uncensored History of America's Top Secret Military Base, is about the secretive Nevada base called Area 51. One chapter offers the new Roswell theory, citing an anonymous source who says Joseph Stalin recruited Mengele and sent the craft into US air space in 1947 to spark public hysteria.

Without this screwball bombshell bolted on to her book, Ms Jacobsen's tome may well have been just another conspiracy ragbag to sit on the shelves alongside all the others. That said, reading the many online, one-star reviews by ordinary readers, who seem to possess a level of genuine scientific knowledge that Jacobsen appears to have ditched in exchange for wild speculation, it becomes evident that the work is riddled with factual errors and scientific anachronisms. But this is the stuff of trash TV and tabloid dreams, Commies + Nazis + UFOs – irresistible! And no publicity is bad publicity.

We'll get on to the Nazis and their supposed UFOs later, but let's briefly examine Jacobsen's theory. This kind of guff might play well with the twenty-first century's dumbed-down conspiracy-obsessed online illiterati, but it seeks to bulldoze through a concrete wall of factual evidence.

- Mengele's movements, from his Nazi Party membership in 1934, his entry into the SS and his work at Auschwitz, from April 1943, right through to his subsequent wanderings as a fugitive war criminal in Germany during 1945–6 whilst the Allies were still searching for him are all officially well documented. Everything you need to know is also included in *Mengele: The Complete Story* by Gerald Posner and John Ware (1986).
- Under a stolen identity, "Fritz Hollmann", at the time he is supposed to have been developing Jacobsen's "aliens" from July 1945 until May 1949, worked as a farmhand in a small village near Rosenheim, Bavaria, staying in contact with his wife and his old friend Hans Sedlmeier, who arranged Mengele's escape to Argentina.
- To develop the "grotesque, childlike aviators" between the time Mengele fled from Auschwitz and the Roswell crash just two years later would make the "Angel of Death" one of

the most phenomenally skilled physicians and biologists of all time. Even if he had been in the USSR, with his retrieved, so-called "research" files he'd taken from Poland, he would have required massive medical facilities to create Jacobsen's proposed "aliens". To create his perverted alien-esque kiddies he would have needed to start the project in the 1930s. Instant biology might make overnight clones in Hollywood, but in the real world living organisms take their own pace. The theory becomes more ludicrous at each level of consideration.

- If Stalin had planned to use such a crackpot method employing a craft designed by decommissioned Nazi engineers, why crash it in the middle of a mainly unoccupied desert – a good idea would have been to drop the thing where someone *actually lived*. How did they manage to invade US air space, in an area utilized by elite elements of the USAF?

- Stalin would not have needed a sadistic Nazi eugenics nut if he had planned the Roswell fiasco. He already had a man capable of the job. His name was Ilya Ivanov, one of Russia's top animal-breeding scientists, who had been chosen by Uncle Joe to make "the perfect soldier". Mr Ivanov's claim to fame, after his failure to cross-breed humanity with apes in Africa during the 1920s, was the establishment of the world's first centre for the artificial insemination of racehorses.

There are many chapters still to be written on Roswell and despite the repeated official denials they will mostly adhere to the myths and legends already firmly established. Another part of the sinister heritage of claim, counter-claim and disinformation is the legendary Majestic 12 (or MJ-12). This was the US government's official code for a covert committee formed in 1947 of military leaders, scientists and other assorted government officials, on an executive order by US President Harry S. Truman. The story goes that MJ-12 was assembled to look into the Roswell crash. The committee has become one of UFO lore's sacred conspiracy tenets and its existence hinges on the appearance in 1980 of a large quantity of supposedly official documents, all hotly debated in the UFO community. The twelve-man MJ-12 committee included, among others, Dr Vannevar Bush, President of Carnegie Institute, Washington, DC, wartime chairman of the Office of Scientific Research and Development, the post-war Joint Research and Development Board (JRDB) and later the Research and Development Board (RDB). The documents, which instigated a tsunami of excitement among ufologists, give instructions on what to do when meeting an alien, including diagrams of UFOs, information on maintaining security, and the President's statements concerning UFO-related issues. Then it gets a little silly, as some pages bear the signatures of Albert Einstein and Ronald Reagan. The general consensus is that all these documents were fakes that had been surreptitiously slipped into the archives. The last batch of MJ-12-related paperwork was released in 1997. Their authenticity will always remain uncertain.

However, in 1978 Canadian documents dating from 1950 and 1951 were uncovered. These also pointed to the existence of a top-secret Pentagon UFO study group with a familiar name in the chair – Dr Vannevar Bush. Some ex-government scientists have given testimony that the group did exist. So, either the MJ-12 documents are entirely bogus (we know at least some of them are, based on the forensic evidence – wrong paper, wrong type styles, various anachronisms) or, more tantalizingly, if a fraction of them are genuine, and MJ-12 *was* set up because of something inexplicable at Roswell … it's that weak candle of possibility which will always flicker in the dark, cold New Mexico night.

Of course, if you're a dedicated disciple at the Temple of Roswell, it helps to check-in your common sense at the door. Roswell rumour is a self-propagating fungus and nothing can prevent it spreading. But the UFO crash was never enough; we had to have the dead ufonauts, too.

THE ROSWELL STORY 2:
ALIEN AUTOPSY

On 5 May 1995, a film producer named Ray Santilli, based in London, revealed what he alleged to be genuine footage of an alien autopsy taken in Roswell in 1947. It was shown at first at the London Museum to media representatives and UFO researchers. Santilli is an interesting character. As well as being a musician and record producer, he certainly knew his way around the promotion business, and the list of musical acts he'd worked with, both British and American, is impressive, from Jerry Lee Lewis and Kid Creole & The Coconuts, to Ian Dury, Hot Chocolate and Boy George. The story Santilli and his business partner Gary Shoefield tell goes as follows.

On a trip to the United States in 1992 they saw twenty-two cans of film shot in 1947 by a US Army cameraman in Roswell. Each can contained film of about four minutes in length. The subject was an alien autopsy. Two years passed before they went back to try and buy the footage, but due to humidity and heat it had degraded, leaving only a few frames intact. What transpired immediately after this remains a little foggy, but after some serious international media negotiations, on 28 August 1995 the resultant Santilli film was broadcast by Fox TV. The advance publicity was enormous, with BBC national radio proclaiming that the showing of the film around the globe could change the way we think about our life on earth. With or without the possibility of authenticity (the broadcast was titled *Alien Autopsy: Fact or Fiction*), Santilli had skilfully played the media moguls at their own game – sensation – and won. The comments reached new, lofty heights when *Time* magazine compared the film's importance to the Abraham Zapruder film shot at JFK's assassination.

One broadcast wasn't enough. The second showing of the film in November 1995 was watched by millions more viewers around the world. The sceptics were on the case from the beginning, looking for those telltale signs of a fake. Yet everything in the shaky monochrome footage seemed to ring true, at least the setting and the equipment. The telephone on view was definitely a 1946 model, and although some people questioned the phone having a spiral cable, they had been available on US phones since 1938 and were standard for US Army phones. The microphone in the film is a 1946 model. Even the wall clock is American, dating from 1938. Viewers with medical knowledge, although far from convinced by the unorthodox, roughshod methods of the biohazard-suited "pathologists", could see that the surgical instruments, such as the bone hammer, the Bunsen burner and the pathology table were correct for their purpose, facts which were confirmed by the ex-President of the American Academy of Forensic Sciences, Professor Cyril Wecht. Some queried the fact that some sequences in the autopsy were pixelated, but this was claimed by the producers to be a device to mask some scenes of a more graphic nature. Although in black and white, the parts where the chest cavity is opened and the removal of the brain (with the deft use of a handsaw), for example, were grisly to say the least. The film also included a statement read out by an elderly gentleman who was verifying the footage as real – because he claimed to be the original military cameraman who shot it.

There was even a section purporting to show alien artefacts from the Roswell wreckage, including six-finger control panels (the alien corpse had six fingers on each hand) and some metallic beams bearing strange symbols. The response was divisive. Even in the UFO community, many were driven to absolute scepticism after watching what they loudly declared as a massive hoax.

But Ray Santilli and Gary Shoefield had carved their names in intergalactic history, and although the furore and debate over their global success eventually died down, within a decade a few home truths began to emerge. By the time the green light was given for the US-funded 2006 feature movie, *Alien Autopsy*, the dubious duo were forced to face the music, a situation with which Ray Santilli had no problems. The feature film is well made, funny and highly entertaining, and the parts of Santilli and Shoefield are played with brio by Britain's favourite light comedy entertainment duo, Ant and Dec (Anthony McPartlin and Declan Donnelly). As part of the movie's promotion, on 4 April 2006, UK TV presenter Eamonn Holmes was on the case with a Sky TV documentary, *Eamonn Investigates: Alien Autopsy*. Holmes asked the questions many had been raising since 1995. Santilli came clean. Apparently, there was real, original footage, as claimed, of an alien autopsy, but all that remained of the 1947 stock was a few blurry seconds. Therefore Santilli and Shoefield decided to "restore" the remaining film stock by building around it their own "simulation" of the real, full footage they had originally witnessed in 1992. They claimed that some of the frames in the TV production were 1947 originals (yet they don't tell us *which* frames are real).

Although the movie, *Alien Autopsy*, comes across as a fast-moving comedy, one can only assume that the alien-building methods it portrays are pretty close to what actually happened. Santilli revealed that they built a set in the living room of an empty flat in Rochester Square, Camden Town, London. They employed an artist and sculptor, John Humphreys, giving him three weeks to make two alien bodies. He used casts filled with sheep brains in raspberry jam. S. C. Crosby, Wholesale Butchers at London's Smithfield meat market, supplied knuckle joints and chicken entrails. The "character" or "pathologist" was played in the film by the artist, Humphreys. Assembling the footage took two separate attempts. The "corpses" were later chopped up and disposed of in bins around London. The old man reading the statement that he had been the original camera-man was a homeless bum they'd picked up on the street in Los Angeles. Humphreys also created the "alien artefacts", six-finger control panels and alien "symbols".

Disappointing as all this is to a genuine ufologist, one has to reluctantly admire the inventive duo's chutzpah in putting all this together, and the wall of silence maintained by all those involved. It was one of the best, most entertaining hoaxes of all time, and by still maintaining that 5 per cent of the film was indeed genuine and dated from 1947, then the Roswell disciples still have something to cling on to. As to the "autopsy" itself, here's what Joseph A. Bauer, a surgeon from Cleveland, Ohio, had to say after seeing the broadcast:

Only two conclusions are possible from this film: either this is the work of beginners attempting to create a hoax to resuscitate the corpse of Roswell crash lore; or, if the film is intended to portray an actual autopsy of an unusual humanoid body (a proposition untenable and entirely unsubstantiated), then it is a documentation of the crime of the millennium – the brutal butchery, devastation, and destruction of unique evidence and an unparalleled opportunity to gain some understanding about this deformed creature, regardless of its origin. I hope that this critique will not guide someone to produce a more believable alien autopsy film.

So that's Roswell. Tourist attraction supreme; great fun, always in motion, never over.

QUICK! GET THE KODAK!
THE McMINNVILLE,
OREGON, PHOTOS

Evelyn Trent and her husband Paul lived on a farm nine miles (15 km) from the Oregon town of McMinnville. At 7.30 p.m. on 11 May 1950, Evelyn had been out in the backyard feeding their rabbits. As she made her way back to the house, she spotted what appeared to be a metallic disk in the sky, moving slowly towards the farm from the northeast. Naturally, she shouted for her husband Paul to come outside and take a look. He came out and looked then dashed back in to get his Kodak camera. He took two shots of the object before it shot off in a westerly direction.

One might expect after such an experience that the Trents might have immediately dashed into town and got the film developed. They didn't. They waited about three days (until Mother's Day) to finish off the roll of film. The chronology gets murky here; according to the scientific researcher, Dr Bruce Maccabee (http://brumac.8k.com/trent2), who analysed the photos between 1977–81, the photos were processed:

> probably during the following week, they took the film to a local drugstore to have it developed. It probably took a week or more for the film to be returned. The Trents showed the pictures to their family and some friends, and, in particular, to a boyfriend of one of Mr Trent's nieces. This young man, Andy Horness, was in the Army and about to travel to Korea (he was killed on the way). He apparently took an interest in the photos and suggested that Mr Trent take them to the local banker, Mr Frank Wortmann.

UFO lore is famous for its embroidery, so some accounts one will read of this event state that the roll of film was left in a drawer for weeks or even months. The banker, Frank Wortmann, was so intrigued by the pictures he displayed them in the bank's front window in McMinnville.

This aroused the interest of a local reporter, Bill Powell, who asked Mr Trent to loan him the negatives. Soon, the photos became internationally famous. They were reprinted in *LIFE* magazine and numerous newspapers, and for half a century have been regarded as genuine by most of the UFO community. The Trents never received a penny for them, despite the fact that after their inclusion in *LIFE* the photographs appeared in media all over the world, and probably made a lot of money for a lot of publications. The Trents' original negatives went missing for some years, until they were discovered in a press archive. Yet the sceptics were soon on the case. Despite the detailed scientific positive analysis of the pictures by Dr Bruce Maccabee, the arch party-pooper of all things UFO, the late Philip Julian Klass (1919–2005), an American journalist and UFO researcher, decided that the Trent photographs were a hoax. He even went so far as to suggest that the Trents had manufactured their own UFO and suspended it on a wire. Razor-sharp and keen-minded, Klass, regarded by some as the "Sherlock Holmes of ufology" was hugely admired by his disbelieving peers, although respected ufologist Jerome Clark wrote in 2003 that Klass was "an obsessed crank who contributed little to the UFO debate except noise, strange rhetoric, pseudoscientific speculation, and character assassination". Subsequent detailed analyses of the photos have maintained Maccabee's original deliberation – they are real. If they were innocent of hoaxing, then one can only feel for the now departed Evelyn and Paul Trent, simple farming folk who were pestered for years by cranks and harassed by phone calls, whilst their pictures brought them nothing but vilification from the likes of Klass and piles of profit for the media.

THE UFO COLLISION MYSTERY

Air Force C-118 Aircraft Has Airborne Collision and Then
Crashes – Killing Crew of Four
Headline from Seattle Post Intelligencer, 2 April 1959

On 1 April 1959 a military C-118 cargo plane collided with what was described by witnesses as a UFO, and crashed near Orting, Washington, after bursting into flames. All four crew members were killed. The plane had taken off from McChord AFB (near Tacoma, Washington) at about 6:30 p.m. on a routine training mission and the collision occurred about ninety minutes into the flight. Bob Gribble (founder of the National UFO Reporting Center) investigated the case. His efforts to reach the crash site were thwarted by police and military personnel. Two witnesses interviewed by Gribble described a "brilliantly glowing" UFO moving rapidly northwards in the vicinity of the aircraft. Apparently, just prior to the crash the pilot radioed that, "We've hit something or it's hit us," just before the plane struck the ground.

Such rumours hang around for years, but twenty-five years later, documentation released by the Air Force under the Freedom of Information Act, despite certain areas of the text being blacked out, put an end to the speculation. The plane's wing had cuffed a tree and the supposed UFO reported by witnesses was, in fact, the burning plane as it passed by on its rapid and deathly descent.

I include this hitherto unexplained item to demonstrate the fact that when information is not generally available to the public

– especially when military connections are involved – it is then that the rumours begin, and over the years they gather that moss of mystery, a careless patina of embellishment that detracts so much credibility from the UFO lobby.

THE REAL X-FILES

It is almost a century since J. Edgar Hoover (1895–1972) was appointed Director of the Bureau of Investigation in 1924, which became the FBI (Federal Bureau of Investigation) in 1935. The Bureau's mission in the early days was to tackle the rash of interstate bank robberies, mob corruption, bootlegging and the increasing crime of kidnapping. Hoover maintained his grip on the FBI for five decades. He became an immensely powerful player on the US political scene, serving under no fewer than seven US Presidents. As the FBI's power increased, it took on other areas of investigation, such as counterespionage and counterterrorism. Fans of the highly successful TV series, *The X-Files*, might be disappointed to know that the files Special Agents Scully and Mulder were investigating didn't take up too much of Hoover's time. For just a brief period between 30 July and 1 October 1947, the Army Air Force (later USAF) enjoyed the assistance of the FBI in its investigation of flying saucers following a special request by General George Schulgen. (The saucers didn't become "UFOs" until the USAF coined the acronym in 1950.)

In 1977, using the Freedom of Information Act, UFO researcher Dr Bruce Maccabee got hold of the first batch of 500 pages of declassified FBI UFO files. These documents were not quite as exciting as had been anticipated. Maccabee discovered that 40 per cent of the files were unimpressive Air Force reports and obvious hoaxes, but he was intrigued to discover that another 40 per cent included teletype reports and transcripts of more significant, officially authentic UFO reports.

When the Air Force had asked Hoover for help, he wrote an internal memo on 15 July 1947, which, in subsequent decades, would propel the Roswell conspiracy club into a "cover-up" tail-spin. This is what Hoover wrote regarding helping the Air Force: "I would do it, but before agreeing to it we must insist upon full access to discs recovered. For instance in the La. case the Army grabbed it and would not let us have it for cursory examination."

Hoover's scribbled memos have become known among researchers as "blue gems". This particular azure nugget convinced many Roswellites that he was referring to the New Mexico crash. The Army "grabbed" a disc? Proof! Perhaps. Was "La." his secret FBI code for Roswell? But as any good American knows, it's simply an abbreviation for Louisiana. During that crucial year of flying-saucer activity, 1947, an unusual aluminium disk with a diameter of just sixteen inches (41 cm) had been discovered in Shreveport, Louisiana, on 7 July. As the artefact was belching smoke, it certainly looked like a crashed saucer, although with its limited dimensions it might have been piloted by leprechauns. However, it was retrieved and taken away by the Army, and later declared to be nothing more than a rough hoax. But General Schulgen, meeting with Hoover, was still keen to have the Bureau's help, informing the FBI that in future his officers would be told "that all cooperation be furnished to the FBI and that all discs recovered be made available for examination by the FBI agents". It is always those words "discs recovered" that continue to tantalize a wide range of UFO researchers. On 30 July the FBI issued Bulletin No. 42 which read: "You should investigate each instance which is brought to your attention of a sighting of a flying disc in order to ascertain whether or not it is a bona fide sighting, an imaginary one or a prank ... The Bureau should be notified by teletype of all reported sightings and the results of your inquiries." And so the agents began collecting data and, in those early "flap" years, there was plenty to collect.

The first hint that there was something called an "X" file came with a report from an FBI special agent in Portland, Oregon, of a sighting which took place on the same day Kenneth Arnold had reported his ground-breaking experience. It was a memo, dated 17 September 1947, addressed to Hoover and headed: "Subject: Reports of Flying Discs – Security Matter-X." However, at that stage of FBI history anything designated "X" signified a counter-intelligence operation. It was nothing to do with the paranormal, unexplained phenomena or UFOs. The cold war was raging, and as a rabid anti-communist, anything Hoover couldn't explain was obviously part of a red plot. The FBI files were stuffed with ongoing investigations into some of the most unlikely potential Soviet infiltrators – anyone who played jazz, various authors and journalists, people who espoused a philosophy of peace, even major scientific figures such as Albert Einstein and all manner of Hollywood players with a liberal attitude. They all had their own shelves in the FBI filing system – "Sabotage', "Internal Security" – with the prominent heading "Security Matter-X". Anyone remotely interested in UFOs could well instigate the opening of a special file. The FBI were not looking for little green (or grey) men; they were looking for big red subversives. As well as the prominent "contactee" of Space People fame, George Adamski, who had been visited twice by special agents, who were rattled by his intergalactic pacifist views and instructed him to shut up, the FBI kept a dossier on prominent UFO writer Major Donald Keyhoe (1897–1988). Keyhoe was an American Marine Corps naval aviator, who wrote extensively on aeronautical subjects (and penned science fiction for magazines such as *Weird Tales*) as well as managing promotional tours for aviation pioneers, including Charles Lindbergh. And here's a hint for TV *X-Files* fans: Hoover also had a file on Hollywood's famed left-wing society columnist, the author of the first UFO book, *Behind the Flying Saucers* (1950). His name was Frank Scully. There was probably an agent Mulder somewhere in the FBI, but he remains hidden.

Whatever good flying-saucer hunting relationships the FBI had with the US Air Force, these were irretrievably wrecked when Hoover discovered a letter from Col. R. H. Smith of the Air Defense Command, which stated, "the services of the FBI were enlisted in order to relieve the Air Force of the task of tracking down all the many instances which turned out to be ash-can covers, toilet seats and whatnot". In other words, the military only had its eyes on the genuinely interesting and inexplicable cases, whilst the FBI received all the rubbish. As the far from amused J. Edgar Hoover was concerned, the USAF had just hammered another nail into the X-Files coffin. He wrote to Maj. Gen. George McDonald at the Pentagon on 27 September 1947, quoting Colonel Smith's "toilet seat" quip: "In view of the apparent understanding by the Air Force, I cannot permit the personnel and time of this organization to be dissipated in this manner. I am advising the Field Divisions … to discontinue all investigative activity regarding the reported sightings of flying discs." Agents read the new instructions in the *FBI Bulletin* No. 57 on 1 October 1947.

However, this wasn't quite the end of the X-Files, because this was the age where there was a red under every bed, and Senator Joe McCarthy was already on the prowl. There was a desperate undercurrent to the burgeoning UFO problem – what if flying saucers were some kind of communist plot? Yet try as they may, Hoover and his men could not make a connection between Lenin, Stalin and the space brothers. Even the hapless witnesses to UFO waves could not be tarred with the commie brush. Thus, the FBI's interest began to wane. With regard to a sighting of a flying disk over the Cascade Mountains, the FBI's Assistant Director Ladd issued a memo: "The results of the investigation conducted by the Bureau Field Offices in this matter have failed to reveal any indications of subversive individuals being involved in any of the reported sightings." The Bureau continued to collect a few items of UFO material over the years until the mid-1960s and kept tabs on various UFO researchers and others, including George Adamski, who still warranted quite a hefty file, but Hoover had certainly distanced himself from the "toilet seats".

When it came to prominent and widely reported UFO flaps which could not be ignored or thoroughly explained, such as the 1950 Oak Ridge, Tennessee, event, when fighter aircraft were scrambled, the Bureau logged sixteen unidentified radar targets and visual observations by security patrols and other witnesses. All were interviewed and their depositions filed. Yet even with all the evidence and a commission of scientific advisors, the event remains unexplained and, more importantly, none of the witnesses were found to be "subversives".

This residue of FBI interest in UFOs came under the heading "The Protection of Vital Installations", which was the Bureau's mandate to keep spies and saboteurs away from sensitive government sites. The FBI investigated a similar UFO incursion in 1950 at the Hanford AEC Plant in Washington State. Two years later, in 1952, the nosey aliens were back again, snooping over South Carolina's Savannah River plant. Once again, the FBI reached no conclusions and didn't find any communists. For Hoover, flying saucers seemed to be a political dead-end. He did, however, have continuing worries about George Adamski's anti-nuclear stance. Anyone opposed to the idea of obliterating humanity beneath a rain of forty megaton H-bombs was naturally deemed un-American, and Adamski's penchant for quoting official and USAF sources in his lectures really rankled with the military.

On 17 March 1953, FBI and USAF agents paid Adamski a visit at his home in Palomar Gardens, California. He was instructed to put his signature to a statement saying that neither the USAF nor the FBI "have approved material used in my speeches". Foolhardy as ever, or brave, Adamski regarded the official visitation as a propaganda gift. At his subsequent lectures he would wave the document aloft as proof of government interest in his ongoing relationship with the "space brothers". Hoover was outraged. In December 1953, two FBI agents and an agent from AFOSI (the Air Force Office of Special Investigations) arrived once more on George's doorstep. The FBI's San Diego office issued a telex, which stated: "Adamski was emphatically admonished that he was immediately to cease and desist in referring to the FBI or OSI as having given him approval to speak on flying saucers ... Adamski was advised that legal action would be taken against him if he persisted in inferring or making these statements."

Yet even three years later, it seems obvious that Adamski was having none of this. His un-American opposition to nuclear weapons kept him under constant surveillance as a subversive. For example, when in 1954 a fledgling Detroit UFO club booked Adamski for one of his enlightening talks, local FBI agents reanimated the X-Files with one of their own marked "Detroit Flying Saucer Club: Espionage-X."

But Hoover had had enough. There was no anti-communist mileage to be had from the space brothers. He issued the order to "stop obtaining from captioned club or its members, material concerning flying saucers". As the 1960s dawned, the Bureau's interest in UFOs became sporadic and all but fizzled out. As the subject comes under most governments' classification systems today as "above top-secret", if there is intelligence about ET contact, chances are even the CIA are in the dark. If "black operations" really exist, there's an agency out there above and beyond the law in charge of all the secrets. The FBI is, after all, an organization set up to fight crime. Fortunately for us all, at least for the time being, hunting for UFOs and aliens remains a legal activity.

THEY'RE ON THE GROUND! FACE TO FACE WITH THE MEN FROM SPACE: THE ANOMALOUS LIFE OF GEORGE ADAMSKI

The publication in 1953 of *The Flying Saucers Have Landed* by George Adamski and Desmond Leslie was a sensation. For my generation, no one has been more influential in inspiring a life-long fascination with the unexplained than the peculiar George Adamski. I was only ten years old when it came out and did not stumble upon it until 1956 in the Boulevard Library in Hull, Yorkshire, England. Science fiction from masters such as Ray Bradbury, Robert Sheckley and Isaac Asimov was thrilling enough, but Adamski's story was not presented as fiction; this was real. It had actual *photographs* of real, alien spacecraft! After all the romantic speculation, here was proof that people were living on other worlds and, better still, they were visiting us to offer their help and advice. Over half a century later, my grati-tude to Adamski survives, but my adolescent faith in his veracity has taken a severe beating.

Dunkirk, in Chautauqua County, New York, was originally settled by Europeans in the early 1800s. The New York and Erie Railroad Company first entered the area in the 1850s. It was incorporated as a city in 1880 and named after the French port city of Dunkerque. Of all the Europeans to settle in this pleasant corner of the state, young George Adamski must have been one of the oddest. He was born in Poland on 17 April 1891. When he was two years old, the family decided to immigrate to the United States. As George grew up in the bustling metropolis, he became deeply interested in nature. He was, by all accounts, a sensitive child. Although not Christians in the traditional sense, his parents were devoutly religious. They seem to have been homespun creationists, rather than being affiliated to any particular Church. This family devotion to God's creation would become an influence in George's later life. He had a wide, cosmic view of the universe; to him the sky above was a vista of infinite wonder.

He enjoyed little formal education, which included only a few years of grade school. The Adamskis were poor and at an early age George had to work to help them maintain an income. But they were Americans now and proud of it. When he'd reached the age of twenty-two, in 1913, he joined the US Army's 13th Cavalry and served against Pancho Villa on the Mexican border. At the height of the First World War, on Christmas Day 1917, he married his sweetheart, Mary Shimbersky, and when the war ended, was honourably discharged from the Army in 1919.

The economically difficult 1920s were his wilderness years, wandering from place to place seeking work. But during this time, with his parents' faith as a basis, he read much and developed his own theories about the cosmos and universal brotherhood. He would often impart his ideas to others, even though he sometimes felt self-conscious about his own lack of formal education. As the 1930s dawned, he was a long way from New York, and decided to settle in the balmier climate of California at Laguna Beach. Here, his broad interest in the cosmos took on a new intensity to the point where he soon became known to a growing number of people who showed a keen interest in his ideas. He would speak to them about brotherhood and the mysteries of the universe, and before long had gathered a group of faithful followers, enough to give this group a name; he called it the Royal Order of Tibet. California was the ideal place for the development of cults and it had many. The Royal Order of Tibet was based on Adamski's notion that the Buddhist monks of that distant land had access to all the secrets of the universe hidden in their monasteries.

Soon hundreds of people were avid followers, keen to hear his ever-developing views on philosophy. This led to his first book being published in 1936, *Wisdom of the Masters of the Far East.*

Soon radio stations such as KMPC in Los Angeles and KFOX in Long Beach were keen to have his lectures on air. Then one day an appreciative student gave him a gift; a six-inch (15.2 cm) reflecting telescope. Now he began studying the heavens more closely. Soon, some technically minded friends provided him with various attachments they'd made that enabled him to use his telescope to take photographs. By the end of the 1930s he had begun developing some inexplicable shots of strange, airborne objects. He submitted some to observatories to see if astronomers might be able to explain what he'd seen. They told him that the photographs lacked detail and distance, so they remained a puzzle.

In 1940 he moved with some of his followers from Laguna Beach to a settlement called Valley Center just off the highway to Palomar Mountain, famed for its observatory. In 1944 the Valley Center was sold, and to get closer to the firmament Adamski moved his coterie further up the mountain where he opened a small café. There, he managed to build his own small observatory and installed a new, fifteen-inch (38.1 cm) telescope. It was the perfect location, above the weather, where he could devote much of his time to scanning the cosmos.

It was here that the real Adamski saga began. There was a heavy shower of meteors in 1946 and during this celestial display everything George had spoken about to his devoted followers seemed suddenly to bear fruit as in amazement they watched, at close range, a huge, cigar-shaped object that hung motionlessly above them. Was this some harbinger of Cosmic Brotherhood?

In 1947, the year of Roswell, Kenneth Arnold and Maury Island, George Adamski had his own experience as an observer of the new phenomena. Together with his wife and a few friends he watched a breathtaking formation of strange objects move across the sky from east to west. It was time for another book. In 1949 the Leonard-Freefield Company in Los Angeles published his work of fiction, *Pioneers of Space*. It featured large cigar-shaped craft piloted by humanoid aliens. In his fantastic story George accompanies these angelic beings who invite him to travel through the solar system to Venus and Mars. They have a large base, a kind of alien service station, on the moon. Contrary to what we now know, Adamski's Venus is no infernal, sulphurous nightmare planet, but a globe rich with vegetation. He dines and wines with the kind and affable Venusians and the Martians and basks in their advanced wisdom.

However, fiction for George was too much like dreaming. The scenarios in *Pioneers of Space* needed to be part of reality, and his next foray into publishing would be his attempt to make them so. Four years later, in 1953, the British Book Centre in New York published *Flying Saucers Have Landed*. He had decided to write of his experiences following an amazing event that took place on Thursday, 20 November 1952. For the first time he had met the occupant of a UFO and they had actually enjoyed a conversation.

His co-author in the project is often listed as an Englishman or British. His name was Desmond Leslie, an Irishman, and his own background is well worth inspection. Desmond was from the Old World's top-drawer aristocratic stock. His father was an Irish-born diplomat, novelist and writer, Sir John Randolph Leslie, 3rd Baronet, generally known as Shane Leslie (1885–1971). A supporter of Irish Home Rule, he had converted to Catholicism in 1908. He was also first cousin of Britain's wartime Prime Minister, Sir Winston Churchill. In 1908, Leslie converted to Roman Catholicism. It is said that F. Scott Fitzgerald dedicated his novel *The Beautiful and Damned* to Leslie.

With the son of a man like this on board, George Adamski was in good hands. Desmond Arthur Peter Leslie was just thirty-three, educated, energetic, well connected and no stranger to the sky above. During the Second World War he'd been a Spitfire pilot in the RAF, and had another career as a pioneer of electric music. In media terms, in England at least, he would become infamous a few years later in 1962 when he punched the haughty theatre critic Bernard Levin in front of eleven million viewers during *That Was the Week That Was*, Britain's top live satirical TV show.

Leslie had a lifelong interest in UFOs and a keen nose for amassing fascinating background material to accompany George's fantastic claims. *Flying Saucers Have Landed* was a massive hit. The strange photographs, showing a bell-shaped saucer with three-ball landing gear and a cigar-shaped "mother ship" disgorging what were referred to as Venusian "scout" craft, fascinated millions of readers. In the book, George said that his first contact with the alien simply involved a conversation, and that he was not invited on board the nearby craft.

Flying Saucers Have Landed was in two parts. The first half was Leslie's work, where he trawled back through history looking for UFOs in ancient times. Sure enough, the Book of Ezekiel was included, along with all kinds of unsubstantiated claims about the Egyptians moving stone blocks for the pyramids with secret alien methods (magic rods, apparently) and similar suggestions about Britain's Stonehenge. Of course, the Brahmins and their Vimanas were prominent. Leslie claimed that UFOs had been visiting the earth since the year (take a deep breath) 18,617,841 BC! Such precision was amazing but, according to Leslie, this incredible bit of dating was "calculated from the ancient Brahmin tables in 1951". Eat your heart out, Stephen Hawking ...

As a softening-up process, a tasty entree to prepare the reader for George Adamski's main course, Leslie's quasi-academic style was fairly compelling, although had he been more scientifically rigorous in his research he might well have saved some embarrassment. A good example of his scatter-gun approach was his inclusion of what had become a favourite "ancient UFO" story among the growing celestial crockery brigade. This was the Ampleforth Abbey sighting, said to have occurred way back in 1290. Leslie aims at authenticity by quoting the "original" text from the old monks in Latin, then gives a translation in English. He gives credit for the supply of this edifying nugget to a man with a name one might only expect to see in a black-and-white 1940s British public information film – Mr A. X. Chumley. It tells the story of two Ampleforth monks, Wilfred and John, and their abbot, Henry. They are roasting sheep when the crucial line of the Ampleforth Latin appears, with the sudden announcement: "*res grandis, circumcularis argenta, disco quodum had dissimilis*" ("Lo! A large round silver thing like a disk flew slowly over them").

In his assessment for the Condon Report on UFOs for the University of Colorado, Samuel Rosenberg goes into some detail with his incisive dissection of ancient UFO sightings. For example, the Ampleforth Abbey "sighting" morphs bizarrely into the "Byland Abbey Sighting" as subsequent, post-Adamski authors clamber on to the gravy train. Whoever Mr A. X. Chumley was, he certainly had a sense of humour, for as the archivist at Ampleforth would have told Leslie (had he bothered to check the story), the "large round silver thing like a disk" and the rest of the "monks roasting a sheep" yarn turns out to be a joke perpetrated in a letter to *The Times* on 9 February 1953 – in a scurrilous communication sent in by two Ampleforth schoolboys. They made it all up.

As an example of how these sincerely presented snippets of ersatz "history" gather the proverbial moss, we must turn to one of Adamski's flying-saucer contemporaries, the colourful Gabriel Green (1924–2001). Among the least well-known of the 1950s "space people" contactees, he was a United States Presidential candidate on two occasions. Claiming to have a PhD in physics from Berkeley in 1953, it transpires that he only attended Woodbury Business College in Los Angeles. He worked as a photographer for the Los Angeles school system. He also met the Space Brothers (with whom he maintained continual telepathic links) who hailed from the planet Korender, orbiting the triple star Alpha Centauri, and enjoyed rides in their spacecraft. He formed his Amalgamated Flying Saucer Clubs of America, Inc. in 1957. His 1960 Presidential campaign was on behalf of the Universal Flying Saucer Party, on a platform of "United World Universal Economics". He also ran in 1962 for the US Senate in California, gathering 171,000 votes. He didn't get in. In Iowa he ran for US President again, in 1972, gaining 200 votes; the panic was over for Nixon and McGovern. Green left the scene for a few years and moved to Yucca Valley, California.

Then, on 29 June 1984, he gathered together the Amalgamated Flying Saucer Clubs of America, and channelled a message from Sananda. Apparently, the "galactic" interpretation of Sananda is "the Master Jesus" as referred to by the devotees of Ashtar. Their faith decrees that Jesus/Sananda shares a spaceship with Ashtar, heading the flying-saucer fleet. So, according to Ashtar's disciples, the Second Coming will be via a flying saucer. No dates were given. Watch the skies ... check the internet ... the Ashtar crew are still active!

Although Desmond Leslie had the wisdom to remove the hilarious Ampleforth yarn from the revised 1970 edition of *Flying Saucers Have Landed*, Green's 1967 opus, *Let's Face the Facts about Flying Saucers* has a nicely restructured version of Ye Merrie Monks of Ampleforth tale wherein the proclamation reads; "Yo Ho! Behold the silver saucer in the sky!" All harmless fun, of course.

In 1955 Adamski's book, *Inside the Space Ships*, was published by Abelard-Schuman. It includes visits on board both cigar-shaped and disk craft. The first are said to have taken place on 18 February 1953 with a further visitation on 12 April 1953, with further contact with space beings in September that year, when the friendly visiting ufonaut joined Adamski for lunch in a Los Angeles restaurant.

Then things become fuzzy. We don't have the date, but he is taken on board a saucer. The following year, on 23 August 1954, he climbed aboard for the fourth time for a farewell banquet. There was no further contact except for Adamski "requesting" permission to take photos of the spaceships, which he attempted on 24 April 1955. Apparently his camera was too crude to pierce the force fields around the saucers. His fame during his 1950s heyday was worldwide. He had international tours arranged for him, addressed packed, spellbound audiences, and met influential leaders and rulers, including Queen Juliana of the Netherlands.

In 1961 Adamski's *Flying Saucers Farewell* was published by Abelard-Schuman. This allowed him to lay out his stall of philosophy, answer the many questions he'd received about his accounts thus far and mount some defence against a growing barrage of criticism.

As science advanced and many other interpretations of the UFO phenomena flooded the market, Adamski's star began to fade. His quaint ideas and fantastic claims had had their day. A growing number of people accused him of being a fraud. Apart from Desmond Leslie's historical howlers there were some laughable items in the books. For example, the encounter in the Mojave Desert with a blond, long-haired alien wearing a ski suit might have been credible, but the only evidence that the cosmic master provided of his race's supreme wisdom was etched into the soles of his intergalactic shoes! Adamski provides a diagram of the symbols on the alien's space boots, and tells us how he immediately made a plaster of Paris cast of them. After all, when you're about to wander into a hot, hostile desert on the off chance that aliens might land, failing to remember that one vital item on your survival checklist – a bag of plaster of Paris, with enough water, a trowel and a bucket – you could be in trouble.

During his final years he claimed to have enjoyed trips to Mars and Saturn and further contact by his cosmic friends, but no one was listening. On 24 April 1965 he died in Silver Spring, Maryland, leaving no will. He was seventy-four.

In retrospect, he seems like a kind, wise soul with good intentions, an entrepreneurial self-proclaimed blue-collar prophet of limited education who made something of his life. Fraud or no fraud, today our lives are ruled by far more disingenuous malefactors than George Adamski. He will always have my affection and gratitude for firing my generation's imagination and curiosity.

An Uncanny Epilogue ...

At 3.30 p.m. on Friday, 6 June 1980, an off-duty coal miner from Lofthouse Colliery in Yorkshire, England, set out to buy some potatoes. He was looking forward to the wedding of his god-daughter the following day. He never made it; five days later, on Wednesday, 11 June, at 3.45 p.m., twenty miles (32.2 km) away in the town of Todmorden, his body was found next to a railway line in Tomlin's coal yard. The son of the yard's owner, Trevor Parker, said that the yard had not been used since 11 a.m. that morning and that the body had not been there at that time. At 4.10 p.m. two policemen, one of whom was Alan Godfrey, came to investigate. A post-mortem was carried out at 9.15 p.m. in Hebden Bridge by Dr Alan Edwards, a consultant pathologist at the Royal Halifax Infirmary. He ascertained that death took place between 11 a.m. and 1 p.m. that day. It was found that the miner had died of a heart attack and had peculiar burns on his neck and shoulders. The burns had been there two days before his death, and a peculiar ointment that forensic scientists could not identify had been applied. Although his clothes were in a decent condition, his shirt had gone, along with his watch and his wallet. The dead man's name was Zigmund *Adamski*.

Five months later, the policeman Alan Godfrey, who had visited the coal yard, witnessed a UFO whilst on duty in his patrol car on 28 November on Burnley Road in Todmorden – just one mile (1.6 km) from Tomlin's coal yard. He could not account for fifteen minutes of his time. Hypnotized by the UFO research group Manchester UFO Research Association (MUFORA) in 1981, he claimed he had been abducted. On 27 September 1981 the *Sunday Mirror* made this their front page story.

Further investigation in 2005 by John Hanson and David Sankey of the British UFO Research Association (BUFORA) established through Adamski's relatives that at the time of his death there had been a family feud, and that an unnamed relative may have been responsible for Zigmund's death. There the trail ends ... yet after we express sympathy to the poor man's family, the semi-romantic whiff of pale possibility remains – did another generation of aliens find the wrong man, but with the right name? If they did, they didn't display the benevolence that George had enjoyed, and with all their intelligence and advanced technology required to traverse the universe, they were too dumb to spot the difference between Adamski the Yorkshire coal miner and Adamski, their Californian PR man.

LITTLE GREEN MEN ... EVOLVING ALIENS AND OTHER ENTITIES

There are literally thousands of worldwide UFO reports spanning every decade since the first major "flap" in the late 1940s and 1950s. I have tried to offer a flavour of this wide-ranging and esoteric subject. The constantly open logbook of UFO sightings probably tells us as much about human behaviour as it does about potential aliens. One could question the fact that our increased international fascination with strange things in the sky coincided with the dawn of the atomic age and the era of new writings in science fiction, through authors such as Isaac Asimov, Robert Sheckley and Ray Bradbury. Are the aliens real or did we invent them? Alternatively, could they be, as described by Whitley Strieber, who wrote of his own abduction in the best-selling *Communion*, beings that connect to us through our minds? There are so many permutations to consider. Historically, the cold war had its influence; for "alien" we could always read "communist" and anything unexplained, foreign or scientifically advanced could be seen as a threat. There has always been variety in the descriptions of UFOs. From the early "airship" sightings to Adamski's cigar-shaped "mother ship" we have moved on to all manner of shapes, the current mystery item being the ubiquitous "flying triangle". Even the "aliens" themselves have evolved over the past half-century.

I was just nine years old when my mother took me to see *The Man from Planet X*, a 1951 science-fiction film directed by Edgar G. Ulmer, who had directed the very first film that teamed up Bela Lugosi with Boris Karloff in 1934, *The Black Cat*. Back in the early 1950s I found *The Man from Planet X* utterly terrifying.

To begin with, the sinister alien visitor who lands near a lonely observatory on the Scottish moors is definitely one of the very first "little green men". He was played by a dwarf actor called Billy Curtis, who had already enhanced his dramatic stature as a Munchkin in *The Wizard of Oz* and would go on years later to star as Mordecai, a small chap supporting Clint Eastwood in *High Plains Drifter*. When the man from Planet X, clad in a gold-fish-bowl helmet and a hastily assembled "space suit" courtesy of the Army and Navy surplus stores, emerged from the fog around the side of his spherical spacecraft I was in dire need of fresh underwear. I seem to recall that he had no other way of communicating other than a series of musical notes, which leaves one wondering if Spielberg had adapted the concept for *Close Encounters of the Third Kind*. I can't recall the full plot details; something about his planet needing to be on an orbit similar to earth's to prevent his race dying. As far as I was concerned, he could pack up and leave as soon as he liked. Yet I know he could well have been the prototype for what became known as the "greys" and all the other gangling, spindle-shanked, bulbous-headed, almond-eyed ETs that followed. Adherents to the Roswell legend will believe differently, of course, as the legendary alien autopsy images predate *Planet X* by four years.

However, in addition to the so-called "greys", the "little green men" have made some memorable, scary appearances. One of the most perplexing cases, the Kelly–Hopkinsville encounter (aka the Hopkinsville Goblins Case and the Kelly Green Men Case) took place in the autumn of 1955 at the remote farm occupied by the Sutton family, at the hamlet of Kelly close to the small city of Hopkinsville, Christian County, Kentucky. After flashing lights had begun to appear in the area, the Suttons were visited on their farm late at night by a gang of small, goblin-like creatures, around three feet tall (0.9 m). They were silvery, or wearing something silver, and had small, spindly limbs and tall, pointy ears. These entities scared the Sutton children by leaping up at the windows, and as the inquisitive intruders seemed reluctant to go away, the Suttons eventually decamped to Hopkinsville police station. Twenty officers went out to the farm and found extensive damage. There were similar reports in the area, and other witnesses included local policemen and state troopers. The case was subsequently investigated by the United States Air Force. Two decades later, at Dyfed, Wales, the same creatures, loitering near their landed craft, appeared to a dozen schoolchildren and three of their teachers, and the goblins have been amongst other sightings elsewhere.

THE ZAMORA SIGHTING

The Zamora sighting, although subsequently superseded by similar events, has long been one of ufology's favourites if for no other reason than that he was a New Mexico policeman. Lonnie Zamora (1933–2009) reported a UFO sighting while on duty on Friday, 24 April 1964, near Socorro, New Mexico. He was in pursuit of a speeding car when he noticed a strange craft with a loud, flaming exhaust moving overhead. He immediately gave up chasing the car and drove to the top of a hill where he had seen the craft. In a gulley below, the startled patrolman was amazed to see two small humanoid entities standing by an egg-shaped craft. When the entities spotted Zamora they quickly boarded the craft and it ascended, displaying a fiery exhaust, which ceased once the craft had risen a short distance. It then flew quickly and silently away. As a reliable, well-documented account, and one which persuaded one of the US Air Force's primary UFO investigators, astronomer Professor J. Allen Hynek, to take the subject more seriously, it has been debunked in recent years as a possible covert experimental craft from a nearby airbase. One aspect that may give this theory some credence is the "fiery exhaust" (not the usual ET propulsion method) yet the presence of the "small humanoid entities" remains a mystery.

Whether or not US Presidents, including Eisenhower and Kennedy, did meet up with ETs, as some ufologists maintain, is a debatable point. Officialdom, in the form of the military, has a strong track record for dismissing UFO sightings and denying the existence of aliens. Yet if the top brass were so convinced that the subject of flying saucers was so much hooey, we might ask why they spent so much time, manpower and resources looking into it.

UFOS AND THE MILITARY: THE "OFFICIAL" PROJECTS

From January 1948 to January 1949 the US Air Force ran Project Sign as its official investigation of UFOs. The public knew about this, referring to it as "project saucer". Project Sign investigated just 243 US and thirty foreign sightings. Out of these, about thirty-six cases remained in the "unexplained" category. The conclusion was that the flying objects were unlikely to be "interplanetary". The story goes that, at first, the report did hint at some extra-terrestrial possibilities, but the Air Force Chief of Staff at the time, General Hoyt Vandenberg, had all personnel involved in writing the report reassigned, turning their initial results down whilst requesting a more "mundane" explanation.

However, Project Sign was just the beginning. On 11 February 1949 it went on to become Project Grudge: "Final Report: – December 27, 1949. Report prepared by US Air Force (Air Materiel Command – Wright-Patterson Air Force Base)". This investigated 237 cases of which 23 per cent remained as unexplained. In March 1952 Project Grudge entered a new transformation, becoming Project Blue Book. Project Blue Book would carry on for a further seventeen years, to be wound up in 1969. The reason for its closure was a report from the University of Colorado, known as the Condon Report, which concluded that "further extensive study of UFOs probably cannot be justified in the expectation that science will be advanced thereby".

However, the inner workings of Project Blue Book reveal a more realistic attitude developing in the ranks of Air Force top brass. Within a year of Blue Book's launch, the staff handling the main project got the "easy" reports whilst the more "difficult" and perplexingly unexplained sightings would be passed over to the 4602 AISS (Air Intelligence Services Squadron). This move implemented Air Force Regulation 200-2 (AFR 200-2), which stated that information of value regarding UFOs must *not reach the public.* This kind of action has provided the conspiracy theorists with enough meat to chew on for decades. Yet we must ask – why must such information be classified? What, indeed, are we not being told? Project Blue Book was the final government-sponsored investigation of UFO sightings – at least, as far as we know. Over the period of Blue Book several thousand reports were filed, yet when *Project Blue Book* was finally edited by Brad Steiger and published by Ballantine Books in 1976, it only deepened the mystery. It revealed that 13,000 sightings had been logged during the project's existence. The twenty-page appendix headed "The Unidentified" is an astonishingly short account of the genuine mysteries over seventeen years, providing the reader with just dates and locations, so we'll never know what was really hidden behind the security screen.

In Britain, the largest disclosure of declassified documents released to date online by the National Archives has been a release of over 8,000 pages of documents detailing UFO investigations, eyewitness testimonies and military concerns about possible extra-terrestrial visitors. They include thousands of close-encounter reports that have been built up over several decades. Nick Pope, who was head of the British government's UFO project for the Ministry of Defence from 1991 to 1993, now lectures on the subject. He told the press on the release of the files: "These documents show absolutely beyond a doubt that over many, many years, Ministry of Defence officials, government ministers and defence intelligence staff have treated the UFO issue seriously. The Ministry of Defence's position was: We don't know what these things are, we don't believe they're of any defence significance. But it remained open-minded about the possibilities of extra-terrestrial life."

Reports of UFO activity throughout the world have proliferated since the 1950s. Some have been particularly bizarre. For example, in France there were forty-six "creature" reports between 10 September and 27 October 1954. They mainly involved dwarf-like beings and frequently a light beam was sighted and the witnesses would become temporarily paralysed. As the decades rolled on, other strange alien-associated reports came in; strange "moth men", something that mutilates cattle on remote ranches and even bizarre mutilations on smaller, European farms. Today, the UFO field is wider and weirder than ever.

On 8 January 2008, hundreds of people in Stephenville in Texas observed several types of UFOs, the descriptions ranging from triangular craft to discs. Some were described as the size of a football field, while others estimated they were up to a mile (1.6 km) long. The news story was covered extensively by CNN's Larry King in the days following the incident, and according to one witness, Steve Allen, a private pilot, the object he saw was travelling at a high rate of speed at 3,000 feet (915 m). Allen said it was, "About a half a mile wide and about a mile long. It was humongous, whatever it was."

On 23 January, after initially denying that any aircraft were operating in the area for operations' security purposes, the US Air Force said that they had ten F-16 Fighting Falcon jets in the region on training flights from NAS JRB Fort Worth. Disgruntled *Empire-Tribune* journalist, Angelia Joiner, who reported on the story during this period, resigned from the Stephenville paper when it ceased covering the topic. However, according to the Mutual UFO Network (MUFON), radar information from the Federal Aviation Authority shows that it tracked the F-16 flight paths as well as *an unknown object* in the same area and time as it was seen by multiple witnesses. The USAF would not comment.

Observed in the skies over the US states of Arizona and Nevada, and the Mexican state of Sonora, on 13 March 1997, the "Phoenix Lights" (sometimes referred to as the "Lights over Phoenix") were a series of widely reported UFOs of various kinds seen by thousands of people between 7.30 and 10.30 p.m. across about 300 miles (483 km), from the Nevada line, through Phoenix to the edge of Tucson. They included a triangular formation of lights plus a series of stationary lights seen in the Phoenix area. The USAF identified the second group of lights as flares dropped from an A-10 Warthog on training exercises at the Barry Goldwater Range in southwest Arizona. These events were also seen by the State Governor, Fife Symington, who referred to the objects he had witnessed as "otherworldly". The Phoenix Lights reappeared in 2007 and 2008, but on both occasions the USAF soon put out the story that they were "military flares dropped by fighter aircraft" at Luke Air Force Base and "flares attached to helium balloons released by a civilian". See *The Phoenix Lights* by Lynne D. Kitei (2004).

The most studied and memorable event in the UK took place in 1980. The Rendlesham Forest Incident involved the USAF's Bentwaters and Woodbridge Air Force Bases (according to Timothy Good, more nuclear weapons were stored at Bentwaters than anywhere else in Europe). On 27 December 1980, in the early hours of the morning, two of Woodbridge Air Force Base's security officers investigated some strange lights in Rendlesham Forest. At first, they thought an aircraft had crashed. However, one of the officers came across a strange craft, the like of which he had never seen before, which had landed. He was brave enough to go up to it, take some rough measurements and even touch it. It then suddenly took off and zoomed away, disappearing above the treeline. Two nights later, the lights returned and the second-in-command of the Woodbridge base, Colonel Charles Halt, went out with other officers to investigate. He took a tape recorder and recorded the night's activities. What he saw astonished him and defied explanation. The Colonel and his men saw a light land in a field. A light was beamed down from a craft above, close to their position, seemingly attempting to communicate with the party. Landing marks were left on the ground and the following day the base's team found that radiation levels were ten times higher than expected within the landing marks. As one of the most documented and unexplained incidents involving US military interaction with UFOs, the Rendlesham Forest case has been the subject of continuing controversy ever since, with the case featuring in *UFO Briefing Document* by Don Berliner (2000) and Timothy Good's *Above Top Secret: The Worldwide UFO Cover-up* (1987).

On 29 December 1980, several thousand miles from Rendlesham Forest, another intriguing UFO incident occurred. Betty Cash, her friend Vickie Landrum and her grandson Colby were driving towards Dayton, Texas. They noticed a bright, fiery object with shooting flames, which stopped and hovered about 135 feet (41 m) directly ahead of them. They got out of the car to look at the object. Betty stayed outside the longest. The object then departed and was accompanied by several helicopters (subsequently identified as Chinook helicopters). Betty followed the object with her car for a while and then dropped off her passengers. She then returned home. She immediately developed severe symptoms that were later attributed to radiation exposure. The other two witnesses also had symptoms, but to a lesser degree. Betty eventually succumbed to cancer several years later. It is not known if this incident contributed to her cancer illness. Betty Cash and Vickie Landrum sued the US government over this incident, but eventually the case was thrown out of court due to lack of evidence. This case is considered one the most significant physical effects cases relating to UFOs, and is featured in most current published UFO works.

From October 1989 throughout 1990, hundreds of reports of illuminated, triangle-shaped objects were recorded in the Belgian Sighting Wave. On several occasions, Belgian Air Force jets pursued these objects to no avail. The objects were frequently observed simultaneously by both airborne and ground-based radars. They remain unexplained, but the Belgian government has cooperated fully with the press and disclosed all details known about these sightings.

In South America, especially in Mexico and Brazil, sightings reached a new zenith in the twenty-first century. There have been mass sightings over Mexico City, simultaneously filmed by numerous members of the public. All we need to do today is log on to YouTube and be astonished. What has been filmed and photographed by ordinary, unsuspecting members of the public can be truly amazing, even allowing for the obvious CGI fakery of some dedicated nerds angling for a job with George Lucas.

Every continent has its mysterious visitors. On 2 July 2011, a group of glowing orbs was seen floating over an area of Moscow, and on a video that captured them, they appear to change back and forth from white to orange. A new prop in the UFO debunker's armoury is the floating Chinese lantern, which has become popular at barbecues and outdoor events in recent years. Yet Chinese lanterns tend not to make sudden, right-angled turns, whizz around at high speed, or switch themselves on and off.

ALIEN ABDUCTIONS

If only a small percentage of the many recurring stories around alien abduction are true, then we may well have to ditch the idea that these airborne intruders are benign. Charles Fort expressed the opinion that, as humans, "we are property" – but the chilling question is *whose* property? The range and nature of alien abduction events is varied, and it includes everything from nocturnal visits, with victims taken aloft on tractor beams, to a more cerebral invasion where time stands still. There are numerous recorded instances of abductees having minute, strange implants inserted into their bodies. Once on board an alien craft, a rectal examination often seems de rigueur. Whatever it is the aliens are looking for, they sure look in some odd places. Locking your bedroom window doesn't seem to help, either. There are reports of abductions in the United States as far back as the 1920s and 1930s, but the real history of alien abduction as we now know it begins with one celebrated, classic case.

In the autumn of 1961 Betty and Barney Hill were driving home from a vacation. They had stopped off at a diner in Colebrook, New Hampshire. At 10.05 p.m. they left the diner, driving south along US Route 3. Barney was amazed as they watched a large, glowing object that approached their car. He pulled up so that they could observe this phenomenon. They heard a kind of beeping sound. The next thing that they remembered was driving thirty-five miles (56 km) south near Ashland and arriving home two to two-and-a-half hours later. They'd heard another beeping sound when "waking up" near Ashland. Barney's back and neck were sore and some warts appeared on his groin. There were mysterious circles on the trunk of the car which later proved to be quite magnetic.

Later, in 1964, a Boston psychiatrist Dr Benjamin Simon put the Hills under hypnosis. Duly mesmerized, what they revealed was a terrifying ordeal where they had been taken by strange beings aboard a spacecraft. They were subjected to a physical examination. This was all very disturbing to the Hills and it soon attracted media attention. In 1965 a series of articles appeared in *Look Magazine* recounting their experience. This is the first publicized account of an alien abduction, and it resulted in a 1966 book by John Fuller, *The Interrupted Journey*. Such events have been continuously reported ever since, becoming the subject of numerous books.

Whatever secrets our governments may be concealing regarding aliens, "reverse" abductions – reported instances of ordinary, "unofficial" humans actually abducting aliens – are thin on the ground, but here's an example from October 1996. Dr Jonathan Reed was on a hiking trip in the Snoqualmie Falls area east of Seattle, Washington. He claims to have encountered an alien while hiking. The creature killed his dog. Reed responded in kind, killing the entity, which he carried for several miles down the trail and eventually to his house. Reed then stored the creature in his freezer. Allegedly the creature came to life and escaped or, as some reports indicate, it was "taken away". As ever, there was a mysterious aftermath when Reed was threatened by authorities and allegedly a lady friend was killed, although it remains unclear why. Reed has video footage of his run-in with the alien, but as well as being blurry it presents more questions than it answers. In the United States the TV show *Fact or Faked: Paranormal Files* dissected Reed's video on Thursday, 11 November 2010, and "recreated" some of the scenes, including those featuring the leathery, crinkly alien who had supposedly killed Reed's dog. With regard to the killing of the dog, one might ask why Reed did not video the poor animal's corpse as evidence. (Apparently the alien sliced it in two.) Although many ufologists continue to question this story, nonetheless it received international attention and led to the publication of a book, *Link – An Extraterrestrial Odyssey*. However, when considering most of the controversy around the video, one has to remember that the footage came to light not long after the comedy movie, *Alien Autopsy* – and even clips from that hilarious film are being shown on some UFO sites as "genuine" Roswell footage. If the event took place in 1996, why has it taken over a decade for the videos to appear? The website UFO Watchdog set out to prove that Dr Reed's true name is John Bradley Rutter and that the title "Dr Reed" is an alias. So, is Reed genuine? The jury's out, though many ufologists continue to investigate this case, and no amount of meticulous debunking will ever persuade true ET believers that their classic cases could be anything but the untrammelled truth.

Official debunking is part and parcel of ufology, even when there are numerous reliable witnesses to an anomalous event. On 9 December 1965 a fireball was witnessed in the skies over eastern Canada, Ohio and Michigan. It was seen by several observers to crash in the woods around Kecksburg, Pennsylvania at 5 p.m. Local police and fire brigades were despatched to the site but the military wasted no time in arriving at the scene. However, before the military arrived, the firemen had seen the object that had come down in the woods. It was shaped like an acorn and displayed hieroglyphic symbols on its side. When the military arrived the firemen were told to leave. Other witnesses testified that the object, covered with a tarpaulin, had been hauled away on a truck. One witness saw the hieroglyphic characters exposed below the tarpaulin. The USAF's Project Blue Book informs us that three military officers were dispatched to the area, but nothing was found. Blue Book concluded that "the object was a meteor".

Debunking abduction reports isn't as easy for officialdom. You can't send a nuts and bolts uniformed Air Force squad out to someone who claims to have been spirited away for a couple of hours in the night by inquisitive aliens. The best way to deal with abduction stories is to ridicule them and suggest that the abductee is dreaming or on narcotics (undoubtedly true in some cases). For example, in its approach to alien abduction, the sceptical side of show business, ably represented by the skilful magic duo, Penn and Teller, carried out an entertaining but condescending hatchet job on anyone claiming to have been abducted, in their 2003 TV documentary series, aptly entitled

Bullshit. Here's Penn's summing up after the duo had attended an abductee convention:

> There's no evidence that these people had any unusual experiences. They're just like all the rest of us with dreams and fantasies. We all need a little attention … The abductees are just people who pathologically need a little attention like … well, like us. You want to stop all this alien bullshit? Just pay attention to the people around you. Say hi. Humans are desperate for human contact. Let's not make our fellow travellers spend sixty bucks an hour to some pig-dog (meaning the abductee therapist) to be the centre of attention. People shouldn't have to convince themselves they have a reptilian lover in outer space to get a few minutes of your time. P & T are siding with the creeps. We always have. We love them. We are them. There are enough earthly reasons to be interested in each other. The alien business gets in the way.

OK, point taken … yet many abduction reports can't be simply dismissed with such supercilious, know-it-all arrogance.

On 11 October 1973 Calvin Parker, aged nineteen, and Charles Hickson, forty-two, sat on a pier in Pascagoula, Mississippi, enjoying a spot of fishing. Suddenly, behind them, they heard a loud buzzing noise. They turned to see, about 12 metres away, a glowing egg-shaped object, approximately 3 metres wide and 2.5 metres high, hovering above the ground, displaying blue lights. Drop-jawed, they watched a door open and three grey-skinned creatures "floated" out. They were about 1.2 metres tall, without necks, round-footed, with claws for hands, with heads shaped "like bullets yet having no eyes". Their mouths were slits, and for ears and noses they had odd conical protuberances. Two of these entities grabbed Hickson, while the third grabbed Parker. Parker fainted. Hickson remained conscious. He reported that the creatures levitated them both into a brightly lit chamber aboard the UFO. Whilst there, a strange "electronic eye" suspended above them, yet unconnected to anything visible, examined them both. Twenty minutes later, the stunned Hickson and Parker were returned to the pier. The UFO rose straight into the air and, at immense speed, shot out of sight. So, either these two characters made all this up, or they both fell asleep on the pier and had an identical dream, or they were genuinely "abducted".

On the same day, a very loud "sonic-type boom" was heard across several states from Ohio onwards, progressing to the East Coast. The sound was first reported at 8.41 p.m. in Ohio and later at 8.53 p.m. in Pennsylvania. Contacts with NASA and the USAF ruled out a meteor or Air Force jets. The boom was followed by a high number of UFO reports across the area. For example, on 17 October 1973, police in Franklin County, Ohio, received a record 150 UFO reports and officials in Wheeling, West Virginia, received 100 reports. You can read the full story in *UFO Contact at Pascagoula* by Charles Hickson and William Mendez (1983). As abduction testimonies go, this is a plain, honest account without the usual alien spiritual embroidery, concerning two ordinary men whose lives were changed by an extraordinary experience.

The 1975 Travis Walton abduction case has been under intense scrutiny for four decades and it remains a classic of the genre. In the northeastern mountains of Arizona on the night of 5 November 1975, a group of loggers witnessed a strange and unusually bright light in the sky. One of the lumberjacks, Travis Walton, whose curiosity got the better of him, hopped out of their truck to take a closer look. As he drew closer to the light, a "beam of energy" knocked him to the ground. Terrified, his companions fled. After summoning up the courage to go back, they discovered both Walton and the craft were gone. When they reported the event to local law enforcers, it seemed so incredible that initially they were suspected of murder. However, five days later Walton turned up, naked and disoriented, near a highway several miles from where he had been taken. He recounted a terrifying experience whereby he had been abducted and carted away on a craft by strange creatures. To this day this remains one of the most documented alien abduction cases. His book, *Fire in the Sky: The Travis Walton Experience* is unfortunately out of print, but the 1993 film made of the story, *Fire in the Sky*, is still available on DVD.

One of the most celebrated (and, sales-wise, successful) abductees is Whitley Strieber, whose book *Communion: A True*

Story, dealing with his 1985 abduction by "non-humans" in New York, topped the bestseller lists in 1987 and, like some of his other works, such as *The Wolfen* and *The Hunger*, became a successful movie. *Communion* was his first UFO/abductee work. The film, starring Christopher Walken as Strieber, came out in 1989. UFO fans often take everything in the book as true, although Strieber himself displays some vagueness on the subject of his abduction. If asked if the encounters in his books "really happened", he says he is not sure. An article by Lee Spiegal in the July 2011 edition of the online *Huffington Post* gives a further view of Strieber:

Certainly, sceptics could have a field day with someone like Strieber; the author first offered readers an account – "Communion" – of being abducted in upstate New York by non-human beings in 1985. But Strieber also has a reputation as a well-respected, rational individual who spends considerable time and effort investigating the things he writes about.

"For more than two decades, I have been interacting with Whitley Strieber and found him to be one of the most intelligent and thoughtful researchers in the field," said John B. Alexander, PhD, former Green Beret commander, developer of weapons at Los Alamos, NM, and author of numerous books, including *UFOs: Myths, Conspiracies and Realities*.

The whole alien abduction phenomenon has kept some psychologists and psychiatrists busy for decades. At the University of Wyoming in Laramie, the psychologist Dr Leo Sprinkle was one of the first to use hypnotism with abductees. He's reached the conclusion that the whole abduction process is part of the evolutionary process that will enable humanity finally to connect with the rest of the cosmos. Still active in his eighties, Dr Sprinkle's extensive work in the field of the paranormal is well respected among his peers.

However, beyond academia, many sceptics will point out that what are often bizarre dreams can easily be interpreted by the dreamer as something else, something more "real". There is the strong Jungian argument that such events might represent some deep, hidden psychological element in our brains, and that such occurrences might be triggered by some kind of coincidence or synchronicity. Other professed abductees could be disingenuous; an eventful, colourful abduction yarn can garner much publicity and media interest, resulting in books and films. There are, however, many abductees, including ordinary people with no desire for publicity and no previous interest in ufology, who remain stunned by their experience, with heartfelt wishes that they'd never told anyone.

SHOOTING STARS: CELEBRITIES AND UFOS

CAMEL, n. A quadruped (the Splaypes humpidorsus) *of great value to the show business. There are two kinds of camels – the camel proper and the camel improper. It is the latter that is always exhibited.*

Ambrose Bierce (1842–1914)

Due to the level of disinformation on UFOs put out by the military and intelligence communities, in media terms anyone reporting having seen an airborne anomaly could be placed in the "nutty" category with ease. Thanks to Hollywood, we have an image of the kind of person, usually a blue-collar American, who sees flying saucers. The event generally takes place in some Midwestern hick town you've never heard of, the kind of place where old men still sit on porches chewing tobacco, muttering "Yup!" or "Yes Siree!" or "Doggone!" The guy usually wears a baseball cap and dungarees and drives a battered 1970s pick-up truck. He'll tell some nasal blonde local TV reporter in her smart two-piece suit something like, "Dang it! Thing came down, all shiny like – took off with my best hound dawg ..." Yet the type of person claiming to have seen a UFO or interested in the phenomenon is rather more wide-ranging.

It's been a long tradition, since the dawn of rock 'n' roll, especially in the United States, for the conservative adult "establishment" to refer to anyone occupying the territory known as pop culture as "the kids". Of course, as rock stars begin to age, they become the establishment, but sometimes they still get a word of support from the previous generation. Colonel Philip Corso is the Former Head of Foreign Technology at the US Army's Research and Development Department at the Pentagon. For four years he was Director of Intelligence on President Eisenhower's White House National Security Staff. He had a message for "the kids":

> Let there be no doubt. Alien technology harvested from the infamous saucer crash in Roswell, in July 1947 led directly to the development of the integrated circuit chip, laser and fibre optic technologies, particle beams, electromagnetic propulsion systems, depleted uranium projectiles, stealth capabilities, and many others. How do I know? I was in charge! I think the kids on this planet are wise to the truth, and I think we ought to give it to them. I think they deserve it.

With statements such as this, the perception of UFOs is changing, and beyond all the ordinary Joes who've seen one, quite a few prominent celebrities have been taken by surprise by a visitation.

Robbie Williams

In 2008 British pop star Robbie Williams made the announcement: "I'm stopping being a pop star. I'm going to be a full-time ufologist." He claimed that he had encountered a UFO at least three times. The former boy band Take That star (successfully reunited with the band during 2010–11), after a spell in America looking for UFOs, insists that the first time he saw a UFO was when he was a kid in Britain. His second sighting was above a hotel in Beverly Hills. "I was lying on my sun lounger outside at night. Above me was a square thing that passed over my head silently and shot off." Robbie also claims that a third UFO appeared as he stood on his bedroom balcony after writing a song about alien contact. "This big ball of gold light turned up. On my life!"

He was briefly attracted to Scientology and reckons ghosts "are other worlds". He based his 2006 Close Encounters solo concert tour on UFOs. As he approaches forty, one wonders if he will indeed opt for a career as a ufologist. He's not alone in the entertainment world in having such a deep fascination with the subject.

Dan Aykroyd

Cynical sceptics might justifiably say that Tinseltown, wacky as it is, is the perfect base for a dedicated ufologist. But the surviving half of the Blues Brothers, Dan Aykroyd, is not only deeply involved in UFO research (he's Hollywood's consultant to MUFON, the Mutual UFO Network), he's actually had Men in Black experiences of his own, and those black suits, Ray-Bans, black ties and white shirts worn by the late John Belushi (Jake) and Aykroyd (Elwood) Blues in the *Blues Brothers* film are certainly a wary homage to the MIB. When filming the TV series *Out There* in New York City he was disturbed to see, on leaving the studio, a pair of the black-clad, sinister interlopers waiting across the road. On his DVD, *Dan Aykroyd Unplugged on UFOs*, produced by David Sereda, a former US Defense analyst, he tells the spooky story. He'd been phoned by Britney Spears, who had invited him to appear on *Saturday Night Live*. He then spotted a parked black Ford sedan across the street on 8th Avenue and 42nd Street. Inside sat the two MIBs, and one of them climbed out of the car and gave him a steady stare across the street. Dan tried to make out the license plate but couldn't. He turned away for a couple of seconds, but when he looked back the car and the MIB had vanished.

Aykroyd also states: "I am a Spiritualist, a proud wearer of the Spiritualist badge. Mediums and psychic research have gone on for many, many years ... Loads of people have seen spirits, heard a voice or felt the cold temperature. I believe that they are between here and there, that they exist between the fourth and fifth dimension, and that they visit us frequently." His great-grandfather, a dentist by occupation and a mystic, corresponded with author Sir Arthur Conan Doyle on the subject of spiritualism. On 29 September 2009, Dan's father, Peter Aykroyd, published a book, *A History of Ghosts*, chronicling the family's historical involvement in the spiritualist movement.

Dwight Schultz

Best known for his roles as Captain "Howling Mad" Murdock on the 1980s action show *The A-Team*, and as Reginald Barclay in *Star Trek: The Next Generation* and *Star Trek: Voyager*, William Dwight Schultz (born 24 November 1947) is an American stage, television and film actor. He's one of those actors who seem to gravitate towards movies with sci-fi plots. He's also in *Star Trek: First Contact*. He's the Mad Scientist Dr Animo in the *Ben 10* series, and enjoys such dramatic roles as Chef Mung Daal in the children's cartoon *Chowder* and Eddie the Squirrel in *CatDog*. Schultz has plenty to say about UFOs. For example:

> The Roswell incident, for instance, had over three hundred witnesses – some describing the bodies, some the craft, some the military procedures. Were they all perpetuating their own lives in a myth? The atom was unleashed in 1946, right when all this stuff was occurring. And the bomb's incredible release of energy and light may have signalled somebody in a dimension which is sharing space with us very closely.

Billy Ray Cyrus

One of the most persistently irritating pop chart hits towards the end of the twentieth century was Billy Ray Cyrus's *Achy Breaky Heart*. The fifty-year-old country singer, who is father to superstar Miley Cyrus, had an ET sighting of his own in 2011, and he even put it out on Twitter, where he wrote to Miley: "OK … my first U F O sighting. Looks like 5 or 6 disk like shapes hovering. Special moment 4 DAD." Prior to this, his interest in the subject had been noted by the SyFy channel in September 2010, announcing that along with his son Trace, Cyrus had been slated to host a debunking show dismissively titled *UFO: Unbelievably Freakin' Obvious*, which would offer a totally sceptical view of UFO sightings. The show hasn't surfaced, but now that Billy Ray's seen his own UFO, will he be able to dismiss his sighting along with all the others?

Sammy Hagar

Sammy Hagar, the lead singer for rock outfit Van Halen, has his own music publishing company called Nine Music. He claims at least three contacts with aliens, and has decided that they emanate from the ninth dimension – hence Nine Music. He reported seeing a UFO as long ago as the summer of 1968. According to an interview in *Guitar* magazine (quoted in Michael C. Luckman's highly entertaining book *Alien Rock*, 2005), Hagar said, "When I was about eighteen or nineteen, they downloaded everything that was in my head … when it was over … I was sick to my stomach, it was so scary." His continuing communication with the aliens has turned his life on end. According to Hagar, the aliens did some sort of a mind meld with him and he knew they were in some sort of space craft, while he was unable to move and bathed in a white light. He's established that there's no other life in our solar system and that the aliens come from somewhere else.

John Lennon

It was during 1974 when John Lennon, standing naked on his New York balcony, was taken aback by the sudden appearance of a flying saucer outside his window. He was standing alongside his assistant and part-time girlfriend, May Pang (this was a period when he was temporarily parted from Yoko Ono), when a saucer-shaped object came into view. According to Pang, when they reported it to the police they were told that they were not alone in seeing the UFO as others had called in, and that they should not panic. John frequently mentioned the event and incorporated it into song lyrics, for instance, the posthumously released "Nobody Told Me" from the album *Milk and Honey* (1984), recorded shortly before his murder in 1980. A line in the song is, "There's UFOs over New York and I ain't too surprised", and he also refers to this in the liner notes to his 1974 album, *Walls and Bridges*, with the message: "On the 23rd August 1974 at 9 o'clock I saw a U.F.O. – J.L."

Elvis Presley

Elvis Presley (1935–77) was almost abducted very early in his career in the 1950s. Together with his crew, including his hefty bodyguard, Lamar Fike, he was camped out in the desert when they all looked up and saw a massive, cigar-shaped object hanging in the sky. Elvis said it made an electrical buzzing noise, and they all experienced a prickling sensation as the hair on their neck and arms rose, as Elvis related: "Like when you have two people put their hands over the top of your head and then lift you off the floor and you're real light, go up fast like an elevator … Well, I thought they were going to take me, man!" The occasion was more memorable because the craft's presence caused bodyguard Lamar to collapse face down in the desert sand. Everyone thought he was dead, his heart had stopped, but they managed to resuscitate him. By that time the UFO had flown away. There were several other occasions when the Presley crew saw UFOs, with one actually hovering over the King's Bel Air mansion in California in 1966. Elvis, like a number of artists of his calibre who had reached the peak of celebrity, always claimed that his purpose on earth was to spread some kind of healing spirituality. Judging by the universal reverence in which he is still held, this seems to be the case.

Jackie Gleason

A giant of mid twentieth-century US TV comedy, Jackie Gleason (1916–87) earned himself the sobriquet "The Great One" with his nationwide television series, *The Honeymooners*, and many other TV hits as well as numerous movie appearances. As the UFO puzzle reached new heights in the 1960s, Gleason began to take a deep interest. According to The Great One's second wife, Beverly, as a close friend of President Richard Nixon, his obsession with the subject led to Nixon offering Gleason the chance to see some alien bodies in 1973, the result of a saucer crash in the southwest. (The actual crash location was not mentioned.) Gleason was flown to Homestead Air Force Base in Florida. Beverly tells us that her husband was taken to an unmarked building where he saw four embalmed bodies. He reported that the corpses were very small with large ears and bald heads. There needs to be a note of caution here, because this story originally ran in the less-than-serious *National Enquirer* – not a publication many believe in, although it is highly enjoyable in a comical way. Gleason, who had a fascination with all things paranormal and a large library on such subjects, became one of the world's leading collectors of UFO information and several of his friends confirm that the story was true.

Jimi Hendrix

When we look back at this phenomenal artist and examine his creativity, and even the cover art of his albums, it should come as no surprise that this guitar legend was totally fascinated by UFOs. According to his school friends in Seattle, Jimi Hendrix (1942–70) was into everything space-related even before his teens. Of course, in the so-called "swingin' sixties" we didn't necessarily need to be abducted by aliens to go off on a trip. There were plenty of those available via handy chemicals. Hendrix once told a *New York Times* reporter that he was from Mars. David Henderson, in his book *The Life of Jimi Hendrix* (1978), tells us that Jimi believed in life on other solar systems and that the aliens were peaceful. Michael Luckman devotes several pages to Hendrix's UFO encounters in his book *Alien Rock*. On 30 July 1970, not long before his untimely death, Hendrix played a concert on the rim of a live volcano in Maui, Hawaii. During the concert a large number of people, Jimi included, reported seeing UFOs flying overhead. Apparently the events were filmed, but I've been unable to find a clip.

Walter Cronkite

Walter Cronkite (1916–2009) was perhaps America's greatest twentieth-century news voice. He told the US public when men landed on the moon, and as the CBS network's premier newsman, he was the first to announce the assassination of John F. Kennedy. Cronkite was the voice of Middle America, so much so that when he began to criticize the American involvement in the Vietnam

War, President Lyndon B. Johnson was dismayed, saying, "If I lost Cronkite, I've lost Middle America."

Cronkite was witness to a major UFO event in the 1950s. In his capacity as journalist, he'd been invited with other reporters by the Air Force to see the testing of a new missile. However, as the projectile was about to take off, a large flying saucer arrived at the launch site. According to Cronkite, the noise of the rocket, which was firing up ready for take-off, obliterated any noise which the UFO might have made. He said that the disk was a grey colour, and once the missile had left the launch pad, the UFO projected a blue beam of light at the weapon, which held it in place about seventy feet (21 m) off of the ground. This all happened in the space of five minutes as stunned guards and their dogs were rooted to the spot while watching the strange event unfold. The missile exploded and the saucer disappeared. Amazingly, the Air Force explained that this had all been an experiment to see the reaction UFOs would have on reporters, but Cronkite thought differently. As was the custom, Men in Black style, the assembled newshounds were told not to speak of the event, which is curious when one realizes that they had been invited as part of the media to witness it! Ever the good American, Cronkite obeyed and only revealed this in an interview with a UFO expert, Bill Knell, in 1973. Since then, the disinformation machine has been in overdrive, attempting to trash Knell's interview. Knell, however, made his public statements whilst Cronkite was still alive and the newsman never refuted the conversation.

David Bowie

"Ground control to Major Tom" … *Ziggy Stardust and the Spiders from Mars* … "Loving the Alien" … if there was any cultural icon you'd expect to take an interest in UFOs, then it would be David Bowie, who, as I write this, is celebrating his sixty-fifth birthday. There's an odd story about Bowie's birth (he was born David Robert Jones on 8 January 1947). Apparently, according to his mother, the midwife proclaimed, "This child has been on this earth before." A cryptic remark, perhaps, yet there is certainly something "otherworldly" about Bowie's career. He told reporters in the 1970s that his mother had seen a flying saucer, and apparently on his US tours he even kept a telescope in the back of the limousine so that he could scan the cosmos for ET through the open sunroof.

Bowie's had his fair share of sightings, too. Back in the 1960s he actually edited a UFO publication. He regularly scanned the night sky and on some occasions saw as many as six UFOs per night. There are many alien connections in his work. He starred in the film adaptation of abductee Whitley Strieber's book, *The Hunger*, and was the "star man" in Nicholas Roeg's *The Man Who Fell to Earth* in 1976. The filming location was suitably New Mexico, the sky above which, in UFO terms, could be called "saucer alley". Bowie and the film crew were not disappointed – they had several sightings whilst on location. David Bowie and alien life – the words seem almost interchangeable and there are many more of his UFO-related events worth looking up.

The above names are just a small sample of the many celebrities and personalities who have an abiding interest in the paranormal and UFOs. Many more could be listed here, from Ringo Starr and George Clinton to Carlos Santana and Johnny Rotten. The mystery of what might be "out there" transcends the trappings of fame and fortune, for this is a subject devoid of class and status that will always attract those of us who keep asking that old question – are we alone? The astronauts such as *Apollo 14*'s Captain Edgar Mitchell know, but even they have their questions: "We all know that UFOs are real. All we need to ask is where do they come from, and *what do they want?*"

DIGGING DEEPER: CLOSE ENCOUNTERS OF THE DANGEROUS KIND

Common sense is often buried beneath the mountain of obstinate claims by dedicated UFO hunters that our governments have had contact with ETs and have been granted access to the workings of intergalactic technology. Military and security organizations are by their nature highly secretive, and whilst their reluctance to reveal their true deliberations on the UFO enigma can be frustrating, organizations such as America's CIA and NASA or European intelligence bodies will always act as one would expect; they keep their cards close to their medals. Some researchers, however, display a more polished, professional persistence. A prime example is Britain's Timothy Good. There is a cool, methodical balance to his thorough research and writing, which is hardly surprising when one considers his terrestrial day job. Born in London, he was educated at the King's School, Canterbury. He studied violin at the Royal Academy of Music, winning prizes for solo, chamber and orchestral playing. In 1963 he joined the Royal Philharmonic Orchestra, and went on to spend fourteen years with the London Symphony Orchestra. He has also played with, among others, the English Chamber Orchestra, London Philharmonic Orchestra, the Mantovani Orchestra and the Philharmonia Orchestra. In recent years he has worked as a freelance musician on movie soundtracks, commercials and TV dramas, as well as playing on records by George Michael, George Harrison, Phil Collins, Elton John, Paul McCartney, Rod Stewart and U2. When one compares this glittering career to Good's alternative occupation as a dedicated writer and researcher on the subject of UFOs, it may seem incongruous. However, one could argue that the emotional ambiguity of musical genius – the staggering talent and ability of composers like Beethoven, Mozart or Mahler – can propel us into an almost paranormal dreamscape every bit as mysterious as that eternal idea that "we are not alone".

The titles of Good's books tell us what his aims are; *Need to Know*, *Above Top Secret* and *Unearthly Disclosure* all deal with the same basic query: what do "they", i.e. officialdom, know and why won't they tell us? Timothy Good gives maximum attention to those who have outstanding experiences to relate. Some of the material he has collected from contactees in *Unearthly Disclosure*, for example, especially reports of bizarre beings (with chilling photographic evidence) leaves you in no doubt that something exceedingly strange is going on.

Good tells of his ambiguous liaisons with America's AFOSI (Air Force Office of Special Investigations). He concluded from anecdotal evidence that the UFO cover-up is as tightly clamped down and operative as ever in the Pentagon. What Good tells us often seems too fantastic to be true. For example, that the sheer technological capability of some races of aliens who are making their home here on earth can be regarded as a threat, yet their presence remains of paramount importance to the US government in its lust for new technologies. Such information will always get the tongue-in-cheek jokey treatment from officialdom and parts of the media. Yet one hapless character in England has realized that behind the hollow laughter there's a chain-mailed fist protecting the truth.

While searching for evidence of anti-gravity and UFO technologies, forty-six year-old Gary McKinnon hacked into ninety-seven NASA and Pentagon computers between February 2001 and March 2002. Besides finding the US military had a very lax computer security network, McKinnon found proof not only of UFO-based technology, but evidence of what apparently was a secret American military unit operating in outer space. So what else did he unearth? In 2006, McKinnon told Wired.com the following:

A NASA photographic expert said that there was a Building 8 at Johnson Space Center where they regularly airbrushed out images of UFOs from the high-resolution satellite imaging. I logged on to NASA and was able to access this department. They had huge, high-resolution images stored in their picture files. They had filtered and unfiltered, or processed and unprocessed files. My dialup 56K connection was very slow trying to download one of these picture files. As this was happening, I had remote control of their desktop, and by adjusting it to 4-bit colour and low screen resolution, I was able to briefly see one of these pictures. It was a silvery, cigar-shaped object with geodesic spheres on either side. There were no visible seams or riveting. There was no reference to the size of the object and the picture was taken presumably by a satellite looking down on it. The object didn't look manmade or anything like what we have created. Because I was using a Java application, I could only get a screenshot of the picture – it did not go into my temporary internet files. At my crowning moment, someone at NASA discovered what I was doing and I was disconnected. I also got access to Excel spread sheets. One was titled "Non-Terrestrial Officers". It contained names and ranks of US Air Force personnel who are not registered anywhere else. It also contained information about ship-to-ship transfers, but I've never seen the names of these ships noted anywhere else.

During the cosy relationship between Tony Blair's New Labour government and the George W. Bush administration, Britain's Home Secretary, David Blunkett, shamefully put his signature on an extradition agreement (under the umbrella of the "War on Terror") that allows British subjects to be extradited to the United States, but the agreement is not reciprocal. American subjects wanted for crimes in the UK can stay safe in their homeland. For a decade McKinnon, banned from accessing a computer or going online, has been fighting an intricate legal battle against extradition to the United States for his "crime", where he faces a term of seventy years in jail. Neither the Bush government nor the ostensibly more "liberal" Obama regime have been willing to forgive, forget and drop the case. Who says UFOs aren't dangerous?

FLIEGE HEIL!
THE NAZIS AND UFOS

The idea of the SS and the Luftwaffe developing technologically advanced flying disks at the end of the Second World War continues to occupy the nerdier, more youthful end of the UFO fraternity. What's needed here is a better grasp of aviation history. Despite all the fanciful artistic images of massive, swastika-emblazoned disks hovering above SS parade grounds, as leather-coated *Gruppenführers* gaze admiringly upon the Reich's handiwork from beneath their peaked caps, what would all sit well in an Xbox game does not, unfortunately, match the historical reality. The whole Nazi flying-saucer mythos (which also includes underground bases in the Arctic and Antarctic, a continuation of another popular Nazi myth – the "Hollow Earth" theory) originates with two innovative German brothers who worked on aircraft designs for the Luftwaffe.

Walter Horten (1913–98) and Reimar Horten (1915–94), known to the UFO fraternity as the Horten brothers, were members of the Hitler Youth and Nazi Party. They were German aircraft pilots and enthusiasts. Their formal training in aeronautics or related fields was minimal, to say the least. During the 1940s, the Hortens, however, were creative innovators, designing some of the Third Reich's most advanced aircraft, including the world's first jet-powered flying wing, the Horten Ho 229.

The severe Treaty of Versailles at the end of the First World War, which Hitler blamed for just about everything, limited the construction of German military aeroplanes in the interwar years. As a result, German military flying became semi-clandestine, taking the form of civil "clubs" supervised by decommissioned First World War veterans who trained students in gliders. As teenagers, the Horten brothers became avid flying-club members. They admired German aircraft designer Alexander Lippisch, whose influence led them away from the dominant design trends of the 1920s and 1930s. The brothers began experimenting with alternative airframes – building models and then filling their parents' house with full-sized wooden sailplanes. By the time Hitler became Chancellor in 1933, the brothers were in the Hitler Youth and their glider was in the air. Extremely aerodynamic and simple, the Hortens' glider designs were characterized by a huge, tail-less albatross-wing with a tiny cocoon of a fuselage, in which the pilot lay prone. What was impressive about the design, however, was the extremely low parasitic drag of their airframes. They were "slick" and scalable to high speeds.

By 1939, Adolf Hitler had got Versailles out of his system, and the Luftwaffe admitted Walter and Reimar to serve as pilots. (They had another brother, Wolfram, who was killed flying a bomber over Dunkirk.) Even in the Third Reich, with its National Socialist ideology, there was snobbery afoot in the Luftwaffe and the German aircraft industry, and as design consultants, the elite of the aeronautical community tended to look down their noses on the Hortens, regarding them as cultural inferiors. Walter had success as a pilot in the Battle of Britain and managed to shoot down seven British aircraft.

By 1942 the Luftwaffe supressed its snobbery and gave enthusiastic support to a Horten-designed twin-turbojet-powered fighter/bomber, designated under wartime protocols as the Horten H IX. The triumphant brothers were awarded 500,000 Reichmarks for their completion of the Ho 229 proto-types. The Horten Ho 229 was the world's first jet-powered flying wing and the turbojet-equipped H IX V2 approached astonishingly high speeds in trials. The supersonic delta-wing H.X, designed as a hybrid turbojet/rocket-fighter with a top speed of Mach 1.4 was one of the first "stealth" designs, as it had a special carbon layer that was able to reduce the radar range detection. The Hortens were certainly moving ahead in the right direction, but history was against them. They also worked on the Horten H XVIII, an intercontinental bomber that was part of the Amerika Bomber project. What was left of the Reich's war effort was being poured into the V2 weaponry but, by 1944, it was becoming obvious that the war was lost. The Ho 229, a fighter jet with great potential, arrived too late to see service. It was captured by the US Army at the end of the Second World War.

So what became of these inventive aeronautical brothers? Reimar emigrated to Argentina where he designed and built gliders and a twin-engine flying-wing transport, which was a commercial failure. Walter stayed in Germany and served as an officer in the post-war Luftwaffe. Reimar died on his ranch in Argentina in 1994, while Walter died in Germany in 1998.

The "did the Nazis invent UFOs?" mystery started after the war. In the late 1940s, before they knew more about the reality of UFOs, Project Sign, the US Air Force's flying-saucer investigation, seriously considered the possibility that UFOs might have been secret aircraft manufactured by the USSR based on the Hortens' designs. Perhaps the following document will put this genie back in the bottle.

SECRET

HEADQUARTERS BERLIN COMMAND
OFFICE OF MILITARY GOVERNMENT FOR
GERMANY (US)
BERLIN, GERMANY

S-2 Branch
APO 742, US ARMY
16 December 47

Subject: Horton Brothers (Flying Saucers)

To: Deputy Director of Intelligence
European Command, Frankfurt
APO 757, US Army

(SOURCE: A-2)

5. As far as the "flying saucer" is concerned, a number of people were contacted in order to verify whether or not any such design at any time was contemplated or existed in the files of any German air research institute. The people contacted included the following:

Walter Horten
Fraulien von der Groeben, former Secretary to Air Force General Udet
Guenter Heinrich, former office for research of the High Command of the Air Force in Berlin
Professor Betz, former chief of Aerodynamic Institute in Goettingen
Eugen, former test pilot

All the above mentioned people contacted independently and at different times are very insistent on the fact that to their knowledge and belief no such design ever existed nor was projected by any of the German air research institutions. While they agree that such a design would be highly practical and desirable, they do not know anything about its possible realization now or in the past.

[signed]

HARRY H. PRETTY
Lt Col GSC S2 Telephone BERLIN 44715
Copy furnished: Director of Intelligence, OMGUS

Smoke screen? Disinformation? Who knows? This is ufology and nothing is ever as it seems. It is interesting that this US Intelligence document originates in that seminal year, 1947, the year of Kenneth Arnold and Roswell – it even uses the new lingua franca "flying saucer". Timothy Good tells a story about a woman who was at the head of MI6, who, attending a conference, overheard a conversation in an adjoining hotel room regarding a German professor involved in Second World War aeronautics. When asked how the Nazis had made such rapid technical progress in aircraft design towards the end of the war, the cryptic reply was, "We had help." The indication was that the "help" came from elsewhere. Some of rocket ace Werner von Braun's comments seem to back this up. Yet whatever "help" was offered, we're still staggering along with old-fashioned jet propulsion and space vehicles launched on massive Roman candles of combustible fuel, and we're still struggling with the secret solution to one element, which the aliens seem to keep to themselves – gravity.

DREAMLAND: AREA 51

We can't set the controls and levitate away from ufology before taking a brief look at that ultimate conspiracy magnet, the place where everyone believes our interplanetary visitors are ensconced as they help the evil military/corporate illuminati to master the secrets of interstellar travel. If you want to go to the fountainhead and ask the US government about Nevada's Area 51, this is a sample of the reply you will receive:

Department of the Air Force
Washington DC 20330-1000

Dear (Enquirer)

This responds to your letter to the secretary of the Air Force regarding "Area 51". Neither the Air Force nor the Department of Defense owns or operates any location known as "Area 51". There are a variety of activities, some of which are classified, throughout what is often called the Air Force's Nellis Range Complex. There is an operating location near Groom Dry Lake. Specific activities and operations conducted on the Nellis Range, both past and present, remain classified and cannot be discussed publicly.

We hope this information is helpful.
Sincerely

JEFFREY A. RAMMES, Major, USAF
Chief, White House Enquiry Branch
Office of Legislative Liaison

That's all they'll tell you and the rest is speculation. However, the term "Area 51" is used in official CIA documentation. What we do know, courtesy of Wikipedia, is the following:

Area 51 is a military base, and a remote detachment of Edwards Air Force Base. It is located in the southern portion of Nevada in the western United States, 83 miles (133 km) north-northwest of downtown Las Vegas. Situated at its centre, on the southern shore of Groom Lake, is a large military airfield. The base's primary purpose is to support development and testing of experimental aircraft and weapons systems. The Groom facility appears to be run as an adjunct of the Air Force Flight Test Center (AFFTC) at Edwards Air Force Base in the Mojave Desert, around 186 miles (300 km) southwest of Groom, and as such the base is known as Air Force Flight Test Center. Other names used for the facility include Dreamland, Paradise Ranch, Home Base, Watertown Strip, Groom Lake, and most recently Homey Airport. The restricted airspace around the field is referred to as (R-4808N), known by military pilots as "The Box" or "The Container".

The intense secrecy surrounding the base, the very existence of which the US government did not even acknowledge until July 14, 2003, has made it the frequent subject of conspiracy theories and a central component to unidentified flying object folklore.

When it comes to keeping secrets, we have to admit – these guys are good at their job.

There are hundreds of other UFO cases that could have been studied in this overview, and names or books have been omitted, such as Major Donald Keyhoe's original 1958 work, *Flying Saucers Are Real*. It's essential reading, a cornerstone of ufology. Keyhoe sums up the official wall of obfuscation he always faced from his government: "It has been a complicated jigsaw puzzle. Only by seeing all parts of this intricate picture can you begin to glimpse the reasons for this stubbornly hidden secret. The official explanation may be imminent. When it is finally revealed, I believe the elaborate preparation – even the wide deceit involved – will be fully justified in the minds of the American people." Seven decades on, and we're still waiting. You can read Keyhoe's book at http://www.gutenberg.org.

I always imagine that one day soon my own sighting will arrive. January 2012 has been exciting for UFO fans here in north Nottinghamshire. Just three miles (4.8 km) up the road from me in Rainworth, outside Mansfield, there's been a major sighting in recent days, and a colour picture of the glowing, cigar-shaped object in our local paper, and another correspondent has written in to say he'd seen the same thing in the area a year ago. I know they're up there – they're simply playing hide and seek. Come on, chaps, don't you know there's a bloke down here *writing* about you? *Show yourselves!*

The UFO is the greatest unexplained phenomenon of our age. There is also a very peculiar and disturbing branch of ufology that we will delve into in the maritime mysteries section: the USO (unidentified submarine objects). Research has revealed the incredible possibility (and there are some staggering witness reports) that, fantastic though it sounds, the aliens have huge bases beneath our planet's oceans. From David Bowie to Davy Jones, it seems that those frustratingly concealed, perplexing ufonauts can direct our attention to wherever they wish, except to the truth.

That's the trouble with flying saucers; the more you learn, the less you know.

PART 3:

BEYOND THE VEIL

The thought of death leaves me in perfect peace, for I have the firm conviction that our spirit is a being of indestructible nature: it works on from eternity to eternity; it is like the sun, which though it seems to set to our mortal eyes, does not really set, but shines on perpetually.

Johann Wolfgang von Goethe (1749–1832)

LIFE AFTER DEATH?

*Why do people embrace God? In my opinion, belief in God and
an afterlife is a necessary extension of man's need to feel that this
life does not end with what we call death.*

Robert Vaughn, actor (1932–)

In our rational, tactile modern world of technology and science,
many find it easier than ever to poke continual fun at most
aspects of the unexplained. Aliens and flying saucers still
remain a huge joke to serious astronomers and scientists; old-
fashioned spiritualism, which we're about to examine, wouldn't
pass muster in today's mechanized world. Ghosts still raise
many a sceptical smile and the Loch Ness Monster may not
even exist.

The erudite writer Peter Brookesmith, elegantly commenting
on spiritualism in the *Fortean Times* in 2002, expressed his
opinion of the more gullible fans of Forteana thus:

In that thick square book, whose pages are of granite and
whose bindings are of brass, titled The True Believer's Bible,
or Ten Thousand Rules for Swallowing Rubbish Whole,
there is an article of faith that runs: "If a man of science supports your claim, it must be true." Thus, flying saucers must
be real because some Americans with PhDs think so, and
crop circles must be made by aliens, despite the repeated
admissions of large numbers of male humans who, stoically
facing middle age, can think of no better ways to meet girls
and while away their weekends.

In many ways, I concur; it's a vigorous view, but a valid dismissal of the often credulous hordes clogging up the internet. But nowhere in the landscape of phenomena is the word "however" more apt as a prefix than with the subject of death.

When that branch of compassionate humanity to whom we can almost apply the term "gods" – dedicated doctors and surgeons – are so overcome with the odd, inexplicable events arising from their efforts to save their patients, we cannot simply sneer at their MD, FRCS or PhD and lump them all together with David Icke. Such people tackle this great final taboo on a daily basis, and those who sacrifice their own time to detailed research and analysis of the subject deserve respect.

The psychiatrist Elisabeth Kübler-Ross, MD, passed away on 24 August 2004. One of triplets, she was born in Zurich, and in 1957 graduated from the University of Zurich's Medical School. In 1958 she moved to the United States to work in a New York hospital, where she became acutely concerned over the treatment of terminal patients. "They were shunned and abused, nobody was honest with them," she said. She decided to give up her time to sit at the bedsides of the dying, listening to their fears and concerns. This thoughtful activity, voluntarily attending to what these terminal patients were going through, led to her developing a deep curiosity around that unanswerable question – what happens when we die?

In 1969 she published the classic *On Death and Dying*, a work which brought Dr Kübler-Ross international renown. "My goal was to break through the layer of professional denial that prohibited patients from airing their innermost concerns," she wrote. She went on to write a further twenty books on the subject, translated into more than twenty-five languages, and throughout her life lectured regularly to packed audiences. She received over twenty honorary doctorates. In 1995 she suffered a series of major strokes, which left her paralysed and facing her own death. At the time she said, "I am like a plane that has left the gate and not taken off. I would rather go back to the gate or fly away." This experience inspired her to write a somewhat different book with David Kessler, *On Grief and Grieving*, with a strap line bound to intrigue; "Life Lessons: two experts on death and dying teach us about the mysteries of life and living." "I wanted," she said, "to finally write a book on life and living." This moving work is her final legacy, completing the circle of her life's research.

Her work with terminal patients and her ongoing investigations inspired other physicians, and by 1975 the young psychiatrist Dr Raymond Moody (who coined the term "near-death experience") had carried out his own research recording and comparing the experiences of 150 persons who had died, or almost died, and then recovered. His 1975 book, *Life after Life*, with a foreword by Dr Kübler-Ross, brought the near-death experience to a wider public attention. It remains a bestseller, and he wrote more works on the subject: *The Light Beyond*, *Reunions*, *Life after Loss*, *Coming Back*, *Reflections* and *The Last Laugh*.

Whether or not you have a faith or a religion, death takes no prisoners. Our short biological existence as humans is a mere infinitesimal flickering pinprick against the eternal black backdrop of the universe. The fact that we seem to cram so much into our few decades is amazing, and most of us cannot begin to imagine what, if anything, comes after. If there are clues, then they come from those many individuals who have straddled the threshold between this life and death, only to come back after being spared. I see neither rhyme nor reason why anyone should make these stories up. Most have a worldwide consistency and they number in their many thousands, but it is only during the past century that the more open-minded practitioners in medicine have employed empirical methodology to study what is a genuine phenomenon.

Unaware of Dr Moody's work at the time, in 1978 another researcher was embarking on her own study of near-death experiences. Doctor P. M. H. Atwater is not a "medical" doctor in the accepted sense. She was already a successful writer, journalist and author. She earned her Letters of the Humanities (LHD) doctorate from the International College of Spiritual and Psychic Studies (ICSPS) in Montreal, Quebec, Canada, on 19 May 1992. The ICSPS is an interfaith seminary and college for the study of transformative spiritual and psychic experiences. In 2005 the Medicina Alternativa Institute awarded her an honorary PhD in Therapeutic Counselling.

The Institute was formed in 1962 under the policy objectives of the World Health Organization (WHO). In 1962 the WHO and UNICEF sponsored an international conference in the USSR at Alma Ata, at the University of Kazakhstan. The Alma Ata Declaration was a global strategy for public health and preventive medicine under the banner "Health for All by 2000 AD", utilizing all available orthodox and traditional healing methods. Guided by the WHO, Medicina Alternativa became an international society with membership limited to those who had attended the Alma Ata meeting, which included delegates from forty-six countries. It is affiliated to the Open International University for Complementary Medicines in Colombo, Sri Lanka. Also in 2005, the International Association for Near-death Studies (see www.iands.org) presented Dr Atwater with an Outstanding Service Award and the National Association of Transpersonal Hypnotherapists gave her a Lifetime Achievement Award. This organization was formed in 1990 by Anne Salisbury. Its website (www.transpersonal hypnotherapy.com) tells us, "The Transpersonal Hypnotherapy Institute is approved and regulated by the Colorado Board of Education. The curriculum of THI is based in Transpersonal Psychology, and it utilizes powerful psychotherapy, hypnotherapy and spiritual techniques."

I provide brief outlines of all the above spiritual establishments because they are the kind of organizations, "approved and regulated" or not, which enrage the loftier reaches of academia, as represented by such esteemed establishments as Harvard, Oxford, Cambridge and Princeton. Above all, regarded as they are as "fringe" organizations dabbling in health matters, they aggravate a large section of the orthodox medical establishment. This understandable attitude often leads to fully trained practising physicians, psychiatrists and psychologists who go out on a limb to study in medicine's no-man's-land of spirituality being derided for what seems to be regarded as almost a dereliction of duty. This is logical, but if those of us who are unfortunately untutored are searching for answers the test tube and the microscope can't provide, we can but give the mavericks, both within orthodox medicine and on its fringes, their voice.

Science v. Quackery

Behind the medical scenes, for a century or more there has been an ongoing battle between "orthodox" scientific medical practice and what we now refer to as alternative medicine. One only has to look at a website such as www.quackwatch.com and we can see an extension of that same antagonism that continues to rage between scientific sceptics and believers in the paranormal. Medicine, referred to through its long history as "the healing arts", has many diverse branches, from shamans to transplant surgeons. Today's American doctors, known generally as "physicians", are educated in and follow the allopathic tradition. Their training is as a result of early twentieth-century reforms instigated by Canada's Sir William Osler (1849–1919). Pathologist, physician, educator, bibliophile, historian, author and renowned practical joker, Osler, known as "the father of modern medicine", was instrumental in the creation of the Johns Hopkins University School of Medicine. American medical practice also owes much to the "Flexner Report", *Medical Education in the United States and Canada*, published in 1910 on behalf of the Carnegie Foundation. It was written by the professional educator Abraham Flexner (1866–1959). This wide-ranging study still exerts great influence over the present-day American medical profession.

Before Osler and Flexner brought science to medical practice, allopathic medicine utilized a large variety of patent medicines that can be compared to what we now call herbal remedies. Some were toxic, many were dubious, but they were nonetheless heavily marketed palliatives, their labels proclaiming relief from "fatigue, malaise, fever, cold, sore joints" etc. By 1920, however, the number of medicines the new generation of physicians were using had dropped dramatically. The thousands of previous concoctions were reduced down to a tiny number of effective medicines. New research and testing soon developed fresh and effective additions to the physician's pharmacopoeia. Some were unprecedented discoveries, but many still had their genesis in the old herbal remedies – for example, quinine. The majority of Osler and Flexner's twenty-first-century devotees continue to regard many alternative therapies related to yoga, t'ai chi and psychic channelling as mere placebos, and in some cases dangerous; in fact, there are campaigns run by some practitioners to regulate such practices as acupuncture and reiki healing. Although it is estimated that perhaps half of US physicians may use alternative therapy, it remains controversial because it is based on historical or cultural traditions, rather than on scientific evidence. Its critics maintain that the terms "complementary" and "alternative" medicine are deceptive euphemisms meant to give an impression of medical authority. Therefore, if you are a qualified medical doctor, stop reading here. We are about to leave science's safe trenches and enter no-man's-land.

Near-Death Experiences

I have chosen Dr Atwater's work due to its depth and breadth and because of her genuine dedication to her subject. Also, she is the only researcher known who went out and did her own independent study of near-death states, having never heard of Raymond Moody, his book or the now famous (but incomplete) "classical model" of the near-death experience (NDE).

As one of the original researchers in the field of near-death studies, she spent almost four decades holding sessions with nearly 4,000 adult and child experiencers. She has written ten books on her findings, runs a blog (www.atwaterndenews.blogspot.com) for questions and answers on the subject, and features on YouTube. Her book *Near-Death Experiences: The Rest of the Story* (2011) summarizes her work for the last thirty-three years. She gives maximum importance to the NDE's pattern of physiological and psychological after-effects – as it is the after-effects that validate the experience, not the other way around. That pattern, in most cases, becomes lifelong. Some of her work has now been verified in clinical, prospective studies, including a study in the Netherlands published in the *Lancet* medical journal.

The following material is reproduced, with her permission, from two of Doctor Atwater's books – *Beyond the Light: The Mysteries and Revelations of Near-Death Experiences* (1994) and *We Live Forever: The Real Truth about Death* (2004). It is based on first-person commentaries from over 3,000 adult experiencers of near-death states.

What It Feels Like to Die

Any pain to be suffered comes first. Instinctively you fight to live. That is automatic.

It is inconceivable to the conscious mind that any other reality could possibly exist beside the earth-world of matter bounded by time and space. We are used to it. We have been trained since birth to live and thrive in it. We know ourselves to be ourselves by the external stimuli we receive. Life tells us who we are and we accept its telling. That, too, is automatic, and to be expected.

Your body goes limp. Your heart stops. No more air flows in or out. You lose sight, feeling, and movement – although the ability to hear goes last. Identity ceases. The "you" that you once were becomes only a memory. There is no pain at the moment of death. Only peaceful silence … calm … quiet. But you still exist.

It is easy not to breathe. In fact, it is easier, more comfortable, and infinitely more natural not to breathe than to breathe. The biggest surprise for most people in dying is to realize that dying does not end life. Whether darkness or light comes next, or some kind of event, be it positive, negative, or somewhere in-between, expected or unexpected, the biggest surprise of all is to realize you are still you. You can still think, you can still remember, you can still see, hear, move, reason, wonder, feel, question, and tell jokes – if you wish.

You are still alive, very much alive. Actually, you're more alive after death than at any time since you were last born. Only the way of all this is different; different because you no longer wear a dense body to filter and amplify the various sensations you had once regarded as the only valid indicators of what constitutes life. You had always been taught one has to wear a body to live.

If you expect to die when you die you will be disappointed. The only thing dying does is help you release, slough off, and discard the "jacket" you once wore (more commonly referred to as a body). When you die you lose your body. That's all there is to it. Nothing else is lost.

You are not your body. It is just something you wear for a while, because living in the earth-plane is infinitely more meaningful and more involved if you are encased in its trappings and subject to its rules.

What Death Is

There is a step-up of energy at the moment of death, an increase in speed as if you are suddenly vibrating faster than before. Using radio as an analogy, this speed-up is comparable to having lived all your life at a certain radio frequency when all of a sudden someone or something comes along and flips the dial. That flip shifts you to another, higher wavelength. The original frequency where you once existed is still there. It did not change. Everything is still just the same as it was. Only you changed, only you speeded up to allow entry into the next radio frequency on the dial.

As is true with all radios and radio stations, there can be bleed-overs or distortions of transmission signals due to interference patterns. These can allow or force frequencies to coexist or commingle for indefinite periods of time. Normally, most shifts up the dial are fast and efficient; but, occasionally, one can run into interference, perhaps from a strong emotion, a sense of duty, or a need to fulfil a vow, or keep a promise. This interference could allow coexistence of frequencies for a few seconds, days, or even years (perhaps explaining hauntings); but, sooner or later, eventually, every given vibrational frequency will seek out or be nudged to where it belongs.

You fit your particular spot on the dial by your speed of vibration. You cannot coexist forever where you do not belong. Who can say how many spots there are on the dial or how many frequencies there are to inhabit. No one knows.

You shift frequencies in dying. You switch over to life on another wave-length. You are still a spot on the dial but you move up or down a notch or two. You don't die when you die. You shift your consciousness and speed of vibration.

That's all death is … a shift.

With many of the other subjects covered in this book, it is easy, in some cases even wholesome, to utter a sceptical snigger. Yet as the saying goes, we're all guaranteed two things; death and taxes. We have nothing to lose by accepting Dr Atwater's uplifting words. We have two choices here: one is to believe that everything we are physically, flesh, blood and bone, comes to an end and decays to dust – but that the rest of our being, our accumulated personality, our cerebral selves – for want of a better word, our souls, live on. The other choice is just as valid; that is to accept that when our lights go out for good, that's it. Nothing. Eternal darkness. I know which choice I've made.

I have been under the knife in the hospital operating theatre on three occasions in recent years. Unlike most innocent patients, with more serious ailments, from heart bypasses to the removal of tumours, my surgery has been the result of self-indulgence; a life of being the soul of the party, overeating, tobacco, Olympic drinking. Then, with advancing age, comes the umbilical hernias, followed by the incisional hernias, leading to the spontaneous emergency of a trapped bowel. Spending twenty-four hours in extreme agony on a trolley in a hospital cubicle, gasping and praying for a nurse to administer that precious morphine, and realizing the acute danger a strangulated bowel presents, as you stare despondently upwards at the fluorescent lamps on the ceiling, thoughts of the real possibility of death insinuate themselves into your psyche. Of course, once they arrive with the morphine you enter the embrace of chemical kindness, and although you don't want to die and leave your loved ones, the extreme peace induced by the drug seems to remove fatality's threat.

Death is still the taboo we avoid discussing. The "end" of our lives is the ultimate mystery. What is it? Where do we go? This pulsating mass of flesh, a beating heart, our active brain, our emotions, our relationships, our walking, breathing existence, all suddenly gone. To where? As Peggy Lee once sang "Is That All There Is?" There is also a delicious moment as we are being prepared for surgery. After twenty-four hours on nil-by-mouth we feel relaxed, lying on our trolley, watching the lamps flash by above as the porter pushes us along unfamiliar corridors to that inner sanctum of surgeons, that brilliant chamber of chrome, stainless steel, pristine cotton and twinkling medical dials in which we will thankfully be unconscious. Then we reach the crossroads as the kindly anaesthetist speaks gently and he sinks that little needle into your vein. Count down: ten … nine … eight … seven … blackness. There is no unconsciousness in my experience as deep and as darkly void as that under anaesthetic. Thus, if and when we come round hours later, still under morphine, we are faced with that mysterious question – that black emptiness – is that what death is like?

Despite the claims of spiritualism and clairvoyance, the usual argument is that no one has ever returned to tell us. However, what this position represents is the fact that, depending on one's faith, Jesus Christ aside, no one who has finally, irrefutably died has been resurrected to describe what life in heaven (or hell) is like. There are those cynics who proclaim, "When I die, I know I'll go to heaven, because I've done my time in hell." But some of us may be granted a brief look into that "other world" from the threshold of a near-death experience.

I have no idea if my following experience counts as an NDE. Perhaps this was arguably more a "near-dream experience". Running it past the experts at the Near Death website, Jody Long responded:

> your experience was more than a dream. I have come to believe that vivid dreams are interactions with spirit, so we don't forget them easily. Your experience is either a possible NDE or at the least a NDE-like experience. The differential would be if the people you saw were alive or had passed over when you saw them. All experiences are valuable. I don't understand why everyone wants to make their experience a NDE. We have so many experiences of all types of consciousness that are just jaw-dropping. It is the subjective feeling and subsequent change of behaviour due to the experience that makes it valuable, in my opinion. Any experience that helps us to be a better human being is phenomenal.

So, here's what happened to me.

After being at home for a few days following surgery in 2007, I had developed a wound infection which required the daily visit of the district nurse to clean it and apply new dressings. I was taking strong painkillers during this period. One night I went to bed earlier than usual and experienced some discomfort. My breathing was difficult (not helped either by the fact that I remained stupidly obstinate as a smoker). Lying on my back in the darkness, I was lamenting the state at which I had allowed myself to arrive. Louis Armstrong's witty observation was running through my mind; "If I'd known I was going to live this long, I would have taken more care of myself." I felt foolish and irresponsible. All this could have been avoided had I lived a better, more sensible life. With a loving wife and children, I felt I had let them all down. I was overcome with great sadness, and it was the worst kind of sorrow – the unforgivable sin of self-pity. Still breathing with difficulty, I eventually drifted off.

What happened next I still find difficult to accept. Although in a deep sleep, I felt as if my heart had stopped. There was a feeling of panic as I struggled to breathe, but this passed, to be replaced with a blissful feeling of calm. I was floating, weightless, surrounded by light; I have heard this referred to as a "tunnel" and although it had those characteristics, the walls themselves were pure light. I was then in an unenclosed landscape of golden light and was pleasantly surprised to see people passing by who I had known during my younger years. Some were old friends, others people I may have argued and fallen out with, yet now there was no enmity. I was then overcome with emotion as my departed mother came into view, smiling. As I moved towards her, I was hoping to speak with her, yet felt myself falling backwards. Suddenly, the light went out and I was awake. I sat bolt upright in bed, gasping for air. Eventually, after much coughing and spluttering, I settled down and switched the bedside lamp on. The feeling of disappointment was immense. I had missed the chance to talk to my mother.

After sitting up in bed for over thirty minutes, I eventually relaxed and began to assess the situation. Rationality kicked in. This was a dream, I told myself. Vivid, yet probably chemically induced by the painkillers. My heart was beating normally. I wasn't perspiring. My chest had cleared and I was able to breathe. Nothing paranormal. Nothing psychic. Yet still that brief episode haunts me. What if ... what if my body had actually shut down – just for a few seconds? Where is the dividing line between a dream and the total switch-off of one's system? Relating this experience to friends and relatives is embarrassing, because it makes me feel something of a spiritual charlatan. Sceptics have suggested that due to my avid interest in such subjects that all the seeds of an NDE were already planted in my subconscious, so that they were poised to enter a random dream. I can accept that. I also accept that my paltry event fades into insignificance when compared to the many real, true reports of NDEs. Yet even if it was simply a dream, its remarkable clarity has left its mark on my view of life and what might come after. There may be two possibilities offered by death, after all; the black emptiness of the operating theatre table or the golden, worry-free bliss of a new dimension, a new start. One thing is for sure – everyone reading these words will one day discover the truth.

However, enough of my deep-slumber imaginings. Time to take another look at the real thing. Doctor Atwater has kindly provided further elements of her research which give us a broader picture of NDEs.

The Four Types of Near-Death Experiences

1. Initial Experience – sometimes referred to as the "non-experience" (an awakening). Involves only one … maybe two or three … elements, such as a loving nothingness, the living dark, a friendly voice, a brief out-of-body experience, or a manifestation of some type. Usually experienced by those who seem to need the least amount of evidence for proof of survival, or who need the least amount of shakeup in their lives at that point in time. Often, this becomes a "seed" experience or an introduction to other ways of perceiving and recognizing reality. Rarely is any other element present.
Incident rate: 76 per cent with child experiencers
             20 per cent with adult experiencers

2. Unpleasant and/or Hell-Like Experience – sometimes referred to as "distressing" (inner cleansing and self-confrontational). Encounter with a threatening void, stark limbo, or hellish purgatory, or scenes of a startling and unexpected indifference (like being shunned), even "hauntings" from one's own past. Scenarios usually experienced by those who seem to have deeply suppressed or repressed guilt, fear, and anger, and/or those who expect some kind of punishment or discomfort after death. Life reviews common. Some have life previews.

Incident rate: 3 per cent with child experiencers

15 per cent with adult experiencers

3. Pleasant and/or Heaven-Like Experience – sometimes referred to as "radiant" (reassurance and self-validation). Heaven-like scenarios of loving family reunions with those who have died previously, reassuring religious figures or light beings, validation that life counts, affirmative and inspiring dialogue. Scenarios usually experienced by those who most need to know how loved they are and how important life is and how every effort has a purpose in the overall scheme of things. Life reviews common. Some have life previews.

Incident rate: 19 per cent with child experiencers

47 per cent with adult experiencers

4. Transcendent Experience – sometimes referred to as "collective universality" (expansive revelations, alternate realities). Exposure to otherworldly dimensions and scenes beyond the individual's frame of reference; sometimes includes revelations of greater truths. Seldom personal in content. Scenarios usually experienced by those who are ready for a "mind stretching" challenge and/or individuals who are more apt to use (to whatever degree) the truths that are revealed to them. Life reviews rare. Collective previews common (the world's future, evolutionary changes, etc.).

Incident rate: 2 per cent with child experiencers

18 per cent with adult experiencers

The Integration Phases Near-Death Experiencers "Grow" Through

Phase One: First 3 years

Impersonal, detached from ego identity/personality traits. Caught up in desire to express unconditional love and oneness with all life. Fearless, knowing, vivid psychic displays, substantially more or less energy, more or less sexual, spontaneous surges of energy, a hunger to learn more and do more. Childlike mannerisms with adults/adult-like behaviours with children, a heightened sense of curiosity and wonder, IQ enhancements, much confusion, challenged with communication. Rebirthing.

Phase Two: Next 4 years*

Rediscovery of and concerned with relationships, family, and community. Service- and healing-oriented. Interested in projects development and work environment. Tend to realign or alter life roles; seek to reconnect with one's fellows, especially in a moral or spiritual way. Unusually more or less active/contemplative. Can resume former lifestyle, but more desirous of carrying out "mission". Retraining.

Phase Three: After the 7th year

More practical and discerning, often back-to-work, but with a broader worldview and a confident attitude. Aware of self-worth and of "real" identity (soul). Tend towards self-governance and self-responsibility. Spiritual development an ongoing priority, along with sharing one's story and its meaning. Dedicated. Strong sense of spiritual values. Reborn.

Phase Four: Around 15th year (with some 12th or 20th year)**

Immense fluctuations in mood and hormonal levels. Often discouraged or depressed while going through a period of "grieving" – reassessing gains and losses from the experience, while fearful that effects are fading. Many problems with relationships, money, and debts. A crisis of "self". If can negotiate "the darkness light can bring", a depth of spiritual maturity and confidence emerges that is unique to the long-term effects of a transformation of consciousness. Born again.

NOTES:
*   Child experiencers in Dr Atwater's study who turned to alcohol for solace (1/3) began drinking during this phase.
** Child experiencers who attempted suicide (21 per cent) did so in this phase.

Physiological After-effects of Near-Death States

Most Common (between 80 to 95 per cent) – more sensitive to light, especially sunlight, and to sound (tastes in music change); look younger/act younger/more playful (with adults) – look older/act and seem more mature (with children); substantial change in energy levels (can have energy surges); changes in thought processing (switch from sequential/selective thinking to clustered/abstracting, with an acceptance of ambiguity); insatiable curiosity; lower blood pressure; bright skin and eyes; reversal of brain hemisphere dominance commonplace; heal quicker.

Quite Common (50 to 79 per cent) – reversal of body clock, electrical sensitivity, heightened intelligence, metabolic changes (doesn't take as long to process food, bowel movements can increase); assimilate substances into bloodstream quicker (takes less of something for full effect); loss of pharmaceutical tolerance (many turn to alternative/complementary healing modalities); heightened response to taste/touch/texture/smell/pressure; more creative and inventive; synesthesia (multiple sensing); increased allergies; preference for more vegetables, less meat (with adults) – more meat, fewer vegetables (with children); latent talents surface; indications of brain structure/function changes (also to nervous and digestive systems, skin sensitivity).

Psychological After-effects of Near-Death States

Most Common (between 80 to 99 per cent) – loss of the fear of death; become more spiritual/less religious; more generous and charitable; handle stress easier; philosophical; more open and accepting of the new and different; disregard for time and schedules; regard things as new even when they're not (boredom levels decrease); form expansive concepts of love while at the same time challenged to initiate and maintain satisfying relationships; become psychic/intuitive; know things (closer connection to Deity/God, prayerful); deal with bouts of depression; less competitive.

Quite Common (50 to 79 per cent) – displays of psychic phenomena; vivid dreams and visions; "inner child" issues exaggerate; convinced of life purpose/mission; rejection of previous limitations/norms; episodes of future knowing common; more detached and objective (dissociation); "merge" easily (absorption); hunger for knowledge; difficulty communicating and with language; can go through deep periods of depression and feelings of alienation from others; synchronicity commonplace; more or less sexual; less desire for possessions and money; service-oriented; healing ability; attract animals (good with plants); aware of invisible energy fields/auras; preference for open doors and open windows/shades; drawn to crystals; laugh more; adults lighter afterwards – children wiser, more serious, bonding to parents lessens.

Afterwards: The Common Traits of a Near-Death Experiencer

The most common traits of healthy (normal) near-death experiencers afterwards, irrespective of age, are as follows. Some exhibit more or less, but this is average. These are based on sessions with 3,000 plus adult and 277 child experiencers.

- Unusually empathetic, rich inner lives, some healing ability.

- Complex, vivid dreams, good recall.
- Highly perceptive, creative, intuitive, strong feelings (especially of love).
- Faculties enhanced, synesthesia (conjoined senses), psychic ability.
- Susceptible to environmental changes, more allergies than before.
- Sense of being able to merge with others and with nature.
- Surplus energy for many (with others less), restless, curious.
- Strong reactions to positive/negative sensory stimuli.
- Much in the way of visuals, aesthetic awareness, knowing.
- Intense focus, love to question, hunger for knowledge.
- Feel things deeply, can have past-life/anomalous memories.
- Identify more with soul than self, mystical awareness.
- Comfortable with things future and otherworldly states/ beings.
- Can at times influence physical objects, electrical sensitivity.
- Out-of-body experiences can sometimes continue.
- Tend towards self-deception, need to relearn basic cautions.
- Tend to identify life as a waking dream.

Dr Atwater comments: "Wake up psychologists and psychiatrists. This is normal for millions of people."

To a great number of surgeons, neurologists and other medical researchers, the idea of the NDE or an OBE (out-of-body experience) having anything to do with the paranormal must be challenged by science. They will say that neurobiological models often fail to explain NDEs resulting from the near proximity of death, when the brain does not suffer physical damage, such as a car accident without cranial injury. They suggest the neurobiological effects could be the result of stress.

Richard Kinseher devised a new theory in 2006, applying knowledge of the Sensory Autonomic System to the phenomenon of the NDE. The autonomic nervous system (ANS or visceral nervous system) is part of the peripheral nervous system. It is a control structure which mainly works below the level of consciousness. It regulates your heart rate, respiration rate, digestion, salivation, perspiration, diameter of the pupils, micturition (urination) and sexual arousal. Kinseher suggests that the experience of approaching death is an exceptionally peculiar paradox to a living organism, capable of triggering an NDE. During this experience, the patient becomes capable of "seeing" the brain scanning our whole life, every event, often all the way back to prenatal. It's like a computer searching a database for a resolution to a problem in the file system, but our mind sees all the events of life as the brain desperately rummages through our hard drive for a solution or some comparison to help cope with impending fatality. Whilst living, we all have memories that we may feel are irretrievably lost, yet people who go through an NDE are flooded with all the events, large or small, that they thought had gone forever. Therefore Kinseher's hypothesis relies upon a theory of memory in which all memories are retained indefinitely.

This research also suggests that OBEs, often occurring in conjunction with NDEs, are a result of attempting to create an overview of the surrounding world whilst assessing the situation. So far, so good, but this does not explain the accuracy of reports by patients of what they have seen during their OBE. They can relate who entered and left the room, the position and posture of their own prone body, often what was said, the way instruments in the operating theatre were laid out; some can even tell us what items were stored on the tops of cupboards or lockers, which would be out of sight from a standing position.

The brain – and the sense of vision – leaving the body? The NDE may well be, as other researchers insist, a malfunction of the brain resulting from the cessation of cerebral blood circulation, and not everyone who temporarily "dies" goes through the experience. But in addition to the many thousands whose NDEs have been logged, there are many others who will not speak of the incident, often with good reason. They would not wish to be stigmatized as some sort of crank or to suggest that their medical experience had in some way had some detrimental effect upon their personality.

Hallucination or not, the effect of an NDE or an OBE is profound and life-changing.

Many male writers are prone to being inspired by the great twentieth-century novelist and man of action, Ernest Hemingway. The kind of man he was is out of fashion now. Fishing, shooting, boxing, even bullfighting, he did it all. He drank like a fish, smoked, worked his way through many tempestuous relationships, yet wrote some of the twentieth century's finest prose. He was no stranger to war – like many journalists and writers of his generation, he saw the great conflicts of his time as massive adventures. When fighting raged in Italy on the banks of the River Piave, near Fossalta, during the First World War, Hemingway, who had enrolled as a Red Cross ambulance driver (he was refused military enlistment due to his eyesight) was wounded by shrapnel. Convalescing in Milan, he wrote a letter home to his family. It contained a cryptic statement: "Dying is a very simple thing. I've looked at death and really I know." Years later, Hemingway explained to a friend what had occurred on that fateful night in 1918 (Dr Atwater quotes this in *Beyond the Light*):

> There was one of those big noises you sometimes hear at the front. A big Austrian trench mortar bomb, of the type that used to be called ash cans, exploded in the darkness. I died then. I felt my soul or something coming right out of my body, like you'd pull a silk handkerchief out of a pocket by one corner. It flew all around and then came back and went in again and I wasn't dead anymore.

This experience enabled him to write more deeply about the subject of death than any other author of the time. The event had a deep and lasting effect, and he was never quite the same "hard man" as he'd imagined he was afterwards. In his classic *A Farewell to Arms*, the character Frederic Henry, like Hemingway, confronts death:

> I ate the end of my piece of cheese and took a swallow of wine. Through the other noise I heard a cough, then came the chuh-chuh-chuh-chuh – then there was a flash, as when a blast-furnace door is swung open, and a roar that started white and went red and on and on in a rushing wind. I tried

to breathe but my breath would not come and I felt myself rush bodily out of myself and out and out and out and all the time bodily in the wind. I went out swiftly, all of myself, and I knew I was dead and that it had all been a mistake to think you just died. Then I floated, and instead of going on I felt myself slide back. I breathed and I was back.

Heaven and Hell

The much hoped-for cosmological or metaphysical afterlife is also known as "Heaven", the "Heavens" or the "Seven Heavens". Heaven is said to be the domain of whatever deity or god your religion worships, the home of the angels and the place wherein we all hope to meet our departed loved ones and venerated ancestors. It's a paradise, the "Higher Place" where most scriptures promise admission only to the good, the pious or the utterly virtuous. Some religions even believe in the possibility of a heaven on earth in a world to come. There are as many passports to heaven as there are religions. Although, for example, the Jewish faith has many references to "the world to come" in general, it is vague about heaven and how to get there, concentrating more on living the life we have as best we can. In Dr Atwater's 2004 book, *We Live Forever: The Real Truth about Death*, she tells us how she defines "the arrangement of heaven and hell, based upon what I have observed in my research, as follows":

Hell refers to levels of negative thought forms that reside in close proximity to the earth plane. The vibration in these levels is slower, heavier, and more dense. It is where we go to work out whatever blocks us from the power of our own light: hangups, addictions, fears, guilts, angers, rage, regrets, self-pity, arrogance. We stay in hell (and there are many divisions to this vibratory level) for however long best serves our development. There is no condemnation here, per se, rather the working out of our own errors in judgement and mistakes, misalignments, or misappropriations (commonly referred to as "sin"). In hell, we have the opportunity to either revel in our folly or come to grips with the reality of consequences:

that every action has a reaction and what is inflicted on another can be returned in kind.

We experience the flip side of our despair or our demands, living through the extremes of whatever we dread. This is not punishment for our sins as much as it is a confrontation with distortions of our values and priorities. We do not leave the realms of hell until we have changed our attitudes and perceptions and are ready for another chance to improve and advance.

Heaven describes levels of positive thought forms that reside in close proximity to the earth-plane. The vibration of these levels is faster, lighter, and more subtle. It is where we go to recognize or enjoy whatever reveals the power of our own light: talents, abilities, joys, courage, generosity, caring, empathy, givingness, virtue, cheer, diligence, patience, thoughtfulness, loving-kindness. We stay in heaven (and there are many divisions to this vibratory level) for however long best serves our development. There is a sense of benefit here, as if one has found one's true home and all is well (commonly referred to as recess or a time of reaping rewards). In heaven, we have the opportunity to assess our progress as a soul, to evaluate pros and cons and outcomes, to remember all truths, including that of our real identity.

We experience the glory of love and the power of forgiveness, and we come to realize our purpose in creation's story: how we fit and what possibilities exist for future learning and growth. We do not leave the realms of heaven until we have advanced as an awakened soul, unified in the spirit and consciousness of love.

Neither heaven nor hell is an end point. Eternity is more vast than either one and far more wondrous. No one knows how vast it is, for all any of us have ever been given are glimpses.

The Buddhists have several heavens, all part of the illusion of reality they call *samsara*. In Buddhism, heaven's a place you pass through en route to possible reincarnation. The Hindus have six levels of heaven. For the good, the devout and well behaved, Islam promises bliss in an afterlife Eden, with the fire of hell for unbelievers, but an even higher ecstatic state for martyrs, the pious and the prophets. The Bible is replete with various descriptions of heaven and hell, and the Christian view has changed and developed with each passing century, but the basics remain the same: obey the "Great Commandment" (see Matthew 22: 37–40), which tells us:

37. Jesus said unto him, Thou shalt love the Lord thy God with all thy heart, and with all thy soul, and with all thy mind.
38. This is the first and great commandment.
39. And the second is like unto it, Thou shalt love thy neighbour as thyself.
40. On these two commandments hang all the law and the prophets.

If you're a Christian, take notice of this and live accordingly, and your passport to heaven's assured.

For the faithful, the thought of heaven offers comfort. But is it all a human construct – a wishful fantasy? The chances are, judging by the nature and broad consistency of the thousands of collected NDE reports, that it could all have some real meaning.

Reported Experiences

You will discover various sources online where people are willing to share their NDE. The most comprehensive website dealing with NDEs, ADCs (after-death communications) and OBEs is a revelation, and includes contributions from hundreds of people around the world (www.nderf.org). Although many "experiencers" are happy to share their own stories in a forum with their peers, tracking down contributors around the globe to seek permission to include them in a commercially produced book is often met with reticence and a natural degree of suspicion. With this in mind I decided to include a couple of genuine experiences from the UK on the guaranteed understanding that I preserve the anonymity of these correspondents who have lived through these truly strange encounters. If you want to absorb the full and fascinating range of experiences, and there are many to choose from, simply visit www.nderf.org and be amazed.

There are numerous NDEs and they share many similar characteristics. Out-of-body experiences usually include perfect visual recall, often from above the body, usually under surgery in an operating theatre, when the patient can describe who was present, what went on and often what was said. Together, these various experiences could fill many books, but here are two samples.

This after-death communication experience, dated 14 November 2011, comes from a forty-eight-year-old man in Birmingham.

It happened during the night. I awoke and felt a sense of absolute peace. Although my daughter had been dead for some months, I had the strange feeling that she was present. I got up and went into the kitchen. She was there, standing by the window, smiling. I had no fear. Looking back, I think I ought to have been shocked or even slightly frightened, but I wasn't. I simply felt very tranquil. We didn't speak; in fact, we didn't need to. There seemed to be some kind of telepathic communication. Although she had died in an unfortunate accident, she displayed no signs of injury. She told me that I should be at peace, and that she was happy, and that she would always be with me and my wife. She then just seemed to fade away, but I wasn't sad. I told my wife about it in the morning, expecting her to disbelieve me, but to my surprise she told me that she had experienced a dream, and seen our daughter, but they had met outside in the sunshine. We don't usually tell many people about this. Some think I simply had a dream and was sleepwalking. But I know it was real, and I now believe that death is certainly not the end.

The following near-death experience took place in Yorkshire. It involves a fifty-eight-year-old woman who had been rushed into hospital in August 2004 with a heart attack.

I remember going in and out of consciousness, and searing pain in my chest and down my arm. I was struggling to breathe; I remember the lights above me in the corridor, then everything went black. Eventually, this blackness turned grey, then became a brilliant, golden light. I have never felt such peace and wonder before or since. I could see what looked like a staircase, which seemed to go along some kind of tunnel, but the tunnel was of the same golden light. I looked up, feeling as if I was climbing, and to my surprise saw my mother, who had left us in 1979. She turned back and smiled at me, and I kept climbing, getting closer and closer. I wanted to reach out and touch her, then suddenly she stopped, turned and said, "You have to go back. It's not time yet." But although I was disappointed, it wasn't that feeling of disappointment we get in everyday life; just a mild sadness, mixed with joy. I think the joy was knowing that whatever this glorious place was, that it existed. The real disappointment was when I came round in the recovery ward. Did I die? The doctors told me that I had "gone" for a couple of minutes, although my experience seemed longer. Did it change my life? Certainly. I have recovered, and every time I think of what happened, I feel great peace. It's helped me to make more of this life, and to look forward to the next.

So, what do we make of all this? The truth is we don't know. Is it evidence of life after death, or something more mundane and "scientific"? With Dr Atwater's and www.nderf.org's kind permission, the following is their conclusion:

The Nine Lines of Evidence from Evidence of the Afterlife: The Science of Near-Death Experiences (www.nderf.org/evidence_afterlife.htm)

1) Crystal-Clear Consciousness. The level of consciousness and alertness during near-death experiences (NDEs) is usually even greater than that experienced in everyday life even though NDEs generally occur when a person is unconscious or clinically dead. This high level of consciousness while physically unconscious is medically inexplicable. Additionally, the elements in NDEs generally follow the same consistent and logical order in all age groups and around the world, which refutes the possibility that NDEs have any relation to dreams or hallucinations.

2) Realistic Out-of-Body Experiences: Out-of-body experiences (OBEs) are one of the most common elements of NDEs. What NDErs see and hear of earthly events in the out-of-body state is almost always realistic. When the NDEr or others later seek to verify what was observed or heard during the NDE, the OBE observations are almost always confirmed as completely accurate. Even if the OBE observations during the NDE included events far from the physical body, and far from any possible sensory awareness of the NDEer, the OBE observations are still almost always confirmed as completely accurate. This fact alone rules out the possibility that near-death experiences are related to any known brain functioning or sensory awareness. This also refutes the possibility that NDEs are unrealistic fragments of memory from the brain.

3) Heightened Senses. Not only are heightened senses reported by most who have experienced NDEs, normal or supernormal vision has occurred in those with significantly impaired vision, and even legal blindness. Several people who have been totally blind since birth have reported highly visual near-death experiences. This is medically inexplicable.

4) Consciousness During Anaesthesia. Many NDEs occur while under general anaesthesia – at a time when any conscious experience should be impossible. While some sceptics claim that these NDEs may be the result of too little anaesthesia, this ignores the fact that some NDEs result from anaesthesia overdose. Additionally, the description of a NDE differs greatly from that of one who experiences "anaesthetic awareness". The content of NDEs that occur under general anaesthesia is essentially indistinguishable from NDEs that did not occur under general anaesthesia. This is further strong evidence that NDEs are occurring completely independently from the functioning of the physical brain.

5) Perfect Playback. Life reviews in near-death experiences include real events that previously took place in the lives of those having the experience, even if the events were forgotten or happened before they were old enough to remember.

6) Family Reunions. During a NDE, the people encountered are virtually always deceased, and are usually relatives of the person having the experience – sometimes they
   are even relatives who died before the NDEer was born.
   Were the NDEs only a product of memory fragments,
   they would almost certainly include far more living people,
   including those with whom they had more recently
   interacted.

7) Children's Experiences. The near-death experiences of
   children, including very young children who are too young
   to have developed concepts of death, religion, or near-
   death experiences, are essentially identical to those of
   older children and adults. This refutes the possibility that
   the content of NDEs is produced by pre-existing beliefs or
   cultural conditioning.

8) Worldwide Consistency. Near-death experiences appear
   remarkably consistent around the world, and across many
   different religions and cultures. NDEs from non-Western
   countries are incredibly similar to those that occur in
   people in Western countries.

9) Aftereffects. It is common for people to experience major
   life changes after having near-death experiences. These
   after-effects are often powerful, lasting, life-enhancing,
   and the changes generally follow a consistent pattern. As
   the NDErs themselves almost always believe – near-death
   experiences are, in a word, real.

The near-death experience is a genuine, puzzling and, in some
ways, exciting phenomenon. It may well provide a real hint of
what awaits us when our bodies finally give up. However, there
are other examples of people dying and being resurrected. These
occasions, where someone can be clinically "dead" for up to
four hours, yet come alive again, are generally referred to as "the
Lazarus syndrome" (see John 11: 53). A feature in the July 2012
edition of the *Fortean Times* by Ted Harrison gives several staggering examples of this phenomenon, the most recent being that
of the footballer Fabrice Muamba, who had collapsed on the
pitch. His heart stopped for seventy-eight minutes and, since
recovering, Muamba and many others have claimed this as a

miracle. So should we fear death? I don't think so. As Samuel Goldwyn is reported to have quipped, "If I could drop dead right now, I'd be the happiest man alive!"

KNOCKING ON HEAVEN'S DOOR: THE SIXTH SENSE

Knowing your own darkness is the best method for dealing with the darknesses of other people.

Dr Carl Gustav Jung (1875–1961)

We've all said it at one time or another: "Scared out of my wits", or, "I was scared witless." Now that we are living in a cruder colloquial age, where vernacular vulgarity has almost become the norm, we'll often hear "I was scared shitless." Today we apply the word "wit" in its dictionary context: "the talent or quality of using unexpected associations between contrasting words or ideas for humorous effect". So a wit, or witty person, is one possessing this talent. But back in Shakespeare's day, "the wits" had a much broader meaning. The Bard would have recognized that there were five "wits", and these were often synonymous with the five senses, which are our five methods of perception, or sense: 1. hearing, 2. sight, 3. touch, 4. smell, and 5. taste. These were regarded as our "outward wits". Today, our familiarity with the paranormal has developed the notion that there is something called a "sixth sense". The poet Stephen Hawes, whose poem "The History of Pleasure or the History of Graunde Amoure" was written in 1506, takes the idea of wits a stage further. He suggests five "inward" wits as: 1. common wit, 2. imagination, 3. fantasy, 4. estimation, and 5. memory. Common wit is what we today know as "common sense", a concept originated by Aristotle as the *sensus communis*, whilst Hawes's "estimation" roughly corresponds to what we now call instinct. Shakespeare would no doubt have recognized the common distinction, where it was made, that there were "five wits" for the inward and "five senses" for the outward. He distinguished between the five wits and the five senses, as can be seen in his Sonnet 141. So if we are scared out of our wits, there are plenty of them to choose from.

The term extrasensory perception (ESP) was coined by Frederic Myers (1843–1901). It refers to a way of receiving information beyond our physical senses, sensed with the mind. Myers was a poet and thinker and one of the founding members of the Society for Psychical Research (SPR), founded in 1882. Still going strong today and based in Kensington, London, the SPR is a non-profit organization whose mission is to understand "events and abilities commonly described as psychic or paranormal by promoting and supporting important research in this area" and to "examine allegedly paranormal phenomena in a scientific and unbiased way". Jung was a member, as was W. B. Yeats and the actor Alastair Sim.

ESP as a term was adopted by psychologist Joseph Banks Rhine (1895–1980) at Duke University, a private research establishment in Durham, North Carolina, founded by Methodists and Quakers in 1838. ESP, often referred to today as "the sixth sense" or the idiomatic "hunch" or "gut instinct", is a term covering psychic abilities such as clairaudience, clairvoyance and telepathy, and their transtemporal operation as precognition or retro-cognition.

ESP is included under the general heading of parapsychology, the scientific study of paranormal psychic phenomena. Parapsychologists claim that the Ganzfeld experiment provides evidence of ESP. The Ganzfeld experiment involves the volunteer, or subject, known as a "receiver", having halved ping-pong balls strapped over their eyes, whilst a red light is shone on them. They sit in a comfy chair in a peaceful room. They also wear headphones that play white or pink noise. This sensory deprivation goes on for around thirty minutes, during which a "sender" observes a randomly chosen target which they attempt to send mentally to the receiver. If the receiver picks any of this mental transmission up, they will tell the sender what they can see. The third participant involved, the "experimenter" who is running the test, can't see the target on which the sender is focusing. The experimenter's task is to take notes or tape-record whatever the receiver reports. Once the receiver's time is up and the ping-pong balls and headphones are removed, the judging procedure offers the receiver a selection of targets to see if they recognize the one on which the sender was focusing. Three of the targets are decoys, so it's hardly surprising that even after many trials, the overall success rate in recognition is only 25 per cent. However, there have been remarkable results, with some receivers scoring as high as 90 per cent, but general science takes a negative view of the Ganzfeld routine. Perhaps the so-called "sixth sense", being part of the mystery of the paranormal, refuses to be quantified by those of us living in our dimension. It remains as inexplicable as everything else beyond the veil, and especially spiritualism.

The penultimate short story of Vladimir Nabokov (1899–1977), "The Vane Sisters", written in March 1951, has been noted in literary circles because of its unreliable narrator. It was first published in both the *Hudson Review* and *Encounter* in 1959, and it can still be read in *The Stories of Vladimir Nabokov* (1995). "The Vane Sisters" deals with the possibility of ghosts intruding into the narrator's world. However, although fiction, the following brief extract amply demonstrates the depth of knowledge the great Russian (sadly known mainly by the general public as the author of *Lolita*) possessed of the history of spiritualism:

I reviewed in thought the modern era of raps and apparitions, beginning with the knockings of 1848, at the hamlet of Hydesville, NY, and ending with grotesque phenomena at Cambridge, Mass.; I evoked the anklebones and other anatomical castanets of the Fox sisters (as described by the sages of the University of Buffalo); the mysteriously uniform type of delicate adolescent in bleak Epworth or Tedworth, radiating the same disturbances as in old Peru; solemn Victorian orgies with roses falling and accordions floating to the strains of sacred music; professional imposters regurgitating moist cheesecloth; Mr Duncan, a lady medium's dignified husband, who, when asked if he would submit to a search, excused himself on the ground of soiled underwear; old Alfred Russel Wallace, the naive naturalist, refusing to believe that the white form with bare feet and unperforated earlobes before him, at a private pandemonium in Boston, could be prim Miss Cook whom he had just seen asleep, in her curtained corner, all dressed in black, wearing laced-up boots and earrings; two other investigators, small, puny, but reasonably intelligent and active men, closely clinging with arms and legs about Eusapia, a large, plump elderly female reeking of garlic, who still managed to fool them; and the sceptical and embarrassed magician, instructed by charming young Margery's "control" not to get lost in the bathrobe's lining but to follow up the left stocking until he reached the bare thigh – upon the warm skin of which he felt a "teleplastic" mass that appeared to the touch uncommonly like cold, uncooked liver.

The story is also famous for its acrostic final paragraph, in which the first letters of each word spell out a message from beyond the grave.

The medium, the psychic, the shaman, the clairvoyant; in the United States and Europe our image of those claiming such titles is often influenced by what we think we know about spiritualism. Darkened rooms, candles, a circle of people holding hands, disembodied spirit voices, peculiar knocking sounds ... and sometimes the Ouija board, scaring everyone rigid. All this and its associated paraphernalia stems from living humanity's morbid fascination with the dead. Despite a century of organized scepticism and repeated debunking, the spiritualist still beguiles us, because as science progresses, the mystery around the spark of life seems to deepen rather than succumb to clarity. How much of spiritualism contains any truth is difficult to ascertain. The French mathematician and theoretical physicist Henri Poincaré (1854–1912) said, "Science is built up of facts, as a house is built of stones; but an accumulation of facts is no more a science than a heap of stones is a house." The facts of spiritualism, riddled as it is with self-delusion at one extreme and sheer fraud at the other, are often plain and unimpressive, but some of this heap of psychic stones continues to enthral us.

Spiritualism is defined by the dictionary as: "the belief that the disembodied spirits of the dead, surviving in another world, can communicate with the living in this world, especially through mediums. Its philosophy is the belief that because reality is to some extent immaterial, it is therefore spiritual." Although the general term "paranormal" might have mystical or even ancient overtones, ("*para*" in ancient Greek refers to "similar to" or "near to") it was only coined in the years 1915–20. The dictionary definition of paranormal is that the term applies to "experiences that lie outside the range of normal experience or scientific explanation". When it comes to such ongoing scientific puzzles like dark matter and dark energy, which we might imagine to be leaning towards the paranormal, the scientists tell us that paranormal phenomena are inconsistent with subjects that have been scrutinized through scientific methodology and empirical observation. This is not to say that, on occasion, the boffins haven't carried out their own research into what we laymen regard as "the unknown". All manner of projects have been mounted, some are still in progress, especially in the fields of spiritualism, alien abduction scenarios and near-death experience. Beyond such challenges stand the massed regiments of the sceptics, and whereas the results of some scientific research often come out as inconclusive, the sceptics, who include many scientists in their ranks, will always tell you that everything in this book is codswallop and hokum. But we're dreamy romantics, so let's press on.

This branch of the unexplained, the spirit world, is just one part of a complex mosaic that, among other elements, includes ghosts, magic, ESP, prediction and an increasing interest in the genuine phenomena of the near-death experience. In 2005 the Gallup Organization carried out a survey of the general population of the United States to establish their beliefs regarding the paranormal: 73 per cent of those polled believed in at least one of the ten paranormal elements presented by Gallup. The poll revealed that 41 per cent held a belief in ESP, 37 per cent believed in haunted houses, ghosts came in at 32 per cent, telepathy 31 per cent, clairvoyance 26 per cent, astrology 25 per cent, the possibility of communication with the dead 21 per cent, a belief in the existence of witches 21 per cent, reincarnation 20 per cent and the possibility of channelling spiritual entities 9 per cent. Only 1 per cent of respondents believed in all ten classifications. Gallup selected the ten categories on the basis that these subjects "require the belief that humans have more than the 'normal' five senses".

The unqualified and untutored can't simply wander into university lecture halls or medical seminars for trainee doctors, as we'd be asked to leave, but if we've an interest in the paranormal there are plenty of organizations happy to have us join, from ghost hunters and magic circles through to the spiritualist Church. Regarding the latter, I have given it a try, but following my first foray into the world of mediums and psychics, I decided to dig a little deeper and discover something about the history of this peculiar interest.

SPIRITUALISM: NOT AS OLD AS YOU THINK ...

You have paid to witness a Demonstration of Mediumship. This demonstration is a form of experiment; no claims are made and the results cannot be guaranteed. You are not guaranteed a personal message. You may see or hear things which you may not have experienced before. If any of you feel you may be vulnerable you should leave now and your entrance fee will be returned.

Spiritualists' National Union,
Model Disclaimer for Evenings of Mediumship

If you attend a spiritualist church in the UK to witness a medium in action – and contrary to what many may think, this *is* a religion – when you enter you'll probably receive a little card containing the above message. In Britain mediums now operate under the constraints of the European Union's consumer legislation. What mediums provide, therefore, would appear to come under goods and services. If you buy a kettle or a TV set and it's faulty, you take it back. If some shyster chemical company tells you that their carpet cleaner will return your worn-out Axminster to its original, pristine state, and it fails miserably to do so, then you report it to your trading standards office. It is doubtful that British legal bureaucracy is much troubled by complaints about dodgy mediums, and I can say from personal experience that the legislation, tough though it may be on a professed religion, seems to be working.

It is easy to think that folks have been sitting around candles in darkened rooms holding hands since time immemorial. No doubt some of the magicians of old, and the alchemists, did something similar, but the idea we have of the spiritualist world today is not all that ancient.

As I have learned to my cost, spiritualism is taken every bit as seriously by its adherents as the Qur'an is by Muslims. After my research for this book, I gave a light-hearted talk about its contents to a small audience in the Midlands. I started my spiel on mediums by rashly stating that, in my opinion, 95 per cent of spiritualism was hogwash. To my surprise, scanning the audience I saw one or two people wince, and one lady at the back stood up and immediately called me to order. "I am sorry," she proclaimed, "but that is wrong. I know – I am a spiritual healer!" I have since felt that my "opinion" hangs by a very thin thread. To many, spiritualism may seem like an elaborate version of parlour magic, but I now realize that it is, without doubt, a religion and, as such, I can see why my bold statement might well qualify me for a spiritual fatwa.

By the mid-nineteenth century, science and religion were ready to pick a fight. Whatever Genesis said in the Bible, the ungodly were on the move to trash it all. Biologists were already tinkering with the new-fangled idea of evolution, something guaranteed to upset the holy applecart. Had Lucifer betrayed God by revealing the ultimate spark of divinity – electricity? Who were these men, challenging the Holy Scriptures with their blasphemous experimentation?

Yet what Bible devotees still hung on to was faith. If they could in some way blend faith with the more astonishing revelations of science, then perhaps religion, in some new form, could keep pace with the boffins. If the men in white coats were demonstrating miracles, there had to be a religious connection. Thus, spiritualism burst on to the scene. Science's by-product had been an unintended attack on biblical faith. It questioned aspects of religious belief, such as miracles. So what better way to reinstate faith was there than to harness the new creed of science to the idea of communication between the dead and the living? The traditional Church's abiding requirement was blind faith, and, apart from the odd appearance every now and then of the Virgin Mary, only offered records of historical "miracles" rather than the real thing. In contrast, the new spiritualists set out to wow their adherents with hard evidence of what lay beyond the veil. The old Church's incense, a prayer, a sermon and a couple of hymns offered no competition to the darkened room, where the spirits of the departed got in touch via levitating tables, spookily talking through mediums, making impromptu appearances in another new medium – photographs – or materializing all manner of artefacts from a trumpet to a bunch of daffodils. And, as was the case with scientific experiments, this spirit world could be "proved" by having ostensibly "independent" adjudicators and observers on hand.

Elizabeth Barrett Browning (1806–61) became a keen spiritualist. In *Sonnets from the Portuguese*, she wrote: "Smiles, tears, of all my life; and, if God choose, I shall but love thee better after death." The world "beyond" was real to her. Floating furnishings were all she needed to show that the dead could talk. She remarked, "Let me see a table move, and I will believe anything … Now the table moves, all Europe witnessing." All this frantic furniture shifting was, to the new faith, confirmation that the achievements of Jesus, with his walks on water, curing the sick and his loaves and fishes routines, were nothing less than the real deal. Science, aligned with faith, had broken through the barrier between our mundane existence and the bliss of the beyond.

In addition, there was nothing wrong with slipping a bit of ancient Greek "science" into the mix to bolster the new faith. The spirits needed their own atmosphere to operate in. In his work published in AD 220, *The Life of Apollonius of Tyana*, Philostratus reports:

And they allowed Apollonius to ask questions; and he asked them of what they thought the cosmos was composed; but they replied: "Of elements." "Are there then four?" he asked.

"Not four," said Iarchas, "but five." "And how can there be a fifth," said Apollonius, "alongside of water and air and earth and fire?" "There is the ether," replied the other, "which we must regard as the stuff of which gods are made; for just as all mortal creatures inhale the air, so do immortal and divine natures inhale the ether."

The idea of ether was propagated because the philosophies of the ancient world found it difficult to deal with the idea of space being a vacuum. *Something* had to be there – there couldn't be absolutely nothing, so ether filled the bill. Therefore, as a further embellishment, the spiritualists saw their "ether" as something that bore light, and this was aligned with the idea of waves. If sound waves travelled through air, and boats travelled through waves on the ocean, and the scientists had demonstrated that light came in waves, then the spirits used waves in the ether to swing their tables and trumpets around.

There are different frequencies of vibration of the ether for electromagnetic waves, radio and X-rays, visible light and heat, with their peculiar frequencies giving them different properties. This adjunct of science dovetailed neatly with the spiritualist idea of the mysterious dimension of the dead, where invisible forces ruled. Spiritualism had to find a link between electromagnetic waves and spirits. Franz Anton Mesmer (1734–1815) was a German physician and part-time astronomer who had a theory that there was a natural energetic transference that occurred between all inanimate and animated objects. He called this "animal magnetism". Other "spiritual forces" were often grouped together, to become known as mesmerism. Mesmer used magnets to produce hypnotic effects harnessing magnetic fluid through pieces of iron and conductive minerals, which he placed upon the diseased areas on his patients' bodies. He claimed "magnetic" effects resulted through the laying-on of hands or even merely by speaking with the patient. And thus modern hypnotism was born (and we still use the term "mesmerized"), although the term "hypnotism" was invented by the English scientist James Braid (1795–1860) in 1843, in an attempt to dissociate himself from "animal magnetism" as he regarded Mesmer's main theory as "pure nonsense".

By combining the science of electromagnetic waves with the theories of Mesmer, the idea of ether and the waiting spirits of the dead, spiritualism was ready to roll. It still gave a healthy nod to faith, yet lacked the stuffiness of the Church, which the mediums had swapped for a kind of scientific authentication. In time, spiritualism claimed that a medium, in the same way that a radio receiver was sensitive to the vibrations of a radio signal, could be equally sensitive to the mysterious vibrations of spirits.

The dark, the mysterious dark … this has always been the utmost requirement of a séance. Why? Because taking their nod from science, mediums came to realize that radio transmissions travelled further in the hours of darkness, so surely this would also apply to the spirits. It took a while to appreciate that this idea was baloney. The reason radio waves are stronger in the dark is due to reflections from the ionosphere after sunset. You can put up the shutters and close the drapes all you like on a sunny afternoon, but that won't create the same conditions as when the earth has turned away from the sunlight. Even the spirits knew this. But the séance in the dark added that necessary phenomenal ambience. It was also perfect cover for the commitment of the many fraudulent moves so-called "mediums" perpetrated throughout spiritualism's heyday. In an age before mass broadcast entertainment, before TV and the cinema, when most of the world's streets were lit by gas and candles and oil lamps were still big business, the music hall was king, but its stages, and those of major lecture halls, were increasingly the domain of the psychics and clairvoyants. There were too many to list here, all with their equally fascinating speciality acts, and those most prominent still occupy the pages of spiritualist history. Here's a sample.

The Fox Sisters

Across the United States and throughout Europe, the second half of the nineteenth century was the age of the spiritualist superstar. Top of the charts were the three Fox sisters from New York: Leah (1814–90), Margaret (aka Maggie) (1833–93) and Kate (1837–92). Maggie and Kate, the younger girls, had to work hard at first to convince their older sister, Leah, that they had established contact with the spirits through the increasingly popular device of "rappings". With spiritualism being the rock 'n' roll of its day, Leah spotted a distinct entrepreneurial opportunity with her talented siblings and took over as their manager, with some success. They maintained their popularity for a number of years, but in 1888 Maggie came clean and admitted that her rappings were simply a hoax. She even showed a confused public how she did it. As is often the case with mediums, the Fox girls realized that unloading their conscience had been bad for business, and the following year Maggie decided to withdraw her admission in a desperate attempt to regain their popularity. But it was too late. The damage had been done, and by 1893 they had all joined the spirit world, with Kate and Maggie passing over in a state of dismal destitution.

Henry Slade

Whatever the Fox girls had confessed to, nothing could dent the popularity of the touring medium shows. Another huge star on the séance circuit was the handsome and charismatic Henry Slade (1825–1905). Slade, with his resplendent moustache, liked to call himself "Doctor" although there is no evidence to suggest he warranted the title. Slade's psychic speciality was his ability, using minute pieces of chalk in the fingers of either hand, to write messages, a feat he even did with the toes of either foot, or with the chalk in his mouth, and he claimed to be able to mirror-write backwards as fast as words were dictated. He offered a reward to the public of $1,000 if it could be proved that his slate writing was the result of trickery rather than the spirits.

It is worth pausing here yet again to consider the mundane methodology the spirit world employs to contact the living. If there is a vast heaven where boundless peace, creativity and intelligence resides, and if the departed really do want to tell us something, we could be forgiven for being far from impressed by nothing more stimulating than rapping on a table, sporadic messages on a slate or a floating trumpet from which emanates illogical and often incoherent messages. What séance attendees were supposed to get from all this remains a mystery, other than that they may have seen their experience as a source of comfort from the confirmation of life beyond physical death.

Slade lived in Michigan, but hit the big time when, en route to the University of St Petersburg in July 1876, he stopped off in London where people queued up to see his act. He also made a fortune from private psychic readings whilst in England.

Awaiting him in St Petersburg was an inspection of his abilities by Madame Helena Blavatsky and Colonel Henry S. Olcott, who would later form the Theosophical Society.

However, during his London stay, everything didn't quite go Slade's way. Apparently, it was claimed that the spirits always preferred to do their writing in the dark. Slade always held the slates out of sight and an eagle-eyed Professor Ray Lancester noticed that the tendons of Slade's wrist moved as he held a slate under the table. Together with another academic, Dr Horatio Donkin, Lancester decided to unmask Slade as a fraud. Whilst attending the next séance, Lancester snatched what was supposed to be a blank slate from Slade's hands and found that, instead of being blank, the slate was already covered in pre-prepared messages from "the spirits".

Lancester's unmasking of Slade was published in the London *Times* on 16 September 1876 and was followed by a legal action by Lancester against Slade for fraud. The case was heard on 1 October 1876. A surprising witness called in Slade's favour was none other than the naturalist D. Alfred Russel Wallace, who despite his parallel work with Charles Darwin on evolution had already defended another medium accused of fraud, Dr Monck. (One of Dr Monck's stock feats was to place a music-box on the table, and cover it with a cigar-box, after which it played or stopped playing at command.) Slade was found guilty of fraud and sentenced to three months in prison with hard labour. However, there was a mistake in the indictment document, and whilst this was being rectified, Slade's manager, Mr Simmonds, quietly spirited his cash cow away to France.

Enraged at Slade dodging the law, Lancester immediately contacted the media in Paris and the subsequent adverse publicity played havoc with Slade's Gallic box-office receipts. The following year the University of Leipzig's Professor Johann C. Zöllner (1834–82) decided to investigate Slade to see if his abilities were genuine. Subsequent reports tell us that Zöllner, although a professor of physics and astronomy, was more than a little naive when it came to dealing with psychic matters. Also, the team he'd assembled to back him up were a veritable "Dad's Army" of unreliable observers. It included the almost blind Professor Fechner, the equally visually challenged Professor

Scheibner (who, to his credit, was not wholly satisfied with the phenomena produced by Slade) and the geriatric Professor Weber who was so out of it that he had no idea of the severe disabilities of the other two. This bumbling quartet was not the best assembly for uncovering the grand possibilities of deception. After testing Slade, Zöllner came to the conclusion that the medium was genuine and possessed "transcendental powers". Zöllner's insistence on the theory of the existence of the fourth dimension as an explanation somewhat weakened the evidential value of the investigation. The professor had made a fool of himself and the critical academic grapevine was soon buzzing. Giovanni Virginio Schiaparelli (1835–1910), the eminent astronomer famous for his mapping of the surface of Mars, commented on Zöllner's fourth dimension idea in a letter to the famous French astronomer and author Camille Flammarion (1842–1925):

It is the most ingenious and probable that can be imagined. According to this theory, mediumistic phenomena would lose their mystic or mystifying character and would pass into the domain of ordinary physics and physiology. They would lead to a very considerable extension of the sciences, an extension such that their author would deserve to be placed side by side with Galileo and Newton. Unfortunately, these experiments of Zöllner were made with a medium of poor reputation.

Schiaparelli may well have been correct about the quality of Slade, the medium, but with the way things are progressing in twenty-first-century science regarding the possibility of other dimensions, who knows – Zöllner might have been on to something.

There was a rumour that Slade sneaked back to London in 1878 under the name of "Dr Wilson". But his painful descent from the top of the bill had begun. Within a decade he was more or less forgotten. At one time he was said to be worth $1 million and was associating with the crowned heads of Europe. After living the high life, in his declining years he was attacked one night and robbed of all the valuables and money he had left, the mugging leaving him paralysed down one side. He ended up giving slate readings at 50 cents a time. According to an 1897 book by Henry Ripley Evans, *The Spirit World Unmasked*, by 1892 Slade was "an inmate of a workhouse in one of our Western towns, penniless, friendless and a lunatic". It may well be a quirky irrelevance, but on 10 March 1892 the *New York World* published a report that Slade was sick in Jackson, Michigan, and that the doctors asserted that he was a woman! This seems to have been confirmed by those working at the sanatorium in Belding, Michigan, where Slade died aged eighty in September 1905. Apparently the doctors there confirmed that the departed medium was indeed a hermaphrodite.

Daniel Dunglas Home

Scottish-born Daniel Dunglas Home (1833–86) gave himself his affected middle name Dunglas. A little self-imposed class dignity never went amiss on a theatre poster, and the choice of "Dunglas" appended to Home (pronounced "Hume") gave Daniel a whiff of Scottish royalty. He knew the history: Francis James Usher bought Scotland's Dunglass Estate from Sir John Richard Hall, 9th Baronet, in 1919. The Hall family occupied Dunglass for 232 years from 1687. Other proprietors were also the Home (or Hume) family from the 1300s to 1516, a line which included the philosopher David Hume and the Lord of Parliament in 1473, Sir Alexander Home. However, it is possible the humble Daniel was related to none of them, although there was some later research that suggested some distant connection.

Aged one, Daniel was adopted by an aunt and they immigrated to the United States. Impressed by the antics of the Fox sisters, Home got himself expelled from school for persistently staging poltergeist demonstrations. He was soon earning a reputation as a medium. After success in the United States, he sailed to England at the age of just twenty-two and then embarked on a mediumship tour of France, Italy and Russia.

In 1858 in Russia, he met a wealthy socialite, the seventeen-year-old Alexandria de Kroll, who soon became his first wife. At his wedding his best man was none other than the author Alexandre Dumas. Alexandria died in 1862, and although

Home expected to inherit her substantial fortune, her family harboured suspicions about his motives and the inheritance was blocked. So he made his way to Britain, where his search for another wealthy woman was soon fulfilled by a very rich widow, Mrs Jane Lyon. Here's where mediumship comes in very handy, because at a séance with his new desire present, he "contacted" her departed husband's spirit, who promptly advised Mrs Lyon to give Home huge sums of money and to adopt him as her son. Although he enjoyed this positive result for some time, everything went pear-shaped when a court convicted him of "improper influence" and ordered him to give his new "Mum" all her cash back. He married again, this time to a wealthy Russian he met in St Petersburg, Julie de Gloumeline, and converted to the Greek Orthodox faith.

Unlike many mediums of his time, despite the fact that he was discovered cheating several times, his misdemeanours were never broadcast to the general public. Home retained the reputation of never having been exposed as a fake, with only an article in the *Journal of Psychical Research* by F. Merrifield suggesting that he carried out frauds by conjuring methods. Home was in total control of all aspects of his séances and never admitted anyone whom he suspected might be challenging or unruly. The existing accounts of his psychic feats vary, but he certainly created his own authentic reputation. As well as the required medium's ability to speak with the dead, producing rapping and knocks at will, Home would amaze everyone during his séances, which were attended by many eminent Victorians, specializing in feats of levitation, his body sometimes rising to the ceiling.

Another of his "turns" was playing an accordion that was locked in a cage under the table at which he sat. It was not the big, sparkly instrument we know today, more of a concertina, a single bellows instrument with a keyboard at one end. With this Home produced "ethereal", somewhat faint, reedy music, all of which seemed terrifically ghostly as it emanated from beneath the table. Were the "spirits" giving impromptu performances? Many thought that to be the case. Home also possessed a huge, shaggily stylish "soup strainer" moustache. Following his death, according to the arch-sceptic and magician James Randi, a number of tiny one-octave mouth organs were found among his séance paraphernalia, and as the great bluesman Sonny Boy Williamson II demonstrated (even without a 'tache) it was quite possible to play a small harmonica hands-free in your mouth – easier if it was concealed by gargantuan whiskers. On top of this, the limited repertoire of the musical phantoms beyond the veil included only two tunes: "The Last Rose of Summer" and "Home, Sweet Home", both perfect because they use just nine notes and are playable with ease on a little one-octave mouth organ.

Wherever one looks, Home's biographical details fluctuate, yet he was undoubtedly one of the most important characters on the spiritualist circuit. Even the bane of all mediums, Harry Houdini, described him as "one of the most conspicuous and lauded of his type and generation". Sadly, we'll never know the truth. The golden age of spiritualism predated the age of film and recording. All we know is that today's "non-spiritual" performers, such as Penn and Teller, David Blaine, David Copperfield and Derren Brown are all capable of reproducing most aspects of the Victorian séance. Yet in retrospect, frauds or not, what those original mediums provided was a totally entertaining sense of wonder and mystery that gave many the hope, forlorn or otherwise, that there was another world where spirits dwelled.

In general, Daniel Dunglas Home's varied abilities as a performer and medium seem to have left a good impression, with the notable exception of the poet Robert Browning (Elizabeth Barrett Browning's husband) who, after attending one of Home's performances, said that he had "never seen so impudent an imposture". Home made the bad mistake of trying to visit Browning, but on arrival the poet threatened to throw "this dungball" down the stairs. In 1864 Browning penned the long and unflattering poem "Sludge the Medium", inspired by Home, where the medium pleads through an increasingly acrimonious dialogue with the writer for his fraudulent activity to be forgiven:

Why should I set so fine a gloss on things?
What need I care? I cheat in self-defence,
And there's my answer to a world of cheats!
Cheat? To be sure, sir! What's the world worth else?

Suffering throughout his life with tuberculosis, the same illness which took his first wife, Home died aged fifty-three on 21 June 1886. He is buried in the Russian cemetery at Saint-Germain-en-Laye in the Île-de-France region in north-central France.

Florence Cook

Eight years after the Fox sisters launched spiritualism on to an amazed world, Florence Cook was born in London's East End in 1856. Even as an infant she claimed that the angels spoke to her. When she was fifteen she was involved in a séance organized by her parents, where she managed to amaze everyone by "tilting" a table. What seems like a mundane feat to us now was a sensation and before long Florence had a growing reputation as a psychic. Inspired by the antics of the Fox sisters, America's new "paranormal" touring act were the Davenport brothers, famous for their "spirit contact" via their speciality, the box illusion. They would be tied up inside a box with some musical instruments. The box would be shut and then the instruments would sound. When the box was reopened, there would be the brothers, still tied up, the inference being that the spirits had provided the tunes, thus leading the audience to believe supernatural forces were at work. Florence was inspired. She had her own "spirit cabinet" built, wherein she would create "spirit faces" whilst bound by her hands, legs and neck to a chair. Attractive, well-spoken and educated, Florence stood out from many mediums because her séances were free, and she even turned down gifts from her many admirers. She soon became a star and added to her catalogue of skills.

Victorian spiritualism's female practitioners had a reputation for their distinct element of eroticism, which often defied the prudery of the time – after all, this was a *spiritual* thing, bordering on religious experience; a bit of flesh here and there revealed by the dearly departed had to be accepted, titillating though it may be.

At one time, when Florence levitated, the "spirits" ripped off her dress. Such a thrill for an audience was bound to increase her popularity, as was the vision of her being tossed into the air by the spirits. Her day job as an assistant teacher at a girl's school came to an abrupt end when the principal, Mrs Eliza Cliff, was forced to sack her due to concerns that her psychic presence might affect the children and damage the school's reputation. Yet Florence had developed such a good act that she was able to slip into the role of full-time medium with ease.

By 1872 Florence had honed her abilities to such an extent that she could "materialize" life-like spirit apparitions. Her most famous visitor from beyond the veil was a certain Katie King. But Katie wasn't a Cook original. This particular wraith was the invention of a disgraced American medium, Jonathan Koons, aka John King, who had been in touch with the spirit of the daughter of the privateer/pirate Captain Henry Morgan. She was one Annie Owen Morgan who was keen, as was her father's spirit, to atone for her sins and had now taken on the form of Katie King. Florence soon adopted Katie, telling her audience that she'd travelled across the ocean to prove the existence of the afterlife to the British. Florence produced an image of the pirate's daughter, a floating deathlike pale face, which, after months of psychic effort, would become a full-body materialization of Katie.

On 9 December 1873 Florence was holding a special séance for such titled guests as the Earl and Countess of Caithness. She was busily impressing the gathering with some full-body materializations, but there was one guest present who was about to cause Florence some grief. His name was William Volckman. Whilst an "apparition" was materializing, Volckman leapt up and grabbed the "spirit" by the wrist. Such a physical intrusion in a Victorian séance was totally beyond the pale and outraged the gathering. It was even thought that it could be fatal to a medium. In the near-darkness Volckman attempted to drag the apparition towards the nearest source of light to examine it, but there was something very worldly about it, as the spirit put up an unexpected fight and left the stunned Volckman with a sore and bloody nose. As the guests homed in on him, dragging him away, the wraith made its exit. When things had calmed down, Volckman unlocked Florence's spirit cabinet, where she still sat, bound in her ropes, but with her dress in serious disarray.

So what inspired William Volckman to commit his desperate act in such esteemed company? The answer was simple

– competition. He was at the time engaged to Mrs Agnes Guppy née Nichol, the widow of Samuel Guppy. Mrs Guppy was no mean psychic herself, and had her own huge fan club. She detested Florence Cook, and as she and William planned to marry not long after the incident, his action must have seemed an apt wedding present. The sceptics went into overdrive, but Florence survived virtually unscathed and determined to appear as authentic as ever in future.

The post-incident séances saw full materializations of Katie King. However, it was very noticeable that Henry Morgan's supposed descendant bore a striking resemblance to a certain Florence Cook.

All this coincided with tests being carried out on Daniel Dunglas Home by the famous scientist William Crookes (1832–1919), who apart from his prowess as a chemist held a strong belief in spiritualism.

Later knighted, he was the co-discoverer of the element thallium, an early pioneer of spectography and is remembered today in the history of the development of television as the inventor of the "Crookes Tube", which he used in a number of experiments that led to the discovery of X-rays by W. C. Roentgen (1895) and of the electron by J. J. Thomson (1897), and was the forerunner of the cathode ray tube. As a scientist Crookes was thorough in his research and experimentation, and whereas today a man of his rigorous empirical methodology wouldn't touch spiritualism with a barge pole, in the Victorian era the psychic world attracted many scientists as a phenomenon worthy of research.

Asking Crookes to carry out tests on her was one of the best moves Florence made. She so impressed him with her materializations of Katie King – especially at the first séance, where Katie took him by the hand and led him behind the curtain to show him Florence lying there – that the stunned scientist made arrangements for Florence to live in his house so that he could study her at length.

Photography was by this time the wonder of the age and Crookes photographed "Katie" fifty-five times. Crooke's family destroyed the majority of the pictures after his death, but you can see a picture of him with Katie King in Cyril Permutt's book *Beyond the Spectrum* (1983). Such pictures seem laughable today; Katie's face is conveniently obscured by an "ectoplasmic shroud" and Crookes's "authentication" that Florence and Katie were two different beings (their pulse rates were different, hair colour and height) proves nothing – other than the "materialization" could well have been another woman standing in. Gilbert Roller's book *Voice From Beyond* (1975) contains an interesting letter concerning Florence from Sir William Crookes, which appeared in various spiritualistic journals in 1874. His faith in her psychic abilities remained undimmed.

The sceptics, however, carried on raising each and every suspicious point they came across. Florence decided it was time to put Katie King to rest. Her departure took place in a private séance with Crookes present to witness Katie embracing Florence and bidding her goodbye for the last time. There does not appear to have been any impropriety whilst Florence stayed with Sir William, because he was married, Florence was engaged and, two months before she left his house, she married. This didn't stop the rumours, though. Florence wasn't the only attractive girl medium under Sir William's roof. He also gave bed and board to another up-and-coming psychic starlet, Mary Showers. The possibility is that the two women worked in tandem; one as Katie King and the other Florence.

Florence took time off to enjoy being married but by 1880 the lure of the spirits drew her back into the limelight. She would have been wiser to have stayed at home. Equipped with a brand new spirit apparition called Marie, she went back on to the séance circuit but hit a huge problem at a sitting on 9 January 1880. Among those attending was Sir George Reresby Sitwell (1860–1943), 4th Baronet, father to Osbert and Edith Sitwell, antiquarian writer and Conservative MP between 1885 and 1895.

The eagle-eyed Sitwell spotted corset stays under Marie's sinuous white dress. Ignoring séance protocol, he grabbed the spirit and bellowed, "Turn on the lights!" Spirit guide Marie, who usually put on a convincing act as a singer and dancer, did not dissolve when Sitwell grabbed her. The figure was revealed to be Florence herself, wearing only her underwear, corsets and a flannel petticoat. Another sitter searched the spirit cabinet and retrieved Cook's discarded outerwear. She had finally been unmasked as a cheat.

The standard defence when this happened to a popular medium was that due to their fading powers, they didn't want to let their audiences down. Florence still had her supporters, but her séances grew fewer and fewer until her death in 1904. Sir William Crookes, being a scientist of genuine ability and fame, was not sullied by his association with mediums, but he was deeply hurt by the harsh criticism it engendered from his peers. Knighted in 1895 for his contributions to the advancement of physics and chemistry, he continued to be a supporter of all things psychic, but abandoned any further research into the subject.

As for Henry Morgan's descendant, Katie King, she was not redundant. Subsequent mediums gave her a place in their act. She cropped up at numerous séances, the last one in Italy in 1974.

So what do the revelations from the great age of the superstar mediums tell us?

By examining this minuscule sample taken from a huge catalogue of cases, it may be easy to imagine that all mediums are frauds. Yet there are records of phenomenal happenings at séances that were not tested by science and remain a total enigma. If Daniel Dunglas Home frequently levitated, at one séance passing through one window a couple of storeys above the street to re-enter floating through another window, how did he do it? How did some mediums, with no prior knowledge of their audience, seem to communicate so accurately with departed relatives? Admittedly, we need to take more than a pinch of salt – a bucketful would be more apt – with the majority of cases, but there have been, and still are, some psychics who remain a tough challenge for sceptics.

Just because one medium was a fraud did not mean that others were not genuine.

Perhaps spiritualism was a valiant attempt to narrow the gulf between religion and science. As we are still discovering in the twenty-first century, science itself is still riddled with phenomena of its own. Many of the good-humoured young boffins at CERN, interviewed late in 2011 on TV after another near miss in their quest for the Higgs boson – the so-called "God Particle" – seemed unable to offer an articulate pronouncement on what it was they were really up to. Was Einstein wrong? Had neutrinos travelled faster than light? Was there a range of dimensions beyond our understanding? Their confused attitude seemed to point to all these incredible possibilities.

In the United States, where one might have expected widespread Christian fundamentalism to have sunk its sharp fangs into such a heresy, free enterprise allows just about anyone the freedom to post an advertisement, a phone number or a sign advertising themselves as a spiritualist medium.

America has millions of believers in spiritualism and they celebrate their faith in some unusual locations. For example, in New York's Leolyn Woods is the virgin forest that surrounds Inspiration Stump on the grounds of the Lily Dale spiritualist community. A stand of enormous trees, some 200–400 years old, gives the location a cathedral-like quality. A fixture in Lily Dale society since 1898, the Inspiration Stump is a very large, old stump in the centre of the forest, where mediums have stood for over a century to deliver their messages from the spirit world. It is believed to be an "energy vortex" in the community, faced by benches that can accommodate approximately 300 people at one time. Mediums communicate with departed spirits twice daily during Lily Dale's summer season, at no charge. However, the spirits act randomly here. They pick you – not the other way around – so you can't put your hand up and ask for a message.

If there's an American capital for spiritualists, then it's probably that place of all things arcane and esoteric, San Francisco. The Golden Gate Spiritualist Church at 1901 Franklin Street sets out its impressive stall with all the information you'll need:

The phenomena of Spiritualism consist of Prophecy, Clairvoyance, Clairaudience, Gift of Tongues (medium, while in trance, communicates from Spirit in foreign languages unknown to the medium), Laying on of Hands, Healing, Visions, Trance, Apports, Levitation, Raps, Automatic and Independent Writings and Paintings, Direct or Independent Voice, Materialization, Photography, Psychometry, and any other manifestation proving the continuity of life as demonstrated through the Physical and Spiritual senses and faculties of man.

That just about covers everything.

On 5 April 1924 the National Spiritualist Association granted the Golden Gate Spiritualist Church its charter, and it developed over the years with the support of a small group of devoted spiritualists. Its founding pastor, principal medium and teacher, Florence Harwood Becker, was born on 16 February 1892. She continued in those roles until she passed to Spirit on 12 July 1970. What the Golden Gate tells us about her service gives us a snapshot of US mediumship:

> Rev. Florence was probably the most outstanding, highly developed medium in Spiritualism's history. She was a dead trance medium. For a few decades, one of her Guides in Spirit, Dr E. J. Briggs, gave trance addresses through her. Another of her guides, a Native American woman in Spirit, Squaw Sally, was the message bearer through her at church services.
>
> In Rev. Becker's séances, trumpets (megaphone-like cones) would float around the circle and the room as Spirit voices spoke through them. She had the gift of direct Spirit voice, where Spirit voices could manifest anywhere in the séance room. As Rev. Becker was in trance during these séances, people from Spirit would also talk through her. Music boxes would float about the séance room, playing.

Perhaps the preponderance of Native American spirit guides throughout mediumship might not include a "Squaw Sally" today. Like the "N" word for African Americans, for Native Americans the word "squaw" has become offensive. For example, when Oprah Winfrey invited the Native American activist Suzan Harjo on to her show in 1992, Harjo shocked viewers when she told the audience that "*squaw* is an Algonquin Indian word meaning vagina". If only the good Reverend Becker had known ...

In those earlier years before TV and CGI, the events at the Golden Gate Church must have been simply awesome. In Britain and Europe, the trumpets and the ectoplasm have receded, to be replaced by a more prosaic, chapel-like spiritualism. When I telephoned my local spiritualist centre to enquire about events, the kind, gentle-voiced lady who answered put my mind at ease: "You do realize we're a religion – but we don't use Bibles and stuff like that …"

On the face of it, for sincere, religious and well-meaning spiritualists to be forced to operate under such Byzantine laws as those of the European Union might seem unfair. However, this branch of religion has a rocky history with its roots going back to Henry VIII's Witchcraft Act of 1542. Before examining this unusual heritage, I decided to check out twenty-first-century spiritualism for myself and seek out local believers to see if I could gather some consoling evidence of the afterlife.

IS THERE ANYBODY THERE?
A NIGHT WITH THE SPIRITS

The only truth was whatever you could make someone believe.
Megan Chance, *The Spiritualist: A Novel* (2008)

Is there a spirit world? I (half) believe there is. I have had some odd experiences that have nudged me in the direction of belief, yet not over the threshold. My mother died at the age of fifty-eight in January 1973 due to complications from a strangulated umbilical hernia. It was a family tragedy that occurred on a dark, icy night not long after Christmas 1972. My son, Martin, was conceived shortly after my mother's death and was born on 24 November 1973. My grandfather, Karl Kohler who died in 1948, was a German. His favourite Christmas carol was the Austrian classic, "*Stille Nacht*" – "Silent Night". It was the one carol which always brought my mother to tears on Christmas Eve. As soon as I hear it each Yuletide I can feel my mother's presence. But when Martin was five years old, on Christmas Eve 1978, as we were getting him ready for bed, excited and happy, preparing for Santa's visit, he was standing by the radio when "Silent Night" came on. He stared at the radio and his chirpy mood changed. He was in tears. I asked him what was wrong; he pointed at the radio.

"That song, Daddy ... making me cry."

I felt a tingle; I like to think that, although he'd never met his Nana, there was a connection. Or am I being unctuously melodramatic?

Some years later, our daughter, Sarah, who was just seven years old when my mother passed on and had spent so many happy hours with her, visited a clairvoyant for a reading. The clairvoyant wasn't one of those "cross my palm with silver" cash-on-delivery types. She was an ordinary housewife with "the gift" who lived on a rundown council housing estate in Grimsby, Lincolnshire. One of the things she told Sarah was that her departed grandmother was her guide, protecting her, and she was offering advice. Sarah was working as a nurse and had remained in Grimsby whilst the rest of us had moved house to Mansfield in Nottinghamshire. Sarah had moved in with her boyfriend at the time. It had been a bad idea and, without prompting, the clairvoyant seemed to know all about it. She told Sarah that the guiding spirit suggested that this relationship was not going to work, and that eventually she would move away and meet another man, who would become the love of her life. She was right. A few weeks later, after several months of trying to live with her boyfriend, things reached an impasse and Sarah had become desperate. She missed us all and phoned me. I went to see her and told her that she could leave Grimsby and come and live with us. And that's what she did. Not long after arriving here and finding a new nursing job, she met our current son-in-law, Ivan. After a long engagement they married in 2005. He's not only the love of Sarah's life, but loved by us all. Does this prove anything? Was it all lucky guesswork? I don't know, but it feels right.

Sarah has always been what we think of as "psychic". When she was in her early teens we were invited by one of my friends to stay for a weekend in a decommissioned old public house in Herefordshire. My wife and I were offered one bedroom and Sarah and Martin were given the one at the end of a short corridor on the first floor. Sarah came to us during the night and said she couldn't stay in the room and that Martin wasn't happy there, either. She said it had a "cold atmosphere" and that there was something "weird" about it. We discovered a few weeks later that there had been a double murder in the building, and that the bodies had been found in that very room. Lingering spirits? Tortured souls? Again, I don't know. But when we moved to our current home in 1987, I had Sarah check it out. "This has been a happy house," was her assessment. So far, that's true.

One final brush with the beyond happened to me one night in 2008 when the whole family were gathered around the table for dinner. The conversation eventually got around to memories of my mother. "Ah, if only she'd lived longer," I said. At that point I turned around abruptly; I had distinctly felt what could only be a hand on my right shoulder, the "fingers" – if that's what they were – giving me an affectionate grip. There was no one at either side or behind me, and Sarah just said, "It's all right, Dad – it's just Nana joining in ..."

So, with these events, either real spiritual connections or simply family sentimentality, permanently etched in my memory, the writing of this book seemed an obvious progression towards seeking further evidence of life beyond the veil. It was with this in mind that I made arrangements in November 2011 to attend an evening of mediumship at my local spiritualist centre.

Make no mistake – spiritualists are nice, kind and thoughtful people. Attend their church and they will make you feel truly welcome.

It was a cold, foggy night before Christmas 2011 and I decided to take Sarah and Ivan along with me. I had the somewhat cock-eyed idea that if indeed there were spirits in the building, Sarah might know. We paid our £4.50 per head admittance fee, bought some raffle tickets and took our place in a cosy, well-decorated chapel-like building that had certain aspects of a church: a raised stage area with a lectern, flowers, etc. The congregation numbered about seventy, and as the room could probably only hold just over 100, it felt reasonably full. There was a special peripatetic medium booked for the event. Checking him out, I learned that he had eleven years of experience both in the UK and internationally as a medium, working halls and theatres, and he had just returned from advanced training at Alpnachstad, near Lucerne in Switzerland. Described as "Clairvoyant, Clairsentient and Clairaudient", he believes that the ability to provide proof to someone that life is eternal is a true blessing from God.

I was unable to find the location our medium had studied at in Switzerland, but there appear to be numerous institutions throughout the world offering psychic training. Psychic schools and spiritual colleges in the United States are big business.

Leading bodies include the Association for Research and Enlightenment (ARE). Founded in 1931 by prominent psychic Edgar Cayce (1877–1945), it develops psychic ability and explores subjects such as holistic health, ancient mysteries, personal spirituality, dreams and dream interpretation, intuition, philosophy and reincarnation. Edgar Cayce helped to found Atlantic University at Virginia Beach in 1930. This is an accredited graduate-level institution and a distance-learning school of higher education open to all qualified students who want to develop psychic ability by understanding phenomena related to spirituality, such as perception beyond the traditional five senses, meditation, dream analysis and mind/body healing. Another leading US organization, calling itself "a psychic kindergarten", is the Berkeley Psychic Institute. If you prefer Florida's sun to that of California, the College of Metaphysical Studies aims "to train and educate prospective leaders for New Age, New Thought spiritual/metaphysical ministries and schools through Distance Learning or On-campus Training".

You can take a degree in parapsychology, paraphysics, neuroscience and quantum mechanics at the University of Alternative Studies. These are just a few samples of America's kaleidoscope of spiritual opportunity. In the UK the Society for Psychical Research has units based in nine different university locations, including Oxford, Edinburgh and Liverpool, offering everything from paranormal to anomaly research. The Guiding Light Centre in South Wales offers training in spirituality, tarot reading and numerology. There's the Centre for Psychic Development at Farnham in Surrey with its own packed menu. With all this training going on, the spirit world ought to be broadcasting loud and clear.

As the lady MC for the night reminded us that there would be no guarantees of a message coming through for anyone in particular, we noticed a man, probably in his thirties, in old jeans and a well-worn checked shirt who had been walking down the aisle earlier and was now by the stage. Ivan nudged me: "Looks like they've got the builders in. Maybe he's the caretaker." It turned out that he was the medium. I found this slightly surprising; I had expected someone at least having the distinction of wearing a suit and tie. But this is spiritualism, and you must leave your Anglican/Catholic sartorial expectations at home.

Upon entering the building we had been given a brochure, a spiritualist "hymnal", so we knew we would be required, as in most churches, to sing. What surprised us was that when we were told to turn to page four, the songs in the hymnal were not hymns, but unfortunately some of the most banal pop lyrics from a variety of chart acts in recent decades. Sure, there was nothing wrong with the sentiments they contained, but as we all began to warble our way through Andrew Lloyd Webber's "No Matter What" (a 2008 chart-topper in the UK for the boy band Boyzone) I was immediately struck by the fact that this was the very same song that is played and sung at the mass gatherings of the shape-shifting lizards conspiracy theory kingpin, David Icke. As my daughter Sarah whispered to me: "I can't *believe* I'm standing in a church having to sing a song by bloody *Boyzone*!"

That said, the lyrics were benign enough and suited to the occasion. I'd probably rather sing them than some of the more doomy, impenetrable stuff one finds in the Anglican canon, with perhaps the exception of "For Those in Peril on the Sea" or "Abide with Me". At least it wasn't "Jesus Wants Me for a Sunbeam" or that socks and sandals liberal vicar's favourite, "Kumbaya". Our medium then read out a prayer, which was one of his own poems from his website. Then we got down to the real business of the night – communing with the spirits.

Soon, the whole edifice of hope came crashing down. I noticed that the first two contacts he made were with two of the church's elders at the back of the hall – the same man and his wife from whom we'd bought the raffle tickets. So they obviously all knew one another. Even so, the gentleman was slightly confused when the medium said, "Are you familiar with someone you know, a gentleman with a heart condition?"

This theme, as with all the evening's contacts, was punctuated with the medium's favourite question; "Does this make sense?" The man wasn't familiar with a heart condition victim, although when prompted, he did suggest that there *might* be someone.

"This man has a very strong influence in your life. Be mindful that this has a big impact on this person – it's the way he's brought that forward ..."

Well, having a heart defect would be a "big impact" on anyone. The man still seemed unable to connect. It seems with mediums that there needs to be much clutching of the temples with thumb and middle finger, as if these provide some kind of antennae to the spirit broadcast. As the audience member ponders over who this strong person in his life with the heart condition might be, the messages take on a more serious tone as the suggestion goes beyond the third party in the spirit world and focuses on the man himself. Shoulder pain is introduced. Does he have some shoulder pain? Yes. The medium begins to feel his own neck and shoulders.

"This shoulder pain you've got – does it travel up your neck? Because as I'm talking to you, the pain is getting worse and worse. I actually feel as if I could do with some painkillers. It is quite severe ..." Now the medium touches his forehead, and we're in touch with the spirit again. "He's focusing up here now ... that shoulder pain – does it cause headaches?"

Before the befuddled subject could respond, the lady sitting next to him came to the medium's assistance.

"I've got shoulder pain shooting up my neck that causes headaches."

"Ah, yes. He's talking about having some treatment, massages and ... does this make sense?"

She says it does. To escape the mundane cul-de-sac of physical health – although it is fertile territory, because almost everyone knows someone with an illness – the focus hits a material object.

"He's showing me a pendant – something silver – it looks like it has wings – an angel? Silver? Does that make sense to you?"

"Yes," replies the woman.

"Well, there's an anniversary around that now." He goes on to tell us that this anniversary is significant, and that the number four is coming up. Does this make sense?

"Well, we live at number four." This minor bombshell is almost on target, but he decides to go for the calendar.

"He's talking about a date in December coming up. About two weeks into December?"

The lady seems to be struggling for a moment, then tells us a birthday happens around that time.

We move on to the introduction of another character into the subject's interrogation. Is she familiar with a short woman, about five feet two inches tall with hip problems, who had difficulty walking? He tells us that: "She's just come forward; she's rocking but she's determined not to use anything to help her with her walking, she doesn't need any help."

It doesn't connect. The woman is puzzled, so the medium paces the stage, clutching his temples, then asks, "Is someone thinking about Dracula?" He then lines this up with Whitby Abbey, mentions Bram Stoker, and sure enough, someone in the congregation mentions that Whitby, a major feature in Stoker's novel, is their favourite seaside resort. It's also mine, but I reckon the spirits are ignoring me this night.

We skirt around Whitby for a few minutes, until another couple are asked if they have metal gates at their house that need oiling. They tell him that yes, they do, but the gates are permanently open. This almost convincing connection does lead one to face the fact that a great many houses have metal gates. Down my own short street, five of the twelve houses have them. If the metal gates question hadn't hit home with this one couple, no doubt it would have resonated with at least one other member of the audience. He rounds this up by telling a woman that the spirit he's talking to has told her that she has been "naive about certain people" and that she should be careful about those people she chooses to be personal friends.

The show lasted around an hour, and if there was some significant, convincing moment, a spine tingle, a bolt from the beyond to secure my belief, I would love to write about it here. Sadly, there was no such experience. At one point a group of three younger women seemed to know someone he had mentioned called Doris, but they told him they knew a Doreen.

"Ah, yes!" he proclaimed, gripping his temples again – "he's corrected it – it is Doreen – I *couldn't read his writing* ..." The spirit went on to mention someone they might have known who suffered stomach ache from eating sour apples. Was there an apple tree close to one of their houses? Of course there was. Then the somewhat salacious spectre, after accusing one of the women of nagging and telling her that if she stopped haranguing her husband, he'd fix the kitchen cupboards anyway, moved on to her underwear. The spirit had observed that she was thinking of sorting out her lingerie drawer, and that some items were "more grey than the white they should be". Hilarity ensued, and this struck home with most of the females in the crowd.

The session ended with another prayer from the medium's own compendium of poems, and although my daughter and her husband were keen to make an exit, I decided to see if my raffle tickets had been blessed by the spirits. They had; number 459 came up, and I took home a nice pot plant as a souvenir, with which my wife was rather pleased. So, not all was lost. I did not feel swindled by the event in any way. The Spiritualists' Disclaimer was fair enough and I'd read it carefully. Rather than feeling cheated, I simply felt very disappointed. I could not help feeling still that there might be a spirit world, but it wasn't evident on this occasion. Perhaps the mysterious "veil" that separates the living from the dead is more scientific than paranormal; it could be another aspect of phenomena related to what they've been up to at the Large Hadron Collider – one of those possible alternative dimensions, with the occasional fissure through which we can see other lives. If that sounds crazy, even in the twenty-first century, imagine how zany the Pope thought Galileo was when he suggested that the earth orbited around the sun.

I'm sure that there are some convincing mediums around. I recall a performance in San Francisco by the Scottish medium, Gordon Smith, wherein what can only be described as his real psychic powers had a profound effect on random members of the audience – with a level of first-time accuracy regarding names, ages and illnesses, Smith's acute reading was superb. If he was using carefully honed stage magic, I have yet to figure out how he was able to connect to people in such a way, unless he was given prior knowledge of individual lives. Yet this kind of thing is plainly possible without spirits or the afterlife being involved.

The British "psychological illusionist" Derren Brown is a brilliant performer who, like his US counterparts David Blaine and David Copperfield, performs mind-bending feats of mentalism using suggestion, psychology, misdirection and showmanship in order seemingly to predict and control human behaviour. His ability, as displayed in his live shows, is truly breathtaking, yet Brown is an avowed atheist and a total sceptic towards all things paranormal. Perhaps it takes a special kind of immoral cunning, a mathematical brain and a sharp, photographic memory to accomplish a medium's remarkable feats. It could be just having the total chutzpah to stand in front of a crowd and hoodwink them into believing that the dead are talking to them – through you.

HOW TO BE A MEDIUM

It's all about a skill known as "cold reading". Once mastered this can be very powerful, but it takes a lot of practice to get it right. The way most people think includes certain areas of weakness, and these are what you will utilize. Surprisingly enough, it works better with intelligent people. Cold reading is a simple concept. It relies on the fact that the truth is so simple it gets overlooked as a possibility. What the majority of mediums do *not* do is provide you with messages from the beyond. They get you, the subject, to feed them with the clues and information they need – then they embroider them and feed them back. It's an impressive and age-old craft. There are four recognized stages in cold reading, which we'll examine; they are Shotgunning, Barnum Statements, Fishing and the Rainbow. Here's what the prominent psychologists P. A. Marks and W. Seeman wrote on the Barnum effect in the *Psychology Record* (no. 12, 1962); these are the kind of suggestions, the "keys" to unlock information, made to their subjects by mediums:

- You have a great need for other people to like and admire you. You have a tendency to be critical of yourself.
- You have a great deal of unused capacity which you have not turned to your advantage. While you have some personality weaknesses, you are generally able to compensate for them.
- Your sexual adjustment has presented some problems for you. Disciplined and self-controlled outside, you tend to be worrisome and insecure inside.

- At times you have serious doubts as to whether you have made the right decision or done the right thing.
- You prefer a certain amount of change and variety and become dissatisfied when hemmed in by restrictions and limitations.
- You pride yourself as an independent thinker and do not accept others' statements without satisfactory proof. You have found it unwise to be too frank in revealing yourself to others.
- At times you are extroverted, affable, sociable, while at other times you are introverted, wary, reserved. Some of your aspirations tend to be pretty unrealistic.
- Security is one of your major goals in life.

They are basic suggestions which could apply to any member of any audience. At the heart of cold reading is a term used in psychology, "cognitive bias". It describes common flaws in human memory, decision-making and perception. Most people will deny these feelings, but even that denial is another demonstration of cognitive bias. Here's a couple of examples:

- Self-relevance effect: personally relevant memories are better recalled than other, similar information.
- Suggestibility: someone else makes a suggestion and you mistake it for memory.
- Confirmation bias: the tendency to seek and interpret information in a way that confirms one's preconceptions. For example, the repeated question "Does this make sense to you?"

By understanding cognitive bias, cold reading can be used by a medium so the subject perceives and later inaccurately recalls events in the way the medium dictates. A medium will ask lots of questions, but make very few actual statements. Statements will be general and flexible to allow for differing responses. There will be a lot of guesswork, starting with general guesses, pausing for feedback before getting specific, but the subject will ignore the inaccurate guesses and pounce on the correct ones. The medium will also look for facial reactions and study body language.

Stage 1: Shotgunning

In this you need rapidly to issue a stream of very general information. As this sinks in with the audience, the medium studies their body language and expressions. For example: "I see someone in your family with a worrying illness; it could be a parent, or a close relative, perhaps a brother or sister ..." As the audience develops their reactions, when one or more members seem to react to one of the suggestions, the medium narrows down the statements to try and draw out more information.

Stage 2: Barnum Statements

We've already looked at these; they're generally applicable to most people (or make up your own).

- You are an independent thinker. You like to check out claims for yourself before you believe what someone tells you.
- You often have great ideas that you just never have the motivation to follow through on.
- You don't like to be told what to do. You have a little bit of an issue with authority.
- You have a fear of rejection.

These ideas are aptly named after Phineas Taylor Barnum (1810–91), America's master showman, businessman, entertainer and scam artist, who carried out celebrated hoaxes as well as founding the Ringling Bros. and Barnum & Bailey Circuses. These statements allow the medium a degree of "wiggle-room" in a reading. If the subject challenges your suggestion, you simply indicate back that they have self-confidence and restructure your further statements. The subject will display some eagerness and seek to connect what you've said in some way to their own lives.

Stage 3: Fishing

The trick is to rephrase the information your subject has presented and then present your subsequent statements as questions. So they like wining and dining? "So, do you often like to go, say, to restaurants, and enjoy good food and wine?" They will then conjure up instances of this activity to match that question. If they give you a positive response, "Yes, I really enjoy wining and dining," then you can come back with, "It's coming through that you seem to be easy to get along with, a very friendly person who enjoys company."

Stage 4: The Rainbow

Specify a particular personality trait but include its opposite. For example, "Most of the time you enjoy company and socializing, but sometimes you feel like being alone and become a little withdrawn." This embraces all possibilities and for most people represents an accurate deduction, no matter how contradictory or even vague it is.

It would be unfair to conclude from all this that all mediums are frauds. There is, however, the strong possibility that many people who consider themselves to be psychics, and have studied these psychological methods, succumb to self-delusion without realizing it. They become so used to the ostensible success of their methodology that they genuinely believe that the dead are talking through them. Combine such practitioners with a largely deluded congregation of followers, weld all this together with unshakeable faith and you have a religion. So where do spiritualists stand when it comes to the Bible?

SPIRITUALISTS, WITCHCRAFT AND THE BIBLE

> *To deny the possibility, nay, the actual existence of witchcraft and
> sorcery, is at once flatly to contradict the revealed word of God in
> various passages both of the Old and New Testament, and the
> thing itself is a Truth to which every nation in the world hath, in
> its turn, borne testimony, by either example seemingly well attested
> or by prohibitory laws, which at least suppose the possibility of a
> commerce with evil spirits.*
>
> Sir William Blackstone, *Commentaries* (1765)

Thomas Judson Brooks, MBE, JP (1880–1958) was a British
coal miner from Yorkshire who became a Labour Member of
Parliament. As a dedicated spiritualist, he campaigned against
what he believed was the outdated Witchcraft Act, which, in
various forms, had been on the British statute since 1542. Due
to his efforts, the Act was repealed and replaced with the
Fraudulent Mediums Act 1951.

Britain's first spiritualist church was set up in Keighley,
Yorkshire, in 1853. Today, with spiritualism designated as a
religion, it would seem wise that the brethren tend not to use the
Bible. "Old Time" religion would probably refer to the following biblical advice.

Leviticus 19:26: "You shall not eat anything with the blood,
nor shall you practise divination or soothsaying." The reference
to blood indicates the old practice, common throughout the
world, of using the entrails and organs of various animals in divination. Thankfully, with the exception of a few locations and the
survival of such practices in voodoo, this is no longer relevant.

Leviticus 19:31 reads: "Give no regard to mediums and familiar spirits; do not seek after them, to be defiled by them: I am the Lord your God."

Leviticus 20:6–8 maintains the hostility against spiritualism: "And the person who turns to mediums and familiar spirits, to prostitute himself with them, I will set My face against that person and cut him off from his people. Consecrate yourselves, therefore, and be holy, for I am the Lord your God. And you shall keep My statutes, and perform them: I am the Lord who sanctifies you."

Leviticus 20:27 issues threats of serious penalties against mediums: "A man or a woman who is a medium, or who has familiar spirits, shall surely be put to death; they shall stone them with stones. Their blood shall be upon them." This brings to mind a verse in Exodus 22: 18: "You shall not permit a sorceress to live." Therefore, taking up the occupation of fortune-telling or occult practices could secure you the biblical death penalty.

Of course, back in the days when the first Witchcraft Act was passed, instigated by Henry VIII in 1542, the great majority of people would not have been able to read Leviticus – reading and writing were largely the domain of monks and priests. There were five Witchcraft Acts between 1542 and 1735, including one issued by Elizabeth I in 1562 with a death penalty and a broadened version in 1604. In 1735, following the ascension of King James, common sense crept in and it was decided that witchcraft was an "impossible" crime. Anyone claiming the power to call up spirits, to predict the future, to cast spells or to suggest the location of stolen goods was to be reprimanded as a vagrant and a confidence trickster, crimes punishable by fines and imprisonment. The Act applied to the whole of Great Britain, repealing both the 1563 Scottish Act and the 1604 English one. Oddly enough, the Act is still in force in Israel, because when the British were in power in Palestine, many aspects of British law were in force and not repealed. Article 417 of the Israeli Penal code of 1977, incorporating much legislation inherited from British and Ottoman times, sets two years of imprisonment as the punishment for "witchcraft, fortune telling, or magic for pay". As the traditional view is that the book of

Leviticus was compiled by Moses, then he would surely be happy with his people for sticking to the law.

In 1944, the Scottish medium Helen Duncan claimed to have made contact with the spirit of a sailor who served on a Royal Navy vessel, HMS *Barham*. The ship was sunk during the Second World War on 25 November 1941 by the German submarine *U-331*; 861 men lost their lives and British military intelligence tried to subdue the fact that the ship was lost, keeping the bad news from the general public. Helen Duncan held a séance in Portsmouth and indicated that she knew about the sinking, and was subsequently arrested and tried, making her the last but one person in England tried under the 1735 Witchcraft Act.

Jane Rebecca Yorke was convicted under the Act later that same year. Yorke was well known as a medium in Forest Gate, London, where the police exposed her after setting up a sting with undercover officers, who fed her false information regarding non-existent family members. Using her access to her "spirit guide" – a Zulu – she had already made a prediction that the war would be over by October 1944. She told one policeman that his brother had been burned to death during a bombing raid. The policeman had no brothers. As well as her Zulu spirit friend, she was also regularly in touch with the departed Queen Victoria. Arrested in July 1944 she was put on trial in September at London's Central Criminal Court, but due to her age, seventy-two, she was placed on good behaviour for three years and fined just £5. She gave no further séances.

Helen Duncan did not fare so well. She was arrested whilst conducting a séance and indicted with seven punishable counts: two of conspiracy to contravene the Witchcraft Act, two of obtaining money by false pretences and three of public mischief (a common law offence). She was given a nine-month prison sentence. It is suspected that some members of the British intelligence services feared that she might reveal the secret plans for D-Day. Duncan had been a noted medium since her schooldays in Scotland and later proved to be a clairvoyant by offering séances in which she appeared to summon the spirits of recently deceased persons by emitting ectoplasm from her mouth. She had six children and worked in a bleach factory. Many supporters, however, publicly supported her and attested to her authenticity as a true medium who had simply made unwelcome revelations during a most contentious and sensitive period – the Second World War.

The Fraudulent Mediums Act of 1951 prohibited anyone from claiming to be a psychic, medium or other spiritualist while attempting to deceive and to make money from the deception (other than solely for the purpose of entertainment). It was repealed on 26 May 2008 and replaced by new Consumer Protection Regulations following an EU directive targeting unfair sales and marketing practices. There were five prosecutions under this Act between 1980 and 1995, all resulting in conviction.

Today there are more than 300 spiritualist churches in Britain that make charges and request donations. In 2006–7 psychic mail-order readings – spiritualist services by post – brought in a hefty turnover of £40 million, according to the Office of Fair Trading, and other psychic services online, via satellite TV and over the telephone still help to keep this branch of enterprise paranormally happy.

TV PSYCHICS:
MOST *NOT* HAUNTED

If you happen to be a convincing medium with a flair for drama (and photogenic attributes can help) then there's a great opportunity waiting for you on TV. Since 2002, the Sky Living Channel has already made fourteen series of the hugely popular *Most Haunted* series, where presenters, accompanied by mediums, stumble about in dark cellars and "haunted" mansions or pubs to which they have previously never been. Their spontaneous, frequently fearful reactions are filmed in that eerie green tint produced by night vision cameras. Productionwise, this must be just about one of the cheapest shows to make, and any creak, bang or off-screen sigh is immediately flagged up as proof of the paranormal. However, all is not as it seems. A report by Matt Roper in the British tabloid, the *Daily Mirror*, on 28 October 2005 exposed a few unwelcome revelations concerning the most over-the-top, melodramatic current medium of them all, Liverpool's Derek Acorah, whose spirit guide happens to be an Ethiopian called Sam. Acorah is no stranger to TV. Despite a constant barrage of scepticism from some quarters suggesting his lack of authenticity as a medium, and a series of parodies by entertainers and comedians from Hugh Laurie and Harry Hill to Peter Kay and Dawn French, Sky and other channels have continued to commission shows featuring Derek Acorah. In November 2009 he appeared in two programmes, *Michael Jackson: The Live Séance* and *Michael Jackson: The Search for his Spirit*. Surrounded by Jacko acolytes and lookalike wannabes, Acorah's version of the dead Prince of Pop made for some of the most hilarious viewing ever. In an online poll of more than 9,000 Yahoo! users the séance was named the worst TV programme of 2009.

Dr Ciaran O'Keeffe, lecturer in the paranormal at Liverpool's Hope University, was drafted on to *Most Haunted* as resident parapsychologist, and made claims in the *Daily Mirror* article that viewers were being hoodwinked by "showmanship and dramatics". O'Keeffe accused Acorah of not only obtaining advance information about locations they would be filming in, but of pretending to communicate with spirits. Together with her husband, producer Karl Beattie, presenter Yvette Fielding was also accused of faking ghostly bumps in the night. O'Keeffe told the press: "I was put in the show to give a professional slant to it, to give it an element of credibility, but the sceptical argument is just swept away. In my opinion, we're not dealing with genuine mediumship. Other crew members have been irked by Derek and what's going on, because it turns what should be a serious investigation into a laughing matter."

Yvette Fielding, however, claimed, "There is no acting in this programme, none whatsoever. Everything you see and you hear is real. It's not made up, it's not acted." Yet the *Mirror* had got hold of footage that had been edited out of the shows in which a cameraman is pushed in the dark, the suggestion being that a paranormal "force" pushed him, and at one point a "sigh", issued by Yvette, makes it into the scene that eventually went on air, as one of the crew spookily asks in the darkness: "What's that noise?"

Karl Beattie's company, Antix Productions, claims the mediums have no idea where they will be filming and have no details about a location's history. Dr O'Keeffe, in speaking out, was in danger of committing media suicide, but he believed viewers should be enlightened as to the real nature of *Most Haunted*. He told the *Mirror*: "I think it's time to open the dialogue about what I've experienced on *Most Haunted*. There have been many incidents with the medium that have been brushed under the carpet."

He became suspicious of Acorah's conduct when they were filming at Castle Leslie, County Monaghan in Ireland. It was there that a seventeenth-century four-poster bed had a reputation for levitation. Dr O'Keeffe recalled: "As we walked into the bedroom, Derek touched the bed and came out with extremely accurate information. He insisted he got all the information just from touching the bed. But it was the wrong bed." He went on to suggest that Acorah must have had prior knowledge of the locations. In an attempt to establish whether or not Acorah was acting deceitfully, Dr O'Keeffe came up with a ruse which he prepared whilst the team were filming at Bodmin Jail (alternatively Bodmin Gaol), an old prison on the edge of Bodmin Moor in Cornwall. This historic building dates from 1779 and was closed in 1927. He invented a long-dead South African jailer called Kreed Kafer – an anagram of Derek Faker.

"I wrote the name down and asked another member of the crew to mention it to Derek before filming. I honestly didn't think Derek would take the bait. But during the filming he actually got possessed by my fictional character!"

O'Keeffe made up another non-existent character for the shoot at Prideaux Place, Cornwall. This time, it was the highwayman Rik Eedles – an anagram of Derek Lies. It didn't take long for psychic Derek to begin talking to the fictional outlaw. Dr O'Keeffe's summing up was pretty devastating: "In my professional opinion we're not dealing with a genuine medium. When Derek is possessed he is doing it consciously – all we are seeing is showmanship and dramatics."

In Scotland, at Craigievar Castle, near Aberdeen, he hoodwinked Acorah again. "I made up stories about Richard the Lionheart, a witch, and Richard's apparition appearing to walk through a wardrobe – the lion, the witch and the wardrobe!" Ignoring the historical fact that Richard I was on the throne 500 years *before* the building of Craigievar Castle, Derek nevertheless regurgitated all of Dr O'Keeffe's misinformation in a dazzling display of spirit contact.

Later, in 2005, the *Most Haunted* crew were in Manchester. David Bull, the presenter, announced that they were broadcasting live from Cheadle's Victorian asylum, a place where many inmates had died in torment. However, unbeknown to Acorah, they were actually in what was left of Barnes Convalescence Home, not a place known for tormented departures.

Dr O'Keeffe recalled: "Derek was communicating with spirits that sounded as if they'd been in an asylum, but it was never an asylum."

Derek Acorah's reaction to the *Daily Mirror* allegations was bold and spirited: "I've worked with Ciaran for many shows and he's got every right to say what he says. However, it does shock and surprise me. Not only do I believe that I am a genuine medium – I live my work 24 hours a day. If I thought that I wasn't a true medium, I wouldn't work as one."

In the face of such shenanigans, it is difficult to retain an open mind on the subject of parapsychology, but there are genuine mediums out there who do not seek fame and fortune, people who do possess uncanny and inexplicable gifts. However, anyone with a developed sense of scepticism is wise to keep their head below the parapet. One website, BadPsychics, is devoted to unmasking spiritual chicanery and dud mediums. Yet the level of vile abuse it receives from "believers" on its forums is shocking. Sceptics have been branded by a host of dumbed-down, near illiterate fans of hauntings and séances as, among other things, being "sexually repressed" and even paedophiles. So be warned – take the mickey out of mediums and the spirits are out to get you. It would be remiss to continue these tales of debunking without reference to the greatest of all sceptics, Houdini, probably one of the most famous magicians in history, and his spiritual battles with one of literature's most intricately inventive minds, Sir Arthur Conan Doyle.

AWAY WITH THE FAIRIES:
HOUDINI v. HOLMES

*You know a conjurer gets no credit when once he has explained
his trick; and if I show you too much of my method of working,
you will come to the conclusion that I am a very ordinary
individual after all.*

Sherlock Holmes in Sir Arthur Conan Doyle,
A Study in Scarlet (1887)

The First World War had a dramatic, heart-rending effect upon
Europe. It expanded the world of spiritualism, with legions of
sad, bereaved relatives becoming desperate to make contact with
their dead loved ones. Sir Arthur Conan Doyle, creator of
Sherlock Holmes, was one of the bereaved; he had lost his son
Kingsley, and was an ardent believer in spiritualism.

In 1917, two young cousins, sixteen-year-old Elsie Wright
and Frances Griffiths, aged ten, who lived in Cottingley, near
Bradford in England, took a series of photographs that they
claimed depicted real fairies living at the bottom of the garden.
The charming pictures eventually came to the attention of
Arthur Conan Doyle, who had been commissioned to write a
feature for the Christmas 1920 edition of the *Strand* magazine.
To Conan Doyle, a committed spiritualist, the girls' pictures
represented clear and visible evidence of psychic phenomena.
With our digital cameras, video and Photoshop today, even the
untrained public eye can immediately spot such obvious fakery.
A reporter from the *Daily Express* traced Elsie in 1966, who

rather teasingly suggested that she believed she had "photographed her thoughts". Yet in the 1980s Elsie and Frances came clean, admitting that they'd used cardboard cut-outs of fairies copied from a children's book. However, Frances continued to claim that the fifth and final photograph was genuine. You can still see them in the National Media Museum in Bradford.

Conan Doyle's credibility in relation to the Cottingley fairies is an apt illustration of the gullible desire of a heartbroken public for hope of the "beyond" following the cruel tragedy of the Great War. It seems strange that a man best known for creating the quintessential detective, who based his deductions solely on reason, would allow himself to be bamboozled by the smoke and mirrors of the so-called "psychics" of his day.

Harry Houdini was born in Hungary on 24 March 1874 as Erik Weisz, and became known later as Harry Weiss. The Weisz family arrived in the United States on 3 July 1878. He was heavily influenced by the brilliant French magician Jean Eugène Robert-Houdin, and when Houdin passed away Harry took on his surname and added an "i". Houdini became the archetypical American magician, a sensational escapologist, fearless stunt performer, actor and, eventually, film producer. He was also a determined sceptic who set out to expose frauds masquerading as supernatural phenomena.

Conan Doyle first met Houdini in 1920, when the magician was touring England. Although their views on the paranormal differed, they became good friends. Houdini had given up on the idea of discovering someone with an interest in spiritualism who he might consider as intelligent, but in Conan Doyle he had found his man. Doyle's enthusiastic adoption of spiritualism had come to dominate his life to the point where his lucrative writing career had been replaced with world tours where he lectured on the mysteries of the psychic world. Houdini had a depth of knowledge of the subject that equalled that of his new friend. Houdini specialized in exposing frauds. He knew from his immensely popular stage act just how easy it was to convince the public that something inexplicably paranormal was happening in the theatre.

Doyle supported the idea of unmasking fraudulent mediums because he believed that their existence brought the movement into disrepute. With his inventive mind and intricate knowledge of illusion and magic, Houdini was able to quickly expose a fake medium. However, although he tried to explain some of the underhand methodology to Doyle, the great author found it difficult to comprehend how a fraud was pulled off. He would tell the magician that he trusted those mediums he knew as honest, reliable souls who could never try and hoodwink their followers. Doyle's attitude was that simply because a spirit's activity could be duplicated, this did not prove that spirits did not exist.

In the spring of 1922 Houdini welcomed Conan Doyle to his home in New York City. During Doyle's visit, Houdini decided to reveal the secrets of one of the mediums' favourite methods of receiving messages from the beyond: slate writing. This was a process where, through the psychic, the spirit writes in chalk across a slate. Houdini instructed his guest to hang a slate from anywhere in the room, allowing it to swing free. He gave Conan Doyle four cork balls, asking him to cut one open to establish that it had not been tampered with. He then had Conan Doyle pick another ball and dip it into a well of white ink. As the ball soaked away, Houdini asked Doyle to leave the house and walk down the street in any direction he chose, taking a pencil and paper with him. Once he'd walked a while, he was to write a question or a sentence, place the piece of paper in his pocket and return to the house. Conan Doyle duly wrote down a riddle from the Bible's book of Daniel, "*Mene, mene, tekel, upharsin,*" meaning, "It has been counted and counted, weighed and divided."

When Doyle re-entered the house, he was in for a shock. Houdini gave him a spoon and asked him to retrieve the ink-soaked ball and place it against the slate. For a breathtaking moment the ball seemed stuck, but then it began to roll around the slate, spelling out "M", "e", "n", "e" to eventually produce the exact words Doyle had written; then the ball dropped to the floor. Doyle was staggered. Houdini's biographers William Kalush and Larry Sloman reveal in their biography *The Secret Life of Houdini* (2006) the confident, methodical logic of a master magician at the top of his trade, telling his puzzled pupil:

Sir Arthur, I have devoted a lot of time and thought to this illusion … I won't tell you how it was done, but I can assure you it was pure trickery. I did it by perfectly normal means. I devised it to show you what can be done along these lines. Now, I beg of you, Sir Arthur, do not jump to the conclusion that certain things you see are necessarily "supernatural", or the work of "spirits", just because you cannot explain them …

The effect on Doyle was not what Houdini was aiming for. His masterful trick, which, apparently, no one has since been able to duplicate, simply strengthened Doyle's conviction that Houdini did indeed possess psychic and supernatural powers. But Houdini was never going to break the magician's code and tell him how it was done.

The two men's friendship continued for a while, despite their philosophical differences, until one day Arthur's wife, Lady Jean Doyle, who was well aware of Harry Houdini's deep love for his departed mother, offered to conduct a séance at his house in an attempt to contact her beyond the grave. Houdini, still hoping to find some truth in Sir Arthur's faith, was willing to let this happen, and together with Lady Doyle and her husband sat around a table with the blinds drawn, armed with pencils and pads of paper. Ruth Brandon, in her 1994 book, *The Life and Many Deaths of Harry Houdini*, relates what the magician had to say: "Sir Arthur started the séance with a devout prayer. I had made up my mind that I would be as religious as it was within my power to be and not at any time did I scoff at the ceremony. I excluded all earthly thoughts and gave my whole soul to the séance."

Conan Doyle, later writing of the occasion, gave his observation: "It was a singular scene, my wife with her hand flying wildly, beating the table while she scribbled at a furious rate, I sitting opposite and tearing sheet after sheet from the block as it was filled up, and tossing each across to Houdini, while he sat silent, looking grimmer and paler every moment."

The series of blunders that followed, compounded by a coincidence, were to eventually deal a fatal blow to the friendship. As a "communication" from Houdini's mother, Lady Doyle's frantic pages of scribbling were couched in very wide, general terms. One fact that Houdini hadn't told the Doyles on the day of the séance,

17 June, was that this was his mother's birthday. There was no acknowledgement of this in the "spirit writing". Another shock to Houdini was that the message, containing such phrases as, "Oh, my darling son, thank God, thank God, at last I'm through … friends, thank you, with all of my heart, for this … I have bridged the gulf – this is what I wanted, oh, so much – Now I can rest in peace," was in English. His mother could not write English, and only spoke broken English. There was an earlier calamity when the "spirit" asked, "Do you believe in God?" and when the affirmative answer was given, she said "then I will make the sign of the cross" and Lady Doyle drew a crucifix at the top of the page. Harry's mother was an Orthodox Jew!

There was little wonder that Houdini was "looking grimmer and paler every moment". He asked Doyle if he could make his own attempt at the spirit writing. Houdini took a pencil and concentrated. He wrote one word, "Powell", and handed it to Sir Arthur. Here, genuine coincidence played a part. A fellow performer of Houdini's, and a close friend, was F. E. Powell, whose wife had recently suffered a paralysing stroke. Unknown to Houdini, however, one of Doyle's close friends, the spiritualist Dr Ellis Powell, had died in England three days earlier. Doyle saw this as a major piece of psychic proof, proclaiming: "I am the person he is most likely to signal to, and here is his name coming through your hands. Truly Saul is among the Prophets."

Shortly after this traumatic event the Doyles sailed for England and Houdini waved them off from the dock. Later that year, however, the outrage he felt after the séance developed into sharp animosity. He wrote a fierce article in the *New York Sun* newspaper denouncing spiritualism and referring to his séance with the Doyles as further evidence of its emptiness. Doyle eventually responded by reaffirming his conviction that what had taken place was a true psychic experience, and wrote to Houdini: "I don't propose to discuss the subject any more with you, for I consider that you have had your proofs and that the responsibility of accepting or rejecting is with you."

Houdini's antagonism towards mediums became fiercer and more pronounced. In December 1922 Orson Munn, the publisher of the magazine *Scientific American*, offered two prizes of $2,500 to anyone who could produce a genuine spirit photograph and to the first person to create a genuine example of authentic psychic phenomena in a séance. In the meantime, Houdini had been spending some of his wealth on his continuing "expose a fraud" campaign. He even bought his own spiritualist church in Worcester, Massachusetts. Part of the deal was that he was entitled to the title of "Reverend", so he inaugurated his wife's niece, Rose Mackenberg, as the Reverend F. Raud. (The F stood for Frances, if anyone asked.) As a cynical, embittered publicity stunt it won his campaign all the column inches he craved. Yet Houdini was about to meet the ultimate challenge of his debunking career. Mina Crandon, the Canadian wife of the rich, high-profile Boston surgeon Dr LeRoi Goddard Crandon, was regarded as possessing extraordinary gifts as a medium and although the Crandons certainly didn't need the prize money, they decided to take up *Scientific American*'s challenge. Mina was Crandon's third wife and this was her second marriage. She was by all accounts a beautiful woman, and so popular at the time in the psychic community that her written prayers were even read out to soldiers in the US Army.

The magazine's judging committee included Dr Daniel Frost Comstock (the man who introduced Technicolor to film), William McDougall, professor of psychology at Harvard, Houdini, Walter Franklin Prince, American psychical researcher, and Hereward Carrington, amateur magician, psychical researcher, author and manager for the Italian medium Eusapia Palladino (who would later be dubbed by the press as "Madame Fakerino"). After various acrimonious arguments with the committee, the ensuing struggle of the great magician to unmask Mrs Crandon, who traded under the stage name "Margery", included a series of rancorous séances. Houdini vehemently claimed, in some detail, that he knew how she continued to make things float in the air, move furniture, and produce voices from trumpets and "spirit hands" poking out through that substance so popular with early spiritualists, ectoplasm. Ectoplasm was claimed to be produced by physical mediums when in a trance state. This material was excreted as a gauze-like substance from orifices on the medium's body and spiritual entities are said to drape this substance over their non-physical body, enabling them to interact in our physical universe. Subsequent scientific tests of ectoplasm have failed to find anything paranormal in the material other than egg white and cheesecloth. Houdini began to include his denunciations of Margery in his stage act, reproducing her routines, and even published a pamphlet describing in detail how she achieved some of her effects.

Spiritualism in the early twentieth century, especially in the United States, certainly had a raunchy and seedier underside, which was evident in the acts of other female mediums as well as the aforementioned Florence Cook. The desirable "Margery", who communicated through the spirit of her dead brother, Walter, was no exception. On some occasions she preferred to perform in nothing more than a flimsy shift and was totally naked beneath. Like many female mediums of the period, she would often produce ectoplasmic effects and materials from her vagina. The ongoing examinations of her psychic talents culminated in Houdini having a special cabinet made in 1924 to house the attractive Mrs Crandon so that only her hands and head were free through holes in the box. Even under this control, she managed to ring a bell that was in a box on the nearby table, with the box falling to the floor. A large, heavy cabinet was tilted over. The table levitated. When the spirit of Walter "came through", he threw a megaphone at Houdini's feet. Mina Crandon was undoubtedly one of the best mediums in the game. Yet to the end, Houdini would maintain Margery was a fraud, although he was highly impressed, at one time writing to the British paranormal researcher, Harry Price: "There is no doubt in my mind, whatsoever, that this lady who has been 'fooling' the scientists for months resorted to some of the slickest methods I have ever known and honestly it has taken my thirty years of experience to detect her in her various moves."

It is difficult to ascertain if Houdini's suspicion was well founded, but Margery did suffer from adverse exposure after she produced a fingerprint on wax. She claimed it came from Walter, her spirit contact, who had also made the chilling prediction that Houdini would be dead in approximately one year. When the Boston Society for Psychical Research examined the fingerprint in detail, it was revealed that it actually belonged to her dentist – the same man who had taught her this method of reproducing fingerprints. Despite the damage to her reputation, and the final judgement by the lofty committee of the *Scientific American* that she didn't pass muster, many still followed her performances religiously until her death, aged fifty-three, in 1941.

Harry Houdini defied Margery's prediction, but only just. He died aged fifty-two of peritonitis from a ruptured appendix at 1:26 p.m. on Halloween, 31 October 1926 at Grace Hospital in Detroit, Michigan. He is buried at Machpelah Cemetery, Queens, New York. There was a plot next to him reserved for his wife, Bess, but as a Catholic she could not be buried in a Jewish cemetery. Bess died in 1943 whilst travelling by train from California to New York, and is buried there at the Gate of Heaven Cemetery. Before Houdini died, he and Bess decided that if indeed there was the possibility of communicating from the afterlife, he would contact her with the secret message "Rosabelle believe", a quote from one of the plays in which she had performed. Throughout the decade 1926–36, upon each Halloween after Houdini's death, Bess attended a séance in the hope that Harry would "come through". He never did, and the confidential message on the table in its sealed envelope remained a secret. She kept a candle burning constantly by his photograph during all those years. In 1936, after a last unsuccessful séance on the roof of the Knickerbocker Hotel, she extinguished the candle, and announced: "Ten years is long enough to wait for any man."

People are still holding séances for Houdini. The "Official Houdini Séance" is currently organized by Sidney Hollis Radner, a Houdini devotee from Holyoke, Massachusetts. Other annual séances are organized at the Houdini Museum in Scranton by magician Dorothy Dietrich and by Neil Tobin, who describes himself as a "necromancer", on behalf of the Chicago Assembly of the Society of American Magicians at the Excalibur nightclub.

The vaudeville stage antics of "mediums" in the first half of the twentieth century, with their table rappings, ectoplasm, spirit slate writings, levitating tables, trumpets, bangs, whistles and noises, seem ridiculous today, although TV's *Most Haunted* comes close. Weird and unsettling though some of these appeared, they should cause the rational among us today to ask questions, the main one being – how on earth did the general public *fall* for this stuff? Another valid enquiry rarely raises its head. This involves the nature and behaviour of the spirits. Trying to contact the dead in a darkened room (always the essential darkness …) seemed only to produce mainly garbled, inconclusive results. As was evidenced during my own attendance at a night of mediumship, their messages seem random, banal and often meaningless. If the powerful world of the beyond exists and its veil can be pierced by our departed loved ones, wraiths in some spiritual Disneyland, then why do we only receive a scattering of evidence in our universe limited to levitating tables, knocks and whistles, spirit scribbling and the occasional cracked drinking glass or flickering candle? Don't they have email over there? What about a psychic telephone? A paranormal text message?

Or how about the *Pataphysical Tape Club*, a fictional radio programme that plays pataphysical sound recordings sent in by listeners. Pataphysics is a philosophy (some call it a "pseudo-philosophy") that attempts to explore what might be beyond the realm of metaphysics. It's a concept created by French writer Alfred Jarry (1873–1907), who called it "the science of imaginary solutions, which symbolically attributes the properties of objects, described by their virtuality, to their lineaments". (This alone probably warrants a text of "WTF?") The pataphysician behind the "Tape Club" radio show is Germany's Felix Kubin (1969–). He's an electronic musician who writes radio plays and is a self-described "dadaist-pataphysicist". He not only introduces these strange recordings on his show but also offers a new method of finding lost objects at home, sings "an amoeba hymn" and interviews a man who approaches women with the help of self-built musical boxes with scary noises. His twenty-five-minute radio play was originally conceived for the Audiotoop festival in Nijmegen. If he helps you to find lost objects then perhaps he's the electronic age's answer to Saint Anthony, Patron Saint of Lost Things and Missing Persons. As we've already strayed into an impenetrable philosophical fog, you may be wondering what metaphysics is. The best I can offer is that it's concerned with explaining the fundamental nature of being and the world, is almost impossible to define and hinges on two basic questions: 1. What is there? 2. What is it like? Confused? Join the club.

However, from finding lost objects to locating lost pooches or pussies isn't a big psychic leap. A regular contributor to the metaphysical website promoting "balance and empowerment", InfiniteQuest.com, is Sonya Fitzpatrick, a British television and radio personality and a pet psychic now living in Texas. She had her own television show, Animal Planet's *The Pet Psychic*. This call-in talk show offered animal advice and animal intuition, and is now available on SIRIUS Satellite Radio Channel 102. Sonya's an ex-model who has walked the best catwalks in Europe. Since childhood, Sonya claims, she's possessed tele-pathic abilities to communicate with reptiles, birds and animals of all kinds. This gift helps her to solve behavioural problems and helps with their physical ailments. She's also had consider-able success in locating lost pets, and her ability enables her to bridge the gap between living owners and their deceased pets. The HBO TV documentary, *To Love or Kill: Man versus Animal*, featured Sonya as part of its exploration into the relationship between humans and animals. Where do all these "abilities" fit? Is there some hinterland between science and absolute scepti-cism? Do we ponder and think well ... maybe, or do we fall about laughing? Perhaps both are valid options. The paranormal is just entertainment until it happens to contact you. That's when you might stop chuckling. None of us can know what sky-diving is like until we jump from the plane.

It is folly to suggest that science answers everything and that just because someone bears the title Doctor or Professor that their opinion on such matters is the truth. However, as a bril-liant magician and illusionist who could fool all the white coats who came after him, including the Mephistophelean brain of the creator of Sherlock Holmes, Houdini's principle nonetheless states that just because something is unexplained does not always mean that it is paranormal, supernatural, extra-terrestrial or conspiratorial. Before declaring that something is not *of* this world, we should establish it is not *in* this world. Annoying though it is for those of us trying to peek behind the veil hiding this life and the beyond, science is grounded in naturalism, not supernaturalism.

MEDIUM RARE: THE SEARCH FOR REAL PSYCHICS

*On the road from the City of Scepticism, I had to pass through
the Valley of Ambiguity.*

Adam Smith (1723–90)

Desiderius Erasmus was a Dutch Renaissance humanist who
lived from 1466 to 1536. His humanism wasn't the godless
humanism we understand today; he was also a priest, but he had
a grip on the mystery of blind faith, saying. "There are some
people who live in a dream world, and there are some who face
reality; and then there are those who turn one into the other."
Perhaps that's the key to the understanding of the world of the
psychic. However, the paranormal is a huge territory and not all
of its edifices can be regarded as mirages. If one seeks to maintain resistance against becoming a 100 per cent sceptic, without
spending days, weeks or months tracking down mediums for
private readings, how can we establish, albeit loosely, the ones
out there who appear to offer something genuinely impressive?
Perhaps the easiest way is through the experiences of their
former clients. The trouble is, when these people place their
endorsements on a psychic's website, one has to question just
how much editing has gone on in order for the medium to maintain their reputation. If they allow the severely critical responses
to sit alongside the glowing testimonials, you could be on to a
winner, but few businesses are likely to trash their image by such
magnanimity.

Psychics and Mediums: What's the Difference?

Psychic: The word's origin is the Greek word "psyche", meaning "breath of life" in connection to a spirit or a soul. Psychics claim contact with their own soul; however, unlike non-psychics, they have access to everyone else's soul. This enables them to indulge in "soul reading", a process where they link through something called your "aura energy field" (which extends beyond our physical body). This gift apparently enables the psychic to log on to your past, present and, in some cases, your future.

Medium: The internet, TV and radio are mediums (we call them "media") so a medium in the spiritual sense is the channel – person – through which a communication is transported or transmitted. Like your TV set or radio, therefore, a spiritualist medium transmits information from the spirit world to that of the living.

Mediumship is a psychic's skills in raising enough spiritual energy to tap in to the spirit world, in the same way that we would search a radio dial trying to tune into a station or flip through our TV channels to find the programme. Mediums claim that this is a very difficult procedure as, like radio signals, the source keeps shifting, and is sometimes made fuzzy by spiritual static, so that might explain why some messages from beyond are garbled and indistinct.

A **Reading** means that the psychic is "reading" you and your aura. Mediums are messengers relaying information from "the other side". If anyone departed does "come through" they might sound as if they're still in this life, so it's up to you to assess whether or not the message makes sense. Apparently, all spiritual mediums are psychic, but not all psychics are mediums.

The Psychic Barber

As you will have gathered from reading this section of the book, finding mediums under the headings "trustworthy" and "authentic" might seem to be an uphill struggle. If you have the showbiz chutzpah and a glimmering of "the gift", then you can make a good living on the clairvoyant/medium circuit. No huge trucks of equipment; just a good mike, a reliable house PA system and decent lighting. It's a self-contained occupation with an eager and willing audience. But there are astounding mediums, and one of them is Gordon Smith, who works as a barber in his native Glasgow. Since earning the nickname "The Psychic Barber", it's been a sobriquet he's found hard to shake off. I have seen him in action and one thing stands out – his compassion. As he says about his gift: "This isn't a *belief*; it's *knowledge* that life goes on." Unlike many of his less skilled albeit colourful competitors, when Gordon addresses a "sitter" he can come up with exact names, addresses, events and descriptions sharply relevant to a person's life and the lives of those they have known. I have seen him offer genuine comfort to the bereaved and he makes no bones about the messages he receives: "You can only give people a glimpse of that life which is to come."

Hailed as "Britain's most accurate medium" Gordon has been featured in numerous television documentaries including the BBC's three-part series, *Mediums: Talking with the Dead*, as well as appearing as an expert guest on various shows such as *Richard and Judy*, *This Morning* and the BBC's *Heaven and Earth*. He also had his own series on the Biography Channel. He's read for celebrities, travelled the globe, and written several books, including *Spirit Messenger* and *The Unbelievable Truth*, all to critical acclaim. Gordon has written regular columns for various magazines and newspapers.

His gift became apparent as a young boy, when he discovered he could sense and hear spirit people, an uncanny ability that sometimes unnerved those around him. As a teenage gymnast, he was good enough to be selected for the Scottish Commonwealth Games squad. When he was twenty-four, in the middle of the night a friend's brother appeared at his bedside, and the gifts he'd noticed as a young lad were rekindled. He later learned that the brother had died that night in a tragic fire. Fifteen years of study and practice followed as Gordon went on to work on his outstanding abilities as a medium or messenger. He developed in a mediumship circle run by the extraordinary Mrs Jean Primrose, an inspirational figure in Scottish spiritualism, and became a close friend of the legendary Albert Best, who was widely acknowledged as one of the best mediums of the last century.

Anyone who has seen Gordon in action will see another side to spiritualism; he seems to adhere to what mediumship really should be at heart – not so much cheap entertainment, but a source of reassurance and comfort. The *Guardian* summed up his contact with the public: "Gordon's gift was to soothe the grief of the heartbroken, to give them hope." He's refreshingly down to earth. He stood out from the flashy, white-suited quasi-evangelist mediums in San Francisco on one of his US visits; cameras caught his American competitors backstage as they stood in drop-jawed envy at his sensitivity and absolute accuracy; he knew the names of sons and daughters in the audience, details of the deceased relatives, their illnesses, their quirky individual characteristics. Of course, the sceptical view could always be that he has some pre-supplied information, but he's been rigorously tested several times, for example by Professor Archie E. Roy, Emeritus Professor of Astronomy, Glasgow University, who has since become a friend, and in this case, any trace of fraud seems highly unlikely. As Professor Roy observed: "The talent Gordon has been blessed with is something most of us can hardly believe, but to see and hear of the help he has given to others in easing their pain is surely his greatest gift. He's also a reasonable barber!"

Rosemary the Celtic Lady™

If you Google "America's greatest mediums" one of the most prominent sites is that of the American Association of Psychics and Healers. One of these practitioners is Rosemary the Celtic Lady™. Based in Colorado, although originating from Glasgow in Scotland, Rosemary McArthur seems to hold sway over the transatlantic mediumship world in a big way. She's the founder of the American, Canadian, and UK Associations of Psychics & Healers™. She is also an author, motivational speaker and "medical intuitive" (that is, an alternative medicine practitioner who uses their claimed intuitive abilities to find the cause of a physical or emotional condition).

Reading the testimonials praising her accuracy in mediumship, clairaudience, psychometry, clairvoyance and clairsentience on her website, it would appear that the Celtic Lady™ has an enviable success rate among her devoted followers. She has many strings to her psychic bow, including that of Reiki Master, developer of AMAHT (Ascended Masters Ancient Healing Techniques™). (Strange how corporate branding, trademarks and all the commercial trappings of intellectual property law dominate the spirit world™.) Reiki is a system of natural healing developed in the 1920s in Japan by the Buddhist Dr Mikao Usui. Oddly enough, although AMAHT™ bears yet another of those insistent, corporate-looking "TM" trademarks, as reiki practised elsewhere has no belief system attached, apparently anyone can receive or learn to give a reiki treatment, the only prerequisite being the desire to be healed.

Of course, all these benign branches of spiritual development appear at first glance to be free of the taint of any form of political or religious extremism. Yet then we read that the Celtic Lady™ is an "Ambassador for Peace with the Universal Peace Federation". Peace around the world is a laudable mission, yet here we step away from the aura of the spirits because the Universal Peace Federation is yet another of the many global enterprises founded by the self-proclaimed Messiah and Second Coming, the Reverend Sun Myung Moon. So, perhaps the spirit world doesn't mind being associated with such extreme right-wing media enterprises as Moon's *Washington Times*, the support of South American Contra death squads and other such sinister, world-dominating interferences with social progress. According to the press, though, Ms McArthur does commune with some impressive spirits. The *Edmonton Journal* stated on 14 April 2008:

The Celtic Lady, Rosemary McArthur when she's not using her professional title, said [Princess] Diana has "channelled" through her to reveal that her 1997 death in a Paris road tunnel was no accident. The self-styled international psychic medium, a Scot living in Colorado, McArthur was in Edmonton on Sunday at the Body Soul and Spirit Expo, a travelling show featuring clairvoyants, healers, card and hair readers, reflexologists and miracle-code practitioners. Diana, who consulted a range of psychics, spiritual healers and astrologers, might have felt at home there. McArthur said that a few hours before meeting Diana in 1993 she fell painfully ill and saw flashes of lights, a black car and heard screeching metal.

"I kept hearing, 'Paris, Paris, Paris'."

Four years later, she endured the same sensations and then heard news of Diana's fatal car crash, Rosemary said. Not long after, Diana "starts channelling through me," saying she was in a better place but "they" had secretly removed a foetus from her body.

Whereas Princess Diana is just one of many prominent personalities who "come through" from the spirit world, the majority of spiritualism's followers seek nothing more than some contact or message from a relative or friend who has "gone over". In the age of the touring celebrity medium, many believers fall for the idea that the bigger the medium, the higher the profile and the more positive the publicity, then this might be a shortcut. As the song goes, "it ain't necessarily so".

Doris Stokes

Doris Stokes (1920–87) was, by all accounts, a nice, homely lady, Britain's most famous medium. Known as the "housewives' clairvoyant", her speciality was necromancy (communication with the dead) and her career in this field spanned over four decades. She knew she had "the gift" as a child. Her choice of inspiration to become a medium herself wasn't all that wise. She'd attended a séance by none other than Helen Duncan, who in 1944 was prosecuted for "conspiracy to pretend that she was in touch with spirits", found guilty and sentenced to nine months. Back then mediums could still get away with issuing "ectoplasm", the ingredients of which sometimes included toilet paper. Yet let's not judge a medium by the company she keeps. Doris went on to develop her powers and rose to international fame, at one time selling out Australia's Sydney Opera House. As well as having contact with her departed father, her large audiences were amazed as she consistently named some of their dead relatives.

However, despite the support and love of thousands of the convinced and the devoted, like most mediums the amiable Mrs

Stokes had a few chinks in her armour. In her book *Voices in My Ear*, she suggested that she'd solved two UK murder cases, one involving some children in Blackpool and another involving a small girl at Kirkham. Yet Detective Chief Superintendent William Brooks of the Lancashire Constabulary made a statement to the effect that Doris had made no contribution to the solving of either murder. But if she could do a spiritual Sherlock in the UK, she could do the same in America, so in Beverly Hills, Los Angeles, she claimed that a local murder victim called Weiss had "come through" to her with details of his murder. The LAPD were unimpressed, stating that all of the dead Weiss's spirit information was readily available to the LA media at the time Doris went public with the "psychic conversation".

She nonetheless gave comfort to many, and donated the proceeds of her books to charity, but any medium always has to keep the radar running for their inevitable nemesis – the professional sceptic.

The continuing controversy – could she or could she not speak with the dead – was the same for Doris Stokes as it is for everyone who claims psychic ability. She was once offered £20,000 by Gerald Fleming, a British millionaire, to prove her ability. But as the accusations of fakery mounted, she refused any requests to be tested under close surveillance, saying, "They have been trying for years to prove that I am a fraud, but they failed because I am not." She was proud that "the thousands of letters I have had from grateful people prove that I have brought comfort to many of the bereaved".

On her 1978 Australian tour she ran into the Lord High Sceptic himself, Canada's master magician, James Randi, the bane of mediums from New York to Newcastle. Doris was appearing on Australian TV's top-rated *Don Lane Show* when Randi boldly called her a liar. Host Don Lane left the set in disgust, later saying that he remained undecided about her powers, but totally disliked the idea of her being insulted in such an ungentlemanly fashion.

But the sceptics were not fooled. Nice lady though she was, Doris was a master of "cold reading". She had that ability to "fish" for information from her audience. If there was an elderly lady in the stalls, on her own, chances are she'd be a widow. Her departed husband, probably an Albert or a George, would no doubt tell her "not to worry". Doris would throw a name out, for example "Little Daniel" and, sure enough, someone out there would probably have a little Daniel. By prefixing the name with "Little" this could of course reveal it was a small child who had "gone over". Did he die in a hospital? The chances are always high that a toddler who has died would do so in hospital. She could join all the dots together with skill and soon a tearfully bereaved mother would be convinced "Little Daniel" was issuing trite and homely messages from kiddie heaven. If you have success enough times with this "fishing" routine, it hardly seems surprising that you will eventually believe that you actually are a true psychic. It's a turning point the great Orson Welles, no mean magician himself, once called "becoming a shut-eye" – where you begin to totally believe in your "psychic" abilities.

Another popular ploy with mediums is the planting of contacts in the audience. In his book, *The After Death Experience* (1978), Ian Wilson exposed Doris Stokes as a fraud when he successfully proved that some of those she called out in the audience were plants. In some cases they had actually been sent tickets for her show, but they had that important element – they were still true believers.

Following her death in 1987, Doris's place in the spotlight was filled by another Doris, a grandmother in her mid-sixties, Doris Collins. She was a skilful successor – and managed by the same agent, Laurie O'Leary. Mrs Collins, like many in her trade, regard sceptics like James Randi as something more than a mere irritant. On Australian TV she actually referred to him and his kind as, "Evil. I know evil when I see it. I'm doing the work of God." Therefore, sceptics = Satan.

However, we can't dismiss the Dorises all that easily. Apparently it was Doris Stokes who, over the dinner table, told notorious press baron and publisher Robert Maxwell intimate details of how he would die. She was proved accurate in every respect. She also appeared on a TV chat show with Stephen Knight (1951–85), the author of *Jack the Ripper: The Final Solution* (1976) and *The Brotherhood* (1984). Both books suggest there is a secret cabal of Freemasons controlling British society. Doris told him, live on TV that he would be "killed for his book". In his work he likened the higher levels of Freemasonry to devil worship. Somewhat paradoxically, it transpires that Knight was a religious follower of the notorious guru Bhagwan Shree Rajneesh and, as a part of this interest, took the name Swami Puja Debal. Doris Stokes was right about his imminent death. A few weeks later Knight was dead from a brain tumour.

There was a humorous coda to all this from Simon Goodley in the *Daily Telegraph* of 16 December 2007:

A week ago my old friend Doris Stokes, the deceased medium who occasionally contacts me offering interviews with dead tycoons, promised to double-check that pensions thief Robert Maxwell really has passed on – a belt-and-braces reaction after we've all recently had cause to re-examine previously held convictions about folk drowning at sea. Well, step down Doris! You've been beaten to it. A reader rings to inform me that Maxwell really is dead as the caller's medium friend says she's spoken to the old fraudster. Sensationally, Bob claims to have been murdered.

From homely psychic British grandmothers scanning for their Little Daniels to the bustling streets of the Big Apple is no great leap for the spirits. But back in the United States, they've really got their act together, and a good medium can easily share a suite in downtown Manhattan with the best of the Mad Men. Take, for example, the highly successful psychic-medium Stephen C. Robinson on 7th Avenue. Stephen uses trance and clairvoyance, and his website www.thenewyorkpsychic.com leaves you in no doubt that you're getting the real deal:

He begins your reading by asking for your questions and your birthday. Next he'll ask for photos of the special people in your life, both dead and alive. Once he has determined your reasons for being here for a reading, he closes his eyes and goes into a clairvoyant, psychic trance as he holds the energy of your object close to his heart chakra. Now the reading begins and he takes you on a psychic journey. With deep respect for your unique pathway, Stephen's psychic abilities allow him to penetrate the veil between today and tomorrow – between this world and the next, to clairvoyantly see details about your life, your future and those who have crossed over. His trance states may take him back to your past-lives as he carefully explains their relevance to your current life. Stephen's voice and his nurturing manner create an air of comfort, safety and trust as you journey with him into the deepest reaches of other dimensions to retrieve information to enable you to create a better life for yourself and others ...

Happy clients are keen to flag up his accuracy:

Mostly his predictions come true in quite surprising and unexpected ways. For example at my first reading he predicted that I would meet and marry a man from South America. At the time I was very much in love with someone else. I left feeling sad. But as things turned out, a friend and I went to a birthday party and I met a guy from Brazil. To make a long story short, Stephen's prediction did come true. My boyfriend found someone else and I fell in love with the South American man and married him ... I have faith and trust in Stephen as a psychic ... He has helped give me reassurance, guidance and hope.

These are the kind of testimonials most mediums would die for.

Michelle Whitedove

America is the mother lode for psychics. In recent years Lifetime TV ran a reality competition featuring sixteen unique individuals from across the country professing the gift of clairvoyance. They all wanted to win the title "America's Number 1 Psychic". They took part in various tough tests, including searching for a man hidden in a hospital, doing a reading with an unidentified person, and demonstrating accuracy with details of a murder scene investigation. Points were awarded based on the number and accuracy of their predictions. It sounds like a good format for a UK show, so it's surprising we haven't had one yet. As each episode ended, the two psychics who had scored the lowest were eliminated, whilst those with the most points entered the next round, which all led to a nail-biting finale to round up the season. The show's winner was Michelle Whitedove, and she was proud to submit her details through a fairly thorough questionnaire to the show's website (www.mylifetime.com/shows/americas-psychic-challenge/cast/michelle-whitedove):

Michelle Whitedove
Age: 30 something
Occupation: Spiritual medium, medical intuitive, author and teacher
State of residence: FL
Marital status: In a relationship
Zodiac sign: Taurus
Describe yourself using 3 adjectives: Honest, Passionate, Perceptive
List your hobbies: Dancing and singing
Who are 3 people you admire most? I admire humanitarians, those people who are out there making a positive impact on the world that we live in. As a positive role model in Hollywood, Angelina Jolie uses her money to fund projects and her status to travel as a UN ambassador and bring awareness to the plights that ravage the citizens of the world. Then there are people like Al Gore and Michael Moore, who are brave enough to step into the spotlight to raise awareness without knowing if their personal truth will be accepted.
Describe your psychic ability: I was born a medium, gifted with sight (clairvoyance) and the ability to communicate with the spirit realm, gaining information through prayer and meditation. Over the years, I have worked to strengthen and fine tune my abilities as a medium and medical intuitive.
When did you realize you had this gift? About the age of eight years old, I came to realize that most people were not seeing the same things that I was or conversing with heavenly beings. I was surprised that people were not acknowledging their unseen support team: guardian angels and spirit guides. I wondered how they could not see them.
Does anyone else in your family have these gifts? If so, who? Not to my knowledge.

Are any of your friends or family sceptics? My family and friends who have seen me in action aren't sceptical. Others prefer to remain in denial, so they won't come to see me at my lectures or classes.

What are your sentiments toward sceptics? It's healthy to be sceptical because there are frauds in every profession. But I am not here to force my beliefs on anyone. When you are ready, then you'll open your mind to the possibility of spiritual phenomena.

Have you ever used your gifts to help people? Explain: Sure, the gift of being a spiritual medium and medical intuitive are only for the purpose of helping others. Every day when I do my readings, the information that is channelled through me is given to benefit another. Personally, my greatest satisfaction comes from helping people solve medical mysteries and counselling children.

What's the best part about having such a gift? Experiencing angels! Helping others! Knowing outcomes! Changing the world, one person at a time, via readings or my books.

What's the worst part about having such a gift? Seeing the negative aspects of people you love.

Refreshing, straightforward, balanced and honest; easy to see why she won the competition.

Psychics for Sale

Psychics, clairvoyants and mediums have in some instances more or less allowed themselves to become a corporate brand. In Britain, for a while we had Lancashire's "Mystic Meg" aka Margaret Anne Lake (1942–) delivering her suitably ominous astrological deliberations on the National Lottery TV show. Allegedly a psychic, today she writes astrology columns for the *Sun* and until its ignominious exit from our news-stands, the phone-hacker's house journal, the *News of the World*, for whom she would provide her "predictions for the year ahead" each January. It is uncertain as to whether or not she predicted the paper would crash and burn in 2011. Some of her failed predictions seem rashly random; for 2006 she said that a new, unknown story by Charles Dickens would be found in a desk in Huddersfield, that a new island would rise from the sea off Australia and that aliens would make contact. Like my lucky Lottery numbers, these didn't come up, although the aliens were probably already here. Mystic Meg is also the owner of several racehorses through her company Mystic Meg Limited, based in Bedford. Her astrological gee-gees have the kind of names one might expect: Astrodonna, Astronangel and Astronova and there are even more celestial names among her equine investments. Here's her prediction for this writer's star sign, Aries, in the *Sun* for 2012: "WIN IT: With lucky Jupiter in your big-money house for the first half of the year you have cool nerve to beat any clock and test any knowledge even with millions at stake. Veto any competitions that trouble your conscience. Your 'win it' number is two and a team in red can come good for you." So it's Manchester United and down to the bookie's to place my bets if Meg's nags are running.

Selfridge's in Oxford Street, one of the most prestigious department stores in the world, introduced the spiritualist "Psychic Sisters" (sole owner, Jayne Wallace) to its store in March 2006.

You can take the weight off your feet and drop by for a reading, and they also offer phone consultations specializing in tarot, clairvoyance, astrology, crystals, palmistry and reiki healing.

America's Psychic Friends Network (PFN) was launched in 1991, with its state-of-the-art phone system and infomercials. PFN's technology allowed the customers to build personal relationships with individual psychics at $3.99 per minute. There was extra kudos to be had because the show, which featured re-enactments of callers' stories, was hosted by singer Dionne Warwick and psychic Linda Georgian. Eventually, the spirits must have lost patience because although the parent company, Inphomation, took in profits of over $100 million their mediums failed to predict the show's looming bankruptcy in 1998, precipitated by a string of lawsuits from several states and the Federal Communications Commission over PFN's dodgy advertising techniques. But the afterworld is kind; Psychic Friends Network is now back, and you can indulge yourself today at its website (www.psychicfriendsnetwork.net) where you'll learn that: "All of our psychics undergo a rigid screening to identify those who really have the psychic gift, as well as to find those psychics who truly care for the wellbeing of the clients, for whom they do their readings."

A Psychic Friends Network shaman became one of America's most colourful self-proclaimed pay-by-the-minute Tarot-reading psychics, the cod-Jamaican Miss Cleo (1962–). Cleo is still a favourite on YouTube, where her infomercials are genu-inely funny. Perhaps her claim to being Jamaican gave her an exotic folksy touch, but she could never quite get the Kingston reggae accent right. In the course of her career Miss Cleo, real name Youree Dell Harris, who was revealed to be a US citizen from Los Angeles, has worked under different names such as "Ree Perris" and "Youree Cleomili". At the height of her fame, everything suddenly fell apart. State attorneys-general and the Federal Trade Commission put legal pressure on her employers for their fraudulent advertising claims. Miss Cleo avoided indict-ment and was known to be still turning over those well-worn tarot cards when she wasn't appearing on television as Cleo in advertisements for a used car dealership in Florida.

There's an extensive list of these mediums, astrologers, shamans and psychics, but we can't omit from this round-up a real witch, Sybil Leek (1917–82) Sybil was an astrologer, psychic and occult author who was dubbed "Britain's most famous witch" by the BBC. She wrote more than sixty books on occult and esoteric subjects. She benefited from the repeal of the 1735 Witchcraft Act in 1951 and was important in helping to re-establish neo-pagan witchcraft, mainly the religion of Wicca, which has thousands of new converts in Britain today.

"EVERYTHING FROM BOWELS TO BEREAVEMENT": POWER, POLITICS, PERSONALITIES AND PSYCHICS

The term clinical depression finds its way into too many conversations these days. One has a sense that a catastrophe has occurred in the psychic landscape.

Leonard Cohen (1934–)

Although this section of this book is headed "Beyond the Veil", the veil itself is not only a curtain between this life and the next. Behind it lurk all the alternative philosophies and accrued mumbo-jumbo that can often seem so attractive to some people that they are prepared to live their lives by its edicts. Spoon-bender Uri Geller once commented that, "Nowadays even presidents, vice-presidents, and heads of big agencies are opening their minds to accept psychic phenomena, because they know it works." A great many people are sifting through the baffling array of spiritual methods on offer to find their own "God particle", through the standard-issue religions or via the assistance of mediums, some of whom are genuine, many of whom are frauds. Out in the shadowy borderlands of sincere spirituality there lurks an affluent army of pseudo-paranormal hijackers, skilled in sales and persuasion, and capable of coaxing even the most skilled international statesmen that they need to suspend their reason and buy their shoddy wares.

Celebrities, pop stars, musicians and even politicians, their wealth and fame never seeming to provide the fulfilment they expect, are quite willing to place their heads above the parapet of expected common sense and expose themselves to a variety of phenomenal New Age baloney; the more outlandish, expensive and peculiar this is, the better. Do the following examples come under the heading "unexplained phenomena"? I think they qualify. The motives of some people, who resell all this to their blinkered clients, their sheer brass neck in plugging into what they perceive to be "psychic" or "spiritual" for personal gain or advancement, are indeed difficult to explain. And without the existence of the phenomena they rely on, they would have to look for a "proper" job.

Of course, politicians and celebrities share the same human genes as the rest of us, so they are just as prone to lose their grip on logic as anyone else. So a successful singer like Britain's Robbie Williams can announce, with no sense of embarrassment, that he's obsessed with UFOs, aliens and conspiracy theories. Madonna, reared as a Catholic, certainly ruffled a few priestly cassocks with her first big hit, "Like a Virgin". It seems odd that she now follows an esoteric adjunct of Judaism: Kabbalah. The word is derived from the root "to receive, to accept", and in many cases is used synonymously with "tradition". An aspect of Jewish mysticism that requires you to wear a piece of string around your wrist, it features speculation on the nature of the creation, divinity, the origin and fate of the soul, and the role of human beings. Other pop stars seem more than willing to join the team on TV's laughable *Most Haunted* to ponce about shrieking in dank cellars, their "gorgeous" features hardly enhanced by night vision cameras. Astrology, weird religions, revelations of psychic beliefs, these are all meat and drink to our tabloid culture, and, from an entertainment standpoint, without them life would be much duller.

One of Ireland's folk/pop family outfit, the Corrs, Andrea, tells us: "I think paranormal experiences are very personal, again, if they are that. Yes, sometimes I've felt that some things I would personally believe enough for me to take action on it ... like, you know, I felt something happen in a hotel once that made me never stay there again."

When our political leaders get involved in all this, we really sit up and take note. These days that paragon of political virtue, ex-UK Prime Minister Tony Blair, has long forgotten his search for mythical Weapons of Mass Destruction. The ongoing disaster of Iraq has been consigned to history's dustbin, along with the tenets of the Labour Party upon whose shoulders he rose to power. He's allegedly making a decent jetset living promoting peace, faith, Louis Vuitton handbags and J. P. Morgan. But at the height of Tony and Cherie Blair's prominence as international political celebs and Bush babies, they were happy to be guided by spiritual "style guru" Carole Caplin. Carole's good at putting important folk in touch with the right psychic practitioners. One that she recommended to Cherie was Lilias Curtin. Mrs Curtin maintains that negative feelings are contained in a "thought field" surrounding the body and those problems are caused by negative patterns known as "perturbations" in the "thought field". You can cure these, says Mrs Curtin, by tapping on certain points on the body in a specific sequence: "By tapping on the correct meridian points in the right order the perturbations are subsumed and the negative emotion disappears," she says.

Mrs Curtin also offers electronic gem therapy. This is a routine where a light is shone through a gemstone on to ailing parts of the body. Also on the menu is magnet therapy, which "helps dislodge toxins" by applying magnets to the body. If none of this works, Mrs Curtin's clinic provides aqua detox therapy, a type of foot spa that she claims flushes out toxins. One might not imagine that a talented entertainer, an impressionist known for his acute satire of everything surrounding the UK government, Rory Bremner, would get sucked into all this, yet he reportedly bought one of the foot spas for £1,800. Mrs Curtin, who lives in Fulham with her lawyer husband Richard and two sons, also offers "voice technology thought field therapy". So, as Britain's National Health Service is doomed to plummet headlong into the private American model, it's good to know we have alternatives available.

In an article entitled "The Weird World of Cherie" in the *Daily Mail* in 2002, Lynda Lee-Potter described Cherie Blair as "gullible, bordering on the cranky when it comes to alternative medicine, homeopathy, gurus and the power of crystals and rocks". We learned that she also had an alleged dependence on "Sylvia", a Dorking-based medium. As Shakespeare asked,

"Who is Sylvia – what is she?" In this case, she's Carole Caplin's mother. However, Sylvia is no mere Doris Stokes. She has a much wider range of talent and ability. She's also a well-regarded dancer and pioneering fitness instructor with some genuinely high-profile celebrity clients, including Mia Farrow and the energetic Jane Fonda, who was choreographed by Sylvia in the film *Julia*. She also worked with Felicity Kendal on *Shape Up & Dance*, the bestselling fitness album. Yet when the body is at rest, the spirits need attention, and Sylvia's holistic approach was more than effective. She referred to some of the sessions she and Carole gave as a "pamper". An "Ayurvedic doctor" had once presented Sylvia with a special questionnaire. When a new client arrived, this was used to investigate all aspects of their lives – diet, work, sexual proclivities. Or, as she told the *Daily Telegraph*, "everything, from bowels to bereavement".

According to another revealing piece by Jamie Doward and Ben Whitford, published in the *Observer* on 21 September 2003, the glamorous ex-model Carole learned her highly persuasive trade in the 1980s working for London-based Programmes Ltd, a secretive telemarketing company that "sought to dominate every aspect of its employees' lives as it transformed them into powerfully persuasive communicators who would be capable of selling anything to anyone". The company appears to have had all the hallmarks of a brainwashing cult. It even established its own school for employees' children, buying up any available property in the vicinity of its offices. Programmes Ltd soon promoted Caplin to Supervisor, and she bought a company flat. If you had the guts to stick it out for more than a year with Programmes Ltd, you were given the privilege of being sent on to the "Exegesis course", described by the *Observer* as "a quasi-psychotherapy programme designed to 're-birth' participants by encouraging them to face up to their inner fears. Its fundamental message was that devotees had to tell the truth at all times, no matter how painful this could be."

Exegesis was run by a former actor and son of a meat salesman, Robert Fuller, who changed his name to the more sophisticated "D'Aubigny". Also on board was record producer Tony Visconti's girlfriend Kim Coe. The Exegesis course had a peculiar element of instruction known as "raising the confront" where attendees were taught argumentative voice techniques and ordered to say what they hated about each other. Staff at Programmes Ltd were instructed never to talk about Exegesis or mention its leader, D'Aubigny/Fuller.

As the boss of Exegesis, Fuller deeply impressed many course pupils with his forceful personality. Some likened his leadership charisma to that of Richard Branson. The multimillion-selling musician of *Tubular Bells* fame, Mike Oldfield, was on the course. The induction period was four days of screaming aloud your worst memories. You were expected to unearth and reveal your "demons" and bring them out into the open. Mike Oldfield said: "I was hyperventilating and I confronted my panic and found out where it came from. I turned into a newborn infant. The memory of that second birth was still there, deep inside my subconscious. I could feel the newness of the air on my skin, on my fingers and on my hair." However, he later added: "It made you very insecure and it made you focus on whatever it was that was bothering you deeply in your subconscious. It sort of pushed you, like doing psychotherapy in three days." What happened after the "second level" of the course is not something ex-members talk about, although there were the usual media allegations involving mind games and even group sex.

By the mid-1980s the hard core who had benefited from Exegesis training formed the heart of a highly focused telemarketing team who could sell just about anything, and they had some big clients, Vodafone among them.

The success of Programmes Ltd was greatly enhanced by its industrious subsidiary agency, the Exhibitionists. There was a particular employment condition if you wanted to be an Exhibitionist. You needed to be a very attractive female. And the majority were ex-models, specifically trained to cajole company directors into placing their telemarketing with Programmes Ltd. Pearl Read, a close friend of Carole Caplin, ran the Exhibitionists. It's alleged that at one time she'd been married to one of London's leading prostitution bosses, a rival to the notorious Kray twins, Joe Wilkins. Like the Krays, he was one of those "good old boy" East End gangsters who was lucky enough in 1976 to be given a conditional discharge after he was collared for helping to run a vice racket. Pearl Read, however, staunchly denied that the Exhibitionists had anything to do with prostitution. However, the Exegesis-trained lovely lady Exhibitionists, by 1985, had managed to swell Programmes Ltd, establishing its capability of making 10,000 sales calls a day and turning it into the UK's biggest telemarketing business. Not bad when you realize that their 1981 turnover was a mere £21,000; by 1990 it was a whopping £6.5 million.

The shareholders loved it, especially the biggest, the Tory MP for Hastings Kenneth Warren, whose day job was parliamentary private secretary to Keith Joseph, Margaret Thatcher's mentor. But cults attract critics and questions were asked in Parliament. David Mellor, then a Home Office minister, condemned the organization as "puerile, dangerous and profoundly wrong" and it was investigated by the police (although no charges were ever brought). Soon Programmes Ltd was no more, but it's still around as the hugely successful telemarketing business, Merchants Group.

Exegesis exploded into a range of various other outfits, whilst Monsieur D'Aubigny joined forces with Visconti to form their own record company.

We're used to the idea of cults being religious-based bodies, and those who escape them usually have very little positive to say about their experience. However, Exegesis was the ideal cult for 1980s yuppies. Those who were in it seem by all accounts to have nothing but happy memories; it was all about sell, sell, sell, and ultimately making money, a movement which seems like the foundation of everything that gets up our noses today, with "greed is good" at the top of the list.

Carole Caplin, brimming with all the positive vibes of the curvaceous Exhibitionists, formed her own New Age companies. Among them was Holistix, devising psychic-styled health and wellbeing exercises for very wealthy clients, who would later include the UK's First Lady, Cherie Blair.

Caplin penned a number of health and wellbeing books and appeared on TV with her own Channel 4 show, *The Carole Caplin Treatment*. According to the press, she was responsible for introducing the Blairs to a range of "spiritual" beliefs. To get close to a Prime Minister one needs to be particularly skilled in the art of persuasion, but before long, she found herself on

holiday with the Blairs in Mexico in 2001. Wearing their swimming costumes, they all gathered in a steam bath and took part
in a "re-birthing" procedure involving smearing mud and fruit
over each other's bodies. Of course, everyone in Britain realizes
that papers like the *Daily Mail* have little good to say about politicians who don't fit their political remit, but in addition to all the
crystals and aroma therapy, with Sylvia's contact with the spirit
world, the all-in-the-tub-together detox bath scrubs, it would be
a shame to leave the Blairs without mentioning this snippet from
Paul Scott at the *Mail Online*, dated 16 May 2008, when Cherie
was on tour promoting her autobiography:

The Strange Case of the Inflatable Trousers
While in Downing Street, Mrs Blair became a regular visitor
to the Mayfair-based therapist Bharti Vyas. Mrs Vyas, who
has no recognized medical qualifications, recommended to
Cherie the wearing of "flowtron leggings" to improve her
wellbeing. Once a month, and helped by Mrs Vyas, Cherie
would climb into the vibrating pants, which resemble a huge
pair of inflatable wetsuit bottoms, which were then filled with
compressed air then deflated at 30-second intervals.

Another unorthodox procedure which Mrs Blair was persuaded to undergo by Vyas was a £35-a-session process called
Magnetic Resonance Therapy. Mrs Vyas, a self-styled
"world-renowned holistic therapist", fitted Cherie with
special goggles which showed a series of kaleidoscopic
colours. She was also given headphones from which came a
procession of strange, rhythmic noises. Barrister and Judge
Cherie was then asked to lie down on a mattress containing a
network of magnetic coils. These, according to Vyas, were
supposed to "rebalance the magnetic field" in her body, while
the "alpha waves" from the goggles were meant to relax her
brain. Surprise, surprise, neither strange therapy merits inclusion in Cherie's memoirs.

Of course, all these stories in the popular press may be highly
entertaining, but from the ordinary reader's point of view, it's
always worth asking the question, "Is this true – or made up?" In
Ms Caplin's case, it would seem that many inventive hacks may

have been having a field day during the Blair years. In an interview (which she claimed would be her last) with David Vincent in the *Observer* on Sunday, 13 May 2012, Carole began fighting back and set about demolishing many of the yarns written about her;

> Bill Clinton asking for a massage at Chequers? "Never happened …" Locking a journalist naked in your bathroom? "Complete fabrication …" Trinny and Susannah claiming they turned you down when you went for a job interview? "Bull." Ran an escort agency called the Exhibitionists? "That was a company which put staff on stands at exhibitions. Duh …" The *News of the World*'s fake sheikh trying to get something on you? "He brought along a sidekick that looked like an Arab version of Jaws from James Bond. You couldn't make it up. Oh, hang on a second, they did …" Had your pass for No 10 revoked? "Didn't have one." Napped in the Blairs' bed? "Made up – the story, not the bed …" Practise primal scream therapy? "No. But if you carry on asking these bloody questions, I might just learn."

Since the revelations about phone hacking and the duplicitous nature of much of Britain's popular press, we're slowly learning to take many claimed "revelations" with a very large pinch of salt. Yet these stories, fiction or fact, continue to entertain us. In many ways, they're similar to UFO lore: 95 per cent can be explained – yet it's that remaining 5 per cent that will always leave us agape and scratching our heads, wondering if these powerful people really do get up to these things.

Iron Lady Margaret Thatcher, who was to the world of the spirit what Orson Welles was to hang-gliding, could hardly be associated with such New Age malarkey, yet it transpires she held secret meetings with an Indian mystic soon after she became leader of the Tory opposition. She conversed with Sri Chandraswamy, a self-declared faith healer and preacher who claimed to be able to "cast spells", in 1975 in her Commons office, where the mystic arrived wearing beads around his neck, an orange shawl and carrying a Gandalf-style staff. This was all revealed by former Indian Foreign Minister Shri Natwar Singh, who was present when these liaisons took place. Apparently the powerful bearded guru so impressed the Meryl Streep-lookalike that she approved a second meeting, wherein she agreed to a couple of his odder requests. One was to wear a shabby amulet he had given her around her wrist and don a special red dress.

Apparently the great guru predicted that she would become Prime Minister and that she would remain in power for over a decade. Of course, Chandraswamy was not your bargain-basement mystic. You need to have top-drawer status to attract clients including the Sultan of Brunei, Nancy Reagan, Elizabeth Taylor and businessmen such as Adnan Khashoggi, whose spirituality encompasses that compassionate branch of commerce, international arms dealing. Surprisingly, clad in crimson and wearing her talisman, Maggie turned up for her second meeting. The guru presented Mrs Thatcher with five strips of paper, asking her to write a question on each, with Mr Singh's help as translator. According to Singh, she displayed "scarcely camouflaged irritation" when Chandrsaswamy closed his eyes and went into a trance. When he came round, prior to unfolding the rolled up strips, he accurately revealed each question she had written.

"Irritation gave way to subdued curiosity," says Mr Singh. "By the fourth question, I thought, she began to consider Chandraswamy a holy man indeed. Chandraswamy was like a triumphant guru and took off his slippers and sat on the sofa in the lotus position. I was appalled but Mrs Thatcher seemed to approve. She asked more questions and, in each case, Chandraswamy's response overwhelmed her." But by then the sun had set, some kind of mystical omen, and the guru made his exit. The rest, as they say, is history.

Curious health routines (at least they seem so to those of us who can't afford them) are certainly the thing you need as an A-list celebrity fighting to keep age at bay. We simply have to take one more glance at Madonna, fifty-three-year-old mother of four, who performed with someone called Nicki Minaj for the capacity crowd at the 2012 Superbowl on 5 February in Indianapolis. Apparently she stipulated that a state-of-the-art "hydraulic yoga mat" with a platform which can be raised to ceiling level, be installed in her room at the Marriott Hotel in where she was booked in prior to her performance. Her instructor accompanied her on the trip, and heat was pumped into the hotel room so that she could do her yoga exercises in comfort. It's not clear as to whether Madonna still follows a strict macrobiotic diet, but later she sent out to Papa John's for fifty pizzas for her and her crew. Madonna had a cheese-free vegetarian version. Staying young seems like hard work, but in Madonna's case she seems to be doing OK. The media company TiVo reported that based on the amount of times that viewers rewound the footage of her Superbowl spot with Ms Minaj to watch again, Madonna's show was 16 per cent more popular than the game itself.

Hydraulics may be one way of raising your game, but the great gurus plug into what they see as "the order of the cosmos" with ease. So it's hardly surprising that another movement should blossom under the banner "cosmic ordering". In the *Scotsman* newspaper on 8 April 2006, British TV viewers got the full story of how the man they thought they'd got rid of, Noel Edmonds, the father of that execrable inflated pink rubber curse of prime time Saturday TV, Mr Blobby, had managed to shoehorn his way back on to our screens after his wilderness years. *Noel's House Party* on BBC1 hit the skids in 1999, but after a variety of other lacklustre shows on various channels, Edmonds, a believer in spiritualism, was introduced by his reflexologist to the book *The Cosmic Ordering Service – A Guide to Realizing Your Dreams* by a German woman, Bärbel Mohr. In case you're wondering, reflexology is an alternative "health" routine involving the physical act of applying pressure to the feet, hands or ears with specific thumb, finger and hand techniques without the use of oil or lotion. So inspired by Fraulein Mohr's helpful hand in guiding him back on to our screens six days per week with a £3 million contract, plus a £10 million dream house in Devon, Edmonds later went on to write his own book, *Positively Happy: Cosmic Ways to Change Your Life*.

According to reports Noel enjoys occasional visits by two melon-sized "spiritual energy balls". They materialize over his shoulders and he believes them to be the spirits of his dead parents. However, the orbs appear only on digital photographs. Cosmic ordering involves writing messages "to the universe" so perhaps we should all get our pens out and give it a try. It's certainly worked for Mr Tidybeard. Whether or not you think cosmic ordering is a heap of bull plop, it is no more sinister or ridiculous than many beliefs. Tom Cruise and John Travolta believe there's an evil alien called Xenu. It hasn't done their income any harm. Former UK MP Ruth Kelly claimed that her support of the Roman Catholic's weird self-flagellation sect Opus Dei was in no way incompatible with her day job as Education Secretary.

Then there's that mythical "special relationship" Britain claims to have with US Presidents such as that retired master of semantics, George W. Bush. One of Dubya's inspirations was a certain evangelical Christian aptly named Arthur Blessitt. Born in 1941, Arthur's life mission was to fulfil a biblical prophecy by carrying the cross to every land on earth, dragging a ten-foot (3 m) long cross behind him, which has kept him occupied from 1969 to 2008. You wouldn't expect a place like Hollywood's Sunset Strip to have an all-night "Christian Night Club", but there was one, with a clientele of hookers, bikers and hippies, eager recipients of Blessitt's advice to ditch downers and acid and "drop a little Matthew, Mark, Luke and John" instead. Arthur has impressed Mr Bush by hauling his cross through over 300 nations. Walking 36,500 miles (58,741 km) from the Orkney Islands to the Vatican, the indefatigable Arthur was welcomed by all as he distributed more of his twenty million "Smile, God Loves You" stickers. His ultimate intention is to launch his publicity into outer space. Whether or not the cross will be included may be down to NASA, but as he only wants to launch a two-inch segment of his burden, the payload might allow it.

Beyond carrying the cross and cosmic ordering the spiritual horizon is wide and studded with many more phenomenal sects and beliefs. How about trying "pranic nourishment" or Breatharianism? This branch of crack-pottery is a movement founded by an Australian, Ellen Greve, born in 1957. She changed her name by deed poll to the more esoteric Jasmuheen. The Breatharians, who number around 5,000 worldwide, believe in living without food or fluid of any sort. You'll find Jasmuheen at many a New Age gathering, and if you pay a fee, you can access her website and buy one of her many self-penned books and recordings. She believes we can live on light and that by avoiding food we can live longer. Apparently she was "told" to change her life by her spirit guide, the Count of St Germain (1712–84). France's mystery man St Germain has inspired her to live on herbal tea and the occasional chocolate biscuit. When the Australian TV programme *60 Minutes* threw down the gauntlet for her to be filmed practising what she preaches, she lasted about forty-eight hours, lost fourteen pounds (6.4 kg) and the whole thing was called off because she was seriously dehydrated. Her cause wasn't helped when one of her keen disciples was caught on camera wolfing down a chicken pie.

At least Jasmuheen is an award winner. She received the Bent Spoon Award by Australian Sceptics in 2000 ("presented to the perpetrator of the most preposterous piece of paranormal or pseudoscientific piffle"). She was the proud recipient in the same year of the Ig Nobel Prize for Literature for her book *Pranic Nourishment — Living on Light*, which informs us that some people do eat food, yet they don't ever really need to. World famine? Smart folk, those Ethiopians. Problem solved – if only Bob Geldof had known …

You wouldn't need to starve if you'd come across the non-denominational Christian Church which teaches first and foremost financial wellbeing, then total life prosperity with the added ingredients spiritual, physical, mental and emotional stability. It's called the Creflo Dollar World Changers Church, or the Creflo Dollar Ministries, formerly the International Covenant Ministries. Founded (where else) in the United States in 1986 by (and it's his *real* name) Creflo Augustus Dollar Jr, it has around 25,000 members. Good ole' Doctor Dollar claims he has the "biblical formula" which will help poor old you to increase your income. It's easy – you give him some money and, like the spiritual gardener he is, he'll plant it and somehow or other your donation will blossom somewhere down the line as you benefit from God's word. It certainly works for Creflo. He lives in a million-dollar home and has two Rolls-Royces. If you want inspiration after sending your donation, just listen to Dr Dollar: "When I'm pursuing the Lord," he says, "those Rolls-Royces are pursuing me."

He even has his own record label, Arrow Records. He's into hip-hop, big style – here's the blurb for a 2011 release: "Stellar and Dove Nominee Canton Jones will keep you bouncing with his smash *Kingdom Business*. Hip Hop Rock artist Shonlock will light your soul with the leading single *Fire Away*. Packed with energy and flavour from hip hop Artists, T-Haddy, Viktory, Big Ran and many more, your thirst and love for hip hop will be quenched!" Hallelujah!

The list of these odd "spiritual" outfits is long and peculiar. Dr Dollar's two Rolls-Royce cars bring to mind the words of wisdom of one of the most successful cult gurus of all time, Bhagwan Shree Rajneesh (meaning: "The Blessed One Who Has Recognized Himself As God") (1931–90), a man whose passion for profitable spirituality put him in almost the same financial bracket as Lehman Brothers, with a not too dissimilar denouement after his acolytes plunged his international cash machine into a long catalogue of misdemeanours. He claimed to be a man of very simple interests. "Believe me," he once said, "richness is far better than poverty." He was "utterly satisfied" with "the best of everything". The Bhagwan, like Dr Dollar, loved his cars; he had no fewer than ninety-three of them, stating;

> The second problem I had with my health was my back ... I cannot sit on an ordinary chair. It may be comfortable, but my back will not fit with it. Similarly I can use only one car. I have used all cars, and the best in the world; but the seat of just one car, one of the models of Rolls-Royce, the Silver Spur, fits with me perfectly. It is not their costliest car; their costliest is the Corniche, then the Carmargue. The third is the Silver Spur. So I tried a Corniche – it didn't work, my back trouble started. But with the Silver Spur it has settled completely.

Gurus are wise enough to make money via their persuasive ways and, if necessary, stay out of politics. But at least they don't resort to voodoo, as some occult-inclined politicians, such as Panama's deposed General Noriega, have been prone to do. Saddam Hussein's mother, Subha Tulfah al-Musallat, was said to be something of a psychic with voodoo tendencies. She named her newborn son Saddam, which in Arabic means "One who confronts", or as the new evangelists studying the Book of Revelation interpret the name, "the destroyer". A domineering woman, she defied the typical status of women in the town of Tikrit, where females were often kept isolated. After her death in 1982, a huge shrine was built in Tikrit at government expense to celebrate the "Mother of Militants".

The trial of Liberian President Charles Taylor has been going on for years, and judging by his arcane beliefs and bizarre autocracy during his reign of terror, he appears to have been born into the wrong century. Dr Fred P. M. van der Kraaij lived in West Africa for over sixteen years both as a university lecturer employed by the government of Liberia and the Dutch Ministry of Foreign Affairs. Here's a sample from van der Kraaij's online blog, liberiapastandpresent.org. The continuing horrors coming out of Taylor's uncanny trial sound like something from the Dark Ages:

> Councillor Fulton Yancy is accused of killing the 7-month pregnant Tomo Allison and pulling the unborn child out, killing the baby too. The circumstances surrounding the discovery of evidence in his home are astonishing. The Liberia National Police used the services of a witch doctor or voodoo priest who reportedly went into Mr Yancy's house and with the "aid of a young girl" discovered two bottles of blood and human parts, and the intestines of the unborn child. The woman and child were reportedly killed four months ago. The use of traditional doctors or voodoo priests to solve crimes is not new. President Samuel Doe hired a Kissi voodoo high priest Contabu who was even officially employed by the Ministry of Internal Affairs. It has been reported that citizens of Bong County are now demanding that traditional priests are employed to solve ritualistic murders in their county.

Every July in Haiti, thousands of believers participate in mass rituals, sacrifice animals and pray to voodoo spirits and the dead for help, as they have done for three centuries. In Mexico, death is a long, rolling festival. Santa Muerte (Holy or "Saint" Death) is a sacred combination of Meso-American and Catholic beliefs.

She's a much venerated figure among Mexicans, who use skeletons in their celebrations to remind themselves of their mortality. Long before the Spaniards arrived, bringing their Catholicism with them, the indigenous populations of Central and South America were indulging in all manner of death-related rituals and processions. What the Church of Rome added was a patina of piety and a splash of additional colour. Mexico's Day of the Dead celebrations, with all their Catholic overtones, take place at the end of October and extend into early November. However, the Santa Muerte cult (she's also known as "Lady of the Night" and "Lady of Shadows") stands beyond the influence or control of the traditional Catholic Church. Many of her followers may not be devout Catholics, yet neither are they atheistic. They include pickpockets and gang members, drug traffickers, mobile vendors, taxi drivers, sellers of pirated merchandise, street people and prostitutes. The cult was clandestine until recently, but in defiance of the Mexican government's various alliances with US drugs and border agencies, the country's poorer criminal elements have defiantly created their own religion that represents the daily violent struggle of their lives. Sinister and scary, Santa Muerte, a skeletal figure, clad in a long robe and carrying one or more objects, usually a scythe and a globe, can grant you wishes; she'll protect you if you work on the street at night, for example as a taxi driver or if you play in a Mariachi band, and you can even petition her to make someone fall in love with you. With over two million devotees, the cult is spreading across the US border and is taking root in America's Mexican communities.

IN THE ARMS OF THE ANGELS: HELP FROM THE HEAVENLY HOST

Make friends with the angels, who though invisible are always with you. Often invoke them, constantly praise them, and make good use of their help and assistance in all your temporal and spiritual affairs.

Saint Francis de Sales (1567–1622),
Bishop of Geneva

My parents failed miserably in their attempts to bring me up as a Roman Catholic. I recall being sent to a Catholic Sunday School when I was ten years old, where we were supervised by psychotic nuns who were utterly and inappropriately named "Sisters of Mercy". As we kids sat there in our austere, unheated classroom we were forced to ingest, parrot-style, something called the Catechism. I recall it contained such indecipherable stuff (I was far more interested in Crazy Horse and the Sioux at the time) as the following:

As St Paul says of the Gentiles: For what can be known about God is plain to them, because God has shown it to them. Ever since the creation of the world his invisible nature, namely, his eternal power and deity, has been clearly perceived in the things that have been made.

And St Augustine issues this challenge: Question the beauty of the earth, question the beauty of the sea, question the beauty of the air distending and diffusing itself, question the beauty of the sky ... question all these realities. All respond: "See, we are beautiful."

And if we didn't immediately chant "See, we are beautiful", then one of the sadistic, carbolic-smelling "merciful" Sisters, wielding a large wooden ruler, would rap our freezing knuckles. This attempt to "Catholicize" me expired after a few months because my dad couldn't afford the bus fares to keep sending me on the ten-mile (16 km) trip, and I always came back with a severe cold from the experience, to say nothing of the bruised fingers. Yet I did learn one thing from the nuns. One day we were visited by an antediluvian Irish Mother Superior called Concepta, in whose presence the vicious, monochrome harpies temporarily suspended their vindictiveness and were transformed into something approaching middle-aged women. We were allowed to ask questions that day, and one of my shivering classmates asked, "What are angels and are they real?"

Concepta was very forthcoming. She described angels in the Bible, and even managed to be magnanimous by mentioning that Muslims have angels, too – even the Protestants had hijacked the concept from Rome. She said that we all had an invisible, guardian angel who was looking over our shoulders from the heavenly realm. Because angels were God's messengers, we should always remember to "praise the Lord" daily and to confess our sins, and the angels would look after us. What sins we had at age ten I can't remember, but the comforting idea of that guardian angel stayed with me.

Twenty-four years later, I was working as a salesman for the international record company, Polydor. My job was to travel the length and breadth of the UK promoting the parent company, the classical label, Deutsche Grammophon. Exceeding the speed limit in my new Ford Cortina, en route to an afternoon appointment to foster sales of Herbert von Karajan's new Beethoven cycle in Edinburgh, Scotland, I reached the top of a hill on the A7 near Bonnyrigg and flew into an unexpected wall of dense fog. I had noticed the roadworks warnings a mile back, but driving over 1,000 miles (1,600 km) per week, I'd become blasé about my motoring skills and quick reactions. But it was too late. At around 60 mph the car left the road and soared through the air like some kind of four-wheeled aircraft. I could see nothing through the windscreen but impenetrable white mist. People say that, during such experiences as this, time slows down. I can verify that; the car's flight may not have been more than a second, yet still I had the sensation of being airborne for much longer. Mahler's *Song of the Earth* was still playing on the cassette player; it had reached a climax and I later checked the translation from the German of the final lyric that was booming from my speakers;

> Oh Death! You are the all-conquering one!
> With wings which I have won for myself
> in fervent striving of love
> I will soar;
> I will die in order to live!

For the tiniest fraction of that flying second I saw the wall of brown earth appear through the fog and the bonnet of the car thumped into it with such violence that, had I not been wearing a seat belt, my head would have smashed like a ripe melon into the windscreen. I blacked out. I can't have been out for long, as I heard voices around me. The car was surrounded by construction workers and the burly foreman pulled the car door open. Breathless, I looked at him. He grinned, shaking his head.

"Och, laddie – ye must have a guardian angel – ye're alive! I've never seen anything like *that* stunt!" Others were muttering words like "Evel Knievel" as they gathered around.

Uninterrupted, the final climactic chords of Mahler ended, and the foreman unbuckled my seat belt and pulled me from the car. I dropped about three feet into soft mud. I was manhandled up an embankment and the fog cleared. I discovered that I had driven through a barrier and soared about fifteen feet across a ten-foot-deep hole (4.6 x 3 m) dug into the road. The car had buried itself in the mountain of displaced earth at the other side, and was stuck there, rear wheels still slowly spinning, like some fat green arrow in nature's dartboard. The chattering roadworkers took me to their lobby and gave me hot tea and a cigarette. I checked myself. My chest was bruised, but nothing broken. They brought a JCB digger, chains and ropes and pulled the car from the mud. They were good men; they got it back on to the road, even brushed it down. The bonnet was crumpled, but everything still worked.

I felt acutely stupid, and rightly so. I thanked them profusely, decided against their advice to rest awhile or call the police, and with the car making some odd noises and looking like something from a mud-caked losing entry in a stock car race, went on to my appointment.

Head office in London was not impressed, but I managed to put a few more Deutschmarks into von Karajan's swollen account. Yet as a brush with death, it was a memorable experience. Everything came back to me when that foreman opened the door. Guardian angels, indeed. The nuns returned in a rapid, flickering approximation of newsreel, which included an incident from my teenage years as a deck hand in the Merchant Navy in 1961. We'd entered a force twelve – a hurricane – in the Pacific and although storms at sea had never frightened me, this one did. Fifty foot (15.2 m) waves, the ship tossed at impossible angles, 3,000 miles (4,800 km) from any help, a purple sky. And then the old Captain, gripping the handrail on the bridge, muttered, "Aye, nothin' to bother over, gentlemen. The angels are with us." On both occasions, they must have been. Just because I didn't die, plus the coincidence of Gustav Mahler's music and the memory of the nuns, is this all melodramatic tosh? I've no problem with readers believing it so. But it made me value life more and become a better driver.

Since starting this book I've discovered that the concept of angels is much wider and deeper among many people than I ever imagined. Although the idea seems even further out of the realms of credulity than aliens or ghosts, perhaps it's the benign nature of angels that appeals to the deep yearning most humans have for some kind of peace and assurance beyond the rigours of this life.

Not usually regarded as an organ of spiritual enlightenment, the *Wall Street Journal* once said that, "angels are incorporeal, sexless, highly intelligent, able to move at the speed of thought, full of warmth and joy, are cooperative not competitive, and often say the same thing: Don't be afraid." One might argue in the twenty-first century that bankers don't deserve the attention of the heavenly host, but even Goldman Sachs and Lehman Brothers probably had souls, so although their angels may have been looking the other way, the rest of us in the avarice-free world could do worse than to rely on our celestial feathered friends.

In medieval angelology, angels are divided by rank into nine orders: seraphim, cherubim, thrones, dominations (or dominions), virtues, powers, principalities (or princedoms), archangels and angels. Christian theologians regard them as divine messengers from God or guardian spirits. The term "angel" is also used by air traffic controllers for an unexplained signal on a radar screen and, of course, it is a fact that all nurses are angels.

Both in the USA and UK, there is a rapidly growing belief in guardian angels. Some people actually believe they enjoy a working relationship with them. Angelology is a big deal. Books, websites, seminars and lectures, thousands of reports on angelic contact, it's all happening. Some of the reports are very odd.

Heavenly Mechanics

Take the case of two elderly sisters, motoring along in the rain on a quiet country road in Iowa. Suddenly, they rumbled to a halt with a punctured tyre. Not the least mechanically inclined, they sat stunned, miles from anywhere, wondering what they would do. Then a car pulled up. Out climbed three tall, handsome, well-suited, blue-eyed, blond young men. Good-humoured, well mannered, one lay prone on the wet tarmac to put the jack in place. The ladies were concerned – the young man was getting his nice clothes dirty. But the other two got the tyre out, replaced it, checked with the stunned women to see if they had any further problems. The ladies offered to pay something for the help they'd received, but these young knights were having none of it. Smiling, they clambered back into their own vehicle and drove away along the quiet road.

What happened next has overtones of the UFO phenomenon, but Aliens or the Men in Black are more likely to stall your car rather than offer a mechanic's services. According to the ladies, they watched the car move away along the highway and it began to shimmer, very brightly. Then it was almost transparent. A brilliant flash of light ensued, and the car simply vanished. The sisters are convinced that the helpful trio were nothing less than angels.

Apparently, there are increasing numbers of similar reports from around the United States of angels rescuing travellers with mechanical faults or punctured tyres. The angels are always handsome, smiling, humorous and young, but whilst changing your wheel they will do so in serious solemnity. Job done, they're off, and their vehicle dematerializes in a magical shimmer.

Britain's leading angelologist is Diana Cooper. She came into contact with the angels whilst at a very low ebb in the early 1990s following her divorce. She says that at the time she was at her lowest – no spiritual energy, no particular belief – and she sat down and said "if there's anything out there, come to me ..." It worked. She was visited by a tall, helpful angel and her life as a spiritual searcher began. She had no further visitations for about ten years, until one night whilst taking a bath three of the winged messengers appeared, which must have been slightly embarrassing. Today, if you visit her website (www.dianacooper.com/angels) you'll discover everything you need to know about the New Age we're living in. Her spiritual books are about angels (she now sees them as "orbs"), archangels, unicorns, all elementals including fairies and Ascended Masters. Her spirit guide is Kumeka, who has given her information about the orbs, Atlantis, the spiritual laws, ascension and enlightenment. Diana tells us that:

> The angels of the 7th dimension are your Guardian Angels and others who help humans. Every single person has a Guardian Angel who protects and looks after them. Your Guardian Angel keeps the divine blueprint for your life, which you agreed before you were born, and he whispers guidance to you to keep you on your chosen spiritual path. Usually we think the whispered guidance of angels is our own inspired thoughts or bright ideas!

She will explain the Keys to the Universe available to humanity for the first time since Atlantis, and offer forecasts for the twenty-year transition to the new Golden Age. She also runs a school, with 600 teachers worldwide, devoted to these subjects: "Our School is dedicated to supporting the creation of the New Golden Age on this planet. All our Teacher Training Programmes, workshops and seminars have been designed to give people the hope, inspiration, wisdom and guidance to move into this new phase with peace, clarity and unconditional love for all life on the planet."

However, she has her critics in the Christian community, who claim that her obsession is at odds with the Bible. Some of her comments ruffle a few celestial biblical feathers, such as this from her book *A Little Light on Angels*: "Religions tell people what to do and what to believe. Spirituality tells people to listen to their own guidance and follow their hearts." And, "Angels of light say, 'Follow your heart. This is your higher purpose.'" But Diana's international mission to show us the light continues. Her diary is full of impressive lecture destinations, such as the Angel Congress in Hamburg, and other seminars in the United States and South Africa. She tells us that all we have to do to meet our own angels is sit down and ask. It hasn't worked for me, but I'll keep trying.

Time magazine ran an article entitled "The New Age of Angels" that stated that 69 per cent of Americans believe angels exist. Writer Nancy Gibbs wrote: "By scriptural tradition, angels pull back the curtain, however briefly, on the realm of the Spirit … in offering a glimpse of the larger universe, they issue a challenge to priorities and settled ways."

You may experience an angel as a comforting presence, or encounter one in a dream, or even in the form of a physical person. Some of the reported incidents seem fantastic, but there is a consistency to most of them. The *Time* article tells of a woman in hospital suffering with uterine cancer who, three days prior to being admitted, was visited by "a tall, dark stranger with deep blue eyes". He told her: "I am Thomas. I am sent by God." He raised his right hand which seemed to emanate heat and a bright white light passed over her body. He then reassured her that her cancer was cured. After she underwent the necessary tests, it was revealed that her cancer was indeed gone. Her doctor believed he witnessed a medical miracle.

Sadly, these celestial beings don't cure everyone, but they do spread some much needed joy and relief at difficult times in people's lives. Another woman reported that her husband was visited by a "pale, white man with icy blue eyes" whilst going through the misery of lymphocytic leukaemia. When the mysterious stranger departed the dying man's whole demeanour changed. His wife revealed that he "seemed lit up, just vibrant". Sadly, however, two days later he died, yet his wife reported that he passed away with an extraordinary peace of mind.

Of course, the sceptical view of these reported encounters with angels is that no proof of such things seems possible. Do these visitations help to mitigate dangerous situations? Those who claim the experience are convinced they do. Others say that even if the visits are not 100 per cent curative, in the case of serious illness, then at least they can lift the danger or totally lighten the sufferer's mood. This may only result in a change in attitude, not circumstance, but those who report such events, as with those who go through a near-death experience, are left with a profound change in their lives. A 2002 study based on interviews with 350 people who have had angel experiences, mainly in the UK, reveals a range of encounters. They include visions, a pleasant fragrance, materializations with multiple witnesses present, warnings, or a sense of being pushed, lifted or touched, all typically to avert a dangerous situation. Many experiences have some connection to someone's death. When angels are actually seen, they come in various forms, such as the classical version, a human with wings, or as entities of light or as truly extraordinarily beautiful or radiant human beings.

In the United States, a 2008 survey by Baylor University's Institute for Studies of Religion found that 55 per cent of Americans believed in guardian angels as compared with 36 per cent who believe in global warming. In Canada, 67 per cent of the population believe in angels. In general, these celestial interlopers seem to be a force for good, although we have to remember that Lucifer was one of the gang before he blotted his copybook.

Perhaps Kurt Vonnegut Jr in his book *The Sirens of Titan* (1959) had it right: "There is no reason why good cannot triumph as often as evil. The triumph of anything is a matter of organization. If there are such things as angels, I hope that they are organized along the lines of the Mafia." Tony Soprano with wings? What a concept! If it exists, then perhaps heaven's radio is playing us a faint song. All we have to do is turn up the volume and listen.

BACK FROM THE DEAD: GHOSTS AND OTHER RESTLESS SPIRITS

The lawn
Is pressed by unseen feet, and ghosts return
Gently at twilight, gently go at dawn,
The sad intangible who grieve and yearn ...

T. S. Eliot (1888–1965), *To Walter de la Mare*

Towards the end of January 2012, Dave Armstrong of building contractors Cox and Allen put his demolition team to work on a derelict Victorian five-gabled building, originally a dentist's back in the early 1900s. In its later life, the not unattractive building, known as Meadowbank House, had been a welcoming guest house in Kendal, England, popular for its easy access to the Lake District. Shortly before the building was knocked down, thirty-eight-year-old Robert Johnson of Heysham, supervising the demolition process, took a photograph of the house.

The wrecking crew had already agreed that there was something a bit odd about the place, an uneasy atmosphere. They'd been through the strange experience of finding a chandelier that suddenly began swinging to and fro of its own accord. This was unsettling, but when they studied the photograph Johnson had taken, they were genuinely disturbed. Apparently, they'd not been on their own working on the building. In the picture there appeared to be a ghost-like figure of a woman, standing staring from the window. Fifty-nine-year-old businessman David Grimshaw, who had once lived in the building, believes that the ghostly woman is his late mother, Frances, making an appearance to protest at the demolition of the home she loved. Mrs

Grimshaw had died a year earlier. After he'd seen the photograph, David, who now lives in Bedford, told the *Daily Mail* on 26 January 2012:

> That is my mother. I'm totally convinced – no one else looks like that. She had glasses and big earrings and she used to wear a dress with a bow at the front and used to stand in that room for hours on the phone – it was the guest house reception and she took bookings from there. She would have been horrified if she had known the house was being demolished because it was beautiful, so maybe that is why she's turned up.

If you're a devout sceptic or a hard-nosed analytical scientist, no doubt you'll be in the "ghosts don't exist" camp. Perhaps they have to been seen, or felt, to be believed. I have seen two, although I was a child at the time, and they may have been the product of the fertile imagination of an eight-year-old. Poltergeists, which we'll get on to eventually, are said to often travel with their innocent victims even when they move house. My first ghost wasn't a poltergeist, but he was in the wrong place, that is if ghosts attach themselves to the locations in which they lived. In 1951, in Hull, Yorkshire, our family and others were moved from our city-centre dwelling to be temporarily housed in an old Army camp next to a suburban golf course, while the post-war Labour Council built us all new houses. Our old house had been surrounded by the unwelcome handiwork of the Luftwaffe; our terrace on Portland Street was one of the last complete blocks of standing housing in the area, and was surrounded by bombed-out buildings and bomb craters.

For a kid born during the war, who had grown up in an adventure park landscape of ruin and rubble, there was fun enough to be had, but when we moved to the old ex-military Nissen huts on Wymersley Road, having a garden, plus access through the hedge to the velvet green golf links, was sheer heaven.

One summer afternoon my mother had been out in our new garden picking some lettuce. I was practising with my catapult, aiming stones at a tin can, when I felt a presence in the vegetable patch. I looked around; it was an elderly, white-haired man standing among a row of cabbages. It was my grandfather, who had died in our previous home two years previously. He smiled back at me. I wasn't afraid, but I turned to look at the kitchen window in the hope that my mother was seeing what I had seen. She wasn't there. When I turned around, Granddad had gone. I raced indoors to tell my mother and she told me not to be silly, but in later years she believed me.

The second apparition came a few months later in the depth of winter. Although we kids loved living in the old Army camp, there was a morose, creepy atmosphere around the place sometimes. I hated going to bed early on the dark winter nights in the old hut. In those days before central heating it was bitterly cold. I shared a bedroom with my younger brother, Alexander. One night, a very frosty night, with a full moon bluely illuminating the foot of my bed, I awoke to find a dim figure standing there. It was indistinct, but appeared to be a soldier, clad in khaki. I watched the figure for a few seconds then, terrified, pulled the blankets over my head. When I dared to peek out again, it had gone. Little Alex slept through it all.

And that's about it for my experiences. Those two small incidents stayed with me, but a jokey attitude and a growing scepticism developed as I grew older, and I dismissed them as a kid's imagination. Now I'm much, much older, and wiser, I feel that they might well have been real.

Since the beginning of recorded history, people have been reporting evidence of ghosts and hauntings. Yet when it comes to investigating their existence, no single theory can provide an explanation. By far the biggest percentage of ghost experiences are made up of anecdotal reports. If you've never had any contact with the paranormal, then the ghost and the haunted house are nothing more than camp-fire stories. But if you've genuinely seen a ghost or had a chilling brush with the spirits, you know they're real. Yet what that "reality" is remains a mystery. Some places have more ghosts than others, yet if they are spirits of the dead, then we die everywhere. It seems odd that ghosts might gather in certain locations.

When Irene Allen, from an organization called Spirit International Rescue (www.spiritrescueinternational.com), was interviewed by the newspaper *Wales on Sunday* in July 2011 she told us that Llanelli is one of the locations where paranormal activity is remarkably prominent. Unfortunately, she reveals, Llanelli's paranormal energy tends to be of the "negative" kind. Irene's a grandmother in her sixties who devotes much of her life to spiritual research, during which she investigates haunted locations and where possible, helps to evict the residing spirits, a process she now calls "clearing". People who devote themselves to this kind of work often do so because they have had direct experiences of the paranormal. With Irene, it was as a five-year-old child. She would play out on the street with her friends. She told *Wales on Sunday*:

> I looked over and saw there was a boy standing there, with blond, curly hair and blue eyes, looking like he was from the 1940s or '50s. He was just watching us. I felt sorry for him and asked him to come and play, but he didn't answer and just kept watching us. I saw him again a couple of days later and asked him if he wanted to play again, but he just gave me this blank stare. When I asked everyone else to tell him to go away, they just thought I was crazy. I thought he was thinking I was stupid and got angry, told him to go away, and he then disappeared. I realized years later that was probably my first clearing.

The spirits even occupy her own home in the form of Annie and Herbert, an Edwardian couple. Spirit Rescue International, however, covers more than just wandering spirits. Irene believes, for instance, that the elusive Bigfoot is an "inter-dimensional being". She plans to find this anomalous beast by remote viewing.

Alton Towers in Staffordshire is a popular location for the public. It's in the UK's premier league of theme parks, built around an old mansion, and by day is a fun place to visit, especially for kids. But on 8 July 2011 an organization called Paranormal Events UK, one of a number of tour companies in the ghost-hunting business, organized an Alton Towers ghost-hunt event. Staff and visitors of the park had reported ghosts and spirits wandering around the grounds. The ghost hunt took place as one would expect, overnight, from 8 p.m. to 3 30 a.m., and cost £35 a head. The punters were divided into two groups who held forty- to forty-five-minute vigils before being fed and watered, then moving on to the next forty-five-minute vigil. Their mission was to encounter the reported ghost of a white lady who roams the rose gardens, the hooded man in the upper floors of the mansion or an aggressive male ghost in the music room, but it is unclear as to whether any of them made an appearance.

So what exactly are ghosts? The popular deduction is that they are souls or spirits trapped in this world following the death of their physical bodies. Some paranormal theorists suggest that a wrongful or traumatic end to a life could leave your spirit adrift between this life and the next, forever wandering and reappearing, tragically unaware that it is a ghost.

Another theory is that they may be echoes imprinted on the environment, recordings from history, some kind of shadow of energy from the past. Whereas "restligeists", residual hauntings, appear to be tied to a particular location or building, poltergeists are a different thing altogether. You could describe them as "haunted people". Often noisy, frightening, violent and destructive, the phenomenon usually attaches itself to one particular person. Because of this some researchers into poltergeist activity (the most frequent ghost phenomenon that is well documented) believe that a poltergeist might be generated internally by individuals under extreme stress. Alternatively, they may be disembodied entities who search for a suitable living person through which they can act, like some phantom parasite.

There are also "intelligent hauntings", ghosts who appear to be able to interact with the living world. Some are thought to be messengers (shades of the angels, here) who offer warnings or may appear in times of need. As if this selection of phantoms wasn't enough, there's something called "living ghosts" – doppelgängers – as well as ghost ships, ghost trains, ghost cars, ghost planes, even a ghost double-decker bus. Needless to say, the sceptics will all tell you that any or all of these manifestations are merely figments of the imagination.

The historical attitude to ghosts has been similar to that shown to most of the paranormal. Like trolls, leprechauns and fairies, they're an entertaining distraction. They make for engaging movies, such as *The Blair Witch Project*, *Poltergeist* and *Paranormal Activity*. One might imagine, reading Dickens, that the idea of phantoms and ghostly apparitions was much more accepted a century ago or longer, and some men of rational thought had a sympathetic view. Even as far back as 1711, Joseph Addison, writing in the *Spectator*, said: "I think a person who is thus terrified with the imagination of ghosts and spectres much more reasonable, than one who contrary to the reports of all historians sacred and profane, ancient and modern, and to the traditions of all nations, thinks the appearance of spirits fabulous and groundless." However, note that Addison said "imagination" of ghosts. The growing annals of ghost lore, and some photographic evidence, would suggest that what many have seen, often with multiple witnesses, falls outside the imagination.

According to a report in the *Daily Telegraph* dated 26 April 2010, there has been a significant rise in reports of what it calls "demonic activity" since 1980. The *Demonic Britain* report was carried out for the DVD release of US TV series *Supernatural*, normally broadcast on the Living cable channel.

British priest and entertainer Reverend Lionel Fanthorpe (1935–) is well known to UK TV viewers as the presenter of Channel 4's series *Fortean TV*. He's a serious Christian priest with an enquiring mind, who has at various times worked as a journalist, teacher, author and lecturer. He gives this reason for the rise in ghost reports: "The present human population is many times greater than it was in the past. Therefore the more people that there are, statistically, the more potential encounters they might have with these unpleasant, non-human entities."

Apparently my native Yorkshire tops the league for such encounters. Some of them are truly weird. They include appearances of ghouls and demons (such as incubus and succubus, which are male and female demons who visit you as you sleep and make sexual contact). As well as more prosaic, standard ghost reports, there are sightings of hell-hounds and werewolves, and instances of demonic possession.

On the road between Northallerton and Leeming Bar in North Yorkshire, a shadow-like, faceless and gruesome hellhound is reported to have collided with a car. In the sea off Filey Bay, also in Yorkshire, what has been described as a spectral "sea demon" has been reported. It has glowing eyes, a long serpentine neck and a huge body. All this and aliens, too.

The mellow-voiced, long-black-coated Yorkshireman Mark Graham is the man you need to take you on the "Original Ghost Walk of York" (theoriginalghostwalkofyork.co.uk). Most ancient major cities will probably have something similar, but a lot of tour guides can be hammy in a failed actor-ish way. Not Mr Graham. He'll guide you through the most haunted city in Britain in a straightforward style, no melodrama, and he knows his stuff. He commences outside the King's Arms, proceeding along the River Ouse. En route he'll tell you about the Cork and Bottle pub where, if you're a female, you should be vigilant when taking a shower; one woman has reported a fruity ghost grabbing her through the soap suds there.

At the York Castle Museum, you'll see the final sights the city's condemned criminals saw: the old cells and the gallows. Their spirits still prowl here, as well as those of ghostly children. Nearby, Clifford's Tower, named after Roger de Clifford (who was hanged there with his corpse on display to rot away for a year in 1322), is an imposingly haunted edifice where Roger's ghost has been frequently sighted. And if you think the Nazis had the franchise on the Holocaust, think again: in 1190, 150 of York's Jews were killed in a pogrom in the castle keep.

Archaeological digs in the city centre in the 1970s unearthed substantial tenth-century Viking remains, which are now preserved in the Jorvik Viking Centre. There are all manner of weird reports from Jorvik: strange presences, assistants reporting things brushing past them, lights going on and off, and the odd bearded Viking has been seen. If you're looking for a place to stay whilst ghost-hunting, there's the notoriously well-haunted Golden Fleece, notable for having no fewer than five regularly reported ghosts, including a hapless Canadian pilot. The *York Evening Press* of 13 July 1994 put his spirit in the spotlight:

> The daughters of a former York landlord today told the haunting tale which led an American family to be spooked by a ghost. They revealed that the globe-trotting spectre that has followed April Keenan and her family from York's Golden Fleece to her home in California is that of a Canadian airman who fell to his death at the pub on Pavement, York. Gloria Cartwright, whose parents Harry & Phyllis Scrivener ran the

pub after the Second World War said the Canadian fell 3 floors to his death after a drinking session. For eight years Gloria slept in the room next to the one the airman fell from but she was always too scared to sleep with the light off. April Keenan yesterday told the *Evening Press* that the ghost touched her as she slept at the Golden Fleece earlier this year. It then reappeared at her home in Quincey, California where she woke up to discover she had written "Geoff Monroe died – The Golden Fleece" on a piece of paper by her bedside.

Apparently the flyer fell out of a window, breaking his neck. Some say he was drunk; others say suicide.

At the rear of the Golden Fleece is Lady Peckett's Yard. Her husband John owned the Golden Fleece and was Lord Mayor of York around 1700. Lady Alice is the hotel's "resident spirit" – seen on many occasions in both the Shambles Room and Lady Peckett's Room, and possibly as a spectral figure observed disappearing through a function-room wall, leaving a pleasant whiff of perfume in the air. There's also a woman in black who walks past a window, and guests in the St Catherine's Room have reported an oppressive presence and a feeling of being pressed down by their shoulders. Of course, in the bar, where the good ale flows, things get a bit more rugged when a seventeenth-century character called One-Eyed Jack makes an appearance, complete with wig, breeches and a red coat.

A short walk away from the Fleece finds us in Mad Alice Lane, named after a woman called Alice Smith, who was wrongly hanged after admitting guilt to crimes that she did not commit. It's an area with yet another ghost called Kay, a bit of a wayward type who was strangled. She's said to have drowned, and appears soaked and bedraggled – in mirrors. There used to be stocks at the Barley Hall, where you'll not only see the "lost boy of York", aged around ten, but the wraith of a laughing, pasty-faced crone. A regularly reported apparition is that of the grinning Sarah Brocklebank, running up and down Stonegate. The story goes that her father, John, was the keeper of the city's keys. Sarah had them at one time and lost them. Her dad was not pleased. When she found them she ran to find him and give them back, but dropped down dead. Then, of course, there's York's magnificent Minster, with a whole catalogue of tragic spirits of its own.

So what are we to make of all this? If you've never seen a ghost, it will be easy to dismiss all these stories as mere myths or threadbare legends. After all, tourists go to Baker Street in London because they believe Sherlock Holmes was real. One researcher, Marc Micozzi, has examined the ghost-spirit phenomena and says:

> Our data show that anomalous perceptions parallel other forms of environmental sensitivity, such as having pronounced or longstanding allergies, migraine headache, chronic fatigue, chronic pain, irritable bowel, even synesthesia (overlapping senses) and heightened sensitivity to light, sound, touch, and smell. Women make up three-quarters of this sensitive population but there are other markers as well: being ambidextrous, for instance, or recalling a traumatic childhood. The more we look at the people who say they're psychic, or who have recurring anomalous experience, the more it seems there's a mix of nature and nurture that predisposes them.

That's one way of looking at it. But the reports keep piling up. Encounters with devils, demons and evil spirits are as widespread today, more so even, as they were in medieval times.

The incubus and succubus accounts seem to bear an uncanny resemblance to the modern trend of alien abduction. However, as the aliens often seem to have a predilection for anal probing and kitting you out with an implant before dropping you back into bed, at least the incubus or succubus seem to have a more straightforward agenda. Victims of incubus or succubus attacks are willing to share their experiences among themselves, often in anonymous online forums. Being interfered with in bed by a supernatural pervert in an act that can only be described as paranormal rape is hardly something you'd want to broadcast down at the pub.

When it comes to reports of demons and werewolves, it seems hardly surprising that many twenty-first-century witnesses interpret their experiences this way. Current TV entertainment, replete as it is with paranormal infantilism, has refused to let go of vampirism and lycanthropy. Shows such as the *Twilight Saga*, *The Vampire Diaries*, *Forever Knight*, *Buffy the Vampire Slayer* and *True Blood* have taken the genuinely creepy, baroque fictional horror of Bram Stoker's 1897 classic, *Dracula*, and morphed it down into an Xbox-styled modern CGI mush which, among a large number of credulous, dumbed-down viewers, seems to be an approximation of reality. I have met university students on film and media courses who genuinely believe that these glamorous vampires are among us and that werewolves exist.

Three decades ago, the innocent Goth culture that sprang up around rock bands such as Bauhaus, with its leather coats, studded belts and surgical boots was laughable enough. There was nothing wrong with a bit of heavy eye make-up and a dog collar. But now we even have something called a "vampire lifestyle". This alternative subculture owes much of its existence to these TV shows and the preponderance of vampires in popular fiction by such writers as Stephenie Meyer. The vampire subculture incorporates elements of sadomasochism, and if you surf the net you'll find many forums constantly discussing its associated eroticism and even bloodletting, as well a selection of magazines devoted to the topic. Take your pick: there's sanguinarian vampirism, which involves blood consumption, or psychic vampirism, whose adepts believe they are drawing spiritual nourishment from "auric or pranic energy". It all makes punk rock or Marilyn Manson seem like a toddler's birthday party.

So, immersed in this fantasy realm 24/7, it might come as no surprise after a herbal cigarette and a few ciders that should one of these bargain basement Buffys see a hapless pensioner on their way home from bingo in the dark, they immediately become the reincarnation of Nosferatu. As for zombies, you could knock one over with a rolled-up newspaper but the movie men insist on inflicting these shambling, flour-and-ketchup non-entities on the eager public. Even though Dracula didn't exist, there are Goths willing to spend a couple of grand going on a pilgrimage to Bran Castle in central Romania, on the border between Transylvania and Wallachia, simply because they believe it to be "Dracula's Castle" (although Poenari Castle and Hunyad Castle claim the same). Research will show that although he knew his Transylvanian fortresses, Bram Stoker never mentioned Bran Castle, which has only tangential associations with the Vlad III "the Impaler" of Wallachia, said to have inspired Stoker as his fictional Dracula. Old Vlad was certainly a cruel and disgusting ruler, but he probably ate garlic every day, preferred steak to stakes, failed miserably to turn into a bat and never wasted his time supping blood – the wine in that region being far superior.

Black dogs, water demons, mysterious chills and shadows, bumps in the night – out of them all, the most mysterious is probably the poltergeist. In an article titled "They're here: The mechanism of poltergeist activity" in the *New Scientist*, 1 April 2008, Zeeya Merali reported: "The sight of small blonde girls watching television is guaranteed to strike fear into the heart of anyone who has watched the movie *Poltergeist*. We're right to be terrified, say physicists. Children generate poltergeist activity by channelling energy into the quantum mechanical vacuum."

Pierro Brovetto, of the Instituto Fisica Superiore, in Cagliari, Italy, together with Vera Maxia, has attempted to get to the bottom of poltergeist phenomena, which results in all manner of items, including furniture, seeming to be tossed around rooms, an exceptionally frightening experience. Brovetto and Maxia maintain that the worldwide reports all have a similarity. The culprit appears to be puberty: "Poltergeist disturbances often occur in the neighbourhood of a pubescent child or a young woman. Puberty is a modification of the child body which involves various organs, chiefly the brain."

They suggest changes in the brain at puberty involve fluctuations in electron activity that, in rare cases, can create disturbances up to a few metres around the outside of the brain. The *New Scientist* explains this hypothesis:

> These disturbances would be similar in character to the quantum mechanical fluctuations that physicists believe occur in the vacuum, in which "virtual" particle and anti-particle pairs pop up for a fleeting moment, before they annihilate each other and disappear again. Brovetto and Maxia believe that the extra fluctuations triggered by the pubescent brain would substantially enhance the presence of

the virtual particles surrounding the person. This could slowly increase the pressure of air around them, moving objects and even sending them hurtling across the room.

At the end of the article, we're informed that Brovetto and Maxia's paper would appear in the journal *Neuroquantology*. Whilst not wishing to end this section of the book on a complicated note, I decided to follow up the research duo's poltergeist investigation in *Neuroquantology*. Sometimes the complete scientific layman has to accept defeat. I got as far as the opening "Abstract". I daren't proceed further because the subject's complexity could well have resulted in furniture flying around my study; here's what it said:

Entropy Increase in Vacuum: A Conjecture about the Mechanism of Poltergeist Phenomenon Piero Brovetto, Vera Maxia
Abstract: Poltergeist accounts concern at least four kinds of strange spontaneous manifestations, such as burn of materials, failures of electric equipments, rapping noises and movements of objects. A simple analysis of phenomenology of these disturbances shows that they might have a common origin, that is, a reduction in strength of molecular bonds due to an enhancement in polarization of vacuum which cuts down the actual electron charge. Arguments based on Prigogine's non-equilibrium thermodynamics are proposed, which show how transformations in the brain of some pubescent children or young women might be the cause of these effects.

The *New Scientist* contacted Nobel laureate physicist Brian Josephson, who is on the editorial board of *Neuroquantology*. His comment? "This looks distinctly flaky to me."

So in the end, discussing ghosts and spirits is about as straightforward as knitting fog. But if you want some poltergeist reassurance, Google Ilya Prigogine or you can peer into the tangled undergrowth of quantum mechanical vacuum yourself (www.neuroquantology.com/index.php/journal/article/view/172). Perhaps there are some things we are simply not equipped to understand ... those who *do* understand have my utmost admiration.

PART 4:

INEXPLICABLE ASTRONOMY

COPY THAT, CAPCOM

So far as hypotheses are concerned, let no one expect anything certain from astronomy, which cannot furnish it, lest he accept as the truth ideas conceived for another purpose, and depart from this study a greater fool than when he entered it.

Nicolaus Copernicus (1473–1543)

If something weird happens in outer space, astronomers and physicists will go into overdrive to explain it. Yet some events are discussed, logged, then filed away, because they remain as unexplained phenomena. The universe is jam-packed with such mysteries and astronomy is always a work in progress. What was science fiction a decade or so ago, the subject of sceptical scientific laughter, has crept into the realms of possibility. For example, physicists are already hypothesizing that there may be more dimensions than the three we know. As already touched upon, theories such as M-theory and string theory suggest physical space has ten and eleven dimensions, respectively, all said to be spatial. Although these extra dimensions are still unproven, it has been suggested that space acts as if it were "curled up" in the extra dimensions on a subatomic scale. In December 2010, the analysis of results from the Large Hadron Collider seemed dismissive of theories with large extra dimensions. But the CERN experiments have continued, and already some physicists and astronomers are positing the idea that even the universe they are studying might not be the only one. There could be other versions of the universe, even another you, another me, existing in parallel worlds.

This might even explain some of the puzzles surrounding out-of-body and near-death experiences; do we step outside ourselves, into a "second self" and look down on version one? But according to professor of physics Max Tegmark at the Massachusetts Institute of Technology, "the key point to remember is that parallel universes are not a theory, but a prediction of certain theories. Whatever the ultimate nature of reality may turn out to be, it's completely different from how it seems." This is all too complex and difficult to contemplate, so for the time being we'll have to concentrate on the dimensions and the universe we know, that which we can see, and in "our" universe there are still many inexplicable things going on.

In late 1991 a strange object approached and passed by the earth, and it came very close indeed in astronomical terms. Stunned astronomers began scratching their heads. The object was catalogued as "1991 VG" and it has caused some disquiet because they still don't know what it was. It was spotted by astronomer Jim Scotti, who was working on the Spacewatch project at Kitt Peak National Observatory, Arizona, on 6 November 1991. Spacewatch is one of a number of projects that look for near-earth asteroids (NEAs).

At first 1991 VG was thought to be an NEO – a Near Earth Object – perhaps an asteroid. Many asteroids pass so close to the earth sometimes that if the public realized their proximity there could well be panic. Scotti estimated that 1991 VG, which he described then as a "fast-moving asteroidal object", was approximately 2,046,000 miles (3,292,718 km) from earth and closing in fast. However, as astronomers paid closer attention to the object, it did not appear to behave like an asteroid at all. Every seven-and-a-half minutes, it "winked" on and off, becoming three times brighter, then dark again. These are the characteristics of artificial satellites. Speculation began; could 1991 VG be some old NASA hardware drifting through interplanetary space, for example, a 1960s or 1970s Apollo moon-launch expired Saturn V booster?

More outlandish ideas cropped up; could it be a Bracewell Probe? A Bracewell Probe is a hypothetical concept proposed by Professor Ronald N. Bracewell, of the Space, Telecommunications and Radio Science Laboratory at Stanford University. He described his idea in the 1960s as "an autonomous interstellar space probe dispatched for the express purpose of communication with one or more alien civilizations, an alternative to interstellar radio communication between widely separated civilizations". It was a hypothesis much loved by science-fiction writers such as Arthur C. Clarke. For example, the black monolith in his story "The Sentinel" (the basis for Kubrick's movie *2001: A Space Odyssey*) is a Bracewell Probe, and Clarke also features one, which he calls the "Starglider", in his novel *The Fountains of Paradise*. Since the 1990s, with improved telescopes, many astronomers have sought to explain 1991 VG away as manmade space junk. However, Dr Duncan Steel of the Australian Centre for Astrobiology (www.aca.absociety.org/aca) wrote a paper analysing the tracking of 1991 VG, and one of the possibilities he came up with is very intriguing:

> None of the handful of manmade rocket bodies left in heliocentric orbits during the space age have purely gravitational orbits returning to the Earth at that time. In addition, the small perigee distance (*perigee* is the point at which an object makes its closest approach to the Earth) observed might be interpreted as an indicator of a controlled rather than a random encounter with the Earth, and thus it might be argued that 1991 VG is a candidate as an alien probe observed in the vicinity of our planet.

Following Scotti's discovery, the strange body steadily proceeded in the direction of the earth. Astronomers at the European Southern Observatory (ESO) in La Silla, Chile, began tracking 1991 VG through a sixty-inch (152.4 cm) telescope. Now the media got hold of the story and press releases had to be issued. ESO's astronomy team, Alain Smette, Olivier Hainaut and Richard West, began the process of measuring the intruder's winking frequency and confirmed that the phenomenon was similar to the pulsations of light observed on reflective, rotating artificial satellites.

On 5 December 1991, it passed 51,000 miles (82,000 km) beyond the orbit of the moon, making its distance from the earth a mere 288,300 miles (463,974 km), very close in astronomical

terms. Then, rather oddly, it began to drift away. It was estimated to be anything between thirty-three to sixty-two feet
(10–19 m) in diameter. Not very big for an asteroid, but more
understandable if it was a manufactured object. It reappeared in
April 1992 on a path similar to earth's orbit around the sun, and
it hasn't been seen since. 1991 VG is just one example of an
astronomical anomaly, but there are many more. Is there
someone out there watching us?

Back in the good old early days of the UFO, as various contactees who claimed to have met aliens let their imaginations
run riot, it wasn't enough simply to report the sighting of a
flying saucer. Leading the way, the irrepressible George
Adamski, as already mentioned, had to bolt sensation on to
sensation by claiming that the handsome space brothers had
actually taken him on a trip to Venus, where he enjoyed a
banquet. Yet since the USSR's Venera programme, with
several unmanned missions and a landing on the planet's
surface, the world of astronomy has come up with a revised
version of Venus. It makes the prospect of a dinner party with
tall, blond Venusian hosts about as likely as the Taliban spending a long weekend in Las Vegas.

The Venera missions have demonstrated that Venus's temperature is much denser and hotter than that of earth. The main
atmospheric gases are carbon dioxide and nitrogen. Other
chemical compounds are present only in trace amounts. It's an
uncomfortable 467 °C (872 °F) at the surface, while the pressure is 93 bar. It supports opaque sulphuric acid clouds making
earth-based observation by telescope a real problem and orbital
observation of the surface impossible. Radar imaging has been
the only way we've learned anything about the topography of
Venus.

Whilst we worry down here on earth about global warming,
we might see our distant future, should we not face up to our
own atmospheric misbehaviour, in the way Venus has ended up.
Some astronomers speculate that around four billion years ago,
Venus's atmosphere was more like that of the earth, with liquid
water on the surface. Some runaway greenhouse effect may have
evaporated the planet's surface water, giving rise to levels of
other greenhouse gases.

So Adamski's Venusian dinner party seems more in the realms of Jules Verne or Ray Bradbury. Yet the cosmos is full of inexplicable weirdness. For every carefully arrived-at conclusion astronomy announces, there are a hundred head-scratching, stubborn background puzzles.

Venus on the surface seems to be nothing less than an inhospitable, toxic cauldron. However, 50 to 65 km above its surface, the atmospheric temperature and pressure is almost earth-like. In fact, even more so than Mars, it's the most earth-like slice of atmosphere in our solar system. With breathable air (21 per cent oxygen, 78 per cent nitrogen) and a pressure and temperature something akin to ours up there in the Venusian sky, who knows what we might find? Some kind of airborne life forms? The bitter, dismissive laughter of astronomers may be rippling through the ether, but on 30 January 2012 SciNews.com presented an interview with one of the scientists who know Venus rather well. No doubt he is hearing that dismissive laughter, too.

Dr Leonid Ksanfomality is a senior researcher and a head of the Laboratory on Photometry and Thermal Radiometry at the Space Research Institute, Russian Academy of Sciences, and a contributor to the Venera missions in the 1970s and 1980s. After months of processing the images from the Venera landings, he's come up with close-up images of three weirdly anomalous objects: a disc, a piece of black rag and a ... scorpion. Over to you, Dr Ksanfomality:

It happened when the first panoramas of the Venus surface were obtained in October 1975. I was at the radio receiving station and working with the data from the Venera-9 and 10 space crafts. One object on the images, looking like a "sitting bird" and measuring about 20 cm, attracted my attention. Later, geologists called it a "strange stone". I had been repeatedly returning to the obtained images, and in 1978, I put a view of this object as a possible inhabitant of Venus in my first popular scientific book *Planets Discovered Anew*.

Dr Y. M. Gektin, one of the scientists involved with the Venera TV experiments, more or less summed up the dilemma astronomers face: "We do not like the hypothesis that life may exist on

Venus. But the problem is that we cannot offer any other explanation to what we see on the Venera panoramas." Having seen the Venera photographs, it's still difficult to come to Dr Ksanfomality's conclusion – a black rag, a disc and a scorpion. The scorpion in particular is bizarre; an elongated speckled blob materializes out of the Venusian soil over a period of minutes, but whether or not it's a life form remains to be seen.

Among the many strange discoveries about our own planet is the conclusion that the earth has a "heartbeat". Winfried Otto Schumann (1888–1974) was a German physicist who predicted the Schumann resonances, a series of low-frequency resonances caused by lightning discharges in the atmosphere. The earth pulses with a special kind of resonant wave. The Schumann resonances have long been dubbed "the earth's heartbeat", and it has only been spotted from below. Recently, however, satellites have found signs of this electromagnetic pulse leaking up into space. Regulated by electricity, this "heartbeat" pulses at about eight cycles per second. As lightning strikes the earth, it creates electromagnetic waves in the atmosphere. It was always thought that the Schumann resonances were confined to the earth, trapped under the blanket of the ionosphere. However, NASA scientists working on the Goddard Space Flight Center have revealed that they have now detected these waves 500 miles (805 km) up. They seem to be leaking, escaping through the boundaries of earth and out into space. The odd thing is that the frequency of this "heartbeat" is speeding up. What this might portend is anyone's guess.

For the non-scientist, the fascinated backyard layperson who sometimes scans the skies on the way home from the pub or watches the odd documentary on the Discovery Channel or BBC, the subject of astronomy remains a complete, jaw-dropping enigma. What we think we know, we know from astronomers. What they know, they have not only learned from the work of previous astronomers, but add to daily by utilizing almost impenetrable mathematics, continuously contributing to the rapid advances in physics and space exploration. The general public can probably grasp only about 10 per cent of their deliberations. One wonders what the results of a survey asking the question "do you understand this?" would be among the many thousands who bought Professor Stephen Hawking's *A Brief History of Time*. Hawking, who was diagnosed with motor neurone disease at the age of twenty-one, is as much in awe of the cosmos as the rest of us but doesn't see anything of the spiritual between humans and the sky above. He said in an interview with Ian Sample in the *Guardian* on 15 May 2011: "I regard the brain as a computer which will stop working when its components fail. There is no heaven or afterlife for broken-down computers; that is a fairy story for people afraid of the dark." It's a stark view, but for a man whose true genius has been so cruelly and physically imprisoned, even the faithful must allow it.

To us mere mortals who stare up at the heavens like kids looking in a sweet-shop window, astronomy is something we can't really argue about. We've been fed a diet of flamboyant science fiction over the past century, much of it written by mathematical buffoons like me. We like to think that the starship *Enterprise* is a feasible prospect, that we can indeed launch a mission to Mars, even though we know little as yet about the almost insurmountable problems this will pose. We can't get our laypeople's heads around the sheer infinity of the universe. Even the idea of it being infinite has been revised. The universe, the cosmologists tell us, is roughly 13.75 billion years old. It is thought to be an expanding sphere, with a diameter of roughly ninety-two billion light years. It contains about a hundred billion galaxies, and a recent study estimated that there are at least 300 sextillion (three followed by twenty-three zeros) stars. Current theories suggest the universe will die out completely in at least another trillion years when the last star burns itself into oblivion leaving nothing but a vast frigid blackness. We may as well enjoy ourselves while we can, but hang on – here are those questions again. If the universe is "a sphere" – what's outside the sphere? If it is expanding, then what is it expanding into? If we could achieve the unimaginable and send a probe to its edge, the sphere's inner wall, would it just come to a stop and nudge it like a pea trapped in a balloon, or would it pierce the shell and go through into … what? Then there's the religious view of the universe. If God created it in a day, where was he and what was he doing the day before? Did he replicate humanity and instal it in various locations around the universe? Or are we kidding ourselves, measuring everything by our human proportions – might we just be busy little microbes in some celestial raindrop?

We might read that astronomers have discovered about twenty-plus planets orbiting around distant stars which might sustain life but we don't stop to think that, really, it's all information infused with futility. We can't get there, and even if the aliens in the earlier part of this book are real and have mastered interstellar travel, they've done so because they're probably technologically at least two millennia more advanced than we are here on the blue marble. If they did try to instruct us on how to develop some interstellar drive, it would probably be like us trying to teach a tortoise to tap dance. *Apollo 11* took three days just to get to the moon. It will take six to ten months to reach Mars. If we set out now to reach our nearest galaxy with current technology, the trip would take several thousand years. So even if we had a spacecraft capable of maintaining a permanent living environment, by the time it reached somewhere like Proxima Centauri, the distant descendants of the original earthling astronauts wouldn't have a clue what they were doing there. After centuries living on board they'd have the insecurity of termites in a mud heap; leaving the ship would terrify them. Their physiology would be nothing like their ancestors. Centuries in space would have made them devolve into spindly weaklings who would probably collapse and die if they left the security of their ship to walk on an earth-like planet with proper gravity. They would possibly die in the same way as H. G. Wells's Martians in *War of the Worlds*: struck down by micro-organisms. Their journey's end would not be a triumph; it would be a bitter tragedy, and the ancient, fading pictures of a green, living earth would have become meaningless.

Of course, there are lots of peculiar theories that we might be able to zip around the universe in giant time/dimension chutes called wormholes, the suggestion being that they might offer a shortcut through space-time. The problem is that no wormhole has ever been observed. They are currently little more than theoretical possibilities.

Good astronomers hate bad astronomers. Bad astronomers are those who cross the line between physics and sci-fi speculation. Good astronomers and physicists like Stephen Hawking,

Patrick Moore and Brian Cox are not prepared to pander to our untutored fantasies. They don't usually give credence to aliens and UFOs. Their quest, their mission, is to apply physics to anomalous phenomena in order to provide reasoned explanations. They don't like people such as the aforementioned Richard C. Hoagland, a former museum space science curator and NASA consultant, who during the historic Apollo missions to the moon was science advisor to Walter Cronkite at CBS. He's the subject of much sceptical internet vitriol because some of his ideas and astronomical interpretations seem too fantastic even for *Star Trek* fans. For example, Hoagland appears to believe that one of the moons of Mars, Phobos, is actually an ancient spaceship. Using available space mission photographs, he also compares Phobos to 2867 Steins, a small asteroid-like object in the solar system which was flown past by the European Space Agency's *Rosetta* mission in the autumn of 2008. Here's what Hoagland has to say about these two celestial bodies on his website (www.enterprisemission.com):

> Steins also turned out to be a ship ... a 3-mile-wide, ancient spaceship orbiting the sun ... and even more remarkably, a ship moulded exactly like a classic diamond. There can be no reasonable doubt: Steins and Phobos were designed by the same "ancient spaceship designer" ... who made full use of the versatile and multi-faceted properties of the "tetrahedral" frame ... in this case, on two very different scales.

This is fantastic stuff. One has to admit, looking at the photographs on Hoagland's extensive and well-illustrated site, that the shapes of both Phobos and Steins are remarkably similar. But so are the shapes of the earth, Mars and the moon. Did the cosmic engineers also decide that planets should be globes? Using copious citation and referencing, Hoagland hammers home his points repeatedly, with an unfortunate resort to that incessant habit of internet conspiracy theorists – the repetitive exclamation mark. Hoagland also champions the "Face" on Mars and the "Pyramids". The NASA *Viking* spacecraft successfully photographed the surface of the planet Mars in 1976 revealing a mile (1.6 km) long, 1,500-foot (457 m) high "humanoid face" discovered in a northern Martian desert known to astronomers as Cydonia. Nearby there are several other objects that have been designated as "anthropomorphic" including several pyramid forms. Various investigators have been studying these anomalies for almost two decades, reaching widely varying conclusions. As with many other astronomical anomalies, they have become the subject of much controversy, and Hoagland summed this up in 1987:

> Either these features on Mars are natural and this investigation is a complete waste of time, or they are artificial and this is one of the most important discoveries of our entire existence on Earth. If they are artificial it is imperative that we figure them out, because they "do not belong there". Their presence may be trying very hard to tell us something extraordinary.

If only George Adamski was around today – he'd be able to reveal all.

When I was a kid I had a map of Mars on my bedroom wall. I drew it myself, copying it from an astronomy library book. It was amazing; it showed a network of straight, interconnecting "canals". I wrote a letter when I was nine years old (which I wish I'd kept) to the British Interplanetary Association asking about Mars. I received a reply; I can't remember what it said, but I do remember the signature; Arthur C. Clarke. I used to imagine the Martian bargees transporting their exotic cosmic produce around the planet, whilst not stopping to think that if they had flying saucers … why did they need canals? The forceful march of astronomy has blown such romance out of the water, but for a time in the late nineteenth and early twentieth centuries, some highly respected "proper" astronomers believed that what they perceived through their inefficient telescopes as long straight lines in the equatorial regions of Mars from sixty degrees north to sixty degrees south were a real canal system. The Italian astronomer Giovanni Schiaparelli called these *canali* in 1877, and was followed by Charles E. Burton, an Irish astronomer, who came up with his own straight lines, although they didn't resemble those of Schiaparelli.

The most convincing proponent (to a prepubescent space cadet) of the Martian waterways was Percival Lawrence Lowell (1855–1916). He was an interesting man, who founded the Lowell Observatory in Flagstaff, Arizona. Mathematician, astronomer, writer and no mean businessman, his name, via his Martian mapping, became synonymous in my little world with a possibly bustling population of tentacled Red Planet boatmen. Lowell may have been way off the mark, but it was he who led the astronomical charge which established, fourteen years after his death, the discovery of Pluto. The name of that cold, distant body means more than a Disney cartoon character; the "p" and "l" in Pluto are Lowell's initials.

As the twentieth century progressed, improved telescopes soon revealed the canals to be non-existent; they had been an optical illusion. Thus a disappointed kid had to grow up and face facts. Space mission cameras with high resolution mapping of the Martian surface would eventually tell a stark truth: craters, dust and seemingly barren lifelessness. But who needs Martian canals when you can have the inspiration of the interplanetary pharaohs?

For the inquisitive with time to spare, if you go online and simply Google "Mars anomalies" you will come up with dozens of sites put together by an international army of amateur astronomers, space fans and computer geeks, all of whom have somehow got hold of photography from various unmanned space missions to the Red Planet. What you'll see on their websites and on YouTube is often nothing like you'll come across on NASA's website. You will begin to believe that there are trees on Mars, Egyptian-style archaeological ruins, glass tunnels, Inca-type cities and mechanical artefacts scattered across the red landscape. It is very difficult to know what veracity any of this "I want to believe" stuff has, but it makes for a long and entertaining winter's night on the keyboard. Is there anything in all this?

The great American astronomer Edwin Powell Hubble (1889–1953) knew how frustrating his vocation was. He said that "the history of astronomy is a history of receding horizons". Unlike Hubble, Richard Hoagland probably won't have a telescope named after him. But – if he's correct in even 10 per cent of his wayward ideas, they might have to build a whole

moon colony in his name. Hubble changed the way we understand the universe. He confirmed the existence of galaxies
other than the Milky Way. He also considered the idea that the
loss in frequency, known as the redshift, observed in the spectra
of light from other galaxies, increased in proportion to a particular galaxy's distance from earth. This distinction is now
known as Hubble's law.

Men like Richard C. Hoagland are extremely entertaining,
but they are also very lucky. They can propagate their theories
around the globe and because of their non-academic status
the worst they can suffer are the poison arrows of the massed
sceptics, such as those who listen to him on America's nightly
Coast to Coast (*C2C*) radio show, hosted by George Noory
(www.coasttocoastam.com). There's even a thread on the *C2C*
online forum where astronomer after astronomer challenges
Hoagland's ideas as totally delusional. His latest revelations
include a cosmic connection between John F. Kennedy and
Barack Obama in relation to the "end of times" in 2012, and
he's come up with some NASA photographs that reveal, he
claims, structures on the moon and a disembodied "robot head"
lying in the dust. It's heady stuff. Some astronauts are willing to
talk about such subjects, but they only issue hints. Try it with
Buzz Aldrin and you're likely to get punched. He takes great
(and justified) exception when faced with those "were the moon
landings a fake?" anoraks who pester him at public events.

So real, university-educated, accredited astronomers, especially those employed by major universities and observatories,
are not going to indulge people like Hoagland if they want to
keep their jobs. And yet ... and yet; deep down many physicists
know that the area they study in encompasses more anomalistic
dead-ends than any other branch of science. Today's mavericks
on their fringes, many of whom we see as crackpots, still have
their place as catalysts, prodding science's rump like a kid with
a stick near a hornet's nest. The primitive present is being transformed into the high-tech future with remarkable rapidity. Our
propensity to believe in everything our technological age can
achieve is based upon drawing-board fantasies that have become
realities. The idea, for example, of Hal the computer or the
videophone in Kubrick's *2001*, or *Star Trek's Enterprise*'s

hand-held communicator devices – harbingers of today's cell phones – were impossible products of a screenwriter's imagination in the 1960s. Now we even have Skype; I can sit here in the English East Midlands and talk face to face with my friends in Dallas or St Petersburg. The kind of "out of the box" thinking that brought all this about is indistinguishable from the heretical free thinking of past centuries, for which many brilliant souls were persecuted.

Galileo died the year Isaac Newton was born (1642). In 1942, the Royal Society of London organized an occasion to celebrate the tercentenary of Newton's birth. However, the Second World War was raging and they had to wait until July 1946 before they could hold the event. It included lectures by some of the great scientists of the time; E. N. da Costa Andrade, H. W. Turnbull, Niels Bohr and Jacques Hadamard. The economist John Maynard Keynes (1883–1946) was booked to speak but in April 1946, three months before the celebrations, he died. A number of Isaac Newton's papers were kept secret until they were up for sale in 1936. Keynes was the first person to see some of these. The economist was fascinated by Newton's writings. On behalf of his deceased brother, Geoffrey Keynes delivered his lecture at the celebrations. What John Maynard Keynes wrote in his preamble to the lecture, entitled "Newton the Man", reveals how many physicists probably feel;

Why do I call him a magician? Because he looked on the whole universe and all that is in it as a riddle, as a secret which could be read by applying pure thought to certain evidence, certain mystic clues which God had laid about the world to allow a sort of philosopher's treasure hunt to the esoteric brotherhood. He believed that these clues were to be found partly in the evidence of the heavens and in the constitution of elements (and that is what gives the false suggestion of his being an experimental natural philosopher), but also partly in certain papers and traditions handed down by the brethren in an unbroken chain back to the original cryptic revelation in Babylonia. He regarded the universe as a cryptogram set by the Almighty – just as he himself wrapped the discovery of the calculus in a cryptogram when he communicated with Leibniz. By pure thought, by concentration of mind, the riddle, he believed, would be revealed to the initiate.

We've already met Galileo (1564–1642) and the trouble he got himself into with the Holy Fathers over propagating the heliocentric ideas of Copernicus (1473–1543). Amazingly, it would be 1981 before the Roman Catholic Church officially "forgave" Galileo. His published works remained on the Roman Church's Index of Prohibited Books until 1835. It seems odd that Galileo should have been castigated for supporting Copernican heliocentric theory six decades after its originator's death. But Copernicus didn't have a telescope, Galileo did, and this was a time when the Roman Catholic Church's Aristotelian views were being challenged. Copernicus may have quietly got away with his theory in 1543, but in 1615 Galileo wrote a private letter outlining his views to the Grand Duchess of Tuscany, Madame Christina of Lorraine, "Concerning the Use of Biblical Quotations in Matters of Science". That letter would come back to haunt him. He should have left the religion alone, but he was unflinching in his defence of logic and science, and he could be very sarcastic and argumentative. In his first trial in 1616 the Church's tribunal used this incriminating letter against him. They directed Galileo to relinquish Copernicanism and to abstain altogether from teaching or defending this opinion and doctrine, and even from discussing it. But for twelve more years he burned the midnight oil honing the Copernican outlook. It was in 1632, with the publication of his *Dialogue Concerning the Two Chief World Systems – Ptolemaic and Copernican*, that he presented all the arguments for and against the two great world systems, the Copernican (sun centred) and the Aristotelian or Ptolemaic (earth centred). When we look today at the seven points Copernicus established, it all makes sense:

1) There is no one centre of all the celestial circles or spheres.
2) The centre of the earth is not the centre of the universe, but only of gravity and of the lunar sphere.
3) All the spheres revolve about the sun as their mid-point, and therefore the sun is the centre of the universe.

4) The ratio of the earth's distance from the sun to the height of the firmament (outermost celestial sphere containing the stars) is so much smaller than the ratio of the earth's radius to its distance from the sun that the distance from the earth to the sun is imperceptible in comparison with the height of the firmament.

5) Whatever motion appears in the firmament arises not from any motion of the firmament, but from the earth's motion. The earth together with its circumjacent elements performs a complete rotation on its fixed poles in a daily motion, while the firmament and highest heaven abide unchanged.

6) What appear to us as motions of the sun arise not from its motion but from the motion of the earth and our sphere, with which we revolve about the sun like any other planet. The earth has, then, more than one motion.

7) The apparent retrograde and direct motion of the planets arises not from their motion but from the earth's. The motion of the earth alone, therefore, suffices to explain so many apparent inequalities in the heavens.

The Roman Curia, the religious authorities, had allowed Greek philosophy to influence its theology by imposing Aristotle's view upon the Bible. Despite increasing scientific observations to the contrary, they steadfastly maintained their traditions and invalid interpretations of scripture.

Condemning Galileo, the Holy Tribunal stated:

the proposition that the sun is the centre of the world and does not move from its place is absurd and false philosophically and formally heretical, because it is expressly contrary to the Holy Scripture. The proposition that the earth is not the centre of the world and immovable, but that it moves, and also with a diurnal motion, is equally absurd and false philosophically, and theologically considered, at least erroneous in faith.

In Galileo's time the Church also believed Aristotle's pronouncement that nature abhorred a vacuum, therefore outer space could not be a void. For many years another Greek notion that space was filled with "the aether" (or as we've seen it with the spiritualist mediums, the "ether"), but Galileo knew that air was subject to gravity, and it eventually became obvious that planets hung on to their atmosphere due to their gravitational pull. So what would the Popes and Cardinals have made of the current bizarre twenty-first century cosmic mystery – dark matter?

DARK MATTER

Outer space is the closest natural approximation to a perfect vacuum. With no friction, stars, planets and moons are able to move freely along their orbits. However, even the deep vacuum of intergalactic space is not devoid of matter as it contains a few hydrogen atoms per cubic metre. Astronomers currently regard dark matter as an undetermined material which nonetheless makes up a large part of the mass of the universe. It doesn't emit or scatter light or other electromagnetic radiation. Because of this strangeness, you can't view it through a telescope. It has been estimated that it constitutes 83 per cent of the matter in the universe and 23 per cent of the mass-energy. It is not at all easy to describe or visualize, but if you dropped a lump of charcoal into a bucket of soot, from a few feet away you probably couldn't see it. It has been speculated that dark matter may be a hitherto unknown type of subatomic particle. So we're back to CERN and the Large Hadron Collider, because the search for this elusive particle is occupying some of the finest brains in particle physics today. Weird stuff in space? There's more.

Part of NASA's Small Explorer programme, the Interstellar Boundary Explorer (IBEX) is a NASA satellite launched on 19 October 2008. Its two-year mission from its orbit about 200,000 miles (322,000 km) above earth is to make the first map of the boundary between the solar system and interstellar space. IBEX has detected matter from outside our solar system. The satellite collects energetic neutral atom (ENA) emissions that are travelling through the solar system to earth that can't be measured by conventional telescopes. These ENAs are created on the boundary of our solar system by the interactions between solar wind particles and interstellar medium particles. IBEX principal investigator David McComas tells us that, "It's the first time that matter from elsewhere in the galaxy has been picked up. This alien interstellar material is really the stuff that stars and planets and people are made of – it's really important to be measuring it."

Although humanity can pat itself on the back for maintaining such eternal and indomitable cosmic curiosity, at the same time the layperson can ask a few valid questions. The search for the Higgs boson, the quest to define the age and birthdate of the universe, has cost billions of dollars while a third of the world starves. So, now that the Higgs boson has been discovered, what are we supposed to do with the results? Is this all to do with the advancement of science and technology? Those who have criticized NASA's space programme will flag up the enormous cost it has entailed over the past half-century. However, space enthusiasts will assure you that there's another case to be made, as statistics reveal that for every US dollar spent on space, $45 have come back in knowledge and progress. Something to think about over our iPads and iPhones.

MARS OR BUST?

Humanity has achieved the aim of travelling to the moon and back. We did it by the skin of our teeth and, if *Apollo 13* is anything to go by, we were lucky to get back to terra firma at all. Hollywood and other studios have all tried their hand at plugging in to the drama of the much longer space voyage. As we increase our knowledge about the challenges space travel will throw up, just how accurate are such movies as *Red Planet* (2000) or *Mission to Mars* (2000)? They look good; the computers are more compact and believable than Kubrick's Hal in 1968 or Ridley Scott's Mother in *Alien* (1979), but they seem to skip past the problems of long periods of zero gravity, radiation and the truth about the real horror awaiting anyone stepping on to another planet's surface.

So, who on earth would want to risk a ten-month interplanetary trip to Mars? Dirk Schultze-Makuch, a professor at Washington State University, and Paul Davies, writing in a special October–November 2010 edition of the *Journal of Cosmology* (JournalofCosmology.com), suggest that a human mission to Mars is technologically feasible, but needs forbiddingly enormous financial and political support. So, how do we cut costs? Easy; make it a one-way trip. Apparently, for the space travel bean counters, the *return* manned mission remains "stuck on the drawing board". So, perhaps, it might be a privately funded, one-way trip blasting off twenty years from now. Surely, no one would volunteer for that? Wrong; 400 readers have volunteered as potential Mars colonists. If you support the mission to Mars, or would like to volunteer to spend the rest of your life there, you are invited to email OnwardtoMars@JournalofCosmology.com.

Just becoming an astronaut takes years of rigorous physical and psychological training, and usually one of the requirements is a brain bordering on Einstein's. What would inspire someone to volunteer for an interplanetary kamikaze expedition?

"I've had a deep desire to explore the universe ever since I was a child and understood what a rocket was," Peter Greaves told FoxNews.com. Greaves is the father of three, and a jack-of-all-trades who started his own motorcycle dispatch company and fixes computers and engines on the side:

> I envision life on Mars to be stunning, frightening, lonely, quite cramped and busy. Unlike Earth I wouldn't be able to sit by a stream or take in the view of nature's wonder, or hug a friend, or breathe deeply the sweet smell of fresh air – but my experience would be so different from all 6 to 7 billion human beings … that in itself would make up for the things I left behind.

Other volunteers included a forty-five year-old nurse and the pastor of the Clarno Zion United Methodist Church in Monroe, Wisconsin, Reverend Paul Gregersen. As a man of the cloth, he feels he'll be needed on the trip: "I have the feeling that spiritual issues would come up among the crew. The early explorers on Earth always took clergy with them." Another was Pasha Rostov, a sixty-nine year-old college student at Texas A&M University and computer programmer. Outlining his qualifications, he said, "I do very well with solitude, I am handy with tools, very good at making things work, have generated my own solar energy, built three houses (with my own hands) and am quite sane and stable." They'd all be happy to wave goodbye to the blue marble – for good.

Spiritual issues? That would be only the half of it. First of all, you would have to let all your family and friends know about your intentions. Unless you were particularly unpopular, this wouldn't go down well. You'd better get Christmas over before setting off. Everything you were familiar with on earth would be consigned to memory the minute you left the launch pad. And if the mission was finally pulled together, what would be the public's reaction? Would there be an explosion of resentful opposition to the idea? Then there's the trip itself. Ten months of close confinement, during which the gravity (or zero gravity) of your situation and your decision to volunteer would finally hit home. There would be that last lingering look at the receding earth as you drift off on to your Mars-bound course. No chance at all of going back. It would be no use radioing Canaveral and saying, "Er ... I've had a change of heart. I think I left the gas on ... forgot to feed the cat ... I'm not getting along with Richard Branson ... if I go EVA, can you send someone to pick me up?"

Then there's the depression which will surely set in, because apart from the comparative safety of your spaceship confinement (if you're not bombarded by micrometeorites), you'll have no idea at all what to expect when you finally land on Mars. If the spacebound Chaplain can't cheer everyone up with a few choice spiritual words of guidance and comfort, chances are you'll be mentally re-running the last twenty minutes of Stanley Kubrick's *2001: A Space Odyssey*. Once on Mars, the problems would really kick in. How are you going to have enough oxygen to last? No doubt there is bio-mechanical research going on to find ways of making breathable air; for example, there could be methods of extracting oxygen from rocks on the moon, but living on Mars and being able to breathe is, as yet, an immense problem.

Science-fiction authors and Hollywood space-opera screenwriters like to flag up the idea of "terraforming" a barren planet. It remains a hypothesis where we "make" an acceptable atmosphere thus rendering a planet fit for human colonization. The assumption is that the environment of a planet can be altered through artificial means. For example, as Mars has significant amounts of frozen water at its south pole, and beneath the surface is permafrost, if this could somehow be made to melt, it would form an ocean around the planet's surface about 12 metres deep, and this would produce clouds. Elemental oxygen in the Martian atmosphere is present as carbon dioxide (CO_2), but we'd need other compounds, ammonia for instance, and the whole job would be an absolutely massive and expensive process where the risk would be that whatever atmosphere we created could wander off and dissolve in outer space. So the feasibility of creating an unconstrained Martian biosphere still shares the drawing board with the financially prohibitive idea of a return trip.

Just to wander around the surface of Mars, the space suit required would be even more complex than anything developed so far. It's the only thing that will save the volunteers' inevitably short lives. Mars' low-pressure atmosphere will be the biggest risk for the astronauts. Air pressure keeps body fluids and blood flowing in a liquid state. If air pressure is too low, your body fluids will boil, lose heat quickly and evaporate. Result: rapid death. As protection from Mars' perilous low-pressure atmosphere, space suits need to be pressurized. Because the Martian atmosphere contains extremely high levels of carbon dioxide, with very low traces of oxygen and nitrogen, they'll require highly specialized breathing apparatus. Take your helmet off, breathe the Martian air and you'd lose consciousness in under twenty seconds and die. Then there are the Mars weather conditions. There can be a discrepancy of temperature on the surface of Mars in the first five feet (1.5 m) above the extremely cold surface, so your suit needs adequate heating. There could be one temperature around your feet and ankles, and another, possibly 20 °C cooler, around your shoulders. So if the designers don't get the space suit just right, you could end up with a combination of burning legs and a frosty chest. And the place is swirling in wind-blown dust, and we have no idea if it is toxic or not.

If you do survive there for a period of time, communication with your loved ones back on earth will be both a frustrating and emotional drain on your patience. Each message you send home will take forty-five minutes to get there, and the replies will take the same. So it could take ninety tedious minutes to find out if your lottery numbers had come up. Once the novelty of being on the Red Planet wears off, every Martian day will seem boringly similar. No trips to the seaside. No lakes and forests. No parks, birds, dogs or cats. Just boulders, craters, red dust and sinister, towering mountains of stark rock. Some say Mars has a pink sky, others claim it is pale blue, depending on how the Mars Rover photography is manipulated.

In the event that some way is found to make enough air to breathe in your colonist's pod, and some method of growing food, you will all have to watch one another get older, weaker and then dying. Should children be produced up there, then should they survive, their human origins to them will be a mystery as they watch time-delayed flickerings of recollected life transmitted from their dead parent's home planet. One wonders if the volunteers have really thought this all through. Despite all this negativity, in the not too distant future, such a pioneering trip may well be the only way the human race can survive. Celebrated physicist Professor Stephen Hawking has said that he believes we may face nuclear Armageddon. It would only take some rabid fundamentalist somewhere in the world (and there seem to be plenty around) with access to the missile launch button to obey their god's whisperings and trigger doomsday. Speaking on BBC Radio 4 as part of a programme celebrating his seventieth birthday, Hawking said, "I think it is almost certain that a disaster, such as nuclear war or global warming, will befall the earth within a thousand years. It is essential that we colonise space. I believe that we will eventually establish self-sustaining colonies on Mars, and other bodies in the solar system, although probably not within the next 100 years." Yet he also warned that if man should meet alien life on our journey into space, the consequences for humanity could be grave. Seems sometimes that you just can't win …

THE ST VALENTINE'S DAY
MARSACRE ...

In the final analysis, going to Mars is too costly for governments, unless they can combine with the commercial sector. NASA's hopes for a manned mission were dashed on 14 February 2012 because they've had to cancel plans for ambitious new missions to the Red Planet. Together with the European Space Agency (ESA), they were arranging a pair of joint missions to Mars that could have made important strides in the search for past or present life.

They had planned to launch the ExoMars Trace Gas Orbiter in 2016 to further explore hints picked up by previous missions of methane in the Martian atmosphere. The ExoMars rover was due to launch in 2018. Its task was to have drilled into the Martian surface seeking clues to past Martian life, for example complex carbon-based molecules. But NASA simply couldn't afford it, leaving the ESA out on a limb. NASA wanted $830 million just for space taxi development alone – getting men and payloads into orbit and down again – in 2013. It asked for a similar amount in 2012, but Congress cut it by more than half, to about $400 million. The bigger financial picture for NASA from the White House is grim, too. Congress needed to approve $17.7 billion for NASA in 2013, about the same as it got in 2012, but around $1 billion less than it had been projecting for 2013 when making plans in recent years. In the meantime, the stranded ESA is reportedly trying to bring the Russian space agency on board instead. Space still seems high on the agenda in

Russia. As a result of these austere times, NASA's Mars budget was slashed. Space is an expensive place – so who else can get us up there?

One man, the same individual who set up something all internet shoppers are familiar with, PayPal, now runs a company which has been placed in the top fifty innovators in the world. His name is Elon Musk and his company, SpaceX (www.spacex.com) builds amazing, economical rockets, with human safety as a leading concern. His Dragon capsule will make the old space shuttle seem like the Wright brothers biplane. There must have been a lot of profitability in PayPal because SpaceX's research and development, its continuing success after several impressive launches and a launch schedule stretching several years ahead, must gobble up the dollars at a rate of knots.

"IT'S LIFE, JIM, BUT NOT AS WE KNOW IT": A QUARTET OF MYSTERY MOONS

Are there other places in the solar system where we might find life? There's a slim possibility, but it would no doubt be a case of "It's life, Jim, but not as we know it."

Europa is a small, icy moon orbiting Jupiter. The *Voyager* and *Galileo* spacecraft have provided us with close-up looks at this intriguing place. Its icy surface is covered with long cracks and fissures, much like the ice floes we see at the poles on earth. The surprising discovery made by astronomers is that Europa's ice "shell" could be floating on top of a deep layer of liquid water below. But it appears to cover the complete moon – a global subsurface ocean. This poses a real conundrum. If there is *liquid* water, there must be *heat* (or high concentrations of salts or ammonia). Put water and heat together, and there's the possibility that something living could be nestling in the warm liquid blackness beneath Europa's icy outer crust. Jupiter's gravity appears to provide enough heat to keep the hidden water liquid and prevent it from freezing. It could well mean an environment similar to the one on the bottom of earth's deepest oceans. It will be a sunless world, but if there are volcanic vents generating heat and minerals, as on earth, it could be occupied by simple life forms. We have plenty of these at the bottom of the Pacific where the sun doesn't shine, so we might come across a whole new race of organic Europa-eans.

Saturn's third largest moon, Iapetus, was discovered in 1671 by Giovanni Domenico Cassini (1625–1712). Iapetus is remarkable for its spectacular "two-tone" colouration. The recent *Cassini* space missions have revealed several strange characteristics. The most inexplicable phenomenon on Iapetus is the equatorial ridge that runs along the centre of the area known as Cassini Regio, about 1,300 km long, 20 km wide and 13 km high. It makes Iapetus look like two halves of a tennis ball stuck together, causing some light-hearted observers to refer to it as the "Death Star". This enigma was discovered when the *Cassini* spacecraft imaged Iapetus on 31 December 2004. The strange ridge has the tallest mountains in the solar system, 20 km-high peaks towering above the surrounding plains, a complex system including isolated peaks, segments of more than 200 km and sections with three near-parallel ridges. Astronomers are puzzling over why it follows the equator almost perfectly. This very odd feature, a prominent equatorial bulge, gives Iapetus the appearance of a massive walnut.

The irrepressible Richard C. Hoagland has devoted quite a number of pages to the photographic evidence of Iapetus and, like his many other deliberations on solar bodies, he's come to the conclusion that something strange is going on up there. He can see architecture, five-sided craters, anomalies including geodesic design, triple straight lines of mountains ... take a look at www.enterprisemission.com/moon2 and put your Charles Fort hat on – you'll need it.

Titan, the largest moon of Saturn, is currently the subject of much scientific discussion and research into the question – could there be life there? With no apparent liquid water on the surface and the fact that Titan is much, much colder than the earth, many astronomers suggest life there is unlikely.

But there are alternative views. Titan appears to have lakes of liquid ethane and/or liquid methane on its surface, as well as rivers and seas, which some suggest could support non-water-based life. Others suggest the possibility of a sub-surface ocean consisting of water and ammonia in which some life forms might survive. Titan has something else going for it; it appears to be the only known natural moon in the solar system with a fully developed atmosphere containing more than trace gases. It's a dense chemically active atmosphere, rich in organic compounds. Whereas this doesn't mean there'll be Titanians striding around there, some speculate that the chemical precursors of life might possibly exist as they did when the earth was forming.

There's hydrogen gas in the mix, too, which offers other possibilities. This gas is cycling through the surface environment and the atmosphere. This has led to the suggestion that micro-organisms known as methanogens could exist. A methanogen produces methane as a by-product of its metabolism. All known methanogens are both archaeans and obligate anaerobes, that is, they cannot live in the presence of oxygen. They're most happy existing in wetlands, gleefully generating methane in the form of marsh gas, and do the same in our own human guts, causing us embarrassing flatulence. Astronauts arriving in this sector of the solar system, therefore, should be prepared for a Titanic fart; the communication "Houston – who cut the cheese?" may gain some frequency.

Then there's another very small icy moon, orbiting Saturn: Enceladus. It's only a few hundred kilometres in diameter, so astronomers thought that any geological activity on such a tiny world would be highly unlikely. But then the *Cassini* spacecraft arrived. What it saw and transmitted back to earth proved yet again that the universe will never cease in changing the minds of the most self-assured physicists. *Cassini* saw geysers and plumes of material erupting from the south polar region through large, warmer cracks, which earned the nickname "tiger stripes". *Cassini* then analysed the composition of the geysers as it boldly flew directly through them. The analysis was astonishing; mostly water vapour, ice particles, salts and organics. The *Cassini* data indicates that these geysers almost certainly originate from a sea or ocean of liquid water below the surface. Warm, organically loaded, salty water; this all sounds familiar to us Earthlings. So could Enceladus harbour some kind of extra-terrestrial life?

Further missions to Europa and the other moons may well be able to answer these questions, and the possibilities are exciting.

INNER AND OUTER LIMITS

We've been used to thinking that there were nine planets in our solar system, but poor little Pluto, out there in the frosty outer limits, has lost its status as a planet, which brings us down to just eight. On 24 August 2006, an organization of professional astronomers, the International Astronomical Union (IAU), revoked Pluto's planetary status when they collectively passed two resolutions. The first of these resolutions is Resolution 5A, which defines the word "planet". Not all astronomers are happy with Pluto's downgrading, and most of us have always taken the definition of "planet" for granted. However, among astronomers, the argument over what is and is not a planet rumbles on.

The IAU's Resolution 5A defines a planet this way: "A planet is a celestial body that (a) is in orbit around the Sun, (b) has sufficient mass for its self-gravity to overcome rigid body forces so that it assumes a hydrostatic equilibrium (nearly round) shape, and (c) has cleared the neighbourhood around its orbit." Some astronomers have questioned the resolution's validity, since relatively few professional astronomers had the ability or opportunity to vote. Here's how the IAU classifies the objects in orbit around our sun:

- Planets: Mercury, Venus, Earth, Mars, Jupiter, Saturn, Uranus, Neptune
- Dwarf planets: Pluto, Ceres (an object in the asteroid belt between Mars and Jupiter), 2003 UB313 (an object farther from the sun than Pluto)

- Small solar-system bodies: Everything else, including asteroids and comets

We've already learned of Percival Lowell's initials being incorporated into Pluto's name, but the state of Illinois was up in
arms over the planet's demotion because the man who eventually discovered the frosty rock was an Illinoisan. So, the noble
leaders of that state rose up, and passed a Senate Resolution;
this is how it read:

SENATE RESOLUTION
1. WHEREAS, Clyde Tombaugh, discoverer of the
planet Pluto, was born on a farm near the Illinois community of Streator; and Dr Tombaugh served as a researcher at
the prestigious Lowell Observatory in Flagstaff, Arizona;
and Dr Tombaugh first detected the presence of Pluto in
1930.
2. Dr Tombaugh is so far the only Illinoisan and only
American to ever discover a planet; and for more than 75
years, Pluto was considered the ninth planet of the Solar
System.
3. A spacecraft called New Horizons was launched in January
2006 to explore Pluto in the year 2015; and Pluto has three
moons: Charon, Nix and Hydra; and Pluto's average orbit is
more than three billion miles from the sun; and Pluto was
unfairly downgraded to a "dwarf" planet in a vote in which
only 4 per cent of the International Astronomical Union's
10,000 scientists participated.
4. Many respected astronomers believe Pluto's full planetary
status should be restored; therefore,
**BE IT RESOLVED, BY THE SENATE OF THE
NINETY-SIXTH GENERAL ASSEMBLY OF THE
STATE OF ILLINOIS,**
5. That as Pluto passes overhead through Illinois' night skies
that it be re-established with full planetary status, and that
March 13, 2009 be declared "Pluto Day" in the State of
Illinois in honor of the date its discovery was announced in
1930.

So, if you look at NASA's website you might see that in some diagrams Pluto is cheekily hanging on to its planetary status. They're an argumentative lot, those astronomers.

If Pluto isn't a planet, would there be anything else out there to qualify as such and bring us back up to nine again? First, let's voyage beyond astronomy's outer limits and meet an Azerbaijani-born American author, Zecharia Sitchin (1920–2010). He was one of those "ancient astronauts" proponents who came to the fore in the 1970s, led by Erich von Däniken. For Sitchin, the origin of humanity could only be explained by the earth being "seeded" by aliens. He also links to David Icke because, like the azure Messiah, Sitchin attributes ancient Sumerian culture to the Anunnaki, that race of shape-shifting lizard folk who, according to most of today's conspiracy-theory fringe, control just about everything, including politics and banking. (Disappointing as it is for the Brownshirt and jackboots brigade, at least lizards makes a change from blaming the Jews …)

But where did this mythical race of extra-terrestrials come from? From an undiscovered planet beyond Neptune called Nibiru. Sitchin claimed the hypothetical Nibiru occupied an elongated, elliptical orbit in our solar system, citing Sumerian mythology in support of his ideas.

Scientists and academics dismissed his theories as pseudo-history and pseudoscience. His work was flawed by lax methodology, the mistranslation of ancient texts, erroneous astronomical calculations and all-round sloppy scholarship. But this never bothered the general X-Files public. His books were worldwide million sellers, translated into more than twenty-five languages. No one has ever found Nibiru and there's no evidence to support Sitchin's suggestion, yet there are still thousands of supporters of his bestselling book *The Twelfth Planet* (1976) and its claim that Nibiru is on a collision course with earth. The collision was originally scheduled for 2003, but as with most "prepare to meet thy doom" prophecies, the "calculations" had to be recalibrated for a new date – this time 2012. If you're reading this, Nibiru has slipped past us and gone on to worry some other planet. Otherwise, these pages are now a pile of ashes floating in a burning cloud of interplanetary detritus.

Nibiru appears to be a fantasy, but there's another sneaky, clandestine planet that has occupied brighter minds than Zecharia Sitchin. We know Vulcan today to be the home of the cogent Mr Spock of the *Starship Enterprise*. But if Vulcan existed, we can't vouch for it being populated by pointy-eared, humourless logicians.

When attempting to explain some irregular and peculiar aspects of Mercury's orbit, the nineteenth-century French mathematician Urbain Jean Joseph Le Verrier (1811–77), who played a part in the discovery of Neptune, hypothesized that Mercury's orbital anomalies were due to the existence of another planet. He called it Vulcan, an apt name for a planet so close to the sun, Vulcan being the god of both beneficial and hindering fire, and the fire of volcanoes. A small body, it was supposed to exist in an orbit between the sun and Mercury. Le Verrier wasn't the only person who claimed the possibility of Vulcan's existence. Edmond Modeste Lescarbault (1814–94) was a doctor and part-time astronomer. Through his 3.75 inch (95 mm) refractor telescope at Orgères-en-Beauce, southwest of Paris, he had observed a small object transiting the sun on 28 March 1859. He already knew of Le Verrier's Vulcan theory, so he wrote to the mathematician, who decided to visit Lescarbault in December 1859. Although Le Verrier seemed ahead of the Vulcan game, it would be Lescarbault who announced the hide-and-seek planet's discovery on 2 January 1860. Lescarbault was duly honoured, and became a Chevalier of the Légion d'honneur. Discovering a planet is a big deal in astronomy. He was soon on the lecture circuit and became popular with numerous learned societies. Let's hope both men died happy, because despite earlier reports and contemporaneous sightings, since then no such planet has ever been found and Mercury's peculiar orbit has now been explained by Albert Einstein's theory of general relativity.

Although that should be the end of the story, Vulcan refused to be extinguished. There were sporadic unreliable reports over the decades following Le Verrier's death, and well into the twentieth century, Vulcan flickered back into life. Together with his academic associates, Henry C. Courten, of Dowling College, New York, whilst examining photographic plates of the 1970 eclipse of the sun, detected a number of objects that appeared to be in orbits close to the sun. These objects were confirmed by a North Carolina observer, while a third in Virginia reported seeing one of the objects. Courten believed that something not quite a planet – but a "planetoid" about 90 to 500 miles (145 to 805 km) in diameter – was orbiting between the sun and Mercury at a distance of about 0.1 astronomical unit. An astronomical unit (abbreviated as AU, au, a.u. or ua) is a unit of length equal to about the distance from the earth to the Sun (92,955,807.3 miles/149,597,870.7 km). Pluto, for comparison, is 39 AU from the sun. Other images on Courten's plates led him to suggest that an asteroid belt exists between Mercury and the sun. But the planet Vulcan? Still illogical, Jim. In argument terms, Vulcan may seem like a rotten old chestnut, but the search for a "Planet X" goes on.

Jan Hendrik Oort (1900–92) was a Dutch astronomer, a pioneer in the field of radio astronomy. The Oort cloud of comets bears his name. Oort postulated a giant cometary sphere surrounding the solar system in 1950. Two astronomers involved in planetary research, John Matese and Daniel Whitmire of the University of Louisiana-Lafayette, claim there's a planet, which they call Tyche, four times the size of Jupiter hiding out in the outer solar system. However, many astronomers say it probably isn't there. Matese and Whitmire have been making a case for Tyche since 1999, and they're stubborn enough to stick with their hypothesis. They believe that the giant planet is lurking in the Oort cloud, out in the far-flung outer limits. Comets arrive in the solar system from all directions, often from as far away as 100,000 AU. If the massive Tyche exists then its presence would explain the unusual orbital paths of some comets that originate there. Matese says, "There's evidence that some Oort cloud comets display orbital peculiarities. We're saying that perhaps the pattern is indicative that there's a planet there." So, watch this space …

As a side note, the word Tyche in Greek means "fortune" or "luck". Tyche was the Greek goddess of fortune and prosperity. It would be easy to interpret the naming of the mystery planet by associating it with the astronomer and alchemist Tycho Brahe (1546–1601), a Danish nobleman whose astronomical and planetary observations were comprehensive and accurate. Tycho lost part of his nose in a swordfight and ended up wearing a selection of copper or silver prosthetic schnozzles for the rest of his life.

THE GOLDILOCKS ZONE

"This porridge is too hot," Goldilocks cried.
So she tried the porridge from the second bowl.
"This porridge is too cold."
So she tasted the last bowl of porridge.
"Ah ... this porridge is just right!" she said happily.
So she ate it all up.

"Goldilocks and the Three Bears",
traditional children's story

As space exploration advances, and with the introduction of newer and more sophisticated telescopes such as the all-revealing Hubble, astronomy has faced up to the possibilities of a universe teeming with life. The chance of solar systems similar to our own, with a planet circling their sun bearing all the characteristics required for developed earth-like biology, is not a wild card. Such planets undoubtedly exist, but it seems doubtful at this stage in human development that we'll ever know much about them beyond the hypothesis. They exist at almost incomprehensible distances from the earth. Some of them, however, already have names. Of course, as we stride forward with our physics and technology, who knows, in a couple of centuries, if we magnify the technical progress we've made in the twentieth century alone by a factor of ten, we may well leap over the hurdle of anti-gravity and develop some amazing new interstellar space drive. The way our planet is going right now, with the challenge of global warming and the possibility of the rising of ocean levels following the melting of polar ice, our descendants may well have to start looking elsewhere in the universe if *homo sapiens* want to carry on. The world population has grown continuously since the end of the Great Famine and Black Death in 1350, when it stood at around 370 million. Current projections show that the global population is expected to reach between 7.5 and 10.5 billion by 2050. That's a whole lot of humanity on a small planet. So if we finally build the starships, then where will we go?

NASA's *Kepler* spacecraft is a space observatory, launched in March 2009 with a planned mission lifetime of at least three-and-a-half years. It was named after the seventeenth-century German astronomer Johannes Kepler (1571–1630). Its mission is to discover earth-like planets orbiting other stars. Forty-eight planet candidates were found in the habitable zones of surveyed stars. The Kepler team estimated that 5.4 per cent of all stars host earth-size planet candidates, and that 17 per cent of all stars have multiple planets. For future generations Kepler-22b, in the constellation of Cygnus, might yet be called home. NASA has suggested that Kepler-22b is the most earth-like planet ever dis-covered. It may be 600 light years away from earth, but it orbits at a distance from its sun-like star that is neither too hot nor too cold to support life, and the astronomers call this the "Goldilocks Zone". No one knows as yet if Kepler-22b is actually habitable. It's there, but could be made of gas.

So is there another potential home for humans somewhere out there across the great galactic divide? Astronomer Dr Ian Griffin, former head of public outreach for NASA's Space Telescope Science Institute, offers a glimmer of hope:

Kepler-22b now shows that there are at least two Earth-like planets in the habitable zones around sun-like stars, which means the number of places where life might be potentially found has doubled overnight. As more data comes in from Kepler over the next few years, the identification of more potentially life-bearing planets will give us a set of targets for the next generation of space telescopes to study.

The problems that lie ahead of us, the mysteries of traversing the black void, do seem to have historical precedents. Columbus and the Pilgrim Fathers imagined that beyond Europe they might fall off the edge of the world and vanish into infinity. When they saw the shores of the Americas they must have gasped in wonder, and the fear of the unknown would have possessed them. But they took the risk. What they did to the world they discovered is not, in retrospect, something of which we can be all that proud. Hopefully, if and when we reach a planet as glorious and beautiful as earth, we'll not make the same mistakes and mess it up. Because of the vast distances, and the need to exceed the speed of light, some have suggested that travelling to the stars will be a form of time travel. NASA's Dr Griffin reminds us of the peculiarities of what we see up there when the sun goes down:

> The light we see from the moon when we look at it at night left its surface just over a second ago; the light we see from the Sun left its surface just over eight minutes ago. Some of the stars that make up the constellations we see in the night sky are hundreds of light years away, which means the light we see left them centuries ago … for me it's astonishing that every time you look up at the night sky you are gazing back through time.

The universe is indeed a bottomless goodie-bag of unexplained phenomena, and everywhere you turn, every week, something strange and new will crop up. For example, an article in the *New Scientist* by Stephen Battersby on 14 April 2010 is the stuff of sci-fi plots. "Mysterious radio waves emitted from nearby galaxy" begins: "There is something strange in the cosmic neighbourhood. An unknown object in the nearby galaxy M82 has started sending out radio waves, and the emission does not look like anything seen anywhere in the universe before. "We don't know what it is," says co-discoverer Tom Muxlow of Jodrell Bank Centre for Astrophysics near Macclesfield, UK." By December 2010, the astronomers were still puzzled. They were still monitoring the object.

The mystery originated in May 2009, when Muxlow's team were monitoring a stellar explosion in M82 using the UK's MERLIN radio telescopes network. The radio emission emerged brightly over a few days, a time period that is more or less warp speed to astronomers. It's been baffling the astronomers ever since. The *New Scientist* elaborated:

It certainly does not fit the pattern of radio emissions from supernovae, with the spectrum of the radiation changing all the while ... they usually get brighter over a few weeks and then fade away. The new source has hardly changed in brightness over the course of a year, and its spectrum is steady. Yet it does seem to be moving – and fast: its apparent sideways velocity is four times the speed of light.

One suggestion is that this might be a black hole, but as this mystery is not right in the middle of the M82 galaxy, where most black holes are found, it could be a smaller scale "microquasar", which occurs after a huge star explodes. Microquasars emit radio waves. They take the form of a black hole up to twenty times larger than the sun. Yet our own galaxy doesn't have anything to match the M82 oddity for brightness. Muxlow also points out another anomaly: microquasars produce X-rays, but this one doesn't. "So that's not right either," he told *New Scientist*.

The mission to explain the myriad mysteries of the universe will arguably occupy physicists until the end of time. Perhaps there will always be things we're not supposed to know.

PART 5:

BIZARRE BIOLOGY

RUBBERNECKS RULE, OK?

Fantasy, abandoned by reason, produces impossible monsters; united with it, she is the mother of the arts and the origin of marvels.

Francisco de Goya (1746–1828)

What's out there in the wild darkness? What do we make of accounts such as this regarding strange "animals" in a roundup of condensed reports logged in the *Fortean Times* in 2003: "Illogan, Cornwall (footage, more than 12 witnesses); near Roseworthy; between Connor Downs and Gwithian; Goonhilly Downs (ginger, spots); near Torpoint (video footage); near Bodmin Moor (initially resembled 'a very short person, entirely black, and wearing flares which swished rhythmically when it walked')." Wearing swishing *flares*? A nocturnal strain of wild hippies? Anomalous animal life is yet another example of our puzzling world's high weirdness. Is there an unknown breed of black panther roaming the moors and woodlands of Britain? Is there some ape-like, seven-foot-tall shaggy creature that remains as elusive as ever in the woods of North America? Does the legend of the Yeti still leave its footprints in the Himalayan snows?

A cryptid is an animal whose existence is not confirmed by science. If you study cryptozoology and wish to seek out these creatures, you're known as a cryptozoologist. Quite often, this is a subject regarded by many with the same disdain as UFO sightings. They may exist, but if you haven't seen one … maybe they don't. However, cryptids have been sighted and documented for centuries.

When she's feeling cruel, Nature herself can produce genuine human oddities and when we've had sight of them, we accept their almost incredible existence. A child mothered by a wolf or apes? It's happened. A man with two bodies? The Elephant Man? Conjoined twins? Two-headed sheep, flea circuses, a singing mouse, horses and dogs who could count, the "bearded lady" of the old time circus, the "Pig-Faced Lady of Manchester Square" … all these have paraded past the inquisitive unafflicted down the centuries. Before peeking into the hidden world of the still-elusive "alien zoo" of the cryptid, it seems sensible to cast a glance at the oddities among *homo sapiens*, those unfortunates who were once referred to as "freaks of nature". Despite the fact that such misunderstood wretches, once a staple of the fairground sideshow, had folk queuing around the block between rides on the dodgems, when it came to presenting them with some kind of real life and personality, the public reeled back in horror. A perfect example was the 1932 American Pre-Code horror film, *Freaks*.

The movie was directed and produced by Tod Browning (1880–1962), who had worked on ten films with the great Lon Chaney (portraying disguised and/or mutilated characters, such as carnival knife-thrower Alonzo the Armless in *The Unknown*, 1927) and successfully directed Bela Lugosi in the 1931 hit, *Dracula*. *Freaks* was based on Clarence Aaron "Tod" Robbins's 1923 short story "Spurs". The opening paragraphs of "Spurs" leave you in no doubt as to what life must have felt like for a circus "freak" in those less enlightened days:

> Jacques Courbé was a romanticist. He measured only twenty-eight inches from the soles of his diminutive feet to the crown of his head; but there were times, as he rode into the arena on his gallant charger, St Eustache, when he felt himself a doughty knight of old about to do battle for his lady.
>
> What matter that St Eustache was not a gallant charger except in his master's imagination – not even a pony, indeed, but a large dog of a nondescript breed, with the long snout and upstanding aura of a wolf? What matter that M. Courbé's entrance was invariably greeted with shouts of derisive laughter and bombardments of banana skins and orange peel?

What matter that he had no lady, and that his daring deeds were severely curtailed to a mimicry of the bareback riders who preceded him? What mattered all these things to the tiny man who lived in dreams, and who resolutely closed his shoe-button eyes to the drab realities of life?

Admittedly, in the context of this book, disability is not an "unexplained phenomenon". The phenomenon is the human weakness of wishing to view these tragic conditions. It's the same macabre magnet that has cars slowing down as they pass road accidents – is there any blood? Dismemberment? What can we see? Thank God *that isn't us*.

Sadly, we still live in a long shadow of that poignant world, where today the ubiquitous Ricky Gervais who, whilst harvesting enough hate mail to start a war by offending parents of Down's syndrome children with his use of the word "Mong", can still stroke the dubious funny bones of the prurient among us by flagging up the "hilarious" difficulties engendered by dwarfism. His TV series *Life's Too Short* was a TV sitcom which had the fine, diminutive actor Warwick Davis in various humiliating scenarios, stuck in a toilet bowl, made to stand in a bin, falling out of cars, unable to reach doorbells. Oh, but those little folk – they're *so funny*. If we also consider the new vogue for morbid TV viewing such as *Embarrassing Bodies* and *Big Body Squad* then our collective role as thoughtless rubberneckers hasn't progressed much since the 1930s.

Freaks, released by Metro-Goldwyn-Mayer, takes us into the strange world of sideshow entertainers. The film's cast is mostly composed of actual fairground performers. Browning could have used prosthetics and make-up, but chose not to pull any punches and hired real people with deformities as the eponymous sideshow "freaks". In his early years, Tod Browning had been a member of a travelling circus. The film draws upon his experiences. There is an honest approach in the screenplay, which presents the physically deformed characters as we would expect "normal" people to be: honourable and trusting. It is the non-afflicted characters, the circus owners, in their conspiracy to murder one of the "freaks", who are the true dark villains. *Freaks* was filmed over three months between October and

December 1931. According to www.imdb.com movie database, in January 1932 the test screenings were so disastrous that one woman claimed the film had caused her to suffer a miscarriage and threatened to sue MGM.

Among the characters featured as "freaks" were the conjoined twins Daisy and Violet Hilton, the limbless Prince Randian aka "The Human Torso", a bearded lady named Olga Roderick, Peter Robinson "the human skeleton", Frances O'Connor and Martha Morris as "the armless wonders", and Schlitzie, played by Simon Metz, a man who suffered such incontinence that he had to wear a dress, although some dispute this. Also featured were Johnny Eck, "the legless man", the intersexual Josephine Joseph, with her left/right divided gender, Elizabeth Green "the Stork Woman" and "Koo-Koo the Bird Girl", who suffered from Virchow-Seckel syndrome or bird-headed dwarfism, and is most remembered for the scene where she dances on the table. Among the microcephalics (referred to as "pinheads") in the film were Zip and Pip played by Elvira and Jenny Lee Snow. The dark, cruel and mysterious heart of biological malfunction is evidenced by the fact that microcephaly is the only proven malformation, or congenital abnormality, found in the children who were born after the bombs fell on Hiroshima and Nagasaki.

Although in its uncut form, the movie had a successful initial run at the box office, when word spread regarding its "offensiveness", the studio cut the picture down from its original ninety-minute running time to just over an hour. Sequences such as freaks attacking the character Cleopatra, as she lay under a tree, the character Hercules, played by the German actor Henry Victor, being castrated, and most of the film's original epilogue were cut. *Freaks* effectively ended Tod Browning's career. Because of the shock to audiences from its deformed cast, the film was banned in the United Kingdom for thirty years. The cut and edited short version finally had a showing in the 1960s and has since become a countercultural cult favourite, popular with midnight audiences. In 1994, *Freaks* was selected for preservation in the United States National Film Registry as being "culturally, historically, or aesthetically significant", and has been ranked fifteenth on Bravo TV's list of the "100 Scariest Movie Moments".

The original author of the story, Tod Robbins, expired almost two decades later after experiencing a horror even he could not have imagined. He left his home in New York to live in the South of France. After refusing to leave during the Nazi occupation, he spent the war in a concentration camp and died in 1949.

Ricky Jay (1948–) is one of America's great stage magicians. He's also an actor and writer. He's celebrated for his card tricks, memory feats and stage patter, and is a sleight-of-hand expert who holds records for card throwing. For example, he can throw a playing card into a watermelon rind, which he refers to as the "thick, pachydermatous outer melon layer", from ten paces. Jay is also a great collector of books and historical ephemera on magic, and one of his own fascinating works is *Learned Pigs and Fireproof Women* (1986). Anyone who loves great movies about the golden age of stage magic such as *The Prestige* (2006) and *The Illusionist* (2006) will be enthralled by his writing – and he also has a role in both films. *Learned Pigs and Fireproof Women* features bizarre reports from the eighteenth and early nineteenth century of unfortunate women born, apparently, with the head of a pig. Regrettably, as photography was still to make its debut, all Jay has to go on are the archaic prints and artists' impressions of these human anomalies produced in the various papers and journals of the time. If these chilling representations have any accuracy, then the girls must have had horrendous lives. The most famous of these unfortunate swine-visage belles (they apparently communicated in grunts and ate "from silver troughs") seems to have been "The Wonderful Miss Atkinson", a twenty-year-old girl from Ireland who resided in London's Manchester Square. Yet the way in which urban myths and European legends were circulated and embellished in the days before mass communication can explain why there were so many reports around of pig-faced women. In the age before the telegraph and the telephone, the wellspring of weird reports was usually some buried nugget of truth which, planted like a seed, grew new branches.

Ricky Jay takes us back to what might be the source of the hog-faced womenfolk reports with a more documented story from the Netherlands around 1640. She was a teenager called Tannakin Skinker from the Rhine town of Wirkham. Naturally, if indeed she did have Miss Piggy features, in those days this surely had to be the result of a devilish curse. In this case Tannakin's pregnant mother rebuffed a beggar woman seeking alms, who "was heard to mutter the Devil's paternoster ... pronouncing ominously 'As the mother is hoggish, so swinish shall be the child she goeth withal'."

As with most of the subsequent pig-faced ladies, they seem to be from well-heeled backgrounds and sums ranging from £1,000 to £40,000 are offered in newspaper adverts to any likely suitor who will take her in wedlock. Those who turn up usually flee in horror. Such stories, if they are real, are the tragedies that paved the way for the confirmation to the general public of the existence of human "monsters" with the arrival on the scene of Joseph Carey Merrick (1862–90), sometimes erroneously named John Merrick, a sad individual with severe deformities who was exhibited as a human curiosity and named the "Elephant Man".

From the Middle Ages onwards there have always been crudely fantastic reports of women giving birth to all manner of animalistic offspring. Many such cases were inevitably linked with devil-worship or witchcraft, and sometimes they appeared very convincing.

Mary Toft (1701–63), an English woman from Godalming, Surrey, caused quite a stir in 1726 when she convinced doctors that she had given birth to rabbits. Pregnant that year, she claimed that after seeing a rabbit, which fascinated her, she miscarried producing various animal parts. A local surgeon, John Howard, looked into it and sought further advice from other physicians, one of whom was in attendance to the Royal Household of King George I, the surgeon Nathaniel St André.

St André was convinced by Toft's claim but the King, duly fascinated by all this, sent yet another surgeon, Cyriacus Ahlers. Ahlers was sceptical, but by this time Mary Toft had become something of a celebrity, and was summoned to London for closer scrutiny and examination. But her bunny-producing days seemed over. She was subsequently imprisoned as a fraud.

Human anomalies and unfortunates suffering from some genetic disorder are not always prone to hiding. But when it comes to those mysterious animals, the cryptids, inconspicuousness is a way of life.

THE ELUSIVE NESSIE

Along with Robert Burns, kilts, shortbread, whisky and bagpipes, the Loch Ness Monster remains one of Scotland's major tourism draws. Probably the worst thing that could happen to this obscured creature would be its true discovery and exposure. As with the UFO phenomenon, Nessie has attracted plenty of sceptics, and true believers haven't been helped in recent years by the fact that new technology has revealed that many of the most famous pictures taken of the monster could be fakes, including the most famous of all, the "Surgeon's Photograph".

In 1993, the stepson of movie-maker and big game hunter Marmaduke Arundel Wetherell (aka "Duke" Wetherell, 1884–1939), Christian Spurling admitted that the "monster" in the famous photo was made by him, for a ruse conducted by his stepfather, with a fourteen-inch (35.6 cm) clockwork tin toy submarine and some plastic. The picture earned its name of the "Surgeon's Photograph" because the man who claimed to have taken it at Loch Ness on 19 April 1934 was a physician named Colonel Robert Kenneth Wilson. Over the years the photograph has undergone various examinations and for decades remained the most convincing "proof" of the existence of what might be a plesiosaur surviving in the loch. The less credulous designated it as an otter head or tree trunk. However, no one ever thought it might be a toy submarine. So where does this leave Nessie? Have the sceptics been proved right? Not really; it would take more than a toy submarine to sink this particular beast. The 1934 picture, important though it once was, is only one of many.

The monster was known long before Duke Wetherell's stunt. Here's a sample of the sightings:

- 1871: A Scottish newspaper reports the first modern sighting, described as a "kelpie", a water-horse of Scottish folklore.
- 1933: Travelling in their car along the banks of the loch, George Spicer and his wife spot what they described as a "dragon or prehistoric animal" carrying another animal across the road in its mouth.
- 1933: The first photograph of the monster is published, taken by Hugh Grey.
- 1960: On 23 April, Timothy Dinsdale (1924–87), an aeronautics engineer, films the monster for over a minute in colour.
- 1972: Dr Robert Harvey Rines (1922–2009) was an American lawyer, inventor, musician (he once played a violin duet with Albert Einstein) and composer. His efforts over thirty-five years to find and identify the Loch Ness Monster are among the most dedicated and persistent. In 1972, he visits Scotland and reports seeing in Loch Ness, "a large, darkish hump, covered with rough, mottled skin, like the back of an elephant". He searched the loch's depths with sophisticated electronic and photographic equipment, mostly of his own design. He came up with multiple theories and several tantalizingly convincing underwater photographs resembling plesiosaurs, including the famous "Flipper Photo", yet was unable to produce sufficient evidence to convince the scientific community of the existence of the fabled monster, even though his submersible sonar scans showed evidence of a large aquatic animal.
- 1975: Sir Peter Scott announces that the monster will henceforth be known by the scientific name *Nessiteras rhombopteryx*.
- 1987: Operation Deepscan begins, overseen by local marine biologist Adrian Shine, using twenty-four sonar-equipped boats on a sweep of the surface. Two significant contacts indicating large moving masses are made, including one near Urquhart Bay at a depth of 600 feet (182 m).

- 1993: Discovery Communications analyses the loch in a study of fish and nematodes (roundworms, phylum *Nematoda*, the most diverse phylum of pseudocoelomates, and one of the most wide-ranging of all animals). A new species of nematode is discovered and the sampling results increase fish population estimates by ninefold.
- 1993: Technical experts at Discovery Communications analyse the 1960 Dinsdale film and detect previously unnoticed shadows resembling the shape of a plesiosaur.
- 2001: Dr Robert Rines and the Academy of Applied Science videotape a V-shaped wake and an object on the loch floor resembling a carcass, in addition to clam shells and fungus suggesting evidence of a connection to the sea.
- 2003: Gerald McSorley trips and falls into the loch and finds a plesiosaur fossil but sceptics claim it must have been moved there from elsewhere.
- 2003: Charity fundraising champion Lloyd Scott, at one time a professional goalkeeper with Watford, Blackpool and Leyton Orient, before becoming a fireman, completes a twelve-day walk along the bottom of Loch Ness in an antique diving suit, breaking the record. Whether or not he met Nessie remains unclear.
- 2004: A Channel 5 documentary team uses movie special effects to construct an animatronic plesiosaur which they dub "Lucy". After mischievously placing it in Loch Ness, it generates 600 sightings but the joke is on the jokers; they lost the robot – it could not be retrieved from the bottom of the loch.
- 2007: Lab technician Gordon Holmes videotapes a fast-moving object he claims was forty-five (13.7 m) feet long.
- 2008: Dr Robert Rines expresses fear that the monster is dead.

Nessie, dead? No, just hiding. After 10,000 years the plesiosaur family have learned how to survive.

Auxiliary coastguard and Drumnadrochit businessman George Edwards has, over the years, seen many strange shapes on Loch Ness. He's been a tour boat operator for twelve years. Now he has opened up a new Loch Ness mystery with the discovery of a huge underwater cavern, which has already been dubbed "Nessie's Lair". Whilst on a coastguard training exercise on the loch he picked up an abnormal signal on his sonar. The loch is around 750 feet (228 m) deep. Edwards made a circular manoeuvre with his boat when he got a reading of 812 feet (247 m) on his sonar equipment. His discovery has been pronounced by experts to be highly significant. George has always believed in Nessie; he thinks that there is more than one creature in the loch and that the cavern could lead to a network of caves. He's since been contacted by a North Sea oil company offering equipment and experts to help him investigate further.

In June 2011, from the exact same vantage point where Timothy Dinsdale shot the best footage of the legendary creature back in 1960, shop and café owners Jan and Simon Hargreaves sighted Nessie whilst enjoying an afternoon break on the store's front decking. Kitchen-worker Graham Baine and Mrs Hargreaves spotted an unusual shape moving on the loch. "We were standing looking out and saw something that looked bizarre, I said to my husband to come and have a look. We stand here all the time and look out and see boats and kayaks but it didn't look like anything we have seen here before." She said it was black in appearance with a long neck which was too long to be that of a seal. "It went under the water and disappeared for probably thirty to forty seconds and then came back up again. It was around for a good four to five minutes. It was just so strange." The Hargreaves are convinced that what they saw was the Loch Ness Monster (www.nessie.co.uk).

Mysterious aquatic monsters are not exclusive to Scotland. In the waterways around London's Olympic Park, there have already been reports of some strange beast in the River Lea that is capable of dragging a hefty sixteen-pound (7.3 kg) Canada goose below the surface for a quick snack. There have been hundreds of reports of such creatures ever since Europeans began exploring the wider world. The "Olympic Beast" is just another addition to the list.

VAN GÖLÜ CANAVARI,
THE LAKE VAN MONSTER

Not reported until 1995, Turkey's "Nessie" has since been sighted by over 1,000 people. Witnesses from all walks of life have described a creature that differs from the one inhabiting Loch Ness. Lake Van is the largest saltwater lake in the world, which makes some kind of sea reptile's existence difficult, because the salt content is so high few fish live there. The Lake Van Monster doesn't have Nessie's dinosaur features, but appears to have a large head, plus fins or spikes on its back. As with Nessie, if you go online you'll find plenty of photos and videos purportedly showing the Lake Van Monster on the move.

MOKELE-MBEMBE

Mokele-mbembe, meaning "one who stops the flow of rivers", is a creature usually described by people around the Congo lakes in Africa as being part dragon and part elephant. Reports of a large, aquatic dinosaur-like creature go back to the seventeenth century. In 1992 a Japanese film crew allegedly captured images of Mokele-mbembe whilst shooting aerial footage from a small plane over Lake Tele as part of a documentary. Noticing a disturbance from something creating a sizeable wake in the water below, the cameraman struggled to maintain focus on the object. He did, however, manage to shoot fifteen seconds of footage, which is available on YouTube today. The "creature" does have overtones of Nessie, but sceptics claim it's either an elephant out for a swim or two blokes in a boat. But the creature has been part of Congo legend and folklore for centuries and reports by the natives are common. Many expeditions have been launched, some quite recent, and although reliable researchers and explorers have reported encounters, the beast remains as hidden as ever.

"CHAMP", THE LAKE CHAMPLAIN MONSTER

No one ever seems able to catch a lake monster, and they seem adept at avoiding cameras. That said, as Lake Champlain is a 125-mile (201 km) long stretch of natural freshwater its mysterious creature has plenty of space in which to hide. Lake Champlain sits within the borders of the United States with Vermont on one side and New York on the other but also straddles the Canada–United States border in the Canadian province of Quebec. Lake Champlain's elusive resident, affectionately known as Champ, has so far evaded capture. Nessie and Champ may be prehistoric hangers-on, but Champ trumps Nessie when it comes to the history of sightings, with legends of a giant lake monster known as "Tatoskok" recorded by two of the nearby Native American tribes. The first newspaper report appeared in 1819. Today, thousands of visitors to the lake claim to have spotted a creature with a bizarre 30 feet (9 m) snake-like neck. A holidaymaker in 1977 took a pretty good picture, but the party-pooper sceptics have dismissed it as a piece of driftwood.

OGOPOGO AND CADDY

Possibly the most frequently described mysterious lake or sea monster, the Ogopogo of Okanagan Lake, in British Columbia, the westernmost of Canada's provinces, is said have an undulating, serpent-like body. It is up to 50 feet (15 m) long, with a horse-like head and long thin neck.

Ogopogo has been reported since the late 1700s. Over the years, hundreds of unsuccessful hunts have been launched to capture evidence. Ogopogo is so popular that it became a mascot for Microsoft Publisher 97 while it was in development.

Another British Columbian creature is the Cadborosaurus, named after Cadboro Bay and affectionately known as Caddy. Said to be one of a pair of aquatic reptiles, Caddy and her "mate", Amy, have been reported on average six times a year since the 1940s. Once again, they're reported as serpents with coils, humps and horse-like heads. During the 1940s a plan was afoot to capture one of the pair as an attraction for Vancouver's swimming pool, but thankfully this was dropped after a campaign by Caddy and Amy's supporters.

BIG PUSSY OR
LURKING LYNX?

ABCs mean more than the alphabet to cryptozoologists: "Alien big cats" cut far more ice with researchers into unexplained phenomena than the mythical "Men in Black" of UFO lore. ABCs are only referred to as "alien" because generally they are animals that are not indigenous to the place of their reported sightings. Arthur Conan Doyle tapped into the macabre attraction of vicious, unseen beasts when he wrote *The Hound of the Baskervilles* (1902), and whereas most people may have heard of the Beast of Bodmin, many may not be familiar with the Surrey Puma, the Fen Tiger or several other big cats frequently reported around the UK. A survey by the British Big Cats Society showed more than 2,000 suspected big cat sightings were reported nationwide between 2004 and 2005, and the level of sightings has been as high as ever since. Devon and Yorkshire lead the league for reports, but in a strong third position is Gloucestershire. The usual attribution for these mysterious beasts is as panthers, and smaller examples are associated with a breed once native to Britain, the lynx. Their freedom in the wild creates much speculation as to their origin: from escaped circus or zoo animals to a mass release in the 1970s after the enforcement of the Dangerous Wild Animals Act of 1976.

CHESHIRE CATS

An ABC report from Cheshire by Oliver Clay in the *Runcorn and Widnes Weekly News*, dated 18 February 2010, is typical:

> Will Hayes, of Runcorn, said he and friends were on a fishing trip when they heard rustling from the bushes in the early hours. He said he saw yellow cat's eyes, much larger than those of a domestic moggie. Will followed the creature which went over to his fishing net before walking away. When he returned in the morning he said the net was ripped, bloodied and had been emptied of fish. He also claims he found paw prints. Will said:
>
> "We first heard noises in the bushes near our tent. I looked with a small torch and could make out two bright eyes looking in my direction, similar to a cat's but much larger. I followed this thing's black body to the water's edge, but it seemed to have no interest in me and moved over to our keep net. I heard rustling and splashing but left it alone and retreated to the tent. In the morning I went to the water's edge and noticed very large feline-like paw marks in the mud."

The *Runcorn and Widnes Weekly News* has been on the ABC case for a while and takes the subject seriously. It reported in 2003 a creature resembling a panther, which soon became known as the "Beast of St Michael's Golf Course". In May 2007 the paper ran the story of Wez Farrington, who spotted a "panther-like cat, bigger than a Labrador" in the town park. Local residents, probably too familiar with Monty Burns's lack of environmental awareness in *The Simpsons*, came to the conclusion that chemical pollution in the borough had been enough in the past to mutate a domestic moggie into something much larger and threatening than a fish-loving Tiddles.

THE BEAST OF EXMOOR

In the wake of the 1976 Dangerous Wild Animals Act reports of large cats rocketed with sightings of beasts in Surrey and Bodmin. As the 1970s drew to a close, Exmoor too had its own ABC. A unique landscape of moorland, woodland, valleys and farmland situated in the southwest of Britain, Exmoor National Park contains an amazing variety of landscapes within its 267 square miles (444 km²).

The descriptions are all similar: a huge animal resembling a cat, black or dark grey, with a long tail; it stands low to the ground, between four to six feet (1.2 to 1.8 m) in length. Occasionally, it may be described as brown in colour.

It began with a motorist's report of such a creature, large and black with dark green eyes, which ran across a road in front of their car. By 1983, the media had dubbed the frequently reported panther-type raider, which was regularly killing livestock, as "The Beast of Exmoor". The legend was helped by eighty sheep being mysteriously slaughtered that year along with evidence of baffling tracks and marks. Now the speculation began as to what this thing could be. Some suggested it might have descended from an escaped leopard that mated with a black puma.

In 1988 the increasing number of sheep killed forced the Ministry of Agriculture on to the scene. They decided on a massive search for the thing and called in the Royal Marines. This amalgamation of bureaucracy and the military only came to the conclusion that a rather ravenous fox was to blame. The local population, especially the farmers, were not placated. The reports are still coming in. As recently as 1995 the Ministry carried out another study, but the beast, like his counterparts across Britain, is still out there.

BIGFOOT AND YETI: HAIRY RELATIVES?

Early in 2011 in Rutherford County in North Carolina, Vietnam War veteran Thomas Byers managed to shoot a grainy five-second video that is one of the latest sightings of one of crypto-zoology's most famous North American quarries, "Bigfoot". The sighting happened in Golden Valley where a Bigfoot nick-named "Knobby", a shaggy, seven-foot- (2 m) tall creature weighing around 300 pounds (136 kg), dashed across the highway. It growled as it waved its bristly arms in the air and propelled itself on shaky legs, leaving behind, according to Byers and his girlfriend Carolyn Wright, a smell something like a mix of road kill and a skunk.

Byers (on www.crazyhorsesghost.hubpages.com) said:

> It was truly one of the most amazing sights I have ever seen. It was at one point only 15–20 foot from me and it happened so fast and shook me up so bad that I really didn't understand what I had seen until it was up the side of the mountain and out of sight. And it did not like the fact that I was there on the road with it. In the video you can hear it snarl or growl at me as it crosses the road.

Even if there's no real evidence that it actually exists, Bigfoot has been the Pacific Northwest's most colourful legend for centuries. Halkomelem is the language of the First Nations people of southeastern Vancouver Island, and it gave us the original name for Bigfoot, "Sasquatch", a large, hairy, bipedal humanoid. It stands on two legs but is covered with fur and, instead of speaking, makes crude animal noises. The most celebrated image caught on camera of this elusive beast was the Patterson–Gimlin film shot by Roger Patterson and Robert Gimlin in northern California in 1967. It may be coincidental but, at the same time, the film *Planet of the Apes* was released. John Landis, who directed the movie, was to go on to accuse John Chambers, the production's costume designer who created the monkey suits, of being the Sasquatch in the Patterson–Gimlin "Bigfoot sighting" footage. However, in 1997, another suspected culprit stepped forward alleging Patterson had offered him $1,000 to don the gorilla suit.

It has to be admitted that most photos and video footage of purported Bigfoots look more than a little dodgy. You can hire a decent gorilla suit these days from any good fancy dress hire company, and being filmed in woodland from a good distance, it would seem relatively easy to convince the growing army of the credulous that the mythical hairy biped is every bit as real as Robin Williams with his shirt off.

However, when it comes to Sasquatch's distant relative, the Yeti, pranksters might be more reluctant to prance around on high mountains in deep snow and sub-zero temperatures.

It seems somewhat unfair to call him the "Abominable" Snowman, because according to those who have met him, the Yeti is really quite amiable, although he prefers women to men. A native of the Himalayan region of Nepal, the Yeti is an ape-like creature similar to Bigfoot. He's also known by the Nepalese and Tibetans as Meh-Teh and is an important part of their history and mythology. Stories of the Yeti first entered Western popular culture in the nineteenth century. Science has little time for him, mainly due to the lack of concrete evidence.

Western interest in the Yeti peaked dramatically in the 1950s. While attempting to scale Mount Everest in 1951, distinguished British Himalayan mountaineer Eric Earle Shipton (1907–77) photographed several large prints in the snow, at about 20,000 feet (6,000 m) above sea level. These photos have been argued over and scrutinized critically for decades. They could be evidence of Yeti's existence or quite an ordinary creature whose footprints have been distorted by the melting snow. There's another element to consider: Eric Shipton was well known for his practical jokes.

In October 2011, the Siberian Yeti Conference in Tashtagol assembled to probe into the mystery further. Almost three million people live in Russia's Kemerovo region in southwestern Siberia. They also have around thirty Yetis. Sightings of the hairy snowmen have risen 300 per cent since 1990. Yeti specialists from Russia, Mongolia, Sweden, the United States, Canada, Estonia and China shared evidence and participated in the three-day event, which included a hike into the surrounding forests and caves looking for clues.

One of the delegates was Jeffrey Meldrum, an anthropologist at Idaho State University. He has absolute faith in the Yeti, but not all the scientists participating assume that the Yeti exists. Chief archaeologist Valery Kimeyev of Kemerovo State University says that some hard evidence is needed to complete the picture: "Until we have found some bones, it doesn't make sense to talk about the yeti. The yeti is not an alien and his life-span is hardly longer than that of a human being – maybe 100 years, but that is debatable. There must be some skeletal remains." However, a researcher in the United States, Loren Coleman, who was invited but didn't make it to Siberia, says DNA evidence from hair and faecal samples suggests that some unknown beast is indeed out there. He says, "Bigfoot, the yeti, the snowman – all of these different kinds of hominids and anthropoids that are unknown – are merely waiting to sort of be found if people have patience."

Meanwhile, Bigfoot and his distant hairy cousin still seem less than keen to step into the limelight, but for those of us who still enjoy a mystery, that's just as well.

HIDING HORRORS:
MOTHMAN,
THE TATZELWURM AND
THE GOAT SUCKER

Mothman is a legendary and quite sinister creature reportedly seen in the Point Pleasant area of West Virginia from 15 November 1966 to 15 December 1967. On 15 November 1966, two young couples from Point Pleasant, Roger and Linda Scarberry and Steve and Mary Mallette, made a report to local police. When their car headlights had malfunctioned, they had seen a large white creature with glowing red eyes. They had been driving through a region of town known as "the TNT area", which was the site of a former Second World War munitions plant. The scary being was said to be a "flying man with ten foot wings" that followed their car. On 16 November 1966 the local paper, the *Point Pleasant Register* featured a report headed "Couples See Man-Sized Bird ... Creature ... Something".

He became known as the Mothman, and was introduced to a wider audience by Gray Barker in 1970 with his book *The Silver Bridge*, then garnered even wider fame later via John Keel's genuinely eerie 1975 book, *The Mothman Prophecies*, claiming that Mothman was related to a wide array of supernatural events in the area and the collapse of the Silver Bridge. Films made from such material rarely achieve the atmosphere produced by the books, but in the case of the 2002 movie *The Mothman Prophecies*, starring Richard Gere and based on Keel's book, all the genuinely disturbing elements of this strange period are preserved. Mothman reports may have declined, but for anyone who takes the time to read Keel's work, the events of 1966–7 in West

Virginia will continue to make us question the high weirdness of our unfathomed universe. From moths to worms is a short step.

Every nation seems to have its own hidden horror, yet one might not expect something as horrible as the Tatzelwurm to be lurking in scenic Switzerland, the land of secret bank accounts, fine chocolate and verdant mountain valleys, the ideal environment for the local pastime of alpine-horn blowing and yodelling. According to the *Fortean Times* (February 2011) "Tatzelwurm" seems to be a central European generic name; it's also known as the *stollenwurm* in Switzerland, *bergstutzen* in Austria, or *basilisco* in Italy.

The Tatzelwurm, like Jack the Ripper or the Beast of Exmoor, is a star player in Europe's underbelly of myth and magic. It is claimed to be a creature completely covered in scales, up to six feet (1.8 m) long. To complete the horror, it has no hind legs but rather a long snake-like body with two front legs, very big bright eyes and feline-like ears. Those unfortunates who have witnessed it say the Tatzelwurm has the appearance of a cat covered in scales rather than fur. Just for good measure, it can apparently expel poisonous fumes that are strong enough to kill a human. The *Fortean Times* feature included a 2009 report by a researcher on the Italian-Swiss border, who seems to have encountered a four-legged version:

> I was not dreaming! I saw it clearly with my own eyes. It approached me, walking on its hind legs. The anterior legs were very small. It resembled a prehistoric velociraptor, and generally it was like a monitor lizard. Yet while monitors move on four legs, this one went upright. Its back was nearly 80 cm above the ground, with the head nearly a metre. I guess it was one and a half or two metres long.

The next time you're in Zurich to open your numbered security box, think on. Buy some chocolate and go home.

Way across the pond in South America, rural communities have their own mythical marauder with which to deal. Known somewhat gruesomely as "the goat sucker", the Chupacabra (from the Spanish *chupar* "to suck" and *cabra* "goat") is a fearsome cryptid with a legendary reputation that has spread across the Americas. More recently, it has been the subject of sightings in its original location, Puerto Rico, where it has been reported since 1995, a somewhat vicious and scary unknown animal; it is also on the rampage in Mexico and certain areas of the United States with Latin American communities. The Chupacabra has an unpleasant habit of attacking and drinking the blood of live-stock, especially goats. Its description varies, but in general wit-nesses report a supposedly heavy creature, the size of a small bear, with a row of spines reaching from the neck to the base of the tail. Reports seem to be spreading, because they have come from as far south as Chile and as far north as Maine, and this particular critter seems to be going international, as new reports of nocturnal goat sucking have appeared from both the Philippines and Russia. Needless to say, science simply views the Chupacabra as a contemporary legend.

The doyen of cryptozoologists, Dr Karl Shuker, a regular contributor to the *Fortean Times*, refers to the Chupacabra in the magazine's *Paranormal Handbook* (2009): "One wag dubbed it as 'Sonic the hedgehog on acid'. That seems as good a descrip-tion as any."

Worldwide, there are many other creatures, some more myth-ical than others, awaiting discovery. The earth is still a place of wonder, where hundreds of new species are discovered every month. As fantastic as the mythical oddities included here might be, if anyone two centuries ago had told us about the Tasmanian Devil, now only extant on that island, we might have written it off as a fantasy.

The size of a small dog, it became the largest carnivorous mar-supial in the world following the extinction of the thylacine in 1936. It moves extremely fast, and can swim rivers and climb trees. Stocky and muscular with its black fur, pungent odour, extremely loud and disturbing screech and keen sense of smell, it possesses the strongest bite per unit body mass of any living mammal and has a penchant for digging up corpses for a quick snack. Put all that together and you could almost call it mythical. But reality is, indeed, often stranger than fiction.

PART 6:

SHIVER ME TIMBERS!
MARITIME MYSTERIES

*There is one knows not what sweet mystery about this sea, whose
gently awful stirrings seem to speak of some hidden soul beneath.*

Herman Melville (1819–91)

DEATHLY DRIFTERS

The western wave was all a-flame,
The day was well-nigh done!
Almost upon the western wave
Rested the broad bright sun;
When that strange shape drove suddenly
Betwixt us and the sun.

Samuel Taylor Coleridge (1772–1834),
The Rime of the Ancient Mariner

The ocean makes up seven-tenths of the surface of the earth. It can be said that we know far less about the depths beneath its rolling waves than we do about outer space. It is a place of wonder and strangeness, a place where you can get lost, or die in unexplained circumstances, a place of extreme heat and icy cold, peaceful calm or deadly storm. Its mysterious horizons surround you beneath wide, star-bright skies, where the air is pure and clean. The sea demands your fear and your respect; in reward it feeds your spirit with water you cannot drink, provides escape, the chance to forget and to meditate.

Passengers on cruise liners, mistakenly thinking that they are spending their dollars on some luxurious floating hotel, will rarely stop to think between the changing shoreline scenery that below the thin steel hull keeping them afloat lies a deep, dark graveyard. Between this cemetery's tragic, tombstone wrecks swim bizarre creatures; things with tentacles, singing whales, chattering dolphins, flying fish, creepy crabs and rapacious sharks, all part and parcel of a variety of earth's biology whose fantastic limits are still unknown. Down there in the darkness the bones of men disintegrate, but the haunted, sunken skeletons of their ships endure.

Born and raised in the port of Hull, a maritime city which had been, in the first half of the nineteenth century, one of the busiest whaling ports in the world, I was brought up on nautical yarns. My grandfather had been a ship's cook, my uncles were all merchant seamen, my cousins trawlermen. So whether I liked the idea or not (I really wanted to go to art college) I was destined for Hull's premier nautical educational establishment, Trinity House Navigation School. Although I could splice a rope, box the compass and steer a boat, I was utterly useless at mathematics, so my chances of fulfilling my parents' dream – by becoming a navigating officer – were doomed from the start. As our navigation tutor told my crestfallen mother: "Put him in charge of a ship and it'll be women and children first ..."

Nevertheless, on my sixteenth birthday, 1 April 1959, I did go to sea. Being a coward, I avoided the dangerous, life-threatening pecuniary blandishments of Hull's vast and successful deep-sea trawling fleet. I chose the Merchant Navy – or, as Hull's fishermen used to call it, the "Big Boats". I served as a steward for six months, then for the final six years as a deck hand. I regret not one minute of my life on the ocean. Herman Melville called a whale ship, "my Yale College and my Harvard". Britain's mighty merchant fleet of the late 1950s and early 1960s was, therefore, my Oxford and my Cambridge.

The seven vessels I sailed on ranged from a ten-year-old 3,000-ton cargo ship carrying twelve passengers to a 5,800-ton tramp built in 1937. They have all died the usual undignified death and have long since been scrapped.

To the landlubber, maritime mysteries will always offer a few creepy chronicles that even those of us living miles from the shore in landlocked safety will recognize. They form an eternal quartet and can be easily listed; the *Mary Celeste*, the *Flying Dutchman*, the Bermuda Triangle and volumes of romantic myth, coincidence and tragedy surrounding the ill-fated *Titanic*. These nautical stories are in many ways similar to the fairy stories and bedtime yarns told to children across the generations. They often have a kernel of truth but, as with the ships involved, they gather barnacles of fanciful fiction onto their already encrusted hulls, and only the rare, hell-bent sceptic with time to spare can usually chip them away with the unprofitable hammer of rigorous research. Often, the solving of one of these mysteries is as entertaining as the puzzle itself, but most of us prefer to leave an unexplained element intact. There are shelves already groaning with tomes on these subjects, so we'll only drop anchor for a short time alongside them and launch a boarding party for a cursory exploration, before sailing off into darker waters.

THE *MARY CELESTE*

We all know this story. Even though it has been examined and debunked time and time again over a century-and-a-half since this enigmatic derelict drifted into paranormal history, it still remains one of the greatest of all maritime mysteries. A silent sinister ship with ragged sails, she drifted towards the Straits of Gibraltar in her own, self-determined erratic way. The apprehensive boarding party found no crew, no passengers; the legend features warm tea in mugs, half-eaten meals, the abandoned ship's cat. So to whom do we offer our thanks for this irresistibly spooky imagery? None other than our old spiritualist friend, the inventor of Holmes and Watson, Sir Arthur Conan Doyle, and his yarn "J. Habakuk Jephson's Statement", published in the prestigious *Cornhill Magazine* in 1883. What gave this early success for Conan Doyle added impact was the fact that it was published anonymously. Apparently, he was paid a hefty fee for the story – enough to pay his house rent for a whole year. Those were the days!

This piece of fascinating fiction was based on the true report of the discovery of the *Mary Celeste* (or as Doyle called it, the "*Marie*" *Celeste*) and it became quite controversial. His tale was mistaken by many to be a factual feature. The US consul Horatio J. Sprague demanded that the *Cornhill Magazine* reveal the origins of what he regarded as "a fraudulent article". Frederick Solly-Flood, Her Majesty's Proctor and Attorney General in Gibraltar, the man who had overseen the salvage of the *Mary Celeste*, declared that "J. Habakuk Jephson's Statement" was "a fabrication from beginning to end", and as such it might easily damage England's international relations. They suspected at one time that the anonymous culprit was Robert Louis Stevenson.

Conan Doyle, however, wasn't bothered by all this. As a writer he felt pleased that his imagination, in print, could be so convincing. The deathly drifter certainly provided a step up in his career.

So what *really* happened to trigger this superlative bit of fictional embroidery?

About 600 miles (966 km) off the coast of Portugal on 4 December 1872, the Canadian cargo ship *Dei Gratia*'s lookout spotted another sail on the horizon. The *Dei Gratia*'s Captain Morehouse decided to approach the vessel with caution. He soon recognized the other ship as the 282-gross-ton American brigantine, *Mary Celeste*. Morehouse was a friend of the *Mary Celeste*'s Captain, Benjamin Briggs. In fact, Morehouse and Briggs had dined together a week before the doomed vessel sailed and they had arranged to meet up in Italy. However, the *Dei Gratia* was still awaiting her cargo and left a week after Briggs had sailed. Briggs was an experienced mariner, who had captained five vessels and owned others. The *Mary Celeste* loaded a cargo of 1,701 barrels of commercial alcohol on New York City's East River on 5 November 1872, then departed from Staten Island for Genoa, Italy, and sailed into nautical history. On board were a seven-man crew – the first mate and the cook were Americans, with four Germans and a Dane, all excellent sailors with impeccable records and fluent in English – plus Mrs Briggs and their two-year-old daughter. Ten souls in all.

As the *Dei Gratia* approached the *Mary Celeste*, Morehouse became concerned; it looked like his friend Briggs was in some kind of trouble. What sails there were flapped in the wind, whilst others were missing, and although they hailed the vessel, there was no reply and, more disturbingly, no one at the helm. She was flying no distress signals. Morehouse assembled a boarding party and they rowed over to the derelict. They discovered that the ship was relatively undamaged. Her cargo was intact. They eventually found the missing sails. There was plenty of food and water on board. The main hatch was sealed, although there was no sign at all of Briggs, his wife, their child and the crew. The *Dei Gratia's* first mate Oliver Deveau stated at the subsequent inquiry that he saw no preparations for eating and there was nothing to eat or drink in the cabin. He reported that "the whole ship was a thoroughly wet mess". Two of her pumps had been dismantled, a third still worked, there was a quantity water between decks and three-and-a-half feet (1.1 m) of water in the hold. Despite these faults, she was still in a seaworthy condition. In the Captain's cabin they found her logbook, but all of the ship's other papers were missing. The compass was damaged and the clock was stopped. Personal belongings and supplies were still on board.

The fore hatch and the lazarette (a storage locker used for gear or equipment) were both open. The ship's sextant and marine chronometer were missing. The *Mary Celeste*'s lifeboat had gone. A rope had been tied sturdily to the ship, its frayed end trailing aft in the sea. Had there been a hasty evacuation?

Morehouse was puzzled; what would make an experienced Captain order such a hurried retreat from a seaworthy ship? And there the legend begins, and endures, because none of the ten people who sailed on the *Mary Celeste* was ever found.

In Conan Doyle's version, the ship was taken over by a black passenger. He and his fellow mutineers hijacked the ship, sailed to Africa and murdered the passengers and crew. Of course, the designation of the villain as a man of colour would have suited the casual imperialist racism of the late Victorian age. Conan Doyle was a man of his time and foreigners from warmer climes made good, exotic suspects for any manner of crime. For example, writing about Tonga, in the Sherlock Holmes novel *The Sign of the Four*, Holmes refers to his *Gazetteer* in Baker Street, to reveal the Tongans as "naturally hideous, having large, misshapen heads, small fierce eyes, and distorted features. Their feet and hands, however, are remarkably small ... They have always been a terror to shipwrecked crews, braining the survivors with their stone-headed clubs, or shooting them with their poisoned arrows. These massacres are invariably concluded by a cannibal feast." So if the *Mary Celeste* had been off Tonga, fair enough; a cannibal dinner. But she was off the coast of Portugal. So, if it wasn't alien abduction, a UFO, a waterspout, a sea monster or some such phenomena, what did happen? There are three theories.

One is piracy, but this seems highly unlikely. Pirates wouldn't have left the valuable cargo on board. The second sounds more plausible. It was suggested by the ship's major shareholder, James Winchester, that Captain Briggs might not have been too happy with his volatile cargo of 1,701 barrels of alcohol. When the salvagers finally unloaded the cargo, nine barrels were empty. Unlike the full barrels, which were made of white oak, the empty ones were red oak, which is more porous. Could the alcohol have seeped, causing a build-up of vapour in the hold? Had there been friction, due to the movement of the ship, between the barrels' steel bands with the danger of sparks? A marine historian, Conrad Byers, suggests that Briggs may have ordered the hold to be opened. If so, and if the barrels had been leaking, there would have been a violent gush of potentially combustible fumes. Perhaps Briggs, being a good, cautious Captain, hastily ordered everyone into the lifeboat, which they secured to the after end of the ship. They would wait until the fumes dispersed and the danger of an explosion had passed. But the line was not tied securely enough to the boat; a storm blew up, the *Mary Celeste* drifted rapidly away in the gale. Adrift in a wild sea in the clothes they stood up in, with no food and water ... we can imagine their fate.

The third suggestion is a recent one by an American researcher, Captain David Williams. He established that on 5 November 1872 a large subterranean earthquake was recorded, its epicentre in the Atlantic Ocean. As we have witnessed with tsunamis, such events can have catastrophic results, yet there was no mention of this in the Captain's log and the inhabitants of the nearby Portuguese islands of the Azores did not report any rumblings. Therefore, you can take your choice of solutions, or make up your own. A tragedy for those involved, but for subsequent generations the *Mary Celeste* has become an endless source of eerie, romantic fascination.

Even her final days were dramatic. Her owner James Winchester sold the blighted vessel at an enormous loss. She changed hands seventeen times over the next thirteen years, and ended up in a sorry condition. One can imagine the spookiness felt on board by her crews during that time. Her final skipper was a man named Captain G. C. Parker. The old tub, loaded with an overinsured cargo of scrap, including boots and cat food, was making a loss so he decided to wreck her in the Caribbean Sea on 3 January 1885 in a deliberate insurance fraud. Parker ran her on to the Rochelais Reef near Port-au-Prince, Haiti, but she refused to sink. So he set fire to her. She still wouldn't break down, but the ship's log, which contained Benjamin Briggs's entries, went up in the flames. Parker made an exorbitant insurance claim for a non-existent cargo of silver cutlery, 125 casks of Bass beer and 975 barrels of herring. It landed him in jail with a potential death sentence, but he died three months later.

The charcoaled hulk saw out her days on the reef and finally slipped beneath the waves. There she lay until 9 August 2001, when the author of *Raise the Titanic*, Clive Cussler, led an expedition headed by his National Underwater and Marine Agency, and claimed to have discovered the remains of the *Mary Celeste*. Subsequent research by the University of Minnesota disputes Cussler's findings, but it's not easy to argue with a genuine marine archaeologist whose organization has discovered fifty wrecks, including the ship which went to the aid of the *Titanic*, the *Carpathia*, and the first ironclad of the American Civil War, the *Manassas*. So, rest in peace Captain Briggs, family and crew. Whatever your mysterious fate was, you'll be remembered in every fo'c'sle throughout the seven seas forever.

On 17 October 1998 the *Daily Mirror* reported that Prince Edward, with his film crew, filmed a ghost ship as they were shooting a TV documentary in the *Crown and Country* series around the Isle of Wight. The subject was the tragedy of a twenty-six-gun frigate that capsized and sank in Sandown Bay, HMS *Eurydice*. The ship perished in 1878 during a blizzard. It achieved later fame as a phantom vessel, with many sightings reported by sailors over the years. The Prince told the *Mirror*: "We were talking about a ghost ship on the Isle of Wight and how we could illustrate this three-masted schooner that just disappears. Suddenly someone said 'Look, there's one now', and sure enough out to sea there was a three-masted schooner. It was not arranged by us. It simply appeared." He said he watched the mysterious schooner sail towards the coast, then it disappeared. A check of shipping records revealed no sailing ships were known to be in the area at the time.

Like all such sightings, it would inevitably be associated with one of the most documented ghost ships of all: the *Flying Dutchman*.

THE *FLYING DUTCHMAN*

At the height of the Second World War, on 3 August 1942, HMS *Jubilee* was off the South African coast, making her way on a calm sea to the Royal Navy base at Simonstown, near Cape Town. At 9 p.m., a strange phantom sailing ship was sighted. On the bridge on watch was Second Officer Davies, together with the ship's third officer, the author of *The Cruel Sea*, Nicholas Monsarrat. Monsarrat signalled the mystery ship, but there was no response. Filling in his report in the ship's log, Davies recorded that a schooner, of an unrecognized rig, was moving under full sail. This was all rather odd, as there was no wind. To avoid collision, HMS *Jubilee* had to change course. Then the strange ship vanished. Interviewed in later life, at the height of his fame, Monsarrat admitted that the phantom ship was the inspiration for his novel *The Master Mariner*.

The legend of the *Flying Dutchman* is a classic yarn from the days of sail, an age when the Bible was as important as the ship's logbook. An irreverent skipper has trouble on board. He indulges in blasphemy. There's a massive storm, God punishes the ship, the crew all perish and the Master is doomed to a spectral existence for all eternity. The *Flying Dutchman* is South Africa's most famous spook, but the ghost ship can be seen in various locations, for example Goodwin Sands, as well as cropping up in stormy weather off the Cape of Good Hope ... or just about anywhere on the rolling sea. The sightings usually involve a fully rigged sailing ship, sometimes engulfed in a luminescent green mist. Fully lit cabins have been reported, and occasionally there have been reports of a shindig in progress on board, singing, even women laughing. Those saucy spectral sailors … no wonder they got into trouble; never mind the compass, crack open another barrel.

So who was this irresponsible, libidinous mariner who was doomed to scare the bejesus out of future generations of hapless matelots? Richard Wagner (1813–1883) knew who he was back in 1843 when he wrote his opera, *Der Fliegende Holländer*. Four years earlier Captain Frederick Marryat had published his entertaining version of the yarn, *The Phantom Ship* (1839). Marryat has the Dutch skipper's name as Philip Vanderdecken. However, the first reference in print to the ship appears in Chapter 6 of *A Voyage to Botany Bay* (1795) aka *A Voyage to New South Wales*, attributed to a London socialite and skilled pickpocket, George Barrington (1755–1804), who was transported to Australia and is remembered for the line "We left our country for our country's good." Heinrich Heine published a novel in 1834, *The Memoirs of Mister von Schnabelewopski*, which included the story of the *Dutchman*. In the Netherlands, the traditional name for the ship's captain is Falkenbourg. In 1855 Washington Irving wrote a version of the tale calling him Ramhout Van Dam. Another contender is a real seventeenth-century captain called Bernard Fokke. Like the eponymous Second World War German aeroplane, Fokke's ship was noted for its impressive speed, particularly for its voyages between Holland and Java. The name of his ship is not mentioned, but many Dutch mariners actually believed Fokke was in league with the devil. Naturally, when he and his speedy vessel vanished the conclusion was that Old Nick had called in the debt. Although it is easy keeping your tongue in your cheek over the *Flying Dutchman* reports, some, from prominent witnesses, are very convincing.

During the Second World War, the German *Kriegsmarine*'s Admiral Karl Dönitz reported that his U-Boat crews logged sightings of the *Flying Dutchman* off the Cape Peninsula. Seeing the *Dutchman* was an unwelcome omen, and usually preceded disaster for a boat. The ghostly East Indiaman was also seen by numerous witnesses at Muizenberg, a beach-side suburb of Cape Town, South Africa, in 1939. On a calm day in 1941, a large crowd at the Cape coast's Glencairn Beach saw a ship with wind-filled sails, but it vanished just as it was about to crash on to the rocks.

Of course, if a monarch sees a ghost, then it must be true. Prince George (later King George V, 1865–1936) saw the *Flying Dutchman*. The two oldest sons of the Prince of Wales had entered the navy in 1877 and by 1879 it had been decided by the royal family and the government that the two should take a character-building cruise. George was just fifteen when he sailed on a three-year-long voyage aboard the 4000-ton corvette HMS *Bacchante* with his elder brother Prince Albert Victor. Accompanying them was their tutor, Canon John Neale Dalton (1839–1931), who was a chaplain to Queen Victoria. The squadron that set sail was commanded by Prince Louis of Battenburg, great-uncle of today's Prince Philip. Off the coast near Cape Town, George, together with Dalton and other officers on the bridge on 11 July 1881, witnessed the spectral *Dutchman*. George's diary entry describes the encounter, with its grisly aftermath. (Some sources claim this report as that of Dalton):

At 4 a.m. the *Flying Dutchman* crossed our bows. A strange red light as of a phantom ship all aglow, in the midst of which light the masts, spars, and sails of a brig 200 yards distant stood out in strong relief as she came up on the port bow, where also the officer of the watch from the bridge clearly saw her, as did the quarterdeck midshipman, who was sent forward at once to the forecastle; but on arriving there was no vestige nor any sign whatever of any material ship was to be seen either near or right away to the horizon, the night being clear and the sea calm. Thirteen persons altogether saw her … At 10.45 a.m. the ordinary seaman who had this morning reported the *Flying Dutchman* fell from the foretopmast crosstrees on to the topgallant forecastle and was smashed to atoms.

The phantom was seen by other ships in the squadron, *Tourmaline* and *Cleopatra*.

Kings and pirates, deckhands, landlubbers and lighthouse keepers all have reported seeing her. Here's a selection of sightings:

- 1823: Captain Owen, HMS *Leven*, recorded two sightings in the log.
- 1835: Men on a British vessel saw a sailing ship approach them in the middle of a storm. It appeared there would be a collision, but the ship suddenly vanished.
- 1879: The SS *Pretoria*'s crew saw the ghost ship.
- 1881: King George V saw the ship whilst another report from a Captain Larsen of an unnamed Swedish ship tells of a near collision with the phantom, which disappeared. The crewman who spotted her, an English sailor called Landersbury, died shortly afterwards.
- 1911: On 11 January, the whaling ship the *Orkney Belle* almost collided with her before she vanished.
- 1923: An officer aboard a British steamer saw her on 26 January and reported the event to the Society for Psychical Research (SPR). Fourth Officer N. K. Stone wrote an account of the fifteen-minute sighting. Second Officer Bennett, a helmsman and cadet also witnessed the ship. Stone drew a picture of the phantom. Bennett corroborated his account. Stone wrote this: "It was a very dark night, overcast, with no moon. We looked through binoculars and the ship's telescope, and made out what appeared to be the hull of a sailing ship, luminous, with two distinct masts carrying bare yards, also luminous. No sails were visible, but there was a luminous haze between the masts. There were no navigation lights, and she appeared to be coming close to us and at the same speed as ourselves ... when she was within about a half-mile of us she suddenly disappeared. There were four witnesses of this spectacle, the Second Officer, a cadet, the helmsman and myself. I shall never forget the Second Officer's startled expression – 'My God, Stone, it's a ghost ship.'"
- 1939: People on South Africa's Cape shore saw the *Flying Dutchman*. Admiral Karl Dönitz maintained logged sightings by U-Boat crews in the area.
- 1941: People at Glencairn Beach sighted the phantom ship that vanished before she crashed into rocks.

- 1942: In September, four witnesses sitting on their balcony at Mouille Point saw the *Dutchman* enter Table Bay, then vanish behind Robben Island.
- Second Officer Davies and Third Officer Monsarrat, HMS *Jubilee*, saw the *Flying Dutchman*. Davis recorded it in the ship's log.
- 1959: Captain P. Algra of the Dutch freighter *Straat Magelhaen* reported that he nearly collided with the ghost ship.

Of course, as with all reports of unexplained phenomena, amidst all the sense of wonder and credulity that gathers around them over the decades, the fine details of provenance become blurred. For example, "a Swedish ship" – the skipper's name survives, but where's the ship? Then there's "men on a British vessel" – which vessel? Look in the Ships List for "SS *Pretoria*" and you'll not find one in 1879 – the nearest candidate is the USS *Pretoria*. That's not to say these ships did not exist but, as we shall see, some become almost synonymous with the phantom they've reported. Lists are laid down and copied out ad infinitum – going back to sources is often a blind alley, but it doesn't spoil the fun in the long run. These are justifiably the areas on to which the sceptics will eagerly latch. Paranormal atheists, when the chronicles seem fuzzy, may be able to add to their demolition by combining a yarn's historical sloppiness with a hypothetical approach. So, for example, if the *Flying Dutchman* isn't a ghost, what is it?

It could be a mass hallucination, an optical illusion or a mirage. Lights and mist on the horizon can fool the sharpest eyes. A couple of stiff rums and a touch of insomnia on a night-watch on the bridge can produce visual hallucinations. They are all factors worth considering. Dr Frederick Meyers, the respected Society for Psychical Research parapsychologist, interviewed Stone and Bennett, the officers on the 1923 sighting. He came up with an interesting theory, widely rejected by other parapsychologists, that a type of consciousness survives physical death and has the ability to telepathically project images to the living who see them. So could the *Flying Dutchman* be the result of some form of an as yet unexplained energy imprinted in time and space? It seems odd that a tragedy or disaster is usually at the root of a haunting. Yet they are just appearances, apparitions and have no intelligence; might they be an indelible, sporadic projection of permanent grief? Or are we at long last facing a new revelation in physics, CERN style – are we periodically peering through the matrix between our dimensions and the ones awaiting discovery?

Or could the *Flying Dutchman* be a "Fata Morgana", a mirage that occurs in calm weather when warm air rests above dense, cold air close to the sea's surface. The air between the two masses acts as a refracting lens, producing a distorted upside-down image of an upright object. Even though a ship could be over the horizon, the observing crew may see an inverted, blurry image of the "mirage ship" appearing much closer and several times larger than its actual size.

Back to Charles Fort; we offer the data, you decide.

THE UNSINKABLE *TITANIC*

Just before taking his berth on the doomed liner, Thomson Beattie wrote home "We are changing ships and coming home in a new unsinkable boat."

It's hardly surprising if today, when the *Titanic* is mentioned, what's flagged up in people's minds is James Cameron's florid, lumbering epic with its cargo of Oscars, accompanied by the incessant caterwauling of Celine Dion. Without "that song", "My Heart Will Go On", it might just have been bearable. As a piece of history, it had more than a few holes in its double hull. However, that's all a matter of taste.

In 1911, the magazine *Shipbuilder* featured an article on the White Star Line's sister ships *Titanic* and *Olympic*. It examined the construction of the vessels in detail and concluded that *Titanic* was practically unsinkable. The White Star Line never claimed the vessel to be "unsinkable" – we can blame journalism for that. After all, this was the new twentieth century, and technology and engineering skills were racing ahead, neck and neck. People were confident that we might have been on the verge of conquering the elements.

Of course, what makes the *Titanic* story the subject of such eternal fascination, which could be regarded in itself as an unexplained phenomenon, is its sense of catastrophe and grief. Of the 2,200 people on board only 705 were rescued. That must surely, most people think, make this, with 1,445 dead, one of the greatest seagoing tragedies of all time. Sadly, this is way off the mark.

The torpedoing of the *Wilhelm Gustloff* in the Baltic Sea on 30 January 1945 by the Russian submarine *S-13* resulted in over

9,000 tragic deaths. This is a phenomenal figure by any comparison. Half of those who perished were children. Over 9,000 people dead in one maritime tragedy – that's six *Titanics* in one sinking. You could make other comparisons with the marine tragedies of the *Lusitania*, *Empress of Ireland*, the USS *Arizona* and the *Andrea Doria*, but all the deaths combined on those four ships, at 3,430 in all, only add up to just over a third of the *Wilhelm Gustloff*'s deaths. So why are there no Hollywood epics about this ship? There are plenty of easy answers. She was a cruise liner sunk while participating in the evacuation of civilians, military personnel and Nazi officials who were surrounded by the Red Army in East Prussia. It occurred during wartime. It happened to the losing side. The disaster was subsequently subdued by German war guilt. Everyone hated the Nazis and their atrocities, so the USSR's retribution was "justified", and the ship had a "bad" name – Wilhelm Gustloff was leader of the Nazi Party in Switzerland before his assassination. There were no celebrities on board, no rich people, so no Hollywood profile – just a lot of enemy civilians fleeing a terrible situation.

So, let's return to the mighty *Titanic* ...

Swirling around the great ship is a sinister fog of bizarre coincidence and unsettling legend. Three years after she went to the bottom of the Atlantic, on 24 March 1915, a man was found dead in his room at the Alamac Hotel in Atlantic City, New Jersey. He was fifty-three years of age. It is believed that he died of an overdose of paraldehyde, a depressant found to be an effective anticonvulsant, hypnotic and sedative. The dead man, born in 1861, was Morgan Andrew Robertson, a renowned American novelist and writer of nautical short stories who claimed to have invented the most important piece of submarine equipment – the periscope.

In 1898, fourteen years before the *Titanic* set sail, just under a century before Celine Dion began bellowing, he published a short novel entitled *Futility*. It is the story of a massive British passenger liner. Its owners and builders declare it to be unsinkable. It has a serious safety deficiency – too few lifeboats. In the month of April the great ship sets sail, collides with an iceberg and, with the tragic loss of half of all those on board, sinks to the bottom of the Atlantic.

The full title of Robertson's book was *Futility or The Wreck of the Titan*.

Comparing Robertson's novel with what actually happened in 1912, it seems more like clairvoyant journalism than fiction. His description of the *Titan* when compared to the specifications of the *Titanic* is remarkable. There are differences, such as the *Titan* sailing from America to England, not the other way round, and the *Titan* sinks in five minutes, not two-and-a-half hours, and whereas the *Titanic* went down bow first, the *Titan* capsized before it sank.

However – Robertson's description includes the following amazing similarities:

- The *Titanic* was 882 feet (269 m) long, displacing 63,000 tons, the largest luxury liner afloat, described in the press as being practically "unsinkable".
- The *Titan* was 800 feet (244 m), displacing 75,000 tons, described as "the largest craft afloat" and "unsinkable".
- The *Titanic* carried four Engelhardt folding lifeboats and only sixteen conventional lifeboats, less than half the number required for a capacity of 3,000 passengers.
- The *Titan* carried, as written by Robertson, "24 lifeboats – as few as the law allowed', less than half needed for her 3,000 capacity.
- The *Titanic* struck an iceberg on her starboard side when she was moving too fast at just over 22 knots, on the night of 14 April 1912, 400 miles (644 km) off Newfoundland in the North Atlantic.
- The *Titan*, also at night, in April, 400 miles (644 km) off Newfoundland in the North Atlantic, hit an iceberg on the starboard side while travelling at 25 knots.
- *Titanic* sank, and more than half of her 2,200 passengers perished.
- *Titan*, also "indestructible", sank, with the death of half of her 2,500 passengers.

One of the fatalities on the *Titanic* that fateful night was the great pioneering investigative journalist and social campaigner, William Thomas Stead (1849–1912). On various occasions throughout his career he suggested to friends and associates that he would probably die from either hanging or drowning. On 22 March 1886, he published an article in the *Pall Mall Gazette* entitled "How the Mail Steamer Went Down in Mid-Atlantic, by a Survivor", which can still be read at www.attackingthedevil.co.uk. In this story, there is a large loss of life when a steamer collides with another ship, much of the tragedy due to a lack of lifeboats. Stead added a note at the end of his piece: "This is exactly what might take place and will take place if liners are sent to sea short of boats." Six years later, in 1892, Stead published his story "From the Old World to the New" in the December issue of the *Review of Reviews*. This piece features a ship called the *Majestic*, which goes to the aid of another vessel that has hit an iceberg and rescues survivors. Stead was quite a character, and has been called by some "the father of tabloid journalism", and, as we shall see, long after his sorry demise on the great ship, his connection to the *Titanic* endures for other reasons.

These remarkable coincidences would seem to be enough to fire anyone's imagination, but other new, strange mythologies have arisen around the tragedy of the *Titanic*. One is the legend of the Mummy of Amon-Ra.

THE MUMMY TAKES A TRIP

Douglas Murray was an Englishman who is often referred to as an Egyptologist. The story goes that in Luxor, Murray had acquired the mummy of a 1600 BC high-priestess of the Temple of Amon-Ra. She had been buried in a coffin, the lid of which bore her image in gold and enamel. As old-style imperialist Englishmen often did back at the turn of the nineteenth to twentieth centuries, he went hunting up the Nile and the gun he was holding inexplicably exploded in his hand. Shades of the "mummy's curse" were already developing.

Murray was in agony on the boat taking him up the Nile and it was delayed by unusually strong winds. When they finally reached Cairo after a painful ten days, gangrene had set in and his arm had to be amputated. On the voyage home to England, two of his friends died and were buried at sea and, within a year, two of the Egyptians involved in the transportation of the mummy case to the docks also died. In *50 Great Ghost Stories*, edited by John Canning (1988), Frank Usher's contribution, "Ghosts of Ancient Egypt", takes the yarn a stage further:

> When the ship arrived at Tilbury it was found that valuable Egyptian curiosities Murray had bought in Cairo had been stolen. But the mummy-case was there awaiting him. Whatever he had lost, he had not lost that, and he said that when he looked at the carved face of the priestess which was upon it, her eyes seemed to come to life and look at him with a malevolence that turned his blood cold. He promptly gave the fatal mummy-case away to a lady, upon whom disaster

immediately befell. Her mother broke her leg and died after months of prolonged suffering. The lady lost her fiancé, who for no apparent reason declined to marry her. Her pets died and she became ill herself with an un-diagnosable complaint which wasted her away so much that she feared death and instructed her lawyer to make her will.

Her will duly made, she decided it was time that Murray had the accursed mummy case returned to him. But by this time the one-armed adventurer wanted nothing more to do with it, so he presented it to the British Museum. His thinking was that, as an establishment of a more scientific bent, they would be immune from any susceptibility to the paranormal. Apparently he was wrong. When a photographer was commissioned to take pictures of the relic, he died under mysterious circumstances. Those who saw the resulting pictures said that the eyes of the priestess stared back with grim malevolence, and one of the Egyptologists was found dead in his bed. When the museum finally took the mummy case into its collection all manner of strange happenings took place in the Egyptology department. Something akin to poltergeist activity was reported, with stuff flying around and strange noises coming from the gilded coffin.

Now a famous person enters the scene, none other than the legendary occultist, Madame Blavatsky. In the presence of the mummy case she had a fit of the shivers. She was asked, "Can you exorcise this evil spirit?" Her reply was not reassuring.

"There is no such thing as exorcism. Evil remains evil forever. Nothing can be done about it. I implore you to get rid of this evil as soon as possible."

Now the indefatigable William T. Stead arrives. He dismisses all the knocking, banging, wailing and bizarre occurrences at the museum as inconsequential, offers a hefty price for the mummy and after having it removed from the building decides he's going to take it to New York on a brand new White Star liner – the *Titanic*. He was well aware that the mummy had a shifty reputation, and to avert any superstitious controversy arranged for it to be hidden in the ship's hold beneath a new Renault car that was being transported to the United States.

It was not until the fateful night of 14 April, out at sea, that he revealed the story of the mummy and its cursed reputation to his opulent and attentive audience. But the priestess of Amon-Ra had her way with the ship that night, and took Stead with her to the bottom of the Atlantic.

What a great yarn! One might think that the real, prescient writing of Morgan Robertson with all its chilling coincidences was enough to build a lurid psychic superstructure around the sad story of the *Titanic*'s fate. But to the non-questioning and credulous hordes of believers in the unsubstantiated enclaves of the weird and wonderful, the ship had to have a curse, too.

So let's unwrap this mummy.

Was William Stead a passenger on the *Titanic*? Yes. American President Taft had asked Stead to speak at a peace conference. Although Stead was indeed a spiritualist, an investigator into paranormal happenings with a deep interest in mysticism, he was primarily a leading figure in journalism, and probably the most important passenger on board. A tireless social campaigner, his bitter broadside against Victorian child prostitution, "The Maiden Tribute of Modern Babylon", created a national scandal when he described the disgust of being able to procure a thirteen-year-old child prostitute for £5. His fame and influence on journalism and social affairs endure long after his death – just check him out on www.attackingthedevil.co.uk. Yet like most men of his stature and time, he liked to be the centre of attention and loved to tell a good story. The cursed mummy saga, which he and his cod-Egyptologist friend Douglas Murray had cobbled together, was perfect fodder for the well-heeled passengers in the *Titanic*'s luxurious saloon. The dynamic duo had already regaled a bunch of uncritical newspaper hacks with the mummy story following a visit to the Egyptian Room at the British Museum, where they had seen the priestess of Amon-Ra's coffin. The tale would have been received with dumbfounded fascination; this great man, who everyone wanted to hear, must have retired to his cabin on the doomed *Titanic* in fits of suppressed laughter.

To begin with, one of the crucial characters in the mummy saga died of influenza in 1891: the theosophist Helena Blavatsky had been dead for over twenty years before the *Titanic*'s first and final voyage in 1912. Although, of course, her spirit might have been at the museum; anything's possible in the psychic world.

Were there automobiles in the hold of the *Titanic*? According to Cameron's movie, Winslet and DiCaprio enjoy nookie in a Renault. To get to the truth here, one would have to see the cargo logbook, but that went down with the ship. Many researchers have argued that there could have been up to ten cars loaded on board, considering the number of very rich passengers. However, the full list of everything on the ship is in *Titanic: Triumph and Tragedy* (2011) the definitive work by John P. Eaton and Charles Haas. No mummy is included but a car is mentioned – it belonged to a Mr W. E. Carter, a Renault simply listed as "1 case auto". The list also reveals "1 case auto parts" shipped by one G. Prost, but no other cars. Charles Haas just happens to be president of the Titanic Historical Society and has scotched the mummy-on-board *Titanic* tale, saying, "The cargo manifest throws those myths right out the window." But that doesn't stand in the way of the faithful – some will claim the mummy was actually hidden *inside* a car ... that way it might have avoided the cargo manifest.

In the end, that evil priestess of Amon-Ra wasn't content to stay down in the Atlantic, because she's still in the British Museum, where her coffin stands in the Second Egyptian Room, known by its serial number AE 22542. She is, however, known as "the Unlucky Mummy'; a final word on her case is that she is linked to the death of Bertram Fletcher Robinson, a British writer and journalist. During 1904, Robinson worked for the *Daily Express* newspaper and carried out research into the history of the "Unlucky Mummy". He concluded that she had malevolent powers and he died aged thirty-six just three years later from typhoid fever and peritonitis following a visit to Paris.

So are we done with the mummy? Not quite. There is still a tenuous link. Surprisingly enough, there is a weird afterglow here, and into it steps our old spiritualist friend, Sir Arthur Conan Doyle.

Claims had been made that Bertram Fletcher Robinson was poisoned by Conan Doyle to cover up an adulterous affair he had with the journalist's wife and to hide the fact he had stolen the plot of *The Hound of the Baskervilles* from him. In 2008,

Rodger Garrick-Steele, a former driving instructor, wanted to exhume Fletcher Robinson's corpse from its place of rest at Ipplepen near Newton Abbot and test it for traces of poison. The Church refused his request. Sir Andrew McFarlane, the chancellor of the ecclesiastical court, ridiculed Garrick-Steele's research and branded the historian as "totally unreliable". This leaves one with an odd thought: had Sherlock Holmes investigated this, no doubt he'd prove the poisoning. But Conan Doyle's predilections would have led him to one conclusion – the mummy did it!

TRIANGLES IN THE FOG: BERMUDA, RHUBARB AND THE GREAT LAKES

Located in West Yorkshire, England between Wakefield, Morley and Rothwell, the Rhubarb Triangle is a nine-square-mile (23 km²) triangle famous for producing early forced rhubarb. Other notable rhubarb focal points in the triangle are East Ardsley, Stanley, Kirkhamgate, Lofthouse and Carlton. Sadly, as lovers of a good crumble or rhubarb tart will attest, the Rhubarb Triangle has diminished rapidly since 1939. Back then, the expanding rhubarb industry was at its tasty zenith, encompassing a thirty-square-mile (78 km²) area between Leeds, Bradford and Wakefield. The forcing sheds of West Yorkshire once produced 90 per cent of the world's winter forced rhubarb, which is a native of Siberia. In February 2010, "Yorkshire Forced Rhubarb" was awarded Protected Designation of Origin (PDO) status by the European Commission's Protected Food Name scheme.

Swiss-Russian physician, botanist, Central Asia researcher and archaeologist Johann Albert Regel (1845–1909) proposed in 1884 that a fermented wine made of rhubarb stalks may have been the elusive drink, soma, once made by Indo-Iranian peoples dating back at least 4,000 years. Certain Zoroastrian and Hindu branches were known to have used the drink in their religious practices to gain divine insight. Apparently, however, rhubarb has no known psychoactive effects on humans, but it did get us through the Second World War, and its acidic fruitiness might give us the divine insight we need for the following tales.

Before the American writer Vincent Gaddis (1913–97) coined the term "Bermuda Triangle", that area of ocean was arguably just another region of the seven seas where ships vanished, albeit with a higher frequency. Then along came Charles Berlitz's bestseller, *The Bermuda Triangle* (1974), and now we have volumes of "triangle lore". As is the case following Watergate, where any uncovered scandal is immediately suffixed "gate", anywhere else on the globe where a dozen or so unexplained things happen is transformed into a "triangle". It's a buzzword.

There's even a Lake Michigan Triangle. The website zmescience.com provided this odd bit of news on 25 May 2011: "While scanning underneath the waters of Lake Michigan for shipwrecks, archaeologists using sonar techniques found something a lot more interesting than the sunken cars and old boats they bargained for, as they discovered a boulder with a prehistoric carving of a mastodon, as well as a series of stones arranged in a Stonehenge-like manner." Labyrinthina.com has a peculiar story from Kathy Doore covering the same area of mystery, which was taken up by William "Boldly Go" Shatner in his History Channel show *Weird or What* episode, "Lake Michigan Triangle", in October 2011.

In 1978, Kathy, an experienced sailor on Lake Michigan, was part of a skilled team who used three classic wooden sailing boats. They competed against each other and practised their navigation several times a week. She set sail one warm summer night and her crew's boat was suddenly swallowed up in a dense fog. As the boats couldn't see each other, they all became worried about a possible collision, and the wind was behaving in a peculiar manner, seeming to blow in two directions. It was all very strange, yet the water was calm. Then what had been a balmy summer evening turned so cold that Kathy was freezing. The boat was moving on, and she wondered if her crew were as cold as she was, but when she turned to speak to them, they had gone. Peering through the fog she found them all gathered on the after deck and not where they'd been moments before, alongside her in the cockpit. They indicated that it was warmer at the after end of the boat and, showing some concern, beseeched her to join them. She was amazed to discover that no one was steering the boat, yet it was steadily moving ahead. The skipper said he'd not been steering for ten minutes.

Kathy then reports: "Draped in dense fog, the vessel began a curious, aquatic dance. Slowly, but deliberately, she turned on her axis completing three, perfect, 360-degree pirouettes, without ever crossing the wind."

Then the mystery fog lifted, and the other two boats came into view. Both were performing the identical manoeuvre. Eventually they pulled out of this vortex and the three boats began to head back to port in the moonlight, across a flat calm sea. The lead boat of the three reached the anchorage, but when Kathy looked around, the third boat was missing. They scanned the horizon yet there was no sign of a mast or sail, so Kathy's boat set off again into the lake to find the missing craft. Minutes later, they headed back, only to discover that the missing boat was tied up with sails stowed, and the crew were rowing ashore. Kathy maintains that this was impossible in such a short time. There was something odd when she looked at her watch, and later she realized that she and her friends couldn't account for a large part of that evening. There seemed to be three hours amiss somewhere. Days later, none of the rest of the sailors wanted to talk about that night and acted as if the strange events had not taken place.

"I've come to realize," she says, "that the events of that night may very well have been for my benefit alone."

This bears all the hallmarks of the classic "time slip" often reported by abductees in UFO cases.

Such experiences are hard to categorize. Their strangeness is representative of certain locations that often possess their own pall of weirdness. I have had similar feelings in the primeval forest of Brocéliande in Brittany, with its dark, deep lakes and the legendary and atmospheric Valley of No Return, a gateway to so many legends; Morgan le Fay, Merlin, King Arthur – you need to go there on a bright, sunlit day and not alone. It's that kind of place.

Jay Gourley's book *The Great Lakes Triangle* (1977) is a chronicle of the mysterious appearances and disappearances of boats and aeroplanes in the region, similar to accounts recalled in *The Bermuda Triangle*. I have sailed on Lake Ontario, and when we in Britain think of lakes we have a picture postcard image of the verdant Lake District. But the lakes of North

America and Canada are huge; they are more like inland seas. Lake Superior, for example, with an area covering 49,300 square miles (127,700 km²) is the largest of the five Great Lakes of North America. It is bounded to the north by the Canadian province of Ontario and the US state of Minnesota, and to the south by the US states of Wisconsin and Michigan. It is the largest freshwater lake in the world by surface area. Over the years numerous ships and planes – and people – have vanished in the lakes.

According to a report dated 29 April 1937 in the *Cleveland Press*, the strangest and most repeated case is that of the Captain of Great Lakes freighter *McFarland*, George R. Donner. On the night of 28 April 1937, as his ship was making her way due west through the lakes from Erie, Pennsylvania, with a cargo of 9,800 tons of coal, Captain Donner decided to bed down in his cabin. Because of the late-spring ice floes, the voyage was a slow one, but she was steadily making headway towards her destination, Port Washington, Wisconsin. Captain Donner had given his crew instructions to wake him as the ship drew near to port. Three hours later, they were approaching Port Washington, so the Second Mate went to the Captain's cabin to wake him. After knocking on the door, there was no reply. Eventually, when they got the door open, it was discovered that it had been locked from the inside; but the Captain was gone. The ship was searched from stem to stern but they never found him. At the time of Donner's disappearance, the *McFarland* was 30 miles (48 km) northwest of Ludington, Michigan; Ludington is reputed to be the nexus of the Lake Michigan Triangle.

Another disappearance took place in the "Michigan Triangle" on 23 June 1950, and involved Flight 2501 of Northwest Airlines. This DC-4 aircraft with fifty-five passengers and three crew took off from New York City and was due to land at Minneapolis. The last radio contact recorded with the plane was that it was 3,500 feet (1,100 m) over Battle Creek, Michigan. The message indicated that due to bad weather near Chicago, the plane was changing course to a northwesterly path over Lake Michigan. Then the airwaves went dead. No wreckage was recovered, although human body fragments and some light debris were found floating, but divers have never found the plane's wreckage.

Luann Grosscup, writing in the *Chicago Tribune* on 21 October 2007, suggests that:

> According to parapsychologists, a line of energy circles the globe and seems to be a breeding ground for mystical phenomenon. Chicago, according to author and historian Ursula Bielski, is one point on that line. Bielski, and her husband, author and journalist David Cowan, own and operate Chicago Hauntings, and have noted that planes, trains and automobiles have generated a number of interesting stories. "The whole lake is full of ghost stories," said Bielski. "There is a triangle in Lake Michigan that is similar to the Bermuda Triangle, where there are repeated episodes of planes and boats disappearing and sometimes reappearing. People report seeing ghost ships, and boaters have picked up people from the water who say their ship sunk, and then the people disappear."

Frederick Stonehouse, author of *Haunted Lake Michigan* (2006), mentions other aircraft ghosts. Across from Chicago's Calvary Cemetery, the burial ground of so many famous senators, baseball stars and Civil War heroes, hundreds of people have reported seeing the ghost of "Seaweed Charlie". This spectre is thought to be that of Herbert Brown, a naval aviator whose plane crashed in the lake during training exercises in 1943. They found his plane but not his body. Reports have his ghost climbing out of the lake and over the rocks, his soaked flight suit covered in weeds and dripping as he drags himself across the road to the gates of the cemetery, where he disappears.

North of the "Seaweed Charlie" location is the site on the lake where, in 1860, the *Lady Elgin* sank in 1860. She was the most luxurious steamer on the lakes, built in 1851 in Buffalo, New York, at a cost of $95,000. She was named after the wife of Lord Elgin, Canada's Governor General from 1847 to 1854. The ship was returning to Milwaukee, carrying supporters of Lincoln's opponent Stephen Douglas home from a presidential rally in Chicago. It was stormy and a schooner, the *Augusta*, rammed the *Lady Elgin*, holing her below the waterline. Some 300 people died. This tragedy remains the greatest loss of life in one event on the Great Lakes.

Students at Northwestern University on Clark Street, Evanston, Chicago, have reported seeing people rising from the nearby lake, saying that their boat sank and asking for help. Still, we all know what students are like.

There is an added poignancy to some of these Great Lakes stories. Between the end of the Civil War and the beginning of the First World War, Lake Michigan was home to over sixty vessels that were used to carry Christmas trees to Chicago and Milwaukee. In the mid-1880s, the Schuenemann brothers, August and Herman, moved to Chicago. They were sailors and merchants, and 60 per cent of their income came from the transport and sale of Christmas trees. Older brother August died in November 1898 when his schooner S. *Thal* sank in a storm near Glencoe, Illinois. Herman carried on the business. He became known as "Captain Santa" as he plied his trade down on the dock near Chicago's Clark Street Bridge. His billboard read: "Christmas Tree Ship: My Prices are the Lowest." His ship's masts and spars were festooned with the new electric Christmas lights. The mainmast was crowned with a tree, a cheery sight in the icy breeze high above the deck. Mrs Barbara Schuenemann, with their three daughters, also made and sold wreaths, garlands and other seasonal greenery. You could buy a tree for between 50 cents and $1. Captain Schuenemann's schooner, the *Rouse Simmons* was also his last command. On 23 November 1912, she sank with the loss of all hands in a winter storm in Lake Michigan. The *Rouse Simmons* will be forever known as the Christmas Tree ship, and she has become a sad Great Lakes version of the *Flying Dutchman*. Over the years, Great Lakes sailors have reported seeing her ghostly image on moonlit nights, her tattered sails wildly flapping about as if in a gale. As with the *Dutchman*, one moment she is there and the next she has vanished.

In 1924, a wallet belonging to Captain Schuenemann, wrapped in oilskin, was discovered in a fishing trawler's net. Then in 1971, the wreck of the *Rouse Simmons* was discovered by scuba-diver Gordon Kent Bellrichard off Two Rivers, Wisconsin, 172 feet (52.4 m) below the surface of Lake Michigan. Many of the trees that never made it into Chicago's cosy Yuletide parlours were still in the ship's hold. Yet as well as being remembered as a ghost, Captain Schuenemann's charitable tradition of donating trees to needy families continues in his memory. Chicago's Christmas Ship lives on in a scheme that has distributed over 12,000 trees to the less fortunate in the past decade.

VILE VORTICES

The Bermuda Triangle's catalogue of strange events and disappearances has been repeated in various books over and over again. Ships disappearing cannot always be regarded as inexplicable occurrences simply because no wreckage is found, but there is certainly something odd going on. There may be something in the notion raised by some parapsychologists that there are twelve "vile vortices" around the world where things and people have a tendency to disappear. This theory was originated by the writer on the unexplained Ivan Sanderson (1911–73), who asserted that these points are situated along particular lines of latitude. Whether or not they are "vile" will no doubt depend on what might befall us if they swallow us up. So the following are places to avoid when planning your next vacation ...

There are five of these areas in the northern hemisphere. These include the Bermuda Triangle; the Algerian megalithic ruins (south of Timbuktu); Mohenjo-daro ("Mound of the Dead"), an ancient city of the Indus Valley civilization, a supposedly highly radioactive location in Sindh, Pakistan; the Devil's Sea or Dragon Triangle, near Iwo Jima, Japan; and Hamakulia, near Hawaii, a site of heavy volcanic activity, where some ships and planes have disappeared in the past. All five of these vortices fall almost in a line close to the Tropic of Cancer.

There are also five vortices in the southern hemisphere, and these follow the line of the Tropic of Capricorn. They are all sites of ancient cultures and megalithic structures, including Easter Island; Sarawak in Borneo; the ruined city of Nan Madol on Pohnpei Island in the South Pacific; an area of Gabon/

Zimbabwe; and an important site of the Incan culture in South America.

There are two more claimed to exist at the North and South Poles.

These "vortex" areas are said to be the main centres for strange events, disappearances, etc. Some parapsychologists believe that the vortices are linked to something called "subtle matter energy", or those old favourites, ley lines, or something even more inexplicable, which they've dubbed "electromagnetic aberration".

But fear not: if vile vortices are not your cup of tea, there are also supposedly rather kinder, positive vortices that emit healing energy. These include that old focus of paranormal energy, Egypt, and the Great Pyramids at Giza. Further east we have the centre for Tibetan enlightenment, the Himalayas, northeast of Lhasa, Tibet. In the United States there is an area between Sedona in Arizona and Sonora in New Mexico, home to the Hopi and Taqui peoples. All of which could make for a more comfortable holiday experience.

DON'T BELIEVE THE HYPE

Paul Begg is a noted British researcher, writer and author. His major credits include *Jack the Ripper: The Uncensored Facts* and the co-authored *The Jack the Ripper A to Z*, now in its third edition. Begg wrote a series of articles for *Unexplained* magazine, where he criticized the methodology of writers on the subject of unexplained disappearances in so-called vortices. He examined some of the original reports in detail. When it came to ships that it was claimed had "mysteriously disappeared", he often found that the reasons behind their loss were quite ordinary. Some losses were easily explained by storms, but correspondents in the vortex theory, with a literary axe to grind, would claim that the weather was fine at the time, and if it added an extra patina of strangeness, locations of sinkings were adjusted to fit the location of the vortex. In order to keep the weirdness factor at full tilt, stories are often hyped up and adjusted to suit the tastes of the faithful. A case in point is the case of the SS *Raifuku Maru*, cited as a prominent chapter of the Bermuda Triangle mystery.

She was a Japanese freighter that allegedly "vanished" en route from Boston to Hamburg, Germany, in 1925. She had a crew of thirty-eight and was carrying a cargo of wheat. In the creepy version of this yarn, on 21 April 1925 the White Star Line vessel RMS *Homeric* received a cryptic SOS in broken English from the *Raifuku Maru*, which read, "Danger like a dagger now! Come quick!" The *Homeric* is reported to have sailed to the location of the SOS, but there was no trace of the stricken freighter. Of course, the use of the word "dagger" drove the psychic community into paroxysms of speculation – it has all the sinister overtones you might expect from what were regarded back then as "inscrutable Orientals". This must have been a UFO or a waterspout, maybe some towering sea monster. I first read this in Vincent Gaddis's *Invisible Horizons* and it had been regarded as a genuine maritime mystery for decades. However, if one checks the story out with a little extra care and attention, you will find that the message received had no "dagger" in it; it read "Now very danger – come quick." When the ship left Boston on 18 April she was already ploughing through a terrific storm. Not only the *Homeric*, but the British vessel *King Alexander* attempted to reach the *Raifuku Maru*, but neither could get close enough due to mountainous seas and were unable to rescue any crew. The Japanese freighter was listing at a thirty-degree angle, and the *Homeric*'s crew watched helplessly as she went down with all hands, and then sent a message to the Camperdown Coast Guard station which read: "Observed steamer *Raifuku Maru* sink in latitude 4143N longitude 6139W regret unable to save any lives." No bodies or survivors, despite attempts to find any, were found.

The sea does this frequently; sometimes souls are allowed to float, sometimes they sink. You can't argue with the ocean; it does things its own way. Both Gaddis and later Charles Berlitz blatantly peddled the myth of the vessel's "mysterious" sinking, and it soon shared a berth with the *Mary Celeste* and the *Carroll A. Deering*, a five-masted commercial schooner. She was found crewless and, after drifting, ran aground off Cape Hatteras, North Carolina, in 1921. She's a prominent nautical conundrum, and a favourite victim of the Bermuda Triangle. We must not mention the possibility of a mutiny or some form of piracy. The aliens got the crew and that's that.

And lest we forget: Flight 19. The sad tragedy of these missing planes forms the very foundation of Bermuda Triangle lore. Five TBM Avenger torpedo bombers disappeared on 5 December 1945 during a United States Navy training flight from Fort Lauderdale, Florida. All fourteen airmen on the flight were lost (although we were reunited with them when they emerged from the Mother ship in Spielberg's *Close Encounters*). As if this loss of life wasn't bad enough, thirteen crew members of a PBM

Mariner flying boat that was sent out to search for the flight were all killed. It is assumed that their plane exploded in midair. The loss of Flight 19 has never really been adequately solved. It is a strange story; some suggest the aircraft may have become disoriented and ditched in rough seas after running out of fuel. Subsequent expeditions to find and identify wreckage have not been successful.

Some years ago I reviewed a new book on the Bermuda Triangle, *The Fog: A Never before Published Theory of the Bermuda Triangle Phenomenon* by Rob McGregor and Bruce Gernon (2005), for the *Fortean Times* magazine. In retrospect, I was a bit savage and curt, and as science lurches forward via astrophysics into even more bizarre enlightenments, I wonder if I was wrong to be so dismissive. The following is an edited version of my review.

Whatever it was that happened to Bruce Gernon, the co-author of this book, in December 1970, was indeed strange. Gernon's story, of how he took off in his sturdy new Bonanza A36 plane from Andros Island in the Caribbean, is the central pillar of this book around which the theory of "The Fog" has been constructed.

A huge, semi-circular cloud formation which seemed to have a mind of its own required all manner of navigational quick thinking. Eventually the plane was encased by a cloud "tunnel", the interior of which was illuminated by flashes of light. During this bizarre experience Gernon experienced weightlessness, and that standard curse of all Triangle stories, a haywire compass. At one point, having managed to contact Miami Air Traffic Control, the controller told him that there were no planes in that sector on his radar – yet the Bonanza should have shown up. Upon exiting from the tunnel Gernon and his two passengers estimated they had been travelling for almost 32 minutes. Yet there was something wrong; they seemed to have experienced some kind of "time slip". After 47 minutes things became weirder. The trip from Palm Beach to Andros usually took at least 75 minutes; on this particular flight the distance travelled was an estimated 250 miles. The Bonanza's maximum cruising speed was 195 miles per hour

– so how had they managed to travel 250 miles in 47 minutes? Being envious of that wily old fox who made a million out of triangular tosh, Charles Berlitz, I have to note that in this book he enjoys too much uncritical reverence. It's hard to forget Berlitz's other dubious cause célèbre, the so-called "Philadelphia Experiment". In an effort to provide some background on the potential science behind the idea of an electromagnetic fog, the "disappearing destroyer" gets an airing here, tagged on to what appears to be a fanciful outing into the weird world of electromagnetic pioneer Nikola Tesla (1856–1943):

"His equipment, which included Tesla coils, RF generators and van der Graaf generators, was jammed into a small room in his (Tesla's) apartment. He turned on all the devices … he felt a nudge against his shoulder. He turned to see a small piece of metal floating in the air … he began levitating pieces of wood, Styrofoam, plastic, copper and zinc … heavy objects began levitating, including a sixty-pound cannon ball."

If Electrical pioneer Tesla was levitating Styrofoam, then he would have been very old or very dead. He died in 1943 aged eighty-seven. Although polystyrene existed in the 1930s, Styrofoam wasn't brought on to the US market by Dow Chemicals until 1954. The van der Graaf generator was the brainchild of Robert Jemison van der Graaf (1901–1967). If Tesla had several of these in his apartment then he must have had a lounge the size of a Zeppelin hangar. The first van der Graaf generator which was constructed in 1931 did indeed require a disused dirigible dock because it was so huge – like Tesla's electricity bill.

In retrospect I was being sceptical and hostile. McGregor and Gernon have to be applauded for at least offering something new. The theory is that there is a mysterious electronic fog that has weird properties and can affect time, space and the environment. It could be a natural phenomenon or, as the authors suggest, a product of America's naval underwater equivalent to Area 51, AUTEC (Atlantic Underwater Test and Evaluation Centre). The sections of the book that deal with the speculative fog theory are intriguing and interesting. It's the padding that lets things down: Flight 19, the UK's Rendlesham Forest UFO, M. K. Jessup, Atlantis, various UFO scenarios – and the obligatory list of vessels lost in the Triangle since 1948. Had this book come out in the 1970s, when von Däniken was making it big, then the authors could have ordered the champagne. Those days are gone, but at the core of their work, if Gernon's experience was exactly as told in the book, then perhaps the idea of the vortexes may not be as wild as it looks.

That said, between 1960 and 1963 I steered an old tramp steamer through the Triangle no fewer than four times. The oddest thing I saw was a one-legged seagull. We need romantic mystery, that vague desire for "something else" – either good or evil – "out there", controlling us. The Bermuda Triangle fits the bill to perfection. Yet I'd prefer to go along with Lloyd's of London – their official take on the Triangle is that it is statistically no more dangerous a part of the seven seas than any other. Then again, maybe I'm fogging the issue ... missing planes, vanishing people, disappearing ships. In the case of the latter, though, as I have discovered to my cost, sometimes no record of the ship even existing in the first place has been found.

Dead Horses in the Doldrums

Since the time of Columbus, for over three centuries, the name "Sargasso Sea" was synonymous with mariners all over the world with the bad luck of being becalmed. This was said to be a strange area, 700 miles (1,127 km) wide by 2,000 miles (3,219 km) long in the mid-Atlantic, clogged with a choking mass of seaweed. Scary tales were told of ships that had been eternally becalmed in an area about 20°N and 35 °N and 30 °W and 70 °W.

Long before anyone named the Bermuda Triangle there were legends among sailors of a "sea of lost ships". The Sargasso Sea is actually a thin lens of warm water perched on top of much colder water. Portuguese sailors in the fifteenth century named the region after the sargassum seaweed growing there. However, the sea may have been known much earlier to the fifth-century BC Carthaginian explorer Himilco the Navigator. Himilco's written record has vanished, but Rufus Festus Avienus, the fourth-century AD writer, mentions Himilco's report of an area of the Atlantic matted with seaweed, and Christopher Columbus and his men were also familiar with the Sargasso Sea. Since the Middle Ages, this has been known as an area where crewless derelicts have often been found. Sargasso Sea drifters are usually in good condition but unmanned; their crews are missing. There is a report of a slave ship drifting there, but when boarded all that was discovered were the skeletons of the slaves and the crew. Built in 1838 the 222-ton wooden ship the *Rosalie* sailed through the area. In 1840 she was found drifting and deserted but in shipshape condition near the Bahamas.

The areas close to the equator became known as the doldrums because of the stillness of the air. But the ships traversing the Sargasso Sea had another name for the regions: the Horse Latitudes. On their voyages of conquest across the Atlantic the Spanish transported horses by ship to their colonies in the West Indies and Americas. Often becalmed in mid-ocean in this latitude, the voyage slowed to a halt. When freshwater had to be rationed, the first on board to suffer were the horses. The poor animals would either be thrown overboard or eaten.

There are extensive records, which have been kept over the past 200 years, of vessels that have vanished in the Bermuda Triangle. You can find a long list of these right up into the twenty-first century at www.bermuda-triangle.com. For example, between 1780 and 1824, the US Navy listed the following vessels as missing in the region: *General Gates*, *Hornet*, *Insurgent*, *Pickering*, *Wasp*, *Wildcat* and *Expervier*. As the *Expervier* was carrying a peace proposal, her vanishing was responsible for prolonging the war of 1812 between Britain and America. In 1944 Rupert T. Gould, a retired British naval officer who collected many stories about mysteries of the sea, revealed the story of the *Ellen Austin*. As Gould is the only original source for this, it remains as an embroidered tapestry that will always be unpicked and rewoven. Charles Berlitz, for example, in his *Bermuda Triangle*, bolts on all manner of extra details to the yarn and one can only surmise that they are fiction. The *Ellen Austin*, 1,812 tons, 210 feet (64 m) in length and built in Maine in 1854, was one of Grinnell, Minturn

& Company's Blue Swallowtail line of Liverpool to New York packets. In 1881 she came across a deserted schooner (the name of the drifter seems to have escaped history) just north of the Sargasso Sea. The *Ellen Austin*'s skipper sent a prize crew on to the deserted vessel with instructions to sail the abandoned ship back in tandem with them to London, where she would no doubt have provided quite a bonus. A squall blew up and the two ships were parted. (Berlitz even tells us that a second prize crew were sent on board.) When the weather cleared, the schooner had disappeared, the prize crew with her. Neither men nor ship were ever found.

The most famous twentieth-century disappearance is undoubtedly the massive USS *Cyclops*, which vanished in March 1918. At 19,360 tons and 542 feet (165.2 m) long, she carried coal to Brazilian waters to fuel British ships in the South Atlantic, after originally being assigned to the Naval Overseas Transportation Service. She put to sea from Rio de Janeiro on 16 February 1918 and after touching at Barbados on 3–4 March, was never heard from again. Her loss with all 306 crew and passengers, without a trace, remains one of the US Navy's greatest unsolved mysteries.

Inter-island freighter *Jamanic K* disappeared in 1995, near the Bahamas. Another small freighter, *Genesis* went missing in 1999. Although the number of remaining mysteries outnumber the solutions in the Bermuda Triangle, it always pays to follow some stories through. A case in point is the celebrated story of the barque *James B. Chester*.

Southwest of the Azores on 28 February 1855, the merchant vessel *Marathon* came across the *James B. Chester*, which was on an erratic course, as if no one were steering her. The *Marathon* hailed her several times, with no response, so the mate was sent over with a boarding party. She was deserted without a soul on board. It looked as if the crew had made their exit in a hurry, because cabins were ransacked, furniture was in disarray, and clothing and books were scattered around. As with the *Mary Celeste*, the ship's papers were missing and her compass had gone. However, the provisions were still on board, as was her valuable cargo of wool, so the *Marathon*'s skipper put a prize crew on board and they managed to sail the *James B. Chester* to

Liverpool, where she was tied up in the port's Albert Dock to become a ghoulish tourist attraction.

Speculation was rife. Pirates? But there were no bloodstains anywhere. Had the crew mutinied and looted the vessel? If so, why abandon the ship and her valuable cargo in mid-ocean? The old standby "a giant octopus" was mooted while later generations of paranormalists suggested that the Atlantans or a UFO took them; yet no one could offer a valid solution. One of her boats was apparently missing – had some unknown terror driven the men to abandon her? Thus the *James B. Chester* entered the creepy chronicles of Bermuda Triangle lore.

But there's always a sceptical party-pooper to ruin a mystery. In an age before the internet, fax machines and easy international phone calls, before radio and TV, once an inexplicable story settled down it usually remained intact and took on mythical proportions. The answer to the puzzle of the *James B. Chester* lies in the archives of the *New York Times*. A series of reports give a revealing timetable of events.

The news that the *Marathon* had discovered the abandoned *Chester* reached New York on 3 April. Her cargo was valued at $150,000. For some odd reason, the story is that someone tried to bore holes in the ship's hull. Not one, but two of her three boats were missing. It is believed that the crew murdered the Captain and fled. Another article on the same page reports that the crew of the "*James Cheston*" (she has since been erroneously named by some writers as such – it's the *New York Times*'s fault!) were picked up by the Dutch vessel *Two Friends* on 15 March. On 6 April, it's reported that the *Chester's* owners are notified that her master, Captain White, had landed in Wilmington, Delaware.

Then we learn that on 10 April, in Savannah, eight members of the *Chester's* crew had come ashore from the Dutch ship *Two Friends* on 7 April, where they were arrested for murder. On 11 April two of the *Chester's* crew testify that the Captain was sick, he had bored holes into the hull with the mates, offering hush money to the rest of the crew. There had been a claim that there was seven foot (2.1 m) of water in the hold, but a sailor revealed that there was just one foot (0.3 m) of water. Captain White of the *Chester* arrived in Boston and asserted that the crew abandoned the ship because she was in danger of sinking. He denied any knowledge of drilling the holes in the hull.

On 12 April, the *James B. Chester*'s mates Chason and Packwood were arrested along with Captain White for barratry, the legal term for the unlawful breach of duty on the part of a ship's master or crew resulting in injury to the ship's owner. Six crew members testified that there was only one foot of water in the hold and that nothing else was wrong with the ship. There's a veiled suggestion in the *New York Times* that rum may have been to blame for the whole affair. The case sailed on. 13 April: As there was only one foot of water in the hold, the two mates accused the Captain of unnecessarily abandoning the ship, because she was still seaworthy. One sailor referred to the voyage as a "Bacchanalian frolic". I've been on a few of those. What became of the miscreants after this is not known, but no doubt jail terms were in order. I am indebted to the truly wonderful www.bermudatrianglecentral.com for this and other fascinating expositions.

FO'C'SLE FRIGHTENERS

It was whilst serving on board my second ship in the Merchant Navy in 1959 that I became aware of the fact that, just like haunted houses ashore, ships could be equally unsettling. I also realized that sailors were among some of the most superstitious workers. Some would spit into the sea as we left port – that was good luck, as was tossing a coin into the water when coming aboard. A woman on board was deemed unlucky; you never mentioned rabbits or pigs, didn't have flowers on board, never cut your hair or nails whilst at sea or mentioned the word "drowned". I also later learned that in Horatio Nelson's time, children were sometimes born on a warship's gun deck – hence the saying "son of a gun" – although that seemed to cancel out the "woman on board" phobia. We frequently smuggled adventurous females on board around the coast of New Zealand, and as long as the skipper never knew, they were a lot of fun as opposed to bad luck.

As a sixteen-year-old catering boy on board the Ellerman's Wilson Line vessel, the *Borodino*, I enjoyed almost six months voyaging between Hull and Denmark. Ships like the *Borodino* were much sought after by married sailors. They were known as "ten day boats". We would sail for Denmark on Friday night, arrive in Copenhagen on Sunday night, remain there until Tuesday, then sail to Odense, and on Friday load up in Aarhus; we'd arrive back in Hull on the early tide on Monday morning. After docking, we were allowed home on leave until rejoining the vessel on Friday night. It was like having a four-day holiday every ten days. However, sometimes the sailing schedule changed slightly, and on occasion it might be easier to spend a night on board in dock, prior to sailing. The *Borodino* wasn't an old ship. She'd been built in 1950 by the Ailsa Shipbuilding Company in Troon. Although primarily a cargo vessel she offered a luxurious lifestyle for twelve passengers.

One night, to avoid having to catch an early bus to the Albert Dock the next morning, I decided to sleep on board. There was a nightwatchman on board and, out of a crew of over thirty, only about three or four of us bedded down, with the rest due on board by 7 a.m. It was a cold November night, and I'd settled down in my bunk with a mug of cocoa and the latest Hank Janson book. Then I heard a piercing scream along the alleyway. I knew that the only other person on that deck level that night was a junior steward. Shocked by this, I dashed to his cabin, and discovered him standing naked and trembling in the open doorway.

"He came ..." he mumbled. "It was Percy – there was this knock on the door and ... and he was just *floating* there ... no legs ... *horrible* – then he just *vanished*!" I tried to console him or discover more about his experience, but he busied himself getting dressed, then packed his bag and left the ship. I never saw him again. The next morning in the mess room, I told the story to the crew, expecting to be pilloried. Who was this "Percy"? Yet they simply accepted the story. They'd all known about this grisly spectre and seemed used to it. The story went that on the vessel's maiden voyage, an engineer called Percy MacDonald had suffered a terrible accident in the engine room, which had cost him both his legs. To the crew, the possibility of his wraith still haunting the ship was quite normal. It was not so for me. Two trips later I signed off the *Borodino* and I never saw the phantom myself, but legless Percy's weird story wouldn't be the last I'd hear out at sea.

There are fewer oceanic ghosts than those on dry land for the obvious reason that land is more densely populated than the oceans. Nautical apparitions are probably more memorable because of their sparser frequency. When off watch at nights at sea, I listened to tales told by men who were still of that generation who had suffered terribly during the Second World War. The chances of death in the Atlantic or Arctic convoys were high, but their knowledge of sea-lore stretched back much further than that. Their tales were not exclusively of ghosts, yet they were often inexplicable and macabre. A couple which stayed with me came from the days of sail.

THE *OCTAVIUS*

When I first heard this story on a voyage along the Canadian coast in the winter of 1961 the name of the vessel wasn't mentioned. It was one of those yarns spun at sea over a beer in the mess room on cold dark nights. It matched the terrain; icy, cruel winds and snowy, desolate shores. However, in 1965 I came across a book by the late Vincent Gaddis, the American author who coined the phrase "Bermuda Triangle". The book, *Invisible Horizons* (1965), was amazing at the time because it contained some of the weird stories I'd heard at sea, as well as a whole lot more. Sadly, however, as with many works covering the unexplained in the 1960s and 1970s, which would culminate with an avalanche of "was God an astronaut?", ancient technology and alien intelligence tomes, a balanced attitude to more thorough research, citation and reference, along with any hint of scepticism, were often surrendered in exchange for drop-jawed wonder – the staple fodder of the credulous. Vincent Gaddis inserted dialogue into his historical narratives, which he could not possibly verify; for example, he has an eighteenth-century Captain declaring, "She'll pass us within a couple of hundred yards ... we'll hail her," and other conversational exchanges, such as, "Lower the lifeboat – we'll board her" and "an uneasy murmur spread among the crew" with sailors proclaiming, "It's a ghost, there's a curse on it ..." These melodramatic embellishments end up sullying the scant few "facts" there are in already mystifying cases. He could never have known what was said on these ships and in today's forensic literary landscape he'd be keel-hauled for such tinkering.

None of this criticism, however, can spoil the sheer entertainment of a spooky yarn, and no one could dig out these nautical nuggets better than Vincent Gaddis. Misty mythologist or not, like Charles Fort he opened the door to other potential dimensions, and we're still peering into the darkness. Don your sou'wester; we're going to sea.

The merchant sailing vessel the *Octavius* seems as much a phantom on the page as she was when she made her brief appearance back in the eighteenth century. What information there is comes from various scattered versions of the story in numerous books on the sea. The first version of this story appeared in the February 1953 edition of *Fate* magazine. Gaddis bases much of his retelling of the tale on a piece in *Sea Stories* magazine, summer 1964, by a Captain Dod Osborne RNR. The *Octavius* is reported to have left England on a voyage to China on 10 September 1761, and successfully reached her destination the following year. Her Captain must have been something of a foolhardy adventurer for his time, because he appears to have risked a homeward voyage through the then unconquered and hazardous Northwest Passage, a route from the Pacific to the Atlantic through the Arctic from Alaska to Greenland, which would not be fully navigated until the first successful route was discovered by Roald Amundsen, who made the voyage in 1903–6. The *Octavius* left China in 1762 and vanished. She never arrived back in Britain.

Thirteen years later, on 11 October 1775, Captain Warren of the whaler *Herald*, making its way through the icebergs along the Greenland coast in a heavy snowstorm, heard his lookout call out that a ship was visible to the west. The vessel sighted was between several icebergs, and as it drifted towards the *Herald*, the crew could see that all her spars and rigging were heavily encrusted with thick ice. Warren scanned the vessel through his telescope, but could see no sign of life. She drew closer, and the crew began hailing the mystery ship, but there was no response. Warren selected eight men and lowered a longboat for a boarding party. As they rowed closer they could just make out the name of the vessel on her stern: *Octavius*.

The crew no doubt had difficulty clambering on board and, in a superstitious age, this must have been a highly unpleasant

mission. They set about clearing snow drifts from her deck.
Then they wrenched open the door to the fo'c'sle and cau-
tiously entered. There, still fully clothed, swathed in stiff blankets in their bunks, were the preserved, frozen bodies of
twenty-eight men. The horrified crew from the *Herald* went
back on deck and followed Warren aft to the Captain's cabin.
Once inside, another terrible tableau was revealed. They found
the rigid body of the *Octavius*'s Captain at a table, slumped in
his chair. A pen lay just beyond the fingers of his right hand,
and a thin green mould had spread over his face, covering his
eyes. Covered in blankets on a nearby bunk was the perfectly
preserved body of a woman, her eyes open. (Gaddis writes
somewhat fancifully that "her head was resting on her elbow
and it appeared as if she had been watching some activity when
she died".) Warren followed the frozen woman's line of sight
and saw the body of a slouched man sitting cross-legged on the
cabin deck, a pile of wood chippings and a flint at his feet.
Under a nearby reefer jacket they found the brittle, preserved
body of a small boy.

After Captain Warren had retrieved the *Octavius*'s logbook,
his crew appear to have panicked, which seems hardly surprising. Any idea of searching the vessel further was turned down.
There was nothing to do but to get back to the *Herald* as soon as
possible. They eagerly clambered into the longboat. Most of the
frozen pages in the log slipped from their fragile binding into the
icy sea, leaving only the first and the last few pages. The ship's
last recorded position was 75 °N 160 °W.

The final entry in the log reads:

November 11 1762: We have now been enclosed in the ice
seventeen days ... The fire went out yesterday, and our
Master has been trying to rekindle it again but without
success. He has handed the steel and flint to the mate. The
Master's son died this morning and his wife says she no longer
feels the terrible cold. The rest of us seem to have no relief
from the agony.

If indeed the story is true, then the *Octavius* had made a remarkable, thirteen-year posthumous first transit, propelled by winds

and currents, across a whole frozen continent from the Pacific to the Atlantic. After her encounter with the *Herald*, the frozen spectre was never seen again and was, apparently, carried away by the wind and currents the following night.

Of course, there are s a few gaping holes in all of these salty tales. For example, Gaddis tells us that those remaining pages of the *Octavius*'s log now reside with "The Registrar of Shipping in London". Presumably, this is Lloyd's Shipping Register, but the earliest surviving volume of Lloyd's Register dates from 1764. If the quoted "final entry" is genuine, then it was obviously not written by the Captain. So who wielded the pen? Was it so cold that they couldn't get a fire started? On a wooden ship? Then again, if the story is true, I ought not to be so disrespectful. However, almost a century later, at the other end of the planet, the southern hemisphere came up with its own carbon copy of the *Octavius* story. I looked at the website of the Australian Antarctic Data Centre (data.aad.gov.au/aadc) and came up with this frosty gem:

Location: Jenny Buttress United States Gazetteer Id 127087
This name originates from United States of America, but is also called, Jenny Buttress (United Kingdom) and Jenny Buttress (Russia). Named by the UK-APC in 1960 for the sailing vessel *Jenny* from the Isle of Wight which was found drifting in Drake Passage by the whaler *Hope* in September 1840. All her crew were dead and the log was entered up to 1823.

Sounds familiar? The *Jenny* was a British schooner that became trapped in an ice-barrier in the Drake Passage (between the southern tip of South America and the Antarctic South Shetland Islands) in 1823. Her last port of call had been Lima, Peru. She was rediscovered by Captain Brighton of the whaler *Hope* on 22 September 1840, after having been locked in the ice for seventeen years. The severe Antarctic cold had preserved all seven bodies on board. As with the *Octavius*, the boarding party found the skipper, pen in hand, frozen at his desk. There was also a woman on board and a dog. The log was found, with another tragic "last entry" reading: "May 4, 1823. No food for 71 days. I am the only one left alive."

The original report of this discovery has been deemed to be unsubstantiated with maritime researchers but it's become a staple of Antarctic sea-lore. The ship is commemorated by the Jenny Buttress, a feature near Melville Peak on King George Island, named by the UK Antarctic Place-Names Committee in 1960. If both of these stories are true then the coincidences ought not to be surprising – wooden ships, harsh, unforgiving, freezing conditions. No doubt there are still vessels out there awaiting discovery.

Who knows what might appear if the ice keeps melting ...

THE *PAMIR*

Hamburg's Blohm + Voss shipyards launched two stately barques in 1905. They were the *Pamir* and the *Passat*, sailing ships of the German shipping company F. Laeisz, whose fleet was famous among sailors as the "Flying P-Line" as all their ships names began with a "P". The *Pamir* was the last commercial sailing ship to round Cape Horn in 1949. At 275 feet (83 m) in length, with enough sail to cover 45,000 square feet (4,180 m²), these elegant, four-masted monsters were a wondrous sight. After a long, chequered history that included two wars and three nationalities for the vessel, flying the flags of Germany, Finland and New Zealand, by 1957 the *Pamir* had become a sail training ship for the German Merchant Service. In command was Captain Diebitsch with a thirty-five-strong crew augmented by fifty-one sea cadets aged between sixteen and eighteen.

In August 1957 she left Buenos Aires carrying a cargo of 3,790 tons of barley. Around 500 miles (805 km) from the Azores, on 20 September she ran into Hurricane Carrie. Her final message was heard on the airwaves at 8 p.m. on 21 September: "Heavy hurricane – all sails lost – 45 degree list – danger of sinking – need help." When the US freighter *Saxon* arrived at the *Pamir*'s last known position, all they found was a lifeboat with five survivors. The following day one more survivor was picked up, but eighty souls had gone to Davy Jones. So ends a true, genuine tragedy. Yet the *Pamir* would return as a grim reminder of the rapacity of the merciless sea.

Four years later, another sail training vessel, the *Esmereld* from Chile, was battling a gale in the English Channel when she sighted another sailing ship. It was identified as the *Pamir*. Needless to say, those who received the report from the *Esmereld* took it with a large pinch of salt. However, a few months later the renowned yachtsman Reed Byers was sailing off the Virgin Islands. He saw a large sailing vessel – he identified her as the *Pamir*. Other sail training vessels, Norway's *Christian Radich* and Germany's *Gorch Foch* both reported sightings of the *Pamir*, and the US Coastguard ship *Eagle* reported that she'd crossed her path. Some of the reports of her sightings may be fanciful, but they were sincerely made. On various occasions when the spectre was reported, her crew were said to be lined up on deck. On her last materialization, only 20 crew members were counted. Another break in the membrane between this world and another? The eternal imprint of a tragedy? If you're going to sea, keep your eyes peeled.

THE *PORT PIRIE*

In the British Merchant Navy's heyday, for a sailor there were some good shipping lines to sail with, and quite a few bad ones. One of the best (and I can vouch for this – I served on two of their vessels) was a subsidiary of the Cunard Line, their cargo fleet, the Port Line. The *Port Pirie* was a fine British cargo vessel on the run between Canada, New Zealand and Australia. On her Australian run in 1948, her boiler had run dry and exploded, killing a donkeyman. To avoid any hint that we're entering an area of cryptozoology here, the donkeyman is the crew member whose job is to deal with the operation and maintenance of any and all assorted machinery other than the ship's main engines. While at sea "donkey engines" could be used to operate the anchor windlass and bilge pumps. The donkeyman could also be called on to perform the duties of fireman or greaser – hence the designation "donkey greaser". Running steam engines was a dangerous job and his knowledge and skill was of great importance. However, exploded boiler equals dead donkeyman.

A year later the *Port Pirie* was tied up in Sydney with Engineer Peter Jones carrying out maintenance work alone in the engine room. The boiler's feed-pump began to make a violent knocking noise. Jones looked at the gauge but it read "full". To stop the noise, he turned the pump off, but minutes later the knocking began again. Jones was puzzled; it shouldn't make a noise at all when turned off. He inspected the gauge again. It still read "full". Yet the pump continued knocking. Eventually he made a very careful examination of the gauge – and discovered it was faulty. In fact, the boiler was empty and could easily have exploded. Jones mentioned this to the old greasers in the mess room, who informed him that the deceased donkeyman, in his agonized death throes, had sworn that no one would die on the ship in the way he had. A mechanical fluke or a benevolent spirit? Take your pick.

THE MYSTERY OF THE
MARLBOROUGH

Before the opening of the Panama Canal in 1914, a sea voyage to the Antipodes – New Zealand and Australia – was a long, risky affair. It meant either sailing through often ferocious, iceberg-infested waters around Cape Horn or, even though the Suez Canal had opened in 1869, many vessels still braved the gales in stormy waters around the southern tip of Africa, the Cape of Good Hope. Both choices posed a significant risk to life.

The Pacific is a massive ocean. I have sailed across it four times and recall that even after traversing the Panama Canal, the trip between the canal and Melbourne was over 9,000 miles (14,484 km). On an old tramp making an average twelve knots the journey could take anything up to three weeks, and on most voyages the sight of another single vessel en route was a rarity. In seagoing terms, the Pacific was to us the equivalent of the universe out beyond the solar system. Yet for centuries men have travelled across it, hunted whales, traded, fished and fought wars. At some points it is up to seven miles (11.3 km) deep. It is a place where getting lost is easy. Flat calm one day, a hurricane the next. But it is beautiful, mind-expanding, beguiling and utterly mysterious.

During the period 1876 to 1890 the barque *Marlborough*, launched in Glasgow in 1876, was a beautiful ship which had carried immigrants from London to New Zealand over fourteen successful passages. Under Captain Anderson from 1876 until 1883, she carried a crew of twenty-nine. Together with her sister ship the *Dunedin*, she was one of the first refrigerated vessels to successfully transport frozen meat from New Zealand to the

UK. She was subsequently sold to the Shaw, Savill & Albion Company.

In 1884 she had a new Master, Captain Herd. On 11 January 1890, she set sail from the small port of Lyttelton in New Zealand. The *Marlborough* then disappeared without trace. As the months passed, Lloyd's Shipping Register in London posted her as missing, presumed sunk by icebergs after rounding the notoriously violent Cape Horn. Two months after the *Marlborough* left New Zealand, in March 1890 her sister, the barque *Dunedin*, left Oamaru with a crew of thirty-four for her return passage to London carrying cargo of wool and frozen meat. She also vanished and has never been found.

Twenty years passed and slowly but surely the age of sail was giving way to the age of steam. Then in 1919 a strange report appeared in the *Glasgow Evening Post*: the various sources available quote the Glasgow paper itself as the origination of the following story, but I have not managed to verify this, and the first paragraph is confusing, as it goes back nineteen years; the remainder of the report seems to cover a much later period: but here's the text: "It was stated that the crew of a passing ship in 1891, saw men, whom they believed to be British seamen, signalling off one of the islands near Cape Horn but it was not possible to get near them owing to the bad weather." Why the incident was never reported at that time seems strange, but the report continues in the baroque and florid language of the period:

Further details of the discovery of the missing ship come via London. It appears that some considerable time back the sad truth was learned by a British vessel bound home from Lyttelton after rounding Cape Horn. The story told by the captain is intensely dramatic. He says: "We were off the rocky coves near Punta Arenas, keeping near the land for shelter. The coves are deep and silent, the sailing is difficult and dangerous. It was a weirdly wild evening, with the red orb of the sun setting on the horizon. The stillness was uncanny. There was a shining green light reflected on the jagged rocks on our right. We rounded a point into a deep cleft rock. Before us, a mile or more across the water, stood a vessel, with the barest shreds of canvas fluttering in the breeze. We signalled and hove to. No answer came. We searched the 'stranger' with our glasses. Not a soul could we see; not a movement of any sort. Masts and yards were picked out in green – the green of decay. The vessel lay as if in a cradle. It recalled the 'Frozen Pirate', a novel that I read years ago. I conjured up the vessel of the novel, with her rakish masts and the outline of her six small cannon traced with snow. At last we came up. There was no sign of life on board. After an interval our first mate, with a number of the crew, boarded her. The sight that met their gaze was thrilling. Below the wheel lay the skeleton of a man. Treading warily on the rotten decks, which cracked and broke in places as they walked, they encountered three skeletons in the hatchway. In the mess-room were the remains of ten bodies, and six others were found, one alone, possibly the captain, on the bridge. There was an uncanny stillness around, and a dank smell of mould, which made the flesh creep. A few remnants of books were discovered in the captain's cabin, and a rusty cutlass. Nothing more weird in the history of the sea can ever have been seen. The first mate examined the still faint letters on the bow and after much trouble read '*Marlborough*, Glasgow'."

Whoever this imaginative mariner was, he told a good yarn. For example, whoever the correspondent was, he was no sailor. In my expericence, a vessel's home port is written on her stern, not her bows. However, there may be some truth here because in 1913 a Captain Burley, an American pilot from Seattle, in conversation with some skippers of the Shaw, Savill & Albion line, described his own bizarre experience concerning the *Marlborough*. As a young sailor he had been shipwrecked off Staten Island, near Cape Horn. He was one of two survivors, and together they set off in search of a whaling station that they believed to exist on the island. Starving and lost, as they stumbled along the barren Chilean coast, they came across a large ship with painted ports, wedged in a cove, which bore the name *Marlborough*. Lying nearby were the huddled skeletons of twenty men and heaps of shellfish, which told how they had tried in vain to fight off starvation.

Truth or fiction? With all maritime yarns, you either leave them as you find them, thus preserving their utterly atmospheric romance (and I'm as guilty as the next sailor in this), or you cast your net a little wider. Always be prepared for confusion. In the case of the story of the *Marlborough*, we need to refer to one of the greatest of all maritime chroniclers, Basil Lubbock (1876–1944). In his epic two-volume work *The Last of the Windjammers* (1922 and 1935) he refers to the *Glasgow Evening Post* piece as "a good example of a newspaper fake". He does relate Captain Burley's story, which he dates as 23 July 1890. Burley claimed to have been wrecked on Tierra del Fuego in the barque *Cordova*. The survivors attempted to reach Good Success Bay, and en route passed the wreck of a barque named *Godiva*. Although they did not see the *Marlborough*, a few miles south of the wreck of the *Godiva* they found a boat bearing the legend "*Marlborough of London*". (Not Glasgow, then?) The boat was pulled up out of reach of the seas and the oars were all there. Lubbock's telling of the Burley story continues:

> Up above the boat in a sheltered part of the rocks we found a tent, made from the belly of a square sail, and I am inclined to believe that the survivors of the boat from the *Marlborough* had obtained the same from the *Godiva*, although the camp in question was several miles to the southward of the wreck. In the tent were seven skeletons and outside was a pile of a sort of mussel shells, which they had apparently subsisted on. I am inclined to believe that they had perished from exposure and ptomaine poisoning.

Lubbock was an experienced Cape Horner, and knew his navigation, and he criticizes the story from the point that the coast of Tierra del Fuego, inside the Le Maire Straits, would be an unlikely location for a vessel westward bound aiming to round the Horn to end up stranded, or even for one of her boats to make a landing.

There are various debunkings of all these stories, and one has to admire the additional research of such authors as Philip MacDougall, whose *Mysteries on the High Seas* (1994) and *Phantoms on the High Seas* (1991) employ academic historical methodology to get to the bottom of barnacled old narratives. But although Ebenezer Scrooge obviously suffered a time slip and "imagined" his "three spirits", if we empirically deconstructed *A Christmas Carol* then our chestnuts would remain unroasted, and Tiny Tim would have died after all. Some writers remain as unrepentant romantics. Guilty as charged, your honour.

The guilty parties behind the inexplicable and phenomenal atmosphere of many sea stories will always be novelists. Because of Robert Louis Stevenson, pirates now all speak with a West Country accent (even in *The Simpsons*) prefixing every utterance with a hearty "Arrr". Actors are equal culprits. Robert Newton is the only Long John Silver. Captain Bligh will always be Charles Laughton, and although Patrick Stewart signed on the *Pequod*, the best Captain Ahab is still Gregory Peck. Nutty skippers cracking up? That's Bogart in *The Caine Mutiny*. The sea itself is a rolling romance, so we should not be surprised when the horizons of fiction and fact morph into one and appear blurred.

In 2010 a new species of extinct giant sperm whale was announced, *Livyatan melvillei*. It was named in honour of the author of *Moby Dick*, Herman Melville. The palaeontologists who discovered the fossil were all *Moby Dick* fans. On 12 May 1985, the New York City Herman Melville Society gathered at 104 East 26th Street to dedicate the intersection of Park Avenue South and 26th Street as Herman Melville Square. This is the street where Melville lived from 1863 to 1891 and where, among other works, he wrote the unfinished novella *Billy Budd, Sailor*. Melville was a poignant example of how some sea stories and their authors can sink without trace. The lingering oceanic ozone of mystery permeated all his work, nowhere more so than in the epic *Moby Dick*. Yet for his final two decades he remained forgotten and anonymous as a customs inspector for the City of New York. His story of the white whale was critically savaged and was as popular in literary terms as a burning orphanage.

Melville died at his home in New York City early on the morning of 28 September 1891, aged seventy-two. Urban legends are every bit as dubious as maritime ones; one persists that in his short obituary notice in the *New York Times*, he was so unknown that they called him "Henry" Melville. It was decades after his death before *Moby Dick* was recognized as a masterpiece. *Billy Budd* remained unpublished until 1924. Melville knew a lot about the strangeness of the sea; he'd sailed on five different vessels and deserted from two. It was when I began to read and reread *Moby Dick* in depth as a junior ordinary seaman in 1960 that I blundered into my own marine quest; but my white whale was a genuine phantom ship.

DEATH SHIP: THE CURIOUS CASE OF THE *OURANG MEDAN*

This strange yarn began as an obscure, bizarre footnote in nautical history. The story of the *Ourang Medan* was one of those chilling fo'c'sle tales told by old hands over a few beers on long voyages. As with the *Mary Celeste*, a modicum of determined digging can usually strip away the romance and often leave us with the bare, demystified facts.

Not so with the *Ourang Medan*. The more one digs, the more fragments, hints and nuances appear. I first heard the story on board the old Port Line ship, *Port Halifax*, when crossing the Pacific in 1961. It was then included in Vincent Gaddis's *Invisible Horizons* (1966) and years later in various other works such as Damon Wilson's *Big Book of the Unexplained* (1998). The oldest source I could track down was an article by Robert V. Hulse in *Fate* magazine in 1953, yet Hulse, like all the others, only had the bare bones of the yarn.

This is a story with a secret; a secret buried somewhere in the guarded records of maritime officialdom. Turn down the lamp, cue the creepy music ...

In February 1948 (or June 1947, depending on which source one consults) a series of distress calls were sent out by the Dutch freighter *Ourang Medan* in the Straits of Malacca between Sumatra and Indonesia: "All officers including captain dead, lying in chartroom and on bridge, probably whole crew dead ..." This chilling message, accompanied by a spate of desperate SOS calls, was followed by indecipherable Morse code ... then a final message of just two stark words "I die."

Boarding parties found the dead radio operator, his hand on the Morse key, eyes wide open. The entire crew, even the ship's dog, were discovered in the same terrified posture, all dead.

According to a supposed document (the first mention being by Vincent Gaddis) called *The Proceedings of the Merchant Marine Council*, the crew were found "teeth bared, with their upturned faces to the sun, staring, as if in fear ..." Later researchers claim that this document was issued by the US Coastguard Service – although why they would issue a report of something happening in the Malacca Straits is another puzzle.

Following the grim discovery of the fear-frozen cadavers, a fire broke out in the ship's hold.

The boarding parties were forced to abandon her. Shortly after, there was an explosion described in some accounts as so violent the vessel "lifted herself from the water", after which she quickly sank.

So, there you have it. It's a great yarn; but is it just an old seadog's tale? Or perhaps, as some have suggested, a fifty-year-old April Fool joke, composed by some bored tabloid hack?

The trouble is, it refuses to go away. If these men did die in such a bizarre fashion, what killed them? I started with Lloyd's Shipping Register. There was no mention of the case. Then that standby of all maritime researchers, *The Dictionary of Disasters at Sea, 1824–1962*. Everything else was in there – even the *Mary Celeste* – but no *Ourang Medan*. I contacted Britain's best magazine for old sailors, *Sea Breezes*, and discussed the case with their late editor, Captain Andrew Douglas, a retired skipper with decades of service on the oceans of the world. He was fascinated, but knew nothing, although he did place a plea for information in the next issue.

It was time to get "official". I wrote to the Admiralty, the Registrar of Shipping and Seamen and the National Maritime Museum in Greenwich. They all told me the same thing; if the *Ourang Medan* was a Dutch vessel, I would have to go to Amsterdam.

Searching the Dutch shipping records in Amsterdam seemed only to deepen the mystery. There was no mention of the ship at all. There was a *Medan*, but she had been scrapped before the Second World War. And my enquiries to the Maritime Authority in Singapore, which may have been able to help with a Malacca Straits incident, drew a blank. I was facing the distinct possibility that this was simply a hoary old fo'c'sle yarn ... until Professor Theodor Siersdorfer of Essen, Germany, entered the frame. Siersdorfer was a respected marine architect with a long career as a lecturer in all things nautical. He had read the plea in *Sea Breezes* and I suddenly discovered that I was not alone; Siersdorfer had been on the case for forty-five years.

An intriguing parcel of information from Germany opened up new avenues, the most exciting of which was the identity of the two vessels that received the *Ourang Medan*'s SOS calls. One was the *City of Baltimore*; the second was the *Silver Star*, owned by Grace Lines of New York, whose crew allegedly boarded the stricken *Dutchman*.

Here the enigma deepens again. Most of the details of the *Silver Star*'s voyage are contained in a strange, thirty-two-page German booklet written in 1954 by one Otto Mielke (now deceased), entitled *Das Totenschiff in der Südsee* (Death Ship in the South Sea). Mielke seemed to know a lot about the *Ourang Medan*'s possible route and cargo but fails to give further detailed sources; this is a strange omission because his details, right down to the tonnage, engine power and Captain's name of the *Silver Star*, are thoroughly referenced. Professor Siersdorfer also mentioned another marine detective, Alvar Mastin (also searching for the departed Dutch ship), a German who lived in my home town of Hull in the 1950s. I could not track him down, but apparently Mastin had repeatedly attempted to get details from Grace Lines in New York of the *Silver Star* crew list and logbook – yet was met with a stony silence.

Thus the possible fact remains that the *Silver Star* crew did really board the *Ourang Medan* (as Mielke has it, in June 1947). I made several unsuccessful attempts to see if there were still members of that crew alive. But there is still confusion; the Germans cite the *Silver Star* as being the vessel boarding the *Orang Medan*, yet Lloyd's Register shows that, at the time, the *Silver Star* had changed owners and had another name ... *Santa Cecilia*.

What follows is pure speculation, but there is a tantalizing, possible explanation as to her crew's demise and her disappearance from the records. Mielke mentions a mixed, lethal cargo on the *Dutchman*: "Zyankali" (potassium cyanide) and nitroglycerine. How this mixture could have gone unrecorded is a mystery, as the controls on such lethal cargoes, even fifty years ago, would have ensured reams of paperwork.

The Geneva Protocol of 1925 ratified by thirty-three nations outlawed all chemical weapons. As history has shown, the Nazis made horrific use of the extermination gas "Zyklon B" but, according to Albert Speer in his book *Inside the Third Reich* (1995), they also stockpiled a secret gas called Tabun and, as late as 1944, were manufacturing 1,000 tons of this deadly substance each month. According to Speer: "It could penetrate the filters of all known gas masks and contact with even small lingering quantities had fatal effects."

Apart from the Nazis, only one other nation used gas: Japan. They used it in China during the Second World War. In 1935, the brilliant Japanese bacteriologist Shiro Ishi set up the Japanese Army Unit 731 in a remote village in occupied Manchuria. Unit 731's brief was to find a chemical, gas or biological weapon to win the war. Hideous, inhumane experiments were carried out on helpless Australian, American, Russian, Chinese and British prisoners during some of the worst war crimes ever committed. Was there a Nuremberg-type trial for these doctors of death? Far from it. The biochemists' hideous research was too "good" to waste; they pulled off a mysterious secret deal with their erstwhile enemies, appearing to come to an arrangement with General Douglas McArthur's forces. The criminals went free and prospered, leaving the possibility that the Japanese might have stored quantities of nerve gas in Singapore.

To try and explain the obstinate absence of the ill-fated *Ourang Medan* from official records, we must look at the political turmoil that existed throughout Indonesia in the immediate post-war years. Before the war, Java and Sumatra were part of the Dutch empire. In 1945 the Dutch returned, expecting to carry on their rule as before, but found the newly established republics of Southeast Asia had gained wide local support. A bitter, dirty war for control broke out, and in 1947–8 the Dutch carried out major "police actions" in area. After the Second World War, there was a brisk trade in nerve gas and biological agents with repressive governments everywhere.

It was OK to make and sell this vile stuff – as long as you didn't use it. But somebody did, that's for sure. Death has always had its currency. So how was this deadly cargo moved around the South China Sea and through the Straits of Malacca during this troubled period? Not by air; the prospect of a cargo plane crashing with several tons of deadly gas on board was too horrendous to consider. No, you hired an insignificant old tramp steamer, preferably with a low-paid foreign crew, stowed the cargo in disguised oil drums and, like all serious smugglers, hoped for the best as well as a blind eye from authority.

I first heard the *Ourang Medan* story in 1961 within fifteen years of its origin. If we accept, due to the nature of her crew's deaths, that she was carrying deadly gas or chemicals and if indeed she was a Dutch vessel, had this news broken it would have been a major embarrassment for any government involved, especially in the light of the restrictions imposed by the Geneva Convention. Hence the dead-ends faced by any researcher. The story exists because, like the gases, it escaped. But here's another mystery: if a gas leak killed the crew, was the final explosion another accident or an officially ordered scuttling? The crew of the *Silver Star* would have told the tale from that day on in every mess room on every ship they sailed in. Eventually, in a mess room on the British tramp steamer *Port Halifax*, it reached me. Aficionados of *The X-Files* have had a field day with this tragedy, blaming UFOs, sea monsters, and so on, but the possible reality is no less ominous.

The field of the unexplained is littered with red herrings, hoaxes and outright fakery. But if the story of this ship of death is an invention, why manufacture it and who was responsible? What made this common currency in the mess rooms of the old vessels I sailed in the 1960s and why were other, real ships involved in the yarn? Any marine researcher will tell you that even the mighty tomes of Lloyd's Shipping Register can throw up more questions than answers, especially when ships have their names changed frequently.

I then received a letter from the Dutch Royal Navy that asked me for information on the *Ourang Medan* case. Why? I could tell them nothing.

In the UK, the Ministry of Defence have irresponsibly destroyed all records of poison gas dumps that are over twenty-five years old. Over 100,000 tons of deadly Tabun and Sarin nerve gases were deliberately loaded on to ships at the end of the Second World War and sunk in the North Sea, the Baltic and Atlantic. In 1998, a Swedish fishing vessel landed an unusual catch: a net full of mustard gas canisters. The crew spent a long time in hospital with serious burns.

Professor Siersdorfer sent me copies of photographs taken by a German captain from Hamburg. I was the first person to see these in fifty years. They revealed a terrifying story. Shortly after the end of the Second World War, a number of commandeered elderly German merchant vessels were used by the Royal Navy in conjunction with the Merchant service. These captured ships were loaded with thousands of tons of canisters and shells of Nazi poison gas, and sailed out into the North Sea, where explosive charges were set. The ancient hulks, bursting with contamination, were then blown up and sunk.

It's a nice, creepy Fortean thought that the hapless sailors of the mythical *Ourang Medan* were visited by a UFO or a giant squid, which was so scary it literally "frightened them to death". That may have been a fine prognosis in the nutty, sci-fi 1950s. Yet humanity is capable of far more sinister behaviour than any intergalactic visitor to Roswell. Whatever solution that can reveal what killed the crew on that sinister Dutch ship lies somewhere at the bottom of the Malacca Straits.

BRUNEL'S FOLLY: THE CURSED *GREAT EASTERN*

Is continuing bad luck an unexplained phenomenon? As the old blues song goes, "If it wasn't for bad luck, I'd have no luck at all", and you could well apply this to one of the unluckiest of cursed ships ever launched.

Isambard Kingdom Brunel (1806–59) came very close in a BBC poll to being voted the greatest Briton of all time. Winston Churchill got the accolade, but Brunel was a worthy contender. Already famous for his work on railways, his innovative passion for steam-powered ships knew no bounds. The *Great Eastern* was the third of his huge shipbuilding projects. The first was a wooden paddle steamer, the *Great Western*, the first steamship to make regular crossings of the Atlantic Ocean. The second was the *Great Britain*, the first large iron steamship; at the time it was the largest ship afloat and the first big ship to use a screw propeller. (There were historical precedents for large ships. For example, in the fifteenth-century Chinese empire, where the 300 treasure ships of Zheng He were each 440 feet [134 m] long, the fleet carrying a crew of 37,000.) However, with the *Great Eastern*, poor Isambard bit off more than he could chew.

Iron was still quite a new material for shipbuilding. Tens of thousands of metalworkers were employed to build his ships. The riveters built the hull from iron plates fixed to a frame. It was immensely strenuous work. "The Great Ship", as it became known, consumed three million rivets, but a riveting team could only fit 100 to 140 rivets in a ten-hour shift. She had four steam engines for the paddles and an additional engine for the propeller.

Because these early steamships could never find enough hold space for the coal they needed for a passage, they still required masts and sails. The *Great Eastern* had six masts, so that the ship could sail on even if all the coal ran out. Brunel designed her to carry 4,000 passengers, or 10,000 soldiers when carrying troops, with enough space in ten huge bunkers for a voyage to India or Australia without requiring coaling stations on the way. The ship would be able to return home even if there was no coal at its destination. But if ever a ship was jinxed, then it was the *Great Eastern*.

She was built in Millwall at the London yard of John Scott Russell and Company. At 19,000 tons she was the world's largest vessel. The strains of construction and the escalating cost soon drove Russell into bankruptcy and decimated Brunel's own hard-earned fortune. At the same time, Brunel's health was taking a serious toll.

Against all advice, the "Great Ship" was designed by Brunel to be launched sideways on iron rails into the Thames. Despite his fame, Brunel was a practical man and wished to avoid publicity for the launch, so he was appalled that word had got out and thousands of spectators turned up in the area around the site for the event. In addition to this, he was dismayed to discover that the shipyard directors had sold 3,000 tickets for spectators actually to enter the yard for a better vantage point.

On 3 November 1867 Brunel and the directors manned the rostrum. Presented with a list of potential names for the vessel, he wearily quipped "Call her Tom Thumb if you like". At 12.30 p.m. Henrietta, the daughter of Henry Thomas Hope, one of the fundraisers for the vessel, named the ship *Leviathan*, even though she was known as the *Great Eastern* – and would be renamed as such in July the following year.

Voices rang out; "She moves, she moves!" Then the winch controlling the launch spun out of control, tossing its operators into the air like rag dolls. Four men were seriously injured and John Donovan, aged seventy-four, died from severe internal injuries. The *Leviathan* had indeed moved – just three feet. Brunel's humiliation is hard to imagine. The winches and equipment that were supposed to push the vessel into the river were totally inadequate.

Over the next three months Brunel attempted several other launches, one with Prince Albert and the Prince of Wales in attendance, using hydraulic rams to move the ship, but without success. She was finally launched at 1.42 p.m. on 31 January 1858, using more powerful hydraulic rams supplied by the Tangye company of Birmingham. At long last the *Great Eastern* was in the water, but getting her there had taken a man's life, injured others and cost a staggering £170,000. From then on, Brunel decided to forego his own fees and ended up paying the men working on the project out of his own pocket. What floated before him on the wintry Thames was an incomplete £750,000 iron hull with no machinery and no funds to fit any. Spring and summer passed, more funds were raised, work continued, but the strain on Brunel became increasingly evident.

After being fitted out at Deptford, the ship was ready for its trials on 5 September 1859. Brunel made a final inspection visit, but after stepping on board he collapsed with a stroke. He died on 15 September. As Brunel had lain dying, on 9 September 1859, the *Great Eastern* was on her sea trials off Hastings. A heater attached to the paddle engine boilers exploded. Six firemen died an agonizing death, scalded by the hot steam. Others were seriously injured as the funnel exploded; some jumped overboard and drowned. The ship's opulent grand saloon was devastated.

On 21 January 1860 her Captain, William Harrison, while sailing from Hythe to Southampton in the ship's boat, was capsized during a squall near the Southampton dock gates. When taken from the water he was found to be dead. The accident also took the lives of the fourteen-year-old son of the *Great Eastern*'s purser, Captain Ley, and the boat's coxswain. Captain Harrison had already suffered some appalling luck, as he had recently become surety for a friend, by whose sudden death the savings he had accrued from a life at sea were lost. He was buried in St James's cemetery, Liverpool, on 27 January, when over 30,000 people followed his body to the grave.

Brunel's innovative design featuring compartments with watertight bulkheads had kept his huge ship afloat and limited the explosion's damage. Yet his grand scheme carried another curse; there were few, if any, docks and harbours in the world that could accommodate a vessel six times larger than anything the shipping world had known. In addition, the usually fraught prospect of the long trip around the Horn of Africa, which Brunel had factored into his design, diminished with the opening of the Suez Canal in 1859. The canal had shortened journeys to India by thousands of miles, yet there was doubt that due to her width and twenty-eight-foot (8.5 m) draught, the *Great Eastern* would be able to use the canal.

Instead, she was left with the much shorter Atlantic voyage, Southampton–New York. Her maiden voyage began on 17 June 1860 with just forty-three passengers, not, as had been hoped, 3,000, and eight of these were "dead heads" – non-paying company directors. She was due to sail shortly after the passengers came on board on 14 July, but many of the crew of 418 were blind drunk and needed at least twenty-four hours to sober up. Once at sea, passengers were put off by the sickening rolling of the ship in the Atlantic storms. Among the passengers were two American friends, Zerah Colburn (1832–70) and Alexander Lyman Holley (1832–82). Zerah Colburn was a brilliant American steam locomotive engineer, technical journalist and publisher. We can't exactly blame the *Great Eastern*, but his demise is in its shadow; he eventually took to laudanum and alcohol, committing suicide aged thirty-eight. He was found near death by two boys taking their dog for a walk in Tudor's Pear Orchard, Belmont, Massachusetts, with a Deringer pistol in his hand. Alexander Lyman Holley, a mechanical engineer considered the foremost steel and plant engineer and designer of his time, despite having a much-disparaged monument in Manhattan's Washington Square Park, has been doomed to obscurity – most New Yorkers jogging past his statue have no idea who he was.

There were other accidents. A sailor fell in the paddle wheel and was killed, another disappeared overboard. A two-day excursion off the American coast turned into a near disaster when the ship drifted 100 miles (162 km) into the Atlantic. The thrill-seeking tourists on board got more than they bargained for.

In September 1861 she made another transatlantic crossing with 400 passengers. It was not exactly uneventful. The ship ran into a hurricane. The large waves caused the ship to lean and this submerged the paddle wheel on one side. That paddle wheel was shut down, but this restricted her propulsion and manoeuvrability became a serious problem. She was unable to turn into the wind and a great wave removed the other paddle wheel. Her damaged rudder became useless and she could not steer. On top if this, the flapping rudder began smashing into the screw propeller, so the propeller had to be shut down. As the force twelve raged, the ship floundered. Eventually, after long and dangerous effort, brave members of the crew immobilized the rudder and the propeller was started again. The *Great Eastern* limped back to Britain, but the cost of repairing the damage was the then gargantuan sum of £60,000.

In August 1862 she was carrying 1,500 passengers when she again ran into a violent storm. Off Long Island the ship passed over a submerged rock that cut a gash, eighty-five feet long and five feet wide (25.9 x 1.5 m), in the bottom of the outer hull. The inner hull was not damaged but the repair of the bottom of such a large ship was no easy matter. During the extensive repairs, at a cost of £70,000 and which lasted until December, workers heard strange knocking and tapping sounds coming from within the hull.

Although she made a few more trips she was running at a heavy loss, totalling £20,000. After costing almost £1 million to build, she was finally auctioned off and brought a price of only £25,000. She was converted and adapted into an oceanic cable layer and leased to the Atlantic Telegraph Company for £50,000. In July 1865 the *Great Eastern* began to lay cable from Ireland to Newfoundland. After laying a thousand miles (1,610 km) of cable, worth £700,000, the cable end was lost in about 6,000 feet (1,829 m) of water and could not be recovered. A further attempt was made in July 1866 with stronger cable and this time it was successful. Her rare success was embellished when the ship navigated to where the first cable had been lost and the old cable was retrieved.

Her end, beached off Liverpool as a curiosity, was ignominious, and she was finally broken up in 1888. The ship was of such robust construction that it took 200 men working around the clock almost two years to take her to pieces. It was during this process that the macabre story emerged that the skeletons of two missing riveters were found trapped in the double hull. The noises which men working on her in New York in 1862 had heard were later claimed to be the ghosts of the trapped "bashers". Whilst many have attempted to debunk this legend, two workers had gone missing during her construction. At the end of one of the best books on the vessel, James Dugan's *The Great Iron Ship* (2003), the author reports that a David Duff wrote to him stating that a skeleton was found inside the ship's shell and the tank tops. It was the skeleton of the basher who was missing, and the frame of the bash boy was found with him.

The skeletons story could be true, although the same thing has been said of the *Titanic* (a ridiculous suggestion – apart from the crushing pressure all human remains would have quickly decomposed) and the Hoover Dam, but you'll only find these in Rick Riordan's fantasy novel, *Titan's Curse*. Some maintain that the inspection hatches in the *Great Eastern*'s inner hull would have provided an easy escape. She featured in the BBC documentary series *Seven Wonders of the Industrial World*, which presented the story of two dead bodies, including a child worker, in the hull as fact. An episode of *Haunted History* also offered the unfortunate bashers as fact. The narrator read out an article from the period when the *Great Eastern* was being scrapped. Some reports claim two men and an apprentice had been sealed in the hull by accident. Of course, if this is true – who got the bones and where are they? But there are a couple of bits of the old ship still around. Her flagpole stands at the Kop end of Liverpool Football Club's ground, and one of her funnels is alongside Brunel's SS *Great Britain* in Bristol.

Many vessels are said to be haunted, such as the *Queen Mary*, now a hotel and tourist attraction moored at Long Beach, California. She seems to be host to several ghosts. One is thought to be the spirit of a seventeen-year-old crewman, John Pedder, crushed to death by a watertight door in 1966: unexplained knocking has been heard from behind the door. One tour guide has reported that she saw a darkly dressed figure where Pedder had died. She remembered the spectre's face; she checked old photographs and recognized Pedder. A mysterious woman in white has been sighted who disappears behind a pillar. Another ghost, sporting a long beard and dressed in blue-grey overalls, has been spotted in the shaft alley of the engine room. Around the ship's swimming pool, ghostly voices and laughter have been heard. One employee claims to have seen the wet footprints of a child appearing on the pool deck.

Ships can be creepy places. Some just seem to have an aura of misfortune around them. The ship might be fine, but occasionally some imperceptible vestige of threat rubs off on her crew. Launched in November 1890 at the shipyard of Russell & Co., Greenock, for Shaw Savill & Albion, the four-masted steel barque *Hinemoa*, as well as carrying general cargo, was one of the first sailing ships with freezing-machinery enabling her to carry 20,000 carcases of mutton from New Zealand. Later in her career her freezing facilities were removed and she became an immigrant ship, transporting thousands of immigrants across the globe to New Zealand. So far, so good, but Basil Lubbock, in his book *The Last of the Wind Jammers*, informs us that by becoming the Master of the *Hinemoa* you surrendered to fate. One of her captains went mad, another was dismissed as a criminal, another was such a hopeless drunk that the crew had to take over the running of the ship. A later captain was found shot in his cabin with a revolver by his side. The next skipper also died a violent death. She was eventually sent to the bottom en route from Australia to Britain by a German U-boat on 7 September 1917.

ANATOMY OF A CLASSIC: GHOST BOAT – *UB-65*

In their excellent and informative book, *Lost At Sea* (1994), Michael Goss and George Behe present a refreshing attitude to research for the following story:

> How many accidents occur during the construction of a ship, we wonder? How many injuries or even deaths befall workmen as winches slip or supports buckle unexpectedly? ... we found ourselves speculating that if a researcher was to look back into the early history of any vessel that latterly came to acquire a "hoodooed" reputation, there might be anecdotes of dock-yard accidents and/or mishaps during sea trials – things insignificant in themselves, yet enough to convince hindsightedly wise individuals that the ship in question was doomed and dangerous from the very start. *UB-65* arguably conforms with this pattern.

Gosse and Behe rightfully devote over thirty analytical pages to what is arguably one of the most chilling ghost stories of the sea, a true classic because this is a multifaceted enigma covering not only the paranormal, but hints at espionage and propaganda, with a fascinating character in its sinister shadow pulling the strings. With the advent of the First World War, death at sea, always a grim possibility in peacetime, became far more likely when the conflict took to the ocean. There are several spooky submarine yarns from both world wars and later, but none are as celebrated or weird as the story of the ill-fated German submarine *UB-65*. According to the meticulous and reliable www.uboat.net her details are as follows.

She was built by Vulcan, Hamburg, launched 26 June 1917, commissioned 18 August 1917, and had just one commander during her short career from 18 August 1917–14 July 1918, Kapitanleutnant Martin Schelle. On her six patrols she sank seven allied ships and damaged a further six. She was one of a class of twenty-four submarines especially designed to operate out of the ports of occupied Belgium. It was during construction that bad fortune began to dog this particular boat.

If we are to accept the legend, then the crew of *UB-65* were less terrified of confronting enemy forces at sea than they were of the ghost that haunted their ship. As with most of these yarns, this one has had its fair share of embellishment over the years. The initial "authority" who launched the spectre was one Hector Charles Bywater (1884–1940), a brilliant naval journalist and strategist, a multilingual spy whose ability to speak German passed him off as a native. Bywater is as much of a conundrum as *UB-65* itself. As will be seen, other writers have added layers of spurious "authenticity" to his original exposition. Bywater bases his telling of the saga on a pamphlet published after the war by "the distinguished psychologist Professor Dr Hecht", and a "first-hand account" by an unnamed petty officer who was lucky enough to leave the boat before she sank.

The misfortunes of *UB-65* began whilst she was still on the slipway. A heavy metal girder slipped from the crane tackle as it was being lowered into position to be welded into the hull, instantly killing a German workman and injuring another, who died in hospital a few days later. Before launching, poisonous fumes in the engine room took the lives of three more workers. So before *UB-65* had even put to sea, five men had died building her.

Once out at sea on her trial run, a sailor was sent forward on the deck to inspect the hatches. He was swept overboard and lost. Her first test dive was almost fatal. She should have levelled out at thirty feet (9 m), but a forward ballast tank ruptured and the sub plummeted to the seabed. She remained stuck there for twelve hours, and during this frightening period floodwater seeped into the batteries. The resulting toxic fumes spread among the crew. When, with some relief, the boat finally managed to surface, everyone was violently ill, so much so that two men died in hospital. Could things get worse? Without a doubt, and here the illegitimate elements of this oft-repeated story begin to rear up. Some writers relate that she was commissioned not in August but in February 1917, with the *UB-65* placed under the command of Oberleutuant Karl Honig. Unfortunately, you will not find a commander of this name listed; the records show Kapitanleutnant Martin Schelle as sole commander during the boat's brief life. But back to the story. While torpedoes were being loaded for *UB-65*'s first patrol, a warhead exploded, killing the Second Officer and eight seamen. Nine other sailors were seriously wounded. By this time anyone being assigned to this particular submarine would have something to worry about and, on top of it all, the first ghost made an entry. As she was under tow back to dry dock for repair, a hysterical sailor reported that he had seen the ghost of the Second Officer, his arms folded, standing on the prow. The haunting had begun.

Although Bywater was the first to bring all this to light in his 1932 book, *Their Secret Purposes*, most of the crew names don't crop up until an article on the sub written by Peter King in *Fate* magazine in 1974. The story gathered more trimmings in Raymond Lamont Brown's *Phantoms of the Sea* (1972) and a further *Fate* article by King in 1977. Bywater's source is a "Professor Dr Hecht" and, from somewhere, King pulls a first name out of the bag – now he's "Max" Hecht. This revelation is followed by a previously unidentified sailor who becomes "Petersen", claiming that he also saw the ghost. Petersen wisely decides to jump ship the day before the *UB-65* was to embark on her first patrol. Several men on that initial patrol report seeing the ghost of that Second Officer. One night the duty officer is found sobbing on the bridge, claiming to have seen the ghostly figure, arms folded, standing on the ship's prow. A torpedo man named Eberhard goes berserk and rants about being pursued by the ghost. According to Bywater, he's given a shot of morphine but, despite its relaxing qualities, eventually makes it up on to the deck where he promptly jumps overboard and sinks like a stone. Whilst under attack from depth charges, Lohmann,

UB-65's coxswain, is thrown to the deck, cracks three ribs and dies from internal injuries a week later. "Oberleutnant Karl Honig" is next on the hit list. After patrolling the Dover Straits in February 1918, *UB-65* docks in Bruges just as British aircraft began a bombing raid. Honig is said to have been decapitated by flying shrapnel as he stepped down the gangplank, his headless body propelled backwards on to the deck. His corpse is laid there for a while, covered with a canvas shroud, and that same night an officer and eight crewmen say they saw the Second Officer's ghost again, standing by the cadaver. Now the entire crew of *UB-65* apply for a transfer. Well, you would, wouldn't you?

The German Navy is very concerned, and yet another new name enters the story; he is "a German Naval Lutheran minister, the Rev. Franz Weber", who conducts an exorcism of the ship. A Commodore arrives and investigates. The anonymous chronicler, the petty officer, tells Max Hecht that he missed a trip on the boat due to rheumatism, and the day before she sails he is visited by another crewman called Wernicke, who bids him a somewhat ominous farewell. New names, including "Richter", keep attaching themselves like limpets to this story and the 1974 *Fate* article identifies the Commodore as "Michelson" (Lamont Brown has him as "Admiral Schroeder"). We'll examine the potential origins of these names later on.

By midsummer 1918, Germany was losing the war. U-boat losses were such that none could be unnecessarily laid up, so *UB-65* was put back into service. On 30 June she set out on what was to be her last patrol. The story goes that while patrolling off the coast of Ireland, the US submarine *L-2*, operating as part of an American flotilla based at Bantry Bay, was travelling at periscope depth when she spotted *UB-65*. The American skipper, Lt Foster (or Forster) got into position and was about to fire torpedoes at the enemy ship. What followed adds another phenomenal twist to the story. Before *L-2* could act, her Captain was amazed as *UB-65* blew up before their eyes and sank. The American submarine never fired a shot. Was that the end of it all? Not quite.

Goss and Behe offer a tantalizing follow-up, which I have unfortunately not been able to track down, but it adds a nice spooky coda. They tell us that on 10 July 1968, almost exactly fifty years to the day (give or take three days, depending on which report of *UB-65*'s death is accurate), a man from Baltimore called Sven Morgens-Larsen and his wife June were enjoying a cruise on their yacht *Grey Seal* off the Irish coast close to Cape Clear. In the late afternoon they were approaching Fastnet Rock. At 6.30 p.m. they heard a muffled explosion. The sea, a few hundred feet from them, churned and up popped a submarine's conning tower. As the rest of the craft emerged from the foam, they saw the number "65" on her side ... and a stationary figure standing on her prow. The whole apparition, submarine, figure, everything, then dissolved and was gone. Apparently Morgens-Larsen knew nothing of the legend until he'd returned to Baltimore where he looked up the story in the archives at Johns Hopkins University. Fact or premeditated fancy? Who cares? Those pesky U-boat men just won't stay down.

Yet even this peculiar report has a precedent. The large American nuclear submarine USS *Thresher* went down with all hands on a deep test-dive 220 miles (354 km) off Cape Cod on 9 April 1963. Her loss in peacetime, with 129 men, was a major maritime tragedy. Fast forward to the summer of 1967 when the Schulz family with their three children are enjoying a cruise on their yacht the *Yorktown Clipper*, again about 200 miles (322 km) off Cape Cod. Suddenly, to their amazement, to starboard, a massive submarine surfaces. She looks damaged, with a gash in her hull. There are two uniformed US Navy men, one standing on her walkway and one on her bows, staring back at the *Yorktown Clipper* through telescopes. This encounter lasted a few minutes, and climaxed dramatically as the sub reared up out of the water and broke apart amidships, then vanished beneath the waves. The two figures did not budge. As she went down, the Schulzes maintain that they saw the name "*Thresher*" on her side.

Perhaps in the watery hereafter, the spirits juggle around with earthbound officialdom because the real nuclear submarine would not have had her name written on her side, just her number, 593, from her official designation SSN-593. So, with the *Thresher* tragedy still painfully fresh to a seagoing family just four years after it occurred, was this some psychic hallucination triggered by a collective memory? The Schulzes were in the area where the tragedy had occurred. If one person had reported this vision, it could be questionable, but a married couple *and* their three children? Would a family conspire to make things up? We don't know – but there's a distinct possibility that Hector C. Bywater may have done so with *UB-65*.

Goss and Behe suggest the story of the jinxed sub may have been part of a British destabilizing propaganda drive to unnerve German sailors. On the other hand, Bywater's *Their Secret Purposes* (1932), which includes the haunted U-boat, is ample evidence that this inventive, talented man liked spinning a meaty yarn. Bywater was no stranger to intelligence work and had worked behind enemy lines in Germany. He is also famous for his 1925 "faction" book, *The Great Pacific War*, written whilst he was naval correspondent for the *Daily Telegraph*.

It is a startling but true fact that Bywater prophesied in uncanny detail the Japanese Pacific campaign of the Second World War. He has been dubbed among some historians as "the man who invented Pearl Harbor". His book opens with Japan's seizure of Manchuria, Formosa and Korea. "But in thus pursuing a policy which aimed at the virtual enslavement of China, Japan had inevitably drawn upon herself the hostility of the Powers," wrote Bywater. Much more so than Morgan Robertson's eerie predictions in 1898 concerning the *Titanic*, Bywater's book is replete with so many accurate predictions that it could well have been the handbook used for Pearl Harbor by the Japanese Imperial Navy. *The Great Pacific War* was published while Isoroku Yamamoto – the admiral who masterminded the Japanese naval strategy in the Second World War – was an attaché with the Japanese embassy in Washington, DC. It was featured in the *New York Times*'s popular book section in 1925, and although the Japanese embassy registered an official protest over the review, declaring it "provocative", the book would have been essential reading for any Japanese naval officer. Yet despite all this, as a kind of Robert Harris of his day, Bywater was making it all up, but magnificently so, due to his thorough knowledge and grasp of naval affairs.

So, what about all those names mentioned in the *UB-65* story? Let's deal first with the very foundation of Bywater's version

– the mysterious "pamphlet" of "Professor Dr Hecht". The pamphlet does not exist. Checking online I find that there was a Max Hecht. He was born in 1857 and is listed as a "psycho-semasiologist". He dealt with semantics and the study of language, and doesn't seem to fit the bill as a renowned, well-known psychologist. Lamont Brown however, refers to him as such, and states that his "unpublicized" report on *UB-65* exists in the Staatsbibliothek der Stiftung Preussicher Kulturbesitz in Marburg. Goss and Behe went to much trouble to have this document and supposed others dug out from the relevant German archives, yet found that they did not exist. They are left only with speculation as to whom Bywater based his mysterious "Professor Dr Hecht" upon. They hint that he might have been based on the journalist and screenwriter Ben Hecht (1894–1964), the first screenwriter to be awarded an Oscar. It seems unlikely. There was indeed a Submarine Commodore called Andreas Michelsen, who had commanded the light cruiser *Rostock* in the Battle of Jutland in 1916, and in June 1917 took over command of U-boats. With no crew list for *UB-65* available, the names Lohmann and Eberhard evade us. Then we have the crewmen Petersen and Wernicke, the man who said goodbye to the unnamed petty officer. There's nothing on Petersen, but there is a Fritz Wernicke (1885–1918), who commanded *UB-42* and *UB-66* (which is one number away from 65), but *UB-66* went down with all hands, with Wernicke in command, on 18 January 1918 in the eastern Mediterranean. There are a couple of other names left hanging; some crewman called Richter and the exorcist, Lutheran Minister, Revd Franz Weber. These appear in versions of the story in the 1970s. *Fate* magazine became a magnet for these stories, and although in its later incarnation (prior to its demise in 2009), it wasn't afraid of debunking a subject, in earlier times many features didn't have to be too academically inclined with sources and footnotes. We were also in the heyday of aliens and the UFO, subjects which could impregnate any other paranormal happening like a virus.

So who were Franz Weber and the mysterious Richter? If you were looking for some German names to slot into a U-boat story – how does Franz Weber-Richter sound? To discover who he was, we only have to look at an article in *Der Spiegel* dated

8 February 1961, entitled "Men from Another Planet". He was Germany's own George Adamski. Together with his interplanetary associate, Charles Mekis, Weber-Richter had managed to convince a growing army of followers that an invasion of earth by the Venusians was imminent. His leaflets and publications delivered an income, but living in South America provided an added opportunity to raise funds. It may have been tough convincing people that he had spent several months living with aliens on Mercury, but Franz Weber-Richter claimed to be Hitler's son, an assertion just slightly more credible than "the Venusians are coming" but sufficient to gain sympathetic handouts from ageing, fugitive Nazis. *Der Führer* would have been proud.

Whatever "the truth" is about the doomed *UB-65*, it doesn't really matter, except for the fact that thirty-seven families in Germany lost their sons, husbands and fathers to an unimaginably horrible death. Time and our imagination have built this into an immortal story and we need such romance in our lives. The careful researchers at www.uboat.net mention nothing of her haunting. Her loss is reported thus: "14 Jul 1918 – Lost by accidental cause (marine casualty) off Padstow, Cornwall on or after July 14, 1918. 37 dead (all hands lost)." And she has now been found as the following report states on both Facebook and Wikipedia:

An expedition mounted in 2004 as part of the Channel 4 *Wreck Detectives* underwater archaeological TV series to survey a previously unidentified U-boat wreck that had been located earlier at 50.611 °N 5.005 °W, during a routine survey by the Royal Navy, confirmed the identity of the boat as *UB-65*. Inspection of the wreck by nautical archaeologist Innes McCartney and U-boat historian Dr Axel Niestlé (through identification of design features such as the type of deck gun, and identification numbers that were stamped on one of her propellers) proved conclusively that the wreck was that of *UB-65*. A survey of the wreck showed no obvious indication of weapon attack being the cause of loss (although this could not be ruled out; shock damage from a depth charge attack could have caused loss through failure of internal seawater systems and hull penetrations that would not be obvious from an external examination). The aft hatches are open indicating a possible attempt by at least some of the crew to escape from the vessel. Consideration of the various observations of the wreck, along with historical observations regarding depth control and handling difficulties on diving experienced by other boats of the class, led to a conclusion that she was most likely lost through accidental causes on or after 14 July 1918, the date of the sinking of a Portuguese vessel in the Padstow area. All of her crew of 37 were listed as lost. Having been identified as *UB-65* the wreck was given protected place status under the Protection of Military Remains Act 1986 on 1 November 2006.

R.I.P. Petersen, Lohmann, Richter, Eberhard and all your other shipmates, real or imagined.

THE DARK OCEAN

Metaphysics is a dark ocean without shores or lighthouse, strewn with many a philosophic wreck.

Immanuel Kant (1724–1804)

Is there a lonelier, more isolated job than that of a lighthouse keeper? For those seeking solace, with time to meditate, surrounded by the high seas, without the inherent dangers involved in being a mariner, then perhaps the lighthouse with its daily routines is as close as you'll get to a monastic life. Yet the strange and the inexplicable are always keen to poke their icy fingers into the lives of isolated men.

The Biminis are a group of small islands about 50 miles (80 km) east of Miami, Florida. There's a lighthouse there which is a familiar landmark for cruise-ship passengers en route to Nassau from Florida. It's unmanned now, although equipped with an automatic light, but the Great Isaac lighthouse is the scene of a famous lighthouse mystery. On 4 August 1969 (some sources claim 22 December) when the relief crew was sent out to change shifts, the light station was discovered to be abandoned. This was very odd, because everything in the building was undisturbed. The two lighthouse keepers had simply vanished and have never been found. Due to its location, the Great Isaac mystery has become yet another curio in the catalogue of Bermuda Triangle mysteries.

Around the world's remote and dangerous coastlines there are many abandoned lighthouses, often complete with stories of hauntings. One such location is the Point of Ayr lighthouse, which has stood, in various incarnations, since 1776 on Talacre Beach in Wales. This isolated yet cheery red-and-white sentinel rising from the sands has no doubt saved many a sailor's life as it guided their ships across Liverpool Bay from the Welsh town of Llandudno. It was abandoned in 1840. Although since then it has at times seemed derelict and neglected, it was refurbished in 1994, but remains unoccupied, standing as a lonely watchman in front of the bay's offshore wind farm. But as with many such buildings, the Point of Ayr lighthouse is known to be haunted. Occasional visits to the location by spiritualist mediums have resulted in claims that the spirit of a lonely man, known to locals as Raymond, who died of a broken heart, haunts the light. There have been sightings of a ghostly lighthouse keeper walking around the top of the tower. Some tourists report feeling unwell and disturbed when they've been there. Now the broken-hearted phantom has been commemorated by local artist Angela Smith, whose seven-foot-tall sculpture made of hundreds of pieces of highly polished, medical-grade stainless steel, named *The Keeper*, stands on the walkway at the top of the tower, the wind whistling through his open metallic ribs like some otherworldly wind chime.

Sometimes notions of "curses" attached to lighthouses have been solved with the appliance of science. A so-called "cursed" lighthouse for a while was the Ship John Shoal lighthouse, off Delaware. The US Congress decided that a light was needed there in 1850, but the sheer logistics of erecting the building became a huge challenge, and it took twenty-seven years to build the iron tower, which was not finished until 1877. Its name derives from a wrecking at the location of the lighthouse in 1797, when the ship *John*, en route from Germany to Philadelphia, ran aground on Christmas Eve. This misfortune put paid to the Yuletide expectations of her German crew who were looking forward to festivities at their planned destination. Thankfully, the cargo and crew were all saved and the men enjoyed the unexpected seasonal hospitality of sympathetic families along the Cohansey River. As well as other peculiar legends around the lighthouse, it was commonly believed that the place was cursed in the 1880s. This took the form of a persistent illness that left several keepers sick or paralysed after extended stays.

The curse went on for years, until it was discovered that the structure's red leaded paint was seeping into the rainwater tanks. All the old paint was stripped away and replaced with a coating of tar. Problem solved; the curse was lifted. However, 3,000 miles (4,828 km) away across the stormy Atlantic, the new lease of life the Ship John Shoal Lighthouse crew enjoyed may well have been welcomed by a trio of their ship-guiding peers. Sadly, even a coating of tar on their abode would not have saved the Scottish lighthouse-men Donal Macarthur, James Ducat and Thomas Marshall.

THE MYSTERY OF
EILEAN MOR

Eilean Mor is one of the principal islands in the Flannan Isles, also known as the Seven Hunters, a lonely cluster about 20 miles (32 km) west of the isle of Lewis in the Outer Hebrides of Scotland. Although it means "Big Island" in Gaelic, at thirty-nine acres this isn't a massive place, but for sailors it's a forbidding one. It rises 288 feet (87.7 m) above the Atlantic Ocean, with perilous sheer cliffs up to 150 foot (45.7 m) high. It was here in 1895 that work began on a seventy-five-foot (22.9m) high lighthouse, and from 1899 it commenced beaming a guiding light to sailors up to twenty-five miles (40 km) out at sea. In 1971 the last crew of keepers left and the light was automated, and it still shines on today.

More fiction and speculation has been churned out over this genuinely strange story of vanished lighthouse-men than any other island-bound maritime mystery. I was cajoled by some of its less steadfast aspects when writing about it several years ago, relying on versions told by such romancers as Vincent Gaddis in his nonetheless fascinating *Invisible Horizons*. Some of what has been passed off as fact for the past century appears to be anything but real. This is regrettable because the story needs no such embellishment – its truth stands alone in its genuine weirdness. As well as Gaddis and others, we can blame the colourful imagination of Wilfrid Wilson Gibson (1878–1962), a prolific poet and close friend of Rupert Brooke. His 1912 ballad, "Flannan Isle", lies at the root of much of the unnecessary detritus this puzzle has gathered down the decades.

Yet, as we crowded through the door,
We only saw a table spread
For dinner, meat, and cheese and bread;
But, all untouched; and no-one there,
As though, when they sat down to eat,
Ere they could even taste,
Alarm had come, and they in haste
Had risen and left the bread and meat,
For at the table head a chair
Lay tumbled on the floor.

There are shades of Conan Doyle's fictitious rendering of the *Mary Celeste* here, and things are not helped by a later stanza which goes:

And how the rock had been the death
Of many a likely lad:
How six had come to a sudden end,
And three had gone stark mad:
And one whom we'd all known as friend
Had leapt from the lantern one still night,
And fallen dead by the lighthouse wall

Eerie hints of creeping madness, shifting personalities, the wages of loneliness and isolation ... meat and drink to a poet. The three keepers, James Ducat, Donald McArthur and Thomas Marshall, were at the end of a fourteen-day shift in December 1900 but had been prevented from leaving the island due to bad weather. A passing ship, the steamer *Archtor*, had found it odd on the night of 15 December that the lighthouse, which was normally visible for twenty-five miles (40 km), was unlit. When the relief tender, the *Hesperus*, set off to the island, the weather, with mountainous seas, had been so bad that they had to stand off for some time, but when they did finally get a man ashore, the truth became evident, as this telegram of 26 December 1900 reveals. It was sent by Captain Harvie, the Master of the *Hesperus*:

A dreadful accident has happened at Flannans. The three Keepers, Ducat, Marshall and the occasional have disappeared from the island. On our arrival there this afternoon no sign of life was to be seen on the Island. Fired a rocket but, as no response was made, managed to land Moore, who went up to the Station but found no Keepers there. The clocks were stopped and other signs indicated that the accident must have happened about a week ago. Poor fellows they must been blown over the cliffs or drowned trying to secure a crane or something like that. Night coming on, we could not wait to make something as to their fate. I have left Moore, MacDonald, Buoymaster and two Seamen on the island to keep the light burning until you make other arrangements. Will not return to Oban until I hear from you. I have repeated this wire to Muirhead in case you are not at home. I will remain at the telegraph office tonight until it closes, if you wish to wire me.

   Master, HESPERUS

All the real, genuine documentation of this case, including the above, is available at the Northern Lighthouse Board's website (www.nlb.org.uk). However, you'll not find any of the other revelations that have clung to the yarn as told by Gaddis and others. One of the strangest is Gaddis's inclusion of entries from the log kept by the lighthouse-men, the source of which he attributes to an article by Ernest Fallon in the August 1929 edition of *True Strange Stories* magazine. It was by repeating these entries when writing this story some years ago that I incurred the displeasure of the Northern Lighthouse Board. Regrettably, the following words are still being peddled by many "unexplained" websites today:

12 December: Gale north by northwest. Sea lashed to fury. Never seen such a storm. Waves very high. Tearing at lighthouse. Everything shipshape. James Ducat irritable. (Later:) Storm still raging, wind steady. Stormbound. Cannot go out. Ship passing sounding foghorn. Could see lights of cabins. Ducat quiet. McArthur crying.

13 December: Storm continued through night. Wind shifted west by north. Ducat quiet. McArthur praying. (Later:) Noon, grey daylight. Me, Ducat and McArthur prayed.
15 December: Storm ended, sea calm, God is over all.

There are distinct echoes of Gibson's poem here: "And three had gone stark mad". Gaddis and others claim that these entries were all written in Marshall's handwriting. The archives of the Northern Lighthouse Board do not corroborate this at all: the handwriting in the log was by Ducat, and the log seems to have only been kept up to 13 December. There were some final brief notes about weather conditions written by Ducat in chalk on a slate at 9 a.m. on 15 December. Whatever befell the men possibly occurred between then and the night of the 15th. Nautical logs are not personal diaries. Any man writing about praying or God, passing facile comments about his shipmate's moods or even using phrases such as "sea lashed to a fury" would have faced more than a few questions from his practical, no-nonsense superiors ashore. Vincent Gaddis was a decent and highly entertaining writer, but his penchant for invention included such contrived conversations as "'Looking forward to shore leave?' asked the skipper, smiling. 'Aye,' Moore answered, 'It'll be good to be back on land for a space where you can see people, talk, and have a drink or two. 'Tis pretty lonely there some times.'" Gaddis wasn't there; how could he describe a "smiling" captain or report conversations? These little verbal excursions in his work might add colour, but they're bogus, and none of these words appear in any of the documents held by the Northern Lighthouse Board.

My original resort to the creepy logbook entries had another result. In 2006 I was contacted by none other than Cyril Nicholas Henty-Dodd (1935–2009), better known as Simon Dee, onetime high-profile British television interviewer and disc jockey who hosted a twice-weekly BBC TV chat show, *Dee Time*, in the late 1960s. (Some suggest that Dee was the model for the Mike Myers character Austin Powers.) Dee was keen to produce a documentary about the Eilean Mor mystery, but when I stripped it back to its factual basics, mysterious though they are, he expressed his "bitter disappointment" and I heard nothing more.

The mystery of the log entries remains. Where did Ernest Fallon get these from? We must conclude that they are an invention. If not, and somewhere they exist, then they are genuinely strange. But Fallon wasn't alone in his embroidery. Children's author Carey Miller in his 1977 *Mysteries of the Unknown* includes the story that when the man, Moore, is sent on to the island from the *Hesperus*, when he "opened the door of the lighthouse three huge birds of an unknown species flew out to sea from the top of the light". There is no evidence to support this. As ever, for the newspapers of the time this sinister event presented a field day for inventive journalism. It began with a report in the *Scotsman*, dated 28 December 1900, stating that one of the cranes on the island had been swept away by the severe weather. The official report contradicts this. Then the *Oban Times* weighed in with three details on 5 January 1901. It reported that there was a half-eaten meal on the table in the lighthouse (other reports even tell us that it was mutton and potatoes), that a chair had been pushed back as if its occupant had arisen in haste and that there was an oilskin found trapped in the wreckage of the island's west crane. The first two claims are entirely spurious and the third appears nowhere else; in any case, even if the sea had swept away one of the keepers, the loss of his oilskin seems unlikely.

So the question will remain forever: what really happened? All manner of suggestions have been presented down the years. The paranormal lobby have been busy creating legends of the "strange atmosphere" and peculiar history of the island. Even piracy has been suggested – although they would have been a pretty dumb bunch of Jack Sparrows to attack Eilean Mor. The inevitable sea monster has been cajoled from the deep, along with time slips, other dimensions and the evergreen favourite, alien abduction. What a bunch of Venusian tourists would want with three horny-handed Scottish lighthouse keepers is beyond imagination. If their disappearance was not supernatural, then the culprit must surely be the sea. Even though the lighthouse stood over 300 feet (91 m) above sea level, the sea at Eilean Mor was so violent at times that spray lashed the top of the light. The jetty was reported as battered and the rails were twisted. Perhaps two men had gone out in a storm and a third had seen a huge wave coming and gone out to warn them, with tragic results. We'll never know. Freak waves are not restricted to Pacific tsunamis. When I sailed through a hurricane in the Pacific, I had no idea how high the waves were, but they towered above the ship like mountains. Two vessels in the South Atlantic in 2001, the *Bremen* and *Caledonian Star*, both encountered 98 foot (30 m) freak waves. Bridge windows on both ships were smashed, and all power and instrumentation were lost. In 2004, the US Naval Research Laboratory ocean-floor pressure sensors detected a freak wave caused by Hurricane Ivan in the Gulf of Mexico. From peak to trough it was around 91 feet (27.7 m) high and around 660 feet (200 m) long. The open sea can be a terrifying place.

The mystery of Eilean Mor continues to inspire creative writers and musicians. Part of Gibson's poem is quoted in "Horror of Fang Rock", an episode in the *Dr Who* series (complete with the misspelling "Flannen"). The Genesis song "The Mystery of Flannan Isle Lighthouse" is featured on the band's compilation *Archive 1967–75*. The missing men inspired Hector Zazou's song "Lighthouse", subsequently performed by Siouxsie Sioux on the album *Songs from the Cold Seas*, and the opera *The Lighthouse* by Peter Maxwell Davies is also based on the incident.

In 2000, exactly 100 years after the keepers disappeared, silence fell for one minute on nearby Breasclete, west of Lewis, in honour of the three men, in an event covered by the BBC in Scotland. A reporter with BBC Radio nan Gàidheal in Stornoway, Alasdair Macaulay, who had researched the incident, said:

I have heard about a woman at Crowlista in Uig who had been hanging out her washing on that day. She was said to have seen a massive wall of water coming in from the west. She apparently ran back to the house as this large wave hit the shore. Her washing and washing line were said to have been swept away.

Such is the all-consuming power of the sea; merciless, inhuman and forever mysterious.

VANISHING ACT: THE PHILADELPHIA EXPERIMENT

For any hoax to succeed it has to be believable and relevant.
Those that endure, resisting even the absolute proof, the definitive
exposure of the culprits and their methods, are endowed with
additional qualities. They resonate with deep-seated imagery in
the minds of the masses and of the educated public.
Jacques F. Vallee (1939–), *Journal of Scientific Exploration*,
Vol. 8, No. 1, 1994

It is always a sad occasion when a ship is decommissioned. Like buildings, they become the temporary homes for generations of men. They carry their cargo around the world, play their role in history and become the receptacles of many memories, happy or sad. Such was the case in Greece on 15 November 1992 when the Hellenic Navy finally said goodbye to its trusty old destroyer, the *Leon* (D54). She hung around for seven years, neglected and rusting in the Piraeus dockyards, until in November 1999 V&J Scrap Metal Trading Ltd bought her for breaking up as scrap. She'd been afloat on the world's oceans for fifty-seven years. Who knows what ghosts still lurked in her old superstructure, or what tortured phantoms infested her hull? According to her legend, many more than we'd care to think.

The *Leon* was transferred to Greece from the US Navy under the Mutual Defense Assistance Program. She was put to service for her new country in January 1951 by Vice Admiral D. Foifas to patrol the azure Aegean Sea as a training vessel for officer cadets and midshipmen. The *Leon*'s new life in the balmy waters of the eastern Mediterranean was a stark contrast to her earlier duties in the cold Atlantic. The *Leon* spent the first eight years of her life with a different identity, as the destroyer USS *Eldridge* (DE-173). Her keel was laid down on 22 February 1943. She was built by the Federal Shipbuilding and Drydock Company, Newark, New Jersey, and launched on 25 July 1943.

In the heat of the Second World War, the *Eldridge* could simply have been just another of the many US Navy destroyers, yet a brief period in her first year afloat has become the subject of several books, films and documentaries. The story goes that the US government managed to make the *Eldridge* invisible – an experiment that had an unexpected bonus in the teleportation of the whole vessel from one port to another. If you ask the US Navy about all this, (and many do), this is an example of the reply you'll receive.

DEPARTMENT OF THE NAVY
OFFICE OF NAVAL RESEARCH
ARLINGTON, VIRGINIA 22217

08 September 1996
Information Sheet: Philadelphia Experiment

Over the years, the Navy has received innumerable queries about the so-called "Philadelphia Experiment" or "Project" and the alleged role of the Office of Naval Research (ONR) in it. The majority of these inquiries are directed to the Office of Naval Research or to the Fourth Naval District in Philadelphia. The frequency of these queries predictably intensifies each time the experiment is mentioned by the popular press, often in a science fiction book.

The genesis of the Philadelphia Experiment myth dates back to 1955 with the publication of The Case for UFO's by the late Morris K. Jessup.

Sometime after the publication of the book, Jessup received correspondence from a Carlos Miguel Allende, who gave his address as R.D. #1, Box 223, New Kensington, Pa. In his correspondence, Allende commented on Jessup's book and gave details of an alleged secret naval experiment conducted by the Navy in Philadelphia in 1943. During the experiment, according to Allende, a ship was rendered invisible and teleported to and from Norfolk in a few minutes, with some terrible after-effects for crew members. Supposedly, this incredible feat was accomplished by applying Einstein's "unified field" theory. Allende claimed that he had witnessed the experiment from another ship and that the incident was reported in a Philadelphia newspaper. The identity of the newspaper has never been established. Similarly, the identity of Allende is unknown, and no information exists on his present address.

In 1956 a copy of Jessup's book was mailed anonymously to ONR. The pages of the book were interspersed with hand-written comments which alleged a knowledge of UFO's, their means of motion, the culture and ethos of the beings occupying these UFO's, described in pseudo-scientific and incoherent terms.

Two officers, then assigned to ONR, took a personal interest in the book and showed it to Jessup. Jessup concluded that the writer of those comments on his book was the same person who had written him about the Philadelphia Experiment. These two officers personally had the book retyped and arranged for the reprint, in typewritten form, of 25 copies. The officers and their personal belongings have left ONR many years ago, and ONR does not have a file copy of the annotated book.

Personnel at the Fourth Naval District believe that the questions surrounding the so-called "Philadelphia Experiment" arise from quite routine research which occurred during World War II at the Philadelphia Naval Shipyard. Until recently, it was believed that the foundation for the apocryphal stories arose from degaussing experiments which have the effect of making a ship undetectable or "invisible" to magnetic mines. Another likely genesis of the bizarre stories about levitation, teleportation and effects on human crew members might be attributed to experiments with the generating plant of a destroyer, the USS Timmerman. In the 1950's this ship was part of an experiment to test the effects of a small, high-frequency generator providing 1,000hz instead of the standard 400hz. The higher-frequency generator produced corona discharges, and other well-known phenomena associated with high-frequency generators. None of the crew suffered effects from the experiment.

ONR has never conducted any investigations on invisibility, either in 1943 or at any other time (ONR was established in 1946). In view of present scientific knowledge, ONR scientists do not believe that such an experiment could be possible except in the realm of science fiction.

The Philadelphia Experiment is the meat and pickle in a fat, juicy hamburger, sandwiched in a very crusty old bun. The top slice of bread is the well-toasted conundrum of a man called Carlos Miguel Allende (1925–86); the bottom slice is a slightly mouldy and equally confusing character named Al Bielek (1927–2011). The hapless customer who bit into this mephitic smorgasbord and released its toxic spores into conspiracy's fertile greenhouse was Morris K. Jessup (1900–1959).

The Case for the UFO by Morris K. Jessup was published in 1955. Jessup was an astronomer with a sideline in astrophysics, as well as being involved in archaeological work in Mexico, and his book was a genuine attempt to discuss the possible means of propulsion used by flying saucers. The UFO was all the rage at the time and, as he lamented the continued use of rocketry, the possibility of some kind of anti-gravity drive using electromagnetism constantly occupied Jessup's keen mind. He was prescient in emphasizing that a breakthrough revision of Albert Einstein's unified field theory would be critical in powering a future generation of spacecraft. Yet the wilder your thoughts become out on the fringes of science, the greater the chance of becoming a nut magnet.

13 January 1955 was a red letter day for Jessup. The mailman brought him a bizarre, rambling letter from a man who identified himself as one "Carlos Allende". Accompanied by two scrappy newspaper clippings, Allende's dispatch spoke of something called the "Philadelphia Experiment", and called upon Jessup to support new research into the "UFT" – Einstein's unified field theory. The letter contested the general knowledge that Einstein's theory was incomplete. The suggestion was that the great Albert had in reality completed the theory, but because he believed humankind was not ready for its consequences, he had supressed it. Einstein had, apparently, shared this conclusion with none other than the great British philosopher and mathematician Bertrand Russell (1872–1970).

Whilst serving as a seaman on board the SS *Andrew Furuseth*, a merchant ship, Allende claimed to have witnessed the USS *Eldridge* vanish and reappear as part of an experiment based on Einstein's theory, carried out by the Navy. He also claimed to know surviving members of the destroyer's crew. The unified field theory aims to describe mathematically and physically the interrelated nature of the forces that comprise electromagnetic radiation and gravity. It would appear that it has not progressed far beyond the theoretical stage; we're still using aviation fuel to fly and rockets to get into orbit, so it can be argued that thus far no single theory has successfully expressed these electromagnetic radiation and gravity relationships in viable mathematical or physical terms, yet that mission is probably still in motion at Area 51 in Nevada.

Jessup, asking for evidence and corroboration, sent Allende a postcard. It was several months before a reply arrived, but this time the signature was a certain "Carl M. Allen". At this point Jessup saw sense because "Allen" said he couldn't provide the required information, but might be able to unearth it if he could be hypnotized. The correspondence was discontinued.

Conspiracy theorists today, forever intent on flogging dead horses, suggest that Carl Allen (as opposed to Allende) was a replacement: a CIA agent trained to occupy and impersonate Allende's original wacky role, planted into the saga because the US government had been intercepting Carlos Allende's mail. The aim was to ridicule the Philadelphia Experiment as the government was concerned that its "secret" may have escaped. Subsequent events would seem to blow large holes in this theory.

Jessup got on with his life, but in the spring of 1957 the Office of Naval Research (ONR) in Washington, DC, contacted him. They had received a rather odd package, the contents of which they wanted him to examine. In a manila envelope marked "HAPPY EASTER" was a copy of Jessup's UFO book, extensively annotated by hand in its margins. The ONR wondered if Jessup recognized the handwriting. To his surprise, he did: it was that of Carlos Allende.

The annotations, in three different coloured inks (Jessup decided that although they seemed to come from three commentators, they were all Allende's work) and resorting to odd capitalization, weird punctuation and peculiar grammar, represented a detailed and lengthy discussion of the merits of various suppositions that Jessup makes throughout his book, with various mentions of the Philadelphia Experiment. Today we would immediately exclaim "Crank!", but the Navy seemed to believe that some of the comments warranted study and had over 100 copies made of the book, complete with the colourful comments. Jessup was now carrying a burden that would eventually weight him down. The ONR later told Jessup that the return address on Allende's letter to Jessup was an abandoned farmhouse.

On 29 April 1959, Dr Manson Valentine, an oceanographer and zoologist, invited Morris Jessup to dinner. Jessup wanted Valentine to discuss a draft document which dealt with the Philadelphia Experiment. The oceanographer was the last person to see Jessup alive. Valentine said that his friend had been "in a depressed state of mind". The next day, Jessup's body, dead from carbon monoxide poisoning, was found slumped at the wheel of his station wagon at Matheson Hammock Park in Dade County, near Miami. A rubber hose had been neatly attached to the exhaust and fed through the open rear window, sealed with a damp rag. No documents or manuscripts were found inside the car. This sad event is one of the enduring pillars of faith among conspiracy theorists.

What then, is supposed to have happened to the USS *Eldridge*? The details are as follows.

The required equipment was installed on board at the Philadelphia Naval Shipyard. In the summer of 1943 testing began, apparently with limited success. On 22 July 1943, the *Eldridge* was, apparently, surrounded by a greenish fog and rendered almost completely invisible. Crew members supposedly felt sick and nauseous afterwards. Then the horror really kicked in. As the green mist cleared and the *Eldridge* reappeared, some sailors were embedded in her metal structure. One seaman had his hand embedded in the steel hull and had ended up on a different deck level. The Navy was forced to limit its original objective of total invisibility and restrict the experiment solely to rendering the *Eldridge* invisible to radar.

So far, so bizarre, but it becomes even more fantastic. "Experts" on the story (and there are many) allege that the secret equipment on board was not properly recalibrated, and despite the terrible results of the earlier effort, the experiment was repeated on 28 October 1943. As before, the ship achieved invisibility, but with an added bonus; in a flash of blue light, she physically vanished from the dock and was teleported to Norfolk, Virginia, over 200 miles (320 km) away. She had been in full view of crew members – including Carlos Allende – aboard the merchant ship SS *Andrew Furuseth*, who then witnessed the *Eldridge* reappear in Philadelphia back at her original berth. Another claim is that during this process she travelled back in time by about ten seconds. There is also the curious story that some of the sailors from the *Eldridge* dematerialized or vanished whilst enjoying a drink ashore in a bar in August 1943. Such were, apparently, the physical after-effects of the experiment.

The man who popularized all of this and brought it to worldwide attention was Yale graduate and multilinguist Charles Frambach Berlitz (1914–2003). Born in New York, he was the grandson of Maximilian Berlitz, founder of the Berlitz Language Schools. Reading his books one has to remember that Berlitz served for thirteen years in the US Army, mostly in intelligence, which will have undoubtedly contributed to his passion for a good story. His childhood was almost as phenomenal as his appetite for the unexplained; each of the servants in the well-heeled Berlitz household had been instructed to communicate with the young Charles in a separate language. By his teens he was fluent in eight languages, conversing in Spanish with his nanny, in Russian with his grandfather, whilst communicating with his father in German. This must have made him quite a military asset. Following the success of his bestselling 1974 book, *The Bermuda Triangle*, in which he had referred to the Philadelphia Experiment, Berlitz teamed up with ufologist and Roswell aficionado William Moore (1943–), who had been researching into the USS *Eldridge* affair for some time, to produce a new publishing success in 1979, *The Philadelphia Experiment*. Moore would later earn a place in the pantheon of ufology as he became a central figure in the release of the controversial Majestic 12 documents, which purport to reveal evidence of a massive cover-up of what occurred at Roswell in 1947. Berlitz and Moore's book makes no bones in its introduction about the possibility of the Philadelphia Experiment being nothing more than an elaborate myth, but its general thrust certainly aims to convince the reader that all of these weird things actually happened. Such was the book's success that the inevitable eponymous movie came out in 1984, with two fictional sailors getting even more from the experiment than invisibility and teleportation. They experience time travel, ending up in the future – naturally, in 1984.

Four years later, this lacklustre piece of sci-fi celluloid found its niche on late night TV and a new chapter in the saga opened up another new chronicle, even more bizarre than the original. Watching the film that night in 1988 was Al Bielek. To understand this man's story, you need to accept that Al Bielek claimed to retain all of the lifetime memories (starting from babyhood) of another man, Edward A. Cameron. Ed Cameron, along with his brother Duncan Cameron, was alleged to be a first-hand participant in the Philadelphia Experiment of 1943. Pay attention at the back, there, because this is difficult. Al claimed that as he viewed the movie, he started to recover fragmented memories of his involvement in the Philadelphia Experiment. So let's stand back for a moment and examine this: Al Bielek was the walking receptacle of another man's life, Ed Cameron, who was supposed to have been a crew member of the USS *Eldridge*. You might be forgiven for falling about in hysterics if someone told you that such a claim would be widely accepted, but we're in paranormal land here and anything goes. Bielek enjoyed a substantial career on the phenomena circuit, guested on many radio and TV shows, produced CDs and DVDs, all because the uncritical, credulous hordes continued to accept that he was the reincarnation of a 1943 sailor. As one supportive website suggests:

> The idea of a separate consciousness inhabiting, at least temporarily, someone else's body is a well-known phenomenon as is the case when a channeller or a medium brings in a spirit to speak through him or a person is possessed by a demonic spirit. It is also possible for a spirit or consciousness to transfer into a different body during a "single" life. This is essentially what occurred to Al Bielek, when the consciousness of Ed Cameron was "transferred" into the body of one-year-old Alfred Bielek in 1927.

Bielek still has many devoted disciples, and whilst it's not fair to kick the dead when they've gone, there's also an extensive and critical website (www.bielek-debunked.com), which potential dupes should study. The whole "Ed Cameron" edifice crumbled when the debunkers contacted Alexander Cameron IV, the living descendant of the family to which Bielek claimed to have belonged in an alternative existence. Bielek's claims appeared to fall like dominoes (one brother had died as a child and the other had never been in the Navy) and the last thing the current Cameron said on the matter was, "I think poor Al has smoked one too many."

Bielek needed more than the Camerons and the USS *Eldridge* to prop up his epic existence. In order to strengthen his media magnet, he claimed involvement in not only the Philadelphia Experiment, but the Montauk Project and other so-called government-backed "black" operations. This allowed him to claim that he'd been subjected to mind control (that's what the New World Order does to us when we know too much). Such a process would wipe his mind clean of all memories of his involvement in sinister projects. The Montauk Project is a legendary series of secret US government operations carried out at Montauk Air Force Station, Long Island, to develop psychological warfare techniques ... and even time travel. That's another trip Bielek has enjoyed and pontificated upon on radio and DVD – he claims to have travelled to the year 2147, but couldn't be bothered to ask who the president was then.

If one studies the transcripts of some of Bielek's lectures, there are more than a few anomalies. Along with Berlitz, he sometimes refers to the Philadelphia Experiment as "Project Rainbow". However, Project Rainbow was the CIA's designation for a research project aimed at reducing the radar cross-section of the Lockheed U-2 to make the plane undetectable by Soviet radars during its flights over the USSR.

Some of the scientific luminaries who Bielek claims were associated with control of the USS *Eldridge* invisibility project include Nikola Tesla and Gustav Le Bon. Of course, if we allow for reincarnation and time travel, maybe these men were involved. However, since the experiment occurred in July 1943 and Tesla died on 7 January 1943 in New York City, his participation seems almost as unlikely as that of the French social psychologist, sociologist and amateur physicist Gustav Le Bon. As he was born in 1841, if he'd been hanging around the Philadelphia docks in 1943, he would have been 102. The possibility is that his ghost was in charge, seeing as he actually died in France in 1931.

You can't keep those persistent Nazis out of these scenarios, either. Another version of the yarn is that, based on Einstein's attempts to understand gravity, the hidden powers were collecting magnetic and gravitational measurements of the sea floor to detect anomalies, which are conveniently linked to "secret anti-gravity experiments" in Nazi Germany led by an SS-Obergruppenführer Hans Kammler (1901–1945?). *The Diaries of Joseph Goebbels*, edited by Hugh Trevor-Roper (1978), contain two references to Hans Kammler, discussing his expansion of duties regarding air armaments in an entry of 11 March

1945 and again on 30 March, after he was made "Plenipotentate of Turbojets". We'll save the tasty morsel of Herr Kammler for later on, but in the meantime you can see him in probably one of the most entertainingly ridiculous movies ever made, *Iron Sky* (2012). How he relates to the USS *Eldridge* is a futile cul-de-sac to be avoided.

So let us leave the late Al Bielek in heavenly peace, where he is no doubt still adding new topics into his storyline as fast as he hears them, claiming, as he often did, that his "memory suddenly came back on that". The last word on the Philadelphia Experiment has to be that of a man who genuinely served in the US Navy's destroyers at the time the alleged "project" happened. What that "experiment" involved was something that happened to many vessels during the war. Named after Carl Friedrich Gauss (1777–1855), an early researcher in the field of magnetism, "degaussing" is the process of decreasing or eliminating an unwanted magnetic field. The term owes its origins to Commander Charles F. Goodeve, RCNVR (1904–80) during the Second World War, who tried to counter the German magnetic mines that continuously threatened the British fleet.

In 1994 one of ufology's more balanced and scientific researchers, Jacques Vallee (who is portrayed by François Truffaut in Spielberg's *Close Encounters of the Third Kind* as the character "Claude Lacombe") interviewed Edward Dudgeon, born in 1927, who produced his identification and his discharge papers from the US Navy. He had served on destroyers alongside the USS *Eldridge* in 1943. Be warned, however: debunkers attract their own "anti-debunkers" and as far as they're concerned, Vallee is a disinformation agent employed by the dark forces of the New Order and Edward Dudgeon is a paid stooge of the Navy's Office of Naval Research. As Mr Fort says, yet again; here's the data, you decide. The following are extracts from the Vallee/Dudgeon interview which you can read in full at www.scientificexploration.org/journal/jse_08_1_vallee.pdf.

Dudgeon: "I am a sixty-seven year old retired executive. I was in the Navy from 1942 through 1945. I was on a destroyer that was there at the same time as the *Eldridge* DE 173. I can explain all of the strange happenings as we had the same secret equipment on our ship. You must realize that in '43, the Germans had been sinking our ships as fast as they came out of the harbours into the Atlantic, which they called 'the Graveyard'. I was just a kid then. In fact I falsified my birth certificate in order to join the Navy in 1942. I was only sixteen at the time, turning seventeen in December of 1942."

Vallee asked Dudgeon what the procedure for degaussing a ship was.

Dudgeon: "They sent the crew ashore and they wrapped the vessel in big cables, then they sent high voltages through these cables to scramble the ship's magnetic signature. This operation involved contract workers, and of course there were also merchant ships around, so civilian sailors could well have heard Navy personnel saying something like, 'they're going to make us invisible', meaning undetectable by magnetic torpedoes, without actually saying it."

Vallee: "What about the smell of ozone?"

Dudgeon: "That's not unusual. When they were degaussing you could smell the ozone that was created. You could smell it very strongly."

Vallee: "What about the luminous phenomena?"

Dudgeon: "Those are typical of electric storms, which are very spectacular. St Elmo's fire is quite common at sea. I remember coming back from Bermuda with a convoy and all the ships being engulfed in what looked like green fire. When it started to rain the green fire would disappear."

Vallee also asks about the observed disappearance of the destroyer from the harbour, and what actually happened in the tavern when men supposedly disappeared in early August 1943.

Dudgeon: "That's the simplest part of the whole story. I was in that bar that evening, we had two or three beers, and I was one of the two sailors who are said to have disappeared mysteriously. The other fellow was named Dave. I don't remember his last name, but he served on the DE 49. The fight started when some of the sailors bragged about the secret equipment and were told to keep their mouths shut. Two of us were minors. I told you I cheated on my enlistment papers. The waitresses scooted us out the back door as soon as trouble began and later denied knowing anything about us. We were leaving at two in the morning. The *Eldridge* had already left at 11 p.m. Someone looking at the harbour that night might have noticed that the *Eldridge* wasn't there anymore and it did appear in Norfolk. It was back in Philadelphia harbour the next morning, which seems like an impossible feat: if you look at the map you'll see that merchant ships would have taken two days to make the trip. They would have required pilots to go around the submarine nets, the mines and so on at the harbour entrances to the Atlantic. But the Navy used a special inland channel, the Chesapeake-Delaware Canal that bypassed all that. We made the trip in about six hours. Norfolk is where we loaded the explosives ... the Navy loaded ships twenty-four hours a day. They could load a destroyer in four hours or less. I know that's where the *Eldridge* went, and she wasn't invisible, because we passed her as she was on the way back from Virginia, in Chesapeake Bay. The *Eldridge* never disappeared. All four ships went to Bermuda in July 43 and came back together in early August. During that time we were also caught in a storm that created a display of green fire accompanied by a smell of ozone. The glow abated when it started raining."

On 24 March 1999, fifteen members of the *Eldridge*'s crew reunited in Atlantic City, New Jersey, for the first time in fifty-three years. Naturally, the controversy of 1943 was a hot topic of conversation. Robert Scheer, who joined the ship as a machinist mate in March 1945 commented: "It's my impression it's from someone with a very good imagination. It's strictly science fiction." Bill van Allen, the ship's executive officer at the time of the "experiment" claimed to have "no knowledge of anything like that happening ... I can't even conceive how the rumour got started."

In the final analysis, if the "PX" happened, so what? The fact is that if there are any invisible ships out there today, we can't see them in any case. As for conspiracies, people need to think very, very carefully when they go to the ballot box. As Erich Fromm (1900-1980) remarked: "If you want a Big Brother, you get all that comes with it."

PART 7:

PANIC AND PARANOIA

I told myself: "I am surrounded by unknown things." I imagined man without ears, suspecting the existence of sound as we suspect so many hidden mysteries, man noting acoustic phenomena whose nature and provenance he cannot determine. And I grew afraid of everything around me – afraid of the air, afraid of the night.

Guy de Maupassant (1850–93)

SCARED WITLESS

Fear defeats more people than any other one thing in the world.
Ralph Waldo Emerson (1803–82)

If you are British, Canadian, European or American, pause for a moment and look around you. You may not be rich; in fact, you might be poor. Yet the chances are you're not all that hungry. Within a few metres of where you are there will be running water at the turn of a tap. Unless the power or gas company have turned you off, you'll have light and be able to cook. If you don't have a car, you could well use public transport to get to where you need to be. The roads will be fairly maintained, with drains and sewers. You can flick on the TV or radio and get the news. You will have domestic worries, yet there will also be bright spots in your day. It may not be a good life, but it's a damn sight better than many. Yet our kids come home, throw their school-bags and coats into the hall and say "I'm starving." No; we're not *starving*; we're "peckish". There are places around the world in Africa and Asia where women have to walk five miles (8 km) to get one gallon of dirty water in a plastic bucket. In Sudan and Somalia, well-fed soldiers laugh as they dismember starving infants. Diseases we thought were long dead still ravage whole populations. Kids are dying of malnutrition every second you are reading these words, whilst we fly into a panic because the prices have gone up at our local filling station.

Yet what would happen if suddenly all the Walmarts, Tescos and Sainsburys suddenly faced closure? What would happen if the water and sewage system suddenly collapsed, we ran out of gas and electricity was rationed? What if the bubonic plague returned? These seemingly unlikely calamitous scenarios are obscure threats hiding way over a dark horizon. Yet on that long dark highway between us and that apocalyptic vision malevolent manipulators lurk. Panic and paranoia are good for business, but those who trigger them off will not feel their effect; they'll just watch them on their laptops on their yacht moored off St Tropez.

As I write this today on a sunny late March afternoon in England, a mass buying panic is in progress just streets away. The truckers who deliver diesel and petrol have threatened to go on strike. There are long lines of cars queuing up at filling stations and one dumb British politician even made the stupid suggestion that people should stock up by filling five-gallon jerrycans to avoid a shortage. Fearing resultant fires, the fire brigade soon pointed out his error and he was forced to apologize, but the damage was done. Yet the Transport Union have not yet even decided whether to strike or not. In the same week the British government decided it would increase the cost of postage stamps by a whopping 30 per cent. One drugstore chain offered "pre-increase" stamps at 5 per cent off. The queue formed outside the shop almost as the news was breaking. Suddenly, everyone has letters to write. So there seems to be an increasingly delicate hair-trigger which, with the slight breeze of a rumour, fires off the panic and paranoia starting pistol. With the rise of global mass communication, today, these wildfires spread rapidly, but they are far from new. I recall a supermarket panic in the UK back in the 1970s which, for some bizarre reason, had something to do with toilet tissue. My late brother-in-law arrived home with forty-five four-roll packs of toilet paper. His family had the cleanest derrieres in Yorkshire for almost two years.

Yet apart from retail panics, the worst examples of paranoia waves are those connected with contagion, bugs and inexplicable mass social behaviour. All of these are meat and drink to the media, which today has become a virus unto itself. The odd thing is that we seem to enjoy scaring ourselves witless. Nowhere is this truer than in Hollywood. It is surprising just how many movies have been made over the past fifty years that deal with epidemics and post-nuclear apocalypses, to say nothing of unstoppable waves of zombies. The movie internet database website www.imdb.com/list features just 100 of their favourites.

They include every fear imaginable, from asteroids hitting the earth in *Deep Impact* (1998) to worlds ravaged by disease in *Doomsday* (2008), *28 Days Later* (2004) and *Carriers* (2009), and many other permutations such as *The Book of Eli* (2010), the relentlessly grim *The Road* (2009), the threat of global warming in *The Day After Tomorrow* (2004) and the inevitable threat posed by the Mayan calendar, *2012* (2010). Because we are surrounded by our comfortable "reality" we can reach the final credits, leave the cinema or our living room, savour the memory of the great CGI and then go to bed.

But then something horrible can happen – flesh-eating viruses, SARS, bird flu, swine flu, a plague of bedbugs, an abused new drug, Satanic child abuse. We learn that the world's bees are dying off – a harbinger of the end of days, a confirmation of the Book of Revelation. Those 500-foot waves may not be breaking over the Empire State Building just yet, but something just as scary can suddenly pull the panic trigger.

In August 2011 the film *Contagion* scored big at the box office and soon grossed $80 million by the end of the year. It tells the grisly yarn of a deadly transmissible virus as it progresses through the international community. The race is on to tackle the escalating health concerns, whilst the global social order falls apart. Implausible? Not really. It may only be a movie, but it does address the problems we might face when social panic suddenly spreads during an infectious disease outbreak. The global village is just that – in the twenty-first century we are all rubbing shoulders with one another. Gone are the days when you had your injections then spent a month on a steamship sailing to some exotic location. The borders of East and West have meshed together; every nation mingles with every other nation via air travel and immigration. Urbanization and transnational population mobility have given modern infectious diseases a virile new agility. Before we look at some of the panic and paranoia, past and present, we should remember the dawn of the AIDS panic, quickly dubbed "the gay plague", when many thought that even a kiss was enough to condemn you to a slow, ugly death. AIDS was and still is bad. But we grew to understand it. Many have lived through it. Thus when we panic, we surrender ourselves to the enemy – and that enemy is fear itself.

THE ZOMBIE BUG

In 1994, confirming their panic-mongering heritage, a British tabloid ran the headline "Flesh-eating bug ate my face!" The story went into national overdrive and soon we had descriptions of melting faces and limbs rotting in front of people's eyes. This was the United Kingdom's new bacterial threat. Necrotizing fasciitis (NF), commonly known as flesh-eating disease or flesh-eating bacteria syndrome, is a nasty ailment, yet a rare infection. It affects the deeper layers of skin and subcutaneous tissues, spreading rapidly. Yet the term "flesh-eating bacteria" is a misnomer. The bacteria don't "eat" the tissue. They ravage muscle and skin by releasing toxins. But the threat wasn't new at all. The press set it up as a new bug, but we already knew it during wartime as malignant ulcer, hospital gangrene and putrid ulcer. Necrotizing fasciitis has a very long history. It killed King Herod and reports of it throughout history have been sporadic. The plague of rotting zombies staggering along our high streets did not happen. Those most susceptible were people with poor hygiene and weakened immune systems. It wasn't until the Fleet Street tabloids heard about a small cluster of the illness in the south of England in the spring of 1994 that the panic began.

The UK's doctors responded to the publicity by maintaining that the cluster was simply an unlucky coincidence. The underlying rate of occurrence of the disease had not changed. Neither the British nor the US government saw it as a threat. Its prevalence today remains the same, but since 1994 we've had other overblown scares to worry about. Sadly, however, when there are high-profile patients, the tabloids will hang in there. NF took

Melvin Franklin (1942–95), bass singer for the Temptations. The Canadian science-fiction author and marine-mammal biologist Peter Watts (1958–) is one of the latest victims, contracting NF early in 2011. On his blog (www.rifters.com/crawl) Watts reported, "If there was ever a disease fit for a science-fiction writer, flesh-eating disease has got to be it. This fucker spread across my leg as fast as a *Star Trek* space disease in time-lapse." Although he gave the ailment one of its best ever descriptions, today's media have other bugs to boil.

SARS:
THE CONSPIRACY VIRUS

Severe acute respiratory syndrome (SARS) is a respiratory disease caused by the SARS coronavirus (SARS-CoV). Between November 2002 and July 2003, there was an outbreak of SARS in Hong Kong that was giving the media pandemic palpitations. After a few weeks SARS spread from Hong Kong to infect individuals in thirty-seven countries in early 2003. The World Health Organization (WHO) then issued an emergency warning, declaring the sickness "a worldwide health threat". Soon, anyone with flu symptoms was panicking.

In March 2003 the BBC World News reported:

> So far, there have been four deaths related to the pneumonia and another five in an outbreak of a similar infection in a province of China, although the two have not yet been definitively linked. Around 200 people are also believed to have been infected world-wide in the last week alone. In the latest cases reported, authorities in Geneva said that two people were in isolation in a hospital after exhibiting symptoms similar to those of the disease, Reuters news agency said. A British man returning from Hong Kong has been admitted to hospital with a suspected case – the UK's first. And in Australia two women who had recently travelled to China have been hospitalised with symptoms, French news agency AFP reported, although doctors stressed there was no proof they were suffering from the illness.

It was time for the big panic and the big scary stuff. The Prime Minister of New Zealand, Helen Clark, told a news conference that WHO experts believed it might rival "Spanish flu" in 1918 – which *killed at least 20 million* and possibly double that number. Professor John Oxford, Queen Mary's College London, stepped in: "If it was influenza, I expect we would have heard this by now. That's certainly rather reassuring."

Once the subject dropped off the media radar, it was reported that the spread of SARS had been fully contained, with the last infected human case seen in June 2003 (disregarding a laboratory-induced infection case in 2004). But just to keep the fear factor flickering, we were told that SARS has not been eradicated (unlike smallpox), as it might still be present in its natural host reservoirs (animal populations) and may potentially return into the human population in the future. Yes, it was unpleasant. Yes, throughout the world, 916 people died. Yet 2,800 children die each and *every day* from malaria. But not us in the West. SARS is still considered a relatively rare disease, with 8,273 cases as of 2003. It was the usual story of tabloid drama; exaggerated information and panic during the outbreak was totally disproportionate to the level of risk. Even in places with virtually no SARS risk, people were wearing surgical masks, cancelling holidays, and indulging in all kinds of ineffective and dangerous self-medication. There were cases of people who had visited the Far East who were not allowed back into their own country. A poll in Taiwan revealed that the Taiwanese population had reached the conclusion that the public response to the SARS "threat" and its accompanying media coverage encouraged panic and was unnecessarily overstated. But there was something more sinister; was it a conspiracy?

In 2003, the head of Moscow's epidemiological services, Nikolai Filatov, made a comment that the SARS virus was probably manmade. This was added to by a member of the Russian Academy of Medical Sciences, Russian scientist Sergei Kolesnikov, who suggested that the SARS coronavirus was a synthesis of mumps and measles. He said it was a combination that could not occur in nature. Therefore, the SARS virus must have been produced in a laboratory. China's internet chat rooms and discussion boards lit up like a Christmas tree, with widespread speculation that the Pentagon might be behind the manufacture of SARS as a biological weapon, an idea which was further fuelled by the failure to track down the source of the outbreak. If it wasn't the United States, determined to curtail China's rising commercial and influential superiority, then others suggested some evil individual or other rogue government might be the culprit.

Then some circumstantial evidence arose that Asian palm civets, also known as "Toddy cats" or "civet cats", an animal eaten as a delicacy in China's Guangdong area, might have carried SARS and because of human contact the virus had crossed over. As if the Toddy cat didn't have enough problems. The oil extracted from small pieces of its flesh kept in linseed oil in a closed earthen pot is used indigenously as a cure for scabies, and the little critters have another use. Kopi Luwak is the most expensive coffee in the world; it is prepared using coffee beans that have been eaten by the animal, partially digested and harvested from its faeces. But the hapless moggie's link to SARS was disputed. To round things off, the Taiwanese and some Americans reversed the speculation – SARS might be a Chinese biological weapon. This was soon dismissed. SARS has an average mortality rate of around 10 per cent around the world, but in the United States there were only 100 reported cases and it didn't kill any Americans.

In 1998 a Chinese lawyer, Tong Zeng, had volunteered in a Chinese–American medical cooperation programme. He published a book in October 2003, *The Last Defence Line: Concerns about the Loss of Chinese Genes*. Zeng, an activist for Chinese patriotic causes with no medical background, made the front page of the *Southern Metropolitan Daily*, one of the most popular newspapers in Guangzhou. His book revealed that in the 1990s, American researchers collected thousands of DNA and blood samples and specimens, which included 5,000 DNA samples from Chinese twins living on the mainland. When SARS broke out, it did not seriously affect the provinces of Yunnan, Guizhou, Hainan, Tibet and Xinjiang – but it took off in the same twenty-two provinces where the samples had been taken. Tong Zeng also points a finger at Japan. In the 1990s Japanese factories in Guangdong insisted on compulsory annual blood tests. It would have been usual for workers to go to local hospitals for blood tests and a proper physical examination, but this didn't happen. What these blood tests were for and where they ended up remains unclear. Yet Tong Zeng admits to speculation and has no concrete proof. Still, SARS was an impressive panic while it lasted.

Since then, each time winter draws near the media gets hold of another stealthily advancing terror containing the potential message in its looming shadow, "You're all going to DIE!" These health concerns are hard to pin down, and what always makes them more sinister and seemingly unstoppable in the well-fed West is that they appear to have their roots in foreign, unknown cultures. So we get "Asian flu" and "Spanish flu" and in the past, just to show what clean-living, upright chaps we British are, syphilis gave us a chance to have a dig at our Gallic neighbours by referring to it as "the French disease". However, in central Europe in the Middle Ages, in addition to the pandemics of smallpox, syphilis and even leprosy, a new disease known as "the English sweat" swept through the area. It's always handy to have someone to blame, the more remote and sinister the source the better.

When we really need to be scared witless we can do a little background research. For example, we discover that Ebola virus disease (EVD) (or Ebola haemorrhagic fever, EHF) is a human disease which may be caused by any of four of the five known Ebola viruses. These four read like something straight out of an old Johnny Weissmuller *Tarzan* movie: Bundibugyo virus (BDBV), Ebola virus (EBOV), Sudan virus (SUDV) and Taï Forest virus (TAFV, formerly and more commonly Cote d'Ivoire Ebolavirus or Ivory Coast Ebolavirus, CIEBOV). EVD is a viral hemorrhagic fever (VHF) and is clinically nearly indistinguishable from Marburg virus disease (MVD). It's nice to see that with the name Marburg virus we haven't forgotten our old sparring partners, the Germans. There doesn't seem to be a Middlesbrough virus or Tunbridge Wells flu around. If it's not Johnny Foreigner spreading the panic, then blame the animal kingdom; in the past there's been dog flu, horse flu and, more recently, widespread paranoia with bird flu and swine flu. It's a wonder anyone is left standing.

In addition to all these peculiar viral mysteries, there are self-inflicted panics when it comes to drugs. Ecstasy began quietly enough with clubbers seeking a further high whilst dancing. It went on to a menu of "leisure drugs" until the odd death here and there transformed it into Satan's aspirin. Now it almost ranks alongside heroin and crack cocaine in the media's perception, and every year a new dreaded drug wave erupts. These are, in many cases, serious cause for concern, but their potential danger is still written about in the same "killer plague" rhetoric as one might expect with the Black Death. The latest drug wave in the US appears to be OxyContin and other prescription medications. It cuts across social classes, wealth, ethnicity or status. For example, in Florida, it's the number one killer of the twenty-five and younger age group in Sarasota County. This plague knows no boundaries. Oxy has become the illegal drug of choice amongst young people. It's an extremely dangerous and highly addictive drug, with concerned parents claiming that their kids are being transformed into "Oxy-Zombies". We live in a scary world indeed.

FOLK DEVILS AND MORAL PANIC: SATANIC ABUSE

If your view of the world is a biblical one, you could be forgiven for believing that Satan was afoot. When it comes to panic and paranoia, as we've seen in recent years, Old Nick is a past master. As a subject of cinematic entertainment, if "devil worship" is your thing, then you've no doubt seen *Rosemary's Baby*, *The Omen* and *The Exorcist*. Yet there are many who accept that satanism is a real threat. What might let this notion down is the fact that most of its methodology – and its exorcism – is based on a foundation of the Holy Bible and Christianity in particular. I have always wondered how Bram Stoker's Van Helsing would have defeated Dracula if the thirsty count had been Jewish or Muslim; would the ubiquitous crucifix have worked then? Yet the fear of satanism has remained strong enough to enable it to be added to a long list of moral panics.

When a population reaches an intense climax of feeling about any issue that appears to threaten the social order, moral panic kicks in. The term was first mentioned by Stanley Cohen in his book *Folk Devils and Moral Panics* (1972). In the UK, for example, back in the 1950s as rock 'n' roll arrived on our shores, it was Teddy boys, a new section of youth who dressed in a vaguely Edwardian style (hence "Teddy"). Most Teddy boys (and girls) just wanted to bop, booze, smoke and have a good time. To the press, rock 'n' roll was an unfathomable banner, the Jolly Roger of indecency. When the movie *Blackboard Jungle* came out in 1955, with soundtrack contributions by the portly, kiss-curled ageing ex-country star, Bill Haley, who had managed to hijack black rhythm-and-blues to provide his own anodyne version of "rock 'n' roll", there were isolated incidents of Teddy boy audiences reaching unparalleled heights of ecstasy. When *Blackboard Jungle* played at a cinema in Elephant & Castle, south London, in 1956 the teenage audience ran riot, dancing in the aisles and tearing up seats. From then on, the conventional wisdom was that all Teddy boys were highly dangerous, they all carried knives and rock 'n' roll was their satanic soundtrack. Compared to the twenty-first century's crack-addled gang culture, Teddy boys were a bunch of Cistercian monks. But they caused a moral panic, in the same way as did their later descendants, the mods and rockers, who stormed Brighton's seafront in the 1960s. A decade later, the two subcultures had faded from public view and the focus of two new moral panics emerged: the hippies and the skinheads.

When the fear of a threat to prevailing social or cultural values arises, those who start the panic – usually those agents of moral indignation, the media, are known by researchers as "moral entrepreneurs", while those perceived to be threatening the social order have been described as "folk devils". Youth culture has always been an easy target, but when the media goes with the flow and picks up on something everyone can hate with a passion, such as paedophilia, the press can create a mob mentality last seen when torch-bearing villagers chased Boris Karloff in the *Frankenstein* movies. One UK newspaper decided to print the location of known paedophiles, which in some areas resulted in a witch-hunt with the result that, in some episodes, even innocent people listed as *paediatricians* were targeted. Behind this dark and utterly distasteful subject, however, something even more evil was thought to lurk.

Throughout the English-speaking world during the 1980s and 1990s a moral panic arose around alleged satanic ritual abuse. This was ostensibly much more serious because social workers, Christian fundamentalists, the police and psychotherapists were propagating the idea that throughout Britain, Australia and the United States there were covens of satanists, witches and black magicians who were using innocent children for their rituals. As the reports rolled in, more stories of abuse or murder, all with satanic elements, began to emanate from countries such as Brazil and Argentina.

This moral panic had many tragic consequences. Hints and rumours in tight-knit communities had social workers taking children into care and many parents, some no doubt innocent, in places as remote as the Orkney Isles to urban conurbations such as Nottingham and Rochdale faced arrest and extremely humiliating court appearances. The salacious nature and grim imagery of satanism kept these stories alive for months. While there were genuine revelations of sickening child abuse, the devils concerned were not the horned, cloven-hoofed variety. Anthropologist Jean La Fontaine subsequently spent years researching a selection of the more high-profile cases from the period 1988 to 1991, and in her 1998 book, *Speak of the Devil*, she concluded that the goal of the abusers was sexual gratification rather than anything ritualistic or religious. The only rituals she uncovered were those invented by child abusers to frighten their victims or justify the sexual abuse. In the end, there wasn't a highly organized cabal of black-hooded devil worshipers well-read in the black arts; just a bunch of sick, nasty people with uncontrollable urges who definitely deserved locking up. As for summoning Lucifer, they wouldn't know where to start, but no doubt many of them will be forced to face Old Nick eventually.

In a piece by David Brindle, Social Services Correspondent for the *Guardian*, on 10 February 2000, it was revealed that two psychotherapists, Valerie Sinason and Rob Hale, had received a £22,000 government grant to produce evidence of ritual abuse. Ms Sinason, who was based at the Tavistock Clinic in London with psychiatrist Dr Hale, claimed forty-six of her patients said they had witnessed the murder of children or adults during ritual abuse ceremonies involving up to 300 people at a time. Some 70 per cent of the reported abuse was carried out by paedophiles and the rest by satanists.

Interviewed on BBC radio, Professor La Fontaine accused Ms Sinason of being "out of her depth" and unable to produce any hard evidence for her beliefs. Sinason and Hale's report on the subject was never released to the public, and the Department of Health stated in response to an enquiry by a reporter that they did not believe the unreleased Sinason–Hale report rendered La

Fontaine's published report invalid. After studying Jean La Fontaine's research, the then Conservative Health Secretary Virginia Bottomley declared that the report had exposed satanic abuse as a myth.

No doubt there are satanists out there. The latest grim stories of "possession" are as tragic as ever. They too involve the ritual torture and beating of children, currently practised by some people from African locations including Nigeria and Congo. Africa's blend of fundamental Christianity, imposed upon ancient cultures by Protestant Western zealots, combined with a residue of localized gods, demons and folk beliefs, seems to survive even in highly urbanized cities such as London and New York. In November 2011, an extreme example of these archaic dogmas arose on a boat packed with illegal immigrants en route to Italy. Five people were arrested on suspicion of murder after more than a dozen innocent victims were thrown from the vessel in a voodoo ritual to calm stormy seas. The Captain, a Nigerian, allegedly picked the victims on ethnic origin or nationality. Horrified survivors told Italian police how human sacrifices were picked from a ship crammed with 400 people after the engine failed. Apparently, some women performed a deathly "magic dance" before the victims were flung overboard to placate the devil and calm the seas.

Mass psychogenic outbreaks are nothing new, and the further back we delve the stranger they get. Religion is often their trigger. One Christian Church legend warned that if you provoked Saint Vitus, a Sicilian martyred in AD 303, there would be plagues of compulsive dancing. In Strasbourg in July 1518, a woman called Frau Troffea began get down and boogie in the street. She was shaking her booty for six days. Before she ran out of energy, thirty-four others had joined. It got worse; by August over 400 more were dancing around. Many expired and died from heart attack, stroke or sheer exhaustion. There have been all manner of weird epidemics. They include the Tanganyika laughter epidemic (1962), fainting schoolgirls in Blackburn, England (1965), the West Bank fainting epidemic in Palestine (1983) and the strange "Strawberries with sugar virus" in Portugal (2006). And let us not forget the bizarre and widespread infestation of New York by bed bugs in 2009–10. We'll always have panic and paranoia, and unless animals and insects have their way, the majority of them will be manmade.

Hopefully, there is no devil. Maybe Tom Waits got it right: "Don't you know there ain't no devil, it's just God when he's drunk ...'

PART 8:

COMBING THE FRINGE: FUN, FORT AND FINE ENTERTAINMENT – A MISCELLANY OF MYSTERIES

Now there are so many scientists who believe in dowsing, that the suspicion comes to me that it may be only a myth after all. My own notion is that it is very unsportsmanlike to ever mention fraud. Accept anything. Then explain it your way.

Charles Fort (1874–1932)

BIZARRE ARCHAEOLOGY

The search for the Grail is the search for the divine in all of us.
But if you want facts, Indy, I've none to give you. At my age,
I'm prepared to take a few things on faith.

Marcus Brody, character in
Indiana Jones and the Last Crusade (1989)

One of the many strongly held beliefs of the paranormal/psychic/ET community is that whatever technology we possess today in the twenty-first century, then the "Ancients" had their own equally impressive versions millennia ago. On a wall in the Temple of Osiris, Abydos, Egypt, there's a hieroglyphic relief panel that the "Was God an Astronaut?" fans believe shows that the ancient Egyptians had helicopters, planes, a flying saucer and even a submarine. There are carvings depicting a bulb-like object beneath the Temple of Hathor at Dendera, which, some have suggested, is evidence of a "Crooke's Tube", in effect, an early light bulb. Of course, the fact that over two or three millennia, the original detail in stone carvings can be worn down to alter their detail is unacceptable debunkery.

Yet there are genuinely mysterious artefacts with inexplicable provenance. Scattered through the jungles of Costa Rica are perfect ancient stone spheres, known as the "Giant Balls of Costa Rica". Their manufacture would seem to demonstrate a level of skill beyond our comprehension, as does the brilliant work of the South American stone masons who put together the intricate walls of Machu Picchu. There have been other Fortean oddities, too, such as coal miners, deep below the earth, who have chipped open blocks of coal, from which have emerged entombed frogs, springing back to life. Some discoveries challenge the belief that our technology is a result of our exploratory science over the past two centuries. There is the so-called "Baghdad Battery", 2,000 years old and dating from the Parthian period (approximately 250 BC to AD 250), found in Khujut Rabu just outside Baghdad. It's a clay jar with a stopper made of asphalt. Protruding through the asphalt is an iron rod surrounded by a copper cylinder. When filled with vinegar or another electrolytic solution, the jar produces about 1.1 volts. What it may have been used for is not clear, but some researchers believe it could have been used to electroplate items, such as putting a layer of one metal (gold) on to the surface of another (silver), a method still practised in Iraq today. If this really is a battery, then it predates the first battery made by Allesandro Volta (1745–1827) in 1798 by 1,500 years.

There are hundreds of bizarre reports from the Victorian and Edwardian period concerning archaeological anomalies, but we need to remember that the Fourth Estate was as duplicitous back then as it is today. We are still living through a media age where a national newspaper, the Sunday Sport, could come up with headlines such as "World War II Bomber found on The Moon" and a similar story concerning a London bus. According to numerous reports of sightings, Elvis is still alive, although he's probably had a pelvis transplant by now. As with the UFO phenomenon, the serious archaeological academics strive, often with success, to demolish the fanciful reports collected by Charles Fort almost a century ago. Thus, in tandem with our sense of wonder, we need to temper our drop-jawed amazement with a dash of common sense.

These inexplicable items are found around the globe, and here's a selection from the kind of items Charles Fort spent his long days digging out of newspapers and periodicals in the British Library. These are very popular pillars of faith among fans of the "ancient advanced technology" hypothesis, and I'm not going to spoil their arcane mystery by debunking them. If you want to know what real archaeologists think to all this, visit www.badarchaeology.com where you can have your sensations of shock and awe surgically removed.

- Ancient nanotechnology. East of Russia's Ural Mountains between 1991–3, men prospecting for gold on the Narada River discovered unusual, mostly spiral-shaped objects, the smallest measuring about 1/10,000th of an inch. Their composition seems to be copper and the rare metals tungsten and molybdenum. Tests revealed the objects to be between 20,000 and 318,000 years old.
- Prehistoric spark plug. A "spark plug" in a fossil-encrusted geode was found in the Coso Mountains on 13 February 1961, by Wallace Lane, Virginia Maxey and Mike Mikesell, who were looking for minerals to sell in their gift shop in Olancha, California. Using a diamond saw, they cut the geode in half to discover an object inside that was obviously artificial. The object had a metal core surrounded by layers of a ceramic-like material and a hexagonal wooden sleeve. X-rays reveal something very like a modern spark plug. Yet the geode had been covered with fossils and was estimated to be 500,000 years old.
- The million-year-old nail. The *Illinois Springfield Republican* reported in 1851 that a local businessman, Hiram de Witt, whilst visiting California, found a fist-sized chunk of auriferous quartz, estimated to be one million years old. When he accidentally dropped it, it split open and out fell a cut-iron nail.
- The rock with a gold thread. An 1844 report in the London *Times* reveals the story that whilst working in a quarry near the River Tweed in Scotland, a group of workers discovered a piece of gold thread embedded in the rock eight feet (2.4 m) below ground level.
- The chain in the coal. The *Morrisonville Times* of 11 June 1891 features the story of Mrs S. W. Culp, of Morrisonville, Illinois, who was breaking up coal into smaller pieces for her kitchen stove one cold day, when she noticed a chain, about ten inches (25.4 cm) long, stuck in the coal. She had it examined and it was found to be made of eight-carat gold, given the description as being "of antique and quaint workmanship". Subsequent investigations concluded that, as some of the coal still clung to the chain, it had not simply been recently dropped into the coal. The section of coal

separated from it still bore the impression of the encased chain.

- Ancient modern tools. The *American Journal of Science and Arts* in 1820 reported that several anomalous quarrymen's tools were found during limestone quarrying near Aix-en-Provence (France) between 1786 and 1788. Workers came to a bed of sand about fifty feet (15.2 m) below ground level. In the layer of sand, they discovered the stumps of stone pillars and fragments of half-worked rock. Digging further, they found the petrified wooden handles of hammers, coins and pieces of other petrified wooden tools. The layer of limestone was dated at 300 million years old.

- Mysterious vase. According to a 5 June 1852 account in *Scientific American*, reprinted from a report from the *Boston Transcript*, during rock blasting at Meeting House Hill in Dorchester (Massachusetts), a metallic vessel was found a short distance south of a meeting house established by the Revd Nathaniel Hall (1805–75). The rock strata, known as Roxbury conglomerate, was claimed to be Precambrian. The artefact was found at a depth of around fifteen feet (4.6 m). The metallic vessel was found in two parts, thought to have been broken by the explosion. The bell-shaped vase, with figures of flowers in bouquet arrangements on its sides, and inlaid with pure silver, measured four-and-a-half inches high and six-and-a-half inches wide at the base (11.4 x 16.5 cm). The estimated age of the rock out of which it came: 100,000 years.

- Anomalous ancient screw. In 1865, in a piece of feldspar, calculated to be twenty-one million years old, unearthed in Nevada at the Abbey Mine in Treasure City, there was a two-inch (5 cm) metal screw that had long ago oxidized, but its form – particularly the shape of its threads – could be clearly seen in the feldspar.

More anachronisms are listed below. It is claimed that these unusual artefacts tell a story of ancient civilizations, mysterious technological advancements and Pre-Columbian transoceanic expeditions, and ET often creeps into these stories, too. Many of these archaeological discoveries challenge both religion and science, although everything on this list has at one time or another been accused of being an elaborate hoax.

The Acámbaro Figures

In July 1944 Waldemar Julsrud was out horse riding in Acámbaro, Guanajuato, Mexico, when he began finding a series of small ceramic figurines. Julsrud became aware that there were more of these around the area and paid a local farmer to dig up the remaining figures, with a fee for every object he discovered. The farmer seemed to be on to a good thing, because with hired local help, he eventually turned up 32,000 figures. These represented everything from dinosaurs to people from all over the world. Oddly enough, they cover several ancient civilizations, such as the Egyptians, Sumerians and bearded Caucasians, plus a large variety of dinosaur species. The theory of evolution suggests that humans did not live in the time of the dinosaurs, so the figures were a boon to creationists who immediately proclaimed the artefacts to be legitimate.

A researcher named Don Patton has suggested radiocarbon dates for the figures ranging from 6,500 years to 1,500 years. Other scientific attempts to date these figures have included thermoluminescence dating, which has produced a date of approximately 2500 BC. Yet unlike other objects found in that area of Mexico, the figures do not seem to display much ageing or wear and tear after being in the rocky soil. Most archaeologists or palaeontologists are reluctant to accept their validity, yet literal interpreters of the Bible see them as proof that men lived alongside the dinosaurs, thus trashing Darwin and his theory of evolution (www.acambaro.gob.mx/cultura/julsrud.htm).

The Riddle of the Dropa Stones

In 1938, in the Bayan-Kara-Ula mountains on the China–Tibet border, an archaeological expedition arrived to explore what was then a little-known area. High in the mountains, caves were discovered. The walls of the caves displayed peculiar artwork depicting images of the stars, the moon and sun, as well as unusual figures with elongated heads. Graves were also excavated that revealed the remains of ancient beings. The skeletons, with unusually large skulls, were a little more than three feet (1 m) tall. The tombs also contained a collection of 30 mm-diameter stone disks, each with a hole at the centre and a groove on the surface of the disk, which spiralled outwards from the hole to produce a double spiral. When the grooves were examined more closely, they revealed a series of small carvings or signs.

The disks became known as the Dropa Stones, of which it is claimed that 716 were eventually found. Among the numerous academics who studied the stones was Professor Tsum Um Nui (or, in some versions of the story, Chi Pu Tei) of the Beijing Academy for Ancient Studies. He decided that the tiny carvings in the disks' grooves represented an unknown language. By 1962, after much work and research, the Professor had managed to translate the language. No one has suggested why, but the story has it that the Peking Academy of Prehistory forbade the Professor from publishing anything about the Dropa Stones. However, after many years of debate he eventually published his hypothesis.

Tsum Um Nui suggested that 12,000 years ago an alien spacecraft piloted by the Dropa race crashed in the Bayan Har Shan region. Back then finding spare parts on earth was a no-go, so the poor Dropas were forced to try and live out the rest of their lives in the mountains. However, they hadn't allowed for the local Ham tribesmen's lack of hospitality and most of the stranded aliens were hunted down and killed. The suggestion is that the Dropa intermarried with the locals, thus adding further complications for the archaeologists examining the skeletons. There is a disputed claim that the Beijing Academy forced Tsum Um Nui to resign. Sadly, the Dropa Stones are not available for public viewing at any museum, as they seem to have disappeared, although you'll find many photographs of dubious provenance on the internet.

On 30 March 1960 Mikhail Borisovy Chernenko and Valentin Isaakovich Rich published an article entitled "Hypotheses, assumptions and guesses: does the trail lead into space?" in Volume 12, Number 9 of the *Current Digest of the Russian Press*, an American Russian language publication popular among Russian émigrés, which had been published since 1910. The same article had originally appeared in *Literaturnaya Gazeta* on 9 February 1960, examining the speculations of a Russian-born ethnologist and mathematician, Matest M. Agrest (1915–2005), who in 1959 proposed that certain monuments of past cultures on earth have resulted from contact with an extra-terrestrial race. The Dropa Stones story enjoyed a further airing in the July 1962 edition of a German vegetarian magazine, *Das Vegetarische Universum*, supposedly penned by a Reinhardt Wegemann and entitled "UFOs in ancient times? The hieroglyphs of Bayan Kara Ula". The story's source was said to be a Japanese news agency, DINA, based in Tokyo, but although many researchers have looked into this, no agency called DINA ever existed. There is a very capable Egyptian belly dancer called Dina, and a DINA that was run by that cruel old despot, General Pinochet, the Dirección de Inteligencia Nacional (the former Chilean national intelligence agency), yet the only aliens he chased were communists. Creaky tales such as this became the bedrock material for writers such as Erich von Däniken, yet unless someone made it all up in the 1950s, the golden age of flying-saucer flappery, who knows, there might still be something in it.

The Horned Human Skull

In the borough of Sayre, fifty-nine miles (95 km) northwest of Scranton in Bradford County, Pennsylvania, "sometime in the 1880s", a large burial mound was discovered. Some very weird human skeletons were unearthed. They were human but for the fact they were over seven feet tall (2.1 m) and possessed odd bony projections located about two inches (5 cm) above the eyebrows. Human skulls with horns? This called for the experts. Once Alanson B. Skinner of the American Investigating Museum, Dr G. P. Donehoo, the Pennsylvania state dignitary of the Presbyterian Church, and W. K. Morehead of Phillips Academy, Andover, Massachusetts, got on the case, they estimated that the bodies had been buried around AD 1200. During the nineteenth century giant horned skulls had been found elsewhere in the United States near El Paso, Texas, and near Wellsville, New York. Of course, now the trail goes cold. Although you'll find a photo of one of these horny devils online, the Sayre bones were allegedly sent to the American Investigating Museum in Philadelphia and someone stole them. The word on the grapevine is that they were ETs but there's an interesting article from 1916 (www.spanishhill.com/articles/horned.htm) where the *Elmira Star Gazette* carries a statement by Professor Skinner. He outlines that what they actually uncovered were some Native American skeletons buried near deer antlers. Needless to say, other horned skulls are said to exist in Europe, but as the Sayre bones were never seen again, many people claim the discovery to be a hoax.

The Map of the Creator

Professor Alexander Chuvyrov of Russia's Bashkir State University made an unusual discovery in 1999. A man named Vladimir Krainov had unearthed an odd stone slab in his backyard. The artefact weighed over a ton and measured 5 feet (1.52 m) high, 3.5 feet (1.06 m) wide, 5 feet (1.52 m) thick and took over a week to dig out. Professor Chuvyrov had been searching for similar slabs which he'd seen mentioned in historical manuscripts. After some research and investigation, the slab was named the Dashka Stone, and seemed to be a three-dimensional relief map of the Ural region. The way the intricate carvings represented elevation and terrain made it similar to maps used by the present-day military. It appears to represent dams, irrigation systems and civil engineering work. The discovery was later titled the Map of the Creator.

It also bears numerous inscriptions that were first thought to be of ancient Chinese origin, although it turned out to be an unknown hieroglyphic-syllabic language. There have been wild estimates as to the slab's age, some suggesting 100 million years, but details of what methodology was used are not given. Many have suggested that, if the Map of the Creator is genuine, then it would suggest the existence of an ancient highly developed civilization, and that such an artefact may have been used for navigational purposes. Both these suggestions are contentious. If the people who made it were so advanced, what were they doing carving stone slabs? Unless it was some kind of signpost, a one-ton lump of stone was hardly a portable navigational device.

However, it remains a mystery, and the Dashka Stone, which for some reason is not available for public viewing, continues to undergo scientific testing. There is a detailed article on the subject from *Pravda* online (www.bibliotecapleyades.net/arqueologia/esp_map_creator02.htm).

The Aluminium Wedge of Aiud

Here's another of those items that the space brothers among us claim to be proof that aliens visited the earth. The Aluminium Wedge of Aiud is a wedge-shaped object found on the banks of the Mures River in 1974 just over a mile (1.6 km) east of Aiud, Romania. It was unearthed from beneath thirty-five feet (10 m) of sand and accompanied by two mastodon bones. It looks like a hammer head. What happened to it is unclear, although some reports state that it went to the Archaeological Institute of Cluj-Napoca for further research. It was found to have been manufactured from an alloy of aluminium and encased in a thin layer of oxide. The alloy contains twelve different elements. Aluminium was not discovered until 1808, when Humphry Davy (1778–1829) identified the existence of the metal base of alum, and was not produced (in an impure form) until 1825 by Danish physicist and chemist Hans Christian Ørsted (1777–1851); it was not produced in quantity until 1885 so its existence alongside prehistoric mastodons, which would make it at least 11,000 years old, is anomalous. Although it naturally occurs within some minerals, aluminium requires heat of more than 1,000 °C to be produced. Once again, and for no clear reason, the Wedge of Aiud is not on display to the public and remains in a secret location. However, pictures of it exist online.

The Los Lunas Decalogue Stone

Hidden Mountain stands near Los Lunas, New Mexico, about 35 miles (56 km) south of Albuquerque. In 1933 Professor Frank Hibben, an archaeologist from the University of New Mexico, was led to Hidden Mountain by an old man who claimed to have seen a strange artefact there as a boy in the 1880s. What Hibben discovered has become known as the Los

Lunas Decalogue Stone, a large boulder that bears a regular inscription carved into a flat panel. This inscription has been claimed by some researchers to be in a form of Paleo-Hebrew, and is possibly an abridged version of the Decalogue or Ten Commandments. A group of letters suggesting the tetragrammaton YHWH, or "Yahweh", appears four times. The Paleo-Hebrew alphabet was an offshoot of the ancient Semitic alphabet, identical to the Phoenician alphabet, dating from the tenth century BC or earlier. It was used by the Israelites, both Jews and Samaritans. Those with an "ancient unknown civilization" wish-list will claim that if the information on the Los Lunas Decalogue Stone (which weighs 80 tons) is accurate, it could not be a forgery because the Paleo-Hebrew script was "unknown to scholars in the 1880s". However, in the *New York Times* of 15 June 1855, there is a feature entitled "The Newly Discovered Phoenician Inscription". Did some Los Lunas wag reach for his masonry chisels? The apparent use of Modern Hebrew punctuation has caused some scholars to doubt its authenticity but other researchers suggest the artefact could be Pre-Columbian, proving early Semitic contact with the Americas and evidence that Israelis could have settled in America. Because of its size, the Los Lunas stone remains in its original location and visitors can take a look by purchasing a Recreational Access Permit from the New Mexico State Land Office.

The Piri Reis Map

The Ottoman sultans reigned for 600 years. For 400 years of that reign, from 1465 to 1856, they occupied the magnificent Topkapı Palace in Istanbul, Turkey. In 1929 the palace became a museum. It was during the building's refurbishment that numerous ancient items were found, and among them was the Piri Reis Map. Drawn on gazelle skin, it is regarded as one of the earliest maps of America, compiled in 1513 by the Ottoman-Turkish military cartographer, Admiral Piri Reis (*c*.1465–*c*.1555). It is the only map from the sixteenth century that shows South America in its correct longitudinal position in relation to Africa. The surviving half of the map displays the western coasts of North Africa and Europe, and the coast of Brazil. It also shows islands in the Atlantic, including the Canary Islands and Azores, plus a mythical island called Antillia and possibly even Japan.

History tells us that the first confirmed sighting of Antarctica happened in 1820 on the Russian expedition of Mikhail Lazarev and Fabian Gottlieb von Bellingshausen. In this respect the Piri Reis map is genuinely puzzling as it not only shows a land mass near present-day Antarctica, but it depicts Antarctica in great detail with elaborate topography and not hidden by ice. Yet estimates suggest the region has been ice-bound for at least 6,000 years. Here, pseudoscience kicks in, with some suggesting that the Ottoman Empire had knowledge of an ancient Ice Age civilization.

Academics prefer to suggest that the Antarctica on the map is more likely Patagonia or the Terra Australis Incognita (Unknown Southern Land), undiscovered at the time, yet believed to exist before the southern hemisphere was fully explored. The map also credits Christopher Columbus, who is thought to have drawn his own map while he was in the West Indies, but historians have searched for this "lost map of Columbus" for years without success.

Regrettably, the Piri Reis map is not on display to the public, but is stored away in the library of the Topkapı Palace.

Giants of America

"Giant" human remains are classified as any bones representative of a person between seven and twelve feet (2.1–3.7 m) in stature. In giant skeleton yarns, size definitely matters. There are claims, for example, that a skeleton twelve feet tall was unearthed in 1833 at Lompock Rancho, California, by soldiers digging a powder magazine pit. Not only was he a big guy, but he had two rows of teeth and was buried with numerous stone axes, carved shells and porphyry (a variety of igneous rock consisting of large-grained crystals) blocks bearing mysterious symbols. In 1856, a skeleton measuring ten feet nine inches (3.3 m) tall was ploughed up by vineyard workers in West Virginia. In 1928, a farmer digging a rubbish pit near Waterproof, Louisiana, revealed a nine-foot-eleven-inch (3 m) skeleton. In Ohio in 1895, twenty skeletons were discovered in a mound near Toledo. They had massive jaws and teeth and were all sitting down and facing east, so with the absence of the remains of a bus shelter, what they were waiting for remains uncertain.

The giant skeletons list is an extensive one. Some claim they may have been the bones of early Sasquatch or Bigfoot, or a giant race of unknown humans. The more these stories roll along down the years, the more barnacles they gather due to sloppy repetition by the ostrich-like credulous who refuse to take their head out of the paranormal sand. A good example is the city of Moberley in Missouri. Although I have no doubt Moberley is a pleasant place, visit its tourism page and you'll not find all that much to entice you there. Yet it ought to be, according to the "ancient unknown civilization" camp, one of the most important archaeological sites in the world. You can verify this by reading a stunning article titled "Missouri's Buried City: A Strange Discovery in a Coal Mine Near Moberly", published on 9 April 1885 in the New York Times (www.nytimes.com). Here's a sample of the amazing revelation:

> The city of Moberly, Mo. is stirred up over the discovery of a wonderful buried city, which was discovered at the bottom of a coal shaft 360 feet deep, which was being sunk near the city. A hard and thick stratum of lava arches in the buried city, the streets of which are regularly laid out and enclosed by walls of stone, which is cut and dressed in a fairly good, although rude style of masonry. A hall 30 by 100 feet was discovered wherein were stone benches and tools of all descriptions for mechanical service. Further search disclosed statues and images made of a composition closely resembling bronze, lacking luster.

In the days before mechanical shovels those miners must have worked in huge gangs around the clock, shifting earth by the ton back up the access shaft, because the story gets even better:

> A stone fountain was found, situated in a wide court or street, and from it a stream of perfectly pure water was flowing, which was found to be strongly impregnated with lime. Lying beside the fountain were portions of the skeleton of a human

being. The bones of the leg measured, the femur four and one-half feet, the tibia four feet and three inches, showing that when alive the figure was three times the size of an ordinary man, and possessed of a wonderful muscular power and quickness.

Apparently this was all verified by a Mr David Coates, the Recorder of the City of Moberly, and Mr George Keating, City Marshal, who were members of the exploring party. It took a long time for news to travel across the states in those days – often a week or more. So take a look at the date of the *New York Times* article; was there a bit of April tomfoolery going on here?

You will also see repeated on various ersatz archaeology sites the story that, "In a Nevada state newspaper in 1947, a strange article was posted titled 'Atlantis in the Colorado River Desert'." That paper was the *Hot Citizen*, dated August 5 1947, but it is actually that day's edition of the *San Diego Union* that makes for more fascinating reading:

TRACE OF GIANTS FOUND IN DESERT

LOS ANGELES, Aug 4. (AP) A retired Ohio doctor has discovered relics of an ancient civilization, whose men were 8 or 9 feet tall, in the Colorado Desert near the Arizona-Nevada-California line, an associate said today.

Howard E. Hill of Los Angeles speaking before the Transportation Club, disclosed that several well-preserved mummies were taken yesterday from caverns in an area roughly 180 miles square, extending through much of southern Nevada from Death Valley, Calif. across the Colorado River into Arizona. Hill said the discoverer is Dr F. Bruce Russell, retired Cincinnati physician, who stumbled on the first of several tunnels in 1931, soon after coming West and deciding to try mining for his health.

MUMMIES FOUND
Not until this year, however, did Dr Russell go into the situation thoroughly, Hill told the luncheon. With Dr Daniel

S. Bovee, of Los Angeles – who with his father helped open up New Mexico's cliff dwellings – Dr Russell has found mummified remains together with implements of the civilization, which Dr Bovee had tentatively placed at about 80,000 years old. "These giants are clothed in garments consisting of a medium length jacket and trouser extending slightly below the knees." said Hill. "The texture of the material is said to resemble gray dyed sheepskin, but obviously it was taken from an animal unknown today."

There are supposed to be thirty-two underground caves close to the Nevada and California border within a 180-square mile (466 km²) radius. The mysterious "Dr Russell" vanished, as has all evidence of this amazing discovery of giants wearing early zoot suits. Claims have been made that the evidence of this historic find was either stolen by the Smithsonian Institute, and rests in some deep secret vault along with the Ark of the Covenant, or it was suppressed and covered up by Darwinian scientists to protect the theory of evolution. It would make a great movie, though.

Long before giants were found in the United States, back in the 1700s, this entertaining myth was alive and well in Europe. When, in 1766, Captain John Byron returned home after circumnavigating the world in HMS *Dolphin*, the historian and writer Horace Walpole published *An Account of the Giants Lately Discovered*. Stories abounded that the crew of the *Dolphin* had seen nine-foot (2.7 m) giants in Patagonia, South America. It didn't take long for Walpole to get his story out, because Byron only docked in May and the thirty-one-page publication came out in July. Walpole poked a little fun at the story by suggesting that Britain might "import" a few of the giant women "for the sake of mending our Breed". However, in, 1773, an official account of Byron's voyage was published and told a less sensational tall story. Yet the Patagonians still stood head and shoulders above the weedy Brits. The first volume of John Hawkesworth's lengthily titled *An Account of the Voyages Undertaken by the Order of His Present Majesty for Making Discoveries in the Southern Hemisphere and Successively Performed by Commodore Byron, Captain Wallis, Captain Carteret, and Captain Cook* ... (1773) tells us:

> When we came within a little distance from the shore, we saw, as near as I can guess, about five hundred people, some on foot, but the greater part on horseback ... one of them, who afterwards appeared to be a Chief, came towards me: he was of a gigantic stature, and seemed to realize the tales of monsters in a human shape ... If I may judge of his height by the proportion of his stature to my own, it could not be much less than seven feet ... Mr Cumming (one of Byron's officers) came up with the tobacco (a gift), and I could not but smile at his astonishment which I saw expressed in his countenance, upon perceiving himself, though six feet two inches high, become a pigmy among giants; for these people may indeed more properly be called giants than tall men ... the shortest of whom were at least four inches taller.

Many websites repeat the story that Captain Cook made an entry in his log that he'd captured a giant and tied him to the mast, but the big chap wriggled free of the ropes and escaped. If this is true, then good for him. Presumably, along with all the other legendary enormous beings, he vanished into the fog of history.

The Kensington Runestone

Kensington, a settlement in Douglas County, Minnesota, is where Olof Öhman, a Swedish–American farmer, discovered a large stone, which was attached to the roots of a small tree, when clearing his land 1898. It weighed a hefty 200 pounds (90.7 kg). It was thirty-one inches (71 cm) high, sixteen inches (40 cm) wide and six inches (15.2 cm) thick, and displayed ancient writing and carved text. There was something unusual about the object so he took into town to see if he could raise an educated opinion on his find. It wasn't until 1907 that Hjalmer R. Holand from Wisconsin University finally deciphered the writings on what became known as the Kensington Runestone. He claimed that the text read:

8 Goths and 22 Norwegians on exploration journey from Vinland over the west. We camp by 2 skerries one day-journey from this stone. We fished one day. After we came home, 10 men red with blood and tortured. Hail Virgin Mary, save from evil. Have 10 men by the sea to look after our ship, 14 day-journeys from this island year 1362.

Holand's findings instigated much controversy. Had Scandinavian explorers, 130 years before Christopher Columbus, reached the middle of North America in the fourteenth century? Sadly, most experts in runes and linguistic specialists considered the artefact to be a hoax. Yet the stubborn belief exists among many that Vikings were in central Minnesota in 1362.

In November 2000, geologist Scott F. Wolter, the author of a number of books on the Kensington Runestone, suggested, after detailed study, that the stone had undergone a natural weathering process in the ground of a minimum of 50 to 200 years. Now some old friends enter the scene – the Knights Templar – but not any old Knights Templar: these are Viking Knights Templar who seem to have had some vague connection to the stone, according to Wolter, in 1362.

It's a dramatic suggestion, but by 1362 the Knights Templar had been disbanded and scattered to the four winds for five decades. We owe the "bad luck" legend of Friday the 13th to the Knights Templar. It was on Friday 13 October 1307 that the Church of Rome had finally had enough of this elite force of zealous fighters. With the blessing of Pope Clement V, King Philip of France had drawn up a highly dubious charge sheet against the Knights which listed their misdemeanours as homosexuality, the black arts, necromancy and abortion. Philip's armies seized the Templars, interrogated, tortured and burned them. Some ships of the Templar fleet managed to find safe haven in Scotland. Also, by the time of the date of the Kensington Runestone, 1362, the Viking age had well and truly ended. It began to fall apart with the failed invasion of England by the Norwegian King Harald III (Harald Hardrada), who was roundly defeated in 1066 by Saxon King Harold Godwinson at the Battle of Stamford Bridge. The Öhman family still maintain that their grandfather was not telling lies, and the artefact rests in the Runestone Museum in downtown Alexandria, Minnesota. It remains a genuine mystery.

The Shroud of Turin: Christ or Leonardo?

Italy's Shroud of Turin has been the inspiration for more books, articles and documentaries than almost any other relic. It's a linen cloth bearing the image of a man, who most people believe to have been Jesus Christ. He appears to have suffered the extreme physical trauma of crucifixion. Wrapped in red silk, since 1578 the shroud has been preserved in a silver chest in the Chapel of the Holy Shroud in the Cathedral of St John the Baptist in Turin.

The ancient linen, which measures fourteen feet three inches (4.34 m) long by three feet seven inches (1.9 m) wide, bears the eerie image of a full male body. The shroud's origins and its image have occupied scientists, historians and researchers in continuing controversy for centuries. As the image on the shroud seems to represent all the artistic representations of the body of Jesus Christ created since his death, the Church firmly believes, as do many Christians, that the face on the shroud is the Holy Face of Jesus. But in 1988 radiocarbon tests were carried out on the linen and results indicated the cloth was dated much later than the time of Jesus, and was probably woven between 1260 and 1390. This would postdate the crucifixion of Jesus by more than a millennium.

Unravelling its history is problematic. The shroud appears to have been in Lirey, France, in 1390 when Bishop Pierre d'Arcis wrote a memorandum to Robert of Geneva (1342–94), who was elected to the papacy by French cardinals who opposed the election of Pope Urban VI. This made him (Anti-)Pope Clement VII, the first Avignon antipope of a nasty split in the Church of Rome that became known as the Western Schism. Bishop Pierre d'Arcis's letter to Clement VII declared that the shroud was a forgery and that the artist had confessed. The history from the fifteenth century onwards is clearer. In 1453 Margaret de Charny gave the shroud to the House of Savoy. In 1578 the shroud was transferred to Turin. If these dates are correct, and the shroud already existed, then some of the current claims about its origin face difficulty.

The Catholic Church has neither formally endorsed nor rejected the shroud, but in 1958 Pope Pius XII approved the image in association with the Roman Catholic devotion to the Holy Face of Jesus. The first photograph of the shroud was made by Secondo Pia on 28 May 1898. Pia, an amateur photographer, was taken aback when he studied the negatives, because they gave the appearance of a positive image, thus implying that the shroud itself is some kind of photographic negative. When scientists at NASA's Jet Propulsion Laboratory carried out their own research, they found that rather than being simply a photographic negative, it could be decoded into a 3-D image. However, this property could not be replicated by researchers.

The shroud has gathered many theories, but the latest hypothesis is the most intriguing.

It suggests that the Shroud of Turin was faked by Renaissance artist Leonardo da Vinci (1452–1519) using pioneering photographic techniques and a sculpture of his own head. Lillian Schwartz, graphic consultant at the School of Visual Arts in New York, used computer scans in the 1980s and matched the face of the *Mona Lisa* to a Leonardo self-portrait and showed that the face on the shroud has the same dimensions as da Vinci.

A UK Channel 5 TV documentary suggests the linen may have been stretched over a frame in a blacked-out room, then coated with silver sulphate, which was available in fifteenth-century Italy. This would have made the cloth light-sensitive. Da Vinci was an innovator in many ways, and if he is behind the creation of the shroud's image, he may have used a primitive version of the camera obscura (Latin: *camera* is a "vaulted chamber/room" and *obscura* means "dark", so combine the terms and we have "darkened chamber/room"). It was one of the inventions that eventually led to photography. It consists of a box or room with a hole in one side. An image is projected on to a screen in the box by an external light source shining through the hole. The image is reproduced upside down, but keeps its perspective and colour. It became popular with many artists because a chosen image or scene could be projected on to your canvas or paper, enabling the creation of an image or scene with great accuracy. The camera obscura has a long history dating back to ancient China and it is featured in the writings of

Aristotle. If da Vinci did figure out the application of silver sulphate, his facial shape would have been projected on to the linen on its frame when the sun's rays passed through a lens in one of the walls, creating a permanent image.

Lynn Picknett, who has written extensively on the shroud and carried out much research said:

> The faker of the shroud had to be a heretic, someone with no fear of faking Jesus' holy redemptive blood. He had to have a grasp of anatomy and he had to have at his fingertips a technology which would completely fool everyone until the 20th century. He had a hunger to leave something for the future, to make his mark for the future, not just for the sake of art or science but for his ego.

So, if da Vinci provided the Catholic Church with one of its most treasured relics, was he a religious man? Apparently not. The first edition of Giorgio Vasari's biographical essay on da Vinci (1550) tells us that, "his cast of mind was so heretical that he did not adhere to any religion, thinking perhaps that it was better to be a philosopher than a Christian". Interestingly, this note was not found in the second edition (1568). *Leonardo*, a biography by Marco Rosci (1976), notes that Leonardo, "adopted an empirical approach to every thought, opinion, and action and accepted no truth unless verified or verifiable, whether related to natural phenomena, human behaviour, or social activities". So if he made the Turin shroud image, he may well have had a sly laugh about it all.

However, the director of the Turin Shroud Centre of Colorado, Professor John Jackson, still believes the item dates from the time of Jesus's crucifixion. He dismissed the Channel 5 documentary's hypothesis, stating that, "the earliest known record of the shroud appears on a commemorative medallion struck in the mid-fourteenth century and on display at the Cluny Museum Paris; it clearly shows clerics holding up the shroud and is dated to around 100 years before Leonardo was born. There is no evidence whatsoever that Leonardo was involved in the shroud."

The shroud has become the perfect example of science versus faith in divinity, an eternal argument making dialogue very difficult. It will forever be one of the most mysterious artefacts in the world.

SKULLDUGGERY

> *There is great treasure there behind our skull and this is true about all of us. This little treasure has great, great powers, and I would say we only have learnt a very, very small part of what it can do.*
>
> Isaac Bashevis Singer (1902–91)

VJ Enterprises was founded in 1991. Its website (www.v-j-enterprises.com) tells us that it is: "A New Age organization whose goal is to share with the public the best information which describes the prophesied Golden Age. Our services include various types of public lectures and workshops focusing on such subjects as the Crystal Skulls, UFOs, Peru, Crop Circles and the Bible Code and the Manifestation of the Aquarian Age."

The phenomenon of crystal skulls remains a controversial archaeological mystery. We're informed by skull fans that thirteen crystal heads have been discovered in various locations around the world, from Tibet to the United States. Joshua "Illinois" Shapiro, who runs VJ Enterprises, leaves their importance in no doubt: "I personally feel that the Crystal Skulls are not only here to share ancient knowledge and wisdom, but to assist in awakening our race to higher spiritual laws and understanding of itself ... If the Crystal Skulls were not brought by extra-terrestrials then certainly we must conclude there have been civilizations much more technologically or spiritually advanced than our own today."

The most famous of these glittering noggins is the "skull of doom', allegedly discovered in 1924 by Anna Le Guillon Mitchell-Hedges (1907–2007). The discovery of the skull, allegedly found beneath an altar in Mayan temple ruins, is said to have taken place on Anna's seventeenth birthday. She was on an archaeological dig at the ancient Mayan city of Lubaantun ("place of fallen stones") in British Honduras (now Belize) with her adoptive father, the adventurer Frederick A. "Mike" Mitchell-Hedges (1882–1959). Mitchell-Hedges had travelled to Belize on a mission to find the ruins of Atlantis. This clear quartz skull weighs about eleven pounds (5 kg) and measures 5¼ inches (13.3 cm) high. It is reminiscent of stone skulls made by the Aztecs. However, Aztec skulls are stylized, and the Mitchell-Hedges skull is more realistic, complete with a detachable jaw.

The controversy over this artefact goes all the way back to its claimed day of discovery. You might think that the biggest gem ever found would have been the prime success of the dig. Yet despite the repetition of the story in later decades, Mike Mitchell-Hedges never mentioned it at the time. It only appeared in his 1954 autobiography, *Danger My Ally*, and it is dispensed with quickly, vanishing altogether in later published editions. As to the ownership of the skull, the passage in the book seems cryptic: "How it came into my possession I have reason for not revealing." He goes on to give it a brief description, that scientists believe that it took 150 years to make, it's 3,600 years old and "the embodiment of all evil". In fact, the whole entry in the 1954 book only covers thirteen lines, which, if the artefact is so important, seems curious.

Legend has it that the skull of doom was used by Mayan high priests to not only focus on death, but to will it. It has gathered a reputation as a malevolent relic. Apparently, if you take the mickey out of the skull, you could die and, with further shades of the popular "mummy's curse", others are supposed to have been struck down with serious illness. Yet the controversy about how the skull was discovered is based on the suspicion that Anna Mitchell-Hedges, who lived to be 100 (a bonus which caused her to redesignate her cranial find as "the skull of love" rather than "death'), may not have even been on the expedition at all in the 1920s, and only visited Lubaantun for the first time many decades later for a TV documentary. Earlier versions of the "discovery" involve the suggestion that her father "planted" the skull beneath the altar, so that she could find it inside a deep hole or cave beneath or inside a pyramid, and enjoy the experience as a birthday present. The man behind all the myth and legend-making is Mike himself. Explorer, gambler, author and soldier with Pancho Villa in the Mexican Revolution, he was quite a character.

Much of Mitchell-Hedges's life was taken up as a deep-sea fisherman. He wrote numerous articles and books complete with that usual fisherman's braggadocio about the size of "the one that got away". But he didn't refer to his sport as such; he called fishing "deep sea research" and expanded his yarns for the Randolph Hearst newspaper empire into more mystical marine territory, which included sea monsters, epic struggles with giant fish and the obligatory courageous reports of struggles with man-eating sharks. He would sail off to the Caribbean at weekends, where his penchant for tales of danger and discovery were embroidered with claims to have discovered lost continents on the seabed as well as island tribes who had never met the white man before.

So what happened to the skull of doom once Anna was supposed to have unearthed it? According to her own version, her dad gave it to the Mayans as a gift, and apparently they "loved him" for bringing them medicines and clothing. That's a neat cover for it not appearing again in the family for another twenty years. The Mayans had it. So, how did it come to be in a collection of artefacts belonging to a London art dealer? Anna's explanation is as follows.

When explorers in the first half of the twentieth century went off on long expeditions, it was not unknown for them to leave valuable items back home in the care of friends, to beat the burglars. The skull was, apparently, left with an old school friend of Mike, Sidney Burney. But in 1943, Mike was horrified to discover that Burney had put the skull up for sale at Sotheby's in London. Learning of this skulduggery the day before the sale, Mitchell-Hedges was, apparently, "so furious that for a while he was unable to speak". He tried to get in touch with Burney but failed, so arose at 5 a.m. on the day of the sale and headed for London, hell-bent on getting his skull back. What transpired when the rage-muted Mitchell-Hedges arrived at Sotheby's is not clear, but apparently it was Sidney Burney's son selling the skull, not Burney Senior. Sotheby's allegedly refused to withdraw it from the sale, so Mitchell-Hedges must have quelled his wrath with the realization that the only way he'd get the skull back was to buy it. This he did at a cost of £400. It seems an odd solution, because if someone had purloined your property and put it up for sale, the first thing you'd do is call the police. However, the sceptics believe that far from being "stolen" by Burney, in fact this was the first time Mitchell-Hedges had come into contact with the contentious crystal noggin. According to the July 1936 issue of the British anthropological journal *Man*, the skull was owned at that time by Burney. Its history prior to the sale at Sotheby's, from the 1920s onwards, begins to look like another of Mitchell-Hedges's tall tales. Sidney Burney, and those who were on the Lubaantun expedition, denied that Mitchell-Hedges found the skull.

After her father's death, the skull became Anna's property. She maintained that Burney only had the piece as collateral against a debt Mitchell owed Burney. So why didn't he simply pay off his debt rather than travelling to London and forking out £400 – a huge sum in wartorn 1943?

Anna occasionally put it on display, claiming it was kept in Atlantis before it was brought to Belize, and that it came from outer space. You can view it for a fee. Today, it is owned and cared for by her widower, Bill Homan, who continues to perpetuate its mystical properties.

So, what about the history of the skull itself? Is it ancient? Does it have paranormal properties? In 1970, Anna allowed a crystal carver and art dealer named Frank Dorland to examine it. Scrying (also called seeing or peeping) is a magic practice that involves seeing things psychically in a medium, usually for purposes of obtaining spiritual visions and less often for purposes of divination or fortune-telling. Dorland pronounced the skull as excellent for scrying. He claimed that, depending on the position of the planets, it emitted sounds and light. He stated that it came from Atlantis. And it gets better; those popular old rascals, the Knights Templar, had carted it around with them during the Crusades. Frank Dorland borrowed the skull from Anna Mitchell-Hedges. One of his acquaintances was the supervisor of the Hewlett-Packard (HP) advertising account, Richard Garvin. Because HP have advanced scientific facilities as leaders in the manufacture of crystal oscillators, Dorland took the skull for tests to the Hewlett-Packard laboratory in Santa Clara.

At the laboratory, the skull was immersed in a tank of benzyl alcohol, which has the same refraction index as quartz crystal. In a benzyl alcohol solution, it would almost disappear. By passing polarized light through the skull and rotating it, it would be possible to locate the axis and observe "twinning". This is a splitting of the direction of crystal growth, which happens under strong impact. It can happen to a single crystal or to separate ones that can twin and grow together. Noticeably darker stress marks that appeared on the Mitchell-Hedges skull showed this process around the eyes, nose and jaw area. Dorland had suspected the skull was composed of separate pieces of quartz, but the technicians at Hewlett-Packard reported that the skull, and its jawbone, was "almost certainly a single crystal of quartz, rather than a composite of three crystals". Mitchell-Hedges had already suggested that the artefact could have taken 150 years to make, so his daughter must have been over the moon when the HP boys suggested it may have taken "300 man-years of effort".

The lab found that the skull had been carved against the natural axis of the crystal. Modern crystal sculptors always take into account the axis or orientation of the crystal's molecular symmetry, because using lasers and other high-tech tools, carving against the grain will shatter the crystal. These were wonderful additions to the skull's growing mystique, and even more so when HP could find no microscopic scratches on the crystal indicating the use of metallic tools. Dorland's hypothesis was that it had been hewn out with diamonds, with the finer details achieved with a combination of water and silicon.

Armed with such potent, high-tech facts, the paranormal road was open to add as many psychic attributes to the skull as you wished. Dorland, who had it for quite some time, began to experience visionary phenomena. He claimed to be able to see buildings and architecture from various historical periods by looking into the eye sockets of the skull. He claimed it had an "aura" that he found fascinating. It was said to give off the sounds of chimes, bells and other assorted noises, including chanting or singing human voices. When he had it in his bedroom overnight, he could hear what he claimed to be the sound of a jungle animal – a big cat – on the prowl.

According to the encouragingly thorough *Strange Magazine* (www.strangemag.com), there was an even weirder and more disturbing episode during Dorland's possession of the skull. Anton Szandor LaVey (1930–97) was a writer, occultist and musician who founded the Church of Satan in San Francisco. He wrote *The Satanic Bible* and established LaVeyan satanism, a synthesized system advocating materialism and individualism. Oddly enough, he described his Church as "atheistic", possessing no belief in God or the Devil, a claim which must have surely narked the Fallen One. As LaVey once quipped, "It's hard being evil in a world that's gone to hell," but he did his best. It was a big mistake by Frank Dorland to allow LaVey into his house. The Frisco Lucifer, always looking for publicity, was accompanied by the editor of an Oakland newspaper. LaVey said that the skull had been made by Satan himself and therefore must be the property of his Church. Apparently Dorland had a hard time getting LaVey to leave. The "churchman" was also a musician, and as Dorland happened to have an organ in his house, LaVey stubbornly sat at the keyboard to practise his demonic skill.

The skull should have been kept in its special vault, but on the day of LaVey's visit it was out of its usual sealed environment and on display in the house. Eventually the bargain basement Beelzebub departed, and Dorland and his wife put the skull away and went to bed. It was not to be a happy night. Dorland recalled that, "All night long there were lots and lots of sounds," yet he searched around and could find nothing. The next morning the sleepless couple discovered that their possessions lay scattered around, although doors and windows remained locked, and there was no sign of a break-in. "We had a telephone dialler," said Dorland, "that had been moved from the telephone at least thirty-five feet to the front door – and it lay right across the front door threshold. I never believed that this happened until it happened to me." What in fact "happened" seems to have been classic poltergeist activity. Needless to say, Dorland thought that LaVey's strong, evil "vibrations" had interacted with the psychic power of the skull, and said, "I think there was a conflict of one type of energy against another type of energy which interfered somehow with physical objects." Eventually Anna Mitchell-Hedges took the skull back and it remained with her until her death.

The greatest expert on the world's crystal skulls, Nick Nocerino, died in 2004. Nocerino devoted his life to studying crystal skulls, claiming that no one knows how they were made and that they are impossible to duplicate. He founded the Society of Crystal Skulls International, an organization that uses some unusual research methodology, including remote viewing, psychometry and scrying, and it owns a collection of crystal skulls from around the world.

Some skulls made of stone are genuine Meso-American cultural artefacts from such civilizations as the Aztecs. They are known as "death heads" or skull masks. That's too prosaic for New Agers. As far as they're concerned, these skulls are either from Atlantis or extra-terrestrial in origin. They are claimed to have magical powers, emitting weird noises, and can spontaneously produce holographic images. This is good enough reason for the purveyors of paranormal trinkets to ensure that their stalls have a good selection of skulls in all materials – crystal, steel, wood, stone, resin; there are thousands available around the world today.

At least thirteen other skulls have made their debut over the years, many said to have magical healing powers and mystical origins. The British Museum in London has one. However, in 1966 the museum carried out a study and survey of these artefacts. Utilizing electron microscopes, it was revealed that two of the skulls examined possessed straight, perfectly spaced surface markings that indicated that they'd been subjected to a modern polishing wheel. The hand-polishing process on genuine ancient objects would reveal tiny irregular scratches. The British Museum's conclusion was that the skulls were made in Germany during the past 150 years. This would explain how they were manufactured with tools unavailable to the ancient Mayans or Aztecs.

In 1992 the Smithsonian Institute received what was insisted to be an "Aztec" crystal skull from an anonymous source, who said it was bought in 1960 in Mexico City. Research by the

Smithsonian concluded that there was a crucial link between the skulls so popular with New Agers. He was a dubious character named Eugène Boban.

Eugène Boban (or Boban-Duvergé, 1834–1908) was the official archaeologist at the court of Maximilian I of Mexico (1832–67). Regarded as a serious French antiquarian, he was also a member of the French Scientific Commission in Mexico. He appears to have possessed a number of crystal skulls, most of which he sold; one now resides in the Musée du Quai Branly in Paris and another in the British Museum. The Paris skull is said to represent the Aztec god of the dead, Mictlantecuhtli, yet does not seem to offer any occult powers.

Perhaps Boban's post as the Emperor's official archaeologist paid well, but even so it must have been a short-lived career. Viennese-born Maximilian was only Emperor of Mexico from 1864 to 1867, his throne provided by Napoleon III's occupying French forces. After just three years, in 1867, the French left, but Maximilian was reluctant to give up his imperial life, mistakenly believing that the people of Mexico supported him. With his armies gone, he refused to go home. He was captured by Benito Juárez's republican forces and executed by firing squad on 19 June 1867.

This disaster must have left Eugène Boban high and dry and strapped for cash, but he carried on dealing in antiques in Mexico until 1880. The conclusions reached by Jane MacLaren Walsh of the Smithsonian Institute in *Crystal Skulls and Other Problems* (1996) were similar to the findings at the British Museum: the crystal skulls were only manufactured between 1867 and 1886. It appears that Boban acquired his skulls not from ancient Meso-American sites but from a source in that nineteenth-century hothouse of engineering technology, Germany.

In the 27 May 2010 online edition of *Archaeology* (www. archaelogy.org), Walsh states that she:

> had two opportunities to examine the Mitchell-Hedges skull closely and to take silicone moulds of carved and polished elements of it, which I have analysed under high-power light and scanning-electron microscopes ... The microscopic

evidence presented here indicates that the skull is not a Maya artefact but was carved with high-speed, modern, diamond-coated lapidary tools ... It is not unreasonable to conclude that the Mitchell-Hedges skull, which first appeared in 1933, (when it came into Sidney Burney's possession) was also created within a short time of its debut.

The crystal skull you can see in the British Museum today first appeared in Eugène Boban's Paris shop in 1881. Four years later, in Mexico City in 1885, he tried to sell it as an Aztec skull, but this ruse was thwarted by the curator of a Mexican museum who denounced it as a fake. The resourceful Boban soldiered on and, according to the *New York Times*, 19 December 1886, he managed to flog it off at an auction at Tiffany & Co. in New York City. Just over two years later, it was bought by the British Museum where it still resides in the Wellcome Trust Gallery.

This is the museum's caption for the exhibit:

A life-size carving of a human skull made from a single block of rock crystal (a clear, colourless variety of quartz). It was acquired by the Museum in 1897 purporting to be an ancient Mexican object. However scientific research conducted by the Museum has established that the skull was most likely produced in the nineteenth century in Europe. As such the object is not an authentic pre-Columbian artefact.

As for the skull of doom/love, if we accept the Smithsonian study, everything seems to point to it being carved in Europe, probably as a copy of the British Museum skull sometime between 1900 and the early 1930s. Who created it or sold it to Burney is unknown. Boban died in 1908 so he cannot be implicated. The real mystical legend seems to have begun when Sydney Burney finally sold the skull in London to Mitchell-Hedges at Sotheby's on 15 October 1943. It remains a terrific yarn and as such it's no surprise that Spielberg got a film out of it. Trust the paranormal to offer top-line entertainment every time.

Other so-called ancient crystal skulls gather their own mythos yet often appear to be as ambiguous as the British Museum or the Mitchell-Hedges skull. Allegedly found in Guatemala early in this century, both the Amethyst Skull and the Mayan Skull have a connection to the late Nick Nocerino. He stated that while travelling in Mexico in 1949 he met a shaman and was introduced to a Mayan priest. The priest said that as his village was poor and needed money, he had permission to sell the skulls. Nocerino declined to buy them, but he "scientifically" studied them, coming up with some amazing discoveries. The skulls seemed to possess all the psychic visionary powers of the skull of doom/love. Another skull in the Nocerino collection, nicknamed "Max" was supposedly given to the people of Guatemala by a Tibetan healer. Like the Knights Templar, those Tibetans certainly got around.

The latest adventures into skulling involve a Canadian Hollywood A-lister we have already met in the UFO section of this book. Dan Aykroyd appears to be a firm believer in all the psychic histories of the world's crystal skulls. He has done us all a service, because if you want a crystal skull of your own, you can now buy one, and it will give you a genuine visionary experience, because it's filled with a litre of the best, purest vodka ever made. It's a bottle you will not be recycling because it is carefully crafted by the best glass craftsmen into a replica of the spookiest crystal skull. Aykroyd came over to London in March 2012 especially to launch his new extrasensory brew, and I for one can't wait to get my hands on a bottle, but regrettably the beverage's website (http://crystalheadvodka.com/about) doesn't give a price. So, when I get mine, I shall raise a glass to Mr Mitchell-Hedges and get ready to experience the infinite.

Bones of Contention (and Other Body Parts ...)

If you're searching for tangible evidence in the murky fog of conspiracy theories, New World orders and secret societies, facts, figures and names are slippery eels. However, beyond the myths and legends surrounding the Bilderberg Group, the Illuminati and the Freemasons, in the leafy Ivy League enclaves of Yale University there is one perceptible organization, obsessed with death; the Skull and Bones Society, dating back to 1832. This secretive group, whose members are known as

Bonesmen, has been populated by some of America's most influential industrialists, politicians, bankers and Presidents, among them George H. W. Bush, George W. Bush and the failed Presidential candidate John Kerry. Whereas their membership list is no secret, their saturnine rituals, performed in the Skull and Bones Hall, otherwise known as the windowless, red stone Newhaven "Tomb", certainly are. One of the Bonesmen's morbid fascinations has been the acquisition of body parts.

Geronimo's Skull

In 1986, Ned Anderson, chairman of the San Carlos Apache tribe in Arizona, led a campaign against the Skull and Bones Society for the return of the skull of none other than the great warrior, Geronimo, who died of pneumonia in 1909. The story goes that in 1918, a group of six well-heeled Bonesmen stationed at Fort Sill, Oklahoma, robbed Geronimo's grave and removed the chief's skull and some bones. According to a centennial history of Skull and Bones by a 1923 initiate, Francis Otto Matthiessen, there exists a 1919 logbook featuring the skull, which is apparently now displayed in a glass case in the Skull and Bones Hall. Matthiessen names the grave robbers, among them one Prescott Bush, the father and grandfather of the US Presidents. Over the past decade twenty of Geronimo's descendants have tried desperately through the US Courts to have the skull returned, but in 2010 Judge Richard Roberts dismissed the lawsuit against Skull and Bones and Yale, saying the plaintiffs cited a law that applies only to Native American cultural items excavated or discovered after 1990.

Mussolini's Brain

The sad theft of Geronimo's remains is just one example of the melancholic fascination with the possession of purloined body parts. In 2009, for a few hours on eBay, you could bid for three glass vials containing a dictator's brain and blood. The initial asking price was 15,000 euros, $20,000 or £13,000. At the end of the Second World War, after he was shot with his mistress Claretta Petacci by anti-fascist partisans, the body of Benito Mussolini (1883–1945) was strung up on a lamp post close to a petrol station near Milan. The Americans, no doubt interested in how the mind of a dictator works, removed his remains and kept the interesting bits. Mussolini's wife, Rachaele, expressed her horror in her memoirs, and in 1966 America returned part of *il Duce*'s brain to his widow. Yet the macabre story didn't end there. Forty-three years later, Mussolini's granddaughter Alessandra discovered what was left of her granddad being peddled on eBay and the auction was abruptly aborted.

Anne Boleyn's Heart

You could drive through Erwarton in Suffolk, England, and hardly realize you'd been there. The village, in the parish of Babergh nine miles (14 km) south of Ipswich on the Shotley peninsula, has a population of just over 100 and a pub, The Queens Head, which closed in 2009. Yet like many seemingly insignificant villages, Erwarton has an interesting little thirteenth-century church, St Mary's. The church organ dates from 1912 and it bears a curious attachment: a copy of a drawing by Holbein of Anne Boleyn together with the legend: "after her execution in the Tower of London, 19 May 1536, it was recorded that her heart was buried in this church by her Uncle, Sir Philip Parker of Erwarton Hall". It goes on to reveal that in 1837 a lead casket was discovered in the church, believed to contain the hapless Anne Boleyn's heart, yet the casket had no inscription. Historian Alison Weir points out that "heart burial had gone out of fashion in England by the end of the fourteenth century" and identifies the uncle in question as Sir Phillip Calthorpe of Erwarton, who was married to Amy (or Amata) Boleyn, Anne's aunt. The story of the heart reverberated around the world for decades after the discovery, and an article in the *New York Times* dated 13 November 1881 confirms Weir's correction and tells us that Erwarton's parish clerk, James Amner, who died in 1875, was present with the rector, Revd Ralph Berners, when workmen restoring the church found the heart-shaped lead casket behind the north wall. It was opened and contained what appeared to be a pile of dust. It was reburied in the Cornwallis vault, beneath where the organ now stands.

The Remains of Thomas Paine

America's independence owes much to Thomas Paine, born in Thetford, England, on 29 January 1737. A great revolutionary and the author of *Rights of Man* and *The Age of Reason*, he inspired Washington's Army during the Revolution of 1776. As his service to America had been at his own expense, in 1784 New York State gave him a confiscated Royalist farm in New Rochelle and Congress awarded him $3,000. Paine died in New York City on 8 June 1809, and only six mourners, including two freed slaves, attended the funeral. He was buried on his farm.

Britain's William Cobbett, political activist and author of *Rural Rides* – another "dangerous man" – was at one time Paine's rival but had come to admire him. He dug up Paine's remains without permission and brought them to London with ambitious plans for a memorial, which never materialized. Paine's bones, in a series of boxes, were handed down through the generations of Cobbett's descendants. What became of them is uncertain, although it is claimed that there is a rib in France, some of his bones were made into buttons and, in 1987, a Sydney businessmen bought Paine's skull while on holiday in London. It was sold to another Australian named John Burgess, reputed to be a descendant of an illegitimate child of Paine. The last bit of news on the tale was that Burgess's wife was trying to raise $60,000 for DNA testing. Is it Paine's skull? Both Gary Berton, president of the Thomas Paine National Historical Association and the New Rochelle Citizen Paine Restoration Initiative have been on the trail. Berton said the skull was the right size and has some incised markings which are believed to have been made by Cobbett and his son.

However, all that definitely remains in New Rochelle of the great man are his mummified brain stem and a lock of hair, kept in a secret location.

Napoleon's Penis

He may have ruled Europe with a rod of iron, but Napoleon Bonaparte's sometimes floppier physical extremity, much enjoyed by Josephine, seems to have suffered the ultimate indignity. The unkindest cut of all, the removal of Bonaparte's penis, is said to have been carried out by his physician when the

Emperor died in exile on St Helena in 1821. The doctor may have given it to the priest who gave him the last rites. The priest's descendants, the Vignali family in Naples, crop up in an article by Guy Lesser about a rare book dealer, A. S. W. Rosenbach, in the January 2002 issue of *Harper's Magazine*. Sadly, the fleshy relic does not seem to have been well preserved. Lesser writes:

> Rosenbach evidently had been fond of showing off his collection of Napoleon relics to his most favoured clients, acquired in the mid-1920s, from the Vignali family of Naples, the descendants of Napoleon's chaplain and last confessor on St Helena. The relics included hair, cutlery, clothes, and, as the piece de resistance, so to speak, a short length of dried leather, kept by Rosenbach in a small blue morocco box – and delicately referred to, in his day, as "Napoleon's tendon". The "thing" had been quietly sold by Rosenbach in the mid-1940s.

The wayward willy has been compared at various times to a piece of leather, a shrivelled eel or a bit of beef jerky. In 1927 it went on display in Manhattan, when *Time* magazine likened it to a "maltreated strip of buckskin shoelace". In 1977, Dr John Lattimer of New Jersey, the world's leading urologist who had treated Nazi war criminals awaiting trial, reputedly forked out $3,000 for the battered baguette (some sources claim it was $38,000) and stored it under his bed where it stayed until his death in 2007. His daughter inherited it as a probably unexpected bonus in her father's will and has had offers up to $100,000.

At least that's a more dignified sum for an Emperor ...

St Francis Xavier's Toe

When the faithful go in search of a miracle, they can have no better reward than a body that refuses to decompose. At the age of forty-six, the zealous Catholic missionary St Francis Xavier, worn out from his various Asian sea voyages, died on Saturday, 3 December 1552 on the Chinese island of Shangchuan. The body remained buried – and fresh – for ten weeks in a coffin full of lime. It was then transported on a decorated galleon to Goa as the saint himself had wished to go there. Huge crowds, accompanied by the nobility, gave the cadaver a royal welcome.

On 14 March 1554 the corpse, in a wooden coffin with damask lining, was taken to the church of Ajuda at Ribandar. Dead or not, Xavier just kept on travelling. Two days later he was delivered to the church of S. Paulo in Goa on 16 March 1554 and the strange life of a relic began when the little toe on the right foot was bitten off by Dona Isabel de Carom, a Portuguese woman, who claimed she was anxious to have a relic of the future saint. Apparently, it gushed blood. Three other toes were later removed from his right foot. One of the purloined extremities ended up at the saint's birthplace, the Castle of Xavier in Navarre.

After sixty years of not mouldering in the grave, the ecclesiastic souvenir-hunters were at it again. On 3 November 1614, Father General Claude Aquaviva instructed that the right arm was to be cut off at the elbow. It arrived in Rome the following year, where it remains in a silver reliquary in the church of Gesu. Today, St Francis Xavier is spread far and wide. As well as the toe, displayed in a silver reliquary in a Goa cathedral, one of his hands is in Japan, there's yet another relic elsewhere in Goa (a diamond-encrusted fingernail) and, for all we know, he may have a toe in the door at other clerical locations.

The Maori Heads

Back in less enlightened times, when Britain, France and Germany had empires, many branches of non-European humanity were seen simply as biological curiosities. The intervention in such cultures back then must have had all the characteristics of today's "alien abduction" phenomenon. Even as late as the 1960s, touring fairgrounds, alongside their two-headed sheep, often had their ten-foot (3 m) mummified South Pacific giant or a brace of tiny, unfortunate mummified little characters doubling as either Polynesian pygmies or even "captured leprechauns". However, the abduction of hapless tattooed Maoris developed into a grisly business for collectors of the exotic. Around the world today about 500 intricately tattooed Maori heads are either hidden away in dusty vaults or stored in boxes in various museum stockrooms. The sad thing about this repugnant trade is that many Maoris were kidnapped from New Zealand, forcibly tattooed, then beheaded. In May 2011 the head of one such unfortunate warrior was handed back to the Maoris in Rouen, northern France, where it had languished in the city's museum for the past 136 years. According to museum director Sebastien Minchin, up until 1966 the head had been displayed as part of the museum's prehistoric collection. Although the Maoris and the New Zealand Consul were pleased with the handover, there are still an estimated fifteen of these heads awaiting return throughout France. In recent years 300 heads have returned home from countries around the world.

"El Negro"

In the same dark, colonial collector's netherworld that led to the exposition of decapitated Maoris lies the story of two opportunistic mid-nineteenth-century French taxidermists, the Verreaux brothers who, finding themselves at a burial site in the Kalahari Desert, decided to take a break from stuffing lions and rhinos and exhume the body of a recently buried African man. Soon they had him well stuffed and suitably embalmed, and before long the morbidly curious of Europe were queuing up to see their handiwork. As the two maladjusted stuffers were a bit disappointed with their victim's light skin, they decided on their own method of making him "African" by adding a layer of black polish. He eventually came to rest in Spain at a Catalonian town called Banyoles, where, known to locals as "El Negro", he resided for a century in the Darder museum until 1992, when Alphonse Arcelin, a local doctor of Haitian descent, raised objections. The town fought to keep the corpse and even issued boxes of chocolates commemorating his presence, but common sense eventually triumphed: he was finally laid to rest in a dignified burial ceremony in Botswana in 2000.

Santa's Sticky Bones

Traditionally, St Nicholas may squeeze down your chimney on Christmas Eve, but the jolly old redcoat's mortal remains might put Rudolf right off his carrots.

The Middle Ages were the high watermark for the lucrative Christian business of attracting pilgrims to holy body parts and possible miracles. The long-dead, real St Nicholas was originally lying in peace in a grave in Myra, Turkey. However, in 1087 the wily elders of the Italian town of Bari, looking for a suitable, cash-raising religious attraction, hit upon the wheeze of hiring a gang of pirates (some called them "privileged mariners") to nip over to Turkey and raid the Myra crypt and bring Father Christmas to Bari. The mission was a success, and the buccaneering blag is celebrated every year with a massive parade followed by a firework display. Commissioned by Abbot Elia in 1087, the Romanesque basilica of St Nicholas in Bari now attracts thousands of pilgrims who hope to benefit from the strange liquid called "Manna" which oozes from St Nick's casket and is said to cure various illnesses.

The King's Head Goes Home

King Badu Bonsu of Ghana's Ahanta tribe seems to have pushed the invading Dutch over the edge in 1838 when he decided to lop off the heads of two Dutch emissaries and use them to decorate his throne. When Major General Jan Verveer discovered what had happened, he promptly had the King hanged and then decapitated, and took his head back home to Holland. Its modern location, the Leiden University Medical Centre, was revealed by Dutch novelist Arthur Japin, who was researching his latest work. For decades, the poor old monarch had been staring out through the glass from a dusty jar of formaldehyde in a store room in the centre's anatomical collections department. In July 2009 the Dutch government received a deputation from Ghana to arrange the head's return. The ceremony was not a particularly joyful occasion, despite the ceremonial tipple of Dutch gin and the red robes of the visiting Ahanta tribesmen. They were still angry; the King's great-great-grandson, Joseph Jones Amoah exclaiming, "I am hurt, angry. My grandfather has been killed ..." The party were also displeased as they thought they had only come to identify the relic, not return it, as they would first have to adhere to tribal protocol by reporting back to their chief. However, the King's head went home a few days later, with the Dutch hoping that they'd righted a wrong.

Lenin Gets a New Suit

It had been sixty years since Vladimir Illych Ulyanov – Lenin (1870–1924) – had a visit from the tailor. However, in 2004, in readiness for the eightieth anniversary of his death and embalming in January 1924, the former Soviet leader received a sartorial overhaul between 10 November and 29 December. He was originally laid in his glass-topped coffin wearing a military uniform, but shortly before the Second World War, Joseph Stalin decided a civilian outfit would better suit communism's most famous corpse. The re-dressing process involved the efforts of a team of twelve Russian scientists, although the style and cut of Lenin's new threads remain distinctly retro.

Embalming specialist Yuri Denisov-Nikolsky, who also nips over to Vietnam from time to time to check on Ho Chi Minh's cadaver, says the Lenin Mausoleum and sarcophagus were never built to be bombproof so during the Second World War, fearing a direct hit by the Nazis, Soviet authorities secretly shipped Lenin – codenamed "Object No. 1" – to a warehouse in central Russia. They put him back on display in March 1945.

The controversy over the legendary cadaver's resting-place continues to occupy many of Russia's top politicians. Boris Yeltsin had definite plans to close down the Mausoleum in Red Square and have Lenin buried next to his mother in the Volkovoe Cemetery in St Petersburg. However, Lenin had requested that he be buried next to one of his early lovers, Inessa Armand, in Moscow. Despite the wishes of Nadya, Lenin's wife, in 1924 Stalin had other plans. Even as Lenin lay dying at his house in Gorki, Stalin announced to the Central Committee: "he will soon be no more … Modern science is capable of preserving his body for a considerable time, long enough at least for us to grow used to the idea of his being no longer with us".

With the founding of the "Committee for Immortalization", Stalin appointed two scientists, Boris Zbarsky and Vladimir Vorbiov, to come up with a successful method of preserving Lenin's corpse. He'd been on ice for two months in the newly erected Mausoleum (a wooden construction, the current marble edifice being built in 1930). His ears had crumpled up and the left hand was turning black but Vorbiov concocted a secret mix of alcohol, glycerin, potassium acetate, water and quinine chloride that soon had the body looking lifelike again. An electric pump was at one time installed in the corpse to maintain constant humidity. Zbarsky looked after the cadaver for over twenty-five years until he was dismissed from his post. When Stalin died on 5 March 1953, he too was embalmed and lay in state for three days. It is estimated that in the density of the distraught crowds wishing to view the dead dictator, around 500 people lost their lives in the chaotic crush.

Stalin was moved to the Lenin Mausoleum on 9 March 1953, where Zbarsky spent several months on the same preservation technique used on Lenin. By November 1953, Stalin had been laid alongside Lenin in his own glass-topped coffin. But not for long. In 1961, as part of his "de-Stalinization" campaign, Soviet Premier Nikita Khrushchev had Stalin's body removed from Lenin's side and buried by the Kremlin wall under several feet of concrete – "to prevent him ever rising again". As for Lenin, he remains in Red Square, despite the fall of communism. He is still a popular tourist attraction, but when interviewed on the thorny subject of his removal in 1999, Mikhail Gorbachev commented: "I'm in absolute favour of burying Lenin's body if this is approached in a humane and Christian way." Considering Lenin looked upon Christianity as "spiritual oppression" he would no doubt turn in his new grave. Current Russian President Vladimir Putin prefers to keep the founder of the USSR where he is: "The people of this country associate their lives with Lenin. To take Lenin out and bury him would say to them that they have worshipped false values, that they lived their lives in vain ... I will try not to do anything which will upset civil calm."

The ages of imperialism, communism and colonialism may be long past, but the lamentable enthralment with bits and pieces of the departed, or even the whole body, is still with us. The frozen cadaver of the "Prince of Pop", Michael Jackson, remains unburied in a bare brick room in a gold casket encased in a clear fibreglass container. Jackson's eighty-year-old mother can't bring herself to have him buried for fear that grave robbers might moonwalk into the cemetery and, like a scene from "Thriller", make off with a Jacko souvenir.

It's a pity all those religious zealots, fairground barkers, taxidermists and Lenin's 1924 embalmers didn't know anything about the modern science of cryonics. If the old chestnut about Walt Disney's frozen noggin is true, saints and sinners could, like baseball legend Ted Williams, whose body was frozen in 2002, become major live attractions in the years to come.

HIMMLER'S HOLY LANCE

> *The characteristic thing about these people [modern-day followers*
> *of the early Germanic religion] is that they rave about the old*
> *Germanic heroism, about dim prehistory, stone axes, spear and*
> *shield, but in reality are the greatest cowards that can be*
> *imagined.*
>
> Adolf Hitler (1889–1945), *Mein Kampf* (1926)

There are probably many people who think that Dan Brown's *The Da Vinci Code* is real history. There are others who get what history they know from Indiana Jones, and when it comes to the Nazis and the occult, a man called Trevor Ravenscroft, who we shall meet eventually, has much to answer for.

The Third Reich, which Hitler proclaimed would last 1,000 years, ended in ruins in just less than fifteen years. One would think, when considering the number of books, films and documentaries it has spawned over the past seventy years, that what Hitler actually meant was that we'd no doubt *remember* the Reich for a millennium. Black SS uniforms and swastikas continue as entertainment dynamite. There is nothing in humanity's vast lexicon of evil-doing to match 1933–45; the period remains as an inexplicable phenomenon of the first order.

However, the melodramatic portrayal of the Nazi regime, due to such strategic military innovations as the blitzkrieg and the cinematic propaganda of Leni Riefenstahl (1902–2003), gives new generations of viewers the impression that the Third Reich was a highly organized, tight-knit machine that, had it not been for the last massive push of D-Day, might well have seen us all speaking German today. The reverse is arguably true. Each member of that gang of inglorious bastards – Himmler, Bormann, Heydrich, Eichmann, Hess *et al.* – occupied their own nasty individual spheres of competing influence, each man played off against the other by Hitler. Germany's early military success was down to a combination of rapid and efficient rearmament, conscription and an audacious, traditional generation of dedicated patrician generals and field marshals who obeyed orders. If their arrogant leader had only listened to them, he might not have ended up as a crispy corpse outside his bunker in 1945. The Führer himself may have swayed the masses with his vitriolic oratory, but if we take a closer look, it becomes apparent that once he'd achieved power, he became a lazy man. He slept in late during his many retreats to his hideaway, the Berghof at Obersalzberg, where he spent many hours watching cowboy films. When German troops on the coast of Normandy saw the massive D-Day armada approaching, the High Command tried frantically to inform Hitler in Berlin, but was told by his staff that he was in bed and they didn't dare to disturb him. Hitler was probably dreaming, something he had done ever since leaving the trenches in the First World War. Unfortunately, his charismatic messianic abilities transformed his nocturnal reveries into a waking nightmare for the world.

Much has been written and filmed about the Nazis and the occult, and even I believed a lot of it until recently. But as new research and documentation comes to light, it seems that much of the "Hitler possessed by demons" literature is nonsense. He was just a very bad man. Yet there is one undeniably central character in the regime that lingers on as the very epicentre of all the stories of Nazi mysticism, and he remains as fascinating as ever: Heinrich Himmler (1900–1945).

His Swedish masseur, Felix Kersten (1898–1960), was probably as close to the Reichsführer-SS as anyone in the Reich. Yet Kersten held no misapprehensions about the nature of his client. In his memoirs, *The Kersten Memoirs, 1940–1945* (1956), he gives a chilling description of the architect of the Final Solution:

His eyes were extraordinarily small, and the distance between them narrow, rodent-like. If you spoke to him, those eyes would never leave your face; they would rove over your countenance, fix your eyes, and in them would be an expression of waiting, watching, stealth ... his ways were the ophidian ways of the coward, weak, insincere and immeasurably cruel. Himmler's mind was not a twentieth-century mind. His character was medieval, feudalistic, Machiavellian, evil.

Apart from his predilection for mass murder, many of this failed chicken farmer's hobbies would sit easy with today's generation of "New Age" enthusiasts. He was well into the legend of Atlantis, a vegetarian who thought he was the reincarnation of Germany's King Heinrich "The Fowler" (876–936), and was a dedicated believer in homeopathic and herbal medicines. He saw to it that Germany's entire mineral-water bottling and distribution industry was nationalized under the SS economic administration department. He inflicted a diet of porridge and leeks on his Aryan SS corps, and made sure that every concentration camp had a herb garden.

The Nazi view of science is, in retrospect, ridiculous. They replaced psychology with an occult gumbo that mixed a helping of the mysticism of George Gurdjieff (1877–1949), the theosophy of Madame Blavatsky (1831–91) and all the archetypes of Nordic mythology. Albert Einstein's theory of relativity was utterly discounted for one main reason – it was "a Jewish theory" and therefore had no value. Newtonian physics were rubbished and were substituted by a cosmic force called *vril*, with a nutty geological concept known as "the hollow earth theory" and the central pillar of National Socialist pseudoscience, the wacky doctrine of eternal ice. The immensely popular *Welteislehre* (World Ice Theory), also known as *Glazial-Kosmogonie* (Glacial Cosmogony), was proposed by Austria's Hanns Hörbiger (1860–1931), a much-respected steam-engine designer, engineer and inventor. In 1894 Hörbiger patented a new design for a blast-furnace blowing engine, replacing the old and easily damaged leather flap valves. His device had a steel valve that eliminated all the drawbacks of existing valve designs. This invention led to efficient steel production and greater productivity in mining. Both the global network of gas exchange and high-pressure chemistry would have been impossible without the

Hörbiger valve and consequently it made him a rich man, able to indulge himself in flights of fancy of a much less sound scientific nature.

Hörbiger received his World Ice Theory in a "vision" in 1894. The hypothesis was that ice was the basic substance of all cosmic processes, and ice moons, ice planets, and the "global ether" (also made of ice) had determined the entire development of the universe. After his "vision" he claimed "I knew that Newton had been wrong and that the sun's gravitational pull ceases to exist at three times the distance of Neptune." Together with a schoolteacher and amateur astronomer, Philipp Fauth, who he met in 1898, he worked on the theory which was published as *Glazial-Kosmogonie* in 1912. It had millions of followers, even in the UK. Both Adolf Hitler and Heinrich Himmler were ardent world ice supporters, and even after Hörbiger's death in 1931, *Welteislehre* retained its place on the Nazis' mad menu of rancid philosophical, racial and quasi-scientific dishes. However, there is evidence that, despite Himmler's closeness to Hitler and his position as the second most important Nazi in the regime, in private the Führer had little time for the SS leader's fascination with research into the ancient past, and especially with his imposition of so much mysticism on to the SS. Himmler had been hell-bent (with some success) on transforming the Black Corps into a society of "Teutonic Knights" complete with pagan rituals. Church weddings were replaced with SS wedding ceremonies, and grooms had to seek Himmler's permission to marry. The Christening ceremony was substituted with an SS equivalent, with salt and bread among the pagan trimmings. Hitler once commented that his Reich had gone to all the trouble of shedding and destroying Christian religious mythology yet now his "True Heinrich" wanted to substitute it all with more "nonsense". According to Albert Speer, Hitler once joked that, "To think someday I might be turned into an SS Saint! I would turn in my grave! We really should do our best to cover up this primitive past."

Yet Himmler had worked long and hard building up the formidable SS and whatever crackpot schemes he wished to develop went ahead. As the man with a card index on just about everyone and anyone who crossed his sinister path, he had the power and the facilities, and as his organization led the field in the biggest state-sponsored robbery in history, the dispossession of millions of Jewish families, he had the funds.

Himmler's favourite brainchild, which he founded with Herman Wirth and Richard Walther Darré on 1 July 1935 was the Ahnenerbe. It was an SS offshoot which promoted itself as a "Study Society for Intellectual Ancient History". Its aim was to research the anthropological and cultural history of the Aryan race. Himmler's aim was to prove that mythological and prehistoric Nordic populations had ruled the world. This led to various Ahnenerbe expeditions to the most unlikely places, such as Tibet and Antarctica. One of the aspects of history that fascinated Himmler involved holy relics, and one of the most important was the so-called "Holy Lance", later to be dubbed by British writer Trevor Ravenscroft as "The Spear of Destiny".

This is supposed to be the spear with which the Roman centurion, Longinus, pierced the side of Christ during the crucifixion. Naturally, to fit Nazi ideology, Longinus, who is not mentioned in the Bible, would be declared a German, and the weapon he used to ease Christ's suffering on the cross would be passed from hand to hand among the high and mighty throughout history. It would become connected to the careers of German and European leaders like Frederick Barbarossa, Charlemagne, Napoleon and Otto the Great, among others. The legend has it that anyone who held possession of the "Holy Lance" held power over the world.

Today Longinus is a saint and has two days when he is remembered: 16 October in the Eastern Orthodox Church and Catholic Church (Latin and Eastern Rites); and 22 October in the Armenian Apostolic Church. Although his name does not appear in any works until the fourth century, the following passage from the King James Bible (John 19: 31–7) describes his merciful act:

31. The Jews therefore, because it was the preparation, that the bodies should not remain upon the cross on the Sabbath day, (for that Sabbath day was an high day,) besought Pilate that their legs might be broken, and that they might be taken away.

32. Then came the soldiers, and brake the legs of the first, and of the other which was crucified with him.

33. But when they came to Jesus, and saw that he was dead already, they brake not his legs:

34. But one of the soldiers with a spear pierced his side, and forthwith came there out blood and water.

35. And he that saw it bare record, and his record is true: and he knoweth that he saith true, that ye might believe.

36. For these things were done, that the scripture should be fulfilled, A bone of him shall not be broken.

37. And again another scripture saith, They shall look on him whom they pierced.

Whereas you'll not find Longinus by name in the Bible, you can see him in the 1965 biblical epic movie *The Greatest Story Ever Told* where he's played (somewhat hilariously, as an unnamed Roman soldier) by none other than John Wayne. In the movie he doesn't have a spear, but in a Death Valley drawl utters, "Truly this man was the Son of God", making this one of cinema's most memorable moments …

Trevor Ravenscroft (1921–89) served as an officer with the Commandos in the Second World War and spent four years in Nazi prison camps after he was captured attempting to assassinate General Erwin Rommel in North Africa in 1941. Later, as a journalist and historian, he devoted much of his time to researching arcane and occult subjects, and was fascinated by the early life of Adolf Hitler. He said his feeling for history was a result of achieving transcendent "higher levels of consciousness" in Nazi concentration camps – perhaps not the best academic foundation for the work he produced. Yet those bleak years led him to study the legend of world destiny that has grown up around the spear of Longinus. He was also fascinated by the influence of black magic and wrote a further book on the quest for the Holy Grail.

His greatest influence, and much of his contested information, came via a Viennese exile called Dr Walter Johannes Stein (1891–1957). Here's where it becomes a little creaky; Stein was undoubtedly a scholar, but he claimed to use "white magic" to "clairvoyantly investigate" historical events. When your primary sources become disembodied spirits, then anything can happen. His 1928 book, *The Ninth Century: World History in the Light of the Holy Grail*, was of great interest to Ravenscroft, and the possibility that Stein had known Hitler in his lost years in Vienna from 1909 to 1913 was the missing link in the occult chain he was attempting to complete. Ravenscroft firmly believed that Dr Stein, whilst a student at the University of Vienna, was deeply into the occult and had met with Hitler, who was supposedly living in a flophouse and surviving off the proceeds of his lacklustre watercolours.

The trouble with Ravenscroft's *Spear of Destiny* (1973) is that when it was published, by the suitably named publisher Neville Spearman, he would have preferred it to have come out as a novel. Yet it contained so much ostensible "research" that it was issued as a history book. That said, it has been a massive bestseller and remains a fascinating read, with some genuinely dark, dramatic scenarios. The problem is that a lot of the "facts" don't stack up.

The Vienna Hitler experienced in his so-called "destitute" years was a great centre of intellectual activity. It was the workshop of Freud and the philosopher Wittgenstein, the place where Gustav Mahler composed and conducted one of Europe's greatest orchestras. Yet the rising tide of anti-Semitism lapped around their ankles, forcing Freud to escape to London whilst Mahler denied his Jewish ancestry by converting to Catholicism. Vienna was the perfect place for a dedicated student of the black arts to practise and prosper, and one such specialist in the darker side of ancient pan-German folklore was Guido von List (1848–1919). List crops up from time to time in the various legends about the occult roots of the Nazi Party, but later members of his circle fell out with the Nazis because List's mystical views on Aryan history did not match those of Himmler. List's ideas and his research into ancient runes (the "sig" rune, ⚡ became the emblem of the SS. ⚡⚡) were used to found a Masonic society, which later embraced National Socialism. Subsequently, numerous members of the Nazi Party embraced List's ideas and writings in furthering their own political agendas.

Trevor Ravenscroft suggests that List was the inspiration for Hitler when, in the 1920s, the imprisoned Führer designed the

Nazi flag with the swastika. However, it was already in use by the mystical Thule Society. Between 1919 and 1921 Hitler frequented the library of a dentist from Sternberg, Dr Friedrich Krohn, a very active member of the Thule Society. Dr Krohn was named by Hitler in *Mein Kampf* as the designer of a flag similar to the one he conjured up.

According to Ravenscroft, Dr Stein's connection with Hitler is alleged to have taken place through an occult Viennese bookseller, Ernst Pretzche, in whose shop, "in the old quarter by the Danube", the future Führer was a regular browser. It was there that Stein found a copy of Wolfram von Eschenbach's *Parzival* (*Parsifal*), which Dr Stein found very useful as he was researching the same story for his work on the ninth century. In the book's margins were handwritten annotations; looking them over Dr Stein was both fascinated and repelled:

> This was no ordinary commentary but the work of somebody who had achieved more than a working knowledge of the black arts! The unknown commentator had found the key to unveiling many of the deepest secrets of the Grail, yet obviously spurned the Christian ideals of the Knights and delighted in the devious machinations of the Anti-Christ. It suddenly dawned on him that he was reading the footnotes of Satan!

These mysterious scribbled footnotes were, apparently, by Hitler.

Ravenscroft tells us that Dr Stein and Hitler went to see the Spear of Destiny together in Vienna's Hofburg Imperial Museum. Stein was no stranger to the relic; he'd seen it before and was always deeply moved by it, claiming that it inspired in him the emotion expressed in the motto of the Knights of the Holy Grail: *Durch Mitleid wissen*, "Through compassion to self-knowledge".

Now it gets strange again. Ravenscroft, when writing about Stein's research regime, foregoes the usual haunts of the historians, such as archives and libraries. He informs us that Stein studied in something named the "Cosmic Chronicle", a place where past, present and future were united in a higher dimension of time. So whatever this psychic location was, Ravenscroft, in his introduction, maintains that the peculiar Viennese boffin taught the same techniques to him, thus clearing the way to issue forth of a stream of unverifiable data. As you can't footnote or cite clairvoyance, whatever Ravenscroft wrote we have to take on extremely fragile trust. Here then, is an amalgam of his and other researchers' knowledge of the Holy Lance's history. However, a word of caution: legends of the Holy Lance are scattered across history like shrapnel, and what makes the story a source of utter confusion is that, in all probability, the Holy Lance which Himmler and Hitler got their hands on is not the real thing. According to sources such as *The Catholic Encyclopedia* (www.newadvent.org), there are at least three contenders for the title "Spear of Destiny", like the "true cross" of the Crucifixion. The "true cross", should you be able to reassemble all the bits and shavings of this relic that are held in reliquaries around the world, would arguably be big enough to crucify Moby Dick. There's a lance in Armenia, a bit in Paris, an important element in the Vatican … it goes on. This is not quantifiable history by any stretch of the imagination, but myth and mystery. Therefore my attempt at a "chronology" only makes even the vaguest sense if you accept that each of the following entries may well apply to any of the lances languishing in the vaults of Europe or beyond.

The Holy Lance: A Chronology

Constantine the Great (272–337, also known as Constantine I or Saint Constantine), the first Roman Emperor to convert to Christianity, was Roman Emperor from 306 to 337. Constantine gave his mother, Helena, unlimited access to the imperial treasury in order to locate the relics of Judeo-Christian tradition. In 326 Helena made her way Palestine. Legend has it that she excavated a site where she discovered three different crosses. According to various Roman sources, Helena was looking for solid proof that the crosses she'd discovered were those used at Christ's crucifixion. She selected a woman who was close to death. There are echoes of Goldilocks and the Three Bears here: apparently, the sick woman touched the first cross, no luck …

then she touched the second cross, no sign of improvement in her health. But the third and final cross was just right; whatever her ailments, she suddenly recovered fully. And so Helena declared the third cross to be the True Cross. It must have been absolutely enormous, because today there are purported bits of it in churches all around the globe. Constantine ordered the building of the Church of the Holy Sepulchre on the site of the discovery, and wherever Helena made more finds churches were also built. There were other claims that Helena also found the nails used in the crucifixion. Due to their supposed miraculous power, she allegedly had one placed in the bridle of Constantine's horse and another in his helmet.

The Spear of Longinus was unearthed by Helena at the same time and place as the Holy Nails and the True Cross, and was later buried at Antioch to prevent its capture by the Saracens. It had become transformed into a prime religious relic, which had pierced the flesh and absorbed the blood of Jesus, and seemed to be ample proof of Christ's death and his subsequent resurrection.

According to Ravenscroft, Hitler visited the Hofburg many times following his first sight of the lance with Stein: "He was excited to find that in century after century the astonishing legend of the Spear had been fulfilled for good and evil." Although Himmler had employed scholars to research the history of the lance, their results were not as thorough as those gained through Dr Stein's "unique method of historical research involving 'Mind Expansion'". So the richly textured history of the Spear of Destiny issuing forth from Stein's "Cosmic Chronicle" offers some startling revelations. This "historical" information from beyond the veil is doubtlessly rich fodder for Xbox or PlayStation games, but its veracity remains dubious. However, it's dark, sinister fun, so let's continue.

Apparently Mauritius, Commander of the Theban Legion (now venerated as St Maurice), held the spear in his hand when he was martyred for refusing to serve the gods of Rome in 287. Then the Roman Emperor Theodosius (347–95) tamed the Goths with the spear's assistance.

One of the Holy Lance's other early owners appears to have been Attila the Hun (c. 405–53). How it came into his possession is unclear. Whilst campaigning in Italy, when his Army was starving, he seems to have realized the relic wasn't all it was cracked up to be. Apparently he rode to the gates of Rome and hurled the lance at the feet of the Roman generals, shouting, "Take back your Holy Lance! It is of no use to me, since I do not know Him that made it holy."

In 529 the Emperor Justinian (482–565) is claimed to have brandished the spear aloft as he closed down the School of Athens, an event that is often cited as "the end of Antiquity".

It was not until the "Anonymous Pilgrim of Piacenza" St Antoninus of Piancenza visited Jerusalem in 570 that the Holy Lance appeared again. In his itinerary, *Itinerarium Antonini Placentini*, he wrote that he saw in the basilica of Mount Sion, "the crown of thorns with which Our Lord was crowned and the lance with which He was struck in the side". Then comes the first mention of Longinus. In the Laurentian Library in Florence there is a manuscript from the year 586, illuminated by one Rabulas, detailing the opening of Christ's side. The accompanying illustration of the Roman soldier thrusting his lance has above it, in Greek characters, "LOGINOS".

In 615 a lieutenant of the Persian King Khosrau II captured Jerusalem and spirited away the holy relics, including the cross and spear. According to the seventh-century Greek Christian chronicle of the world, the *Chronicon Paschale*, the point of the lance was broken off and somehow came into the possession of Nicetas, the Patriarch of Constantinople, who took it there and deposited it in the church of St Sophia. Now we have two potential bits of the lance, which somewhat confuses the story. And the legend starts to become very German. Hitler must have been over the moon when he discovered that his early favourite military hero, General Charles Martel (686–741) aka "The Hammer" had held the Holy Lance and actually used it as a weapon in the Battle of Poitiers in 732, which defeated the Arabs and curtailed the spread of Islam throughout Europe. The Hammer's grandson, Charlemagne (742–814), the first Holy Roman Emperor, later dubbed by the Vatican "the Father of Europe", is supposed to have slept with the spear at his side and carried it into forty-seven victorious battles.

If Hitler was thrilled by all this, Heinrich Himmler must have suffered moist palpitations when he discovered that the spirit that possessed the Reichsführer-SS as a reincarnation, King Henry the Fowler (876–963) (like Himmler, another chicken fancier), ruled with the spear, as did his successor Holy Roman Emperor Otto the Great (912–73). Then it became the property of Frederick I Barbarossa (1122–90), who had held the spear in his hands as he kissed the feet of the Pope in Venice. Here the other part of the legend surfaces – lose hold of the spear and you die. Barbarossa dropped it when he was crossing a stream in Sicily and duly expired.

Next are the colourful chronicles of the First Crusade and the lance gets a mention on two important dates (which vary slightly depending on sources).

10 June 1098: Peter Bartholomew, a peasant serving in Count Raymond of Toulouse's Army, had gone to the Holy Land from Provence. He claimed St Andrew had appeared to him in several visions wherein he revealed the location of the lance. He informed the sceptical spiritual leader of the Crusade, papal legate Bishop Adhémar of Le Puy, but he wasn't impressed. However, Bartholomew led Count Raymond to the Cathedral of St Peter in Antioch and after a day of strenuous, unproductive digging, leapt into the hole and produced a piece of iron, which he announced as the lance. Raymond was awestruck, regarding it as an authentic relic, and the Crusaders, who were being besieged in Antioch by Emir Kerboga, Attabeg of Mosul, had their confidence renewed and carried it with them into battle against the Muslims.

28 June 1098: at the Battle of Orontes in Antioch, the Crusaders held the lance aloft as they drove back the Turkish army of Emir Kerboga, who failed in his mission to recapture the city. The 75,000-strong Muslim Army, split by internal dissent and poor morale, was defeated by just 15,000 ill-equipped and worn-out Crusaders. The Holy Lance's reputation was growing.

The larger Constantinople relic eventually fell into the possession of the Turks and Sultan Bajazet II (1447–81) gave the lance to Pope Innocent VIII (1432–92) as a peace offering because the Pope was holding Bajazet's brother Zisim as prisoner. It has been in the Vatican ever since, preserved under the dome of St Peter's. Pope Benedict XIV (1675–1758) sent to Paris for an exact drawing of the broken-off point of the lance; when this was compared with the larger St Peter's relic, the Pope was satisfied that the two relics had once formed one single blade.

Previously, the second, smaller piece of the lance had been incorporated into an icon and centuries in 1244, it was presented by Baldwin II of Constantinople to the only canonized King of France, Louis IX (1214–70). Louis built Sainte-Chapelle in Paris to house the Holy Lance, the crown of thorns, a fragment of the True Cross, relics of the Virgin Mary and even the Holy Sponge, which had been dipped in vinegar at Christ's crucifixion. As for the larger bit of the lance, there are reports that in 670, various scribes saw it in the Church of the Holy Sepulchre at Jerusalem. Ravenscroft even has the spear in England at one point, in a story told by William of Malmesbury of the giving of the Holy Lance to King Athelstan of England (893–939). The Athelstan Museum at Malmesbury (www.athesltanmuseum.co.uk) tells us that:

> Duke Hugh of the Franks, when seeking the hand of Eadhild, Athelstan's half-sister, sent Athelstan relics which included the Lance of Charlemagne which had pierced the side of Jesus. He also gave him the Sword of Constantine which had fragments of the cross including a nail set in crystal in the hilt. Athelstan gave these relics to Malmesbury abbey. Others, more bizarre, like the head of St Branwaladr or St Samson's arm he gave to other churches.

The trail goes cold for a while until Sir John Mandeville, in *The Travels of Sir John Mandeville*, an Anglo-Norman French book circulated between 1357 and 1371 that relates his supposed travels, said that when he was in Paris and Constantinople in 1357, he saw the blade of the Holy Lance in both locations.

In 1411 the son of the Holy Roman Emperor Charles IV, Sigismund of Luxemburg (1368–1467), was made Holy Roman Emperor. In 1424, a lance, believed to have been in the possession of Constantine the Great and enshrining a nail or some portion of a nail of the Crucifixion, became part of the Holy

Roman regalia. In that same year, Sigismund announced: "It is
the Will of God that the Imperial Crown, Orb, Sceptre, Crosses,
Sword and Lance of the Holy Roman Empire must never leave
the soil of the Fatherland." The relics became known collectively as the *Reichkleinodien* or Imperial Regalia (and this version
of the lance, seemingly unrelated to the Vatican lance, was destined to become known as the Vienna lance or Hofsburg spear).
They were taken from Prague, Sigismund's capital, home to his
birthplace, Nuremberg. The regalia seemed safe for a couple of
centuries, but war was never far away.

In the spring of 1796 Napoleon Bonaparte was rampaging his
way across Europe and heading in the direction of Nuremberg.
The city council became concerned for the safety of the Imperial
Regalia. If the spear fell into Bonaparte's hands – what then?
Therefore the treasures were moved to Vienna, where they were
entrusted to a certain Baron von Hügel on the understanding
that he would return the objects as soon as peace had been
restored.

The Holy Roman Empire was officially dissolved in 1806, but
of course Bonaparte still had unfinished business. In the meantime, Baron von Hügel had pulled off a fast one. Whilst arguments raged over the ownership of the relics, he flogged the
entire collection, including the spear, to the Habsburgs. It wasn't
until Napoleon had been defeated at Waterloo that Nuremberg's
confused and angry councillors realized what had occurred and
asked for their treasures back, but the Austrians hung on to
them. And there they stayed until the Anschluss, when Adolf
Hitler incorporated Austria into his Reich and took the Spear of
Destiny for himself.

Ravenscroft's telling of the night of 14 March 1938 when
Hitler and Himmler purloined the Holy Lance and the rest of
the regalia is intriguing. He writes as if he were actually there,
which he patently was not – and neither was his oracle Dr Stein,
who had fled to England in 1933 to escape Himmler's arrest
warrant. Thus it remains difficult to prove this is what actually
took place. When Hitler returned from visiting his home town,
Linz, he moved into his palatial suite at Vienna's Imperial Hotel.
Himmler and a few SS officers had arrived days before to clear
the way for taking over Austria by arresting prominent members

of the First Republic. The SS rounded up Jews, communists, Social Democrats and any political dissenters they could find and packed them all off to concentration camps. By 12 March, 70,000 people had been arrested. Himmler had been on the case of the Holy Lance from the day he arrived and organized troops of the elite SS-Liebstandarte Adolf Hitler, as well as Austrian SS platoons under the command of Ernst Kaltenbrunner, to form a ring of steel around the Weltliche Schatzkammer museum in the Hofburg. Every member of the museum staff right down to the cleaners were "interviewed" by Gestapo officials and went into Himmler's sinister card index. If the bona fide Vienna police force sought to intervene in any way with enquiries regarding the constitutionally illegitimate cordon around the Hofburg, the SS had carte blanche to shoot to kill.

Just after midnight on 14 March, Hitler left the Imperial with Himmler and they made their way to the Hofburg where they were met by the General Secretary of the Ahnenerbe, Wolfram Sievers, the Nazi's internal "legal" expert (and Martin Bormann's father-in-law), Major Walter Buch and Kaltenbrunner. Hitler and Himmler went inside to be alone with the lance, and allegedly Hitler remained in solitude with it for an hour before leaving. Together with Himmler, he now believed he held the key talisman for successful conquest. In October 1938 the treasures of Charlemagne were loaded on to a sealed SS train and returned to Germany to end up on display in Nuremberg.

Now the legend is bent and shaped to suit every "Nazi occult" nerd's fantasies. Website after website will tell you the following, usually repeated word for word: "During the final days of the war in Europe, at 2:10 p.m. on 30 April 1945, Lt Walter William Horn, serial number 01326328, of the United States 7th Army, took possession of the spear in the name of the United States government." Of course, that "serial number" makes it all very official; and 30 April fits in neatly with the Spear of Destiny legend – it's the same day Hitler committed suicide. Ravenscroft also tells a colourful yarn about General Patton handling and inspecting the spear and barking at those gathered around him, berating German officials who can't answer his questions. But for the story of the rediscovery of the Holy Roman regalia we need better sources: one of the finest books on the mass theft of

European art, Lynn H. Nicholas's *The Rape of Europa* (1994). What happened is as follows.

Mayor Liebl of Nuremberg was a dedicated Nazi whose brief was to protect the Reich's treasures in the city. After heavy bombing in 1944, he consulted Himmler on the security of the treasures. Convinced that they might be discovered by the advancing US Army, Liebl had elaborate bunkers built eighty feet (24 m) beneath the eleventh-century Kaiserburg. The bunkers were well disguised because their entrance was through the back of what appeared to be a prosaic little shop on a side street. These tunnels stretched out beneath the city's streets. Special copper containers were constructed to contain the treasures and were soldered shut. They were then walled up in great secrecy in one of the passages on 31 March 1944 by two city officials, Dr Lincke and Dr Friese, in the presence of Mayor Liebl. They were even meticulous enough to build what they thought would be a convincing cover story, that the relics had been taken from the city to Austria, where the SS had sunk them in Lake Zell. To add weight to this smokescreen, they got two SS members to move boxes into a truck and drive away. This way they probably hoped witnesses might verify their story.

On 16 April 1945 US troops entered Nuremberg. Perhaps still in fear of Himmler and losing his confidence over his stewardship of the treasures, Mayor Liebl, fanatical Nazi to the last, burned all his documents and on 19 April committed suicide. He no doubt thought that at least if he was dead, then the treasures might never be discovered.

When it came to storing money or valuables and committing robbery for Himmler, SS General Josef Spacil (1907–67) was very busy as the Reich crumbled around him. He knew where all kinds of cash was buried. But as the Americans were now everywhere, on 8 May 1945 he changed into a plain Wehrmacht uniform and tagged along with the retreating 352 Volksgrenadier Division who were surrendering to US troops. For a while he got away with calling himself "Sergeant Aue", but under intense interrogation his true identity soon came out. The American Counter Intelligence Corps (CIC) officers encouraged him to reveal the location of various caches of cash, gold and buried treasure.

By June 1945, the CIC in Nuremberg knew there was something amiss. It was known that this city was where Charlemagne's holy relics had been stored and they suspected that Eberhard Lutze, director of the German Museum, knew more than he was telling. He was taken for rough interrogation at Ellingen where he told the Liebl cover story about the SS men removing the treasures. Spacil had told the same tale, but after listening to other SS prisoners the intelligence men were not buying the story. Some had stated that Himmler planned use the Holy Roman relics as symbols of a new German resistance movement. This idea did not sit well with the Americans. SHAEF (Supreme High Command Headquarters, Allied Expeditionary Force) had gathered together an impressive crew of art and monuments experts known as the MFAA (Monuments, Fine Arts, and Archives), and they knew their business and what to look for.

It was at this point that Lieutenant Walter Horn arrived, a German-speaking member of MFAA who exercised his prodigious interrogation expertise in Nuremberg. He focused on one of Mayor Liebl's cronies, Dr Friese, and played him off against Josef Spacil. Horn banged Friese up for a night of solitary confinement with the threat that he would have to face Spacil the next day. Friese cracked. The Nazis and the SS, the whole Reich, were finished. Himmler was no longer a threat: on 25 May he'd bitten on his cyanide capsule and had gone to hell as the greatest mass murderer in history. Dr Friese had nothing more to gain by keeping the location of the treasures secret. Not long after, he led the Americans to the secret entry off Panier Platz, and deep below the street the Holy Roman Empire's regalia was finally revealed.

So the much repeated story of Hitler dying on the day of the discovery is simply untrue. The Führer had been dead almost two months when the Holy Lance was revealed again. And where was Patton's Third Army in April 1945? Not beneath the streets in Nuremberg. They were miles away at Kronberg Castle in Frankfurt, where they had ordered the Hesse family, including Queen Victoria's granddaughter, Princess Margaret Hesse, to pack up and move out so that the castle could become a HQ and officer's club. No doubt Patton, who had a great feeling for poetry and world history, eventually viewed the relics; with regard to the spear, there is a curiously oblique reference in the first verse of one of his own poems entitled "Through a Glass Darkly":

Perhaps I stabbed our Saviour
In His sacred helpless side.
Yet I've called His name in blessing
When in after times I died.

So whilst the massed ranks of internet based paranormal/psychic/occult webmasters pass around the legend of the Holy Lance from site to site, complete with all its warts, you can make what you will of the main oracles of all this colourful mythology, Trevor Ravenscroft and his mentor, the psychic Dr Stein. Without doubt, the true history of the Spear of Destiny is still bizarre and engrossing.

Christoph Lindenberg (1930–99) was a lecturer at the University of Tübingen and a prominent German writer and academic whose specialized work was his biography of Rudolf Steiner (1861–1925). Steiner was a philosopher and social reformer who also spent a great deal of his life studying spiritualism and mysticism. When Trevor Ravenscroft's *The Spear of Destiny* came out in 1973, it was natural that one of its main reviews would be by a German specialist, and Christoph Lindenberg gave the book all the scrutiny he could muster in the journal *Die Drie*. One of Lindenberg's main criticisms was that he doubted whether Dr Stein met Hitler at all, and seemed dubious about his relationship with Ravenscroft. Stein died in 1957 and *The Spear of Destiny* didn't surface until 1973. Because of all the psychic/cosmic/higher consciousness stuff in the book, if you believe in such things, then we have to assume that at some time Stein was dictating to Ravenscroft from the grave.

The main problem is that it is easy to believe that Ravenscroft really did intend his book to be simply an historical fantasy novel, yet it was promoted and issued as "real" history, and a dyed-in-the-wool academic like Lindenberg may not have grasped this. Lindenberg was an expert in the social, mystical and political scene in early twentieth-century Vienna, so it's hardly surprising that he blows huge holes in Ravenscroft's narrative about Hitler. Lindenberg really went to town on research for his review by scouring the Vienna records office. Ravenscroft's story, for example, features Adolf Hitler at the Vienna Opera House in the winter of 1910–11, naturally, to fit in with the "tramp" image, in the "cheap seats", sympathizing with the character Klingsor as he watches Wagner's *Parsifal*. That might be fine for Quentin Tarantino, but Lindenberg reveals that it was impossible; the first performance in Vienna of Wagner's opera did not take place until 14 January 1914, three years later than in Ravenscroft's version. Although Ravenscroft/Stein even describe its proprietor in a suitably macabre way, "a malevolent-looking man with a bald pate, a partly hunched back and a toad-like figure," there's a problem with the bookshop run by Herr Ernst Pretszche. Lindenberg combed Vienna's police records and business directories covering the period 1892 to 1920 but found no such shop.

Nicholas Goodrick-Clarke is professor of Western Esotericism at the University of Exeter and author of several books including *The Occult Roots of Nazism* (1985). He also demolishes much of Ravenscroft's work. For example: "The fictional nature of the whole episode surrounding the annotated copy of *Parsifal* is suggested by the similarity of Pretzsche's obscure bookshop to the one described by Sir Edward Bulwer-Lytton in *Zanoni* (1842), which probably served Ravenscroft as a literary model."

Then there's the image of the early Hitler. The media, past and present, has always loved rags to riches, impotent-to-powerful stories, and the thought of the pre-First World War Führer as described by Stein as he sits by the window in Vienna's Demel Café near the Hofburg Palace (it's still in business today – great chocolate and fine coffee), reading Hitler's scribbled notes in the copy of *Parsifal* – "the footnotes of Satan" – fits the bill. Stein glances through the window and sees "the most arrogant face and demonical eyes he had ever seen". It was Hitler, clad in "a sleazy black overcoat, far too big for him", a starving, ragged pavement artist, flogging postcard size watercolours, toes poking through his tattered shoes "beneath frayed trouser ends".

If we take on board the comments of the book's erudite critics, then there appear to be more inaccuracies than you can shake a stick at. Ravenscroft has Stein going to search out Hitler in the "flophouse" he's living in on Vienna's Meldemannstrasse in August 1912. But when he asks the hostelry's manager, Herr Kanya, about Hitler's whereabouts, Kanya informs Stein that Adolf had gone to Spittal an der Drau where an aunt had left him a legacy. Thereafter, Hitler dressed well. But as Christoph Lindenberg points out in his review, whilst it's true that Johanna Pölzl, Hitler's aunt, did leave him a legacy, he'd collected it in March 1911, not August 1912.

The most thorough work on Hitler's early years is by a German, Werner Maser (1922–2007), who in some detail collected all ascertained facts of Hitler's youth. Among several works covering the period, his 1973 *Hitler: Legend, Myth and Reality* offers many revelations, although other works on the Führer by John Toland and Ian Kershaw are equally absorbing. Maser's research reveals that Hitler was not impoverished and always had enough money. The so-called "flophouse" on Meldemannstrasse was more of a hotel than a Salvation Army hostel, and Hitler paid for a comparatively expensive room at fifteen Kronen a month. He was also particular about his appearance. So the tragic image of a Chaplinesque gutter figure, trying to sell his pictures, is misleading. Yet as a myth to engender empathy with the destitute German proletariat years later, it was ideal.

The Holy Lance: More than One Destiny?

Alan Baker, author of *Invisible Eagle: The History of Nazi Occultism* (2000), thinks Hitler's quest for the Hofburg loot was more about its cash value than its occult power. There are also those who insist that the real Holy Lance is not in the Hofburg today, but is in the possession of a secret German society who call themselves the Knights of the Holy Lance, and that a fake lance was constructed and returned to the museum.

In Kracow, there's another contender for the title Holy Lance. Although it is alleged to have been there for eight centuries, its earlier history is unknown. Professor of Medicine at Tulane and then Louisiana State University, Dr Howard A. Buechner, MD, served in the Second World War and is a retired colonel with the US Army. He's written extensively on the spear and states that the Vienna lance is a fake. He claims that he was contacted by a U-boat commander, using the pseudonym "Capt. Wilhelm Bernhart", who told him that the genuine spear was sent with other Nazi treasures by Hitler to Antarctica on a mission commanded by a "Col. Maximilian Hartmann". In 1979 Hartmann allegedly recovered the treasures. Buechner received a logbook from Bernhart detailing this expedition with pictures of the objects recovered, claiming that, after the Spear of Destiny was recovered, it was hidden by a Nazi secret society somewhere in Europe. Among others Buechner contacted to enquire about the alleged expedition was Hitler Youth leader Artur Axmann. Buechner remains convinced that the story is true.

Another theory is that German U-boat *U-534* was carrying the spear. Although Admiral Karl Dönitz had ordered all his U-boats to surrender as from 8 a.m. on 5 May 1945, on that same day *U-534* was underway heading north towards Norway in the Kattegat sea, northwest of Helsingor, Denmark, when she was attacked by the RAF. She was commanded to stop, yet for some unknown reason *U-534* refused to do so. She was badly damaged and began to sink by the stern. Forty-nine of her fifty-two-man crew survived including five who escaped via a torpedo hatch as she lay on the seabed. Her commander, Kapitänleutnant Herbert Nollau, committed suicide in 1968.

In August 1993 the wreckage was raised from the seabed in the hope of finding hidden treasure on board – even perhaps the Holy Lance. Today you can visit the U-boat as a museum in the UK at Birkenhead. There were some advanced secret torpedoes on board, but no treasure, according to Danish businessman Karsten Ree who financed *U-534*'s salvage. No Spear of Destiny.

Vienna? Cracow? Antarctica? The Knights of the Holy Lance? We may never know what's true and that's an essential factor in maintaining a truly engrossing mystery.

Those who have analysed the artefact state that the so-called Spear of Longinus is not the spear that pierced the side of Christ and has been dated to around the thirteenth century. But there is something about the nail, purported to be from the cross … just maybe …

As for the Spear of Destiny giving the owner "power over the world", Austria was hardly a world power in 1938, nor is it today. The Third Reich was already powerful by the time Hitler got his hands on it. And if General Patton did get hold of it, with the atomic bomb under her belt, America was already powerful enough, although Patton didn't last much longer than the Führer. Aged sixty, he died twelve days after a car crash in Germany of a pulmonary embolism in the afternoon of 21 December 1945. Sadly, not the kind of glorious death "Old Blood and Guts" had probably envisaged.

Just a couple of other myths about *der* demonic Führer. There's a great line in the Mel Brooks movie, *The Producers*: "Hitler! *There* was a painter – he could do a whole apartment, two coats, in one afternoon!" Adolf was never a house painter. The jury may still be out on whether or not he only had one testicle, but the general academic consensus is that he had the full set.

URBAN LEGEND GOES UNDERGROUND: A VICTORIAN RAILWAY MYSTERY

There are mysteries which men can only guess at, which age by age they may solve only in part.

Bram Stoker (1847–1912)

Everyone at some time comes into contact with an urban legend: the "Granny on the roof rack", the murderous hitch-hiker's severed finger stuck in your car door handle or drugged holiday-makers waking up in some Marrakesh flophouse minus a vital organ ... Urban myths are modern folklore. They are stories told to us by people who seem sincere, yet privately we don't fully believe them. The sources of such yarns are always obscure; start asking and they'll tell you they'd heard it from "a friend of a friend", and thus the story becomes known as a "FOAF". Yet once they're in circulation, there's no stopping them and they're great to roll out when enjoying a few drinks with friends ... and friends of your friends.

Originating in Fairfax County, Virginia in 1970, the Bunny Man is an urban legend that has spread across the Washington, DC, area. Its location is a concrete tunnel at a Southern Railway overpass on Colchester Road in Clifton. The bridge over the tunnel has become known as "Bunny Man Bridge" because the story involves a man wearing a rabbit costume. But he's no Ronald McDonald™. This particular Buggsy attacks you with an axe and likes to dismember bodies. At one time, over four decades ago, some people did see a strange figure there dressed as a rabbit and an axe was found. Today, this sinister little underpass tunnel has become famous every Halloween when the "Bunny Man Ghost", looking a bit crusty with his advancing years, supposedly appears. Perhaps this Hammer Horror version of *Watership Down* is no more sinister than the tooth fairy or leprechauns, but there are some weird myths where the book remains open ... there just might be something in there.

The following is a description of the plot for a 1974 British movie called *Death Line*, starring Donald Pleasence:

At the turn of the century, a group of diggers were lost during a cave-in of part of the London Underground tube-train network. They managed to live for a lifetime trapped in a crevice, but now there is only one family left. The half-human father heads to the Underground station to pick off lone passengers for food, while a London police detective investigates the mysterious disappearances.

Sounds good as creepy entertainment, but where on earth would a writer get such an idea? Tunnels and anything subterranean are definitely spooky, and there's nothing more eerily enigmatic than a closed and abandoned subway station. Most of the major London tube stations have their own peculiar ghost stories, some of which are quite recent. When the system is closed during the night, it seems to get pretty weird down there.

In 1998 I read a book, *Railway Ghosts*, published in 1985 by a British author, Barry Herbert. One of the stories really stood out and it fascinated me so much that I travelled to see Mr Herbert at his home in Grimsby, Lincolnshire, to see if I could glean anything further. The original cited report is apparently in the *London Evening News* of 29 September 1978, but I've not been able to track it down. Unfortunately, Mr Herbert died in 2011, so I am now unable to pursue this further. However, here are the basics of his story.

Nineteen-year-old Pamela Goodsell was referred to as "a student". In 1978 Miss Goodsell was walking through bushes in Sydenham Park, near the site of the old Crystal Palace in southeast London, when suddenly, the ground gave way beneath her feet and she found herself tumbling down a twenty-foot (6 m) shaft and landed with a thump on a hard surface. In the almost pitch darkness, she could not see, so took out a box of matches and struck one. She leaned over and realized that she was on the roof of an old train carriage. Inside, to her horror she saw the skeletal remains of passengers, still clad in Victorian clothes, some men sporting top hats, and all lying in some disarray on the mouldering floor. The train appeared to have been sealed up in an underground tunnel. Pamela was horrified by her discovery yet very puzzled that the local authorities hadn't exhumed the remains, and thus brought to light the fact of the mystery. It's not known how she managed to escape back up the vertical shaft. She eventually made enquiries with London Transport, whose response was: "Completely preposterous. There is no record of an underground crash in the area. We don't lose trains and passengers like that, not even in Victorian times." Miss Goodsell later returned to the park, but could not find the shaft. However, according to Mr Herbert, she remained quite unshakeable in her account of the horrific experience and the legend of an abandoned underground train appears to have held sway in Sydenham for some time.

Later, in 1998, I decided to try and track Miss Goodsell down through a friend, Warren Grynberg, a Blue Badge tourist guide in the City of London. He had a regular history spot at one time on Radio London, and we flagged up the story, asking if Miss Goodsell was out there, but we had no result. Barry Herbert had mentioned that the story had been looked into by the "Norwood Historical Society", but no such organization exists. There is a Norwood Society, but the train yarn doesn't feature on its website. Unfortunately, Mr Herbert hadn't managed to actually meet Miss Goodsell and had just relied on the original press report.

I vaguely remembered that there had been some kind of railway activity around Crystal Palace in the 1860s, so a bit of further digging revealed some important background. The legend of the forgotten train suggests that it had been shunted into a tunnel after a tragic engineering mistake and some suggest that the relevant documents appertaining to the mystery were lost during the last war. You will also find "reports" online suggesting that the non-existent Historical Society had sought permission to sink bore holes into Sydenham Park in an effort to get to the bottom of this puzzle, although one would think that the real Norwood Society might have made such events a major story; they are not mentioned. But there *was* a railway there, and a tunnel.

The Crystal Palace pneumatic railway (also known as the Crystal Palace atmospheric railway) was designed by Thomas Webster Rammell (?–1879), a close friend of Henry Austin, son-in-law of Charles Dickens. The line was built near Crystal Palace Park in south London in 1864. Rammell had already built a similar atmospheric line for the London Pneumatic Despatch Company, which was used to deliver mail. The principle of the pneumatic railway involved an airtight tunnel measuring ten feet (3 m) by nine feet (2.7 m). Carriages, which seated thirty-five passengers and had sliding doors at each end, were equipped with a large "collar" at one end, and the train was "sucked" along the tunnel by air pressure provided by a steam-engine-driven enormous fan, twenty-two feet (6.7 m) in diameter. To send the carriage back along the tunnel and create the necessary vacuum, the fan's rotation would be reversed, and when the carriage needed to stop, the guard applied the brakes.

Rammell's tunnel was 600 yards (550 m) long, negotiating a difficult bend along the line between the Sydenham and Penge entrances to the park. Trains ran between 1 p.m. and 6 p.m. and the journey time was just fifty seconds. Tickets for the journey cost sixpence each, so the likelihood of any of the non top-hat wearing labouring classes using the line seem slight. Rammell had a laudable career in public works and remains an unsung railway hero, who is buried in an unmarked grave in Watford. The element of mystery remains because it's not clear what became of the line, as there appears to be no record of when it ceased to operate. Railway researchers suggest that Rammell had originally constructed the tunnel as a pilot scheme for a larger atmospheric railway planned to run between Waterloo and Whitehall. The Sydenham tunnel, despite a trial excavation some years ago by BBC TV, has never been found and many believe it may have been destroyed by construction work for the Festival of Empire celebrations in 1911. If you're still out there, Pamela Goodsell, I'd love to hear of your experience first-hand, although I have heard that the legend was already current during the 1930s. This would, however, still make a fascinating project for the UK's Channel 4 *Time Team*.

Stumbling across an unknown abandoned subway tunnel? It's happened before. In 1869, Alfred Ely Beach (1826–96) was famous as an inventor, publisher and patents lawyer. The successful publisher and editor of the widely read magazine, *Scientific American*, Beach invented an early typewriter for use by the blind. Following the Civil War, he founded the Beach Institute, a school for freed slaves in Savannah. In 1912, as they dug beneath the Big Apple's streets, workers were busily excavating a new line (the BMT Broadway Line) for what everyone thought was New York's first subway system, part of which had opened in 1904. They were staggered as they suddenly opened up an unknown tunnel containing the remains of a subway carriage and the tunnelling shield used during a forgotten railway's initial construction. Also revealed was an opulent, lavishly decorated reception hall with a fountain. This amazing discovery halted work for a while. For the assembled navvies, this must have provided all the wonder of discovering a new tomb in the Valley of the Kings.

The workers had found the abandoned "Secret Subway", the Beach Pneumatic Railway, a system based on T. W. Rammell's original ideas. Beach had demonstrated the same system at the American Institute Exhibition in 1867. He was an honest, upright man of some wealth yet New York was run by the indomitable crook, Boss Tweed, a corrupt manipulator surrounded by his own council of payola-dealing opportunists. Beach knew that if he built a subway for New York, he would have to pay Tweed a hefty bribe, so he decided he would build his subway in total secrecy. How he did it is an amazing story, which you can read in full at www.klaatu.org. Beach put up $350,000 of his own money to bankroll the project. Workers entered through the basement of a Broadway building and worked by night, beginning the project towards the end of 1869 and constructing a pneumatic subway line beneath Broadway. The truly grand project was completed in only fifty-eight days. It had a single tunnel, 312 feet (95 m) long and 8 feet (2.4 m) in diameter, running under Broadway from Warren Street to

Murray Street. It opened in 1870. Boss Tweed was in for a shock when the *New York Post* of 26 February 1870 announced the project in glowing terms:

> On descending the steps at the corner of Warren Street and Broadway, the visitor finds himself in a neatly oil-clothed room, on the left of which appears the top of the rotary blower neatly painted. Advancing a few steps, the visitor turns to the right and descends three more steps, when he finds himself in a handsome and brilliantly lighted saloon. In the centre is a fountain with jetting water and gold-fishes swimming in the basin. The ceilings and sidewalls are hand-finished, and with neat striping about the gas brackets, present an attractive appearance. The floor is covered by oil-cloth, and the windows are hung with damask curtains and cornices. The surbase is of alternate stripes of walnut and white pine, and about the room are arranged settees and easy-chairs. A piano also adds to the attractiveness of the apartment.

Although Beach put forward plans for a full subway system, Tweed's corrupt influence defeated him and the Boss's own elevated railway was passed by the legislature. Beach's project was shut down, the tunnel entrance was sealed and the station, built in part of the basement of the Rogers Peet Building, was reclaimed, but was devastated by fire in 1898. Beach's tunnel was absorbed within the limits of the present day City Hall Station under Broadway. Building a subway system in fifty-eight days – in secret, without planning permission? Try *that* in the twenty-first century!

THE LAUGHTER OF
THE GODS

*Man is a credulous animal, and must believe something; in the
absence of good grounds for belief, he will be satisfied with bad
ones.*

Bertrand Russell (1872–1970)

In Chapter 1 of his *Book of the Damned*, Charles Fort states that
the ideal is to be neither a true believer nor a total sceptic but
that "the truth lies somewhere in between". The amount of
reading, viewing and web-surfing involved in completing this
book have revealed to me a vision of a clandestine world that
exists beyond the humdrum existence the majority of us are
bound to accept. The mundane panoply of work, routine, the
rolling news media, entertainment, the weather, relationships,
families and health plus our everyday acceptance of advancing
technology fill the majority of people's lives to the brim, leaving
little time for speculation. Those with a religion or a faith might
feel themselves lucky, because they seek to surrender their sense
of frustration and confusion to a higher entity, a spiritual force
above and beyond humanity, a being who knows what's best for
us, yet is so omnipotent that he/she is never required to answer
the most important question of all: "Why?"

Having staggered outside the enclave of normality I now
realize there exists a hinterland of alternative beliefs, far beyond
the many permutations of the great religions and their warring
factions. Yet even out here in this strange land, which I have
dubbed Anomalica, the spiteful gods are looking over the fence
and laughing. Mahatma Gandhi (1869–1948) said that anger

and intolerance are the enemies of correct understanding. Nowhere has that statement been more apt during the many hours I have spent criss-crossing the dark valley between credulity and scepticism. For example, the level of vitriolic hatred on some pro-psychic/anomaly websites that arises when the appliance of science and well-grounded fact demolishes a long-held paranormal conspiracy theory is shocking. Simply trying to retain a tongue-in-cheek Fortean "believer/sceptic" posture, as I have done throughout this project, is enough to brand me, through the internet weapons of lax spelling, dodgy punctuation and BLOCK CAPITALS, as a "disinformation" agent or a dupe of the CIA, the illuminati and the New Order.

As I hope I have verified in this book, there are still enough genuine mysteries in the world to go around that we can afford to lose a few by reaching valid solutions. But no. Roswell, Philadelphia *et al.* thou shalt not touch; the pillars of belief are indestructible. Thus, we are left with the argument from ignorance, which insists that a story must be true because it has not been proven false. Personal incredulity can also play its part: because I cannot imagine a natural explanation, there isn't one. If there is an infuriating blank file in our mental database, then rather than leave it barren some people will fill the gap with a solution or belief of their own, which eventually morphs into an article of faith. Thus do natural phenomena become supernatural, normal puzzles become paranormal, anything unknown in the sky is driven by aliens, major world events become conspiracies.

As a child, credulity is our strength. In those years from birth to around ten, innocence is all. It is a wonderful thing, and having spent four Yuletide seasons as a professional Santa Claus, the memories of those wonderful bright-eyed kids for whom the fantasy of reindeers, gifts and sheer magic were nothing less than real have often brought me to tears. A little credulity at that age is harmless enough. Yet once you realize that there is no tooth fairy and that the man with the sack who ate the milk and cookies is your dad, you surrender your spiritual fantasy to blunt materialism, unless, of course, you accept religion. If you have a god and a bible, be it the Holy Bible, the Qur'an, the Dhammapada or the Bhavagad-Gita, you will laugh at Santa Claus, dismiss his reindeers and replace the tooth fairy with a much larger catalogue of "grown-up" mysticism and permanently unshakeable belief. As the Bhavagad-Gita tells us, "neither in this world nor elsewhere is there any happiness in store for him who always doubts".

However, outside organized religion there is a phenomenon called the "New Age". No one is quite sure what this is, but it's been on the cards for a while, ever since all those naked actors in the musical *Hair* were prancing around singing about "the Age of Aquarius" back in the 1960s. New Age philosophy offers a long, pick 'n' mix menu, a kind of expanded spiritual version of a Pizza Hut™ salad bar. This exotic melange has to encompass flavours from around the world and it's preferable for them to have an ancient foundation. No doubt they keep thousands of people happy, especially those who have taken up the commercial opportunities the New Age market can offer. Meditation and yoga are ancient physical routines that work, as does t'ai chi, but there are all kinds of other goodies on offer as long as you're prepared to believe. One of the strangest beliefs among those who can afford it is that which involves fashion: wearing the right "brand" can make you happy. Here's an example from Oprah Winfrey:

I have a special pair of poop shoes under my desk. Whenever I need to drop a deuce, I slip them on and scurry to the restroom, and no one ever knows it's me. Like, if I'm wearing Louboutins that day, and my producer sees Earth shoes in the stall... well, you get the idea. It was truly a light bulb moment when that came to me ...

Obviously, women who wear Louboutins (the Louboutin Metal Nodo 150 water snake sling-backs cost £1,395 as opposed to Earth's Union black shoes at £98) must never be known to have disgusting bodily functions.

Then there's the religion of going to the gym and spending ninety minutes each day walking on machines, which provide the same exercise as walking down the street, and bicycles which go nowhere. The contract gym industry therefore will not be pleased now that Dr Michael Mosley, in a BBC documentary in

March 2012, has demonstrated that few relatively short bursts of intense exercise, amounting to only a few minutes a week, can deliver many of the health and fitness benefits of hours of conventional exercise, according to extensive new research. But forget physical exertion and shopping – there are other, phenomenal New Age ways of feeding energy into your chakras.

Crystal Balls

The use of crystals in divination goes back to the Celtic druids. During Europe's medieval age, the crystal ball became the divination item of choice among occultists, fortune-tellers, wizards and gypsies. For some arcane reason, these people claim that they can see both the past and the future in a crystal ball. They were "the stones of power" to the Highlanders in Scotland and, even today, whilst you're crossing a gypsy's palm with silver in her caravan, there'll probably be a crystal ball in the vicinity. Crystals also possess aesthetic properties that have long made them attractive in jewellery. A crystal is a solid formed by the solidification of chemicals, with a regularly repeating internal arrangement of atoms and molecules, bounded by external plane faces. Crystal particles form a variety of geometrical shapes due to their internal compressions. They are also used in many areas of modern technology.

To New Agers, however, the crystal has magical healing and mystical paranormal powers. It is believed by many that crystals channel good "energy" and ward off bad "energy". This belief is promoted among occultists and psychics. But the sceptic would say that this conviction only offers a placebo effect, based upon wishful thinking, selective thinking, subjective validation, sympathetic magic and communal reinforcement. What we don't have is scientific evidence that crystals are conduits of healing and protection, emitting magical energies, or that they in some way can tell the future.

According to the pervasive crystalline marketeers, their products resonate with healing "frequencies" from "vibrations" to help balance your yin and yang whilst working wonders with your chakras (said to be "force centres" or energy whorls permeating from a point on the physical body). A whole branch of pseudoscience has built up around crystals, which are said to affect the emotions and can be used not only for physical healing, but for sensitive problems. The list of crystal advantages goes on: bolstering your immune system, healing, self-expression and creativity, and assisting meditation. Or you can buy a "crystal wand", utilized to heal auras in aura therapy.

Another claim made by the crystal sales folk is that, if properly arranged, they'll deliver protection against harmful electromagnetic forces. What might these threatening forces be? In addition to other people, you are under threat from hairdryers, microwave ovens, power lines, computer monitors and cellular phones. What you really need is Charles Brown's BioElectric Shield®. Brown, a chiropractor from Montana, claims to have had visions whilst he lay in bed and heard voices in his head instructing him to arrange crystals in the shape of a flying saucer. By so doing, he would be protected. You can buy a BioElectric Shield® from the bargain model at $139 to well over a thousand dollars. Allegedly, Cherie Blair, wife of ex-Prime Minister Tony Blair, sports one of these magical pendants. They are said to be "medically proven" and even "based on Nobel Prize winning physics".

Trust the scientists and the medical profession to try and foul up a ray of New Age hope with their meddling. In research supported by the Perrott-Warrick Fund, Trinity College Cambridge, the BioElectric Shield® was tested, and the full results can be seen at www.susanblackmore.co.uk. The summing up would not have gone down well in Montana:

> The widespread use of expensive and ineffective devices is not a trivial concern. We need research to find out which claims are true and which are false. The results should then be publicized to help people make informed choices about how to spend their money and to prevent false claims. On the basis of our results, we believe that the BioElectric Shield® is ineffective.

One aspect of crystals is that they produce an electrical charge when compressed, which offers the New Age dealers the hope that crystals can harness and direct energy. This is known as the piezoelectric effect and was discovered in 1880 by Pierre and Jacques Curie. So does the piezoelectric effect give crystals healing or protective power? In spite of evidence to the contrary, in the New Age and neo-pagan occultist boutiques they'll tell you that they do. In the end, if people want to pay out their hard-earned money for a placebo that provides imaginary calmness, with the bonus of fully charged chakras, that's their business.

As for fortune-telling, crystals are arguably no better use than animal organs for divining the future, although a crystal ball is more humane and sanitary than the divination practice of "reading the innards" – the disembowelling of innocent creatures who don't know yesterday from tomorrow.

But there's much, much more to the mystery of crystals than prosaic "spiritual" jewellery. As Indiana Jones discovered, the bigger the crystal, the greater the inscrutability.

In 1949, in the Republic of Czechoslovakia, an inventor, Karel Drbal of Prague, applied for a rather odd patent. It took a decade, but Patent File Number 91304 Method of Maintaining Razor Blades and the Shape of Straight Razors was granted. Drbal had reached the conclusion that placing razor blades within the pyramid shape could resharpen them and, on a larger scale, cure some illnesses.

We're not too clear on how he arrived at this assumption but, apart from the ceremonial goatee beards on most ancient Egyptian statuary, we must assume that the pharaohs and their courts were no strangers to the razor. Indeed, it seems that the Egyptians were the original hairless elite. The tombs of Egyptian royalty often contain personal care items such as manicure tools, razors and other cosmetic implements. Egyptian works of art suggest that their attitude to hairy folk was that those who were hirsute were little more than peasants and slaves or uncouth plunderers. The top of the hairy-faced hit list were criminals and mercenaries. So, did they keep their razors sharp in a mini-pyramid?

Following Drbal's patent, he launched the Cheops Pyramid Razor Blade Sharpener. But this was only a beginning ... eventually some people decided to try sleeping in a larger version of a pyramid, but according to reports, some sleepers awoke dehydrated whilst others said they had experienced scary nightmares. Others claimed physical and mental rejuvenation and increased energy levels. As part of his arcane formula, Drbal was careful to insist that it was important that the dimensions of the pyramid scale matched those of the Great Pyramid at Giza. He even explained the ratios and provided an easy formula for getting one's measurements right, although we'll not go into the mathematics here. However, if you want to give it a try, here's what you need to do:

- Cut four equilateral triangles from heavy paper or cardboard. The dimensions can be changed depending on what size you need, as long as all sides are equal length.
- Construct a pyramid by taping the sides together.
- (Optional) Make a false floor that fits inside the pyramid.
- Align the pyramid so that the baselines point at magnetic north and south. Use a compass to find these directions.
- The pyramid must align exactly to magnetic north-south, so don't forget to take the magnetic declination of your particular locality into consideration.

So, you've made your pyramid – now, it's time to give it a test run.

- Put as many used razor blades as you wish on the false floor of the pyramid so that they point east to west. Leave the razor blades overnight and see if they have gotten any sharper by being in the pyramid.
- Some people claim the shape has the power to dehydrate organic material. Flowers are a good test of this claim. Place fresh, live flowers inside the pyramid for twenty-four to forty-eight hours and see if they dry out.

Short-term though such fads have been, they have never been short of takers. Trawl across the internet and you'll find that "serious" research into pyramid power is still in full swing. Of course, over in Tinseltown, home to the enlightened scientologists, there are more customers for this kind of thing than one can wave a crystal at.

Movie star Gloria Swanson slept with a miniature pyramid under her bed and claimed that "every cell in my body tingled". The late James Coburn had his own "pyramid tent" in which he meditated. After a session communing with his inner self, it was the cat's turn. He put his cat and her kittens to bed over a nest formed of tiny pyramids because he'd heard that pyramid power meant that kittens could well grow up in a "special" way. A Houston doctor placed microbes under a pyramid and revealed that they lived sixty-four hours longer than other microbes that were denied pyramid power. The list of such oddities is a long one. A few years ago, before the familiar Gillette razor blade made way for the now ubiquitous disposable razor, Max Toth, president of the Toth Pyramid Co. of New York, boldly declared that his cardboard Pyramid Razor Blade Sharpener was a good investment as the money saved on razor blades might far exceed the modest $3.50 price of a Toth Pyramid. A company in Canada, Evering Associates, marketed Toth's products and added another level to the sales spiel by claiming that the pyramid could dehydrate tropical fish for display purposes. Dried fish and a good shave are one thing, but Patrick Flanagan, who had another pyramid business in Glendale, California, inadvertently utilized the ultimate sales persuader – he said that the pyramid increased his "sexual sensitivity".

New mystical claims surfaced in the 1970s after Wilhelm Reich created his "orgone box" thirty years previously. This bizarre invention, albeit the product of sincere benevolence, is often lumped together with the geometric pyramid form, and some "experts" even think that the focused energy of a pyramid was just the thing a mummy needed to keep those bandages fresh.

Seventy years ago French researchers claimed that if a dead cat was placed inside a pussy-sized plywood pyramid, it simply dehydrated, rather than decaying, thus becoming "mummified". This in turn inspired Karel Drbal's Cheops Pyramid Razor Blade Sharpener. Another claim was that it could freshen vegetables. If this was the case, each branch of Tesco today would look like a Giza theme park.

Following Max Toth's acquisition of Drbal's US rights, he was joined by professor of "creative electronics" Eric McLuhan of Fanshawe College in Ontario. As the son of media guru Marshall "the medium is the message" McLuhan, a patina of kudos was added to all these pyramid claims. McLuhan the younger published his account of meat-dehydration experiments. This involved bite-sized chunks of moist hamburger which, depending on their placement inside a pyramid, dried out at varying rates. Needless to say the pharaohs of the food could see the possibility of a fast buck. Before long eggs, fish and flowers were all stinking away under little pyramids and folks were trying to make stale coffee fresh again, hoping to ripen fruit quickly, add quality to cheap wines and even make cigarettes taste better.

Entering into this circus was the inventive electronics prodigy, twenty-eight-year-old Patrick Flanagan. His Pyramid Energy Generator had a metal base upon which was assembled a collection of one-inch- (2.5 cm) high pyramids. It was available by mail order and as the orders dropped through the mailbox, he expanded his catalogue to include the $25 opaque vinyl Cheops Pyramid Tent. This was, apparently, just the thing for dedicated New Agers as the perfect energy-packed space for yoga, "biofeedback" and the Maharishi's ubiquitous transcendental meditation. However, despite his earlier mention of his improved sexual sensitivity gained whilst snoozing in his tent, he went along with the more prosaic researchers, claiming that, "The most immediate use of the pyramid may well be in the area of food storage," stating that the geometric shape "acts as a focus or lens, through which flows energy created by the earth's magnetic field".

Pyramids, McLuhan discovered, must be aligned precisely on magnetic north. He discovered that if they were in the vicinity of fluorescent lights, TVs, radiators, windows, radios, perhaps even your washing machine or Hoover, then the power of ancient Egypt was dissipated. Even when avoiding all these pitfalls, McLuhan was honest enough to state, "If you do all that, it may or may not work. If you don't, it certainly won't work."

There is no scientific evidence to prove or disprove pyramid power. If there is an effect, it appears to occur primarily inside the pyramid, yet the same force is also said to emanate from the pyramid. Pyramid power is, unfortunately, one of those areas of research that trained, experienced scientists tend to avoid as a cul-de-sac subject yet, at the same time, anyone not schooled in science would soon realize that, as a research project, it would require the kind of dedication and precision that only comes with years of rigorous academic practice. This situation provides the ideal climate for pseudoscience to flourish and thrive, and by doing so, provide us with hours of innocuous entertainment.

Coincidence and Synchronicity

*I am open to the guidance of synchronicity, and do not let
expectations hinder my path.*

Dalai Lama (1935–)

One pleasant August day in 1985 I was walking along Charing Cross Road in London. I was only visiting, on my way to find Dobell's Jazz Record Shop. Thinking of jazz my thoughts went back to an old friend I'd known in the 1960s up in Hull. We'd shared a love of jazz and blues and had lost contact with one another in the mid-1970s. I fancied a coffee, walked into a café and there, sitting in the corner smoking a cigarette and enjoying a mug of tea, was my old jazz-loving friend. Of course, if you add up the possibilities – he'd moved to London, I was visiting, we shared the same tastes and we were in the vicinity of a record shop – there is an outside chance of something like this happening. But if I hadn't thought of him, would he have appeared? These coincidences are unlikely conjunctions of events. They happen to most people. They possess a serendipity that often startles us and they are truly inexplicable.

Researching a naval biography in 1999 I had to make a special trip to the British Library to take photocopies from a long out-of-print book from 1918, Meriel Buchanan's *Petrograd: The City of Trouble*. When I arrived back home in Nottinghamshire later that night, there was a parcel waiting for me from photographer Graham Harrison, a close friend who had worked with me in Russia. It was a copy of the same book. He'd found it the day before in a charity shop.

We sometimes call coincidence by another name: synchronicity. It's a concept Carl Gustav Jung (1875–1961) came up with in the 1920s. Two or more events that are apparently causally unrelated or unlikely to occur together by chance are observed to occur together in a meaningful manner. There have been many famous coincidences and they often seem incredible. Sceptics will tell us that it's simply down to the law of averages and selective perception. Jung thought differently – could this be a secret glimpse of a hidden dimension of the universe? We've all experienced the phenomenon of déjà vu, that odd feeling that you know exactly what's about to happen, or a place seems oddly familiar, or you know what someone is about to say. Is this a rip in the cosmic curtain?

Jung observed three kinds of synchronous events: premonitions, dreams of some future happening; the "gut feeling" of some event that happens outside your thoughts; and thoughts about events which actually happen at a distance. Psychics and those with a taste for the paranormal have suggested events linked to precognition and clairvoyance may be associated with synchronicity. The scientific community have linked all this to quantum physics, chaos theory and even something called fractal geometry. Whatever it means, synchronicity is fascinating, and maybe we're not meant to understand it all.

Some coincidences, as we have already seen with those surrounding the *Titanic*, come together after a period of time. One of the most famous examples is the strange connections between two assassinated Presidents, John F. Kennedy and Abraham Lincoln. This is the commonly repeated version. Both were elected a hundred years apart, with Lincoln in 1860 and Kennedy in 1960. After their murder, they were both succeeded by men with the same surname, Johnson, and both were Southerners. They too were both born a hundred years apart; Andrew Johnson in 1808, Lyndon B. Johnson in 1908. Lincoln and Kennedy's assassins were also born a hundred years apart – John Wilkes Booth in 1839 and Lee Harvey Oswald in 1939 – and both were dead before they could be brought to trial. Lincoln was murdered in a theatre and Booth was cornered in a warehouse, while Kennedy's fatal shot came from a warehouse with Oswald captured later in a theatre. Kennedy was assassinated riding in a Ford Lincoln, and Lincoln was shot in Ford's Theatre. Kennedy had a secretary named Evelyn Lincoln; Lincoln's secretary was named Kennedy. Sure, the hundred-year thing is weird, but it is just as easy to compile a list of absolute differences between the two men. I'll not spoil things by doing so, but John Wilkes Booth was *not* born in 1839 – he was born in 1838, and you could spend a long time in the White House archives trying to find a Lincoln secretary called Kennedy; his private secretaries were actually John G. Nicolay and John Hay.

This is what happens in the internet age. You set up a para-normal/cosmic/conspiracy website and someone else thinks they can make a better job of the graphics and sets up their own version. Before long there are hundreds of such sites spreading like fungus, all repeating the same legends and, in many cases, tweaking what "facts" there are to suit the spooky factors. Kennedy died on 22 November 1963. Yet still there is fun to be had when you read that a month before Lincoln was shot he was in Monroe, Maryland, and a "month before Kennedy was shot he was with Marilyn Monroe". (Actually, Marilyn had died in August 1962, but that doesn't bother the mystery nerds.) The list goes on from there and has been the source of considerable debate ever since. Needless to say, the rational mind of the mathematician will explain all these anomalies away; their con-nectivity can be worked out using the right formula. Yet even allowing for the slipshod embroidery, they are strange, maths or no maths. But we're not done with Abe Lincoln yet; the cosmic tumblers had one more surprise

A few months before Lincoln was shot, there was another odd occurrence. Lincoln's son, Robert Todd Lincoln (1843–1926), whilst awaiting a train in Jersey City, New Jersey, on a crowded station, tripped over and fell on to the track beneath a train that was just picking up speed. Suddenly a man leapt to Lincoln's rescue and the President's son was saved. He thanked the man who had pulled him out of danger. The hero was none other than the brother of John Wilkes Booth – Edwin Booth, the famous actor of his day. What are the chances of this scenario – the son of a President saved by the brother of that President's assassin? For Robert Todd Lincoln, his father's murder must have been in his thoughts in later life when the 200-day presi-dency of James A. Garfield (1831–81) ended abruptly when he was shot by assassin Charles J. Guiteau. Robert Lincoln, who was Garfield's Secretary of War at the time, was present – as he was twenty years later at the Pan-American Exposition in Buffalo, New York, at the invitation of President William McKinley (1843–1901), when McKinley was shot by anarchist Leon F. Czolgosz on 6 September 1901. Yet again, the conspiracy anoraks get it wrong – yes, Robert Lincoln was there in Buffalo, but *not present* at the assassination, another phoney "fact" that is always repeated. Nevertheless, it seems like the Lincoln presence had its own aura of bad luck.

Some coincidences are better documented, such as the death in 2002 of a pair of seventy-year-old identical twin brothers from Raahe, Finland. Both were out riding their bicycles in a snowstorm. They were both killed on the same stretch of road within two hours of one another and both were hit by trucks. As the second brother wasn't aware of his sibling's earlier death, he obviously didn't commit suicide. Coincidences between identical twins are a regular occurrence. Even those who were separated at birth, if they rediscover one another, often find that they might dress the same, have similar jobs, similar tastes in food or music and have corresponding habits. There are cases where they have married spouses with identical names. But perhaps that's a repeated genetic code. There might even be something called fate that decided that the Finnish twins had to die on the same day.

Some coincidences can get you into trouble. A retired school teacher, Leonard Dawes, for over twenty years had been compiling crossword puzzles for London's *Daily Telegraph*. An innocent enough pastime, but in May 1944, his crossword clues accidentally managed to include two D-Day landing beaches, Utah and Omaha. That was bad enough, but other clue words for the quiz were top-secret codewords, Mulberry, Overlord and Juno. The only people who knew these words and their crucial significance were on General Eisenhower's staff. Poor old Dawes was hauled in as a German agent but after some serious interrogation the security boys realized his random choice had been innocently made. The odds against five top-secret codewords being chosen at such a delicate juncture in the Second World War must be astronomical.

In 1984, writer/director Sandor Stern, whose main claim to fame was the screenplay for *The Amityville Horror* (1979), was slated to direct a TV movie for NBC entitled *John and Yoko: A Love Story*. As everyone knows, John Lennon was gunned down by a crazed, schizophrenic loner in front of the Dakota Apartment Complex in New York City in December 1980. Once casting had got under way, it soon became apparent that the actor who'd landed the role of Lennon might not have been a good choice. There was a problem – his name was the same as the murderer who had settled in to life at Attica Prison in upstate New York: Mark Chapman. He was dropped from the cast. Actually, the underrated actor's full name is Mark Lindsay Chapman, who has since managed a decent career – he played Chief Officer Wilde in James Cameron's *Titanic*. Still, his Lennon credentials finally landed him the Beatle role in a 2007 flop called *Chapter 27*, where the real assassin, Mark Chapman, was played by Jared Leno, who had to put on seventy-two pounds (33 kg) to get the role.

George Feifer, journalist, novelist and translator, is the author of nine books, including the bestselling *Moscow Farewell* (1976) and *The Girl from Petrovka* (1971). In 1973, actor Anthony Hopkins had landed a lead role with Goldie Hawn to appear in the filmed version of Feifer's *The Girl from Petrovka*. With the US hardback copy of the book unavailable in Britain and the paperback not yet published, Hopkins could not find a copy of the book anywhere in London. Yet as he went to sit on a bench at a train station, he saw that some kind reader had left a book. Not only was it *The Girl from Petrovka*, it was actually George Feifer's own annotated, personal copy, which the author had lent to a friend and which had subsequently been stolen from his friend's car.

Erdington is a small area five miles (8 km) from the centre of Birmingham in England. It was the site of two murders, separated by 157 years, of two twenty-year-old girls, Mary Ashford and Barbara Forrest. They were both raped and strangled, their bodies found on the same day – 27 May in 1974 and 1817. The site of their bodies was only 300 yards (274 m) apart. Both girls had visited their best friend on the evening of Whit Monday and on the evening of each girl's death, they had done the same things: attended a dance while wearing a new dress. The man accused of Mary Ashford's murder in 1817 was a bricklayer named Abraham Thornton. The man accused of Barbara Forrest's 1974 murder was Michael Thornton, a child care officer. Both professed their innocence and both were acquitted. Mary Ashford and Barbara Forrest both shared the same birthday.

Edgar Allan Poe's chilling 1838 novella, *The Narrative of Arthur Gordon Pym of Nantucket*, told the tale of four shipwreck survivors adrift in an open boat. After many days without food, lost on the wide ocean, the decision was made that they would have to kill and eat one of their number, the poor cabin boy, Richard Parker. Sometimes reality follows fiction with startling results. Poe (1809–49) had been dead thirty-five years when, in 1884, a vessel called the *Mignonette*, a yawl commanded by a Captain Tom Dudley, left Southampton, England. Unfortunately, she foundered in a hurricane in the South Atlantic. Four survivors were cast adrift in a lifeboat: Dudley, the mate, Edwin Stephens and two deck hands. They were 1,600 miles (2,575 km) from land. After nineteen days adrift, with no food or water, desperation overtook them. The youngest of the four drank seawater and became delirious, so the others decided to kill and eat him. The lad's carcass kept them alive for twenty-five more days. He was the *Mignonette*'s cabin boy. His name was Richard Parker. Had the opium-smoking Poe, back in 1837–8, peeked through his own self-generated darkness to report some grim future tableau?

As coincidence stories go, the following is a classic and it's one of my favourites as it involves food. Every time I have Christmas pudding, I think of Monsieur de Fortgibu. *Bon vivant* Monsieur de Fortgibu, enjoying life in 1805, met the French writer Émile Deschamps (1791–1871). Deschamps had never met Fortgibu before, but he would remember the stranger's kindness because he had given some plum pudding to the famous writer. Ten years later, in 1815, Deschamps was examining the menu in a Paris restaurant and he noticed plum pudding was available. Yet when he tried to order some, the waiter told him the last helping had already been served to another customer. It just happened to be the same Monsieur de Fortgibu. Years *sans* plum pudding passed, until in 1832 Émile Deschamps attended a dinner, where, to his delight, he was once again offered plum pudding. Naturally, the gregarious writer told his amused hosts the story of his two previous plum duff episodes, dating from twenty-seven years and ten years earlier, and laughingly finished off by suggesting that only the mysterious de Fortgibu was missing to make the setting complete. Who should then enter the room but Monsieur Fortgibu himself? Perhaps there's something paranormal about plum pudding.

There are many such entertaining stories, some amusing, many quite chilling, and they all possess that undercurrent of strange ambiguity. These human events seem to have their naissance somewhere beyond the boundaries of our understanding, and as such, they leave that gap between scepticism and credulity open just wide enough for us to peer into the darkness beyond.

Citadel of Secrets: The Mystery of Edward Leedskalnin

There are no rules of architecture for a castle in the clouds.
G. K. Chesterton (1874–1936)

In 1986, one-time British punk rock star Billy Idol (1955–), now living in the United States, released a bestselling album on the Chrysalis label, *Whiplash Smile*. One of the tracks, which he also penned, was the country-influenced "Sweet Sixteen". The song was inspired by the poignant story of a man named Edward Leedskalnin, whose sixteen-year-old fiancée, Agnes Scuffs, jilted him on the night before their wedding. Billy Idol filmed the video for "Sweet Sixteen" in the remarkable, rambling monument of Florida's Coral Castle, sometimes called the Eighth Wonder of the World, which Leedskalnin built, single-handedly, in memory of his lost love, between 1919 and 1951, quarrying and sculpting an estimated 1,100 tons of fossil coral. In one of his publications, he claimed, "I have discovered the secrets of the pyramids, and have found out how the Egyptians and the ancient builders in Peru, Yucatan and Asia, with only primitive tools, raised and set in place blocks of stone weighing many tons." He stated he had, "rediscovered the laws of weight, measurement, and leverage," stating that these laws, "involved the relationship of the Earth to celestial alignments".

Edward Leedskalnin was born in Riga, Latvia, on 12 January 1887. Details of his childhood are not known. His family, who were stonemasons, were poor and his education very basic. Engaged at the age of twenty-five in 1912 to the sixteen-year-old Agnes Scuffs, whom he referred to as his "sweet sixteen", he suffered a major psychological blow when she jilted him the night before the wedding. The reason she gave was his age. Dismayed and heartbroken, after a few years he left Latvia and crossed the Atlantic, first working in lumber camps in Canada before moving to the United States to work in California and Texas. In 1920 he was diagnosed with tuberculosis and decided to move to a warmer climate, buying some land in Florida in the small settlement known as Florida City.

Over the next twenty-seven years, Leedskalnin worked solidly to construct his masterpiece, dedicated to his lost love, Agnes. This skinny, short man, weighing just a hundred pounds (45 kg), lived and worked around the clock on this bizarre ten-acre monument, originally known as Rock Gate Park. Over the years, as he added to it, working totally alone during the night, this strange, industrious man's weird working methods began to attract all manner of wild speculation. Some regarded him as a mechanical genius, others as some kind of magician who could defy gravity.

After being violently attacked by thugs who believed he had some kind of treasure on the site, one night, during the 1930s, he decided to move everything, lock, stock and barrel, a few miles away to the safer Florida location of Homestead. Various megaliths weighing a total of three million pounds (1,340 tons) were moved with the help of a local trucker. Leedskalnin never owned a car and went into town on his bicycle. The odd thing is, although the stones were transported on the truck, neither the truck driver or anyone else was allowed to see them being loaded or unloaded.

The new site became known as the Coral Castle (http://www. coralcastle.com) and for ten cents Leedskalnin was pleased to show people around. Apparently he was quite the host, and using his self-made "pressure cooker" often cooked hot dogs for visiting children. His most remarkable carving is the huge nine-ton stone door, through which he drilled a hole, top to bottom, aligned with the stone's centre of gravity. Through the hole rests a shaft on an automobile gear, ensuring the door's perfect balance is such that it can be easily pushed open with one finger by a five-year-old. The door fits within a quarter of an inch of the walls on either side. Many modern engineers, examining this door, have puzzled over how it was put into place by one man.

As people passed through the hefty "Nine Ton Gate", they were impressed by the sheer weight and size of some of the blocks and slabs erected around the site. Journalists and visitors would frequently question Leedskalnin's construction methods, which have remained a mystery. When asked, "How did you build the castle?" he would shrug this off with, "It's not difficult really. The secret is in knowing how." In the five technical booklets he wrote during his time working on the castle, he focused mainly on the nature of magnetism. He claimed to see beads of light on objects, displaying the physical presence of nature's magnetism. His hypothesis was that the knowledge of atomic structure and electricity then held by scientists was incorrect. According to Leedskalnin, all forms of existence were made up of three components: neutral particles of matter and north and south poles. Yet his writings have failed to reveal the full breadth of arcane knowledge, which was hinted at during his verbal utterances over the years.

Although it remains unclear what training he may have had, he appears to have been a skilled electrical engineer who quite openly generated his own electricity. He built his own AC generator, and was quite pleased to discuss this with his immediate neighbours. However, it was his cryptic explanations, contained in his writings completed between 1945–51, of the laws of magnetism and electricity that, he claimed, made it possible for him to construct his immense, rambling Coral Castle.

He could be very secretive when it came to opening up the discussion around his building methods. If anyone tried to spy on him working during the night, he would immediately cease work until they left. Those undiscovered snoopers who did witness his nocturnal labours issued some very strange reports. Rocks were seen to move by themselves and one of his neighbours claimed that he'd seen Leedskalnin place his hands on the huge stones and sing to them, whilst another group of observers reported seeing "coral blocks floating through the air like hydrogen balloons".

Working alone, he also quarried, moved and erected a thirty ton, forty-foot- (12.2 m) tall obelisk. He carved a three-ton "rocking chair", which could be set in motion with your index finger, and a heart-shaped, 5,000-pound (2,268 kg) coral rock table with a red blooming *Ixora coccinea* plant growing in the middle. From one piece of stone, he built a spiral staircase leading down to a subterranean refrigerator. Astronomical rules and mathematics appeared to guide Leedskalnin in the layout of his castle and its various components. He created a twenty-five-foot- (7.6 m) high, thirty-ton telescope, aligned to the North Star, as well as a handy sundial – accurate to two minutes – calibrated to noon of the winter and summer solstice. Elsewhere in his labyrinth were carvings of planets, the solar system and three eighteen-ton pieces of coral rock representing the full moon and its first and last quarters. The fossilized Florida coral beds Leedskalnin worked on were up to 4,000 feet (1,220 m) thick. It seems incredible that he moved these huge blocks alone, using only hand tools, although on one occasion he did actually invite a quarrying contractor to cut a stone from his quarry. The contractor used a 600 horsepower crane and a diamond-tipped power saw, yet was puzzled by Leedskalnin's ability. The contractor, after cutting the four vertical sides of the stone, had to break it away at the base to release it. Leedskalnin had a method of slicing it free by cutting across the base horizontally. Perhaps having a visiting contractor was a way for Leedskalnin to polish his reputation as a local enigma.

Although he welcomed paying tourists on fine Florida days, at all other times Ed Leedskalnin was a very private man and the walls to his castle, which he finished erecting in 1940, prove this. They are eight feet tall and three foot thick (2.4 x 0.9 m), weighing 125 pounds (57 kg) per cubic foot with a combined weight approaching 58 tons. Reports that stones were being levitated as Leedskalnin sang led some researchers in the field of acoustics and levitation to suspect that he was nullifying the power of gravitation by the use of a vibrating and condensed sound field.

This has remained a popular theory among those who believe the Great Pyramid at Giza was built in this way. A tenth-century Arab historian, Abu al-Hasan Ali ibn al-Husayn ibn Ali al-Mas'udi, records that the Egyptians moved large stone blocks by the use of magic spells and wrote: "In carrying on the work, leaves of papyrus, or paper, inscribed with certain characters, were placed under the stones prepared in the quarries; and upon being struck, the blocks were moved at each time the distance of a bowshot (which would be a little over 200 feet), and so by degrees arrived at the pyramids."

An acoustics engineer who once worked for NASA, Tom Danley, has developed an acoustic device, capable of levitating small objects. Its 1991 patent reads: "An acoustic levitator includes a pair of opposed sound sources which have interfering sound waves producing acoustic energy wells in which an object may be levitated. The phase of one sound source may be changed relative to the other in order to move the object along an axis between the sound sources." Tom Danley also became interested in the Great Pyramid and was invited to Egypt by the producers of the 1993 NBC documentary *The Mystery of the Sphinx* to measure sound in the pyramid's King's Chamber. *Fate* magazine reported on Danley's visit:

> In the Great Pyramid in the King's Chamber an F-sharp chord is resident, sometimes below the range of human hearing. Former NASA consultant Tom Danley feels the sound may be caused by wind blowing across the ends of the air shafts and causing a pop-bottle effect. These vibrations, some ranging as low as 9 hertz down to 0.5 hertz, are enhanced by the dimensions of the Pyramid, as well as the King's Chamber and the sarcophagus case inside. According to Danley, even the type of stone was selected to enhance these vibrations.

Another "acoustic levitation" enthusiast, Christopher Dunn, proposed that the Great Pyramid could be compared to a huge musical instrument. He believed that the pyramid had a harmonic relationship to the earth and was capable of responding sympathetically with the earth's resonance. In the chapter

"Diamagnetic Gravity Vortexes", found in the book *Anti-Gravity and the World Grid* by David Hatcher Childress (1987), it is suggested that the area of South Florida at Coral Castle, considered part of the Bermuda Triangle, "is a powerful diamagnetic levitator ... Leedskalnin demonstrated magnetism and the mechanism of levitation by applying the natural Earth Grid principles of diamagnetism. Leedskalnin could levitate huge pieces of coral by using the centre of mass for the needed slight uplift launching pressure."

In December 1951 Ed Leedskalnin became ill. He left a sign stuck to the castle door, which read "Going to the Hospital", and went by bus to Miami's Jackson Memorial Hospital. He had stomach cancer. Three days later he died from malnutrition in his sleep at the age of sixty-four. No one was privy to his secrets, although he did leave a peculiar plaque hanging over his bed – it bore the legend: "THE SECRET TO THE UNIVERSE IS 7129 / 6105195."

Ed had a nephew in Michigan who inherited the castle. He sold the site in 1953 to a family from Illinois. After Ed's death, relatives discovered a box that contained various clues leading to a hidden cache of $3,500, the somewhat meagre savings he'd made from visitor tours and the sale of his pamphlets. Also, because US Highway 1 passes Ed's castle, he was able to sell some land at a small profit.

So, did Ed Leedskalnin rediscover some arcane acoustic levitation system? Or was he simply just an extremely clever and adaptable little man who worked out every move with mathematical precision? We may never know. Yet the Coral Castle, like the Taj Mahal, is a solid testimony to the power of love. However, the Taj Mahal was built by a rich king's workforce – the Coral Castle was built by a simple, skinny, little, solo working man.

EPILOGUE: THROUGH THE REVOLVING DOOR

Do not expect to arrive at certainty in every subject which you pursue. There are a hundred things wherein we mortals must be content with probability, where our best light and reasoning will reach no farther.

Isaac Watts (1674–1748)

The enjoyable experience of writing this book has been in some ways equivalent to being trapped in a revolving door. At one side the portal opens on to an interior of utter scepticism whilst the other ejects one on to a busy, alien street in a foreign city of puzzlement and wonder. Of all the subjects covered, life after death remains the most impressive, with the eternal UFO conundrum a close second. The landscape of unexplained phenomena is a wide one, and there are undoubtedly areas I have omitted.

In Charles Dickens's 1853 novel *Bleak House*, the rag and bottle merchant and collector of papers, Krook, dies horribly in flames. This was an early mention of spontaneous human combustion, a possibility Dickens firmly believed in, yet he was severely criticized by the English essayist George Henry Lewes (1817–78) who denounced Krook's fictional death as "outlandish and implausible". Spontaneous combustion occurs when an object, or a human, bursts into flame from an internal chemical reaction, apparently without being ignited by an external heat source. In most cases the victim is almost completely consumed, usually inside their home, while little to no damage is recorded in the room. So, had George Henry Lewes been alive today he might have to eat his words. There have been hundreds of cases of spontaneous human combustion over the last 300 years, and Dickens would have felt vindicated had he read this report by Josie Ensor from the London *Telegraph* of 23 September 2011:

> Michael Faherty, 76, was found lying face down near an open fire in his living room in Galway, Ireland. Apart from his body, investigators could find no other damage in the house. Dr Kieran McLoughlin, the West Galway coroner, said it was the first time in his 25-year career that he had returned a spontaneous combustion verdict, which is believed to be the first in Ireland.

Investigators checked the fireplace, but that wasn't the cause of the fire. Only the man's body had burned. There was no trace of a combustive accelerant or evidence of foul play. The medical opinion in the report says it all: "Dr McLoughlin said he had consulted medical textbooks and carried out other research in an attempt to find an explanation. 'This fire was thoroughly investigated and I'm left with the conclusion that this fits into the category of spontaneous human combustion, for which there is no adequate explanation,' he said."

So perhaps the reality of such a strange phenomenon is determined not by what mainstream science believes, but by what the evidence reveals. Can a man or woman's body become a ball of fire that burns only the flesh and bones and nothing else around it? It would appear so, yet the eye sees only what the mind is prepared to comprehend. Perhaps, when it comes to the many narratives of paranormal and psychic events, deep down we might tend to think that everyone is at best deluded or at worst a potential liar. Yet we have that old saying, "I take as I find", and, for example, I take the stories of near-death experience very seriously, as I've had what seemed like a tenuous glimpse into that subject myself.

When it comes to UFOs and aliens, there are authorities on the subject who stand out like reliable beacons in a 90 per cent fog of fantasy and fallacy. Of all the UFO researchers I have encountered whilst writing this book, one man towers above all the others. I may have a soft spot for him because he is a truly great musician, but when Timothy Good speaks or writes, he always grabs your attention and leaves you pondering rather than laughing. Leonardo da Vinci once said that there are three classes of people: those who see, those who see when they are shown and those who do not see. Once you step into the arena of unexplained phenomena, you have to look at what you are shown and then try to see. Truth or imagination? In a BBC TV show hosted by the comedian Frank Skinner, *Opinionated*, broadcast in March 2012, Timothy Good was in the audience in Norwich. Skinner asked the audience if anyone had experience of aliens. This is what Good said:

Scepticism is warranted because 90 per cent of all UFOs can be explained in conventional terms. But aliens have made formal and informal contact in all walks of life. In 1967 I was with the London Symphony Orchestra in New York. I had heard from several people about their encounters with some of these people, the more human types of aliens who look similar to us. I had heard that they were highly telepathic and that sometimes you could initiate meetings. This was my second experience; I was sitting in the lobby of New York's Park Sheraton Hotel one afternoon and I sent out a message – in my mind – that if "any of you guys are around please come and sit down next to me and prove it". After about half an hour a man came in and there was something about him which immediately struck me. He was about five feet ten and dressed immaculately in a charcoal-grey suit. He came and sat down beside me. He had an attaché case, from which he pulled out a copy of the *New York Times*, and turned the pages over slowly, one by one. He then folded the newspaper, put it back in the case and just sat there. So I said – *in my mind* – "Right; if you are who I think you are, would you take your right index finger and hold it to the right side of your nose?" And immediately, he did. People say, "Why didn't you speak to him?" Well, I didn't, that's the fact of the matter and I regret it. He sat and looked at me for a while and then he left.

As Timothy Good's dedicated research consistently aims at uncovering the truth about UFOs, I have no reason to think that he was lying. Why would he? When he told Frank Skinner that President Eisenhower had actually been taken to a US air force base to meet aliens, Skinner was amazed, exclaiming, "*Hang on!* How did we miss this? Why wasn't it publicized? This is a *huge* story!"

"Well," said Good, "I've written about it before so it obviously isn't."

Good's reply probably explains more about the public's perception of the unexplained than a dozen books or documentaries. The human brain can only take so much. Just dealing with our everyday physical and social existence is enough of a challenge – everything else is white noise and wallpaper. But if we look beyond the wallpaper and listen behind the white noise, sometimes we get a brilliant little insight into where we're going.

In a TV documentary about the RAF, an old man in his late eighties, who as a pilot in the Second World War survived a bomber crash over Germany, told the terrifying story of being hit by flak over the most heavily defended city in the Reich, Essen. His Lancaster bomber lost a wing and began plummeting to earth in a spiral. The centrifugal force pinned him and his comrades to the interior of the fuselage. He said, "Yet I was consumed by a great, sudden feeling of peace. I was only twenty-two, but I thought, I am going to answer the question every man has – I am going to discover if there really is life after death." Somehow, he managed to force himself to the open plane door and parachuted to the ground. All his crew died in the crash. He hadn't panicked – that tranquillity had possessed him in that brief space between this life and the potential of something else. What that "something" is, we shall all discover in the end.

The wonderful author of *The Hitchhiker's Guide to the Galaxy*, Douglas Adams (1952–2001) could well have summed up everything in the pages of this book when he said: "There is a theory which states that if ever anybody discovers exactly what the Universe is for and why it is here, it will instantly disappear and be replaced by something even more bizarre and inexplicable. There is another theory which states that this has already happened."

This has been an adventure, and I hope you have enjoyed it as much as I have. If we meet again, hopefully it will be on that staircase in the golden tunnel of light – provided the aliens don't take us first.

SELECT BIBLIOGRAPHY

This selection of books does not represent a comprehensive overview of all the subjects covered in this work. The books listed are those I have accessed as hard copy for the purpose of research. A larger portion of my research was carried out online, and hopefully I have cited each website address within the text in most instances. The following books are from my own library collection covering unexplained phenomena.

Introduction/Part 1: The Age of Unreason/Part 8: Combing the Fringe

Bardens, Dennis, *Mysterious Worlds* (London: Fontana, 1972).

Brookesmith, Peter, *Strange Talents* (London: Black Cat/Orbis/Macdonald, 1988).

Calkins, Carrol C., *Mysteries of the Unexplained* (New York: Readers Digest, 1982).

Campbell, Joseph, *Creative Mythology: The Masks of God* (Harmondsworth: Penguin, 1976).

——, *The Power of Myth* (New York: Doubleday, 1988).

Chapman, Colin, *Shadows of the Supernatural* (Oxford: Lion, 1990).

Collyns, Robin, *Did Spacemen Colonise the Earth?* (London: Pelham, 1974).

Drake, W. Raymond, *Gods and Spacemen in the Ancient East* (London: Sphere, 1968).

Enright, D. J., *The Oxford Book of the Supernatural* (Oxford: Oxford University Press, 1995).

Evans, Christopher, *Cults of Unreason* (London: Harrap, 1973).

Eysenck, Hans J. and Carl Sargent, *Explaining the Unexplained* (London: Weidenfeld and Nicolson, 1982).

Fairley, John and Simon Welfare, *Arthur C. Clarke's Chronicles of the Strange and Mysterious* (London: Guild, 1987).

Getting, Fred, *Visions of the Occult* (London: Guild, 1989).

Grant, John, *Great Mysteries* (London: Quintet, 1989).

Icke, David, *The Biggest Secret* (Scottsdale, AZ: Bridge of Love Publications, 1999).

Infield, Glenn B., *Hitler's Secret Life* (London: Hamlyn, 1980).

King, Francis, *Satan & Swastika: The Occult and The Nazi Party* (St Albans: Mayflower, 1976).

King, Francis and Jeremy Kingston, *Mysterious Knowledge* (London: Aldus, 1976).

Knight, Damon, *Charles Fort: Prophet of the Unexplained* (New York: Doubleday, 1970).

MacGregor, Rob and Bruce Gernon, *The Fog* (St Paul, MN: Llewellyn, 2005).

McKnight, Gerald, *The Strange Loves of Adolf Hitler* (London: Sphere, 1978).

Marvels & Mysteries: Mystics and Prophets (Bristol: Orbis/Parragon, 1998).

Michell, John and Robert J. M. Rickard, *Phenomenal: A Book of Wonders* (London: BCA/Thames & Hudson, 1979).

Morgan, Giles, *The Holy Grail* (Harpenden: Pocket Essential, 2006).

Nicholas, Lynn H., *The Rape of Europa* (London: Macmillan Papermac, 1995).

Ravenscroft, Trevor, *The Spear of Destiny* (York Beach, ME: Weiser, 1982).

Sri Rahula, Walpola, *What the Buddha Taught* (Oxford: One World, 1997).

Steinmeyer, Jim, *Charles Fort: The Man Who Invented the Supernatural* (New York: Tarcher/Penguin, 2008).

Suster, Gerald, *Hitler and the Age of Horus* (London: Sphere, 1980).

Sutton, David, (ed.), *The Fortean Times Paranormal Handbook* (London: Dennis, 2009).

Wilson, Colin, *Mysteries* (London: Hodder & Stoughton, 1978).

——, *The Occult* (Falmouth: Mayflower, 1971).

The World's Last Mysteries (New York: Reader's Digest, 1977).

Part 2: Hot Chestnuts – UFOs

Blumrich, Josef F., *The Spaceships of Ezekiel* (New York: Bantam, 1974).

Brookesmith, Peter, (ed.), *UFOs: Where Do They Come From?* (London: Black Cat/Orbis/Macdonald, 1988).

Good, Timothy, *Above Top Secret: The Worldwide UFO Cover-up* (London: Guild/Sidgwick & Jackson, 1988).

——, *Unearthly Disclosure* (London: Arrow, 2001).

Keel, John A., *Our Haunted Planet* (London: Neville Spearman, 1971).

——, *Why UFOs?* (New York: Manor Books, 1970).

Luckman, Michael C., *Alien Rock: The Rock 'n' Roll Extra-terrestrial Connection* (New York: Pocket Books, Simon & Schuster, 2009).

Noorbergen, Rene, *Secrets of the Lost Races* (London: New English Library, 1980).

Pilkington, Mark, *Mirage Men* (London: Constable, 2010).

Randles, Jenny, *UFOs and How to See Them* (London: Brockhampton Press, 1992).

Steiger, Brad, (ed.), *Project Blue Book* (New York: Ballantine, 1976).

Part 3: Beyond The Veil

Addams Welch, William, *Talks with the Dead* (New York: Pinnacle, 1975).

Atwater, P. M. H., *The Big Book of Near-Death Experiences: The Ultimate Guide to What Happens When We Die* (Charlottesville, VA: Hampton Roads, 2007).

——, *Near-Death Experiences: The Rest of the Story* (Charlottesville, VA: Hampton Roads, 2011).

——, *We Live Forever: The Real Truth about Death* (Virginia Beach, VA: ARE Press, 2004).

Brandon, Ruth, *The Life and Many Deaths of Harry Houdini* (New York: Kodansha, 1995).

Cayce, Edgar, *On Dreams*, ed. Dr Harmon Bro (New York: Warner, 1989).

Kübler-Ross, Elisabeth, *Life Lessons: Two Experts on Death and Dying Teach Us about the Mysteries of Life and Living*, with David Kessler (New York: Scribner, 2001).

——, *On Death and Dying* (New York: Simon & Schuster/ Touchstone, 1969).

Marvels & Mysteries: Life after Death (Bristol: Orbis/Parragon, 1997).

Maxwell-Stuart, P. G., *Witchcraft: A History* (Stroud: Tempus Publishing, 2000).

Moody, Raymond, A., *Life After Death* (London: Harper Collins, 2001).

Peake, Anthony, *Is There Life After Death?* (London: Arcturus, 2007).

Permutt, Cyril, *Beyond the Spectrum: A Survey of Supernormal Photography* (Cambridge: Patrick Stephens, 1983).

Spencer, John and Anne, *The Encyclopaedia of Ghosts and Spirits* (London: Headline, 1992).

Stone, Reuben, *Life after Death* (Leicester: Bookmart/Amazon, 1993).

Zolar, *The Encyclopaedia of Ancient and Forbidden Knowledge* (London: Souvenir Press, 1970).

Part 4: Inexplicable Astronomy

Cox, Brian, *The Quantum Universe (And Why Anything That Can Happen, Does)* (Cambridge, MA: Da Capo Press, 2012).

——, *Wonders of the Universe* (London: HarperCollins, 2011).

Feynman, Richard P., *QED: The Strange Theory of Light and Matter* (Princeton, NJ: Princeton University Press, 2006).

Greene, Brian, *The Fabric of the Cosmos: Space, Time, and the Texture of Reality* (New York: Vintage, 2005).

Hawking, Stephen, *The Universe in a Nutshell* (New York: Bantam, 2001).

Krauss, Lawrence M., *A Universe from Nothing: Why There Is Something Rather than Nothing* (New York: Free Press, 2012).

Part 5: Bizarre Biology

Bord, Janet and Colin, *Modern Mysteries of Britain* (London: Grafton, 1988).

Harpur, Patrick, *Demonic Reality: A Field Guide to the Other World* (Harmondsworth: Penguin, 1995).

Jay, Ricky, *Learned Pigs and Fireproof Women* (London: Robert Hale, 1987).

Man, John, (ed.), *The World's Wild Places: The Himalayas* (Amsterdam: Time Life, 1981).

Shuker, Dr Karl, *Karl Shuker's Alien Zoo* (Bideford: CFZ Press, 2011).

——, *The Encyclopaedia of New and Rediscovered Animals* (Devon: Coachwhip, 2011).

Part 6: Shiver Me Timbers! Maritime Mysteries

Berlitz, Charles, *Without a Trace* (London: Granada, 1977).

Berlitz, Charles and William Moore, *The Philadelphia Experiment* (London: Granada, 1980).

Gaddis, Vincent, *Invisible Horizons* (New York: Ace Books, 1965).

Goss, Michael and George Behe, *Lost At Sea: Ghost Ships and Other Stories* (New York: Prometheus, 1994).

Gourley, Jay, *The Great Lakes Triangle* (London: Fontana, 1977).

Honan, William H., *Bywater: The Man Who Invented the Pacific War* (London: Macdonald, 1990).

Lamont Brown, Raymond, *Phantoms, Legends, Customs and Superstitions of the Sea* (London: Patrick Stephens, 1972).

Moore, Steve, (ed.), *Fortean Studies Volume 4* (London: Fortean Times/John Brown, 1998).

Part 7: Panic and Paranoia

Alcabes, Philip, *Dread: How Fear and Fantasy Have Fuelled Epidemics from the Black Death to the Avian Flu* (New York: Public Affairs, 2009).

Bratich, Jack Z., *Conspiracy Panics* (Albany, NY: State University of New York Press, 2008).

Ranger, Terence and Paul Slack, *Epidemics and Ideas: Essays on the Historical Perception of Pestilence* (Cambridge: Cambridge University Press, 1992).

Rosenberg, Charles E., *Explaining Epidemics* (Cambridge: Cambridge University Press, 1992).

Wheen, Francis, *How Mumbo-Jumbo Conquered the World: A Short History of Modern Delusions* (London: Harper Collins, 2004).

——, *Strange Days Indeed: The Golden Age of Paranoia* (London: Harper Collins, 2010).

Essential Books by Charles Fort

The Book of the Damned: The Collected Works of Charles Fort, introduction by Jim Steinmeyer (New York: Tarcher, 2008).

New Lands (New York: Ace Books, 1941), also available in earlier and later editions.

Lo! (New York: Ace Books, 1941), also available in earlier and later editions.

Wild Talents (New York: Ace Books, 1932), also available in later editions.

Complete Books of Charles Fort, introduction by Damon Knight (New York: Dover, 1998).

Magazines

No anomalist or serious seeker after the truly fantastic can be without a monthly dose of the excellent *Fortean Times* magazine. The *Fortean Times* opens your mind; its website (www.forteantimes.com) says it all: "You'll need a sense of adventure, curiosity, natural scepticism and a good sense of humour. Every month, *Fortean Times* takes you on an incredible ride where you'll enjoy learning about the most fantastic phenomena on earth." If you're really dedicated and want to lay out a worthwhile investment, the magazine's whole archive is available on a series of CD-ROMs going back three decades. Hours of fun are assured.

Other magazines worth looking at include:

The Anomalist: Daily review of world news on maverick science, unexplained mysteries, strange talents, unexpected discoveries and more.

Atlantis Rising: Covers ancient mysteries, future science and unexplained anomalies.

Beyond Investigation Magazine: Quarterly chronicle on ghost hunting and other paranormal investigations.

Fate Magazine: The old original and most famous, dedicated to reporting UFOs, alien abductions and other supernatural or paranormal events.

Paranormal News: Source for UFO- and paranormal-related information.

The Skeptic: The UK's only regular magazine to take a sceptical look at pseudoscience and claims of the paranormal.

Surfing the Strange, Combing the Fringe: Websites

For a weekly round-up of everything weird, from ghosts to UFOs and Bigfoot, you'll get a fine fix in your inbox for free every few days by subscribing to "Stephen Wagner – Paranormal Phenomena" (paranormal.about.com/bio/Stephen-Wagner-3374.htm). Stephen Wagner is the About.com guide to paranormal phenomena and every aspect of the unexplained.

To paraphrase Groucho Marx, there are more paranormal/psychic/anomalist websites today than you can shake a stick at. To pick just one out simply doesn't work. All have their good points, but surfers beware, a great number of them are laughably naive in their repetitive credulity. If you're looking for balanced research and investigative courage, once you've spotted a story that takes your fancy, always surrender to the cold shower of healthy scepticism by going to somewhere like www.theironskeptic.com to provide a balanced assessment.

The following are go-to addresses that will link you to hundreds of available paranormal/psychic/conspiracy sites, but again, be warned – they're addictive and much midnight oil will be burned:

http://topparanormalsites.com
www.paranormalpulse.com
www.trueghoststories.co.uk
www.unexplained-mysteries.com
http://paranormal.about.com

INDEX